One-Stop Internet Resources

Log on to jat.glencoe.com

ONLINE STUDY TOOLS

- Chapter Overviews
- Interactive Tutor
- Self-Check Quizzes
- E-Flashcards

ONLINE RESEARCH

- Student Web Activities
- Web Resources
- Current Events
- State Resources
- Beyond the Textbook Features

ONLINE STUDENT EDITION

- Complete Interactive Student Edition
- Textbook Updates

FOR TEACHERS

- Teacher Forum
- Web Activity Lesson Plans
- Literature Connections

World History
JOURNEY ACROSS TIME
The Early Ages
COURSE 2

Jackson J. Spielvogel, Ph.D.

NATIONAL GEOGRAPHIC

Glencoe

New York, New York   Columbus, Ohio   Chicago, Illinois   Peoria, Illinois   Woodland Hills, California

Authors

Jackson J. Spielvogel is associate professor emeritus of history at the Pennsylvania State University. He received his Ph.D. from The Ohio State University, where he specialized in Reformation history under Harold J. Grimm. His articles and reviews have been published in several scholarly publications. He is co-author (with William Duiker) of *World History,* published in 1994 (3rd edition, 2001). Professor Spielvogel has won five major university-wide awards, and in 1997, he became the first winner of the Schreyer Institute's Student Choice Award for innovative and inspiring teaching.

The National Geographic Society, founded in 1888 for the increase and diffusion of geographic knowledge, is the world's largest nonprofit scientific and educational organization. Since its earliest days, the Society has used sophisticated communication technologies, from color photography to holography, to convey geographic knowledge to a worldwide membership. The Education Products Division supports the Society's mission by developing innovative educational programs—ranging from traditional print materials to multimedia programs including CD-ROMs, videodiscs, and software.

About the Cover: Throughout ancient history and across the world, people have built great monuments to their civilizations. Top: pyramids at Giza built by ancient Egyptians; middle left: Praetorian Guards of ancient Rome; middle: female porcelain figurine, Dehua, China; middle right: terra-cotta warriors at the tomb of Qin Shihuangdi in Xian, China; bottom left: monoliths at Stonehenge built by the first peoples of ancient England; and bottom right: the Parthenon built in ancient Greece.

 **Glencoe**

The **McGraw·Hill** Companies

Send all inquiries to:
Glencoe/McGraw-Hill
8787 Orion Place
Columbus, OH 43240-4027

ISBN: 0-07-860310-2

Printed in the United States of America.

1 2 3 4 5 6 7 8 9 10 071/055 09 08 07 06 05 04

Consultants & Reviewers

Academic Consultants

Winthrop Lindsay Adams
Associate Professor of History
University of Utah
Salt Lake City, Utah

Sari J. Bennett
Director, Center for Geographic Education
University of Maryland Baltimore County
Baltimore, Maryland

Richard G. Boehm
Jesse H. Jones Distinguished Chair in
    Geographic Education
Texas State University
San Marcos, Texas

Sheilah Clarke-Ekong
Associate Professor of Anthropology and
    Interim Dean
Evening College
University of Missouri, St. Louis
St. Louis, Missouri

Timothy E. Gregory
Professor of History
The Ohio State University
Columbus, Ohio

Robert E. Herzstein
Department of History
University of South Carolina
Columbia, South Carolina

Kenji Oshiro
Professor of Geography
Wright State University
Dayton, Ohio

Joseph R. Rosenbloom
Adjunct Professor, Jewish and Near
    Eastern Studies
Washington University
St. Louis, Missouri

FOLDABLES Dinah Zike
Educational Consultant
Dinah-Might Activities, Inc.
San Antonio, Texas

Reading Consultants

Maureen D. Danner
Project CRISS
National Training Consultant
Kalispell, Montana

ReLeah Cossett Lent
Florida Literacy and Reading Excellence
    Project Coordinator
University of Central Florida
Orlando, Florida

Steve Qunell
Social Studies Instructor
Montana Academy
Kalispell, Montana

Carol M. Santa Ph.D.
CRISS: Project Developer
Director of Education
Montana Academy
Kalispell, Montana

Bonnie Valdes
Master CRISS Trainer
Project CRISS
Largo, Florida

Teacher Reviewers

Destin L. Haas
Social Studies Teacher
Benton Central Junior-Senior High School
Oxford, Indiana

Anna Marie Lawrence
Social Studies Teacher
Snellville Middle School
Snellville, Georgia

Richard Meegan
Social Studies Department Chair
Masconomet Regional School District
Topsfield, Massachusetts

J. Keith Miller
Social Studies Teacher
Bragg Middle School
Gardendale, Alabama

Beth Neighbors
Social Studies Teacher
Pizitz Middle School
Vestavia Hills, Alabama

Virgina Parra
Social Studies Teacher
Osceola Middle School
Ocala, Florida

Susan Pearson
Social Studies Teacher
The Academy for Science and
    Foreign Languages
Huntsville, Alabama

Nancy Perkins
Social Studies Implementer 1–12
Bonny Eagle Middle School
Buxton, Maine

Beverly Prestage
Social Studies Program Supervisor
Cranston High School West
Cranston, Rhode Island

Julie A. Scott
Social Studies Teacher
East Valley Middle School
Spokane, Washington

Larry W. Smith
Heritage Education Teacher
Massie Heritage Interpretation Center
Savannah, Georgia

Jerry A. Taylor
Social Studies Teacher
Towns County Comprehensive School
Hiawassee, Georgia

Contents

Be an Active Reader xvi

Previewing Your
Textbook xviii

Scavenger Hunt xxiii

NATIONAL GEOGRAPHIC Reference
Atlas R1

NATIONAL GEOGRAPHIC Geography
Handbook . . . GH1

How Do I Study Geography GH2
How Do I Use Maps and Globes? GH4
Using Charts, Graphs, and Diagrams GH11
Geographic Dictionary GH14

Tools of the Historian . . . Tools1

Measuring Time Tools1
Organizing Time Tools2
How Does a Historian Work? Tools4
History and Geography Tools6
What Is a Historical Atlas? Tools8
Links Across Time Tools10

Unit 1

Early Civilizations 1

CHAPTER 1
The First Civilizations 4

Reading Previewing 6
1 Early Humans 8
2 Mesopotamian Civilizations 16
3 The First Empires 26

CHAPTER 2
Ancient Egypt 34

Reading Predicting 36
1 The Nile Valley 38
2 Egypt's Old Kingdom 47
3 The Egyptian Empire 59
4 The Civilization of Kush 68

CHAPTER 3
The Ancient Israelites 76

Reading Main Idea 78
1 The First Israelites 80
2 The Kingdom of Israel 86
3 The Growth of Judaism 93

▼ Ancient Assyrian soldiers

◀ Ancient Egyptian artwork of a funeral boat

Gianni Dagli Orti/CORBIS

Unit 2

The Ancient World 108

CHAPTER 4
The Ancient Greeks 112
Reading Making Connections.................... 114
1 The Early Greeks 116
2 Sparta and Athens 124
3 Persia Attacks the Greeks 131
4 The Age of Pericles 138

CHAPTER 5
Greek Civilization 150
Reading Context 152
1 The Culture of Ancient Greece 154
2 Greek Philosophy and History 168
3 Alexander the Great 174
4 The Spread of Greek Culture 182

CHAPTER 6
Early India 190
Reading Vocabulary 192
1 India's First Civilizations 194
2 Hinduism and Buddhism 202
3 India's First Empires 209

CHAPTER 7
Early China 220
Reading Text Structure 222
1 China's First Civilizations 224
2 Life in Ancient China 232
3 The Qin and Han Dynasties 240

Unit 3

New Empires and New Faiths 254

CHAPTER 8
The Rise of Rome 258
Reading Taking Notes 260
1 Rome's Beginnings 262
2 The Roman Republic 268
3 The Fall of the Republic 277
4 The Early Empire 286

CHAPTER 9
Roman Civilization 298
Reading Responding & Reflecting 300
1 Life in Ancient Rome 302
2 The Fall of Rome 317
3 The Byzantine Empire 327

CHAPTER 10
The Rise of Christianity 338
Reading Sequence Clues 340
1 The First Christians 342
2 The Christian Church 351
3 The Spread of Christian Ideas 358

CHAPTER 11
Islamic Civilization 368
Reading Main Idea.......................... 370
1 The Rise of Islam 372
2 Islamic Empires 379
3 Muslim Ways of Life 387

Appendix 707

Contents

Be an Active Reader xvi

Previewing Your
Textbook xviii

Scavenger Hunt xxiii

NATIONAL GEOGRAPHIC Reference
Atlas R1

NATIONAL GEOGRAPHIC Geography
Handbook . . . GH1

How Do I Study Geography GH2
How Do I Use Maps and Globes? GH4
Using Charts, Graphs, and Diagrams GH11
Geographic Dictionary GH14

Tools of the Historian . . . Tools1

Measuring Time Tools1
Organizing Time Tools2
How Does a Historian Work? Tools4
History and Geography Tools6
What Is a Historical Atlas? Tools8
Links Across Time Tools10

Unit 3

New Empires and New Faiths 254

CHAPTER 8
The Rise of Rome 258
Reading Taking Notes 260
  1 Rome's Beginnings 262
  2 The Roman Republic 268
  3 The Fall of the Republic 277
  4 The Early Empire 286

CHAPTER 9
Roman Civilization 298
Reading Responding & Reflecting 300
  1 Life in Ancient Rome 302
  2 The Fall of Rome 317
  3 The Byzantine Empire 327

CHAPTER 10
The Rise of Christianity 338
Reading Sequence Clues 340
  1 The First Christians 342
  2 The Christian Church 351
  3 The Spread of Christian Ideas 358

CHAPTER 11
Islamic Civilization 368
Reading Main Idea 370
  1 The Rise of Islam 372
  2 Islamic Empires 379
  3 Muslim Ways of Life 387

Unit 4

The Middle Ages 400

CHAPTER 12
China in the Middle Ages 404
Reading Inferences 406
  1 China Reunites 408
  2 Chinese Society 416
  3 The Mongols in China 423
  4 The Ming Dynasty 430

Richard A. Cooke/CORBIS

◀ Anasazi jewelry

CHAPTER 13
Medieval Africa **440**
🔲Reading◤ **Compare and Contrast** **442**
  1 The Rise of African Civilizations 444
  2 Africa's Government and Religion 460
  3 African Society and Culture 468

CHAPTER 14
Medieval Japan **480**
🔲Reading◤ **Cause and Effect** **482**
  1 Early Japan 484
  2 Shoguns and Samurai 491
  3 Life in Medieval Japan 498

CHAPTER 15
Medieval Europe **508**
🔲Reading◤ **Questioning** **510**
  1 The Early Middle Ages 512
  2 Feudalism 522
  3 Kingdoms and Crusades 534
  4 The Church and Society 544
  5 The Late Middle Ages 553

Unit 5

A Changing World **564**

CHAPTER 16
The Americas **568**
🔲Reading◤ **Summarizing** **570**
  1 The First Americans 572
  2 Life in the Americas 582
  3 The Fall of the Aztec and Inca Empires 593

CHAPTER 17
The Renaissance and Reformation **604**
🔲Reading◤ **Analyze and Clarify** **606**
  1 The Renaissance Begins 608
  2 New Ideas and Art 618
  3 The Reformation Begins 633
  4 Catholics and Protestants 642

CHAPTER 18
Enlightenment and Revolution **654**
🔲Reading◤ **Monitor and Adjust** **656**
  1 The Age of Exploration 658
  2 The Scientific Revolution 670
  3 The Enlightenment 680
  4 The American Revolution 690

Appendix

What Is an Appendix? **707**
SkillBuilder Handbook **708**
Standardized Test Practice **726**
Primary Sources Library **736**
Suggested Readings **748**
Glossary **750**
Spanish Glossary **756**
Gazetteer **763**
Index **772**
Acknowledgements and Photo Credits **792**

Features

Primary Source

Course 1
Paleolithic Cave Paintings 10
"Hymn to the Nile" 41
Selecting a New King 71
The Ten Commandments 83
Proverbs 89
The Talmud 102
Athenian Soldier's Oath 122
Herodotus's History 135
Pericles' Funeral Oration 145
Demosthenes' Warning 175
The Poetry of Theocritus 183
Morality in the Eightfold Path 206
The Bhagavad Gita 214

Course 1 and 2
The *Aeneid* 264
A Roman Triumph 270
Cicero Calls for War 282
The Book of Epodes 304
Distrust of Money 320
Rome Is Attacked 322
Theodora Refuses to Flee 330
Sermon on the Mount 348

Royal Caliphs 382
The Mystery of Smallpox 391

Course 2
Defending Confucianism 413
Li Bo 420
Kublai Khan's Park 428
Ghana Profits From Trade 462
The Sultan of Mali 465
Japan's New Constitution 488
Bushido Code 495
Magna Carta 537
Ibn Fadlan Describes the Rus 539
The Franciscan Way of Life 546
The Aztec Defeat 597
Incan Record Keeping 599
The Prince 614
Leonardo's Inventions 621
Knowledge of God 640
Ignatius and Christianity 644
The Law of Nations 682
The Natural Rights of Women 685
The Mayflower Compact 693
The Declaration of Independence 698

Primary Sources Library

Epic of Gilgamesh 738
An Egyptian Father's Advice to His Son 739
Ancient Israelites 739
The *Analects* of Confucius 740
The Rights of Women 741
Song from the *Rig Veda* 741
A Woman on the Throne 742
A Heroic Rescue Attempt 743
The *Quran* 743
The Sultan of Mali 744
The Magna Carta 745
The Tale of Genji 745
Arrival of the Spaniards 746
The Life of Olaudah Equiano 747
Queen Elizabeth's speech 747

WORLD LITERATURE

Course 1
The Prince Who Knew His Fate,
    translated by Lise Manniche 53
"Icarus and Daedalus,"
    retold by Josephine Preston Peabody 164
Course 1 and 2
"A Wild-Goose Chase:
    The Story of Philemon and Baucis,"
    retold by Geraldine McCaughrean 311
Course 2
"Sundiata: The Hungering Lion,"
    retold by Kenny Mann 454
"A Midsummer Night's Dream,"
    by William Shakespeare,
    adapted by E. Nesbit 627

Biography

Course 1

Ötzi the Iceman 12
Hammurabi 22
Hatshepsut 63
Ramses II 66
David 88
Ruth and Naomi 99
Pericles 141
Homer 159
Plato and Aristotle 172
The Buddha 207
Emperor Asoka 212
Confucius 237
Qin Shihuangdi 243

Course 1 and 2

Lucius Quinctius Cincinnatus 273
Augustus 289
Constantine the Great 321
Empress Theodora 331
Jesus of Nazareth 346
Paul of Tarsus 349

Saint Augustine 356
Muhammad 375
Omar Khayyam and Ibn Khaldun 392

Course 2

Genghis Khan 427
Zheng He 434
Mansa Musa 466
Queen Nzinga 471
Prince Shotoku 489
Marasaki Shikibu 502
Charlemagne 517
Thomas Aquinas 551
Joan of Arc 556
Pachacuti 589
Montezuma II and Hernán Cortés 598
Leonardo da Vinci 622
Martin Luther 638
Catherine de' Medici 647
Elizabeth I 665
Sir Isaac Newton 677
John Locke 683

SkillBuilder Handbook

Finding the Main Idea 709
Taking Notes and Outlining 710
Reading a Time Line 711
Sequencing and Categorizing Information 712
Recognizing Point of View 713
Distinguishing Fact From Opinion 714
Analyzing Library and Research Resources 715
Analyzing Primary Source Documents 716
Building a Database 717

Summarizing 718
Evaluating a Web Site 719
Understanding Cause and Effect 720
Making Comparisons 721
Making Predictions 722
Drawing Inferences and Conclusions 723
Recognizing Economic Indicators 724
Interpreting Political Cartoons 725

Features

Linking Past & Present

Course 1

Education 21
Hieroglyphs and Computer Icons 61
Head Coverings 97
The Olympics 128
The Theater 160
Papermaking 245

Course 1 and 2

Living in the Shadow of Mt. Vesuvius 290
Roman and Modern Architecture 325
Missionaries 362
Hijab 390

Course 2

Grand Canal and Three Gorges Dam Project . . . 410
African Music 475
Martial Arts 500
The Jury System 536
Chocolate 595
The Anabaptists, Amish, and
    Mennonites 637
Telescopes 674

NATIONAL GEOGRAPHIC HISTORY MAKERS

Course 1

Dead Sea Scrolls 100
Development of Sanskrit, c. 1500 B.C. 199
The Invention of Zero, c. A.D. 500 215
Chinese Writing 228
Twelve Tables, c. 451 B.C. 273

Course 2

Twelve Tables, c. 451 B.C. 273
Movable Type, c. 1450 620

NATIONAL GEOGRAPHIC The Way It Was

Course 1

Tools 11
From Farming to Food 42
Cats in Ancient Egypt 64
Education in Ancient Israel and Judah 98
Women's Duties 143
Greek Medicine 184
The Role of Women 227
Chinese Farming 234

Course 1 and 2

Roman Dinner Parties 271
Roman Aqueducts 291
Ancient Roman Sports 306
Slavery in the Roman Empire 319
Byzantine Mosaics 333
Christian Catacombs 353
Muslim Carpets and Weavings 389

Course 2

Civil Service Exams 414
Printing 419
Africa's Salt Mines 449
Kente Cloth 474
Samurai 496
Anasazi Cliff Dwellings 578
Mayan Ball Game 584
The Life of a Renaissance Artist 624
Music of the Enlightenment 686

You Decide . . .

Course 1

Hammurabi's Laws: Fair or Cruel? 24
Alexander the Great: Villain or Hero? 180
Was Caesar a Reformer or a Dictator? 284

Course 2

Was Caesar a Reformer or a Dictator? 284
Feudalism: Good or Bad? 532
The Value of City-States 616

Primary Source Quotes

Ed. = Editor	Tr. = Translator	V = Volume

Course 1

Chapter 1
"The Mesopotamian View of Death." From *Poems of Heaven and Hell from Ancient Mesopotamia*. Tr. N.K. Sanders. In *Aspects of Western Civilization*, V1. Ed. Perry M. Rogers. 2000. 33

Chapter 2
"Hymn to the Nile, c. 2100 B.C.E." In *Ancient History Sourcebook*. www.fordham.edu/halsall/ancient/hymn-nile.html 41
Lise Manniche, tr. *The Prince Who Knew His Fate*. 1981 . . .53–58
Egyptian scribe. Quoted in *Barbarian Tides*. Ed. Thomas H. Flaherty. 1987. 63
"Beit Shean Stela of Ramses II." Hieroglyphic translation in *Ancient Near Eastern Texts*. James B. Pritchard. www.reshafim.org.il/ad/egypt/ramesisII_bethshan_insc.htm . . . 66
"The Selection of Aspalta as King of Kush, c. 600 BCE." From *Ancient History Sourcebook*. www.fordham.edu/halsall/ancient/nubia1.html 71
Herodotus. From *The History*. Tr. David Grene. 1987. 75

Chapter 3
Exodus 20:3–17. *The Contemporary English Version* [Bible]. 1995. 83
2 Samuel 23:3–4. *The Holy Bible, 1611 Edition, King James Version*. 2003. 88
Proverbs 10:2, 5, 9. *The Contemporary English Version* [Bible]. 1995. 89
From *The Talmud for Today*. Tr./Ed. Rabbi Alexander Feinsilver. 1980. 102
Josephus. "The Siege of Jerusalem, A.D. 70." In *Eyewitness to History*. Ed. John Carey. 1987. 105

Chapter 4
Plutarch. "Spartan Discipline." In *Aspects of Western Civilization*, V1. Ed. Perry M. Rogers. 2000. 126
Xerxes, as recorded by Herodotus. From *The Persian Wars*. Tr. George Rawlinson. 1942. 135
Pericles, as recorded by Thucydides. From *History of the Peloponnesian War*. Tr. William Smith. 1845. 141
Xenophon. "On Men and Women from Oikonomikos, c. 370 BCE." From *Memorabilia and Oeconomicus*. In *Ancient History Sourcebook*. www.fordham.edu/halsall/ancient/xenophon-genderroles.html 143
Pericles, as recorded by Thucydides. From *History of the Peloponnesian War*. Tr. Rex Warner. 1954. 145
Thucydides. From *History of the Peloponnesian War*. Tr. Rex Warner. 1954. 146
Pericles, as recorded by Thucydides. From *The Peloponnesian War*. Unabridged Crawley Translation 1951. 149

Chapter 5
Josephine Preston Peabody. "Icarus and Daedalus." *The Baldwin Project*. www.mainlesson.com/display.php?author=peabody&book=greek&story=icarus 164–167

Homer. From *The Iliad*. Tr. Robert Fitzgerald. 1974. 159
Thucydides. From *History of the Peloponnesian War*. Tr. Rex Warner. 1954. 173
Demosthenes. "The First Philippic (351 B.C.E.)." From *Orations of Demosthenes*. In *Aspects of Western Civilization*, V1. Ed. Perry M. Rogers. 2000. 175
Michael Wood. From *In the Footsteps of Alexander the Great*. 1997. 180
Arrian. "From Arrian, *The Anabasis of Alexander*." From *The Anabasis of Alexander*. www.luc.edu/faculty/ldossey/arrian.htm 181
Theocritus. "First Idyll." In *The Idylls of Theokritos*. Tr. Barriss Mills. 1963. 183
Thucydides. From *History of the Peloponnesian War*. Tr. Rex Warner. 1954. 189

Chapter 6
From *The Word of the Buddha*. Tr. Nyanatiloka. Ed. Buddhist Publication Society. www.enabling.org/ia/vipassana/Archive/N/Nyanatiloka/WOB 206
Buddha. From *The Dhammapada*. Tr. Eknath Easwaran. 1986. 207
From *Bhagavadgita*. Tr. Sir Edwin Arnold. 1993. 214
"The Buddha's Farewell Address." In *The Teachings of the Buddha*. Ed. Paul Carus. 1915. 219

Chapter 7
Confucius. *Analects*. From *The Essential Confucius*. Tr. Thomas Cleary. 1992. 236
Confucius. In *Familiar Quotations*. Ed. Justin Kaplan. 1992. 237
Laozi. "Higher Good Is Like Water" in *"Tao Te Ching."* From *The Taoist Classics*. V1. Tr. Thomas Cleary. 1999. 239
Qin Shi Huang Di. Quoted in *China: Its History and Culture*. W. Scott Morton. 1980. 243
"A Caveat Against Violence." From *The Tao Te Ching*. Tr. Stan Rosenthal. www.clas.ufl.edu/users/gthursby/taoism/ttcstan3.htm 251

Course 1 and 2

Chapter 8
Virgil. *The Aeneid*. Tr. Robert Fitzgerald. 1981. 264
Zonaras. "A Roman Triumph." In *Aspects of Western Civilization*, V1. Ed. Perry M. Rogers. 2000. 270
Livy. From *The Rise of Rome: Books One to Five*. Tr. T. J. Luce. 1998. 272
Cicero. "The Sixth Oration of M. T. Cicero Against Marcus Antonius." From *The Orations of Marcus Tullius Cicero*, V4. Tr. C. D. Yonge. 1894. 282
Augustus. "Res Gestae: The Accomplishments of Augustus." In *Aspects of Western Civilization*, V1. Ed. Perry M. Rogers. 2000. 289
Augustus. "Res Gestae: The Accomplishments of Augustus." In *Aspects of Western Civilization*, V1. Ed. Perry M. Rogers. 2000. 297

Primary Source Quotes

Chapter 9

Horace. "The Book of Epodes." In *The Complete Works of Horace.* Tr. Charles E. Passage. 1983. 304

"A Wild-Goose Chase: The Story of Philemon and Baucis." In *Roman Myths.* Retold by Geraldine McCaughrean. 1999. 311–316

"Distrust of Imperial Coinage (260 C.E.)." *Oxyrhynchus Papyrus,* no. 1411, V2. Tr. A.S. Hunt. In *Aspects of Western Civilization,* V1. Ed. Perry M. Rogers. 2000. 320

Jerome. "News of the Attacks." In *Aspects of Western Civilization,* V1. Ed. Perry M. Rogers. 2000. 322

Theodora. Quoted in "The Nika Riot (532)" by Procopius. In *Aspects of Western Civilization,* V1. Ed. Perry M. Rogers. 2000. 330

Procopius. "The Secret History of Justinian and Theodora." In *Aspects of Western Civilization,* V1. Ed. Perry M. Rogers. 2000. 331

Gaius. "Legislation Against the Abuse of Slaves" from *Institutes,* 1.53. In *Aspects of Western Civilization,* V1. Ed. Perry M. Rogers. 2000. 337

Chapter 10

Jesus of Nazareth. John 13:46. *The Contemporary English Version* [Bible]. 1995. 346

Jesus of Nazareth. Matthew 5:11–12. From *Good News Bible,* 2nd Edition. 1992. 348

Paul of Tarsus. Acts 20:35. *The Contemporary English Version* [Bible]. 1995. 349

Augustine. *Confessions.* Tr. Henry Chadwick. 1991. 357

Benedict. From *The Rule.* "Of the Daily Manual Labor." In *Sources of World History,* V1. Ed. Mark A. Kishlansky. 2003. 367

Chapter 11

Ibn Khaldun. "The Muqaddimah (1377 C.E.)." From *The Muqaddimah.* In *Sources of World History,* V1. Ed. Mark A. Kishlansky. 2003. 382

Al-Razi. "On the Causes of Small-Pox." In *Aspects of Western Civilization,* V1. Ed. Perry M. Rogers. 2000. 391

Omar Khayyam. From *Rubáiyát of Omar Khayyám.* Tr. Edward Fitzgerald. 1952. 392

Omar Khayyam. From *Rubáiyát of Omar Khayyám: A Paraphrase From Several Literal Translations.* Richard Le Gallienne. 1978. 397

Course 2

Chapter 12

Han Yü. "An Inquiry on the Way (Tao)." In *A Source Book in Chinese Philosophy.* Tr./Ed. Wing-Tsit Chan. 1963. 413

Shên Kua. From *Dream Pool Jottings.* In *The Invention of Printing in China and Its Spread Westward,* 2nd Edition. Thomas Francis Carter. 1955. 419

Li Bo. "Seeing a Friend Off." In *The Columbia Book of Chinese Poetry.* Tr./Ed. Burton Watson. 1984. 420

Li Bo. "Still Night Thoughts." In *The Columbia Book of Chinese Poetry.* Tr./Ed. Burton Watson. 1984. 420

Duo Fu. "Spring Landscape." In *The Selected Poems of Tu Fu.* Tr. David Hinton. 1988. 421

Genghis Khan. Attributed to him in *Genghis Khan.* Brenda Lange. 2003. 427

Marco Polo. "Kublai Khan's Park, c. 1275." In *Eyewitness to History.* Ed. John Carey. 1987. 428

Zheng He. Quoted in *Chinese Portraits.* Dorothy and Thomas Hoobler. 1993. 434

John of Plano Carpini. From *History of the Mongols.* Translated at Stanbrook Abbey. www.accd.edu/sac/history/keller/Mongols/states5a.html ... 439

Chapter 13

J. V. Egharevba. "The Empire of Benin" from *A Short History of Benin.* In *The African Past.* Ed. Basil Davidson. 1964. 450

"Sundiata: The Hungering Lion" In *African Kingdoms of the Past.* Retold by Kenny Mann. 1996. 454–459

Abdullah Abu-Ubayd al Bekri. "Ghana in 1067." In *The African Past.* Ed. Basil Davidson. 1964. 462

Al-Dukhari. Quoted in *Topics in West African History.* A. Adu Boahen. 1966. 462

Ibn Fadl Allah al Omari. "Mali in the Fourteenth Century." In *The African Past.* Ed. Basil Davidson. 1964. 465

Yoruba. "Praise of a Child." Tr. Ulli Beier and Bakare Gbadamosi. In *Poems From Africa.* Ed. Samuel Allen. 1973. 470

Gomes Eannes de Zurara. Quoted in *The Slave Trade.* Hugh Thomas. 1997. 472

Telford Edwards. Quoted in *The Mystery of the Great Zimbabwe.* Wilfrid Mallows. 1984. 479

Chapter 14

Prince Shotoku. "The Seventeen Article Constitution (640 C.E.)." In *Sources of World History,* V1. Ed. Mark A. Kishlansky. 2003. 488

Yamamoto Tsunetomo. From *Hagakure: The Book of the Samurai.* Tr. William Scott Wilson. http://afe.easia.columbia.edu/japan/ japanworkbook/ traditional/bushido_print.html 495

"Twenty-One Anonymous Tanka from the Kokinshū." In *From the Country of Eight Islands.* Ed./Tr. by Hiroaki Sato and Burton Watson. 1986. 501

Murasaki Shikibu. From *The Diary of Lady Murasaki.* Tr. Richard Bowring. 1996. 502

Heike Monogatori. From *The Tale of the Heike.* Tr. Hiroshi Kitagawa and Bruce T. Tsuchida. 1975. 504

Seami Jūrokubushū Hyōshaku. "The Book of the Way of the Highest Flower (Shikadō-Sho)." In *Sources of Japanese Tradition.* Ed. Ryusaku Tsunoda, et. al. 1958. 507

Chapter 15

Charlemagne. Quoted in "The World of Charlemagne" by Norman P. Zacour. In *The Age of Chivalry.* Ed. Merle Severy. 1969. 517

A. E. Dick Howard, ed. *Magna Carta: Text and Commentary.*
1964. 537

Ibn Fadlan. From *Risāla.* In "Ibn Fadlān's Account of the Rūs with
Some Commentary and Some Allusions to Beowulf," by H. M.
Smyser. In *Franciplegius.* Ed. Jess B. Bessinger, Jr. and Robert P.
Creed. 1965. 539

Pope Urban II. Reported by Robert the Monk. Quoted in *The
Discoverers.* Daniel J. Boorstin. 1983. 541

Francis of Assisi. "Admonitions (ca. 1220 C.E.)." In *Sources
of World History,* V1. Ed. Mark A. Kishlansky. 2003. 546

St. Thomas Aquinas. From *Summa Theologiae.* Ed. Timothy
McDermott. 1989. 551

Charles Scott Moncrieff, ed. *The Song of Roland.* 1976. 552

From *Joan of Arc: In Her Own Words.* Ed./Tr. Willard Trask.
1996. 556

King Louis IX. "Legal Rules for Military Service." In *Aspects of
Western Civilization,* V1. Ed. Perry M. Rogers. 2000. 561

Chapter 16

Pachacuti. Quoted in *History of the Incas.* Pedro Sarmiento de
Gamboa. 1999. 589

Juan Díaz. Quoted in "Conquest and Aftermath" by Gene S. Stuart.
In *The Mysterious Maya* by George E. Stuart and Gene S.
Stuart. 1977. 596

From *The Broken Spears.* Ed. Miguel Leon-Portilla. Tr. Lysander
Kemp. 1992. 597

Pedro de Cieza de Léon. "Chronicles of the Incas, 1540,"
from *The Second Part of the Chronicle of Peru.* In *Modern
History Sourcebook.*
www.fordham.edu/halsall/mod/1540cieza.html 599

Bartolomé de las Casas. "Apologetic History of the Indies (1566
C.E.)." In *Sources of World History,* V1. Ed. Mark A. Kishlansky.
2003. 603

Chapter 17

Niccolò Machiavelli. "The Prince (1513 C.E.)." In *Sources of World
History,* V1. Ed. Mark A. Kishlansky. 2003. 614

Leonardo da Vinci. From *The Notebooks of Leonardo da Vinci,* V2.
Ed. Jean Paul Richter. 1970. 622

William Shakespeare. "A Midsummer Night's Dream" In *The
Children's Shakespeare.* Retold by E. Nesbit.
1938. 627–632

Martin Luther. "The Ninety-five Theses (1517)." In *Aspects
of Western Civilization,* V1. Ed. Perry M. Rogers. 2000. 638

John Calvin. *Institutes of the Christian Religion.* In *Sources
of World History,* V1. Ed. Mark A. Kishlansky.
2003. 640

From *The Autobiography of St. Ignatius Loyola.* Tr. Joseph F.
O'Callaghan. Ed. John C. Olin. 1974. 644

Catherine de Medici. Quoted in *Biography of a Family.* Waldman
Milton. 1936. 647

Martin Luther. "The Ninety-five Theses (1517)." In *Aspects
of Western Civilization,* V1. Ed. Perry M. Rogers. 2000. 653

Chapter 18

"Queen Elizabeth's Armada Speech to the Troops at Tilbury,
August 9, 1588." In *Elizabeth I: Collected Works.* Tr. Leah S.
Marcus, et. al. 2000. 665

Sir Isaac Newton. Quoted in *On the Shoulders of Giants.* Ed.
Stephen Hawking. 2002. 677

Charles de Secondat, baron de Montesquieu. From *The Spirit of
Laws.* In *Great Books of the Western World,* V38. Ed. Robert
Maynard Hutchins. Tr. Thomas Nugent. Revised by J. V. Prichard.
1952. 682

John Locke. From *Two Treatises of Government.* 1991. 683

Mary Wollstonecraft. From *A Vindication of the Rights of Woman.*
2001. 685

"The Mayflower Compact." In *Documents of American History.* Ed.
Henry Steele Commager. 1958. 693

"The Declaration of Independence." In *Documents of American
History.* Ed. Henry Steele Commager. 1958. 698

Duarte Barbosa. "The East Coast of Africa." From *The Book of
Duarte Barbosa.* In *Aspects of Western Civilization,* V1. Ed.
Perry M. Rogers. 2000. 703

Primary Source Library

From *Gilgamesh.* Translated from *Sîn-leqi-unninnī* version by
John Gardner and John Maier. 1984. 738

"The Precepts of Ptah-Hotep, c. 2200 BCE." In *Ancient History
Sourcebook.*
www.fordham.edu/halsall/ancient/ptahhotep.html 739

Genesis 12:1–7. From *The Revised English Bible.* 1989. 739

Confucius. *Analects.* From *The Essential Confucius.* Tr. Thomas
Cleary. 1992. 740

Socrates. From *Plato's Republic.* Tr. B. Jowett. 1982. 741

"Night." From *The Rig Veda.* Ed./Tr. Wendy Doniger O'Flaherty.
1981. 741

Anna Comnena. "The Alexiad: Book III" From *The Alexiad.*
Ed./Tr. Elizabeth A. Dawes. 1928. In *Medieval Sourcebook.*
www.fordham.edu/halsall/basis/annacomnena-
alexiad03.html 742

Pliny. *Letters and Panegyricus,* V1, Letters, Books I–VII. Tr. Betty
Radice. 1969. 743

From *An Interpretation of the Qur'an.* Tr. Majid Fakhry.
2000. 743

Ibn Fadl Allah al Omari. "Mali in the Fourteenth Century." In *The
African Past.* Ed. Basil Davidson. 1964. 744

From *Magna Carta and The Tradition of Liberty.* Louis B. Wright.
1976. 745

Lady Murasaki. From *The Tale of Genji.* Tr. Arthur Waley.
1960. 745

From *The Broken Spears.* Ed. Miguel Leon-Portilla. Tr. Lysander
Kemp. 1992. 746

From *The Kidnapped Prince: The Life of Olaudah Equiano.* By
Olaudah Equiano. Adapted by Ann Cameron. 1995. 747

"Queen Elizabeth's Armada Speech to the Troops at Tilbury,
August 9, 1588." In *Elizabeth I: Collected Works.* Tr. Leah S.
Marcus, et. al. 2000. 747

Maps, Charts, Graphs, and Diagrams

National Geographic Maps

NATIONAL GEOGRAPHIC Geography Handbook GH1

How Do I Study Geography? GH2
How Do I Use Maps and Globes? GH4
Using Charts, Graphs, and Diagrams GH11
Geographic Dictionary GH14

Course 1

Unit 1

Early Farming, 7000–2000 B.C. 13
Ancient Mesopotamia 17
Assyrian Empire 28
Ancient Egypt, c. 3100 B.C. 39
Egyptian Kingdoms 62
Kush Kingdom, c. 250 B.C. 70
Ancient Israel 90

Unit 2

Ancient Greece, c. 750 B.C. 114
Greek Colonies and Trade, 750–550 B.C. 121
Sparta and Athens, c. 700 B.C. 125
The Persian Empire, 500 B.C. 132
Persian Wars, 499–479 B.C. 134
The Peloponnesian War, 431–404 B.C. 144
Alexander's Empire, 323 B.C. 176
Hellenistic World, 241 B.C. 179
Geography of India 195
Aryan Migration, 2000–500 B.C. 198
Mauryan Empire, c. 250 B.C. 210
Gupta Empire, c. A.D. 600 213
The Geography of China 225
Shang Empire 226
Zhou Empire 230
Qin and Han Empires, 221 B.C.–A.D. 220 241
Trading in the Ancient World 246

Course 1 and 2

Unit 3

Italy, 500 B.C. 263
Growth of the Roman Republic, 500–146 B.C. 269
The Punic Wars, 264–146 B.C. 274
The Roman Empire: Trade and Expansion 292

Germanic Invasions of Rome, A.D. 200–500 323
The Byzantine Empire, A.D. 527–565 329
Spread of Christianity, A.D. 325 352
Spread of Christianity, A.D. 325–1100 361
The Middle East, c. A.D. 600 374
The Spread of Islam, A.D. 632–750 380
Abbasid Empire, A.D. 800 383
The Expansion of the Ottoman Empire 385

Course 2

Unit 4

Tang Dynasty China, c. A.D. 700 409
Song China, c. A.D. 1200 411
Mongol Empire Under Genghis Khan, 1227 424
Mongol Empire, 1294 425
Ming Dynasty China, 1368–1644 431
Zheng He's Voyages, 1405–1433 433
Geography and Climate Zones in Africa 445
Trade Routes of North Africa 448
Trade in East Africa 452
African Religions Today 463
Bantu Migrations 469
The Slave Trade, c. 1450–1800 473
Geography of Japan 485
Europe's Geography and People, c. A.D. 500 513
Germanic Kingdoms, c. A.D. 500 514
The Frankish Kingdom, c. A.D. 500–800 516
Invasions of Europe, c. A.D. 800–1000 518
Europe, c. 1160 538
Growth of Moscow 540
The Crusades, 1096–1204 542
Jewish Expulsions, c. 1100–1500 548
The Black Death in Asia 554
The Black Death in Europe 555
The Hundred Years' War 557

Unit 5

Migration to America 573
Civilizations of Mesoamerica 575
Civilizations of South America 577
People and Cultures of North America, c. 1300–1500 590

Italy, c. 1500 609
Holy Roman Empire, 1520 639
Religions in Europe, c. 1600 645
European Explorations of the World 662
European Trade in Asia, c. 1700 667

The Columbian Exchange 668
Growth of Prussia and Austria, c. 1525–1720 688
Europeans in North America 691
Thirteen Colonies 694
Colonial Trade Routes, c. 1750 695

Charts and Graphs

Course 1

Unit 1

Comparing the Neolithic and Paleolithic Ages 14
Comparing Mesopotamia to Egypt 44
Alphabets 85
Major Hebrew Prophets 91
Major Jewish Holidays 96

Unit 2

The Greek Alphabet 120
Comparing Governments 140
Greek Gods and Goddesses 155
Greek Philosophers 170
Greek Scientists and Their Contributions 185
Early India's Social System 200
Major Hindu Gods and Goddesses 204
Chinese Numbering System 236
Chinese Philosophers 238
Four Chinese Dynasties 247

Course 1 and 2

Unit 3

The Julio-Claudian Emperors 288
The "Good Emperors" of the Pax Romana 292

Greek and Roman Gods 310
The Decline of Rome 318
Early Church Hierarchy 355
The Cyrillic Alphabet 363
The Five Pillars of Islam 378
The Rightly Guided Caliphs 381

Course 2

Unit 4

Dynasties of China 409
Comparing Africa to the U.S. 446
African Trading Empires, A.D. 100–1600 451
Religion in Africa 463
European Population, A.D. 1300–1500 555

Unit 5

Important European Explorers 663
The Scientific Revolution 676
The Scientific Method 679

Diagrams

Course 1

Archaeological Dig 9
Ancient Egyptian Society 45
Inside a Pyramid 51
Athenian Homes 142
The Trojan Horse 157
The Parthenon 162
Typical Home in Early India 197
Chinese Village 233

Course 1 and 2

Roman Legionary 266
The Roman Colosseum 305
A Roman House 308
Islamic Mosque 393

Course 2

City Life in Tang China 412
The City of Djenne 464

Samurai Armor 494
Feudal Society 523
A Medieval Manor 524
A Medieval Castle 527
Tenochtitlán 586
Florence Cathedral 610
Globe Theater 625
Santa Mariá 661
The Microscope 678

Be an Active Reader

Think about your textbook as a tool that helps you learn more about the world around you. It is an example of nonfiction writing—it describes real-life events, people, ideas, and places. Here is a menu of reading strategies that will help you become a better textbook reader. As you come to passages in your textbook that you do not understand, refer to these reading strategies for help.

1 Before You Read

Set a Purpose
- Why are you reading the textbook?
- How does the subject relate to your life?
- How might you be able to use what you learn in your own life?

Preview
- Read the chapter title to find what the topic will be.
- Read the subtitles to see what you will learn about the topic.
- Skim the photos, charts, graphs, or maps. How do they support the topic?
- Look for vocabulary words that are boldfaced. How are they defined?

Draw From Your Own Background
- What have you read or heard concerning new information on the topic?
- How is the new information different from what you already know?
- How will the information that you already know help you understand the new information?

2 As You Read

Question
- What is the main idea?
- How do the photos, charts, graphs, and maps support the main idea?

Connect
- Think about people, places, and events in your own life. Are there any similarities with those in your textbook?
- Can you relate the textbook information to other areas of your life?

Predict
- Predict events or outcomes by using clues and information that you already know.
- Change your predictions as you read and gather new information.

Visualize
- Pay careful attention to details and descriptions.
- Create graphic organizers to show relationships that you find in the information.

Look for Clues As You Read

Comparison and Contrast Sentences
- Look for clue words and phrases that signal comparison, such as *similarly, just as, both, in common, also,* and *too.*
- Look for clue words and phrases that signal contrast, such as *on the other hand, in contrast to, however, different, instead of, rather than, but,* and *unlike.*

Cause-and-Effect Sentences
- Look for clue words and phrases such as *because, as a result, therefore, that is why, since, so, for this reason,* and *consequently.*

Chronological Sentences
- Look for clue words and phrases such as *after, before, first, next, last, during, finally, earlier, later, since,* and *then.*

3 After You Read

Summarize
- Describe the main idea and how the details support it.
- Use your own words to explain what you have read.

Assess
- What was the main idea?
- Did the text clearly support the main idea?
- Did you learn anything new from the material?
- Can you use this new information in other school subjects or at home?
- What other sources could you use to find more information about the topic?

Previewing Your Textbook

Follow the reading road map through the next few pages to learn about using your textbook. Knowing how your text is organized will help you discover interesting events, fascinating people, and faraway places.

Units

Your textbook is divided into units. Each unit begins with four pages of information to help you begin your study of the topics.

WHY IT'S IMPORTANT

Each unit begins with a **preview** of important events and *Why It's Important* to read about them.

TIME LINE

A time line shows you **when** the events in this unit happened. It also compares events and people from different places.

MAP

This map shows you where the events in this unit happened.

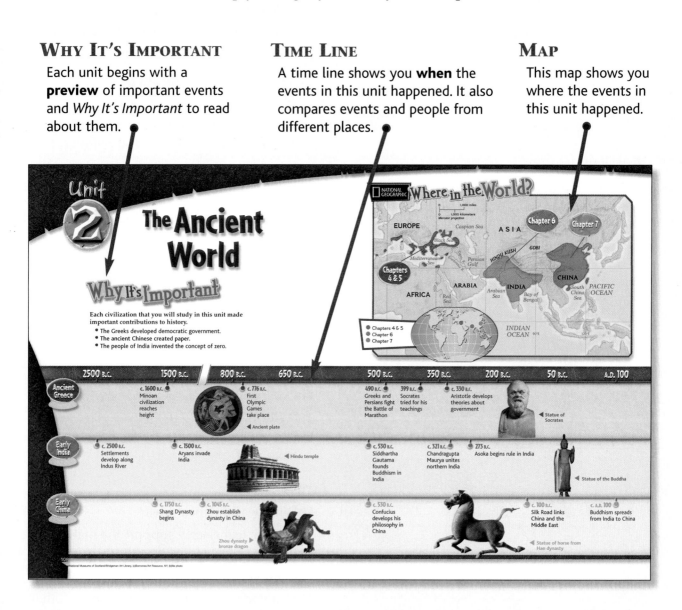

Unit 2
The Ancient World

Why It's Important

Each civilization that you will study in this unit made important contributions to history.
- The Greeks developed democratic government.
- The ancient Chinese created paper.
- The people of India invented the concept of zero.

NATIONAL GEOGRAPHIC Where in the World?

EUROPE — Caspian Sea — ASIA — Chapter 6 — Chapter 7
Black Sea — GOBI
Mediterranean Sea — Persian Gulf — HINDU KUSH — CHINA
Chapters 4 & 5 — ARABIA — INDIA — South China Sea — PACIFIC OCEAN
AFRICA — Red Sea — Arabian Sea — Bay of Bengal
INDIAN OCEAN

- Chapters 4 & 5
- Chapter 6
- Chapter 7

Ancient Greece
- c. 1600 B.C. Minoan civilization reaches height
- c. 776 B.C. First Olympic Games take place — ◀ Ancient plate
- 490 B.C. Greeks and Persians fight the Battle of Marathon
- 399 B.C. Socrates tried for his teachings
- c. 330 B.C. Aristotle develops theories about government
- ◀ Statue of Socrates

Early India
- c. 2500 B.C. Settlements develop along Indus River
- c. 1500 B.C. Aryans invade India
- ◀ Hindu temple
- c. 530 B.C. Siddhartha Gautama founds Buddhism in India
- c. 321 B.C. Chandragupta Maurya unites northern India
- 273 B.C. Asoka begins rule in India
- ◀ Statue of the Buddha

Early China
- c. 1750 B.C. Shang Dynasty begins
- c. 1045 B.C. Zhou establish dynasty in China
- Zhou dynasty ▶ bronze dragon
- c. 530 B.C. Confucius develops his philosophy in China
- c. 100 B.C. Silk Road links China and the Middle East
- c. A.D. 100 Buddhism spreads from India to China
- ◀ Statue of horse from Han dynasty

Time line: 2500 B.C. — 1500 B.C. — 800 B.C. — 650 B.C. — 500 B.C. — 350 B.C. — 200 B.C. — 50 B.C. — A.D. 100

(National Museums of Scotland/Bridgeman Art Library, (c)Borromeo/Art Resource, NY, (l)file photo)

Chapters

Each unit of *Journey Across Time: The Early Ages* is divided into chapters. Each chapter starts by giving you some background information about what you will be reading.

CHAPTER TITLE
The chapter title tells you the **main topic** you will be reading about.

CHAPTER PREVIEW
The **preview** describes what you will be reading about in this chapter.

HISTORY ONLINE
This tells you where you can go **online** for more information.

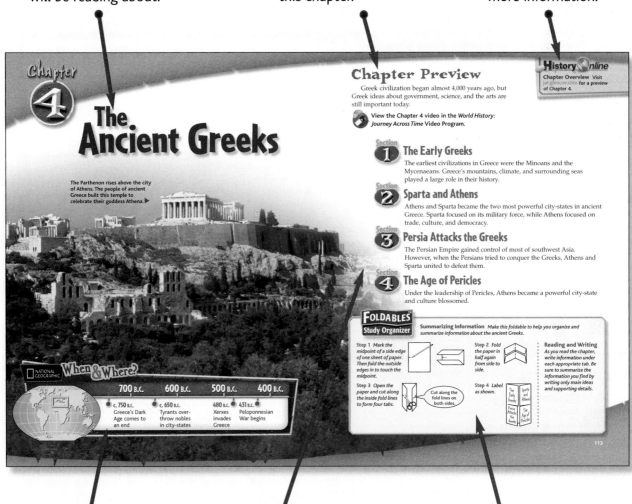

WHEN AND WHERE?
Here you can see **when** and **where** events in this chapter happened.

SUMMARIES
Summary statements give you the **main idea** in each section.

FOLDABLES
Use the *Foldables* to **take notes** as you read.

Previewing Your Textbook

Chapter Reading Skill

Because reading about Social Studies is different than reading a novel or magazine, every chapter offers help with reading skills.

READING STRATEGY
This shows you what *Reading Skill* you will be learning about—**making connections.**

PRACTICE IT!
Next comes an easy-to-follow **practice** activity.

WRITING
Writing about what you read will help you remember the event.

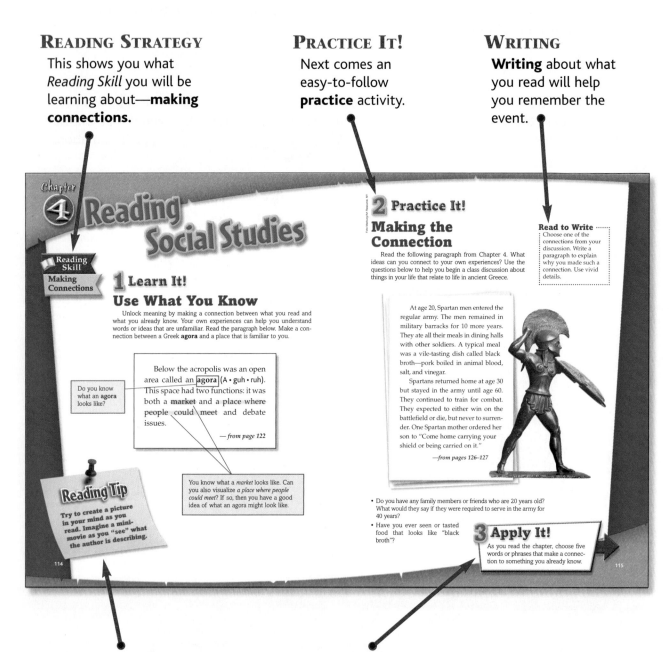

Chapter

4 Reading Social Studies

Reading Skill
Making Connections

1 Learn It!
Use What You Know

Unlock meaning by making a connection between what you read and what you already know. Your own experiences can help you understand words or ideas that are unfamiliar. Read the paragraph below. Make a connection between a Greek **agora** and a place that is familiar to you.

> Do you know what an **agora** looks like?

Below the acropolis was an open area called an agora (A • guh • ruh). This space had two functions: it was both a **market** and a place where people could meet and debate issues.

— *from page 122*

You know what a *market* looks like. Can you also visualize *a place where people could meet*? If so, then you have a good idea of what an agora might look like.

Reading Tip

Try to create a picture in your mind as you read. Imagine a mini-movie as you "see" what the author is describing.

114

2 Practice It!
Making the Connection

Read the following paragraph from Chapter 4. What ideas can you connect to your own experiences? Use the questions below to help you begin a class discussion about things in your life that relate to life in ancient Greece.

> At age 20, Spartan men entered the regular army. The men remained in military barracks for 10 more years. They ate all their meals in dining halls with other soldiers. A typical meal was a vile-tasting dish called black broth—pork boiled in animal blood, salt, and vinegar.
>
> Spartans returned home at age 30 but stayed in the army until age 60. They continued to train for combat. They expected to either win on the battlefield or die, but never to surrender. One Spartan mother ordered her son to "Come home carrying your shield or being carried on it."
>
> —*from pages 126–127*

- Do you have any family members or friends who are 20 years old? What would they say if they were required to serve in the army for 40 years?
- Have you ever seen or tasted food that looks like "black broth"?

Read to Write
Choose one of the connections from your discussion. Write a paragraph to explain why you made such a connection. Use vivid details.

3 Apply It!
As you read the chapter, choose five words or phrases that make a connection to something you already know.

115

READING TIP
This **Reading Tip** tells you more about making connections.

APPLY IT!
Here is an opportunity to **apply** what you have learned.

Previewing Your Textbook

Sections

A Section is a division, or part, of the chapter. The first page of the Section, the Section Opener, helps you set a purpose for reading.

GET READY TO READ!

Read the **connection** between what you already know and what you are about to read.

MAPS

Maps help you learn how **geography** and history are related.

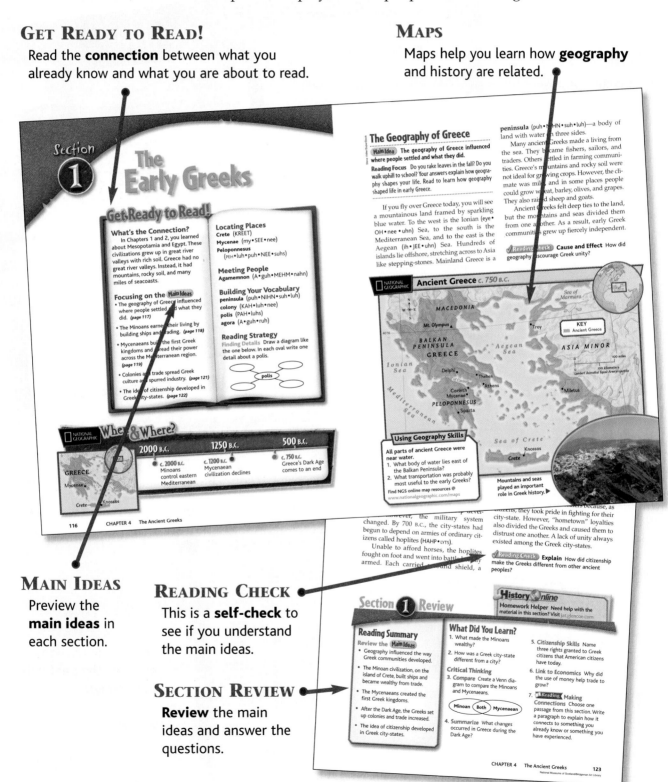

MAIN IDEAS

Preview the **main ideas** in each section.

READING CHECK

This is a **self-check** to see if you understand the main ideas.

SECTION REVIEW

Review the main ideas and answer the questions.

Previewing Your Textbook

Special Features

Look for special features that help history come alive.

YOU DECIDE . . .
Imagine you were there and could give your **opinion.**

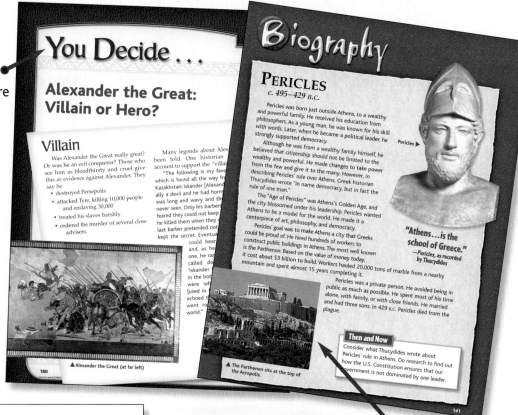

You Decide . . .

Alexander the Great: Villain or Hero?

Villain

Was Alexander the Great really great? Or was he an evil conqueror? Those who see him as bloodthirsty and cruel give this as evidence against Alexander. They say he
- destroyed Persepolis
- attacked Tyre, killing 10,000 people and enslaving 30,000
- treated his slaves harshly
- ordered the murder of several close advisers

Many legends about Alex[ander have] been told. One historian [gives an] account to support the "villain" [view].
"The following is my favo[rite legend] which is found all the way fr[om] Kazakhstan: Iskander [Alexander was] ally a devil and he had horn[s that] was long and wavy and th[ey were] never seen. Only his barbers [knew and] feared they could not keep [the secret so] he killed them when they [knew. The] last barber pretended not [to know and] kept the secret. Eventual[ly he] could bear [the secret no longer] and, as he [could not tell any] one, he ran [to a well which was] called do[wn and shouted] 'Iskander [has horns'] in the bot[tom. The words] were wh[ispered back and] echoed t[hrough the water and] went ro[und the] world."

▲ Alexander the Great (at far left)

180

Biography

PERICLES
c. 495–429 B.C.

Pericles was born just outside Athens, to a wealthy and powerful family. He received his education from philosophers. As a young man, he was known for his skill with words. Later, when he became a political leader, he strongly supported democracy.

Although he was from a wealthy family himself, he believed that citizenship should not be limited to the wealthy and powerful. He made changes to take power from the few and give it to the many. However, in describing Pericles' rule over Athens, Greek historian Thucydides wrote "In name democracy, but in fact the rule of one man."

The "Age of Pericles" was Athens's Golden Age, and the city blossomed under his leadership. Pericles wanted Athens to be a model for the world. He made it a centerpiece of art, philosophy, and democracy.

Pericles' goal was to make Athens a city that Greeks could be proud of. He hired hundreds of workers to construct public buildings in Athens. The most well known is the Parthenon. Based on the value of money today, it cost about $3 billion to build. Workers hauled 20,000 tons of marble from a nearby mountain and spent almost 15 years completing it.

Pericles was a private person. He avoided being in public as much as possible. He spent most of his time alone, with family, or with close friends. He married and had three sons. In 429 B.C. Pericles died from the plague.

◀ Pericles

"Athens...is the school of Greece."
—Pericles, as recorded by Thucydides

Then and Now
Consider what Thucydides wrote about Pericles' rule in Athens. Do research to find out how the U.S. Constitution ensures that our government is not dominated by one leader.

▲ The Parthenon sits at the top of the Acropolis.

141

BIOGRAPHY
Read more about famous **people.**

Greek Drama

Main Idea Greek drama still shapes entertainment today.

Reading Focus Think about your favorite movie. How would you describe it? Is it a tragedy? Is it a comedy? Read to find out how Greek plays still influence our entertainment.

What is **drama** (DRAH•muh)? Drama is a story told by actors who pretend to be characters in the story. In a drama, actors speak, show emotion, and imitate the actions of the characters they represent.

Today's movies, plays, and television shows are all examples of drama.

Tragedies and Comedies The Greeks performed plays in outdoor theaters as part of their religious festivals. They developed two kinds of dramas—comedies and tragedies.

In a **tragedy** (TRA•juh•dee), a person struggles to overcome difficulties but fails. As a result, the story has an unhappy ending. Early Greek tragedies presented people in a struggle against their fate. Later Greek tragedies showed how a person's character flaws caused him or her to fail.

Linking Past & Present
The Theater

THEN Tragedies and comedies were staged at a theater on the slopes of the Acropolis in Athens. The plays included music and dance. Greek actors wore costumes and held large masks. The masks told the audience who the actor was supposed to be—a king, a soldier, or a god. All the actors were men, even those playing female parts.

▲ A modern-day play

NOW Actors today include both men and women—and even children and animals. Special effects and makeup have replaced handheld masks. Music in modern theater is sometimes just as important as the actors' words. *If you watched a Greek play, what might it tell you about life in ancient Greece?*

▲ Ruins of a Greek theater

160   CHAPTER 5   Greek Civilization

The Way It Was
NATIONAL GEOGRAPHIC

Focus on Everyday Life

Women's Duties In ancient Athens, a woman's place was in the home. Her two main responsibilities were caring for the household and raising children. The Greek writer Xenophon (ZEH•nuh•fuhn) recorded a man's explanation of women's duties.

"Thus your duty will be to remain indoors and send out those servants whose work is outside, and superintend those who are to work indoors . . . and take care that the sum laid by for a year be not spent in a month. And when wool is brought to you, you must see that cloaks are made for those that want them. You must see too that the dry corn is in good condition for making food."
—Xenophon, Memorabilia and Oeconomicus

The second floor of ev[ery house held] the women's quarters. An Athenian woman lived there with her children. She was expected to keep her children well and happy. She encouraged them to learn sports and play with toys, and taught them how to interact with friends and family members. Although boys left home at age seven to attend school, girls stayed with their mothers, learning how to care for a house and children.

▲ Greek woman and servant

Connecting to the Past
1. Why do you think women and children lived on the second floor of the home?
2. Over what areas of life did an Athenian woman have authority?

CONNECTING PAST & PRESENT
See the connections between the **past** and the **present.**

Scavenger Hunt

Journey Across Time: The Early Ages contains a wealth of information. The trick is to know where to look to access all the information in the book. If you run through this scavenger hunt exercise with your teacher or parents, you will see how the textbook is organized, and how to get the most out of your reading and study time. Let's get started!

1 What civilizations are discussed in Unit 3?

2 What is the topic of Chapter 10?

3 Who is the topic of the *Biography* on page 272?

4 What *Reading Skill* will you be learning about on pages 340–341?

5 What does the *Foldables*™ *Study Organizer* on page 369 ask you to do?

6 How are the key terms in Chapter 9, Section 2, *plague* and *inflation*, highlighted in the text?

7 There are four types of Web site boxes in Chapter 11. One box previews the chapter, one suggests a Web activity, and one provides help with homework. What does the fourth box provide help with?

8 What do you find on page 365?

9 What is the topic of *The Way It Was* feature on page 389?

10 What is the topic of the map on page 269?

REFERENCE ATLAS

NATIONAL GEOGRAPHIC

World: Political	R2	South America: Physical	R15
World: Physical	R4	Europe: Political	R16
North America: Political	R6	Middle East: Physical/Political	R18
North America: Physical	R7	Africa: Political	R20
United States: Political	R8	Africa: Physical	R21
United States: Physical	R10	Asia: Political	R22
Middle America: Physical/Political	R12	Polar Regions	R24
South America: Political	R14		

ATLAS KEY

SYMBOL KEY

⌐⌐⌐ Canal	∘ Depression	⬮ Below sea level	⬮ Lava
.... Claimed boundary	+ Elevation	⬮ Dry salt lake	⬮ Sand
▦▦▦ International boundary	⊚ National capital	⬮ Lake	⌐⌐ Swamp
	• • ● Towns	⬮ Rivers	

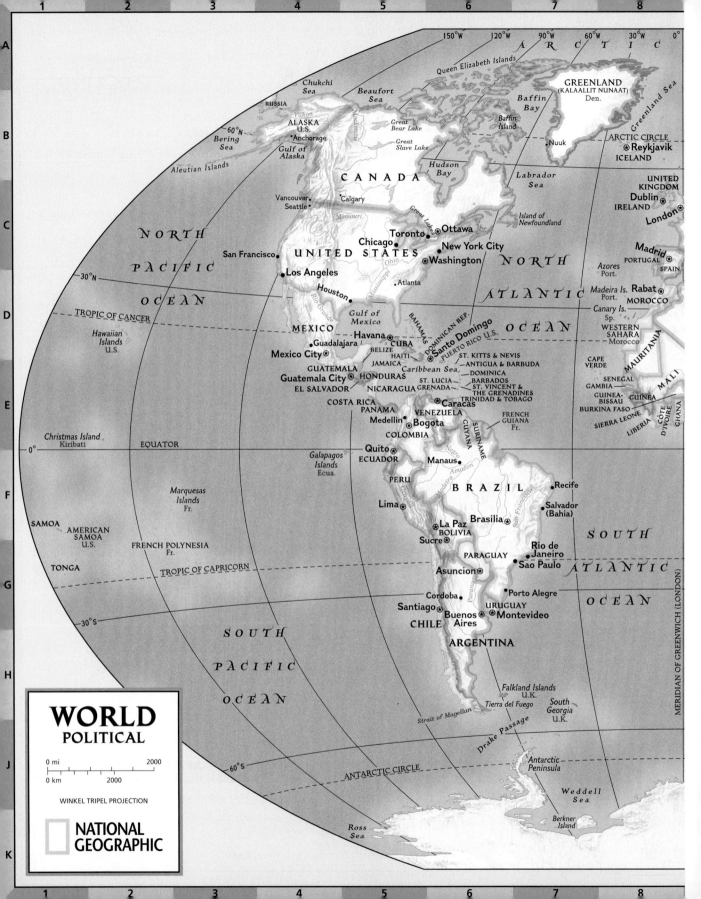

WORLD
POLITICAL

0 mi 2000

0 km 2000

WINKEL TRIPEL PROJECTION

NATIONAL GEOGRAPHIC

A R C T I C

150°W   120°W   90°W   60°W   30°W   0°

Queen Elizabeth Islands

GREENLAND
(KALAALLIT NUNAAT)
Den.

Chukchi
Sea

Beaufort
Sea

Baffin
Bay

Greenland Sea

RUSSIA

Yukon

ALASKA
U.S.

•Anchorage

60°N

Bering
Sea

Gulf of
Alaska

Mackenzie

Great
Bear Lake

Great
Slave Lake

Baffin
Island

Nuuk•

ARCTIC CIRCLE

⊛ Reykjavik
ICELAND

Aleutian Islands

CANADA

Hudson
Bay

Labrador
Sea

UNITED
KINGDOM

Dublin ⊛
IRELAND

Vancouver•
Seattle•

•Calgary

Island of
Newfoundland

London ⊛

NORTH

Missouri

Great Lakes

Toronto• •Ottawa

Madrid ⊛

PACIFIC

San Francisco•

UNITED STATES

Chicago•
Ohio

•New York City
⊛Washington

NORTH

Azores
Port.

PORTUGAL   SPAIN

30°N

Los Angeles•

Mississippi

•Atlanta

ATLANTIC

Madeira Is.
Port.

Rabat ⊛
MOROCCO

OCEAN

•Houston

Rio Grande

Gulf of
Mexico

Canary Is.
Sp.

OCEAN

WESTERN
SAHARA
Morocco

TROPIC OF CANCER

Hawaiian
Islands
U.S.

MEXICO

Havana•

•Guadalajara

Mexico City ⊛

BAHAMAS

DOMINICAN REP.

BELIZE   CUBA
HAITI•
JAMAICA

Santo Domingo
PUERTO RICO U.S.

ST. KITTS & NEVIS
ANTIGUA & BARBUDA
DOMINICA

CAPE
VERDE

MAURITANIA

MALI

GUATEMALA

Caribbean Sea

SENEGAL

Guatemala City ⊛ HONDURAS
EL SALVADOR   NICARAGUA

ST. LUCIA
BARBADOS
GRENADA   ST. VINCENT &
THE GRENADINES
TRINIDAD & TOBAGO

GAMBIA
GUINEA-
BISSAU   GUINEA

BURKINA FASO

CÔTE D'IVOIRE
GHANA

Christmas Island
Kiribati

EQUATOR

0°

COSTA RICA
PANAMA

•Medellin

⊛Caracas

VENEZUELA
⊛Bogota

GUYANA

SURINAME

FRENCH
GUIANA
Fr.

SIERRA LEONE
LIBERIA

Galapagos
Islands
Ecua.

COLOMBIA

Quito ⊛
ECUADOR

Negro

Marquesas
Islands
Fr.

PERU

Manaus•

B R A Z I L

Amazon

Madeira

•Recife

SAMOA

AMERICAN
SAMOA
U.S.

Lima ⊛

La Paz•
BOLIVIA

⊛Brasilia

San Francisco

Salvador
(Bahia)

SOUTH

FRENCH POLYNESIA
Fr.

Sucre•

TONGA

TROPIC OF CAPRICORN

PARAGUAY

Rio de
Janeiro•
•Sao Paulo

ATLANTIC

Asuncion ⊛

Parana

•Porto Alegre

OCEAN

SOUTH

30°S

Cordoba•

URUGUAY

PACIFIC

Santiago•
CHILE

⊛Buenos
Aires

⊛Montevideo

OCEAN

ARGENTINA

Falkland Islands
U.K.

MERIDIAN OF GREENWICH (LONDON)

Tierra del Fuego

South
Georgia
U.K.

Strait of Magellan

Drake Passage

60°S

ANTARCTIC CIRCLE

Antarctic
Peninsula

Ross
Sea

Weddell
Sea

Berkner
Island

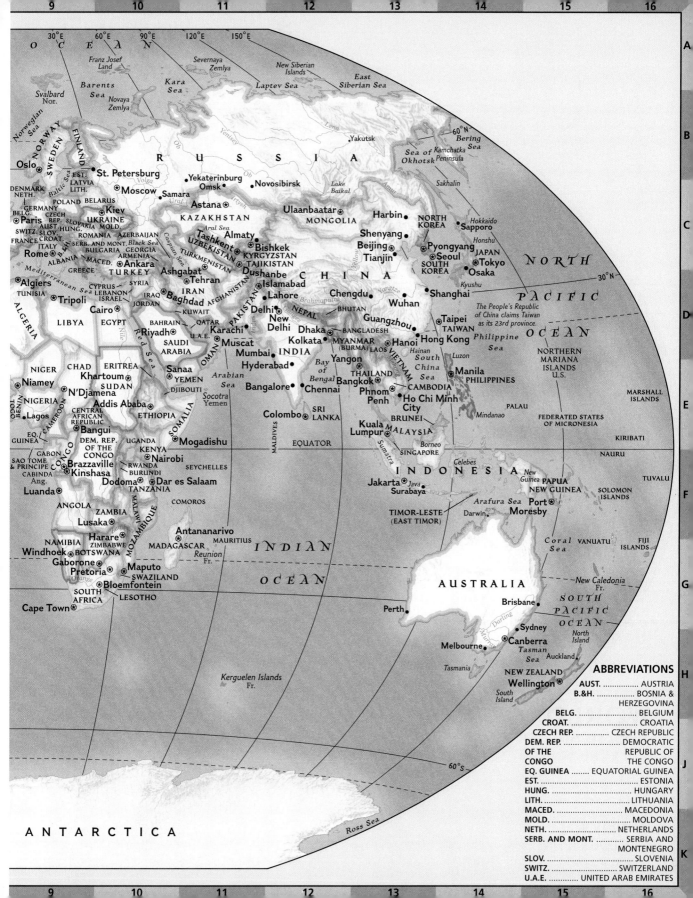

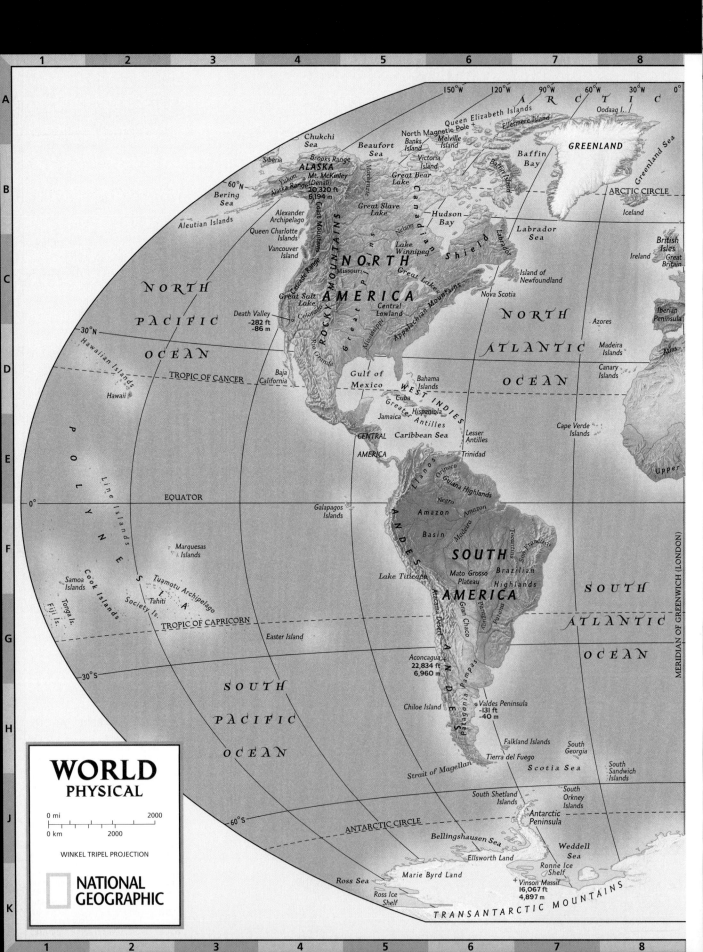

WORLD
PHYSICAL

0 mi   2000

0 km   2000

WINKEL TRIPEL PROJECTION

NATIONAL GEOGRAPHIC

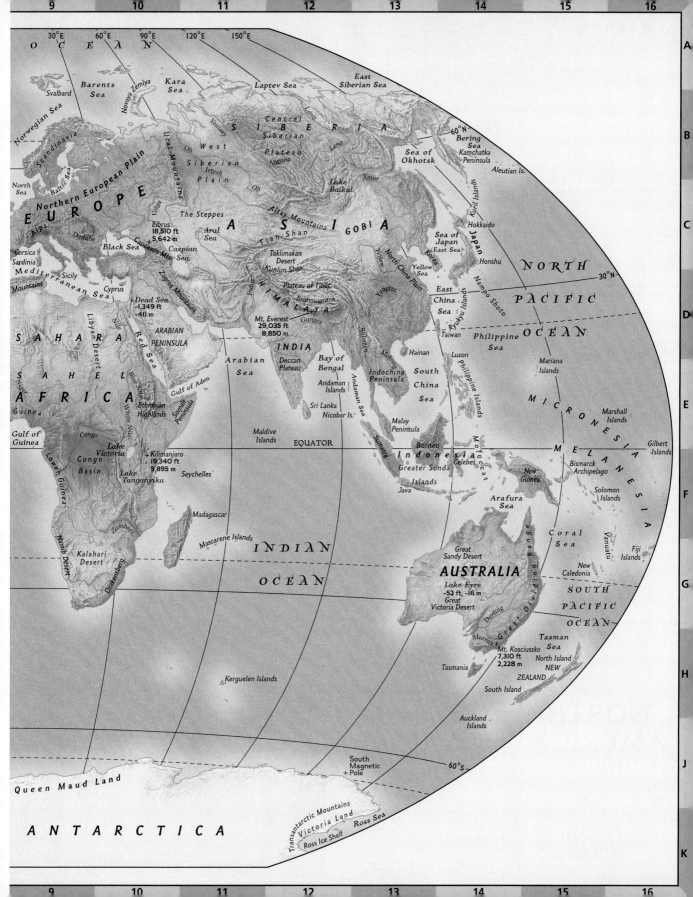

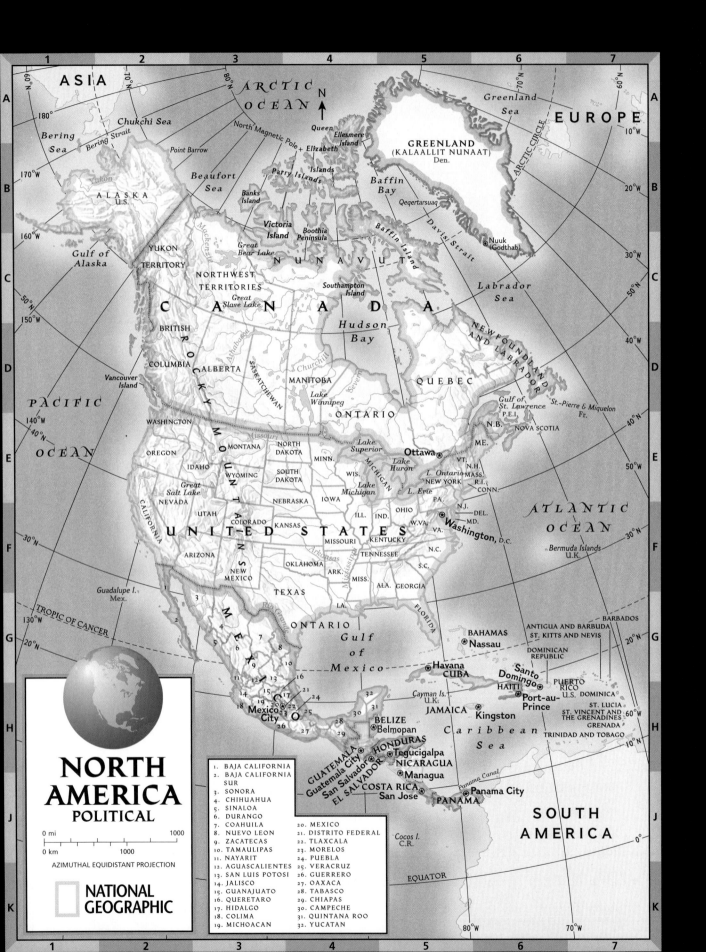

NORTH AMERICA
POLITICAL

0 mi   1000

0 km   1000

AZIMUTHAL EQUIDISTANT PROJECTION

NATIONAL GEOGRAPHIC

1. BAJA CALIFORNIA	
2. BAJA CALIFORNIA SUR	
3. SONORA	
4. CHIHUAHUA	
5. SINALOA	
6. DURANGO	
7. COAHUILA	
8. NUEVO LEON	
9. ZACATECAS	
10. TAMAULIPAS	
11. NAYARIT	
12. AGUASCALIENTES	
13. SAN LUIS POTOSI	
14. JALISCO	
15. GUANAJUATO	
16. QUERETARO	
17. HIDALGO	
18. COLIMA	
19. MICHOACAN	
20. MEXICO	
21. DISTRITO FEDERAL	
22. TLAXCALA	
23. MORELOS	
24. PUEBLA	
25. VERACRUZ	
26. GUERRERO	
27. OAXACA	
28. TABASCO	
29. CHIAPAS	
30. CAMPECHE	
31. QUINTANA ROO	
32. YUCATAN	

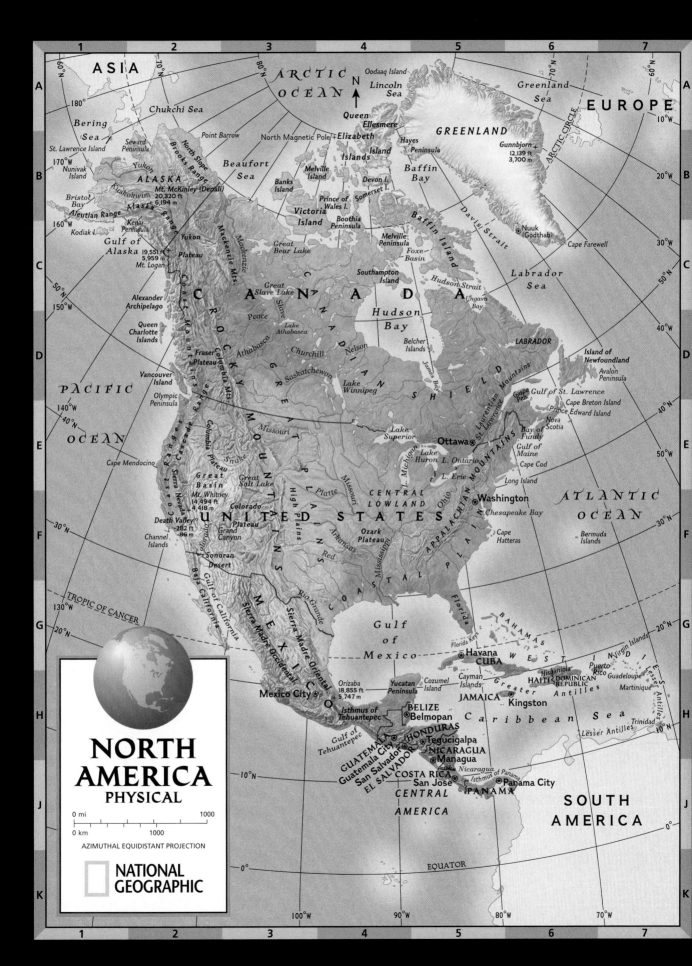

NORTH AMERICA
PHYSICAL

0 mi 1000
0 km 1000

AZIMUTHAL EQUIDISTANT PROJECTION

NATIONAL GEOGRAPHIC

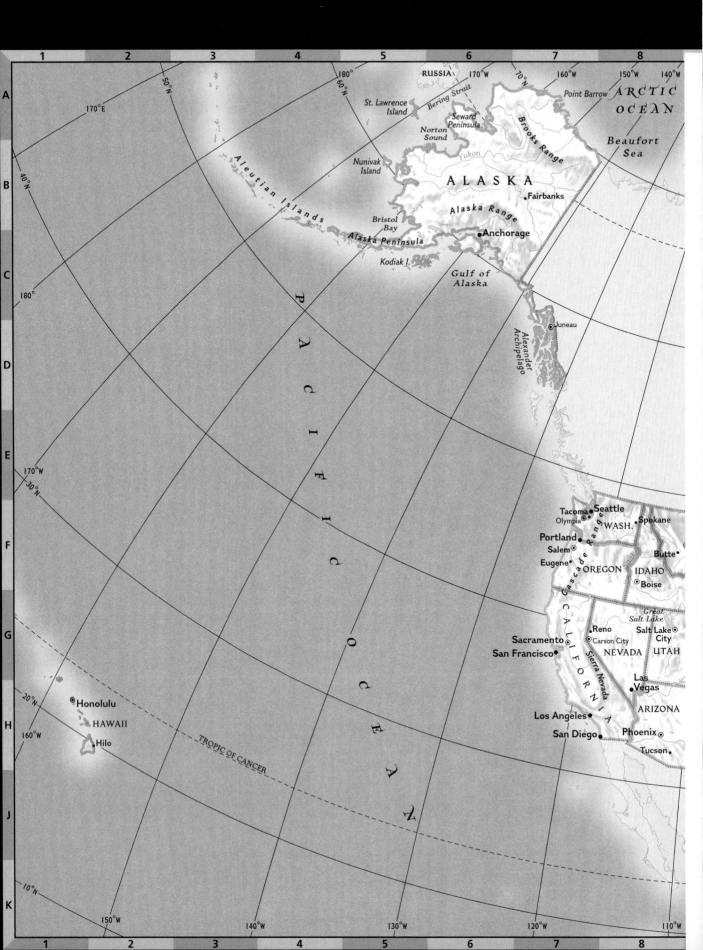

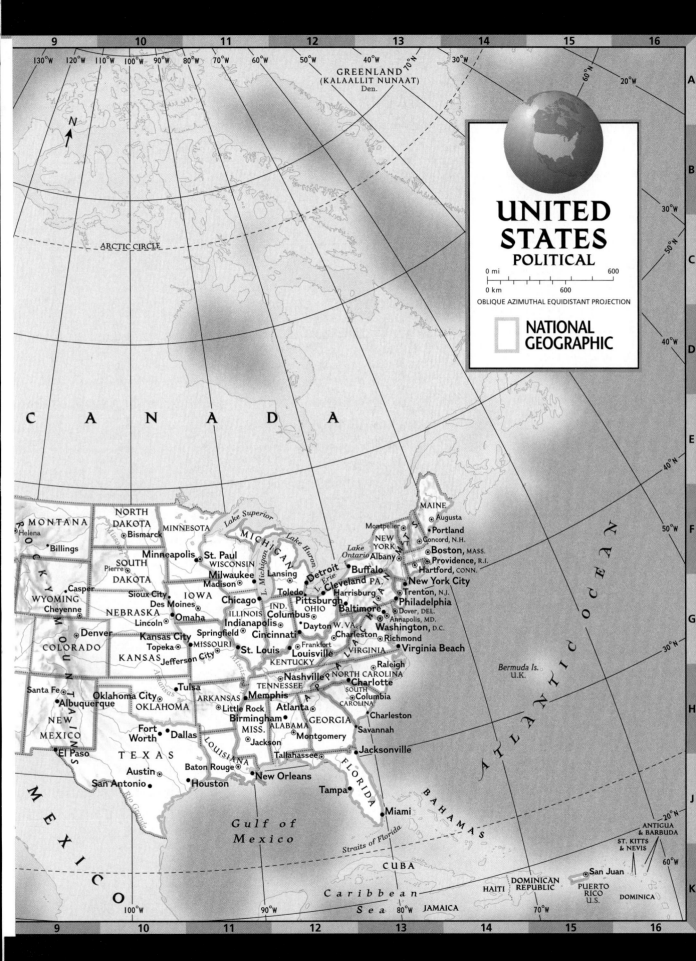

UNITED STATES
POLITICAL

0 mi   600

0 km   600

OBLIQUE AZIMUTHAL EQUIDISTANT PROJECTION

NATIONAL GEOGRAPHIC

GREENLAND
(KALAALLIT NUNAAT)
Den.

ARCTIC CIRCLE

C A N A D A

MONTANA
Helena
Billings

NORTH DAKOTA
Bismarck

MINNESOTA

Lake Superior

MICHIGAN

Lake Huron

MAINE
Augusta

Montpelier
Portland
Concord, N.H.

NEW YORK
VT.
Albany
Boston, MASS.
Providence, R.I.
Hartford, CONN.

SOUTH DAKOTA
Pierre

Minneapolis
St. Paul
WISCONSIN
Milwaukee
Madison

Lansing
L. Michigan
Detroit
L. Erie
Cleveland
Buffalo
PA.
New York City

WYOMING
Casper
Cheyenne

Sioux City
IOWA
Des Moines

Chicago
ILLINOIS
IND.
Toledo
Columbus
OHIO
Pittsburgh
Harrisburg
Trenton, N.J.
Philadelphia

NEBRASKA
Lincoln
Omaha

Indianapolis
Springfield
Cincinnati
Dayton W. VA.
Baltimore
Dover, DEL.
Annapolis, MD.
Washington, D.C.

Denver
COLORADO

Kansas City
Topeka
MISSOURI
St. Louis
Jefferson City
KANSAS

Frankfort
Louisville
KENTUCKY
Charleston
VIRGINIA
Richmond
Virginia Beach

Santa Fe
Albuquerque
NEW MEXICO
El Paso

Oklahoma City
OKLAHOMA
ARKANSAS
Tulsa
Little Rock

Nashville
TENNESSEE
Memphis

Raleigh
NORTH CAROLINA
Charlotte
SOUTH CAROLINA
Columbia

Bermuda Is.
U.K.

Fort Worth
Dallas
MISS.
ALABAMA
Birmingham
Atlanta
GEORGIA
Jackson
Montgomery
Charleston
Savannah

TEXAS
Austin
San Antonio
LOUISIANA
Baton Rouge
New Orleans
Houston
Tallahassee
Jacksonville
FLORIDA

M E X I C O
Rio Grande

Gulf of Mexico

Tampa
Miami

BAHAMAS

Straits of Florida

CUBA

Caribbean Sea

JAMAICA

HAITI
DOMINICAN REPUBLIC

San Juan
PUERTO RICO
U.S.

ANTIGUA & BARBUDA
ST. KITTS & NEVIS

DOMINICA

A T L A N T I C   O C E A N

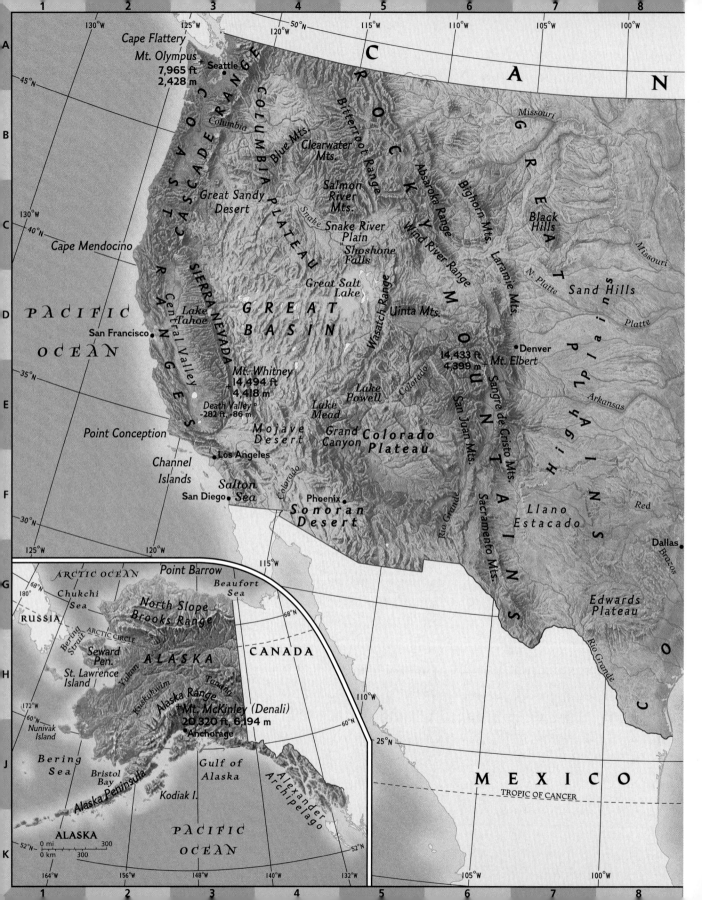

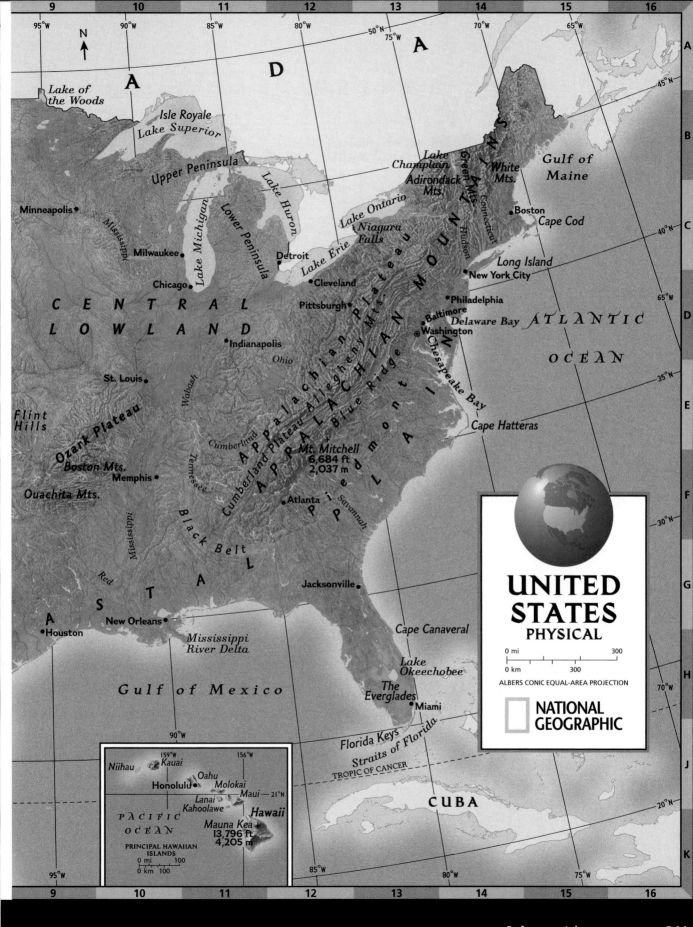

UNITED STATES

STATES PHYSICAL

0 mi   300

0 km   300

ALBERS CONIC EQUAL-AREA PROJECTION

NATIONAL GEOGRAPHIC

Lake of the Woods

Isle Royale
Lake Superior

Upper Peninsula

Minneapolis

Mississippi

Milwaukee

Chicago

Lake Michigan

Lower Peninsula

Lake Huron

Detroit

Lake Erie

Cleveland

CENTRAL

LOWLAND

Indianapolis

Ohio

Pittsburgh

St. Louis

Wabash

Flint Hills

Ozark Plateau

Boston Mts.

Memphis

Ouachita Mts.

Tennessee

Cumberland

Appalachian Plateau

Cumberland Plateau

Allegheny Mts.

Blue Ridge

APPALACHIAN MOUNTAINS

Mt. Mitchell
6,684 ft
2,037 m

Black Belt

Atlanta

Piedmont

Savannah

COASTAL

Mississippi

Red

New Orleans

Houston

PLAIN

Jacksonville

Mississippi
River Delta

Gulf of Mexico

Lake Champlain

Adirondack Mts.

Green Mts.

White Mts.

Gulf of Maine

Lake Ontario

Niagara Falls

Connecticut

Hudson

Boston

Cape Cod

Long Island

New York City

Philadelphia

Baltimore

Delaware Bay

Washington

Chesapeake Bay

ATLANTIC

OCEAN

Cape Hatteras

Cape Canaveral

Lake Okeechobee

The Everglades

Miami

Florida Keys

Straits of Florida

TROPIC OF CANCER

CUBA

CANADA

Niihau

Kauai

Oahu

Honolulu

Molokai

Lanai

Kahoolawe

Maui

Hawaii

PACIFIC OCEAN

Mauna Kea
13,796 ft
4,205 m

PRINCIPAL HAWAIIAN ISLANDS

0 mi   100

0 km   100

Map grid columns: 1 2 3 4 5 6 7 8

Map grid rows: A B C D E F G H J K

UNITED STATES

N

Tijuana
Mexicali
30°N
BAJA
CALIFORNIA
Sonoran
Desert
SONORA
Ciudad
Juarez
Gulf of California
Baja California
Sierra Madre Occidental
Chihuahua
CHIHUAHUA
Rio Grande
COAHUILA
Nuevo
Laredo
BAJA
CALIFORNIA
SUR
DURANGO
SINALOA
M E X
Monterrey
NUEVO
LEON
Matamoros
Gulf of Mexico
La Paz
False Cape
Mazatlan
ZACATECAS
SAN
LUIS
POTOSI
TAMAULIPAS
Sierra Madre Oriental
Ciudad Madero
Tampico
20°N
NAYARIT
AGUASCALIENTES
Guadalajara
JALISCO
San Luis
Potosi
Leon
C
QUERETARO
VERACRUZ
TLAXCALA
Merida
YUCATAN
Yucatan
Peninsula
Coz
Isla
QUINTANA ROO
Revillagigedo Islands
Mex.
GUANAJUATO
COLIMA
MICHOACAN
Mexico City
Popocatepetl
17,802 ft
5,426 m
PUEBLA
O
Orizaba
18,855 ft
5,747 m
Bay of Campeche
CAMPECHE
DISTRITO FEDERAL
MEXICO
HIDALGO
Sierra Madre del Sur
TABASCO
Veracruz
Isthmus of
Tehuantepec
Belize
City
Belmopan
BELIZE
Gulf of
Honduras
MORELOS
Acapulco
GUERRERO
OAXACA
CHIAPAS
Sierra Madre
Gulf of
Tehuantepec
GUATEMALA
Guatemala City
EL SALVADOR
San Salvador
Tegucigalpa
HON
Leon
CENTRAL
AMERICA

MIDDLE
AMERICA
PHYSICAL/POLITICAL

0 mi   400
0 km   400

AZIMUTHAL EQUIDISTANT PROJECTION

NATIONAL
GEOGRAPHIC

PACIFIC

OCEAN

Cocos Island
C.R.

10°N

0°

110°W   100°W   90°W

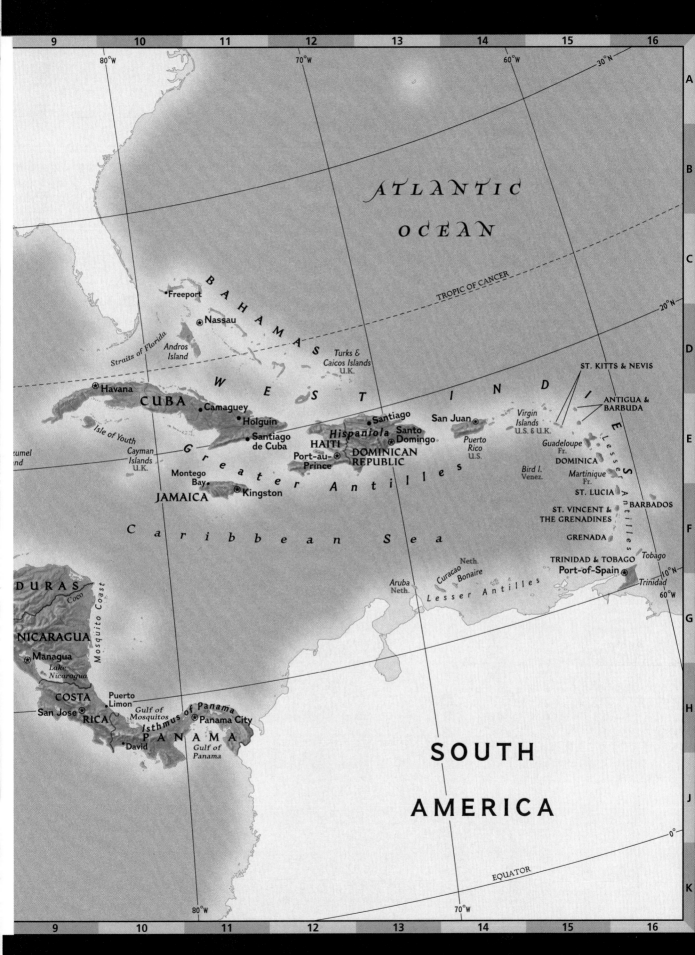

ATLANTIC

OCEAN

TROPIC OF CANCER

30°N

20°N

BAHAMAS

•Freeport

⊛ Nassau

Straits of Florida

Andros
Island

Turks &
Caicos Islands
U.K.

ST. KITTS & NEVIS

W   *E*   *S*   *T*   *I*   *N*   *D*   *I*   *E*

⊛ Havana

CUBA

•Camaguey

•Holguin

•Santiago
de Cuba

Santiago•

Hispaniola

San Juan

Virgin
Islands
U.S. & U.K.

ANTIGUA &
BARBUDA

Isle of Youth

Cayman
Islands
U.K.

*Cumel
nd*

HAITI

Santo
Domingo

*Puerto
Rico
U.S.*

Guadeloupe
Fr.

DOMINICA

Port-au-
Prince

**DOMINICAN
REPUBLIC**

Bird I.
Venez.

*Martinique
Fr.*

Greater

Montego
Bay•

JAMAICA

⊛ Kingston

Antilles

ST. LUCIA

ST. VINCENT &
THE GRENADINES

BARBADOS

C   a   r   i   b   b   e   a   n   S   e   a

GRENADA

Neth.
Curaçao
Bonaire

*Aruba
Neth.*

TRINIDAD & TOBAGO
Port-of-Spain ⊛

Tobago

Trinidad

10°N
60°W

Lesser Antilles

DURAS

Mosquito Coast

Coco

NICARAGUA

⊛ Managua

*Lake
Nicaragua*

COSTA

Puerto
Limon

*Gulf of
Mosquitos*

Isthmus of Panama

⊛ Panama City

San Jose ⊛

RICA

PANAMA

*Gulf of
Panama*

•David

SOUTH

AMERICA

0°

EQUATOR

80°W

70°W

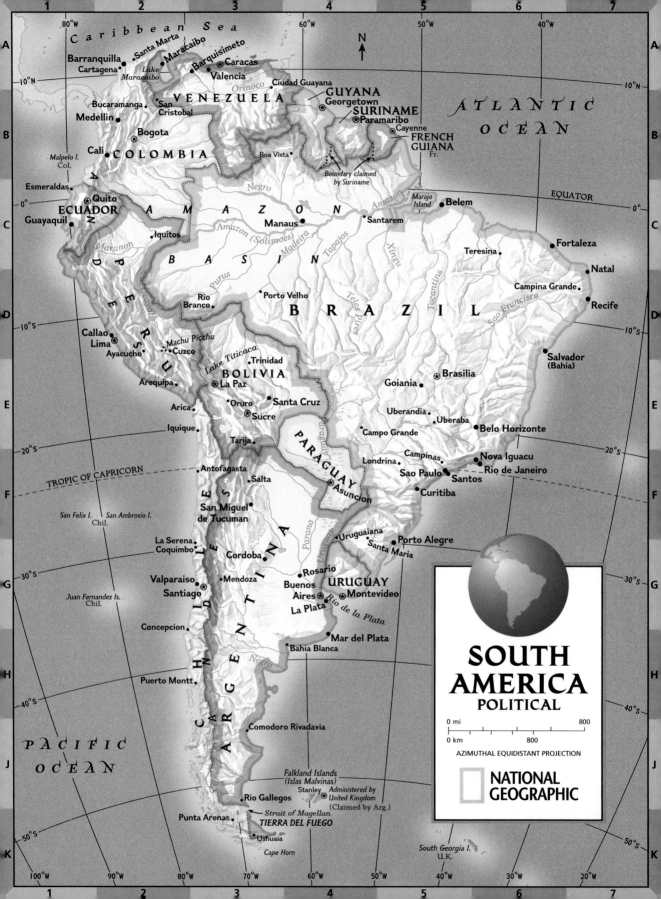

SOUTH AMERICA POLITICAL

Caribbean Sea

80°W

A
Santa Marta
Barranquilla
Cartagena
Maracaibo
Barquisimeto
Caracas
Valencia
10°N
Lake Maracaibo
Ciudad Guayana
GUYANA
Georgetown
SURINAME
Paramaribo
Cayenne
FRENCH GUIANA
Fr.

B
Bucaramanga
San Cristobal
VENEZUELA
Medellin
Bogota
Cali
COLOMBIA
Boa Vista
Boundary claimed by Suriname

ATLANTIC OCEAN

Malpelo I. Col.
Esmeraldas
Quito
ECUADOR
Guayaquil
Negro
Amazon
EQUATOR
0°
Marajo Island
Belem

C
Iquitos
Manaus
Santarem
Maranon
Amazon (Solimoes)
Madeira
Tapajos
Xingu
Teresina
Fortaleza
Natal
Campina Grande
Recife

D
Purus
Rio Branco
Porto Velho
BRAZIL
Teles Pires
Tocantins
Sao Francisco
10°S
Salvador (Bahia)

E
Callao
Lima
Ayacucho
Cuzco
Machu Picchu
Lake Titicaca
Trinidad
BOLIVIA
La Paz
Arequipa
Oruro
Sucre
Santa Cruz
Goiania
Brasilia
Uberandia
Uberaba
Belo Horizonte
Arica
Iquique
Tarija
PARAGUAY
Campo Grande
Campinas
Londrina
Nova Iguacu
Sao Paulo
Rio de Janeiro
Santos
Curitiba
20°S

F
TROPIC OF CAPRICORN
Antofagasta
Salta
Asuncion
San Felix I.
San Ambrosio I. Chil.
San Miguel de Tucuman
Parana
Uruguaiana
Porto Alegre
Santa Maria

G
La Serena
Coquimbo
Cordoba
Mendoza
Rosario
Buenos Aires
URUGUAY
Montevideo
La Plata
Rio de la Plata
30°S
Valparaiso
Santiago
Juan Fernandez Is. Chil.
Concepcion
Mar del Plata
Bahia Blanca

H
Puerto Montt
ARGENTINA
Negro
40°S

PACIFIC OCEAN

J
Comodoro Rivadavia
Falkland Islands (Islas Malvinas)
Stanley
Administered by United Kingdom (Claimed by Arg.)

K
Rio Gallegos
Strait of Magellan
TIERRA DEL FUEGO
Punta Arenas
Ushuaia
Cape Horn
South Georgia I. U.K.
50°S

SCALE:
0 mi — 800
0 km — 800
AZIMUTHAL EQUIDISTANT PROJECTION

NATIONAL GEOGRAPHIC

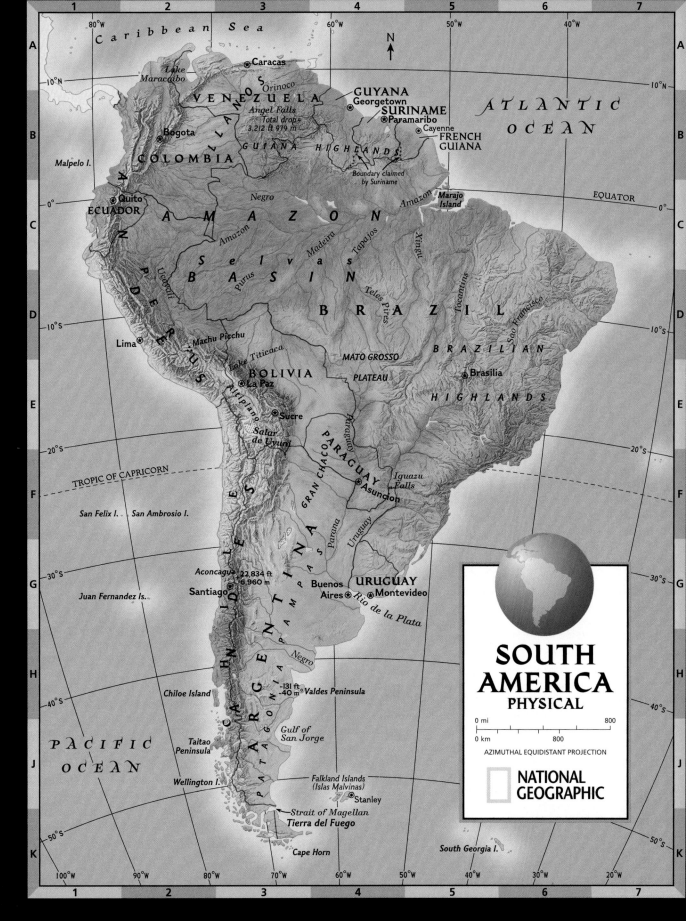

Caribbean Sea

80°W

10°N

Lake
Maracaibo

Orinoco

Caracas

60°W

N

GUYANA
Georgetown

SURINAME
Paramaribo

ATLANTIC

50°W

40°W

OCEAN

10°N

VENEZUELA

Angel Falls
Total drop=
3,212 ft 979 m

GUIANA HIGHLANDS

Cayenne
FRENCH
GUIANA

B

Malpelo I.

COLOMBIA

Boundary claimed
by Suriname

EQUATOR

0°

Quito
ECUADOR

Negro

A M A Z O N

Amazon

Marajo
Island

0°

C

Amazon

Madeira

Tapajos

Xingu

S e l v a s

B A S I N

Purus

Teles
Pires

Tocantins

Sao Francisco

D

10°S

Ucayali

PERU

Lima

Machu Picchu

Lake Titicaca

B R A Z I L

BRAZILIAN

10°S

MATO GROSSO
PLATEAU

BOLIVIA
La Paz

Sucre

Altiplano

Salar
de Uyuni

Paraguay

PARAGUAY

GRAN CHACO

Asuncion

Iguazu
Falls

Brasilia

HIGHLANDS

E

20°S

TROPIC OF CAPRICORN

San Felix I.   San Ambrosio I.

Parana

Uruguay

20°S

F

A N D E S

G

30°S

Aconcagua 22,834 ft
6,960 m

Juan Fernandez Is.

Santiago

P A M P A S

Buenos
Aires

URUGUAY
Montevideo

Rio de la Plata

30°S

H

40°S

Chiloe Island

Negro

-131 ft
-40 m Valdes Peninsula

ARGENTINA

PATAGONIA

40°S

J

PACIFIC

Taitao
Peninsula

Gulf of
San Jorge

OCEAN

Wellington I.

Falkland Islands
(Islas Malvinas)

Stanley

J

Strait of Magellan
Tierra del Fuego

50°S

K

Cape Horn

South Georgia I.

50°S

K

100°W   90°W   80°W   70°W   60°W   50°W   40°W   30°W   20°W

SOUTH
AMERICA
PHYSICAL

0 mi   800

0 km   800

AZIMUTHAL EQUIDISTANT PROJECTION

NATIONAL
GEOGRAPHIC

EUROPE
POLITICAL

0 mi 400
0 km 400

AZIMUTHAL EQUIDISTANT PROJECTION

NATIONAL GEOGRAPHIC

ICELAND
Akureyri
Reykjavik

Faroe Islands
Den.
Torshavn

Rockall
U.K.

Shetland
Islands
Lerwick

ARCTIC CIRCLE

Norwegian Sea

NORWAY
Tromso

Are
Trondheim
Alesund
Bergen
Stavanger
Oslo
Uppsala
Stockholm
Goteborg
Gotland
Sundsvall

MERIDIAN OF GREENWICH (LONDON)

Isle of Lewis
Orkney Islands
Inverness

UNITED
SCOTLAND
Glasgow
Edinburgh
Aberdeen
NORTHERN
IRELAND
Belfast

IRELAND
Dublin
Cork

Irish
Sea

KINGDOM
WALES
Cardiff
ENGLAND
Birmingham

Liverpool
Manchester

North
Sea

Skagerrak

DENMARK
Copenhagen
Arhus
Malmo
Kiel
Hamburg

Baltic

Gdansk
Bydgoszcz

Celtic
Sea
Land's End

London
Southampton

The
Hague
NETH.
Amsterdam

Berlin

GERMANY

POLAND
Lodz

ATLANTIC
OCEAN

English Channel
Brest
Le Havre

Rennes
Paris

Brussels
BELGIUM
LUX.

Bonn
Frankfurt

Rhine

Wroclaw
Prague
CZECH REP.

Oder

Nantes

La Rochelle

FRANCE

Strasbourg

Munich

Bratislava
SLOVAKIA
Vienna

Bay of
Biscay

Limoges
Bordeaux

Zurich
Bern
SWITZERLAND

LIECH.
ALPS
AUSTRIA

Budapest
HUNGARY

A Coruna
Vigo

Donostia-
San Sebastian

Toulouse

Geneva
Lyon

Turin
Milan

SLOVENIA
Ljubljana
Venice
Zagreb
CROATIA

20°W
40°N

Porto
Coimbra

PORTUGAL

Bilbao

Pyrenees

MONACO
Marseille
Nice

Genoa
SAN
MARINO

Adriatic Sea

BOSNIA &
HERZEGOVINA
Sarajevo

Valladolid
ANDORRA
Zaragoza

ITALY

MONTENEGRO

Lisbon

Madrid
SPAIN

Barcelona

Corsica
Fr.

VATICAN
CITY
Rome

Tirana
ALBANIA

Cape
St. Vincent

Cordoba
Seville
Cadiz
GIBRALTAR
U.K.
Malaga

Valencia

Murcia
Cartagena

Palma

Balearic
Islands
Sp.

Sardinia
It.

Naples

Cagliari

Tyrrhenian
Sea

Ionian
Sea

Strait of Gibraltar

Mediterranean

Palermo
Sicily
Messina
Catania

Valletta
MALTA

AFRICA

60°N
40°W
30°W
30°W
50°N

40°N

30°N
10°W
0°
10°E

30°W
20°W
10°W
70°N
0°
10°E

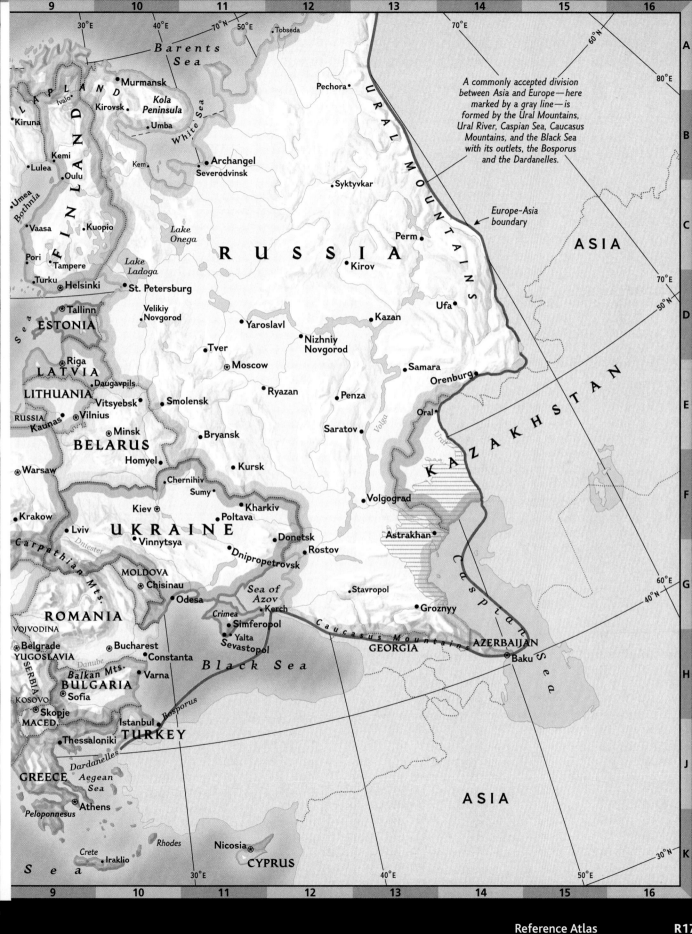

A commonly accepted division between Asia and Europe—here marked by a gray line—is formed by the Ural Mountains, Ural River, Caspian Sea, Caucasus Mountains, and the Black Sea with its outlets, the Bosporus and the Dardanelles.

Barents Sea

• Tobseda
• Pechora
• Murmansk
Kola Peninsula
• Kirovsk
White Sea
• Umba
• Kem
• Kiruna
• Ivalo
LAPLAND
FINLAND
• Kemi
• Lulea
• Oulu
• Umea
Bothnia
• Vaasa
• Kuopio
• Pori
• Tampere
Lake Onega
• Turku
• Helsinki
• St. Petersburg
⊛ Tallinn
ESTONIA
Sea
⊛ Riga
LATVIA
• Daugavpils
LITHUANIA
• Vitsyebsk
RUSSIA
• Kaunas
⊛ Vilnius
⊛ Minsk
BELARUS
• Smolensk
⊛ Warsaw
• Homyel
• Chernihiv
• Sumy
• Krakow
• Lviv
Dniester
⊛ Kiev
UKRAINE
• Vinnytsya
Carpathian Mts.
MOLDOVA
⊛ Chisinau
• Odesa
ROMANIA
VOJVODINA
⊛ Belgrade
• Bucharest
YUGOSLAVIA
• Constanta
SERBIA
Danube
• Varna
Balkan Mts.
BULGARIA
KOSOVO
⊛ Sofia
⊛ Skopje
MACED.
• Istanbul
Bosporus
• Thessaloniki
TURKEY
GREECE
Dardanelles
Aegean Sea
• Athens
Peloponnesus
Sea
Crete
• Iraklio
Rhodes
• Nicosia ⊛
CYPRUS

• Archangel
• Severodvinsk
• Syktyvkar
RUSSIA
Lake Ladoga
• Velikiy Novgorod
• Perm
• Kirov
• Yaroslavl
• Tver
• Ufa
• Nizhniy Novgorod
• Moscow
• Kazan
• Ryazan
• Samara
• Bryansk
• Orenburg
• Penza
• Kharkiv
• Kursk
• Saratov
Volga
• Oral
• Poltava
• Dnipropetrovsk
• Donetsk
• Rostov
• Volgograd
Europe-Asia boundary
ASIA
URAL MOUNTAINS
KAZAKHSTAN
Ural
• Astrakhan
• Stavropol
Sea of Azov
Crimea
• Kerch
• Simferopol
• Yalta
• Sevastopol
Caucasus Mountains
• Groznyy
GEORGIA
AZERBAIJAN
⊛ Baku
Caspian Sea
Black Sea

ASIA

EUROPE

Black Sea

Sea of Marmara

●Istanbul

ANATOLIA

⚝ Ankara

TURKEY

●Tunis

TUNISIA

Taurus Mountains

● Aleppo

CYPRUS

SYRIA

LEBANON—

Beirut ⚝ Damascus

⚝Tripoli

ISRAEL

Syrian Desert

Mediterranean Sea

Jerusalem

●Alexandria

⚝ Cairo

⚝ Amman

El Giza

JORDAN

LIBYA

Sinai Pen.

See inset below

EGYPT

Nile R.

Hejaz

Eastern Mediterranean Area

30°E

TURKEY

N

● Aleppo

CYPRUS

SYRIA

Mediterranean Sea

LEBANON

Beirut ⚝

⚝ Damascus

Sea of Galilee

Golan Heights

Jordan River

Tel Aviv–Yafo ●

West Bank

Suez Canal

Jerusalem ⚝

⚝ Amman

Gaza Strip

Dead Sea

El Giza ● ⚝ Cairo

ISRAEL

JORDAN

EGYPT

SAUDI ARABIA

30°N

Nile River

Gulf of Suez

Gulf of Aqaba

0 mi   100

0 km   100

Red Sea

SAHARA

Aswan High Dam

Boundary claimed by Sudan

Red Sea

SUDAN

AFRICA

⚝ Khartoum

30°E

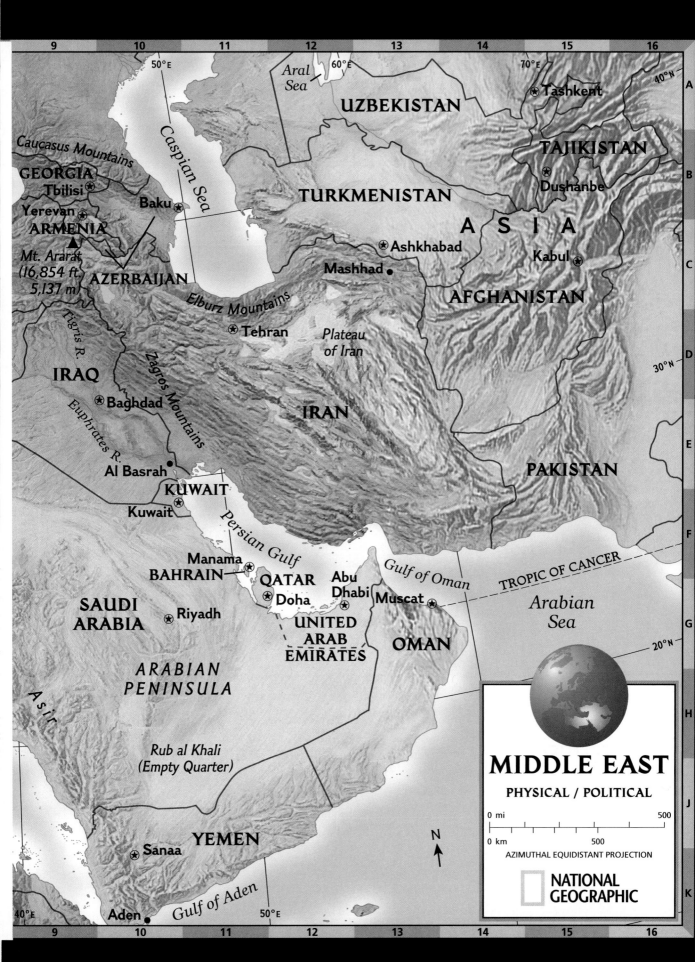

9 10 11 12 13 14 15 16

50°E Aral Sea 60°E 70°E 40°N A

UZBEKISTAN Tashkent

Caucasus Mountains Caspian Sea TAJIKISTAN B

GEORGIA TURKMENISTAN Dushanbe

Tbilisi Baku A S I A

Yerevan Ashkhabad Kabul C

ARMENIA Mashhad

Mt. Ararat (16,854 ft.) 5,137 m) AZERBAIJAN AFGHANISTAN

Elburz Mountains

Tigris R. Tehran Plateau of Iran D 30°N

Zagros Mountains

IRAQ IRAN PAKISTAN E

Euphrates R. Baghdad

Al Basrah KUWAIT F

Kuwait Persian Gulf Gulf of Oman TROPIC OF CANCER

Manama Arabian Sea 20°N G

BAHRAIN QATAR Abu Dhabi Muscat

SAUDI ARABIA Riyadh Doha

UNITED ARAB EMIRATES OMAN

ARABIAN PENINSULA

Asir H

Rub al Khali (Empty Quarter)

MIDDLE EAST

PHYSICAL / POLITICAL

J

0 mi 500

0 km 500

YEMEN N

Sanaa AZIMUTHAL EQUIDISTANT PROJECTION

NATIONAL GEOGRAPHIC

Aden Gulf of Aden K

40°E 50°E

9 10 11 12 13 14 15 16

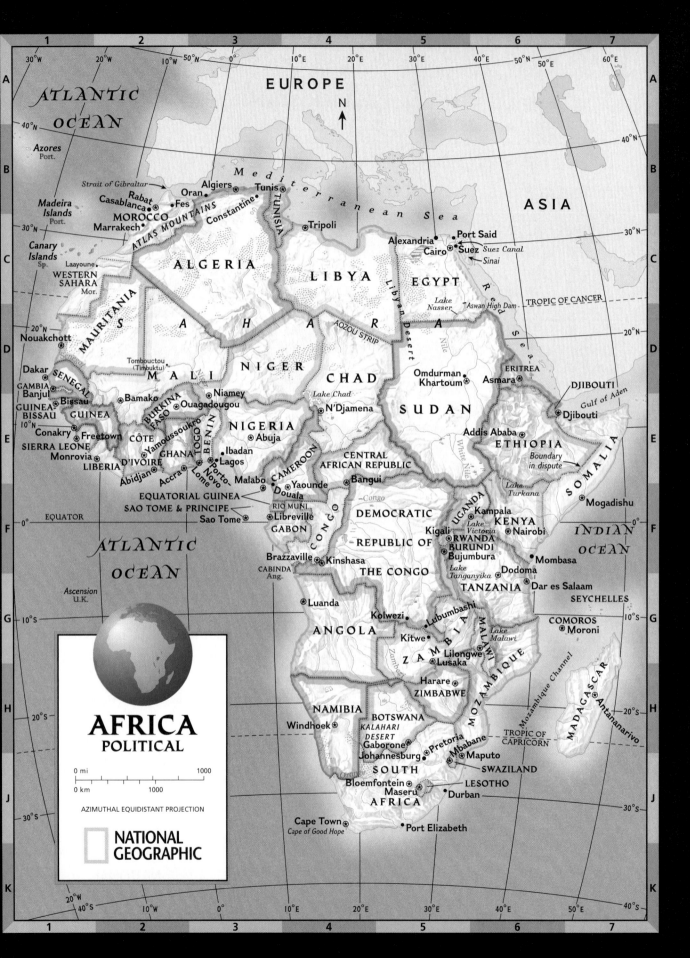

AFRICA
POLITICAL

0 mi 1000
0 km 1000

AZIMUTHAL EQUIDISTANT PROJECTION

NATIONAL GEOGRAPHIC

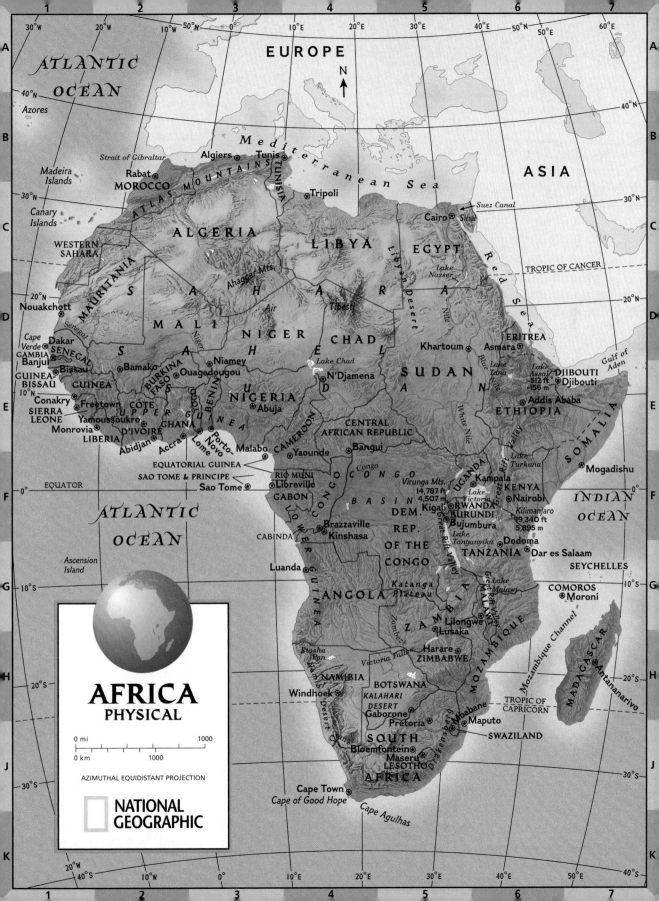

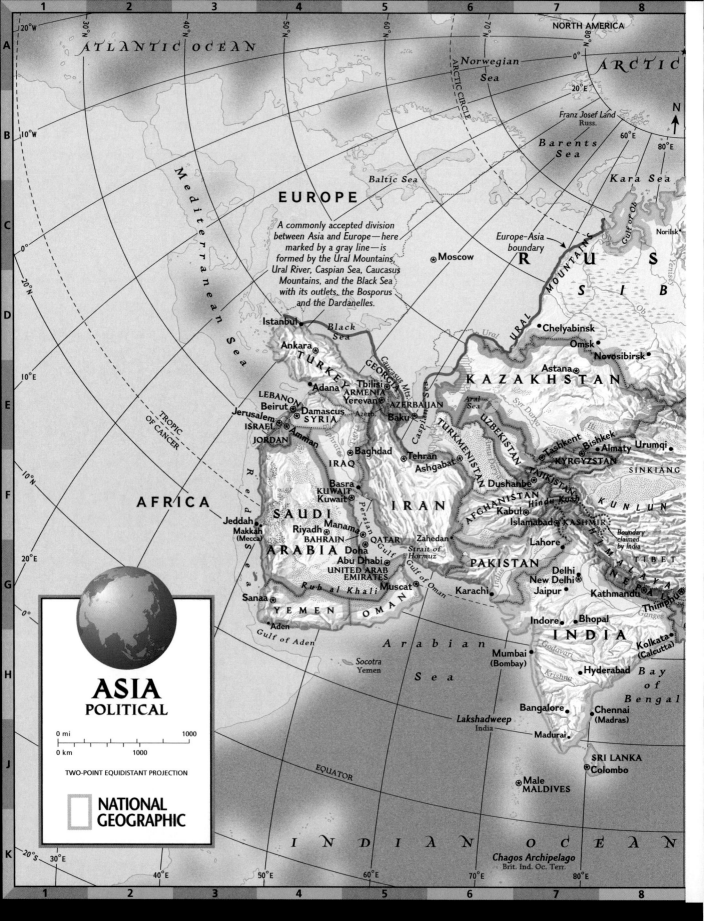

ATLANTIC OCEAN

NORTH AMERICA

ARCTIC

Norwegian
Sea

ARCTIC CIRCLE

N

Franz Josef Land
Russ.

Barents
Sea

Kara Sea

Baltic Sea

EUROPE

A commonly accepted division
between Asia and Europe—here
marked by a gray line—is
formed by the Ural Mountains,
Ural River, Caspian Sea, Caucasus
Mountains, and the Black Sea
with its outlets, the Bosporus
and the Dardanelles.

⊛ Moscow

Europe-Asia
boundary

R   U   S   S

S   I   B

• Norilsk

Gulf of Ob

Mediterranean Sea

Black
Sea

Istanbul

Ankara

TURKEY

Adana

GEORGIA

Tbilisi
ARMENIA
Yerevan

Caucasus Mts.

AZERBAIJAN

Azerb.

Baku

URAL MOUNTAINS

• Chelyabinsk

Ural

• Omsk

Novosibirsk •

Astana •

KAZAKHSTAN

Aral
Sea

Syr Darya

UZBEKISTAN

Tashkent

Ili

Bishkek •

Almaty •

Urumqi •

KYRGYZSTAN

SINKIANG

Irtysh

Ob

Yenisey

LEBANON
Beirut ⊛
Jerusalem ⊛
ISRAEL
JORDAN

Damascus
SYRIA
⊛ Amman

Euphrates

Tigris

⊛ Baghdad

IRAQ

Caspian Sea

⊛ Tehran
Ashgabat ⊛

TURKMENISTAN

Amu Darya

Dushanbe ⊛

TAJIKISTAN

Hindu Kush

KUNLUN

AFRICA

TROPIC
OF CANCER

Red Sea

Basra •
KUWAIT
Kuwait ⊛

SAUDI

Persian Gulf

Jeddah •
Makkah •
(Mecca)

Riyadh ⊛

Manama ⊛
BAHRAIN

QATAR

Zahedan •

IRAN

AFGHANISTAN

Kabul ⊛

Islamabad ⊛

KASHMIR

HIMALAYA

Boundary
claimed
by India

TIBET

ARABIA

Doha
Abu Dhabi ⊛
UNITED ARAB
EMIRATES

Strait of
Hormuz

Gulf of Oman

Lahore •

PAKISTAN

Delhi •
New Delhi ⊛
Jaipur •

Kathmandu ⊛
NEPAL
Thimphu ⊛

Ganges

Sanaa ⊛

Rub al Khali

Muscat ⊛

OMAN

Karachi •

Indus

Indore •

Bhopal •

INDIA

Kolkata •
(Calcutta)

Aden •

YEMEN

Gulf of Aden

Socotra
Yemen

Arabian

Sea

Mumbai
(Bombay) •

Godavari

Krishna

Hyderabad •

Bay
of
Bengal

Bangalore •

Chennai •
(Madras)

Lakshadweep
India

Madurai •

SRI LANKA
Colombo ⊛

EQUATOR

⊛ Male
MALDIVES

I   N   D   I   A   N   O   C   E   A   N

Chagos Archipelago
Brit. Ind. Oc. Terr.

ASIA
POLITICAL

0 mi   1000

0 km   1000

TWO-POINT EQUIDISTANT PROJECTION

NATIONAL
GEOGRAPHIC

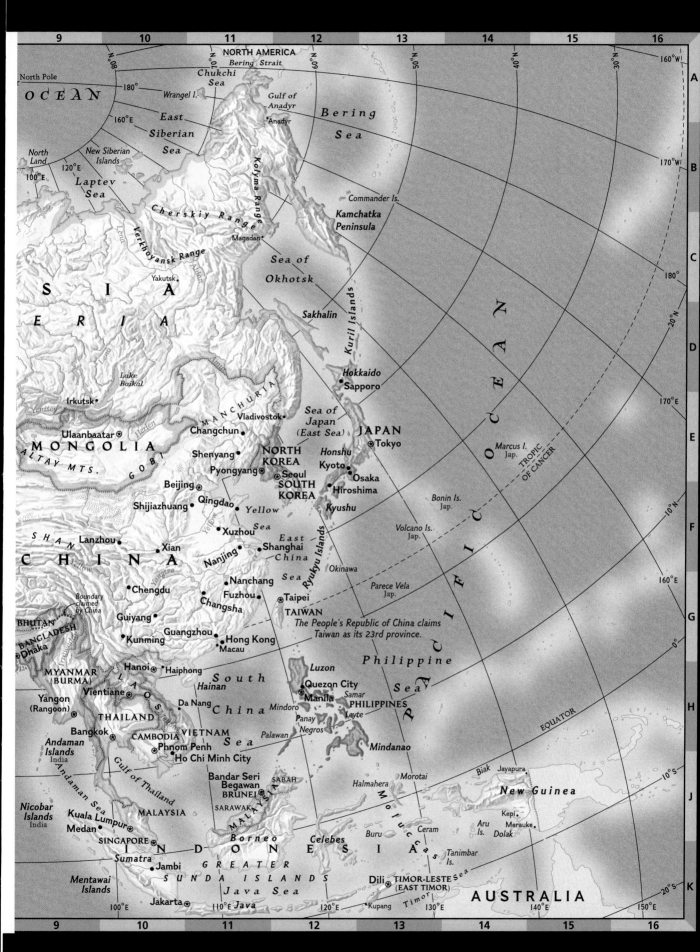

| 9 | 10 | 11 | 12 | 13 | 14 | 15 | 16 |

NORTH AMERICA
Bering Strait

North Pole

O C E A N
180°
Wrangel I.
Chukchi Sea
Gulf of Anadyr
•Anadyr

Bering Sea

160°E
East Siberian Sea

North Land
120°E
100°E
Laptev Sea
New Siberian Islands

Cherskiy Range
Kolyma Range
Commander Is.
Kamchatka Peninsula

Verkhoyansk Range
•Magadan

S I A
Yakutsk•
Sea of Okhotsk

E R I A
Lena
Aldan
Sakhalin
Kuril Islands

Irkutsk•
Lake Baikal
Yenisey
Herlen

Ulaanbaatar⊛
M O N G O L I A
A L T A Y   M T S.
G O B I
MANCHURIA
Vladivostok•
Changchun•
Amur

Hokkaido
Sapporo

Sea of Japan (East Sea)
JAPAN
⊛Tokyo
Honshu

Shenyang•
NORTH KOREA
Pyongyang⊛
Kyoto
Osaka
Marcus I. Jap.

TROPIC OF CANCER

Beijing⊛
⊛Seoul
SOUTH KOREA
Hiroshima
Shijiazhuang•
Qingdao•
Yellow
Kyushu

S H A N
Lanzhou•
Sea
Bonin Is. Jap.

Xuzhou•
Xian•
Yellow
East China
Volcano Is. Jap.

C H I N A
Nanjing•
Shanghai•
Sea
Ryukyu Islands

Chengdu•
Changsha•
Nanchang•
Fuzhou•
Okinawa

Boundary claimed by China
Guiyang•
⊛Taipei
TAIWAN
Parece Vela Jap.

BHUTAN
BANGLADESH
⊛Dhaka
Kunming•
Guangzhou•
Hong Kong•
Macau•
The People's Republic of China claims Taiwan as its 23rd province.

MYANMAR (BURMA)
Hanoi•
Haiphong•
South
Luzon
Quezon City
⊛Manila
Philippine Sea

Yangon (Rangoon)⊛
Vientiane⊛
L A O S
Da Nang•
China
Mindoro
Samar
PHILIPPINES

THAILAND
Bangkok⊛
CAMBODIA
VIETNAM
Phnom Penh⊛
Ho Chi Minh City•
Palawan
Sea
Panay
Negros
Leyte

Andaman Islands India
Gulf of Thailand
Mindanao

Andaman Sea
Bandar Seri Begawan
SABAH
Biak
Jayapura
EQUATOR

Nicobar Islands India
Kuala Lumpur⊛
MALAYSIA
BRUNEI
SARAWAK
Halmahera
Morotai
New Guinea

Medan•
SINGAPORE⊛
Borneo
Celebes
Buru
Ceram
Aru Is.
Kepi•
Merauke•
Dolak

Mentawai Islands
Sumatra
Jambi•
G R E A T E R   S U N D A   I S L A N D S
M o l u c c a s
Tanimbar Is.

100°E
Jakarta⊛
110°E
Java
Java Sea
120°E
Dili•
TIMOR-LESTE (EAST TIMOR)
Timor Sea
130°E
AUSTRALIA
140°E
150°E
Kupang•

P A C I F I C   O C E A N

| 9 | 10 | 11 | 12 | 13 | 14 | 15 | 16 |

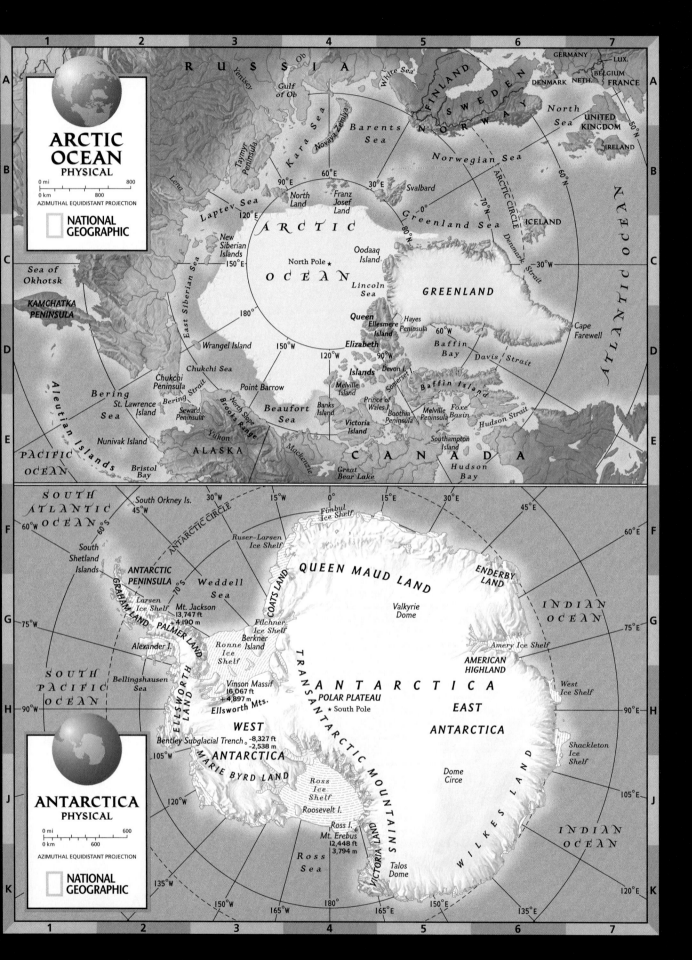

ARCTIC OCEAN PHYSICAL

0 mi 800
0 km 800
AZIMUTHAL EQUIDISTANT PROJECTION

NATIONAL GEOGRAPHIC

ANTARCTICA PHYSICAL

0 mi 600
0 km 600
AZIMUTHAL EQUIDISTANT PROJECTION

NATIONAL GEOGRAPHIC

NATIONAL GEOGRAPHIC

Geography Handbook

The story of the world begins with geography—the study of the earth in all of its variety. Geography describes the earth's land, water, and plant and animal life. It is the study of places and the complex relationships between people and their environment.

The resources in this handbook will help you get the most out of your textbook—and provide you with skills you will use for the rest of your life.

▼ The Gui River, Guilin, China

▲ Saharan sand dunes, Morocco

The Amazon, Brazil ▶

How Do I Study Geography?

To understand how our world is connected, some geographers have broken down the study of geography into five themes. The **Five Themes of Geography** are (1) location, (2) place, (3) human/environment interaction, (4) movement, and (5) regions. You will see these themes highlighted in the Chapter Assessment Geography Skills of *Journey Across Time: The Early Ages.*

Six Essential Elements

Recently, geographers have begun to look at geography in a different way. They break down the study of geography into **Six Essential Elements.** Being aware of these elements will help you sort out what you are learning about geography.

Element 2

Places and Regions

Place has a special meaning in geography. It means more than where a place is. It also describes what a place is like. It might describe physical characteristics such as landforms, climate, and plant or animal life. Or it might describe human characteristics, including language and way of life.

To help organize their study, geographers often group places into regions. **Regions** are united by one or more common characteristics.

Element 1

The World in Spatial Terms

Geographers first take a look at where a place is located. **Location** serves as a starting point by asking "Where is it?" Knowing the location of places helps you develop an awareness of the world around you.

Element 3

Physical Systems

When studying places and regions, geographers analyze how **physical systems**—such as hurricanes, volcanoes, and glaciers—shape the earth's surface. They also look at communities of plants and animals that depend upon one another and their surroundings for survival.

Element 4

Human Systems

Geographers also examine **human systems,** or how people have shaped our world. They look at how boundary lines are determined and analyze why people settle in certain places and not in others. A key theme in geography is the continual **movement** of people, ideas, and goods.

Element 5

Environment and Society

How does the relationship between people and their natural surroundings influence the way people live? This is one of the questions that the theme of **human/environment interaction** investigates. It also shows how people use the environment and how their actions affect the environment.

Element 6

The Uses of Geography

Knowledge of geography helps us understand the relationships among people, places, and environments over time. Understanding geography and knowing how to use the tools and technology available to study it prepares you for life in our modern society.

How Do I Use Maps and Globes?

Hemispheres

To locate place on the earth, geographers use a system of imaginary lines that crisscross the globe. One of these lines, the **Equator,** circles the middle of the earth like a belt. It divides the earth into "half spheres," or **hemispheres.** Everything north of the Equator is in the Northern Hemisphere. Everything south of the Equator is in the Southern Hemisphere.

Another imaginary line runs from north to south. It helps divide the earth into half spheres in the other direction. Find this line—called the **Prime Meridian** on a globe. Everything east of the Prime Meridian for 180 degrees is in the Eastern Hemisphere. Everything west of the Prime Meridian is in the Western Hemisphere.

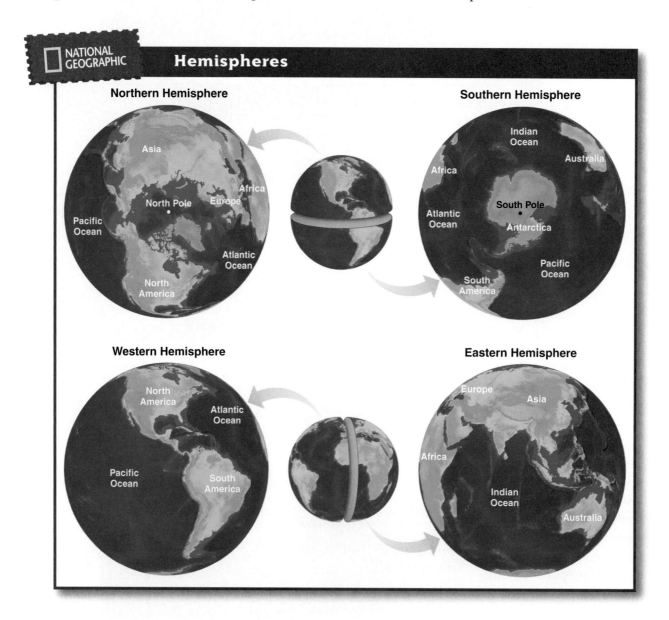

NATIONAL GEOGRAPHIC

Hemispheres

Northern Hemisphere

Asia
Africa
Europe
North Pole
Pacific Ocean
Atlantic Ocean
North America

Southern Hemisphere

Indian Ocean
Australia
Africa
Atlantic Ocean
South Pole
Antarctica
Pacific Ocean
South America

Western Hemisphere

North America
Atlantic Ocean
Pacific Ocean
South America

Eastern Hemisphere

Europe
Asia
Africa
Indian Ocean
Australia

Understanding Latitude and Longitude

Lines on globes and maps provide information that can help you easily locate places on the earth. These lines—called **latitude** and **longitude**—cross one another, forming a pattern called a grid system.

Latitude

Lines of latitude, or **parallels,** circle the earth parallel to the **Equator** and measure the distance north or south of the Equator in degrees. The Equator is at 0° latitude, while the North Pole lies at latitude 90°N (north).

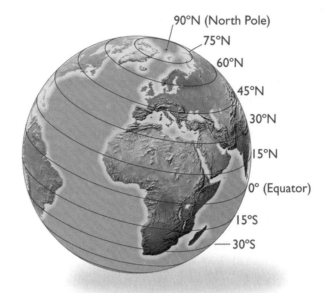

Longitude

Lines of longitude, or **meridians,** circle the earth from Pole to Pole. These lines measure distances east or west of the starting line, which is at 0° longitude and is called the **Prime Meridian.** The Prime Meridian runs through the Royal Observatory in Greenwich, England.

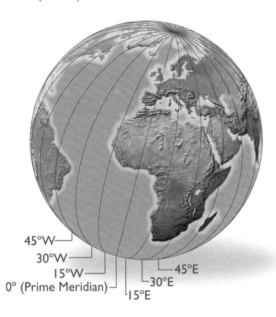

Absolute Location

The grid system formed by lines of latitude and longitude makes it possible to find the absolute location of a place. Only one place can be found at the point where a specific line of latitude crosses a specific line of longitude. By using degrees (°) and minutes (') (points between degrees), people can pinpoint the precise spot where one line of latitude crosses one line of longitude—an **absolute location.**

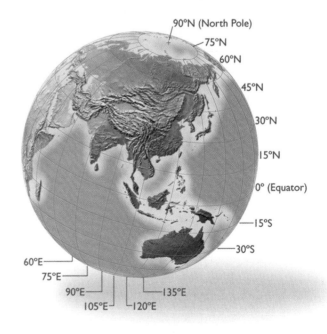

From Globes to Maps

The most accurate way to depict the earth is as a *globe*, a round scale model of the earth. A globe gives a true picture of the continents' relative sizes and the shapes of landmasses and bodies of water. Globes accurately represent distance and direction.

A *map* is a flat drawing of all or part of the earth's surface. Unlike globes, maps can show small areas in great detail. Maps can also display political boundaries, population densities, or even voting returns.

From Globes to Maps

Maps, however, do have their limitations. As you can imagine, drawing a round object on a flat surface is very difficult. **Cartographers,** or mapmakers, use mathematical formulas to transfer information from the round globe to a flat map. However, when the curves of a globe become straight lines on a map, the size, shape, distance, or area can change or be distorted.

Great Circle Routes

Mapmakers have solved some problems of going from a globe to a map. A **great circle** is an imaginary line that follows the curve of the earth. Traveling along a great circle is called following a **great circle route.** Airplane pilots use great circle routes because they are the shortest routes.

The idea of a great circle shows one important difference between a globe and a map. Because a globe is round, it accurately shows great circles. On a flat map, however, the great circle route between two points may not appear to be the shortest distance. Compare Maps A and B on the right.

Mapmaking With Technology

Technology has changed the way maps are made. Most cartographers use software programs called **geographic information systems (GIS).** This software layers map data from satellite images, printed text, and statistics. A **Global Positioning System (GPS)** helps consumers and mapmakers locate places based on coordinates broadcast by satellites.

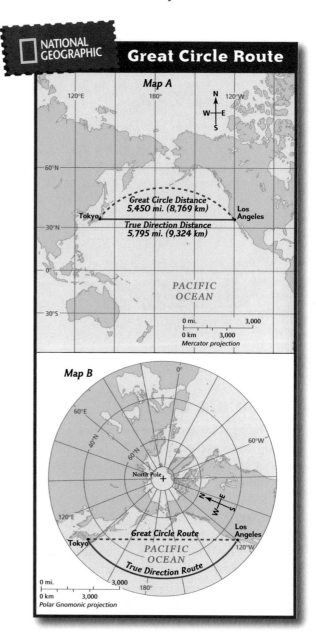

NATIONAL GEOGRAPHIC
Great Circle Route

Map A

120°E · 180° · 120°W

60°N

Great Circle Distance
5,450 mi. (8,769 km)

Tokyo — Los Angeles

30°N

True Direction Distance
5,795 mi. (9,324 km)

0°

PACIFIC OCEAN

30°S

0 mi. — 3,000
0 km — 3,000
Mercator projection

Map B

0°

60°E · 60°W

40°N · 60°N

North Pole

120°E · 60°W

Great Circle Route

Tokyo · Los Angeles

PACIFIC OCEAN · 120°W

True Direction Route

0 mi. — 3,000 · 180°
0 km — 3,000
Polar Gnomonic projection

Common Map Projections

Imagine taking the whole peel from an orange and trying to flatten it on a table. You would either have to cut it or stretch parts of it. Mapmakers face a similar problem in showing the surface of the round earth on a flat map. When the earth's surface is flattened, big gaps open up. To fill in the gaps, mapmakers stretch parts of the earth. They choose to show either the correct shapes of places or their correct sizes. It is impossible to show both. As a result, mapmakers have developed different projections, or ways of showing the earth on a flat piece of paper.

Goode's Interrupted Equal-Area Projection

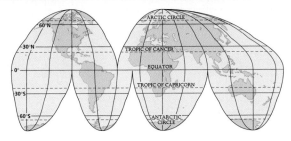

▲ Take a second look at your peeled, flattened orange. You might have something that looks like a map based on **Goode's Interrupted Equal-Area** projection. A map with this projection shows continents close to their true shapes and sizes. This projection is helpful to compare land areas among continents.

Robinson Projection

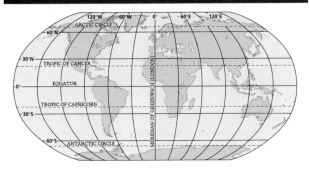

▲ A map using the **Robinson** projection has minor distortions. Land on the western and eastern sides of the Robinson map appears much as it does on a globe. The areas most distorted on this projection are near the North and South Poles.

Winkel Tripel Projection

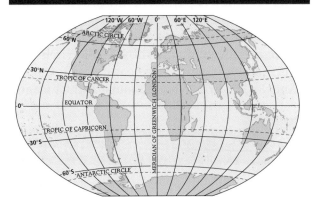

▲ The **Winkel Tripel** projection gives a good overall view of the continents' shapes and sizes. Land areas in a Winkel Tripel projection are not as distorted near the Poles as they are in the Robinson projection.

Mercator Projection

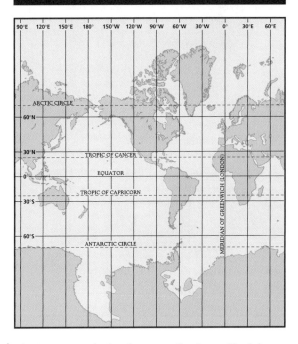

▲ The **Mercator** projection shows true direction and land shapes fairly accurately, but not size or distance. Areas that are located far from the Equator are quite distorted on this projection. Alaska, for example, appears much larger on a Mercator map than it does on a globe.

Parts of Maps

Map Key An important first step in reading a map is to note the map key. The **map key** explains the lines, symbols, and colors used on a map. For example, the map on this page shows the various climate regions of the United States and the different colors representing them. Cities are usually symbolized by a solid circle (•) and capitals by a (✪). On this map, you can see the capital of Texas and the cities of Los Angeles, Seattle, New Orleans, and Chicago.

Climate Regions of the United States

Key
- Desert
- Highland
- Humid continental
- Humid subtropical
- Marine
- Mediterranean
- Steppe
- Subarctic
- Tropical
- Tundra

Scale A measuring line, often called a **scale bar,** helps you figure distance on the map. The map scale tells you what distance on the earth is represented by the measurement on the scale bar.

Compass Rose A map has a symbol that tells you where the **cardinal directions**—north, south, east, and west—are positioned.

Types of Maps

General Purpose Maps

Maps are amazingly useful tools. Geographers use many different types of maps. Maps that show a wide range of general information about an area are called **general purpose maps.** Two of the most common general purpose maps are physical and political maps.

Physical Maps

Physical maps call out landforms and water features. The physical map of Sri Lanka (below) shows rivers and mountains. The colors used on physical maps include brown or green for land and blue for water. In addition, physical maps may use colors to show **elevation**—the height of an area above sea level. A key explains what each color and symbol stands for.

NATIONAL GEOGRAPHIC

Spain: Political

Bay of Biscay

FRANCE

ANDORRA

PORTUGAL

Ebro R.

Douro R.

Zaragoza

Barcelona

Madrid

SPAIN

Tagus R.

Valencia

Balearic Islands

Guadalquivir R.

Seville

Málaga

ATLANTIC OCEAN

GIBRALTAR U.K.

Strait of Gibraltar

Mediterranean Sea

AFRICA

0 mi. 200
0 km 200

Lambert Azimuthal Equal-Area projection

Political Maps

Political maps show the names and boundaries of countries, the location of cities and other human-made features of a place, and often identify major physical features. The political map of Spain (above), for example, shows the boundaries between Spain and other countries. It also shows cities and rivers within Spain and bodies of water surrounding Spain.

NATIONAL GEOGRAPHIC

Sri Lanka: Physical

Point Pedro

Jaffna

Gulf of Mannar

Trincomalee

Bay of Bengal

SRI LANKA

Chilaw

Kattankudi

Matale

Pidurutalagala 8,281 ft. (2,524 m)

Colombo

INDIAN OCEAN

Matara

0 mi. 100
0 km 100

80°E

Elevations

Feet		Meters
3,280		1,000
1,640		500
650		200
380		100
0		0

▲ Mountain peak
⊛ National capital
• Major city

Special Purpose Maps

Some maps are made to present specific kinds of information. These are called **thematic** or **special purpose maps.** They usually show themes or patterns, often emphasizing one subject or theme. Special purpose maps may present climate, natural resources, and population density. They may also display historical information, such as battles or territorial changes. The map's title tells what kind of special information it shows. Colors and symbols in the map key are especially important on these types of maps. Special purpose maps are often found in books of maps called atlases.

One type of special purpose map uses colors to show population density, or the average number of people living in a square mile or square kilometer. As with other maps, it is important to first read the title and the key. The population density map of Egypt shows that the Nile River valley and delta are very densely populated.

Some other special purpose maps such as the one of China's Defenses are not presented in color. They print in black and white. This is an example of a map you might find on a standardized test or in a newspaper.

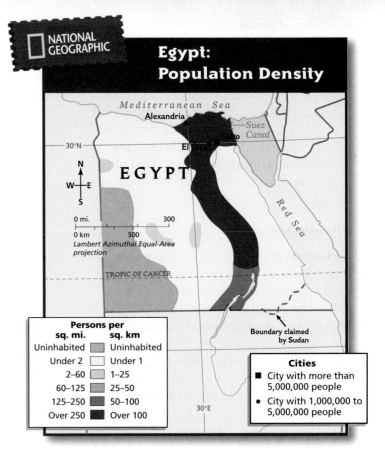

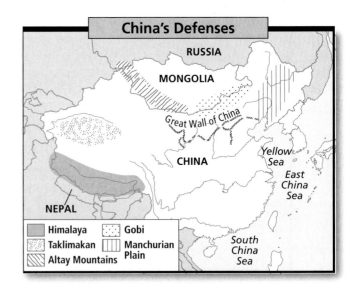

Using Graphs, Charts, and Diagrams

Bar, Line, and Circle Graphs

A graph is a way of summarizing and presenting information visually. Each part of a graph gives useful information. First read the graph's title to find out its subject. Then read the labels along the graph's **axes**— the vertical line along the left side of the graph and the horizontal line along the bottom. One axis will tell you what is being measured. The other axis tells what units of measurement are being used.

Graphs that use bars or wide lines to compare data visually are called **bar graphs.** Look carefully at the bar graph (right) which compares world languages. The vertical axis lists the languages. The horizontal axis gives speakers of the language in millions. By comparing the lengths of the bars, you can quickly tell which language is spoken by the most people. Bar graphs are especially useful for comparing quantities.

Bar graph

A **line graph** is a useful tool for showing changes over a period of time. The amounts being measured are plotted on the grid above each year and then are connected by a line. Line graphs sometimes have two or more lines plotted on them. The line graph (below) shows that the number of farms in the United States has decreased since 1940.

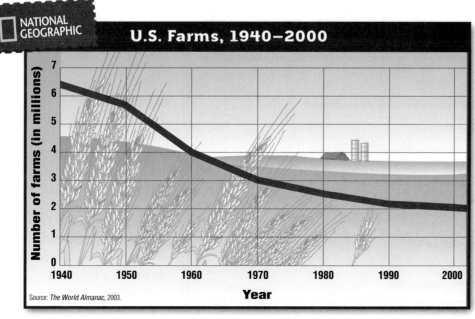

Line graph

You can use **circle graphs** when you want to show how the whole of something is divided into its parts. Because of their shape, circle graphs are often called pie graphs. Each "slice" represents a part or percentage of the whole "pie." On the circle graph at right, the whole circle (100 percent) represents the world's population in 2002. The slices show how this population is divided among the world's five largest continents.

Charts

Charts present facts and numbers in an organized way. They arrange data, especially numbers, in rows and columns for easy reference. To interpret the chart, first read the title. Look at the chart on page 91. It tells you what information the chart contains. Next, read the labels at the top of each column and on the left side of the chart. They explain what the numbers or data on the chart are measuring.

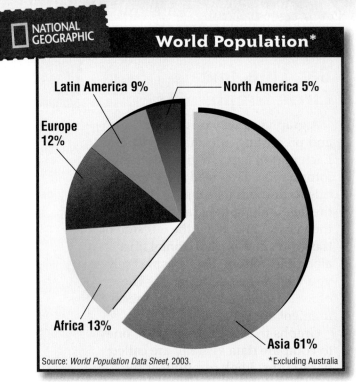

NATIONAL GEOGRAPHIC

World Population*

Latin America 9%

North America 5%

Europe 12%

Africa 13%

Asia 61%

Source: *World Population Data Sheet*, 2003.

*Excluding Australia

Circle graph

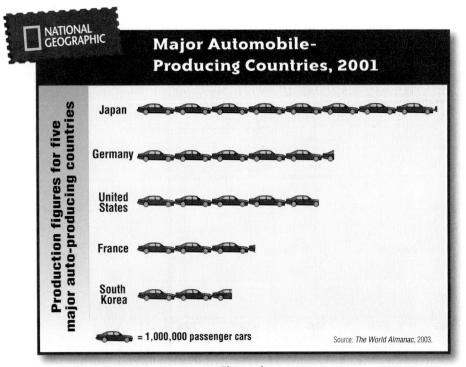

NATIONAL GEOGRAPHIC

Major Automobile-Producing Countries, 2001

Production figures for five major auto-producing countries

Japan

Germany

United States

France

South Korea

= 1,000,000 passenger cars

Source: *The World Almanac*, 2003.

Pictograph

Pictographs

Like bar and circle graphs, pictographs are good for making comparisons. **Pictographs** use rows of small pictures or symbols, with each picture or symbol representing an amount. Look at the pictograph (left) showing the number of automobiles produced in the world's five major automobile-producing countries. The key tells you that one car symbol stands for 1 million automobiles. The total number of car symbols in a row adds up to the auto production in each selected country.

Climographs

A **climograph**, or climate graph, combines a line graph and a bar graph. It gives an overall picture of the long-term weather patterns in a specific place. Climographs include several kinds of information. The green vertical bars on the climograph of Moscow (right) show average monthly amounts of precipitation (rain, snow, and sleet). These bars are measured against the axis on the right side of the graph. The red line plotted above the bars represents changes in the average monthly temperature. You measure this line against the axis on the left side.

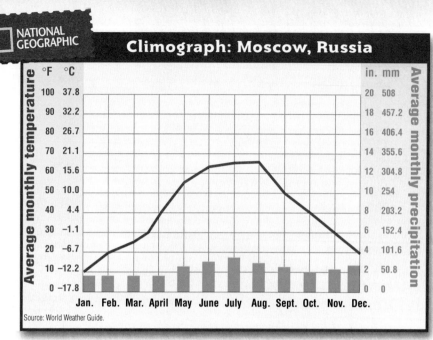

Climograph

Diagrams

Diagrams are drawings that show steps in a process, point out the parts of an object, or explain how something works. An **elevation profile** is a type of diagram that can be helpful when comparing the elevations—or height—of an area. It shows an exaggerated side view of the land as if it were sliced and you were viewing it from the side. The elevation profile of Africa (below) clearly shows sea level, low areas, and mountains.

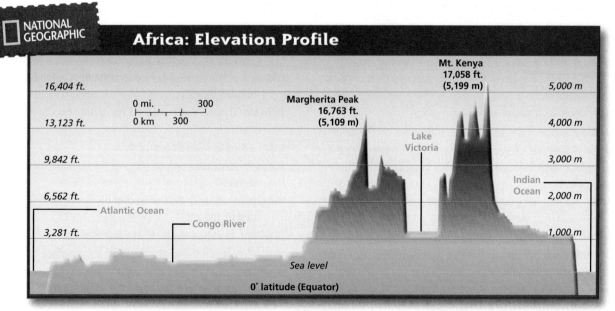

Diagram

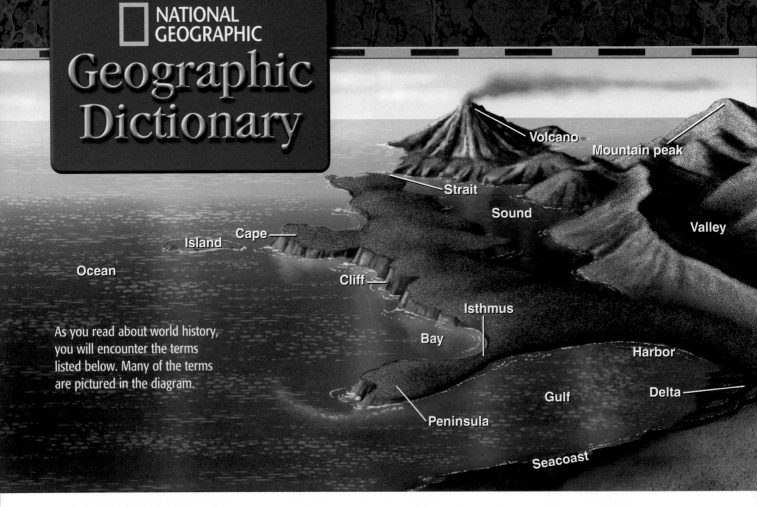

NATIONAL GEOGRAPHIC
Geographic Dictionary

As you read about world history, you will encounter the terms listed below. Many of the terms are pictured in the diagram.

absolute location exact location of a place on the earth described by global coordinates

basin area of land drained by a given river and its branches; area of land surrounded by lands of higher elevation

bay part of a large body of water that extends into a shoreline, generally smaller than a gulf

canyon deep and narrow valley with steep walls

cape point of land that extends into a river, lake, or ocean

channel wide strait or waterway between two landmasses that lie close to each other; deep part of a river or other waterway

cliff steep, high wall of rock, earth, or ice

continent one of the seven large landmasses on the earth

cultural feature characteristic that humans have created in a place, such as language, religion, housing, and settlement pattern

delta flat, low-lying land built up from soil carried downstream by a river and deposited at its mouth

divide stretch of high land that separates river systems

downstream direction in which a river or stream flows from its source to its mouth

elevation height of land above sea level

Equator imaginary line that runs around the earth halfway between the North and South Poles; used as the starting point to measure degrees of north and south latitude

glacier large, thick body of slowly moving ice

gulf part of a large body of water that extends into a shoreline, generally larger and more deeply indented than a bay

harbor a sheltered place along a shoreline where ships can anchor safely

highland elevated land area such as a hill, mountain, or plateau

hill elevated land with sloping sides and rounded summit; generally smaller than a mountain

island land area, smaller than a continent, completely surrounded by water

isthmus narrow stretch of land connecting two larger land areas

lake a sizable inland body of water

latitude distance north or south of the Equator, measured in degrees

longitude distance east or west of the Prime Meridian, measured in degrees

lowland land, usually level, at a low elevation

map drawing of the earth shown on a flat surface

meridian one of many lines on the global grid running from the North Pole to the South Pole; used to measure degrees of longitude

mesa broad, flat-topped landform with steep sides; smaller than a plateau

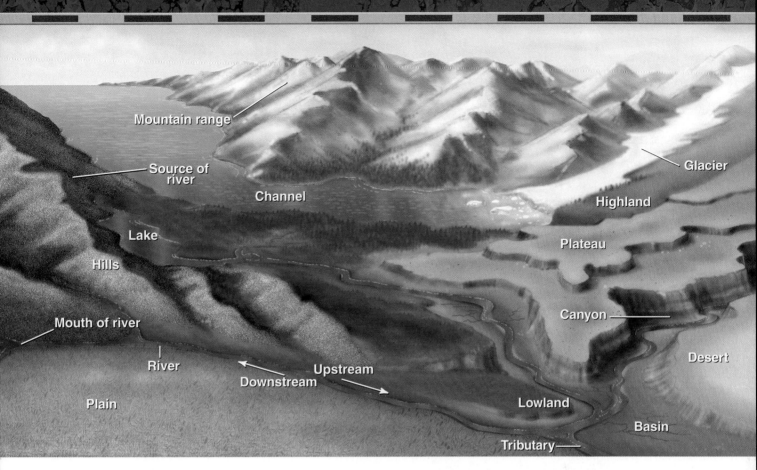

Mountain range

Source of river

Channel

Glacier

Highland

Plateau

Lake

Hills

Canyon

Desert

Mouth of river

River

Upstream

Downstream

Lowland

Plain

Basin

Tributary

mountain land with steep sides that rises sharply (1,000 feet [305 m] or more) from surrounding land; generally larger and more rugged than a hill

mountain peak pointed top of a mountain

mountain range a series of connected mountains

mouth (of a river) place where a stream or river flows into a larger body of water

ocean one of the four major bodies of salt water that surround the continents

ocean current stream of either cold or warm water that moves in a definite direction through an ocean

parallel one of many lines on the global grid that circle the earth north or south of the Equator; used to measure degrees of latitude

peninsula body of land jutting into a lake or ocean, surrounded on three sides by water

physical feature characteristic of a place occurring naturally, such as a landform, body of water, climate pattern, or resource

plain area of level land, usually at a low elevation and often covered with grasses

plateau area of flat or rolling land at a high elevation, about 300–3,000 feet (91–914 m) high

Prime Meridian line of the global grid running from the North Pole to the South Pole through Greenwich, England; starting point for measuring degrees of east and west longitude

relief changes in elevation over a given area of land

river large natural stream of water that runs through the land

sea large body of water completely or partly surrounded by land

seacoast land lying next to a sea or ocean

sea level position on land level with surface of nearby ocean or sea

sound body of water between a coastline and one or more islands off the coast

source (of a river) place where a river or stream begins, often in highlands

strait narrow stretch of water joining two larger bodies of water

tributary small river or stream that flows into a larger river or stream; a branch of the river

upstream direction opposite the flow of a river; toward the source of a river or stream

valley area of low land between hills or mountains

volcano mountain created as liquid rock or ash erupts from inside the earth

Tools of the Historian

A historian is a person who studies and writes about the people and events of the past. Historians find out how people lived, what happened to them, and what happened around them. They look for the reasons behind events. They also study the effects of events.

Have you ever wondered if you could be a historian? To answer that question, you will need to find out how history is researched and written. Historians use a number of tools to research and organize information. You can learn about these tools in the next few pages. As you study this textbook, you will see that these tools will help you understand world history.

Archaeologists are scientists who unearth the remains of the past. Historians depend on their work.

Digging Up the Past

What Do Archaeologists Study?
- Human and animal bones, seeds, trees
- Pottery, tools, weapons
- Mounds, pits, canals

▲ Prehistoric pottery

How Do They Gather Data?
- Surveys on foot
- Photographs taken from airplanes or satellites
- Ground-penetrating radar
- Plot locations on maps
- Dig for evidence with tools from heavy equipment to shovels
- Sonar scanning to find underwater objects

How Do They Interpret Findings?
- Organize artifacts into groups based on similarities
- Compare objects in relation to other objects
- Look for evidence of changes over a period of time
- Date once-living objects by measuring carbon-14 levels
- Use microscopic and biological tests to date objects

Carbon-14 dating ▶

Do Your Own Digging

Research the library and Internet to find information on two archaeological diggings, one past and the other, very recent. Compare and contrast the methods used in each digging. What changes do you notice in tools archaeologists have used over time?

Measuring Time

Main Idea

Historians rely on calendars and the dating of events to measure time.

Reading Focus Have you ever thought about traveling back in time to a place long ago? Historians do just that. Read to see how historians keep track of past events.

Calendars Historians rely on *calendars*, or dating systems, to measure time. Cultures throughout the world have developed different calendars based on important events in their history. Western nations begin their calendar on the year in which Jesus was thought to have been born. The Jewish calendar begins about 3,760 years before the Christian calendar. This is the time when Jewish tradition says the world was created. Muslims date their calendar from the time their first leader, Muhammad, left the city of Makkah for Madinah. This was A.D. 622 in the Christian calendar.

▼ A people called the Minoans made this stone calendar.

▲ About A.D. 500, a Christian monk, or religious person, developed the Western way of dating events.

The dates in this book are based on the Western calendar. In the Western calendar, the years before the birth of Jesus are known as "B.C.," or "before Christ." The years after are called "A.D.," or *anno domini*. This phrase comes from the Latin language and means "in the year of the Lord."

Dating Events To date events *before* the birth of Christ, or "B.C.," historians count backwards from A.D. 1. There is no year "0." The year before A.D. 1 is 1 B.C. (Notice that "A.D." is written before the date, while "B.C." is written following the date.) Therefore, a date in the 100 years before the birth of Christ lies between 100 B.C. and A.D. 1.

To date events after the birth of Christ, or "A.D.," historians count forward, starting at A.D. 1. A date in the first 100 years after the birth of Christ is between A.D. 1 and A.D. 100.

Thinking Like a Historian

1. **Identify** What do "B.C." and "A.D." mean? How are they used?

2. **Dating Events** What year came *after* 184 B.C.?

3. **Comparing and Contrasting** As you read, use the Internet to find out the current year in the calendars mentioned in your text. Why are calendars different from culture to culture?

Organizing Time

Tools made by prehistoric people

Main Idea

Historians organize history by dividing it into blocks of time.

Reading Focus Have you ever thought about the names given to a block of events, such as "summer vacation" or "the baseball season?" Read to see how historians use names to describe different stretches of time in history.

Periods of History Historians divide history into blocks of time known as *periods*, or *eras*. For example, a period of 10 years is called a *decade*. A period of 100 years is known as a *century*. Centuries are grouped into even longer time periods, which are given names.

The first of these long periods is called *Prehistory*. Prehistory refers to the time before people developed writing, about 5,500 years ago. This is followed by the period known as *Ancient History*, ending c. A.D. 500. (c., or *circa*, means "about"). Historians call the next thousand years the *Middle Ages*, or the medieval period. From c. 1500, *Modern History* begins

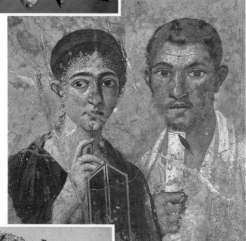

▲ A young couple of ancient Rome

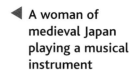

◄ A woman of medieval Japan playing a musical instrument

◄ Educated Europeans of the early modern period discussing new ideas

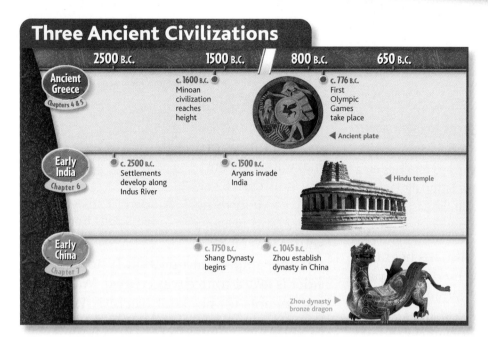

Three Ancient Civilizations

2500 B.C. 1500 B.C. 800 B.C. 650 B.C.

Ancient Greece
Chapters 4 & 5

c. 1600 B.C.
Minoan civilization reaches height

c. 776 B.C.
First Olympic Games take place

◄ Ancient plate

Early India
Chapter 6

c. 2500 B.C.
Settlements develop along Indus River

c. 1500 B.C.
Aryans invade India

◄ Hindu temple

Early China
Chapter 7

c. 1750 B.C.
Shang Dynasty begins

c. 1045 B.C.
Zhou establish dynasty in China

Zhou dynasty ► bronze dragon

and continues to the present day. In this book, you will study the history of the world from prehistory to the beginning of the modern period.

What Is a Time Line? Which came first: the American Civil War or World War II? Did the train come before or after the invention of the airplane? In studying the past, historians focus on *chronology*, or the order of dates in which events happened.

You might be wondering how to make sense of the flow of dates and events. An easy way is to use or make a time line. A *time line* is a diagram that shows the order of events within a period of time.

Most time lines are divided into sections in which the years are evenly spaced. In some cases, however, a spread of time may be too long to show all of the years in even spaces. To save space, a period of time may be omitted from the time line. Where this happens, a slanted or jagged line appears on the time line to show a break in the even spacing of events. For example, the time line above shows a break between 1500 B.C. and 800 B.C.

A time line also labels events. Each event on the time line appears beside the date when the event took place. Sometimes events and their dates are shown on a single time line. In other cases, two or more time lines are stacked one on top of the other. These are called multilevel time lines. They help you to compare events in different places at certain periods of time. For example, the multilevel time line above shows events in three ancient civilizations from 2500 B.C. to 650 B.C. The skill "Reading a Time Line" on page 711 will help you learn to work with time lines.

Thinking Like a Historian

1. **Reading a Time Line** Look over the time line above to get an idea of what a time line shows. What is the title? When does it begin and end? What two features make this time line different from many other time lines? Why are they used?

2. **Understanding a Time Line** Why do you think the dates on the time line are marked with a "c."?

3. **Making a Time Line** Create a time line using the terms B.M.B. (before my birth) and A.M.B. (after my birth). Fill in the time line with five key events that happened before and after you were born. Illustrate the time line with copies of photos from your family album.

How Does a Historian Work?

▲ Scientist studying Dead Sea Scrolls from southwest Asia

Main Idea

Historians study a variety of sources to learn about the past.

Reading Focus Have you ever searched for clues on a treasure hunt? Read to find out how historians look for clues to create a written record about the past.

Where Is the Evidence?
Historians begin by asking questions, such as: Why did two particular countries go to war? What effect did their fighting have on peoples' lives? How does the conflict influence our world today? Such questions help historians identify and focus on historical problems.

Historians generally find evidence in primary sources and secondary sources. *Primary sources* are firsthand pieces of evidence from people who saw or experienced an event. They include written documents, such as letters, diaries, and official records. They also include spoken interviews as well as objects, such as photos, paintings, clothing, and tools. The skill "Analyzing Primary Source Documents" on page 716 will give you a chance to work with written primary sources.

Secondary sources, on the other hand, are created *after* the events by people who played no part in them. Secondary sources are partially based on primary sources. They include biographies, encyclopedias, and history books—even this textbook.

Historians study secondary sources for background information and for a larger view of an event. However, to get new evidence that advances knowledge, historians must turn to the firsthand information found only in primary sources.

Examining Sources
Historians *analyze,* or examine, primary and secondary sources. First, they determine *where* and *when* a source was created. Another important question historians consider is *why* a source was created. Was it a letter meant to be kept secret? Was it a government document published for all citizens to read?

Can the Sources Be Trusted?
Historians examine sources for *credibility,* or truthfulness. This is because each source reflects a *point of view,* or a general attitude about people and life. The creator of a source uses his or her point of view to decide what events were important, which people were key players, and what details were worth recording. Sometimes point of view is expressed as a *bias,* or an unreasoned, emotional judgment about people and events.

Historians try to be aware of point of view and bias both in their sources and in themselves. Therefore, they check new

▲ Ruins of Mayan temple in Central America

The Decline of Rome

Weak Roman Government
- Dishonest government officials provide poor leadership.

Social Problems
- Famine and disease spread throughout the empire.

Declining Economy
- Income and wages fall.
- Wealthy fail to pay taxes.

Reform Fails and Rome Divides in Two
- Government fails to keep order.
- Violence and tension increase.
- Diocletian divides the empire.

Eastern Roman Empire
- Constantinople becomes the new capital.
- The empire survives attacks and prospers.

Western Roman Empire
- Numerous attacks threaten the empire.
- Territory is slowly lost to invaders.

Byzantine Empire
- This empire is created from the Eastern Roman Empire and lasts nearly 1,000 years.

Rome Falls
- The city of Rome falls in A.D. 476.
- The Western Roman Empire is divided into Germanic kingdoms by A.D. 550.

sources and their own ideas against sources already known to be trustworthy. They also examine many sources that express different points of view about an event. In this way, historians try to get a clear, well-rounded view of what happened.

Historians piece together the credible evidence and draw conclusions. In drawing conclusions, they use their own thinking and knowledge of the past to *interpret*, or explain, the meaning of the events.

Cause and Effect

Historical events are linked by cause and effect. A *cause* is what makes an event happen. The event that happens as a result of the cause is known as an *effect.* Historians look for cause-and-effect links to explain *why* events happen.

Usually, one event is produced by many causes. Similarly, one event often produces several different effects. These cause-and-

effect links form what is called a *cause-and-effect chain.* Because so many historical events are related, cause-and-effect chains can become very long and can include events that occur over a long period of time. The chart above shows such a chain of events.

Thinking Like a Historian

1. **Understanding Evidence** Suppose a friend wanted to write a history of your life so far. What primary sources might he or she use to find evidence of your daily activities?

2. **Analyzing Sources** Find two written accounts of a recent event in your town. Which of the two accounts do you think is the most credible? Why?

3. **Recognizing Cause and Effect** Study the cause-and-effect chart on this page. What were three major causes of Rome's decline? What were two important effects of Rome's decline upon history?

History and Geography

▲ Growing rice in China

Main Idea ....

Historians try to understand how climate, landforms, and human activities have shaped past events.

Reading Focus Have you ever had a party or sports event cancelled because of bad weather? Read to find out how historians study the effects of the natural world on history.

....

Geography is the study of the earth's physical and human features. In this text, you will discover how geography has shaped the course of events in world history. Sometimes the study of geography is broken down into five themes. *The Five Themes of Geography* are:

- **location** (Where is it?)
- **place** (What is it like?)
- **human/environment interaction** (What is the relationship between people and their surroundings?)
- **movement** (How do people in one area relate to people in other areas?)
- **region** (What common features bring geographical areas together?)

Location

....

"Where is it?" In using geography, historians first look at where a place is located. Every place has an absolute location and a relative location. *Absolute location* refers to the exact spot of a place on the earth's surface. For example, the city of Atlanta, Georgia, is located at one place and one place only. No other place on Earth has exactly the same location. *Relative location* tells where a place is, compared with one or more other places. Atlanta is northwest of Miami and southwest of New York City.

The Acropolis, Athens, Greece ▶

Place

....

"What is it like?" *Place* describes all of the characteristics that give an area its own special quality. These can be physical features, such as mountains, waterways, climate, and plant or animal life. Places can also be described by human characteristics, such as language, religion, and architecture.

Human/Environment Interaction

....

"What is the relationship between people and their surroundings?" Landforms, waterways, climate, and natural resources all have helped or hindered human activities. People in turn have responded to their environment, or natural surroundings, in different ways. Sometimes they have adjusted to it. At other times, people have changed their environment to meet their needs.

▲ Camel caravan in North Africa

▲ Wall painting showing life in ancient Egypt

Movement

"How do people in one area relate to people in other areas?" Historians answer this question within the theme of *movement.* Throughout history, people, ideas, goods, and information have moved from place to place. Movement has brought the world's people closer together. Transportation—the movement of people and goods—has increased the exchange of ideas and cultures. Communication—the movement of ideas and information—has allowed people to find out what is happening in other parts of the world.

Region

"What common features bring geographical areas together?" To make sense of all the complex things in the world, historians often view places or areas as regions. A *region* is an area that is defined by common features. Regions can be defined by physical features, such mountains and rivers, or by human features, such as religion, language, or livelihood.

Six Essential Elements

Recently the study of geography has been broken down into *Six Essential Elements:*
- The World in Spatial Terms
- Places and Regions
- Physical Systems
- Human Systems
- Environment and Society
- The Uses of Geography

You will learn about the Six Essential Elements in the Geography Handbook on pages GH2–GH3. Knowing these elements will help you in your study of history.

Thinking Like a Historian

1. **Identify** How are absolute location and relative location different?

2. **Analyzing Themes** What characteristics do geographers use to describe a place?

3. **Linking History and Geography** Make a list of the Five Themes of Geography. Under each theme, explain how you think geography has shaped the history of your community.

What Is a Historical Atlas?

Main Idea

Maps give information about areas of the world at different periods of history.

Reading Focus Have you used a map to go from one place to another? Read to find out how you can rely on maps for clues about the past.

Historical Maps An *atlas* is a book of maps showing different parts of the world. A *historical atlas* has maps showing different parts of the world at different periods of history. Maps that show political events, such as invasions, battles, and boundary changes, are called *historical maps.*

Some historical maps show how territories in a certain part of the world changed over time. Below are two maps. One map shows the areas of Europe, Asia, and Africa that were ruled by Alexander the Great in 323 B.C. The other map shows the same region as it looks today. Placed next to each other, the maps help you compare historical changes in the region from ancient times to today.

In the larger map, Alexander's empire stretches from the eastern Mediterranean Sea in the west to the Indus River in the east. There are no political borders. Instead, other things are shown. For example, the arrows on the map represent the movement of Alexander's armies as they conquered new lands. On the smaller map, lines show modern political boundaries in the region today.

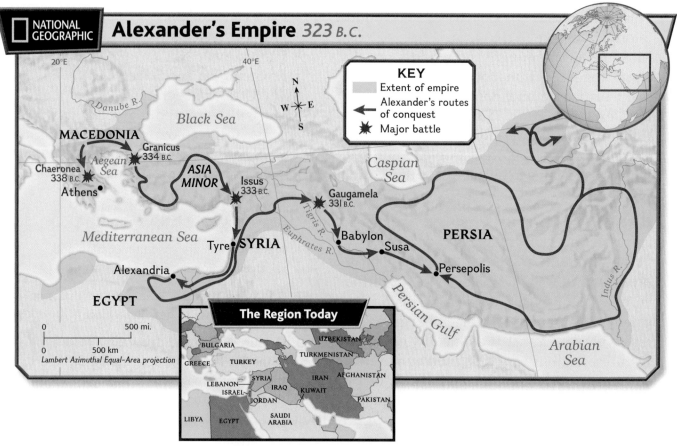

NATIONAL GEOGRAPHIC

Alexander's Empire 323 B.C.

KEY
- Extent of empire
- Alexander's routes of conquest
- Major battle

Danube R.
Black Sea
MACEDONIA
Granicus 334 B.C.
Chaeronea 338 B.C.
Aegean Sea
Athens
ASIA MINOR
Issus 333 B.C.
Caspian Sea
Gaugamela 331 B.C.
Tigris R.
Mediterranean Sea
Tyre SYRIA
Euphrates R.
Babylon
Susa
PERSIA
Alexandria
Persepolis
EGYPT
Persian Gulf
Indus R.
Arabian Sea

0   500 mi.
0   500 km
Lambert Azimuthal Equal–Area projection

The Region Today

BULGARIA
UZBEKISTAN
GREECE
TURKEY
TURKMENISTAN
LEBANON
SYRIA
IRAN
AFGHANISTAN
ISRAEL
IRAQ
KUWAIT
JORDAN
PAKISTAN
LIBYA
EGYPT
SAUDI ARABIA

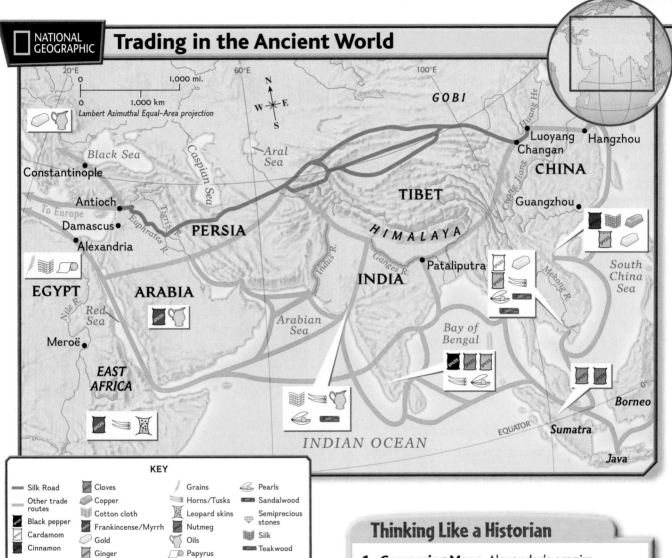

Trading in the Ancient World

KEY

- —— Silk Road
- ---- Other trade routes
- Black pepper
- Cardamom
- Cinnamon
- Cloves
- Copper
- Cotton cloth
- Frankincense/Myrrh
- Gold
- Ginger
- Grains
- Horns/Tusks
- Leopard skins
- Nutmeg
- Oils
- Papyrus
- Pearls
- Sandalwood
- Semiprecious stones
- Silk
- Teakwood

Historical Routes

On some maps, lines may show *historical routes*. These are roads or courses over which people or goods have traveled all through history. Such routes are often colored. On the map above, the purple line shows the Silk Road, the ancient trading route between Asia and Europe.

On maps of historical routes, the key gives clues to what is shown on the maps. This map's key shows the different goods traded throughout the ancient world.

Thinking Like a Historian

1. **Comparing Maps** Alexander's empire included many different territories. In what territory was the city of Persepolis located? What present-day country covers this area today?

2. **Reading a Map Legend** Look at the map of ancient trade routes. What goods came from southern India? How were goods carried from place to place in ancient times?

3. **Analyzing Maps** Select any chapter in your textbook. List the titles of the maps found in that chapter. Beside each map's title, state what kind of symbols are used in each map key and what they represent.

Links Across Time

The people and events of the past have left their mark on our world today.

Reading Focus How have older family members affected your life today? In the same way, many things link past to present in world history. Read about examples of past-and-present links for each of the five units you will be studying in your text.

Unit 1 Early Civilizations

For centuries, people in southwest Asia have fought over scarce land and water. Religious and ethnic differences also have led to wars. Today, one of the fiercest and longest conflicts has been between Palestinian Arabs and Israelis.

▼ Ancient warriors attack walled city

▲ Fighting today between Palestinians and Israelis

Unit 2 The Ancient World

People in ancient civilizations admired the deeds of their heroes. The ancient Greeks held the first Olympic games about 776 B.C. Today the modern Olympics draw athletes from all over the world.

▼ Ancient Greek athletes

▲ Racers in modern Olympics

Unit 3 New Empires and New Faiths

After 500 B.C., strong governments and new religions arose in many parts of the world. The Romans believed that laws apply equally to all citizens. Today, the U.S. Congress is the part of our national government that makes laws. Its upper body—the U.S. Senate—is named after the Senate of ancient Rome.

▲ **Roman Senate**

U.S. Congress ▶

Unit 4 The Middle Ages

The period from about A.D. 500 to A.D. 1500 is known as the Middle Ages. During this time, trade routes expanded, and ideas and goods spread. In medieval China, the Grand Canal increased trade and prosperity. Today, modern China is building the Three Gorges Dam to provide electric power for its growing cities.

Three Gorges Dam ▶

◀ **Grand Canal**

Unit 5 A Changing World

Beginning about A.D. 1500, thinkers developed new ideas about government and began to use scientific ideas to explore nature. One discovery or invention led to another, creating an explosion of knowledge. Advances in science continue today.

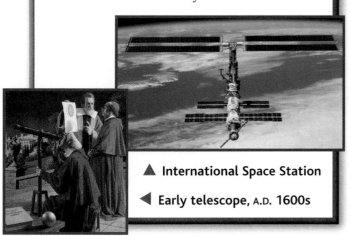

▲ **International Space Station**

◀ **Early telescope,** A.D. **1600s**

Thinking Like a Historian

As you read *Journey Across Time: The Early Ages*, notice how the past affects the present. When you begin each unit, collect newspaper or magazine articles about a current event from the area you are studying. Then, after completing each unit, write down how you think a past event in that region is related to the current event.

Unit 3

New Empires and New Faiths

Why It's Important

Each civilization that you will study in this unit made important contributions to history.

- The Romans invented concrete and used the arch in building.
- The Christians helped shape the West's religious beliefs.
- The Muslims spread the religion of Islam and invented algebra.

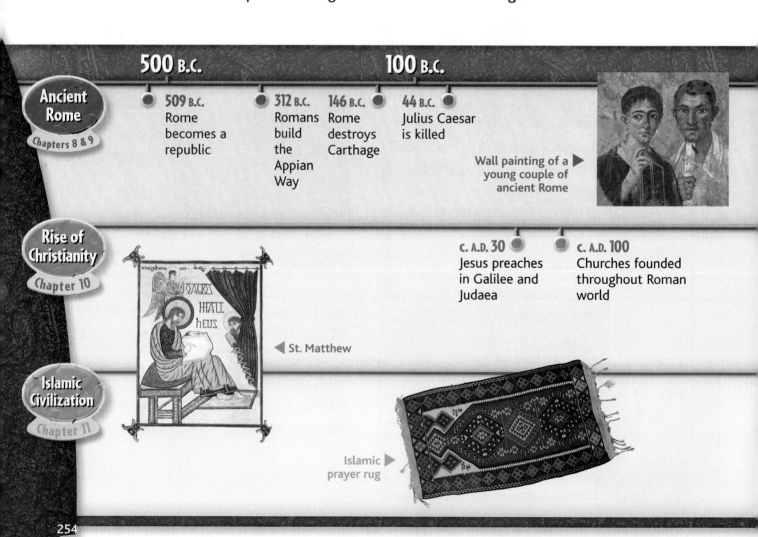

500 B.C.   **100 B.C.**

Ancient Rome
Chapters 8 & 9

509 B.C. Rome becomes a republic

312 B.C. Romans build the Appian Way

146 B.C. Rome destroys Carthage

44 B.C. Julius Caesar is killed

▶ Wall painting of a young couple of ancient Rome

Rise of Christianity
Chapter 10

c. A.D. 30 Jesus preaches in Galilee and Judaea

c. A.D. 100 Churches founded throughout Roman world

◀ St. Matthew

Islamic Civilization
Chapter 11

Islamic ▶ prayer rug

NATIONAL GEOGRAPHIC Where in the World?

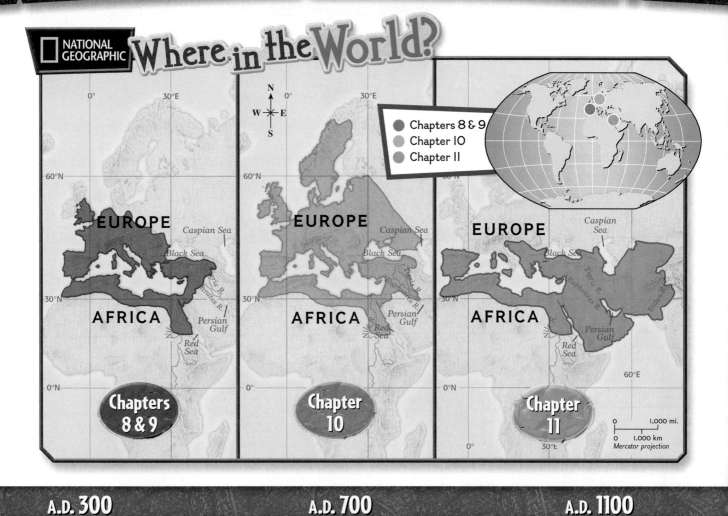

EUROPE

Caspian Sea

Black Sea

AFRICA

Persian Gulf

Red Sea

Chapters 8 & 9

● Chapters 8 & 9
● Chapter 10
● Chapter 11

EUROPE

Caspian Sea

Black Sea

AFRICA

Persian Gulf

Red Sea

Chapter 10

EUROPE

Caspian Sea

Black Sea

AFRICA

Euphrates R.

Tigris R.

Indus R.

Persian Gulf

Red Sea

Chapter 11

0   1,000 mi.
0   1,000 km
Mercator projection

A.D. 300	A.D. 700	A.D. 1100

A.D. 180
Pax Romana ends

A.D. 476
Western Roman Empire ends

A.D. 534
Justinian reforms Roman law

◄ Gladiators in battle

A.D. 392
Christianity becomes Rome's official religion

◄ Church of Hagia Sophia ("Holy Wisdom")

A.D. 1054
Eastern Orthodox and Roman Catholic Churches separate

◄ Mosque in Baghdad

A.D. 624
Muhammad founds Islamic state in Arabia

C. A.D. 830
Baghdad reaches its height as center of Islamic learning

C. A.D. 1200
Muslim rule reaches to northern India

Places to Locate

EUROPE

① ② ③

Mediterranean Sea

④

AFRICA

Roman aqueduct

See Ancient Rome
Chapters 8 & 9

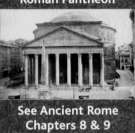

Roman Pantheon

See Ancient Rome
Chapters 8 & 9

People to Meet

Augustus

63 B.C.–A.D. 14
Roman emperor
Chapter 8, page 289

Jesus

c. 6 B.C. –A.D. 30
**Crucifixion led to rise of
Christianity**
Chapter 10, page 346

Paul

c. A.D. 10–65
Christian thinker
Chapter 10, page 349

Constantine

c. A.D. 280–337
Roman emperor
Chapter 9, page 321

ASIA

3 Hagia Sophia

See Ancient Rome
Chapters 8 & 9

4 Mount of the Beatitudes

See Rise of Christianity
Chapter 10

5 Kaaba

See Islamic Civilization
Chapter 11

Arabian Sea

Augustine

A.D. 354–430
Christian
philosopher
Chapter 10, page 357

Theodora

C. A.D. 500–548
Byzantine empress
Chapter 9, page 331

Muhammad

C. A.D. 570–632
Muslims believe Allah
dictated the Quran to
Muhammad
Chapter 11, page 376

Omar Khayyam

A.D. 1048–1131
Islamic poet
and philosopher
Chapter 11, page 392

Chapter 8

The Rise of Rome

◀ Ruins of the Forum in Rome, Italy

NATIONAL GEOGRAPHIC When & Where?

500 B.C.	300 B.C.	100 B.C.	A.D. 100
451 B.C. Romans adopt the Twelve Tables	**267 B.C.** Rome controls most of Italy	**27 B.C.** Octavian becomes Rome's first emperor	**A.D. 96** Rule of the Good Emperors begins

Chapter Preview

While the Chinese civilization arose in East Asia, the Romans created an empire that covered much of the Mediterranean world. Read this chapter to discover how the Romans were able to win control of such a large area.

History Online

Chapter Overview Visit jat.glencoe.com for a preview of Chapter 8.

 View the Chapter 8 video in the *World History: Journey Across Time* Video Program.

Rome's Beginnings

The civilization of Rome began in Italy. Rome grew from a small city into an economic and military power.

The Roman Republic

Rome was a republic for almost 500 years. During this time, it gradually expanded the right to vote. After many years of war and following the destruction of the Carthaginian Empire, Rome took control of the Mediterranean region.

The Fall of the Republic

As Rome's territory grew, the army gained political power. The Roman Republic, weakened by civil wars, gave way to the Roman Empire.

The Early Empire

Augustus and many of his successors governed well. Rome's empire grew larger and wealthier.

FOLDABLES
Study Organizer

Know-Want-Learn *Make this foldable to help you organize what you know, what you want to know, and what you learn about the rise of Rome.*

Step 1 *Fold four sheets of paper in half from top to bottom.*

Step 2 *On each folded paper, make a cut 1 inch from the side on the top flap.*

Cut 1 inch from the edge through the top flap only.

Step 3 *Place the folded papers one on top of the other. Staple the four sections together and label the top four tabs: Rome's Beginnings, The Roman Republic, The Fall of the Republic, and The Early Empire.*

Staple here.

Rome's Beginnings

Reading and Writing *Before reading the chapter, write what you already know about the beginning of Rome, the rise and fall of its republic, and the early Roman Empire under the tabs of your foldable. Also write one question you have on each tab. As you read, summarize what you learn under each tab.*

Chapter 8 Reading Social Studies

Reading Skill
Taking Notes

1 Learn It!

Note Taking

Did you know that when you take notes, you remember more than three-fourths of the information you recorded? That is why it is important to learn to take careful notes as you are reading.

Read this paragraph from Section 3.

Trouble in the Republic

Rome's armies were victorious wherever they went. Yet problems were building at home. Dishonest officials stole money, and the gap between rich and poor was growing. Thousands of farmers faced ruin, and the cities were becoming overcrowded and dangerous.

—*from page 278*

Reading Tip

Authors of textbooks help with note taking by giving you headings and subheadings. If you are not sure of the main topic, it is a safe bet that headings in bold are important.

Here is one method of note taking for the above paragraph.

Main Topic	Important Details
Republic's Problems	1. dishonest officials 2. gap between rich and poor 3. farmers faced ruin 4. cities overcrowded

2 Practice It!

Make a T-Chart

Read the first few pages of Section 2 and use this T-chart as a guide to help you practice taking notes.

Main Topic	Important Details
Rome's government	1.
	2.
Social groups in Rome	1.
	2.
Roman law	1.
	2.

Read to Write ·······

On page 273, read about Rome's first code of laws, the Twelve Tables. Come up with your own 12 Tables of School Law, and explain why each one should be used to govern the students in your school.

3 Apply It!

As you read Section 1, write the names of important people or places on the left column of your note-taking paper. On the right side, list details from your reading.

Section 1

Rome's Beginnings

Get Ready to Read!

What's the Connection?

In previous chapters, you learned about the civilization of ancient Greece. Greek ways did not die with the end of Greece's freedom. They were adopted and spread widely by another civilization, Rome.

Focusing on the Main Ideas

• Geography played an important role in the rise of Roman civilization. *(page 263)*

• The Romans created a republic and conquered Italy. By treating people fairly, they built Rome from a small city into a great power. *(page 265)*

Locating Places

Sicily (SIH•suh•lee)
Apennines (A•puh•NYNZ)
Latium (LAY•shee•uhm)
Tiber River (TY•buhr)
Etruria (ih•TRUR•ee•uh)

Meeting People

Romulus (RAHM•yuh•luhs)
 and Remus (REE•muhs)
Aeneas (ih•NEE•uhs)
Latins (LA•tuhnz)
Etruscans (ih•TRUHS•kuhnz)
Tarquins (TAHR•kwihnz)

Building Your Vocabulary

republic (rih•PUH•blihk)
legion (LEE•juhn)

Reading Strategy

Summarizing Information Use a diagram like the one below to show how the Etruscans affected the development of Rome.

Etruscans	

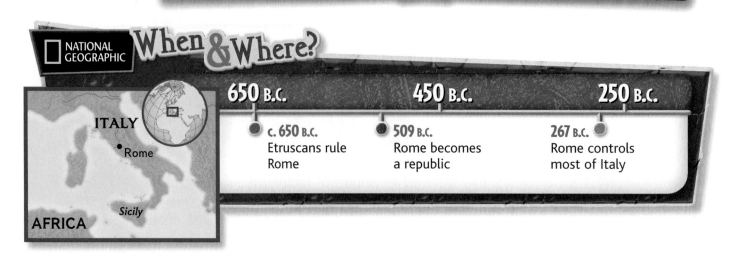

NATIONAL GEOGRAPHIC When & Where?

ITALY
• Rome
Sicily
AFRICA

650 B.C.
c. 650 B.C.
Etruscans rule
Rome

450 B.C.
509 B.C.
Rome becomes
a republic

250 B.C.
267 B.C.
Rome controls
most of Italy

The Origins of Rome

Main Idea Geography played an important role in the rise of Roman civilization.

Reading Focus If you were founding a new city, what natural features would influence your choice of a building site? As you read this section, think about the choices that the early Romans made.

Italy is in an important location in the middle of the Mediterranean region. It is a long, narrow peninsula with a distinctive shape: it looks like a high-heeled boot jutting into the sea. The heel points toward Greece and the toe toward the island of **Sicily** (SIH•suh•lee). Across the top of the boot are the Alps, craggy mountains that separate Italy from European lands to the north. Another mountain range, the **Apennines** (A•puh•NYNZ), runs all the way down the boot from north to south.

The landscape of Italy is similar to that of Greece, but the Apennines are not as rugged as Greece's mountains. They can be crossed much more easily. As a result, the people who settled in Italy were not split up into small, isolated communities as the Greeks were. In addition, Italy had better farmland than Greece. Its mountain slopes level off to large flat plains that are ideal for growing crops. With more capacity to produce food, Italy could support more people than Greece could.

Historians know little about the first people to live in Italy. There is evidence, however, that groups from the north slipped through Italy's mountain passes between about 1500 B.C. and 1000 B.C. Attracted by the mild climate and rich soil, a small but steady stream of newcomers settled in the hills and on the plains. Among these peoples were the Latins, who built the city of Rome on the plain of **Latium** (LAY•shee•uhm) in central Italy.

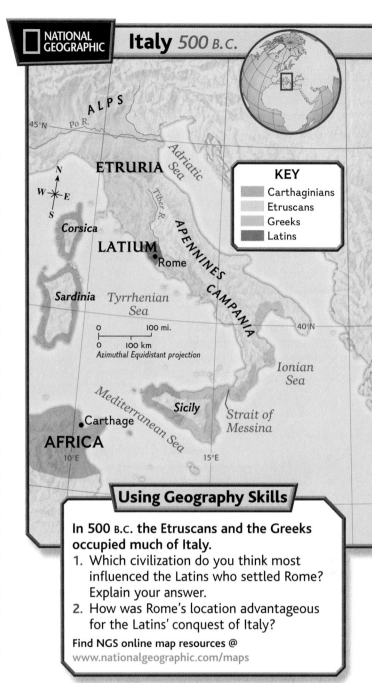

NATIONAL GEOGRAPHIC

Italy *500* B.C.

KEY
- Carthaginians
- Etruscans
- Greeks
- Latins

Azimuthal Equidistant projection

Using Geography Skills

In 500 B.C. the Etruscans and the Greeks occupied much of Italy.

1. Which civilization do you think most influenced the Latins who settled Rome? Explain your answer.
2. How was Rome's location advantageous for the Latins' conquest of Italy?

Find NGS online map resources @ www.nationalgeographic.com/maps

Where Was Rome Located? Geography played a major part in the location of Rome. The site chosen for Rome was about 15 miles (24 km) up the **Tiber River** (TY•buhr) from the Mediterranean Sea. The Tiber River gave the Romans a source of water and a way to the rest of the Mediterranean world. At the same time, Rome was far enough from the sea to escape raids by pirates.

The *Aeneid*

Two legends describe the beginning of Rome. One says that after Troy was destroyed, Aeneas and the other Trojans went in search of another place to live.

"Weeping, I drew away from our old country.... I took to the open sea, borne outward into exile with my people, my son, my hearth gods, and the greater gods.... Now making landfall under the southwind there, I plotted out on that curved shore the walls of a colony—though fate opposed it—and I devised the name Aeneadae for the people, from my own."

—adapted from Virgil, *Aeneid*

▲ Virgil

DBQ Document-Based Question

What type of person do you think Aeneas was to build a new city after having the first one destroyed?

In addition, Rome was built on seven hills. These hills were steep, so the Latins, or Romans as they came to be known, were able to defend their city against enemy attack. Rome was also located at a place where people could easily cross the Tiber River. As a result, Rome became a stopping place for people traveling north and south in western Italy and for merchant ships sailing in the western Mediterranean.

How Did Rome Begin?

Two different legends describe how Rome began. The traditional story is that twin brothers named **Romulus** (RAHM•yuh•luhs) and **Remus** (REE•muhs) founded the city. As babies, the boys were abandoned near the Tiber River. Rescued by a wolf and raised by a shepherd, they decided to build a city in 753 B.C. The twins quarreled, however, and Remus made fun of the wall his brother was building. In a fury, Romulus lashed out at Remus and killed him. Romulus went on to become the first king of Rome, the new city he named after himself.

The seeds of Rome are traced even farther back in the *Aeneid,* a famous epic by the Roman poet Virgil. The *Aeneid* is the story of the Trojan hero **Aeneas** (ih•NEE•uhs). He and a band of followers are said to have sailed the Mediterranean Sea after the Greeks captured Troy. After many adventures, the Trojans landed at the mouth of the Tiber. Through warfare and then marriage to the local king's daughter, Aeneas united the Trojans and the **Latins** (LA•tuhnz), the local people. He thus became the "father" of the Romans.

Historians are not sure how Rome began. They think that Latins lived in the area of Rome as early as 1000 B.C. They built huts on Rome's hills, tended herds, and grew crops. Sometime between 800 B.C. and 700 B.C., they decided to band together for protection. It was this community that became known as Rome.

Early Influences

After about 800 B.C., other groups joined the Romans in Italy. Two of these groups, the Greeks and the **Etruscans** (ih•TRUHS•kuhnz), played a major role in shaping Roman civilization.

Many Greeks came to southern Italy and Sicily between 750 B.C. and 550 B.C., when Greece was busily building overseas colonies. From the Greeks, Romans learned to grow olives and grapes. They also adopted the Greek alphabet, and they

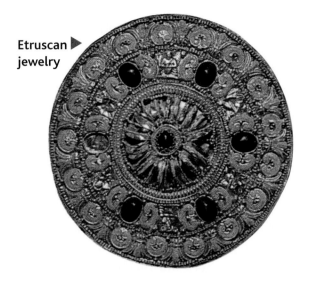

◄ Etruscan jewelry

would eventually model their architecture, sculpture, and literature after the Greeks.

Rome's early growth was influenced most, however, by the Etruscans. The Etruscans lived north of Rome in **Etruria** (ih•TRUR•ee•uh). After 650 B.C., they moved south and took control of Rome and most of Latium.

The Etruscans were skilled metalworkers who became rich from mining and trade. They forced enslaved people to do the heaviest work and made their own lives comfortable. Their tomb paintings show men and women feasting, dancing, and playing music and sports. Some murals also show bloody battle scenes, revealing the Etruscans' pride in their military.

The Etruscans changed Rome from a village of straw-roofed huts into a city of wood and brick buildings. They laid out streets, temples, and public buildings around a central square. Etruscans also taught Romans a new style of dress, featuring short cloaks and togas—loose garments draped over one shoulder. More importantly, the Etruscan army would serve as a model for the mighty army the Romans eventually assembled.

✔ Reading Check **Explain** How did geography help the Romans prosper?

The Birth of a Republic

Main Idea The Romans created a republic and conquered Italy. By treating people fairly, they built Rome from a small city into a great power.

Reading Focus Have you heard the phrase "winning hearts and minds"? It means convincing people to support you rather than just forcing them to obey. Read on to learn how the Romans not only conquered other people in Italy but also won their hearts and minds.

The Etruscans ruled Rome for more than 100 years. Under the Etruscans, Rome became wealthy and powerful. However, the ruling family, called the **Tarquins** (TAHR•kwihnz), grew more and more cruel.

Finally, in 509 B.C., the Romans rebelled. They overthrew the Tarquins and set up a **republic** (rih•PUH•blihk). A republic is a form of government in which the leader is not a king or queen but someone put in office by citizens with the right to vote. In a republic, the citizens have the power. The rise of the Roman Republic marked the beginning of a new chapter in Rome's history.

▲ Etruscan murals often showed lively scenes of daily life, such as religious ceremonies or people enjoying music and feasts. *How did the Etruscans become wealthy?*

At the time Rome became a republic, it was still a small city, surrounded by enemies. Over the next 200 years, the Romans fought war after war against their neighbors. In 338 B.C. they finally defeated the other Latins living nearby. Next they attacked the Etruscans and defeated them in 284 B.C. By 267 B.C., the Romans had also conquered the Greeks in southern Italy. With this victory, the Romans became the masters of almost all of Italy.

Roman Legionary

A soldier's armor was made of iron strips joined by leather ties.

The long iron point on the spear was made to bend after the spear was thrown, preventing an enemy from using it.

Shields were made from sheets of wood glued together and covered with leather or cloth.

At first, the Roman army was made up of ordinary citizens. Later the army contained well-trained professional soldiers and was one of the best fighting forces in the world. *What was a standard, and why did the army carry them?*

Why Was Rome So Strong? Rome was able to conquer Italy because the Romans were excellent soldiers. In the republic's early days, every male citizen who owned land had to serve in the army. Discipline was harsh, and deserters were punished by death. The tough discipline helped mold Roman soldiers into fighters who did not give up easily. In addition, they were practical problem solvers.

For example, Roman armies at first fought like Greek armies. Row upon row of soldiers marched shoulder to shoulder, keeping their shields together and holding long spears. Roman generals soon realized that this way of fighting was slow and hard to control. They reorganized their soldiers into smaller groups called **legions** (LEE•juhnz). Each legion had about 6,000 men and was further divided into groups of 60 to 120 soldiers. These small groups could quickly cut through enemy lines.

Roman soldiers, or legionaries, were armed with a short sword called a *gladius* and a spear called a *pilum.* Each unit also carried its own standard—a tall pole topped with a symbol. In battle, standards helped keep units together because the soldiers could see them above the action.

Shrewd Rulers The Romans were not only good fighters but also smart planners. As they expanded throughout Italy, they built permanent military settlements in the areas they conquered. Then they built roads between these towns. These roads allowed troops to travel swiftly to any place in their growing territory.

To rule their new conquests, the Romans created the Roman Confederation. Under this system, Romans gave full citizenship to some peoples, especially other Latins. They could vote and serve in the government, and they were treated the same as other citizens under the law. The Romans granted other peoples the status of allies.

Allies were free to run their own local affairs, but they had to pay taxes to the republic and provide soldiers for the army. The Romans made it clear that loyal allies could improve their position and even become Roman citizens.

With these policies, the Romans proved themselves clever rulers. They knew that conquered peoples would be more loyal to the government if they were well treated. Rome's generosity paid off. As a result, the republic grew stronger and more unified.

All the same, Rome was not afraid to use force if necessary. If conquered peoples revolted against Roman rule, their resistance was swiftly put down.

✓ Reading Check **Describe** How did Rome rule its new conquests?

▲ This mosaic, or picture made from bits of stone, shows a group of Roman legionaries. *How many soldiers made up a legion?*

History Online
Homework Helper Need help with the material in this section? Visit jat.glencoe.com

Section 1 Review

Reading Summary

Review the Main Ideas

- The Latins settled the region of Rome on the west side of Italy. The region's geography, as well as Etruscan and Greek ideas, helped Rome grow.

- In 509 B.C. the Romans overthrew Etruscan rule and established a republic. By about 275 B.C., Roman legions had conquered most of Italy.

What Did You Learn?

1. Where did the Greeks live in Italy, and how did they influence Roman civilization?

2. Describe the two legends that tell of the founding of Rome. Then describe how and when Rome was actually founded.

Critical Thinking

3. **Geography Skills** Draw a diagram like the one below. List examples of how geography determined Rome's location.

The Location of Rome

4. **Summarize** Describe the Roman conquest of Italy.

5. **Compare and Contrast** How did geography affect the development of civilization in Greece and Italy?

6. **Expository Writing** Write a short essay discussing the reasons Rome was so successful in its conquest of Italy.

7. **Reading** Taking Notes Use the blue subheads in Section 1 to create notes about Rome's beginnings. List each subhead on the left of a T-chart and details on the right.

Section 2

The Roman Republic

Get Ready to Read!

What's the Connection?

Romans had suffered under cruel Etruscan kings. When they had the chance to create their own government, they chose something very different.

Focusing on the Main Ideas

- Rome's republic was shaped by a struggle between wealthy landowners and regular citizens as it gradually expanded the right to vote. **(page 269)**

- Rome slowly destroyed the Carthaginian Empire and took control of the entire Mediterranean region. **(page 274)**

Locating Places

Carthage (KAHR•thihj)
Cannae (KA•nee)
Zama (ZAY•muh)

Meeting People

Cincinnatus (SIHN•suh•NA•tuhs)
Hannibal (HA•nuh•buhl)
Scipio (SIH•pee•OH)

Building Your Vocabulary

patrician (puh•TRIH•shuhn)
plebeian (plih•BEE•uhn)
consul (KAHN•suhl)
veto (VEE•toh)
praetor (PREE•tuhr)
dictator (DIHK•TAY•tuhr)

Reading Strategy

Categorizing Information Complete a chart like the one below listing the government officials and legislative bodies of the Roman Republic.

Officials	Legislative Bodies

NATIONAL GEOGRAPHIC When & Where?

450 B.C. | **300 B.C.** | **150 B.C.**

451 B.C. Romans adopt the Twelve Tables

264 B.C. Punic Wars begin

146 B.C. Rome destroys Carthage

SPAIN · ITALY · Rome · Carthage · GREECE

Rome's Government

Main Idea Rome's republic was shaped by a struggle between wealthy landowners and regular citizens as it gradually expanded the right to vote.

Reading Focus Do you know where our word *republic* comes from? It is made up of two Latin words meaning "thing of the people." Read on to learn about the republican government that early Romans created.

Early Romans were divided into two classes: patricians and plebeians. The **patricians** (puh•TRIH•shuhnz) were wealthy landowners. These nobles made up Rome's ruling class. Most of Rome's people, however, were **plebeians** (plih•BEE•uhnz). This group included artisans, shopkeepers, and owners of small farms.

Both patrician and plebeian men were Roman citizens. They had the right to vote and the responsibility to pay taxes and serve in the army. However, plebeians had less social status. Marriage between members of the two classes was forbidden. Plebeians also lacked an important political right: they could not hold public office. Only patricians could serve in the government.

How Did Rome's Government Work? In the Roman Republic, the top government officials were the **consuls** (KAHN•suhlz). Two consuls—both patricians—were chosen every year. They headed the army and ran the government. Because they served such short terms, there was little risk that they would abuse their power. The consuls also

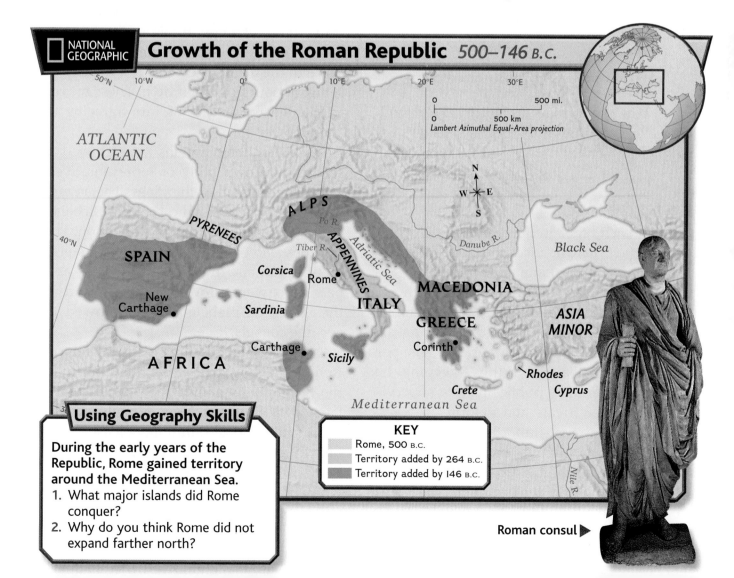

NATIONAL GEOGRAPHIC

Growth of the Roman Republic 500–146 B.C.

500 mi.

500 km

Lambert Azimuthal Equal-Area projection

ATLANTIC OCEAN

PYRENEES

ALPS

Po R.

Tiber R.

APPENNINES

Adriatic Sea

Danube R.

Black Sea

SPAIN

Corsica

Rome

New Carthage

Sardinia

ITALY

MACEDONIA

GREECE

ASIA MINOR

Carthage

Sicily

Corinth

AFRICA

Rhodes

Cyprus

Crete

Mediterranean Sea

Nile R.

Using Geography Skills

During the early years of the Republic, Rome gained territory around the Mediterranean Sea.
1. What major islands did Rome conquer?
2. Why do you think Rome did not expand farther north?

KEY

Rome, 500 B.C.

Territory added by 264 B.C.

Territory added by 146 B.C.

Roman consul ▶

A Roman Triumph

Sometimes military leaders returning to Rome after a victory took part in a great parade called a triumph.

▲ Roman soldiers

"Thus arrayed [decoratively dressed], they entered the city, having at the head of the procession the spoils and trophies and figures representing the captured forts, cities, mountains, rivers, lakes, and seas—everything, in fact, that they had taken.... [When] ... the victorious general arrived at the Roman Forum ... he rode up to the Capitol. There he performed certain rites and made offerings."

—Zonaras, "A Roman Triumph"

DBQ Document-Based Question

Why do you think the military leaders and their troops were dressed decoratively before the triumph?

kept each other in line because each could **veto** (VEE•toh), or reject, the other's decision. The word *veto* is Latin for "I forbid."

Rome had other important officials called **praetors** (PREE•tuhrz). Their main job was to interpret the law and act as judges in court cases. Various other officials performed specialized duties—keeping tax records, handling public finances, supervising public festivals, and so forth.

Rome's most important legislative, or lawmaking, body was the Senate. This was a select group of 300 patrician men who served for life. In the beginning, the Senate only gave advice to the consuls. Over time,

the power of the Senate grew. By the 200s B.C., it could also propose laws, hold debates on important issues, and approve building programs.

Another legislative body was the Assembly of Centuries. It elected important officials, such as consuls and praetors, and passed laws. Like the Senate, the Assembly of Centuries was under the control of the patricians.

Plebeians Against Patricians As you might expect, plebeians complained about having so little power in the Roman Republic. After all, they fought alongside patricians in the army, and their tax payments helped the republic thrive. It seemed reasonable that they should have equal rights.

Eventually, the plebeians took action to bring about change. In 494 B.C. many plebeians went on strike. They refused to serve in the army. They also left the city to set up a republic of their own. These moves frightened the patricians into agreeing to share power.

In 471 B.C. the plebeians were allowed to set up their own body of representatives, called the Council of the Plebs. The assembly elected tribunes who brought plebeian concerns to the government's attention. The tribunes also won the right to veto government decisions. In 455 B.C. plebeians and patricians were allowed to marry, and in the 300s B.C., plebeians were allowed to become consuls.

The most far-reaching political reform came in 287 B.C. In that year, the Council of the Plebs finally gained the power to pass laws for all Romans. Now all male citizens had equal political standing, at least in theory. In practice, a few wealthy patrician families still held most of the power, and women remained without a voice in government. The Roman Republic had become more representative, but it was far from a full-fledged democracy.

Who Was Cincinnatus?

An unusual feature of the Roman Republic was the office of **dictator** (DIHK•tay•tuhr). We define a dictator today as an oppressive ruler with complete control over the state. Roman dictators also had complete control, but they served the people and ruled on a temporary basis during emergencies. The Senate would appoint a dictator in times of great danger. As soon as the danger was past, Roman dictators gave up their power.

The best-known early Roman dictator is **Cincinnatus** (SIHN•suh•NA•tuhs). About 460 B.C., a powerful enemy had surrounded a Roman army. Officials decided that the crisis called for a dictator and that Cincinnatus was the man for the job. The officials found Cincinnatus plowing his fields. A loyal and devoted citizen, Cincinnatus left his farm and gathered an army. He defeated the enemy in short order and returned to Rome in triumph. Although he probably could have continued ruling, Cincinnatus did not want power. Having done his duty, he returned to his farm a mere 15 or 16 days after becoming dictator.

Cincinnatus was widely admired in his own time and in later ages. George Washington, for one, took inspiration from his example. Like Cincinnatus, Washington was a farmer when he was asked to head an army: the Continental Army in the American War for Independence. After leading the Americans to victory, Washington returned to his plantation home. Only later, and with some reluctance, did he agree to become the first president of the United States.

The Way It Was

Focus on Everyday Life

Roman Dinner Parties Before Rome became a powerful empire, Romans ate simple meals of porridge, dried vegetables, and greens. People rarely ate meat or seafood. After Rome's conquests, the dining habits of wealthy Romans changed. Newly rich Romans showed off their wealth with expensive feasts that included exotic foods and lively entertainment for their guests.

At Roman dinner parties, guests reclined on couches. The enslaved servants served the food, which would be carried into the banquet room on great silver platters. Roman dishes might include boiled stingray garnished with hot raisins; boiled crane with turnips; or roast flamingo cooked with dates, onions, honey, and wine.

▼ A wealthy Roman woman reclining on a couch

Connecting to the Past

1. Whose eating habits changed after Rome became wealthy and powerful?
2. Describe how their eating habits changed.

Biography

LUCIUS QUINCTIUS CINCINNATUS

c. 519–438 B.C.

The loyal devotion of Cincinnatus greatly impressed the Roman historian Livy. In his *History of Rome,* Livy advised his readers to listen to the worthwhile story of Cincinnatus, whose virtue rose high above any rewards that wealth could bring.

According to Livy, Cincinnatus lived in Rome but owned and worked a four-acre field on the other side of the Tiber River. On the day that the officials looked for Cincinnatus, they found him hard at work in his field, covered with dirt and sweat. Cincinnatus was surprised when the officials asked him to put on his toga and listen as they explained the wishes of the Roman Senate. Cincinnatus must not have been aware of the danger the Roman army faced, because he asked the officials if everything was all right before calling to his wife, Racilia, and asking her to bring him his toga quickly.

The officials explained the emergency situation to Cincinnatus. He agreed to the Senate's request that he become a dictator. Cincinnatus and the officials crossed the Tiber River to Rome and were greeted by his three sons, other relatives and friends, and members of the Senate. Later they escorted Cincinnatus safely to his home. The next morning, before daylight, Cincinnatus went to the Forum and gathered his forces to attack the enemy.

▲ Cincinnatus is asked to lead Rome.

"The city was in the grip of fear."
–Livy, *The Rise of Rome*

Then and Now

Name a modern-day leader that you think historians will write about with great admiration. Explain why.

Roman Law One of Rome's chief gifts to the world was its system of law. The legal system of the United States owes much to the Roman system.

Rome's first code of laws was the Twelve Tables, adopted about 451 B.C. Before this time, Rome's laws were not written down. As a result, plebeians claimed that patrician judges often favored their own class. They demanded that the laws be put in writing for everyone to see.

The patricians finally agreed. They had the laws carved on bronze tablets that were placed in Rome's marketplace, or the Forum (FOHR•uhm). The Twelve Tables became the basis for all future Roman laws. They established the principle that all free citizens had the right to be treated equally by the legal system.

The Twelve Tables, however, applied only to Roman citizens. As the Romans took over more lands, they realized that new rules were needed to solve legal disputes between citizens and noncitizens. They created a collection of laws called the Law of Nations. It stated principles of justice that applied to all people everywhere.

These standards of justice included ideas that we still accept today. A person was seen as innocent until proven guilty. People accused of crimes could defend themselves before a judge. A judge had to look at the evidence carefully before making a decision.

The idea that the law should apply to everyone equally and that all people should be treated the same way by the legal system

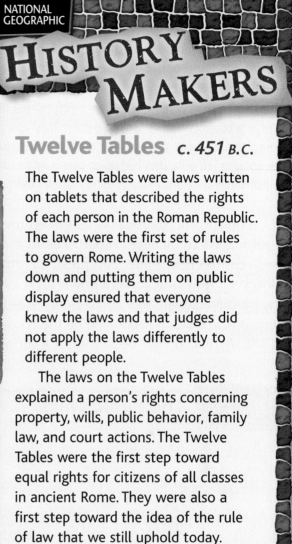

▲ These bundles of rods and axes, called fasces, symbolized the legal authority of Roman leaders.

HISTORY MAKERS

Twelve Tables c. 451 B.C.

The Twelve Tables were laws written on tablets that described the rights of each person in the Roman Republic. The laws were the first set of rules to govern Rome. Writing the laws down and putting them on public display ensured that everyone knew the laws and that judges did not apply the laws differently to different people.

The laws on the Twelve Tables explained a person's rights concerning property, wills, public behavior, family law, and court actions. The Twelve Tables were the first step toward equal rights for citizens of all classes in ancient Rome. They were also a first step toward the idea of the rule of law that we still uphold today.

is called the "rule of law." In the age of Rome, the rule of law was still a new idea. In many lands, people at the top of society often had special privileges and did not have to obey the same laws or use the same courts as people lower down. In some places, people at the bottom of society did not have any legal rights at all. The rule of law is one of the key ideas that the Romans gave to the world. It is still the basis of our legal system today.

✓ **Reading Check** **Contrast** Before 471 B.C., what right did patricians have that plebeians did not?

Rome Expands

Main Idea Rome slowly destroyed the Carthaginian Empire and took control of the entire Mediterranean region.

Reading Focus When you achieve a victory—whether it is in academics, sports, or some other field—do you then strive for more success? That may have been how the Romans felt once they had taken over Italy. Read on to learn how they continued to expand their power.

While Rome developed its government, it also faced challenges abroad. The Romans had completed their conquest of Italy. However, they now faced a powerful rival in the Mediterranean area. This enemy was the state of **Carthage** (KAHR•thihj) on the coast of North Africa. It had been founded around 800 B.C. by the Phoenicians. As you learned earlier, the Phoenicians were sea traders from the Middle East.

Carthage ruled a great trading empire that included parts of northern Africa and southern Europe. By controlling the movement of goods in this region, Carthage made itself the largest and richest city in the western Mediterranean.

The First Punic War Both Carthage and Rome wanted to control the island of Sicily. In 264 B.C. the dispute brought the two powers to blows. The war that began in 264 B.C. is called the First Punic War. *Punicus* is the Latin word for "Phoenician." The war started when the Romans sent an army to Sicily to prevent a Carthaginian

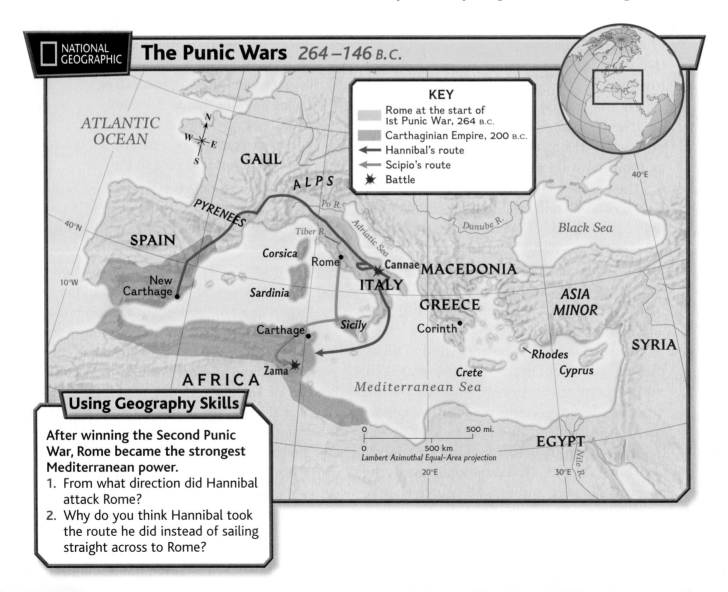

NATIONAL GEOGRAPHIC **The Punic Wars** *264–146 B.C.*

KEY
- Rome at the start of 1st Punic War, 264 B.C.
- Carthaginian Empire, 200 B.C.
- ← Hannibal's route
- ← Scipio's route
- ✳ Battle

ATLANTIC OCEAN
GAUL
ALPS
PYRENEES
SPAIN
Po R.
Danube R.
Adriatic Sea
Black Sea
Tiber R.
Corsica
Rome
Cannae
MACEDONIA
New Carthage
ITALY
Sardinia
GREECE
ASIA MINOR
Carthage
Sicily
Corinth
SYRIA
AFRICA
Zama
Crete
Rhodes
Cyprus
Mediterranean Sea
EGYPT
Nile R.

0   500 mi.
0   500 km
Lambert Azimuthal Equal-Area projection

Using Geography Skills

After winning the Second Punic War, Rome became the strongest Mediterranean power.
1. From what direction did Hannibal attack Rome?
2. Why do you think Hannibal took the route he did instead of sailing straight across to Rome?

takeover. The Carthaginians, who already had colonies on the island, were determined to stop this invasion.

Up until then, the Romans had fought their wars on land. However, they soon realized they could not defeat a sea power like Carthage without a navy. They quickly built a large fleet of ships and confronted their enemy at sea. The war dragged on for more than 20 years. Finally, in 241 B.C., Rome crushed Carthage's navy off the coast of Sicily. Carthage was forced to leave Sicily and pay a huge fine to the Romans. The island then came under Roman rule.

The Second Punic War To make up for its loss of Sicily, Carthage expanded its empire into southern Spain. Roman leaders were not happy about Carthage gaining land near Rome's northern border. They helped the people living in Spain rebel against Carthage. Of course, Carthaginians were angry. To punish Rome, Carthage sent its greatest general, **Hannibal** (HA•nuh•buhl), to attack Rome in 218 B.C. This started the Second Punic War.

Hannibal's strategy was to take the fighting into Italy itself. To do this, Hannibal gathered an army of about 46,000 men, many horses, and 37 elephants. He landed his forces in Spain and then marched east to attack Italy.

Even before reaching Italy, Hannibal's forces suffered severe losses crossing the steep, snowy Alps into Italy. The brutal cold, gnawing hunger, and attacks by

▼ In December 218 B.C., Hannibal's forces and the Roman army met in battle near the Trebbia River in northern Italy. In a well-planned attack, the Carthaginian forces badly defeated the Romans. Hannibal made good use of his elephants in the attack, but most died following the battle. *At what other battle in Italy were the Romans defeated by Hannibal?*

mountain tribes killed almost half of the soldiers and most of the elephants. The remaining army, however, was still a powerful fighting force when it reached Italy.

The Romans suffered a severe loss in 216 B.C. at the Battle of **Cannae** (KA•nee) in southern Italy. Even though Hannibal's army was outnumbered, it overpowered the Roman force and began raiding much of Italy.

The Romans, however, raised another army. In 202 B.C. a Roman force led by a general named **Scipio** (SIH•pee•OH) invaded Carthage. Hannibal, who was waging a war in Italy, had no choice but to return home to defend his people.

At the Battle of **Zama** (ZAY•muh), Scipio's troops defeated the Carthaginians. Carthage gave up Spain to Rome. It also had to give up its navy and pay a large fine. Rome now ruled the western Mediterranean.

More Conquests While Carthage was no longer a military power, it remained a trading center. In 146 B.C. Rome finally destroyed its great rival in the Third Punic War. Roman soldiers burned Carthage and enslaved 50,000 men, women, and children. Legend says that the Romans even spread salt on the earth so no crops would grow. Carthage became a Roman province, or regional district.

During the Punic Wars, Rome successfully battled states in the eastern Mediterranean. In 148 B.C. Macedonia came under Roman rule. Two years later, the rest of Greece became Roman. In 129 B.C. Rome gained its first province in Asia. It was no wonder that the Romans began to call the Mediterranean *mare nostrum*—"our sea."

✓ **Reading Check** **Describe** How did Rome punish Carthage at the end of the Third Punic War?

History **O**nline
Homework Helper Need help with the material in this section? Visit jat.glencoe.com

Section ② Review

Reading Summary

Review the Main Ideas

• During the Roman Republic, the government changed as the plebeians, or lower classes, and the patricians, or ruling class, struggled for power.

• Beginning in 264 B.C., Rome fought and won a series of wars with Carthage and other powers and gained control of the Mediterranean region.

What Did You Learn?

1. Who were the top government officials in the Roman Republic, and what were their duties?

2. What does *mare nostrum* mean, and why did the Romans use the term?

Critical Thinking

3. **Sequencing Information** Draw a diagram to describe the sequence of events from the start of the First Punic War to the start of the Second Punic War.

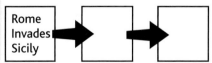

Rome Invades Sicily →

4. **Geography Skills** Where was Carthage located, and why did it compete with Rome?

5. **Summarize** What other conquests did Rome carry out during the period of the Punic Wars?

6. **Evaluate** Why do you think the legacy of Roman law is considered so important?

7. **Persuasive Writing** Write a speech demanding equal rights for plebeians in the early republic.

Section 3

The Fall of the Republic

Get Ready to Read!

What's the Connection?
By the end of the Third Punic War, Rome ruled the Mediterranean world. All was not well, however. Closer to home, the republic faced increasing dangers that would soon lead to its end.

Focusing on the Main Ideas
• The use of enslaved labor hurt farmers, increased poverty and corruption, and brought the army into politics. *(page 278)*

• Military hero Julius Caesar seized power and made reforms. *(page 280)*

• The Roman Republic, weakened by civil wars, became an empire under Augustus. *(page 282)*

Locating Places
Rubicon (ROO•bih•KAHN)
Actium (AK•shee•uhm)

Meeting People
Julius Caesar
  (jool•yuhs   SEE•zuhr)
Octavian (ahk•TAY•vee•uhn)
Antony (AN•tuh•nee)
Cicero (SIH•suh•ROH)
Augustus (aw•GUHS•tuhs)

Building Your Vocabulary
latifundia (LA•tuh•FUHN•dee•uh)
triumvirate (try•UHM•vuh•ruht)

Reading Strategy
Finding the Main Idea Use a chart like the one below to identify the main ideas of Section 3 and supporting details.

Main Idea		
Supporting Detail	Supporting Detail	Supporting Detail
Supporting Detail	Supporting Detail	Supporting Detail

NATIONAL GEOGRAPHIC When & Where?

GAUL
ITALY
SPAIN   Rome•
            ASIA MINOR
      GREECE

100 B.C.   **60** B.C.   **20** B.C.

82 B.C.
Sulla becomes dictator of Rome

44 B.C.
Group of senators murder Julius Caesar

27 B.C.
Octavian becomes Rome's first emperor

Trouble in the Republic

Main Idea The use of enslaved labor hurt farmers, increased poverty and corruption, and brought the army into politics.

Reading Focus Poverty, corruption, unemployment, crime, and violence are problems we hear about today. Read on to learn how the Romans struggled with these same issues 2,000 years ago.

Rome's armies were victorious wherever they went. Yet problems were building at home. Dishonest officials stole money, and the gap between rich and poor was growing. Thousands of farmers faced ruin, and the cities were becoming overcrowded and dangerous.

Rich Versus Poor

As you read in Section 2, most of the people who ruled Rome were patricians—rich people who owned large farms. These rich landowners ran the Senate and held the most powerful government jobs. They handled Rome's finances and directed its wars. Despite some gains for the plebeians, many people became very unhappy about this situation.

Rome had few privileged citizens compared with the many Romans who farmed small plots of land. In the 100s B.C., however, these farmers were sinking into poverty and debt. Why? Many of them had been unable to farm because they were fighting in Rome's wars. Others had suffered damage to their farms during Hannibal's invasion of Italy.

Moreover, small farmers could not compete with wealthy Romans who were buying up land to create **latifundia** (LA•tuh•FUHN•dee•uh), or large farming estates. These rich landowners used a new source of labor—the thousands of prisoners brought to Italy during the wars. By using these enslaved people to tend their crops, wealthy Romans could force owners of small farms out of business.

Faced with debts they could not pay off, many farmers sold their land and headed to the cities, desperate for work. However, jobs were hard to find. Enslaved people did most of the work. If free men were lucky enough to be hired, they earned low wages. These conditions created widespread anger.

▲ This image shows Romans farming their land. *Why were Roman farmers becoming poor in the 100s B.C.?*

Roman politicians were worried about riots breaking out, but they quickly turned the situation to their advantage. To win the votes of the poor, they began providing cheap food and entertainment. This policy of "bread and circuses" helped many dishonest rulers come to power.

Why Did Reform Fail?
Not all wealthy people ignored the problems facing the Roman Republic. Two prominent officials who worked for reforms were Tiberius and Gaius Gracchus (GRA•kuhs). These brothers thought that many of Rome's problems were caused by the loss of small farms. They asked the Senate to take back public land from the rich and divide it among landless Romans.

Many senators, however, were among those who had claimed parcels of public land. Putting their own interests above the general welfare, they fought the Gracchus brothers' proposals. A band of senators even went so far as to kill Tiberius in 133 B.C. Twelve years later, Gaius met the same fate. These were dark days for the Roman Republic, when the people charged with making and upholding the laws could so shockingly violate them.

The Army Enters Politics
Matters only worsened as the Roman army took on a new role. Until now, the army had mostly stayed out of government affairs. Things changed when a military leader named Marius became consul in 107 B.C. Previously, most soldiers were owners of small farms. Now because this type of farmer was disappearing, Marius began to recruit soldiers from the

◄ Tiberius Gracchus (left) and his brother Gaius believed that moving poor Romans from the city to farms would help solve the republic's problems. *What happened to the Gracchus brothers?*

poor. In return for their service, he paid them wages and promised them the one thing they desperately wanted—land.

Marius changed the Roman army from citizen volunteers to paid professional soldiers. The new troops, however, were motivated by material rewards rather than a sense of duty. They felt loyal to their general, not to the Roman Republic. This gave individual generals a great deal of influence and good reason to become involved in politics. They needed to get laws passed that would provide the land they had promised their soldiers.

Marius's new military system led to new power struggles. It was not long before Marius faced a challenge from a rival general with his own army, a man named Sulla. In 82 B.C. Sulla drove his enemies out of Rome and made himself dictator.

Over the next three years, Sulla changed the government. He weakened the Council of the Plebs and strengthened the Senate. Then he stepped down from office. He hoped that the Roman Republic could heal its wounds and recapture its glory. Instead, Rome plunged into an era of civil wars for the next 50 years. Ambitious men saw how Sulla used an army to seize power. They decided to follow the same path.

✓ **Reading Check** **Explain** What change did Marius make to the Roman army?

History Online

Web Activity Visit jat.glencoe.com and click on *Chapter 8—Student Web Activity* to learn more about the rise of Rome.

Julius Caesar

Main Idea Military hero Julius Caesar seized power and made reforms.

Reading Focus Did you know that George Washington, Andrew Jackson, William H. Harrison, Zachary Taylor, Ulysses S. Grant, and Dwight D. Eisenhower all commanded armies before becoming president? Read to learn about a famous Roman who made a similar jump from military leader to political leader.

After Sulla left office, different Roman leaders battled for power, supported by their loyal armies. In 60 B.C. three men were on top: Crassus, Pompey, and **Julius Caesar** (jool•yuhs SEE•zuhr). Crassus was a military leader and one of the richest men in Rome. Pompey and Caesar were not as rich, but both were successful military men. Drawing on their wealth and power, they formed the First Triumvirate to rule Rome. A **triumvirate** (try•UHM•vuh•ruht) is a political alliance of three people.

Caesar's Military Campaigns The members of the Triumvirate each had a military command in a remote area of the republic. Pompey was in Spain, Crassus in Syria, and Caesar in Gaul (modern France). While in Gaul, Caesar battled foreign tribes and invaded Britain. He became a hero to Rome's lower classes. Senators and others back home in Rome feared that Caesar was becoming too popular and might seize power like Sulla or Marius.

After Crassus was killed in battle in 53 B.C., the Senate decided that Pompey should return to Italy and rule alone. In 49 B.C. the Senate ordered Caesar to give up his army and come home. Caesar faced a difficult choice. He could obey the Senate and perhaps face prison or death at the hands of his rivals, or he could march on Rome with his army and risk a civil war.

Caesar decided to hold on to his 5,000 loyal soldiers. He marched into Italy by crossing the **Rubicon** (ROO•bih•KAHN), a

Caesar's Rise to Power

Caesar was part of the First Triumvirate, whose members are shown below.

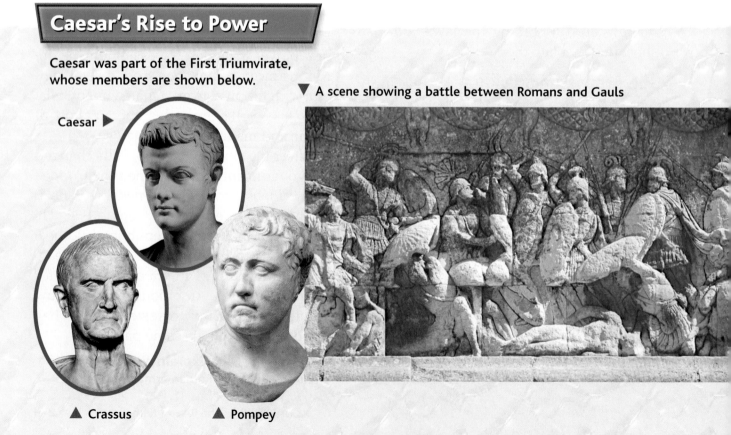

Caesar ▶

▼ A scene showing a battle between Romans and Gauls

▲ Crassus   ▲ Pompey

small river at the southern boundary of his command area. By doing so, Caesar knew that he was starting a civil war and that there was no turning back. The phrase "crossing the Rubicon" is used today to mean making a decision that you cannot take back.

Pompey tried to stop Caesar, but Caesar was the better general. He drove Pompey's forces from Italy and then destroyed Pompey's army in Greece in 48 B.C. After this victory, Caesar was made dictator of Rome for one year.

Caesar's Rise to Power In 44 B.C. Caesar had himself declared dictator of Rome for life. This broke with the Roman tradition that allowed dictators to hold power for only short periods of time. To strengthen his hold on power, Caesar filled the Senate with new members who were loyal to him.

At the same time, Caesar knew that reforms were needed. He granted citizenship to people living in Rome's territories outside the Italian peninsula. He started new colonies to provide land for the landless and created work for Rome's jobless people. He ordered landowners using slave labor to hire more free workers. These measures made Caesar popular with the poor people of Rome.

One reform of Caesar's still affects us today. He created a new calendar with 12 months, 365 days, and a leap year. The Julian calendar, as it was called, was used throughout Europe until A.D. 1582. Our calendar today is only slightly different.

While many Romans supported Caesar, others did not. His supporters believed he was a strong leader who brought peace and order to Rome. His enemies, however, feared that Caesar wanted to be king. These opponents, led by the senators Brutus and Cassius, plotted to kill him. Caesar ignored a famous warning to "beware the Ides of March" (March 15). On that date in 44 B.C., Caesar's enemies surrounded him at the Senate building and stabbed him to death.

✔ **Reading Check** **Explain** Why did Brutus, Cassius, and others kill Caesar?

▼ **Caesar crossing the Rubicon**

Brutus (left) was one of the senators who killed Caesar. Antony (above) supported Caesar and his nephew Octavian and fought against Caesar's assassins.

Rome Becomes an Empire

Main Idea The Roman Republic, weakened by civil wars, became an empire under Augustus.

Reading Focus Have you ever been in a traffic jam and wished that a police officer would show up to get things moving? Read on to learn how Romans welcomed the arrival of a strong new ruler.

Caesar's death plunged Rome into another civil war. On one side were forces led by the men who had killed Caesar. On the other side was Caesar's grandnephew **Octavian** (ahk•TAY•vee•uhn), who had inherited Caesar's wealth, and two of Caesar's top generals, **Antony** (AN•tuh•nee) and Lepidus. After defeating Caesar's assassins, these three men created the Second Triumvirate in 43 B.C.

The Second Triumvirate
The members of the Second Triumvirate began quarreling almost at once. Octavian soon forced Lepidus to retire from politics. Then the two remaining leaders divided the Roman world between themselves. Octavian took the west; Antony took the east.

In short order, though, Octavian and Antony came into conflict. Antony fell in love with the Egyptian queen Cleopatra VII and formed an alliance with her. Octavian told the Romans that Antony, with Cleopatra's help, planned to make himself the sole ruler of the republic. This alarmed many Romans and convinced Octavian to declare war on Antony.

In 31 B.C., at the Battle of **Actium** (AK•shee•uhm) off the west coast of Greece, Octavian crushed the army and navy of Antony and Cleopatra. The couple then fled to Egypt. A year later, as Octavian closed in, they killed themselves. Octavian, at the age of 32, now stood alone at the top of the Roman world. The period of civil wars was

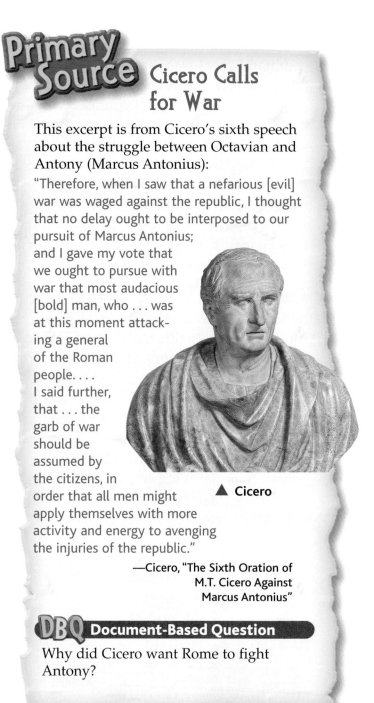

Primary Source — Cicero Calls for War

This excerpt is from Cicero's sixth speech about the struggle between Octavian and Antony (Marcus Antonius):

"Therefore, when I saw that a nefarious [evil] war was waged against the republic, I thought that no delay ought to be interposed to our pursuit of Marcus Antonius; and I gave my vote that we ought to pursue with war that most audacious [bold] man, who . . . was at this moment attacking a general of the Roman people. . . . I said further, that . . . the garb of war should be assumed by the citizens, in order that all men might apply themselves with more activity and energy to avenging the injuries of the republic."

▲ Cicero

—Cicero, "The Sixth Oration of M.T. Cicero Against Marcus Antonius"

DBQ Document-Based Question

Why did Cicero want Rome to fight Antony?

over, but so was the republic. Octavian would lay the foundation for a new system of government—the Roman Empire.

Who Was Augustus?
Octavian could have made himself dictator for life, like Julius Caesar did. He knew, though, that many people favored a republican form of government. One such person was

Cicero (SIH•suh•ROH), a political leader, writer, and Rome's greatest public speaker. Cicero had argued against dictators and called for a representative government with limited powers.

Cicero's speeches and books swayed many Romans. Centuries later, his ideas would also influence the writers of the United States Constitution.

Although Cicero did not live to see Octavian rule, he had supported him, hoping he would restore the republic. In 27 B.C. Octavian announced that he was doing just that.

He knew the Senate wanted this form of government. However, Octavian also knew that the republic had been too weak to solve Rome's problems. Although he gave some power to the Senate, he really put himself in charge. His title, *imperator*, translates to "commander in chief," but it came to mean

▲ At the Battle of Actium, Octavian's forces defeated those of Antony after Cleopatra's ships retreated. *How did the Battle of Actium affect the history of Rome?*

"emperor." Octavian also took the title of **Augustus** (aw•GUHS•tuhs)—"the revered or majestic one." From this point on, he was known by this name.

✓ **Reading Check** **Explain** How did Octavian's government reflect the ideas of Cicero?

History Online

Homework Helper Need help with the material in this section? Visit jat.glencoe.com

Section 3 Review

Reading Summary

Review the Main Ideas

- As the gap between the ruling class and the poor in Rome increased, a number of reforms failed, and generals began to gather power.

- Julius Caesar became dictator and carried out reforms to aid Rome's poor. Later he was assassinated by members of the Senate.

- Caesar's grandnephew Octavian defeated Antony and Cleopatra and became Augustus, the first Roman emperor.

What Did You Learn?

1. What is a triumvirate?

2. Who was Cicero, and how did he influence the writers of the United States Constitution?

Critical Thinking

3. **Understanding Cause and Effect** Draw a diagram like the one below. Fill in the chain of effects that was caused by the thousands of enslaved prisoners that were brought to Italy from Rome's many wars.

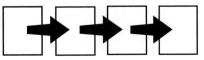

4. **Summarize** What reforms did the Gracchus brothers suggest?

5. **Analyze** What was the "bread and circuses" policy, and how did Roman politicians benefit from it?

6. **Analyze** What reforms did Julius Caesar put in place that increased his popularity with poor and working-class Romans?

7. **Persuasive Writing** Imagine you are a Roman citizen. Decide whether you would have been for or against Julius Caesar's rise to power and his reforms. Then write a newspaper editorial explaining your views. Be sure to include facts to support your opinions.

You Decide . . .

Was Caesar a Reformer or a Dictator?

Great Reformer

During his life, Julius Caesar was greatly admired by many people. He was also hated and feared by many others. Some believed he was too ambitious—exceptionally eager for fame and power—and that his ambition would keep him from acting in Rome's best interest.

Was Caesar a great reformer or an ambitious dictator? Those who saw him as a great leader and reformer said that he

- won the support of his soldiers through his military leadership and strategy
- treated many of his defeated enemies generously and appointed some of them—including Brutus—to government positions
- ended the rule of corrupt Roman nobles
- brought order and peace to Rome
- restored cities that had been destroyed by the republic
- strengthened and expanded the state of Rome
- started public jobs programs to aid the poor
- granted Roman citizenship to people from foreign countries or states.

▲ The assassination of Julius Caesar

Ambitious Dictator

Caesar also had many enemies, including some who had been his friends. They saw Caesar as a dangerous dictator and thought he was taking advantage of his growing power.

They said that he

- became an enemy when he refused to follow the Senate's order to return to Rome
- started a civil war that led to the destruction of the republic
- increased the number of senators to add to his number of supporters
- treated his defeated enemies with cruelty
- punished those who wanted to uphold the traditions and laws of the republic
- weakened the Senate to gain absolute power over Rome
- kept hidden any facts that did not make him look brave and intelligent
- sought glory for himself at the expense of the republic.

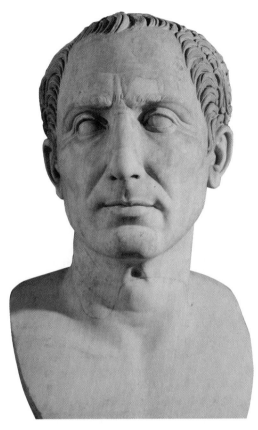

▲ Julius Caesar

You Be the Historian

Checking for Understanding

1. Define *ambition*. Identify some ways ambition can be a positive characteristic and some ways it can be a negative characteristic.
2. What could Caesar have done to show his enemies that he was not abusing his power?
3. Do you think Caesar was a great leader and reformer or an ambitious dictator? Write a brief essay that explains how you view Caesar. Use facts to support your position.

Section 4

The Early Empire

Get Ready to Read!

What's the Connection?

You learned in Section 3 that when Octavian became Augustus, the Roman world began to change. The republic gave way to an empire, and peace and prosperity spread throughout the Mediterranean.

Focusing on the **Main Ideas**

- By expanding the empire and reorganizing the military and government, Augustus created a new era of prosperity. *(page 287)*

- Rome's system of roads, aqueducts, ports, and common currency made the empire rich and prosperous. *(page 290)*

Locating Places

Rhine River (RYN)

Danube River (DAN•YOOB)

Puteoli (pyu•TEE•uh•LY)

Ostia (AHS•tee•uh)

Meeting People

Caligula (kuh•LIH•gyuh•luh)

Nero (NEE•roh)

Hadrian (HAY•dree•uhn)

Building Your Vocabulary

Pax Romana
   (pahks   roh•MAH•nah)

aqueduct (A•kwuh•DUHKT)

currency (KUHR•uhn•see)

Reading Strategy

Cause and Effect Use a chart like the one below to show the changes Augustus made in the Roman Empire and the effect of each change.

Causes		Effects
	→	
	→	
	→	
	→	

NATIONAL GEOGRAPHIC **When & Where?**

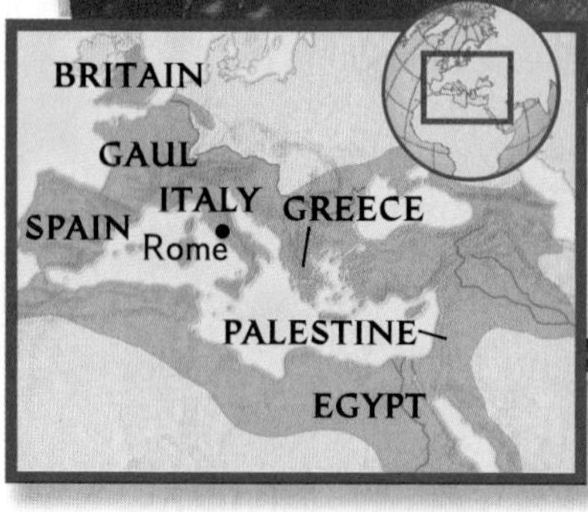

BRITAIN

GAUL

SPAIN ITALY GREECE
      Rome

PALESTINE

EGYPT

A.D. 10

A.D. 14
Augustus dies

A.D. 110

A.D. 96
Rule of the Good
Emperors begins

A.D. 210

A.D. 180
Pax Romana
ends

The Emperor Augustus

Main Idea By expanding the empire and reorganizing the military and government, Augustus created a new era of prosperity.

Reading Focus What makes a good or bad leader? Think about this question as you read about Augustus and other Roman emperors.

Augustus paved the way for 200 years of peace and prosperity in Rome. The emperors who followed him were not all good rulers, but they helped the Roman Empire reach its peak. For centuries, the Mediterranean region had been filled with conflict. Under Augustus and his successors, the region was under the control of one empire. A long era of peace began with Augustus and lasted until A.D. 180. It was called the *Pax Romana* (pahks roh•MAH•nah), or "Roman Peace."

What Did Augustus Achieve? Upon becoming emperor in 27 B.C., Augustus set out to make the empire strong and safe. To provide security, he built a permanent, professional army of about 150,000 men—all Roman citizens. Augustus also created a special unit called the Praetorian Guard.

This force consisted of about 9,000 men in charge of guarding the emperor. The Praetorian Guard later became very influential in Roman politics.

Augustus's legions conquered new territories and added vast stretches of northern Europe to the empire. All of Spain and Gaul came under Roman rule, as did land in what is today Austria, Hungary, Romania, and Bulgaria.

Meanwhile, Augustus rebuilt Rome with stately palaces, fountains, and splendid public buildings. "I found Rome a city of brick," he boasted, "and left it a city of marble." The arts flourished as never before, and Augustus also imported grain from Africa to feed the poor. He knew that a well-fed population would be less likely to cause trouble.

Augustus devoted much of his energy to improving Rome's government. During his reign, more than 50 million people lived in the Roman Empire. To rule this huge population, Augustus appointed a proconsul, or governor, for each of Rome's provinces. These new officials replaced the politicians who had been chosen by the Senate. Augustus often traveled to the provinces to see how the governors were doing.

▲ The city of Rome at the height of the Roman Empire

The Julio-Claudian Emperors

Emperor	Accomplishments
Tiberius	14–37 A.D. Great military leader; regulated business to prevent fraud; kept Rome's economy stable
Caligula	37–41 A.D. Abolished sales tax; allowed people in exile to return; increased court system's power
Claudius	41–54 A.D. Built new harbor at Ostia and new aqueduct for Rome; conquered most of Britain
Nero	54–65 A.D. Constructed many new buildings; gave slaves the right to file complaints; assisted cities suffering from disasters

Understanding Charts

The four emperors who followed Augustus were all relatives of Augustus.
1. Under which emperor was Britain conquered?
2. Conclude Why do you think the Roman Empire remained at peace even with weak emperors such as Caligula and Nero?

Augustus also reformed the Roman tax system. Previously, individual tax collectors paid the government for the right to do the job. To make their investment worthwhile, tax collectors were allowed to keep some of the money they gathered. Many of them, however, were dishonest and took too much. Augustus solved this problem by making tax collectors permanent government workers. This change made the tax system fairer.

Augustus also reformed the legal system. He created a set of laws for people in the provinces who were not citizens. As time passed, however, most of these people gained citizenship. The laws of Rome then applied to everyone, although the legal system generally stressed the authority of the government over the rights of the individual.

Who Came After Augustus?

After ruling for almost 40 years, Augustus died in A.D. 14. No law stated how the next emperor was to be chosen. Augustus, however, had trained a relative, Tiberius, to follow him. The next three emperors—**Caligula** (kuh•LIH•gyuh•luh), Claudius, and **Nero** (NEE•roh)—also came from Augustus's family. They are called the Julio-Claudian emperors. Unfortunately, they were not all fit to lead. Tiberius and Claudius ruled capably. Caligula and Nero, however, proved to be cruel leaders.

Mental illness caused Caligula to act strangely and to treat people cruelly. He had many people murdered, wasted a lot of money, and even gave his favorite horse the position of consul. Eventually, the Praetorian Guard killed him and put Claudius on the throne.

Nero was also a vicious man. Among those he had killed were his mother and two wives. He is best remembered for having "fiddled while Rome burned." According to legend, he was playing music miles from Rome when a fire destroyed much of the city in A.D. 64. Eventually, he committed suicide.

Reading Check Explain What did Augustus do to make the empire safer and stronger?

Biography

AUGUSTUS
63 B.C.–A.D. 14

Octavian was born to a wealthy family in a small Italian town southeast of Rome. During his youth, Octavian suffered a number of illnesses. He refused to let his illnesses interfere with his life, however, showing the determination that would later make him Rome's first emperor.

Octavian's father was a Roman senator, but it was Octavian's great-uncle—Julius Caesar—who first introduced Octavian to public life in Rome. In his late teens, Octavian joined Caesar in Africa and then the following year in Spain. At the age of 18, while Octavian was studying at school, he learned that his great-uncle had been murdered. In his will, Caesar had adopted Octavian as his son. Caesar had also made Octavian his heir—a position that Antony had assumed would be his. Against his family's advice, Octavian went to Rome to claim his inheritance. By the time he reached Rome, however, Antony had seized Caesar's papers and money and refused to give them to Octavian. With remarkable political savvy for someone so young, Octavian turned the situation around in his favor. He won the hearts of Caesar's soldiers and the people of Rome by celebrating the public games that Caesar had started.

In his rise to power and during his reign as Emperor Augustus, Octavian pushed himself and his loyal followers with relentless energy. In his private life, however, he lived simply and quietly and shunned personal luxury. He was devoted to his wife, Livia Drusilla, and spent his spare time with her at their home on the outskirts of Rome.

Augustus ▶

> "I extended the frontiers of all the provinces of the Roman people."
>
> –Augustus, "Res Gestae: The Accomplishments of Augustus"

Then and Now

Augustus overcame the obstacles of illness and political enemies to become a great emperor. Can you think of any present-day individuals who overcame obstacles to excel at something?

Unity and Prosperity

Main Idea Rome's system of roads, aqueducts, ports, and common currency made the empire rich and prosperous.

Reading Focus Do you find that you are more productive when you are not worried about conflicts at home or school? Read to learn how the Roman Empire prospered during its time of peace.

After Nero committed suicide, Rome passed through a period of disorder until Vespasian, a general and one of Nero's proconsuls, took the throne. Vespasian restored peace and order. He put down several rebellions in the empire, including the Jewish rebellion in Palestine. Troops commanded by his son Titus defeated the Jews and destroyed the Jewish temple in Jerusalem in A.D. 70.

During his reign, Vespasian began construction of the Colosseum—a huge amphitheatre—in central Rome. His son Titus, then his other son Domitian, ruled Rome after he died. Both sons oversaw an era of growth and prosperity in Rome. During Titus's reign, two disasters struck the empire. The volcano Mount Vesuvius erupted, destroying the city of Pompeii, and a great fire badly damaged Rome.

Linking Past & Present

Living in the Shadow of Mt. Vesuvius

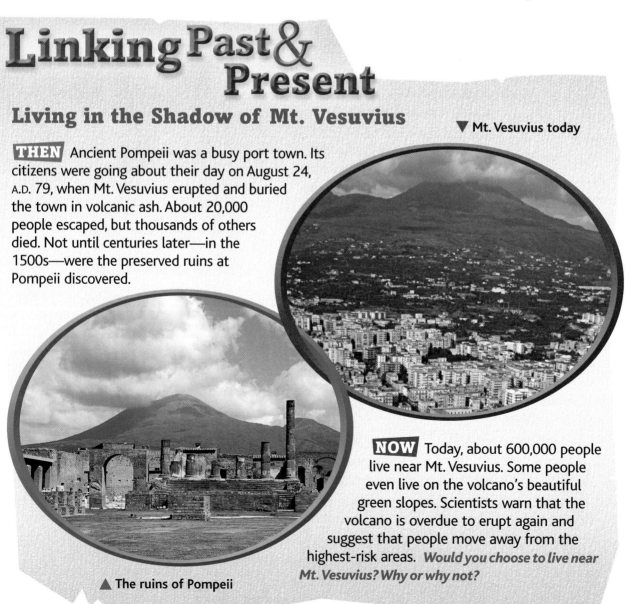

▼ Mt. Vesuvius today

THEN Ancient Pompeii was a busy port town. Its citizens were going about their day on August 24, A.D. 79, when Mt. Vesuvius erupted and buried the town in volcanic ash. About 20,000 people escaped, but thousands of others died. Not until centuries later—in the 1500s—were the preserved ruins at Pompeii discovered.

NOW Today, about 600,000 people live near Mt. Vesuvius. Some people even live on the volcano's beautiful green slopes. Scientists warn that the volcano is overdue to erupt again and suggest that people move away from the highest-risk areas. *Would you choose to live near Mt. Vesuvius? Why or why not?*

▲ The ruins of Pompeii

The "Good Emperors" At the beginning of the A.D. 100s, a series of rulers who were not related to Augustus or Vespasian came to power. These five emperors—Nerva, Trajan, **Hadrian** (HAY•dree•uhn), Antoninus Pius, and Marcus Aurelius—are known as the "good emperors." They presided over nearly a century of prosperity, from A.D. 96 to A.D. 180. Agriculture flourished, trade increased, and the standard of living rose.

During this time, the emperor came to overshadow the Senate more than ever before. The five "good emperors" did not abuse their power, however. They were among the most devoted and capable rulers in Rome's history. They improved Roman life in many ways, naming trained officials to carry out their orders.

Among the achievements of these emperors were programs to help ordinary people. Trajan gave money to help poor parents raise and educate their children. Hadrian made Roman law easier to understand and apply. Antoninus Pius passed laws to help orphans. All the emperors supported public building projects. They built arches and monuments, bridges and roads, and harbors and aqueducts. An **aqueduct** (A•kwuh•DUHKT) is a human-made channel for carrying water long distances.

A Unified Empire
Later emperors continued to conquer new territory for Rome. The empire reached its largest size under Trajan. It spread well beyond the Mediterranean, including Britain in the north and part of Mesopotamia in the east.

Trajan's successors, however, realized that the empire had grown too big to rule effectively. Hadrian began to pull back. He removed troops from most of Mesopotamia.

Science and Inventions

Roman Aqueducts Transporting water is a complex problem. Roman engineers solved it by building aqueducts. Roman aqueducts carried water across a valley or hillside using gravity, aboveground stone arches, and underground pipes made of stone or clay. Between 312 B.C. and A.D. 226, 11 aqueducts were built to bring water to Rome from as far away as 57 miles. Once the water made it to Rome, it was held in collecting tanks. Most people gathered water from these public tanks. Only the rich and high-ranking officials had private water tanks in their homes.

Many Roman aqueducts still stand and are used today. Engineers in ancient Persia, India, and Egypt built similar water systems hundreds of years before the Romans. However, historians agree that the Romans were the greatest aqueduct builders of the ancient world.

◀ **Roman aqueduct**

Connecting to the Past
1. How did the Romans transport water to the city of Rome?
2. Why do you think that only the rich and powerful had private water supplies?

The Roman Empire: Trade and Expansion

Extent of Roman Empire, 146 B.C.

ITALY
SPAIN •Rome
Carthage• ASIA MINOR
Mediterranean Sea GREECE
40°N
N W E S
0 500 mi.
0 500 km
Lambert Azimuthal Equal-Area projection
Black Sea

Extent of Roman Empire, 44 B.C.

ITALY
SPAIN •Rome
Carthage• ASIA MINOR
Mediterranean Sea GREECE
40N
N W E S
0 500 mi.
0 500 km
Lambert Azimuthal Equal-Area projection
Black Sea

Extent of Roman Empire, A.D. 14

ITALY
SPAIN •Rome
Carthage• ASIA MINOR
Mediterranean Sea GREECE
40N
N W E S
0 500 mi.
0 500 km
Lambert Azimuthal Equal-Area projection
Black Sea

The "Good Emperors" of the *Pax Romana*

Nerva	**Trajan**	**Hadrian**	**Antonius Pius**	**Marcus Aurelius**
A.D. *96–80*	A.D. *98–117*	A.D. *117–138*	A.D. *138–161*	A.D. *161–180*
Reformed land laws in favor of the poor; revised taxes	Expanded the empire to its largest size; built many new public works	Built Hadrian's Wall in Britain; made Roman laws easier to understand	Promoted art and science; built new public works; passed laws to aid orphans	Helped unite the empire economically; reformed Roman law

In Europe, he set the empire's eastern boundaries at the **Rhine River** (RYN) and **Danube River** (DAN•YOOB). He also built Hadrian's Wall across northern Britain to keep out the Picts and Scots—two warlike people who lived in northern Britain.

In the A.D. 100s, the Roman Empire was one of the greatest empires in history. It included about 3.5 million square miles (9.1 million square km). Its people spoke different languages—mostly Latin in the west and Greek in the east. They also practiced different local customs. What unified the empire, though, were Roman law, Roman rule, and a shared identity as Romans.

Roman culture had been carried into every province by the soldiers who protected the empire and by the officials sent to govern. The Romans were generous in granting citizenship. In A.D. 212 every free person was made a Roman citizen.

A Booming Economy Most people in the Roman Empire made a living from the land. Small farms dotted northern Italy. In

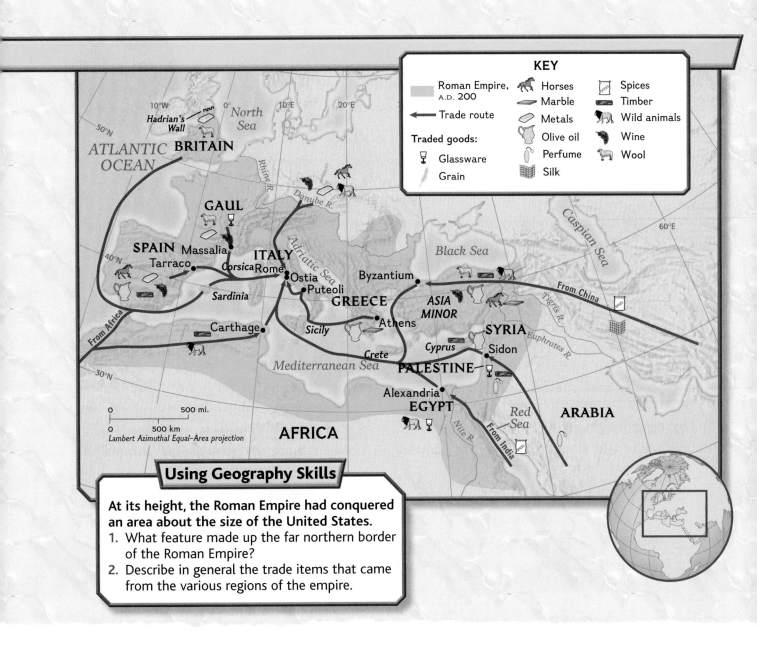

KEY

Roman Empire, A.D. 200

→ Trade route

Traded goods:

🏺 Glassware
🪶 Grain

🐎 Horses
▭ Marble
▬ Metals
🏺 Olive oil
🥚 Perfume
▦ Silk

Spices
Timber
Wild animals
Wine
Wool

Using Geography Skills

At its height, the Roman Empire had conquered an area about the size of the United States.
1. What feature made up the far northern border of the Roman Empire?
2. Describe in general the trade items that came from the various regions of the empire.

southern and central Italy, latifundia, or large estates worked by enslaved people, were common. On these estates and in the provinces of Gaul and Spain, farmers produced grapes and olives. The making of wine and olive oil became big business. In Britain and Egypt, the chief crops were grains. Bountiful harvests from these regions kept Rome's people well fed.

Agriculture was the most important part of the economy, but industry was important too. Potters, weavers, and jewelers produced goods and cities became centers for making glass, bronze, and brass.

Traders came from all over the empire—and beyond—to ports in Italy. Two of the largest port cities were **Puteoli** (pyu•TEE•uh•LY) on the Bay of Naples and **Ostia** (AHS•tee•uh) at the mouth of the Tiber. The docks were lively places. Luxury items, including silk goods from China and spices from India, poured in to satisfy the rich. Raw materials, such as British tin, Spanish lead, and iron from Gaul, went to the workshops of Roman cities.

Roads and Money A good transportation network was vital to the empire's trade. During the *Pax Romana,* Rome's system of roads reached a total length of 50,000 miles (80,000 km). On the seas, the Roman navy helped to rid the Mediterranean of pirates. Goods could be shipped more safely to and from Rome's ports.

Rome's trade was helped by a common **currency** (KUHR•uhn•see), or system of money. Roman coins were accepted throughout the Mediterranean region by A.D. 100. Merchants could use the same money in Gaul or Greece as they did in Italy. The Romans also created a standard system of weights and measures. This made it easier for people to price goods, trade, and ship products.

Ongoing Inequality The Roman Empire's prosperity did not reach all of its people.

▲ Roman coins could be used throughout most of the empire, making trade much easier. *How else did Rome improve trade during the empire?*

Shopkeepers, merchants, and skilled workers benefited from the empire's trade. Rich Romans built great fortunes and lived in luxury. However, most city dwellers and farmers remained poor, and many remained enslaved.

 **Identify** Who were the "Good Emperors," and what did they accomplish?

History Online

Homework Helper Need help with the material in this section? Visit jat.glencoe.com

Section 4 Review

Reading Summary

Review the Main Ideas

- Augustus conquered new lands and created a professional military and a system of proconsuls. He improved the tax system and the legal system, ushering in the *Pax Romana.*

- Under Vespasian, his sons, and the five good emperors, Romans continued to be prosperous. They built an elaborate system of roads and developed a common currency that promoted trade and economic growth.

What Did You Learn?

1. What was the *Pax Romana?*

2. What products came from the farms of Italy, Gaul, and Spain?

Critical Thinking

3. **Organizing Information** Draw a diagram like the one below. Add details about the improvements and changes Augustus made to the Roman Empire during his reign.

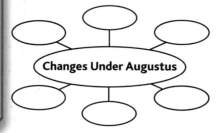

Changes Under Augustus

4. **Sequencing Information** Describe the sequence of emperors who ruled Rome, from Augustus through the "Good Emperors."

5. **Analyze** Why was Rome's creation of a common currency important?

6. **Evaluate** Who do you think was a more important leader, Julius Caesar or Augustus? Explain.

7. **Creative Writing** Write a short play in which several Roman citizens discuss one of the emperors mentioned in this section and his accomplishments.

Section ① Rome's Beginnings

Vocabulary
republic
legion

Focusing on the Main Ideas
- Geography played an important role in the rise of Roman civilization. *(page 263)*
- The Romans created a republic and conquered Italy. By treating people fairly, they built Rome from a small city into a great power. *(page 265)*

Section ② The Roman Republic

Vocabulary
patrician
plebeian
consul
veto
praetor
dictator

Focusing on the Main Ideas
- Rome's republic was shaped by a struggle between wealthy landowners and regular citizens as it gradually expanded the right to vote. *(page 269)*
- Rome slowly destroyed the Carthaginian Empire and took control of the entire Mediterranean region. *(page 274)*

Roman consul ▶

Section ③ The Fall of the Republic

Vocabulary
latifundia
triumvirate

Focusing on the Main Ideas
- The use of enslaved labor hurt farmers, increased poverty and corruption, and brought the army into politics. *(page 278)*
- Military hero Julius Caesar seized power and made reforms. *(page 280)*
- The Roman Republic, weakened by civil wars, became an empire under Augustus. *(page 282)*

Section ④ The Early Empire

Vocabulary
Pax Romana
aqueduct
currency

Focusing on the Main Ideas
- By expanding the empire and reorganizing the military and government, Augustus created a new era of prosperity. *(page 287)*
- Rome's system of roads, aqueducts, ports, and common currency made the empire rich and prosperous. *(page 290)*

Chapter 8 Assessment and Activities

Review Vocabulary

Each of the following statements is false. Replace each word in italics with a word that makes the statement true. Write the correct words on a separate sheet of paper.

____ 1. A *legion* is a form of government in which the citizens choose their leader.

____ 2. *Patricians* included artisans and shopkeepers.

____ 3. The judge in a Roman court case was a *consul*.

____ 4. In early Rome, the role of *praetor* lasted only until a crisis had passed.

____ 5. Large farming estates that used enslaved people to tend crops were called *aqueducts*.

____ 6. A *veto* was a human-made channel for carrying water.

Review Main Ideas

Section 1 • Rome's Beginnings

7. Describe the role geography played in the rise of Roman civilization.

8. How did treating people fairly help Rome to increase its power?

Section 2 • The Roman Republic

9. How did the roles of patricians and plebeians differ in Roman society?

10. Explain how Rome gradually defeated the Carthaginians.

Section 3 • The Fall of the Republic

11. How did slavery weaken the Roman Republic?

12. How did Augustus change the Roman Republic?

Section 4 • The Early Empire

13. Was Augustus a successful ruler? Explain your answer.

14. How did the Roman Empire change during the *Pax Romana?*

Critical Thinking

15. **Compare** In the chapter, Cincinnatus is compared to George Washington. Think of another person or character who is similar to Cincinnatus. Explain how they are similar.

16. **Explain** Why did Caesar fight Pompey?

17. **Predict** What do you think would have happened if Hadrian had tried to further expand the Roman Empire?

Review

Reading Skill | Taking Notes | **Note Taking**

18. Read the following paragraph from page 269. Take notes on the information by making a T-chart.

> Early Romans were divided into two classes: patricians and plebeians. The patricians were wealthy landowners. These nobles made up Rome's ruling class. Most of Rome's people, however, were plebeians. This group included artisans, shopkeepers, and owners of small farms.

To review this skill, see pages 260–261.

Geography Skills

Study the map below and answer the following questions.

19. **Place** Which areas did Rome control after the Punic Wars?

20. **Human/Environment Interaction** What does the building of Hadrian's Wall say about the Picts and Scots?

21. **Region** Why was it important to the Romans to control Mediterranean lands?

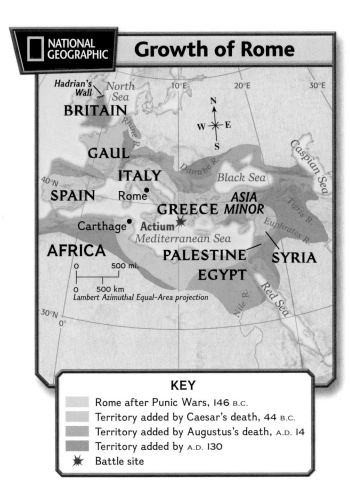

NATIONAL GEOGRAPHIC — Growth of Rome

KEY
- Rome after Punic Wars, 146 B.C.
- Territory added by Caesar's death, 44 B.C.
- Territory added by Augustus's death, A.D. 14
- Territory added by A.D. 130
- ✳ Battle site

Read to Write

22. **Persuasive Writing** Suppose you were working with Tiberius and Gaius to reform Rome. Write a letter or speech that explains why reform is needed and what types of reforms should occur.

23. **Using Your** FOLDABLES Use your foldable to write a series of questions about the chapter. With a partner, take turns asking and answering questions until you have reviewed the entire chapter.

History Online
Self-Check Quiz To help prepare for the Chapter Test, visit jat.glencoe.com

Building Citizenship

24. **Making Connections** Use the Internet and your local library to research the Twelve Tables. Work with your classmates to design a similar series of laws, and record them, using modern language. How is your law code similar to and different from the Twelve Tables?

Using Technology

25. **Creating Promotional Materials** Use the Internet to find at least five places related to ancient Rome that can be visited by tourists. Create a guidebook or brochure on the computer advertising these links to the past and persuading people to visit that area. Share your final product in a report to the class.

Primary Source — Analyze

Augustus wrote a historical document describing his accomplishments. This passage is about his military leadership.

"About 500,000 Roman citizens were under military oath to me. Of these, when their terms of service were ended, I settled in colonies or sent back to their own municipalities a little more than 300,000, and to all these I allotted lands or granted money as rewards for military service."

—Augustus, "Res Gestae: The Accomplishments of Augustus"

DBQ Document-Based Questions

26. Why did Augustus give money to his retired soldiers?

27. Why do you think Augustus did not explain the reasons for his actions?

Roman Civilization

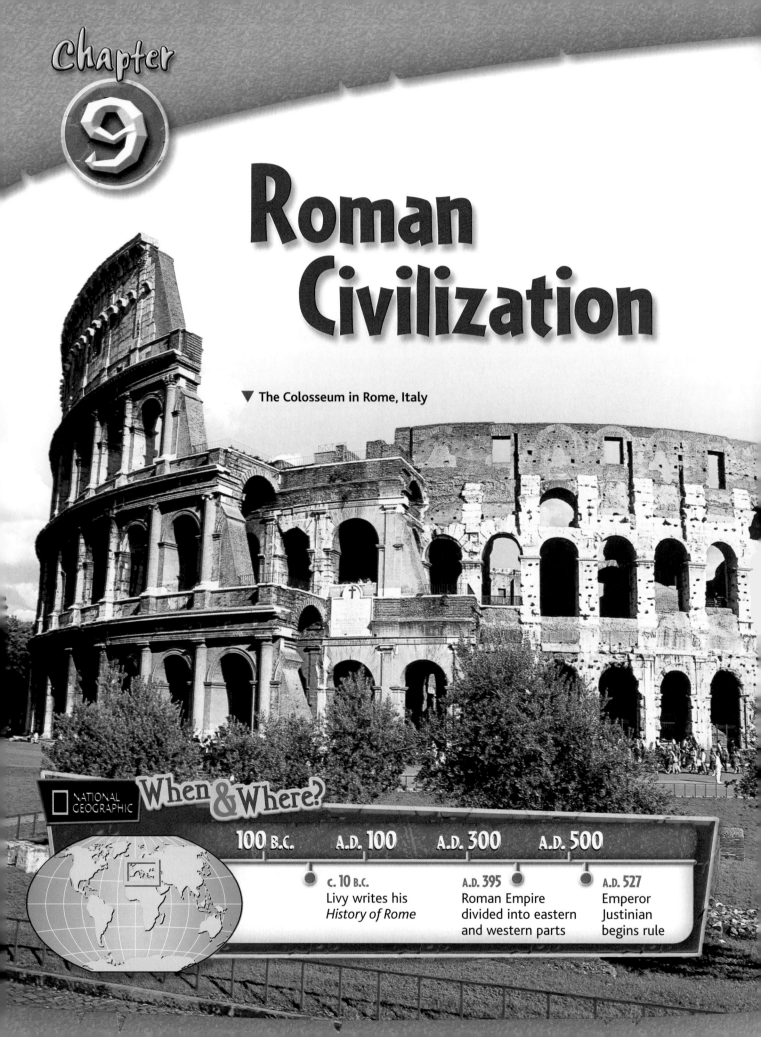

▼ The Colosseum in Rome, Italy

NATIONAL GEOGRAPHIC **When & Where?**

100 B.C.	A.D. 100	A.D. 300	A.D. 500

c. 10 B.C.
Livy writes his
History of Rome

A.D. 395
Roman Empire
divided into eastern
and western parts

A.D. 527
Emperor
Justinian
begins rule

Chapter Preview

The Romans developed a civilization as well as an empire. Read this chapter to find out about Roman achievements that still influence your life today.

 View the Chapter 9 video in the *World History*: *Journey Across Time* Video Program.

History Online
Chapter Overview Visit jat.glencoe.com for a preview of Chapter 9.

 Life in Ancient Rome

The Romans learned from the Greeks but changed what they borrowed to suit their own needs. The lives of rich and poor Romans were very different.

 The Fall of Rome

Rome finally fell when Germanic invaders swept through the empire in the A.D. 400s. Roman achievements in government, law, language, and the arts are still important today.

 **The Byzantine Empire**

As the Western Roman Empire fell, the Eastern Roman, or Byzantine, Empire grew rich and powerful. The Byzantines developed a culture based on Roman, Greek, and Christian ideas.

 **FOLDABLES™**
Study Organizer

Organizing Information *Make this foldable to help you organize and analyze information by asking yourself questions about Roman civilization.*

Step 1 *Fold a sheet of paper into thirds from top to bottom.*

Step 2 *Turn the paper horizontally, unfold, and label the three columns as shown.*

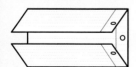

Life in Ancient Rome | The Fall of Rome | The Byzantine Empire

Reading and Writing *As you read the chapter, write the main ideas for each section in the appropriate columns of your foldable. Then write one statement that summarizes the main ideas in each column.*

Reading Social Studies

1 Learn It!

Your Point of View

An important part of reading involves thinking about and responding to the text from your own point of view.

Read the following paragraph about daily life in Rome and look at how one student reflects as she reads.

"Reminds me of a city I visited once"

> The city of Rome was **crowded, noisy, and dirty**. People tossed garbage into the streets from their apartments, and thieves prowled the streets at night. Most people in Rome were poor. They lived in **apartment buildings made of stone and wood. High rent forced families to live in one room.**
>
> —from page 306

"What would that look like? What would it smell like?"

"Were they like apartment buildings today?"

"Sounds like it would be very uncomfortable and crowded!"

Reading Tip

While you do not want to daydream as you are reading, you do want to think about the text. Good readers' minds are busy, almost "talking back" to the text as they read.

2 Practice It!

Reflect and Respond

Read the following paragraph. Take a few minutes to reflect on what you have read and then respond by exchanging thoughts with a partner. Some suggested topics are listed below.

Read to Write ·······

In Section 2, you will read why historians believe the Roman Empire fell. Choose one of the reasons and respond to it, explaining why you think this is the most likely reason for the decline of the Roman Empire.

> Between the ages of 14 and 16, a Roman boy celebrated becoming a man. He would burn his toys as offerings to the household gods. Then he would put on a toga, a loose-fitting robe that Roman men wore. Once he came of age, a man might join his family's business, become a soldier, or begin a career in the government. Roman women did not become adults until they married. A woman usually wore a long flowing robe with a cloak called a *palla*.
>
> —*from pages 307–308*

- Do boys do anything today to show that they have become men?

- What does a toga look like? What does a *palla* look like?

- Why did a woman have to wait until she married to become an adult?

- Why were boys and girls treated so differently?

3 Apply It!

As you read, keep a reader's notebook. Record responses to facts or ideas that you find interesting.

Section 1

Life in Ancient Rome

Get Ready to Read!

What's the Connection?
You have already learned about Rome's rise to power. Life in Rome was not easy, but as the empire grew, its people accomplished many things in art, science, and engineering.

Focusing on the Main Ideas
- In addition to their own developments in science and engineering, Roman artists and writers borrowed many ideas from the Greeks. *(page 303)*

- The rich and poor had very different lives in the Roman Empire, as did men and women. *(page 306)*

Meeting People
Virgil (VUHR•juhl)
Horace (HAWR•uhs)
Galen (GAY•luhn)
Ptolemy (TAH•luh•mee)
Spartacus (SPAHR•tuh•kuhs)

Building Your Vocabulary
vault (VAWLT)
satire (SA•TYR)
ode (OHD)
anatomy (uh•NA•tuh•mee)
Forum (FOHR•uhm)
gladiator (GLA•dee•AY•tuhr)
paterfamilias (PA•tuhr•fuh•MIH•lee•uhs)
rhetoric (REH•tuh•rihk)

Reading Strategy
Compare and Contrast Use a Venn diagram like the one below to show similarities and differences between the rich and the poor in Rome.

Roman Rich | Roman Poor

NATIONAL GEOGRAPHIC **When & Where?**

BRITAIN
GAUL GREECE
SPAIN ITALY
Rome •
• Constantinople
PALESTINE—
EGYPT

100 B.C.   **A.D. 1**   **A.D. 100**

73 B.C. Spartacus leads revolt of enslaved people

c. 10 B.C. Livy writes his *History of Rome*

c. A.D. 80 Colosseum completed

Roman Culture

Main Idea In addition to their own developments in science and engineering, Roman artists and writers borrowed many ideas from the Greeks.

Reading Focus Are there people in your life that you admire? What have you learned from them? Read to find out what the Romans learned from the Greeks.

The Romans admired and studied Greek statues, buildings, and ideas. They copied the Greeks in many ways. However, they changed what they borrowed to suit their own needs. In one important way, the Romans were very different from the Greeks. The Greeks loved to talk about ideas. To the Romans, ideas were only important if they could solve everyday problems.

What Was Roman Art Like?

The Romans admired Greek art and architecture. They placed Greek-style statues in their homes and public buildings. Roman artists, however, carved statues that looked different from those of the Greeks. Greek statues were made to look perfect. People were shown young, healthy, and with beautiful bodies. Roman statues were more realistic and included wrinkles, warts, and other less attractive features.

In building, the Romans also turned to the Greeks for ideas. They used Greek-style porches and rows of columns called colonnades. But they also added their own features, such as arches and domes. Roman builders were the first to make full use of the arch. Arches supported bridges, aqueducts, and buildings. Rows of arches were often built against one another to form a **vault** (VAWLT), or curved ceiling. Using this technique, the Romans were able to build domes from many rings of shaped stone.

The Romans were the first people to invent and use concrete, a mixture of volcanic ash, lime, and water. When it dried, this mix was as hard as rock. Concrete made buildings sturdier and allowed them to be built taller.

Rome's concrete buildings were so well built that many still stand today. One of the most famous is the Colosseum, completed about A.D. 80. It was a huge arena that could seat about 60,000 people. Another famous building is the Pantheon, a temple built to honor Rome's gods. The Pantheon's domed roof was the largest of its time.

▼ **This Roman bridge still stands in Spain.** *In what other structures were arches used?*

The Book of Epodes

In this poem excerpt, Horace praises the lifestyle of those who farm their family's land.

"Happy the man who, far from business and affairs

Like mortals of the early times,

May work his father's fields with oxen of his own,

Exempt [free] from profit, loss, and fee,

Not like the soldier roused by savage trumpet's blare,

Not terrified by seas in rage,

Avoiding busy forums and the haughty doors

Of influencial citizens."

—Horace, *The Book of Epodes*

▲ Horace

DBQ Document-Based Question

According to Horace, what kinds of things does the farmer avoid?

Roman Literature

Roman authors based much of their writing on Greek works. For example, the Roman writer **Virgil** (VUHR•juhl) drew some of his ideas from Homer's *Odyssey*. Virgil's epic poem, the *Aeneid* (uh•NEE•uhd), describes the adventures of the Trojan prince Aeneas and how he came to Italy. Virgil presents Aeneas as the ideal Roman—brave, self-controlled, and loyal to the gods.

Rome's other famous writers also looked to the Greeks for inspiration. Using Greek models, the poet **Horace** (HAWR•uhs) wrote **satires** (SA•TYRZ). These works poked fun at human weaknesses. Horace also composed **odes** (OHDZ), or poems that express strong emotions about life. The

Roman writer Ovid wrote works that were based on the Greek myths. The poet Catullus also admired Greek writings. He wrote short poems about love, sadness, and envy.

Like the Greeks, Rome's historians recorded the events of their civilization. One of Rome's most famous historians was Livy. He wrote his *History of Rome* about 10 B.C. In this book, Livy describes Rome's rise to power. Livy greatly admired the deeds of the early Romans, and he believed that history had important moral lessons to teach people.

Livy celebrated Rome's greatness, but the Roman historian Tacitus took a darker view. He believed that Rome's emperors had taken people's freedom. Tacitus also thought Romans were losing the values that made them strong. He accused them of wasting time on sports and other pleasures.

Also like the Greeks, the Romans enjoyed plays. Roman plays were often based on Greek tragedies and comedies. Playwrights such as the tragedy writer Seneca and the comedy writers Plautus and Terence wrote plays for religious festivals. Romans especially liked plays with humor.

Roman authors influenced later writers in Europe and America, but the language of the Romans, Latin, had an even bigger impact on future generations. Latin became Europe's language for government, trade, and learning until about A.D. 1500. Latin became the basis of many modern European languages, such as Italian, French, and Spanish, and shaped many others. Many of the English words we use today come from Latin as well.

Roman Science and Engineering

The Romans also learned from Greek science. A Greek doctor named **Galen** (GAY•luhn)

brought many medical ideas to Rome. For example, he emphasized the importance of **anatomy** (uh•NA•tuh•mee), the study of body structure. To learn about inner organs, Galen cut open dead animals and recorded his findings. Doctors in the West studied Galen's books and drawings for more than 1,500 years.

Another important scientist of the Roman Empire was **Ptolemy** (TAH•luh•mee). Ptolemy lived in Alexandria, in Egypt. He studied the sky and carefully mapped over 1,000 different stars. He also studied the motion of planets and stars and created rules explaining their movements. Even though Ptolemy incorrectly placed Earth at the center of the universe, educated people in Europe accepted his ideas for centuries.

While Roman scientists tried to understand how the world worked, Roman engineers built an astonishing system of roads and bridges to connect the empire. Have you ever heard the saying "All roads lead to Rome"? Roman engineers built roads from Rome to every part of the empire. These roads were well built, and some have survived to this day.

The Romans also used advanced engineering to supply their cities with freshwater. Engineers built aqueducts to bring water from the hills into the cities. Aqueducts were long troughs supported by rows of arches. They carried water over long distances. At one time, 11 great aqueducts fed Rome's homes, bathhouses, fountains, and public bathrooms. Roman cities also had sewers to remove waste.

Reading Check **Explain** How was the character Aeneas an ideal Roman?

The Roman Colosseum

The Colosseum in Rome could hold some 60,000 people. The arena even had a removable canvas awning to protect spectators from the hot Roman sun.
What was concrete made from?

A system of cages, ropes, and pulleys brought wild animals up to the Colosseum floor from rooms underground. ▼

The Way It Was

Sports & Contests

Ancient Roman Sports Sports were important to the Romans. Paintings on vases, frescoes [moist plaster], and stone show Romans playing ball, including a version of soccer. Roman girls are shown exercising with handheld weights and throwing an egg-shaped ball. Balls were made of different materials such as wool, hair, linen, sponges, and pig bladders wrapped in string.

Some Roman sporting events took place in the Colosseum, amphitheaters, and the Circus Maximus. Wild beast fights, battles between ships, and gladiator contests attracted Roman spectators by the thousands. Chariot racing was held in the Circus Maximus, and the drivers wore team colors of red, white, green, and blue.

▲ Scene showing gladiators in battle

Connecting to the Past

1. How do we know sports were important to the Romans?

2. How are today's sports different from Roman sports? How are they similar?

Daily Life in Rome

Main Idea The rich and poor had very different lives in the Roman Empire, as did men and women.

Reading Focus Do you think there is a big difference in the lives of boys and girls you know today? Why or why not? Read to learn how the lives of Roman boys and girls were very different from each other.

What was it like to live in Rome over 2,000 years ago? Rome was one of the largest cities in the ancient world. By the time of Augustus, over a million people lived there. Rome was carefully planned, as were many Roman cities. It was laid out in a square with the main roads crossing at right angles. At its center was the **Forum** (FOHR•um). This was an open space that served as a marketplace and public square. Temples and public buildings were built around it.

Wealthy Romans lived in large, comfortable houses. Each home had large rooms, fine furniture, and beautiful gardens. In the center was an inner court called an atrium. Wealthy Romans also had homes called villas on their country estates.

The city of Rome was crowded, noisy, and dirty. People tossed garbage into the streets from their apartments, and thieves prowled the streets at night. Most people in Rome were poor. They lived in apartment buildings made of stone and wood. High rent forced families to live in one room.

Roman apartments were up to six stories high. They often collapsed because they were so poorly built. Fire was a constant danger because people used torches and lamps for lighting and cooked with oil. Once started, a fire could destroy entire blocks of apartments.

To keep the people from rioting, the Roman government provided "bread and circuses," or free grain and shows. Romans of all classes flocked to the chariot races and gladiator contests. **Gladiators** (GLA•dee•AY•tuhrz)

▲ Chariot races were held in an arena called the Circus Maximus, one of the largest arenas ever made. *Besides chariot races, what other types of shows attracted Romans?*

fought animals and each other. Most gladiators were enslaved people, criminals, or poor people. Gladiators were admired, much like sports heroes are today.

What Was Family Life Like?

Family life was important to the Romans. Their families were large. They included not only parents and young children but also married children and their families, other relatives, and enslaved servants. The father was the head of the household. Called the **paterfamilias** (PA•tuhr•fuh•MIH•lee•uhs), or "father of the family," he had complete control over family members. For example, he punished children severely if they disobeyed. He also arranged their marriages.

In some cases, the paterfamilias made sure his children were educated. Poor Romans could not afford to send their children to school. Wealthy Romans, however, hired tutors to teach their young children at home. Some older boys did go to schools, where they learned reading, writing, and **rhetoric** (REH•tuh•rihk), or public speaking.

Older girls did not go to school. Instead, they studied reading and writing at home. They also learned household duties.

Between the ages of 14 and 16, a Roman boy celebrated becoming a man. He would burn his toys as offerings to the household gods. Then he would put on a toga, a loose-fitting robe that Roman men wore. Once he came of age, a man might join his family's business, become a soldier, or begin a career

▼ A Roman teacher and student

in the government. Roman women did not become adults until they married. A woman usually wore a long flowing robe with a cloak called a *palla*.

Women in Rome Women in early Rome had some rights, but they were not full citizens. The paterfamilias looked after his wife and controlled her affairs. However, he often sought her advice in private. Women had a strong influence on their families, and some wives of famous men, including emperors, became well-known themselves. For example, the empress Livia (LIHV•ee• uh), wife of Augustus, had a say in Rome's politics. She was later honored as a goddess.

The freedoms a Roman woman enjoyed depended on her husband's wealth and standing. Wealthy women had a great deal of independence. They could own land, run businesses, and sell property. They managed the household and had enslaved people do the housework. This left the women free to study literature, art, and fashion. Outside the home, they could go to the theater or the amphitheater, but in both places they had to sit in areas separate from men.

Women with less money had less freedom. They spent most of their time working in their houses or helping their husbands in family-run shops. They were allowed to leave home to shop, visit friends, worship at temples, or go to the baths. A few women did work independently outside the home. Some served as priestesses, while others worked as hairdressers and even doctors.

A Roman House

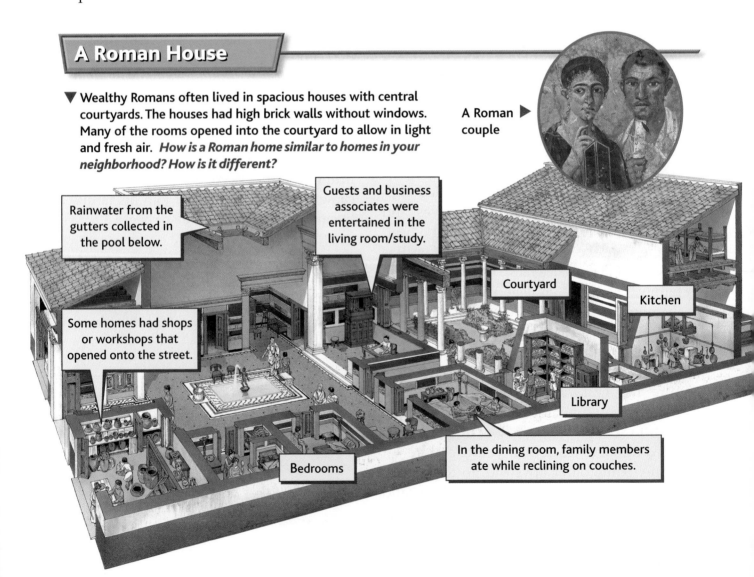

▼ Wealthy Romans often lived in spacious houses with central courtyards. The houses had high brick walls without windows. Many of the rooms opened into the courtyard to allow in light and fresh air. *How is a Roman home similar to homes in your neighborhood? How is it different?*

A Roman ▶ couple

Rainwater from the gutters collected in the pool below.

Guests and business associates were entertained in the living room/study.

Courtyard

Kitchen

Some homes had shops or workshops that opened onto the street.

Library

Bedrooms

In the dining room, family members ate while reclining on couches.

▼ A Roman family at the dinner table

▲ These apartments were built of brick and stone for wealthy Romans. *What sort of buildings did poor Romans live in?*

How Did Romans Treat Enslaved People?

Slavery was a part of Roman life from early times. But the use of slave labor grew as Rome took over more territory. Thousands of prisoners from conquered lands were brought to Italy. Most spent their lives performing slave labor. By 100 B.C., about 40 percent of the people in Italy were enslaved.

Enslaved people did many different jobs. They worked in homes, fields, mines, and workshops. They helped build roads, bridges, and aqueducts. Many enslaved Greeks were well educated. They served as teachers, doctors, and artisans. Enslaved people who earned wages usually were able to buy their freedom.

For most enslaved people, life was miserable. They were punished severely for poor work or for running away. To escape their hardships, enslaved people often rebelled.

In 73 B.C. a slave revolt broke out in Italy. It was led by a gladiator named **Spartacus** (SPAHR•tuh•kuhs). Under Spartacus, a force of 70,000 enslaved people defeated several Roman armies. The revolt was finally crushed two years later. Spartacus and 6,000 of his followers were crucified, or put to death by nailing on a cross.

Roman Religion

The ancient Romans worshiped many gods and goddesses. They also believed that spirits lived in natural things, such as trees and rivers. Greek gods and goddesses were popular in Rome, although they were given Roman names. For example, Zeus became Jupiter, the sky god, and Aphrodite became Venus, the goddess of love and beauty. Roman emperors also were worshiped. This practice strengthened support for the government.

Romans honored their gods and goddesses by praying and offering food. Every Roman home had an altar for their household gods. At these altars, the head of the family carried out rituals. Government officials made offerings in temples. There the important gods and goddesses of Rome were honored. Some Roman priests looked for messages from the gods. They studied

Greek and Roman Gods

Greek God	Roman God	Role
Ares	Mars	god of war
Zeus	Jupiter	chief god
Hera	Juno	wife of chief god
Aphrodite	Venus	goddess of love
Artemis	Diana	goddess of the hunt
Athena	Minerva	goddess of wisdom
Hermes	Mercury	messenger god
Hades	Pluto	god of the underworld
Poseidon	Neptune	god of the sea
Hephaestus	Vulcan	god of fire

◄ Minerva, goddess of wisdom

the insides of dead animals or watched the flight of birds, looking for meaning.

As the empire grew larger, Romans came into contact with other religions. These religions were allowed, as long as they did not threaten the government. Those that did faced severe hardships. You will read about one of these religions—Christianity—in the next chapter.

✔ Reading Check **Contrast** Describe the freedoms of upper-class women that were not available to women of other classes.

History Online

Homework Helper Need help with the material in this section? Visit jat.glencoe.com

Section 1 Review

Reading Summary

Review the Main Ideas

- Roman art, literature, and science borrowed much from the Greeks. Roman engineers made advances, including the development of cement, the arch, aqueducts, and domes.

- Religion and family were important parts of Roman life. Enslaved people carried out many different tasks in Roman society.

What Did You Learn?

1. What were some of Ptolemy's scientific achievements?

2. How were the Roman and Greek religions similar?

Critical Thinking

3. **Compare and Contrast** Draw a chart like the one below. Fill in details to compare and contrast Roman and Greek art and architecture.

Greek Art	Roman Art

Greek Architecture	Roman Architecture

4. **Analyze** Explain the importance of the language of the Romans.

5. **Describe** Describe the education of Roman children.

6. **Conclude** The Romans borrowed ideas from other peoples. Do you think our culture today borrows ideas from other peoples? Explain your answer.

7. **Reading** **Responding and Reflecting** Look at the art showing the Roman house on page 308. Write five things that come to mind as you view this picture.

A WILD-GOOSE CHASE
THE STORY OF PHILEMON AND BAUCIS

Retold by Geraldine McCaughrean

Before You Read

The Scene: This story takes place in ancient Rome in the legendary time when gods visited Earth to interact with humans in person.

The Characters: Philemon and Baucis are the man and woman who welcome guests to their home. Clio is their goose. Jupiter and Mercury are two ancient Roman gods.

The Plot: A husband and wife welcome two guests into their cottage. They have no food for the guests, but they do have a pet goose. As the pair try to provide their guests with food, the guests reveal their identities and reward the host and hostess for their generosity.

Vocabulary Preview

fowl: bird

wielding: controlling

gaped: hung open

quills: feathers

hospitality: friendliness and generosity toward guests

ramshackle: falling apart

disintegrated: broke into small pieces

gilded: decorated with gold

preening: grooming and making pretty

Do you know a person who is always friendly and generous, no matter what the circumstances? In this story, a good-natured husband and wife are rewarded when they receive special guests into their home.

As You Read

Keep in mind that this story is a myth. Like the Greeks, Romans passed myths from one generation to the next to explain some aspect of the world. Often, the stories involved gods and goddesses as well as humans.

A knock at the door. A pair of passing strangers. Philemon and Baucis did not know the two men on their doorstep, but they had never yet failed to offer a warm welcome to anyone who called at their little cottage.

"Come in! Sit down! My wife will cook you supper!" said Philemon.

His wife tugged at his sleeve. She did not need to say more. Both of them knew there was no food in the house. Not a bite. Baucis and Philemon themselves had been living on eggs and olives for days. There was not even any bread.

Philemon smiled sadly at Baucis, and she smiled sadly back. "It's the goose, is it?" he said.

"The goose it is," she replied.

Clio was all they had left. She was more like a pet than a farmyard fowl. And yet, guests are a blessing sent by the gods, and guests must be fed. So Philemon fetched his sharp ax and Baucis began to chase the goose, trying to drive it into the cottage.

Jupiter sat back in his chair and waited patiently for dinner. "Do you think we should help?" he said to Mercury, hearing the commotion in the yard.

"I know we shall have a wait," replied Mercury.

"Here—you try," said Baucis, passing the ax to Philemon.

The goose was squawking, Baucis was yelping, and Philemon was coughing as he ran

about wielding the ax. He struck at Clio, but the goose moved, and he demolished a bush. He swung again and hit the wooden pail. The goose shrieked with outrage, then with terror, and slapped about on her big, triangular feet—plat, plat, plat—skidding into their homemade altar piled high with flowers, into the fish-drying rack,[1] into the washing on the tree.[2] Olives rained down on the roof of the shack.

"Do you think we should go?" said Jupiter, as he and Mercury listened to the wild-goose chase and their hungry stomachs growled quietly.

At last Philemon and Baucis cornered the goose against the cottage door. Her orange beak gaped. Philemon raised the ax . . . and Clio bolted backward into the shack, running around the room like a black-footed pillow fight until she caught sight of Jupiter.

Now, animals are not so easily fooled by disguises, and although Jupiter and Mercury were dressed as peasants, in woolen tunics and straw hats, she instantly recognized the King of the gods and threw herself on his mercy. Neck outstretched, eyes bulging, she ran straight between his knees and into his lap. He was overrun with goose.

"A thousand pardons, friend," gasped Baucis, crawling in at the door, her hair stuck with goose quills. "Won't you take an olive while you wait?"

Jupiter stroked the goose, which stood paddling[3] on his thighs, and spat out a few feathers. "Shield me! Save me! Protect me!" said the goose, in the language of geese.

---

[1]**fish-drying rack:** large wooden structure on which fish are hung to dry
[2]**washing on the tree:** laundry hung on the tree branches to dry
[3]**paddling:** moving its feet

Jupiter tickled it under the beak. "Your hospitality is a marvel, dear Philemon, gentle Baucis. In all my long travels over the face of the world, I have never met such unselfish hosts. Here is your only goose, and you were ready to cook it for us! Your generosity surpasses that of the gods themselves!"

"Now, sir," said Baucis sternly. "You may be a guest, but I'll have no ill spoken of the gods in this house. Though we have little to offer, the gods have been good to us, have they not, my love?"

"They have, they have," said Philemon. Mercury concealed a grin.

"And they shall be good to you ever after!" declared Jupiter, rising to his feet. He rose and rose, 'til his head touched the rafters, and his face brightened 'til the room was light as day. His disguise fell away and Mercury folded it small and smaller 'til it fit inside one fist and was gone.

"As you see, I am Jupiter, King of the gods, and this is my messenger, Mercury. We like to travel the world and visit the people whose sacrificial smoke perfumes the halls of Heaven. But travel where we may and stay where we might, we never met with such hospitality as yours! Name any favor and it shall be your reward. A small kingdom, perhaps? A palace? A chest of sea treasure from the vaults of Poseidon?[4] Wings to fly or the gift of prophecy? Name it!"

Mercury looked uneasy. He had seen the greed and ambition of mortals all too often. This mild-looking couple would probably demand to be gods and to dine at the table of the gods; would ask for immortality or a banner of stars wide as the Milky Way, spelling out "Philemon the Philanthropist,"[5] "Baucis the Beautiful."

Baucis looked at Philemon, and Philemon smiled back and wrung his hat shyly between his hands.

"Almighty Jupiter, you have done our little house such an honor today that we have

---

[4]**Poseidon:** Roman god of the sea
[5]**philanthropist:** someone who is charitable

hardly breath enough to speak our thanks. Our greatest joy in life has always been to worship at our humble little altar—out there in the yard. What more could we ask than to go on doing that—oh, and both to die at the same hour, so that we may never be parted. My Baucis and I."

Jupiter complained of a speck of dust in his eye and went outside. He could be heard blowing his nose loudly. When he ducked back through the door, his eyes were quite red-rimmed. "Come, priest and priestess of my shrine! Your temple awaits you!"

All of a sudden, the drafty, ramshackle little hut disintegrated, like a raft of leaves on a river. Around and above it rose the pillars of a mighty temple. The simple cairn[6] of stones that had served for an altar still stood there, piled with firewood and swagged with flowers, but now it stood on a marble floor, and from that floor rose forty marble pillars cloaked with beaten gold, supporting a roof gilded with stars. The living quarters for priest and priestess were piled with feather mattresses and silken pillows, and priestly robes of soft cotton hung waiting about the shoulders of Carrara[7] statues.

---

[6]**cairn:** mound
[7]**Carrara:** an Italian city known for its white marble
  quarries and statues

Already, from all corners of the landscape, pilgrims were setting out at a run to visit the marvelous new temple of Jupiter, whose red roof signaled to them across miles of open countryside. Philemon and Baucis would be kept busy receiving their sacrifices, tending the sacrificial flame, sweeping up the ashes.

But they thrived on the hard work, just as they had always done. The worshipers brought not only flowers for the altar but baskets of delicious food for the priest and priestess whose fame spread far and wide. Tirelessly they worked until, being mortal, even Baucis and Philemon became exhausted. Watching from the terraces of Heaven, Jupiter saw them pause now, each time they passed one another, and lean one against the other for a moment's rest, Baucis laying her head on Philemon's shoulder.

"They are weary," said Mercury.

"You are right," said Jupiter. "It is time for them to rest."

So instead of breathing in the fragrance from the altar below, he breathed out—a breath that wafted away the white robes of priest and priestess and left behind two noble trees at the very door of the temple. One was an oak, the other a linden tree, and they leaned one toward another, their branches intertwined, casting welcome shade over the threshold.

Clio the goose liked to rest there at noon, preening her . . . feathers and singing.

Responding to the Reading

1. Why do Philemon and Baucis fail to recognize their guests? Which character does recognize them?

2. Jupiter said that he and Mercury like to "visit the people whose sacrificial smoke perfumes the halls of Heaven." Who does he mean?

3. **Cause and Effect** What is the result of Jupiter's gift to Philemon and Baucis?

4. **Analyze** Why do Philemon and Baucis not ask the gods for fame and power?

5. **Reading** **Read to Write** Imagine that friends who live in another town visit you. What would you provide for them? Would it be different from the things you provide for yourself? Imagine you are Philemon or Baucis, and write one or two paragraphs explaining how you would have treated their guests.

Section 2

The Fall of Rome

Get Ready to Read!

What's the Connection?

In Section 1, you learned about Roman life and achievements when the empire was at its height. Over time, however, the Roman Empire began to have problems, and it gradually grew weaker. Eventually, Rome fell to outside invaders.

Focusing on the **Main Ideas**

- Poor leadership, a declining economy, and attacks by Germanic tribes weakened the Roman Empire. *(page 318)*

- Rome finally fell when invaders swept through the empire during the A.D. 400s. *(page 322)*

- Rome passed on many achievements in government, law, language, and the arts. *(page 325)*

Locating Places

Constantinople
(KAHN•STAN•tuhn•OH•puhl)

Meeting People

Diocletian (DY•uh•KLEE•shuhn)
Constantine (KAHN•stuhn•TEEN)
Theodosius
(THEE•uh•DOH•shuhs)
Alaric (A•luh•rihk)
Odoacer (OH•duh•WAY•suhr)

Building Your Vocabulary

plague (PLAYG)
inflation (ihn•FLAY•shuhn)
barter (BAHR•tuhr)
reform (rih•FAWRM)

Reading Strategy

Sequencing Information Create a diagram to show the events that led up to the fall of the Western Roman Empire.

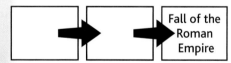

Fall of the Roman Empire

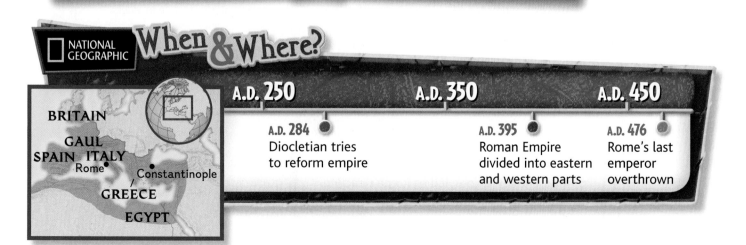

NATIONAL GEOGRAPHIC **When & Where?**

BRITAIN
GAUL
SPAIN   ITALY
Rome •
Constantinople
GREECE
EGYPT

A.D. 250   A.D. 350   A.D. 450

A.D. 284
Diocletian tries
to reform empire

A.D. 395
Roman Empire
divided into eastern
and western parts

A.D. 476
Rome's last
emperor
overthrown

The Decline of Rome

(Main Idea) Poor leadership, a declining economy, and attacks by Germanic tribes weakened the Roman Empire.

Reading Focus What do you do when you face a difficult problem? Do you try to solve it yourself? Do you ask other people for help? Read to learn about the problems the Roman Empire faced and how its leaders responded.

In A.D. 180 Marcus Aurelius died. His son, Commodus (KAH•muh•duhs), became emperor. Commodus was cruel and wasted money. Instead of ruling Rome, Commodus spent much of his time fighting as a gladiator. In A.D. 192 the emperor's bodyguard killed him. Nearly a century of confusion and fighting followed.

After Commodus, emperors called the Severans ruled Rome. Much of their time was spent putting down revolts and protecting Rome's borders. The Severans stayed in power by paying the army well, but they ignored the growing problems of crime and poverty.

Political and Social Problems When the last Severan ruler died in A.D. 235, Rome's government became very weak. For almost 50 years, army leaders fought each other for the throne. During this time, Rome had 22 different emperors.

Poor leadership was not Rome's only difficulty. Fewer Romans honored the old ideals of duty, courage, and honesty. Many government officials took bribes. As problems

The Decline of Rome

Weak Roman Government
- Dishonest government officials provide poor leadership.

Social Problems
- Famine and disease spread throughout the empire.

Declining Economy
- Income and wages fall.
- Wealthy fail to pay taxes.

Reform Fails and Rome Divides in Two
- Government fails to keep order.
- Violence and tension increase.
- Diocletian divides the empire.

Eastern Roman Empire
- Constantinople becomes the new capital.
- The empire survives attacks and prospers.

Western Roman Empire
- Numerous attacks threaten the empire.
- Territory is slowly lost to invaders.

Byzantine Empire
- This empire is created from the Eastern Roman Empire and lasts nearly 1,000 years.

Rome Falls
- The city of Rome falls in A.D. 476.
- The Western Roman Empire is divided into Germanic kingdoms by A.D. 550.

Understanding Charts

Many issues, including a weak government, lack of food, and fewer jobs, led to Rome's decline.
1. According to the flow chart, what occurs after reform fails?
2. **Cause and Effect** What were the final effects of the Roman Empire being split in two?

increased, talented people often refused to serve in government. Many wealthy citizens even stopped paying taxes. Fewer people attended schools, and a large number of the empire's people were now enslaved. Wealthy Romans supported slavery because it was a cheap way to get work done.

Economic and Military Problems

During the A.D. 200s, Rome's economy began to fall apart. As government weakened, law and order broke down. Roman soldiers and invaders seized crops and destroyed fields. Farmers grew less food, and hunger began to spread.

As the economy worsened, people bought fewer goods. Artisans produced less, and shopkeepers lost money. Many businesses closed, and the number of workers dropped sharply. Many workers had to leave jobs and serve in the army. A **plague** (PLAYG), or a disease that spreads widely, also took its toll. It killed one out of every ten people in the empire.

Rome also began to suffer from **inflation** (ihn•FLAY•shuhn), or rapidly increasing prices. Inflation happens when money loses its value. How did this happen? The weak economy meant fewer taxes were paid. With less money coming in, the Roman government could not afford to defend its territories and had to find a way to pay its soldiers and officials. One way for the government to get the money it needed was to put less gold in its coins.

By putting less gold in each coin, the government could make extra coins and pay for more things. People soon learned that the coins did not have as much gold in them, and the coins began losing value. Prices went up, and many people stopped using money altogether. They began to **barter** (BAHR•tuhr), or exchange goods without using money.

The Way It Was

Focus on Everyday Life

Slavery in the Roman Empire Public and private slavery were common in Roman society. Public slaves were owned by the state. They took care of important buildings and served government officials. Educated public slaves were used to help organize the governments of conquered areas.

Private slaves were owned by individuals. They were often forced to work long hours and could be sold at any time. Wealthy Romans had hundreds or even thousands of enslaved people. Most enslaved people worked on farms.

Most enslaved people were men. This was probably because their work required great strength. Some enslaved men also became gladiators. Enslaved women made clothing and cooked for their owner's family.

▼ Roman slaves at work

Connecting to the Past

1. What was the main difference between public and private enslavement?

2. Which jobs were probably considered the most desirable by enslaved people?

Meanwhile, invaders swept into the empire. In the west, Germanic tribes raided Roman farms and towns. In the east, armies from Persia pushed into the empire's territory. As fighting increased, the government could no longer enlist and pay Romans as soldiers. It began using Germanic warriors in the army. However, these Germanic soldiers were not loyal to Rome.

What Were Diocletian's Reforms?

In A.D. 284 a general named **Diocletian** (DY•uh•KLEE•shuhn) became emperor. To stop the empire's decline, he introduced **reforms** (rih•FAWRMZ), or political changes to make things better. Because the empire was too large for one person to rule, Diocletian divided it into four parts. He named officials to rule these areas but kept authority over all.

Diocletian also worked to boost the economy. To slow inflation, he issued rules that set the prices of goods and the wages to be paid to workers. To make sure more goods were produced, he ordered workers to remain at the same jobs until they died. Diocletian's reforms failed. The people ignored the new rules, and Diocletian did not have enough power to make them obey.

Who Was Constantine?

In A.D. 305 Diocletian retired from office. After a period of conflict, another general named **Constantine** (KAHN•stuhn•TEEN) became emperor in A.D. 312. To aid the economy, Constantine issued several orders. The sons of workers had to follow their fathers' trades, the sons of farmers had to work the land their fathers worked, and the sons of soldiers had to serve in the army.

Constantine's changes did not halt the empire's decline in the west. As a result, Constantine moved the capital from dying Rome to a new city in the east. He chose the site of the Greek city of Byzantium (buh•ZAN•tee•uhm). There he built a forum, an amphitheater called the Hippodrome, and many palaces. The city became known as **Constantinople** (KAHN•STAN•tuhn•OH•puhl). Today, Constantinople is called Istanbul.

✔ **Reading Check** **Explain** How did Diocletian try to reverse the decline of Rome?

Biography

CONSTANTINE THE GREAT
c. A.D. 280–337

First Christian Roman Emperor

Constantine was the first Roman Emperor to become a Christian, although he was not baptized until near his death in A.D. 337. He first came to believe in Christianity many years earlier, when he was a military leader. Constantine believed he had seen a flaming cross in the sky that said, "By this sign thou shall conquer." The next day his army was victorious in an important battle. He believed that the cross was a call to the Christian God.

During his reign, Constantine granted new opportunities to Christians and helped advance the power of the early Catholic Church. At the Council of Nicea in A.D. 325, he encouraged discussion about the acceptance of the Trinity (Father, Son, and Holy Spirit). He also boosted the political positions and power of bishops within the Roman government.

Even though Constantine had many political and religious successes, his life was filled with controversy and tragedy. Constantine married a woman named Fausta. His eldest son from a previous marriage was named Crispus. Fausta accused Crispus of crimes and claimed that he was planning to seize the throne. Constantine was so shocked that he had his son killed. Constantine later discovered that Fausta had lied because she wanted her own son to be in line for the throne. He then had Fausta killed.

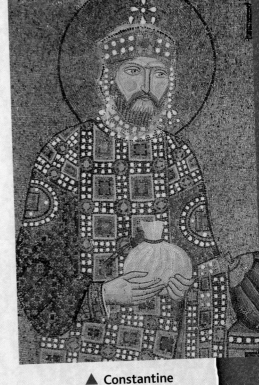

▲ Constantine

▲ Modern-day Constantinople

Then and Now

Constantine believed freedom of religion was important for the success of his empire and made sure that Christians could no longer be persecuted. What part of the U.S. Constitution protects freedom of religion?

Rome Falls

Main Idea Rome finally fell when invaders swept through the empire during the A.D. 400s.

Reading Focus How would you feel if a favorite place—a shop, park, or recreation center—was closed after being open for many years? Read to learn how the Romans had to face an even greater loss when their city and empire fell.

Both Diocletian and Constantine failed to save the Roman Empire. When Constantine died in A.D. 337, fighting broke out again. A new emperor called

Primary Source
Rome Is Attacked

In this excerpt from one of his letters, the Christian leader Jerome describes attacks on the Roman provinces.

"Who would believe that Rome, victor over all the world, would fall, that she would be to her people both the womb and the tomb.... Where we cannot help we mourn and mingle with theirs our tears.... There is not an hour, not even a moment, when we are not occupied with crowds of refugees, when the peace of the monastery is not invaded by a horde of guests so that we shall either have to shut the gates or neglect the Scriptures for which the gates were opened."

—Jerome, "News of the Attacks"

▲ Saint Jerome

DBQ Document-Based Question

Does Jerome think the gates of the monastery should be shut? Explain.

Theodosius (THEE•uh•DOH•shuhs) finally gained control and ended the fighting.

Ruling the empire proved to be difficult. Theodosius decided to divide the empire after his death. In A.D. 395, the Roman Empire split into two separate empires. One was the Western Roman Empire, with its capital at Rome. The other was the Eastern Roman Empire, with its capital at Constantinople.

Rome Is Invaded As Rome declined, it was no longer able to hold back the Germanic tribes on its borders. Many different Germanic groups existed—Ostrogoths, Visigoths, Franks, Vandals, Angles, and Saxons. They came from the forests and marshes of northern Europe.

These Germanic groups were in search of warmer climates and better grazing land for their cattle. They also were drawn by Rome's wealth and culture. In addition, many were fleeing the Huns, fierce warriors from Mongolia in Asia.

In the late A.D. 300s, the Huns entered Eastern Europe and defeated the Ostrogoths (AHS•truh•GAHTHS). The Visigoths, fearing they would be next, asked the Eastern Roman emperor for protection. He let them settle just inside the empire's border. In return they promised to be loyal to Rome.

Before long, trouble broke out between the Visigoths and Romans. The empire forced the Visigoths to buy food at very high prices. The Romans also kidnapped and enslaved many Visigoths.

Web Activity Visit jat.glencoe.com and click on *Chapter 9—Student Web Activity* to learn more about Roman civilization.

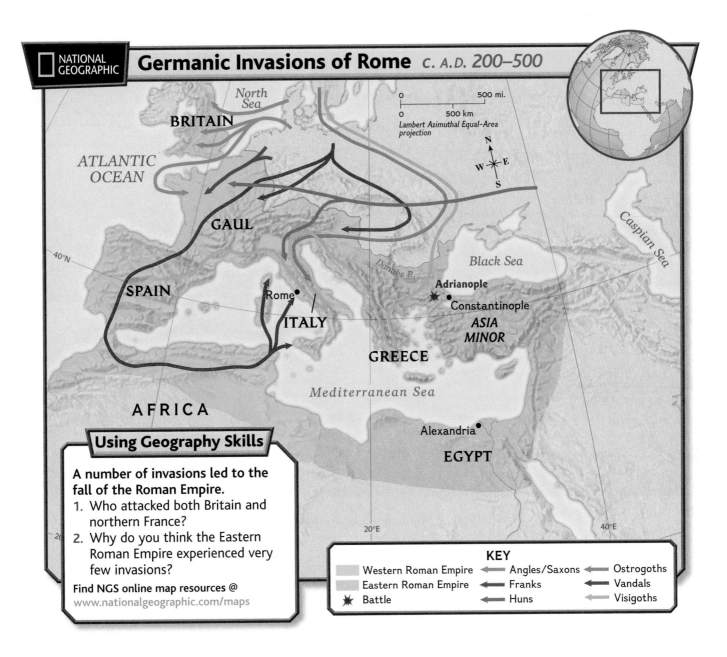

Germanic Invasions of Rome c. A.D. 200–500

NATIONAL GEOGRAPHIC

North Sea

BRITAIN

ATLANTIC OCEAN

GAUL

SPAIN

Rome

ITALY

AFRICA

40°N

Danube R.

Black Sea

Adrianople

Constantinople

ASIA MINOR

GREECE

Mediterranean Sea

Alexandria

EGYPT

Caspian Sea

0   500 mi.
0   500 km
Lambert Azimuthal Equal-Area projection

20°E   40°E

Using Geography Skills

A number of invasions led to the fall of the Roman Empire.
1. Who attacked both Britain and northern France?
2. Why do you think the Eastern Roman Empire experienced very few invasions?

Find NGS online map resources @
www.nationalgeographic.com/maps

KEY

Western Roman Empire	Angles/Saxons · Ostrogoths
Eastern Roman Empire	Franks · Vandals
Battle	Huns · Visigoths

Finally, the Visigoths rebelled against the Romans. In A.D. 378 they defeated Roman legions at the Battle of Adrianople (AY•dree•uh•NOH•puhl). After that defeat, Rome was forced to surrender land to the Visigoths.

The Germanic tribes now knew that Rome could no longer defend itself. More and more Germanic warriors crossed the borders in search of land. In the winter of A.D. 406, the Rhine River in Western Europe froze. Germanic groups crossed the frozen river and entered Gaul, which is today

France. The Romans were too weak to force them back across the border.

In A.D. 410 the Visigoth leader **Alaric** (A•luh•rihk) and his soldiers captured Rome itself. They burned records and looted the treasury. Rome's capture by Alaric was a great shock to the empire's people. It was the first time Rome had been conquered in 800 years.

Another Germanic group known as the Vandals overran Spain and northern Africa. They enslaved some Roman landowners and drove others away. Then the Vandals

▲ An image showing the Visigoths invading Rome. *What leader did the Visigoths overthrow to take control of Rome?*

sailed to Italy. In A.D. 455 they entered Rome. They spent 12 days stripping buildings of everything valuable and burning them. From these attacks came the English word *vandalism,* which means "the willful destruction of property."

Rome Falls By the mid-A.D. 400s, several Germanic leaders held high posts in Rome's government and army. In A.D. 476 a Germanic general named **Odoacer** (OH•duh• WAY•suhr) took control, overthrowing the western emperor, a 14-year-old boy named Romulus Augustulus (RAHM•yuh• luhs aw•GUHS•chah•luhs). After Romulus Augustulus, no emperor ever again ruled from Rome. Historians often use this event to mark the end of the Western Roman Empire.

Odoacer controlled Rome for almost 15 years. Then a group of Visigoths seized the city and killed Odoacer. They set up a kingdom in Italy under their leader, Theodoric (thee•AH•duh•rihk). Elsewhere in Europe, other Germanic kingdoms arose.

By A.D. 550, the Western Roman Empire had faded away. Many Roman beliefs and practices remained in use, however. For example, Europe's new Germanic rulers adopted the Latin language, Roman laws, and Christianity. Although the Western Roman Empire fell to Germanic invaders, the Eastern Roman Empire prospered. It became known as the Byzantine Empire and lasted nearly 1,000 more years.

✓ Reading Check **Identify** Which event usually marks the fall of the Western Roman Empire?

The Legacy of Rome

Main Idea Rome passed on many achievements in government, law, language, and the arts.

Reading Focus Do you know where the words "doctor," "animal," "circus," and "family" come from? These words come from the Latin language spoken by the Romans. Read to discover other things we have borrowed from the Romans.

Our world would be very different if the Roman Empire had never existed. Many words in the English language and many of our ideas about government come from the Romans. The same is true for our system of laws and our knowledge about building. As you will read in the next chapter, the peace and order brought by Roman rule also allowed the Christian religion to spread.

Roman Ideas and Government Today

Roman ideas about law, as first written in the Twelve Tables, are with us today. We, like the Romans, believe that all people are equal under the law. We expect our judges to decide cases fairly, and we consider a person innocent until proven guilty.

Linking Past & Present

Roman and Modern Architecture

THEN Early Romans borrowed architectural ideas from the Greeks, but they also developed their own style. Roman designs often included vaults, columns, domes, and arches. New architectural ideas meant that buildings could be constructed in new ways. Because of concrete and a new design, Roman theaters did not have to be built on natural slopes to have tiered seating.

▼ The Rotunda at the University of Virginia

NOW Columns, domes, and arches still appear in many modern buildings. Banks, homes, and government buildings often use a Roman style. *What Roman architectural styles do you see in your neighborhood?*

▲ The Pantheon in Rome

Roman ideas about government and citizenship are also important today. Like the early Romans, Americans believe that a republic made up of equal citizens is the best form of government. We also believe that a republic works best if citizens do their duty, participate in government, and work to make their society better.

Roman Influence on Culture

Today the alphabet of the Latin language, which expanded from 22 to 26 letters, is used throughout the Western world. Latin shaped the languages of Italy, France, Spain, Portugal, and Romania. Many English words also come from Latin. Scientists, doctors, and lawyers still use Latin phrases. Every known species of plant and animal has a Latin name. Today, we also still admire the works of great Roman writers such as Virgil, Horace, Livy, and Tacitus.

Ancient Rome also left a lasting mark on building in the Western world. We still use concrete today for much of our construction, and Roman architectural styles are still seen in public buildings today. When you visit Washington, D.C., or the capital city of any state, you will see capitol buildings with domes and arches inspired by Roman architecture.

Christianity

As you probably know, Christianity is one of the major religions in the world today. Christianity began in the Roman Empire. When Rome's government adopted Christianity in the A.D. 300s, it helped the new religion to grow and spread. After Rome's fall, many Roman ideas blended with those of Christianity.

✓ Reading Check **Compare** Which aspects of the Roman Empire are reflected in present-day cultures?

History Online

Homework Helper Need help with the material in this section? Visit jat.glencoe.com

Section 2 Review

Reading Summary

Review the Main Ideas

- A series of weak emperors, invasions by outsiders, disease, and a number of other factors led to a greatly weakened Roman Empire.

- Numerous invasions by Germanic peoples led to the fall of Rome in A.D. 476.

- Roman ideas about government and Roman architecture are just some of the legacies of ancient Rome.

What Did You Learn?

1. What social problems helped cause the empire's decline?

2. Why did the Roman government use Germanic warriors in its army?

Critical Thinking

3. **Summarizing Information** Draw a diagram like the one below. Fill in details about Rome's legacies in the areas of government, law, and citizenship.

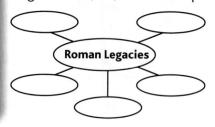

Roman Legacies

4. **Cause and Effect** How did inflation affect Rome?

5. **Describe** Who were the Visigoths, and how did they contribute to the fall of Rome?

6. **Identify** Give examples of Roman ideas in language and architecture that exist today.

7. **Persuasive Writing** Imagine you are living in Rome around the time of the fall of the empire. Write an editorial for a newspaper identifying what you think is the main reason for the decline and fall of the empire, and what might have been done to prevent it.

The Byzantine Empire

Get Ready to Read!

What's the Connection?

In the last section, you learned that even though the Roman Empire in the West fell, the Eastern Roman Empire survived and prospered. It became known as the Byzantine Empire. The Byzantines developed a new civilization based on Greek, Roman, and Christian ideas.

Focusing on the Main Ideas

- The Eastern Roman Empire grew rich and powerful as the Western Roman Empire fell. *(page 328)*

- The policies and reforms of Emperor Justinian and Empress Theodora helped make the Byzantine Empire strong. *(page 329)*

- The Byzantines developed a rich culture based on Roman, Greek, and Christian ideas. *(page 332)*

Locating Places

Black Sea
Aegean Sea (ih•JEE•uhn)

Meeting People

Justinian (juh•STIH•nee•uhn)
Theodora (THEE•uh•DOHR•uh)
Belisarius (BEH•luh•SAR•ee•uhs)
Tribonian (truh•BOH•nee•uhn)

Building Your Vocabulary

mosaic (moh•ZAY•ihk)
saint (SAYNT)
regent (REE•juhnt)

Reading Strategy

Cause and Effect Complete a chart to show the causes and effects of Justinian's new law code.

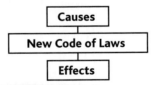

```
┌──────────┐
│  Causes  │
└──────────┘
      │
┌─────────────────┐
│ New Code of Laws │
└─────────────────┘
      │
┌──────────┐
│  Effects │
└──────────┘
```

NATIONAL GEOGRAPHIC

When & Where?

BALKAN PENINSULA
SPAIN ITALY
Rome
Constantinople
ASIA MINOR
PALESTINE
EGYPT

A.D. 525   A.D. 550   A.D. 575

A.D. 527
Emperor Justinian begins rule

A.D. 537
Hagia Sophia completed

A.D. 565
Justinian dies

The Rise of the Byzantines

Main Idea The Eastern Roman Empire grew rich and powerful as the Western Roman Empire fell.

Reading Focus Think of your own community. How have groups of people from different backgrounds contributed to its character? What would your town or city be like without these contributions from all the different groups? Read to learn about the different groups that made up the Byzantine Empire.

The Eastern Roman, or Byzantine, Empire reached a high point in the A.D. 500s. At this time, the empire stretched west to Italy, south to Egypt, and east to the border with Arabia. Greeks made up the empire's largest group, but many other peoples were found within the empire. They included Egyptians, Syrians, Arabs, Armenians, Jews, Persians, Slavs, and Turks.

▲ The ancient walled city of Constantinople

Why Is Constantinople Important? In the last section, you learned that Emperor Constantine moved the capital of the Roman Empire from Rome to a new city called Constantinople. Constantine's city became the capital of the Byzantine Empire. By the A.D. 500s, Constantinople was thriving and had become one of the world's great cities.

One reason for Constantinople's success was its location. It lay on the waterways between the **Black Sea** and the **Aegean Sea** (ih•JEE•uhn). Its harbors offered a safe shelter for fishing boats, trading ships, and warships. Constantinople also sat at the crossroads of trade routes between Europe and Asia. The trade that passed through made the city extremely wealthy.

Constantinople had a secure land location. Lying on a peninsula, Constantinople was easily defended. Seas protected it on three sides, and on the fourth side, a huge wall guarded the city. Later a huge chain was even strung across the city's north harbor for greater protection. Invaders could not easily take Constantinople.

Influence of Greek Culture
The Byzantines at first followed Roman ways. Constantinople was known as the "New Rome." Its public buildings and palaces were built in the Roman style. The city even had an oval arena called the Hippodrome, where chariot races and other events were held.

Byzantine political and social life also were based on that of Rome. Emperors spoke Latin and enforced Roman laws. The empire's poor people received free bread and shows. Wealthy people lived in town or on large farming estates. In fact, many of them had once lived in Rome.

As time passed, the Byzantine Empire became less Roman and more Greek. Most Byzantines spoke Greek and honored their Greek past. Byzantine emperors and officials began to speak Greek too. The ideas of non-Greek peoples, like the Egyptians and the Slavs, also shaped Byzantine life. Still other customs came from Persia to the east. All of these cultures blended together to form the Byzantine civilization. Between A.D. 500 and A.D. 1200, the Byzantines had one of the world's richest and most-advanced empires.

Reading Check Explain Why did the Byzantine Empire have such a blending of cultures?

Emperor Justinian

Main Idea The policies and reforms of Emperor Justinian and Empress Theodora helped make the Byzantine Empire strong.

Reading Focus Do you sometimes rewrite reports to make them easier to understand? Read to learn how Justinian rewrote and reorganized the Byzantine law code.

Justinian (juh•STIH•nee•uhn) became emperor of the Byzantine Empire in A.D. 527 and ruled until A.D. 565. Justinian was a strong leader. He controlled the military, made laws, and was supreme judge. His order could not be questioned.

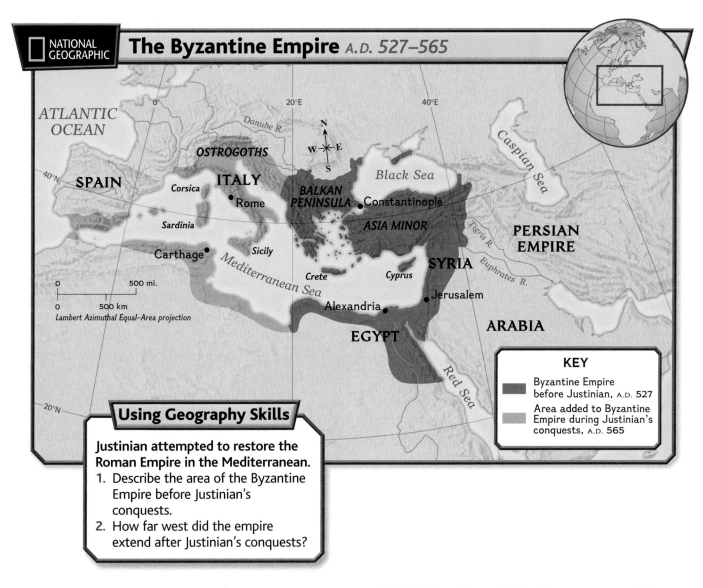

NATIONAL GEOGRAPHIC

The Byzantine Empire A.D. 527–565

KEY
- Byzantine Empire before Justinian, A.D. 527
- Area added to Byzantine Empire during Justinian's conquests, A.D. 565

Using Geography Skills

Justinian attempted to restore the Roman Empire in the Mediterranean.
1. Describe the area of the Byzantine Empire before Justinian's conquests.
2. How far west did the empire extend after Justinian's conquests?

Primary Source

Theodora Refuses to Flee

Justinian's court historian recorded Theodora's opinion about whether to escape or fight during the A.D. 532 revolt.

"My opinion then is that the present time . . . is inopportune [not a good time] for flight, even though it brings safety. . . . For one who has been an emperor, it is unendurable to be a fugitive. . . . May I not live that day on which those who meet me shall not address me as empress. If, now, it is your wish to save yourself, O Emperor, there is no difficulty."

—Procopius, "The Nika Riot"

Theodora ▶

DBQ Document-Based Question

Why did the empress not wish to escape?

Justinian's wife, the empress **Theodora** (THEE•uh•DOHR•uh), helped him run the empire. Theodora, a former actress, was intelligent and strong-willed, and she helped Justinian choose government officials. Theodora also convinced him to give women more rights. For the first time, a Byzantine wife could own land. If she became a widow, she now had the income to take care of her children.

In A.D. 532 Theodora helped save Justinian's throne. Angry taxpayers threatened to overthrow Justinian and stormed the palace. Justinian's advisers urged him to leave Constantinople. Theodora, however, told him to stay and fight. Justinian took Theodora's advice. He stayed in the city and crushed the uprising.

Justinian's Conquests Justinian wanted to reunite the Roman Empire and bring back Rome's glory. To do this, he had to conquer Western Europe and northern Africa. He ordered a general named **Belisarius** (BEH•luh•SAR•ee•uhs) to strengthen and lead the Byzantine army.

When Belisarius took command, he reorganized the Byzantine army. Instead of foot soldiers, the Byzantine army came to rely on cavalry—soldiers mounted on horses. Byzantine cavalry wore armor and carried bows and lances, which were long spears.

During Justinian's reign, the Byzantine military conquered most of Italy and northern Africa and defeated the Persians in the east. However, Justinian conquered too much too quickly. After he died, the empire did not have the money to maintain an army large enough to hold the territory in the west.

Justinian's Law Code Justinian decided that the empire's laws were disorganized and too difficult to understand. He ordered a group of legal scholars headed by **Tribonian** (truh•BOH•nee•uhn) to reform the law code.

The group's new simplified code became known as the Justinian Code. Officials, businesspeople, and individuals could now more easily understand the empire's laws. Over the years, the Justinian Code has had a great influence on the laws of almost every country in Europe.

☑ Reading Check **Explain** What did Justinian accomplish during his reign?

Biography

EMPRESS THEODORA
c A.D. 500–548

Theodora began life in the lower class of Byzantine society but rose to the rank of empress. The historian Procopius recorded the events of her early life. According to Procopius, Theodora's father worked as a bear keeper at the Hippodrome. After his death, Theodora followed her mother's advice and became an actress. A career in acting was not as glamorous then as it is now. It was a job of the lower class, like wool spinning, which was Theodora's other job.

Even though Theodora was of the lower class, she began dating Justinian. Justinian was attracted to Theodora's beauty and intelligence. Because Justinian wanted to marry Theodora, his uncle, the emperor, changed the law that prevented upper-class nobles from marrying actresses. The two were married in A.D. 525.

Justinian considered Theodora his intellectual equal. In his writings, Justinian said he asked for Theodora's advice on laws and policies. At Theodora's urging, he granted more rights to women. Some historians believe Theodora had great power within the royal court, perhaps more than Justinian. For example, nearly all the laws passed during Theodora's reign as empress mention her name. Theodora and Justinian had no children together. When Theodora died from cancer in A.D. 548, Justinian was overcome with grief. He had her portrait incorporated into many works of art, including numerous Byzantine mosaics.

▲ Empress Theodora advises Emperor Justinian.

> "She was extremely clever and had a biting wit."
> –Procopius, *The Secret History*

Then and Now

Name a modern-day female political leader that you think has great influence in making and changing laws. Explain your choice.

Byzantine Civilization

Main Idea The Byzantines developed a rich culture based on Roman, Greek, and Christian ideas.

Reading Focus Do you think a multicultural population adds to a country's interest and success? Read to learn how the diverse groups of the Byzantine Empire contributed to its culture.

The Byzantine Empire lasted approximately 1,000 years. For much of that time, Constantinople was the largest and richest city in Europe. The Byzantines were highly educated and creative. They preserved and passed on Greek culture and Roman law to other peoples. They gave the world new methods in the arts. As you will learn, they also spread Christianity to people in Eastern Europe.

The Importance of Trade From the A.D. 500s to the A.D. 1100s, the Byzantine Empire was the center of trade between Europe and Asia. Trade goods from present-day Russia in the north, Mediterranean lands in the south, Latin Europe in the west, and Persia and China in the east passed through the empire. From Asia, ships and caravans brought luxury goods—spices, gems, metals, and cloth—to Constantinople. For these items, Byzantine merchants traded farm goods as well as furs, honey, and enslaved people from northern Europe.

This enormous trade made the Byzantine Empire very rich. However, most Byzantines were not merchants. Instead they were farmers, herders, laborers, and artisans. One of the major Byzantine industries was weaving silk. It developed around

◀ Sculpture showing chariot racing at the Hippodrome

▲ Byzantine jewelry

▲ The style of the Hagia Sophia, shown here, and other Byzantine churches influenced the architecture of churches throughout Russia and Eastern Europe.
What does the name "Hagia Sophia" mean?

A.D. 550. At that time, Byzantine travelers smuggled silkworm eggs out of China. Brought to Constantinople, the silkworms fed on mulberry leaves and produced silk threads. Weavers then used the threads to make the silk cloth that brought wealth to the empire.

Byzantine Art and Architecture

Justinian and other Byzantine emperors supported artists and architects. They ordered the building of churches, forts, and public buildings throughout the empire. Constantinople was known for its hundreds of churches and palaces. One of Justinian's greatest achievements was building the huge church called Hagia Sophia (HAH•jee•uh soh•FEE•uh), or "Holy Wisdom." It was completed in A.D. 537 and became the religious center of the Byzantine Empire. It still stands today in Istanbul.

Inside Hagia Sophia, worshipers could see walls of beautiful marble and mosaics. **Mosaics** (moh•ZAY•ihks) are pictures made from many bits of colored glass or stone. They were an important type of art in the Byzantine Empire. Mosaics mainly showed figures of **saints** (SAYNTS), or Christian holy people.

Byzantine Women

The family was the center of social life for most Byzantines. Religion and the government stressed the importance of marriage and family life. Divorces were rare and difficult to get.

Byzantine women were not encouraged to lead independent lives. They were expected to stay home and take care of their families. However, women did gain some important rights, thanks to Empress Theodora. Like Theodora herself, some Byzantine women became well educated and involved in politics. Several

The Way It Was

Focus on Everyday Life

Byzantine Mosaics Imagine taking bits of glass and turning them into beautiful masterpieces. Byzantine artists did just that starting around A.D. 330. Roman mosaics were made of natural-colored marble pieces and decorated villas and buildings. Byzantine mosaics were different. They were made of richly colored, irregular pieces of glass and decorated the ceilings, domes, and floors of Byzantine churches.

Byzantine mosaics were created to honor religious or political leaders. The centers of domes—because they were the highest points of the churches—were commonly reserved for images of Jesus. Mosaics were expensive. They were ordered and paid for by emperors, state officials, or church leaders. Many mosaics are still intact and can be seen today inside churches, monasteries, and museums.

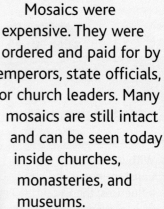

◀ Mosaic from the Byzantine Empire

Connecting to the Past

1. Why do you think the name of the person who paid for the mosaic—rather than the name of the person who made the mosaic—was often recorded in the inscription?
2. What types of art do present-day artists make with glass?

royal women served as regents. A **regent** (REE•juhnt) is a person who stands in for a ruler who is too young or too ill to govern. A few ruled the empire in their own right.

Byzantine Education Learning was highly respected in Byzantine culture. The government supported the training of scholars and government officials. In Byzantine schools, boys studied religion, medicine, law, arithmetic, grammar, and other subjects. Wealthy Byzantines sometimes hired tutors to teach their children. Girls usually did not attend schools and were taught at home.

Most Byzantine authors wrote about religion. They stressed the need to obey God and save one's soul. To strengthen faith, they wrote about the lives of saints. Byzantine writers gave an important gift to the world. They copied and passed on the

▲ This Byzantine religious text is beautifully illustrated. *What did Byzantine boys study at school?*

writings of the ancient Greeks and Romans. Without Byzantine copies, many important works from the ancient world would have disappeared forever.

 **Reading Check** **Identify** What church is one of Justinian's greatest achievements?

History **Online**
Homework Helper Need help with the material in this section? Visit jat.glencoe.com

Section 3 Review

Reading Summary

Review the (Main Ideas)

• With its capital at Constantinople and strong Greek influences, the Byzantine Empire grew powerful and wealthy.

• The Byzantine emperor, Justinian, reconquered much of the land that had been held by the old Roman Empire in the Mediterranean. It also issued a new law code known as the Justinian Code.

• As the Byzantine Empire grew wealthy from trade, art, architecture, and education flourished.

What Did You Learn?

1. What is a mosaic, and where were mosaics found in the Byzantine Empire?

2. How did silk weaving develop in the Byzantine Empire?

Critical Thinking

3. **Organizing Information** Draw a diagram like the one below. Fill in details about Constantinople's location.

Location of Constantinople

4. **Describe** What were some of the trade items that were exchanged between merchants in Constantinople?

5. **Explain** Why were divorces difficult to get in the Byzantine Empire?

6. **Analyze** What important service did Byzantine writers provide to the rest of the world? Explain its significance.

7. **Persuasive Writing** Which civilization do you think was the most advanced—that of the Greeks, the Romans, or the Byzantines? Write a speech explaining your answer.

Chapter 9 Reading Review

Section 1 Life in Ancient Rome

Vocabulary
vault
satire
ode
anatomy
Forum
gladiator
paterfamilias
rhetoric

Focusing on the Main Ideas
- In addition to their own developments in science and engineering, Roman artists and writers borrowed many ideas from the Greeks. *(page 303)*
- The rich and poor had very different lives in the Roman Empire, as did men and women. *(page 306)*

◄ A Roman family at the dinner table

Section 2 The Fall of Rome

Vocabulary
plague
inflation
barter
reform

Focusing on the Main Ideas
- Poor leadership, a declining economy, and attacks by Germanic tribes weakened the Roman Empire. *(page 318)*
- Rome finally fell when invaders swept through the empire during the A.D. 400s. *(page 322)*
- Rome passed on many achievements in government, law, language, and the arts. *(page 325)*

Section 3 The Byzantine Empire

Vocabulary
mosaic
saint
regent

Focusing on the Main Ideas
- The Eastern Roman Empire grew rich and powerful as the Western Roman Empire fell. *(page 328)*
- The policies and reforms of Emperor Justinian and Empress Theodora helped make the Byzantine Empire strong. *(page 329)*
- The Byzantines developed a rich culture based on Roman, Greek, and Christian ideas. *(page 332)*

Chapter 9 Assessment and Activities

Review Vocabulary

Match the definitions in the second column to the terms in the first column.

___ 1. plague
___ 2. anatomy
___ 3. inflation
___ 4. gladiator
___ 5. regent
___ 6. mosaic
___ 7. paterfamilias
___ 8. ode

a. pictures made of many bits of colored glass or stone

b. rapidly increasing prices

c. father of a family

d. emotional poem about life's ups and downs

e. study of the body's structure

f. a disease that spreads widely

g. a person who stands in for a ruler who cannot govern

h. a warrior who fought animals and people in public arenas

Review Main Ideas

Section 1 • Life in Ancient Rome

9. What did the Romans borrow from the Greeks? What did they develop on their own?

10. What were the lives of the rich and poor like in the Roman Empire?

Section 2 • The Fall of Rome

11. What weakened the Roman Empire?

12. What caused the fall of Rome in the A.D. 400s?

Section 3 • The Byzantine Empire

13. What policies and reforms helped make the Byzantine Empire strong?

14. What different groups of people contributed to the Byzantine culture?

Critical Thinking

15. **Cause and Effect** Why did Alaric's capture of Rome shock the Roman people?

16. **Predict** What do you think would have happened if Theodosius had not divided the Roman Empire?

Review Reading Skill Responding and Reflecting **Your Point of View**

17. Read the following paragraph from page 330. Write at least five things you might reflect on as you read this information.

In A.D. 532 Theodora helped save Justinian's throne. Angry taxpayers threatened to overthrow Justinian and stormed the palace. Justinian's advisers urged him to leave Constantinople. Theodora, however, told him to stay and fight. Justinian took Theodora's advice. He stayed in the city and crushed the uprising.

To review this skill, see pages 300–301.

Geography Skills

Study the map below and answer the following questions.

18. **Place** Which areas were conquered by Justinian's military?

19. **Human/Environment Interaction** Why do you think Justinian decided to conquer lands to the west of his empire?

20. **Movement** What made it difficult for the Byzantine Empire to hold on to Justinian's conquests?

NATIONAL GEOGRAPHIC **Byzantine Empire**

ATLANTIC OCEAN
0° 10°E 20°E Danube R.
SPAIN 40°N ITALY
Corsica • Rome
Sardinia Constantinople •
Carthage • Sicily
Mediterranean Sea Crete
30°N
0   500 mi.
0   500 km
Lambert Azimuthal Equal-Area projection

KEY
Byzantine Empire before Justinian, A.D. 527
Byzantine Empire after Justinian's conquests, A.D. 565

N W E S

Read to Write

21. **Descriptive Writing** Suppose you are a newspaper reporter living in the time of the Roman Empire. Write a front-page article about the slave revolt in 73 B.C., the content of Theodosius's will, or the removal of Romulus Augustulus. Remember to include a headline.

22. **Using Your** **FOLDABLES** Use the information you wrote in your foldable to create a brief study guide for the chapter. For each section, your study guide should include at least five questions that focus on the main ideas.

History Online
Self-Check Quiz To help you prepare for the Chapter Test, visit jat.glencoe.com

Linking Past and Present

23. **Analyzing** In the chapter, you learned that the culture of the Byzantine Empire was greatly influenced by the Romans and Greeks, as well as the Egyptian, Slavic, and Persian cultures. Think about the culture of the United States, in which many cultures have blended. Work with a classmate to identify aspects of the U.S. culture that were originally part of other cultures.

Building Citizenship Skills

24. **Analyzing** Growing political and social problems helped set the stage for Rome's final fall. Traditional Roman ideas of duty, courage, and honesty lost their importance. Why do you think duty, courage, and honesty are important in keeping a society and political system strong?

Primary Source **Analyze**

The Roman Empire did have some laws to prevent the extreme abuse of slaves.

"At the present time neither Roman citizens nor any other persons who are under the rule of the Roman people are permitted to treat their slaves with excessive and baseless [reasonless] cruelty. . . . A man who kills his own slave without cause is ordered to be held just as liable as one who kills another's slave."

—Gaius, "Legislation Against the Abuse of Slaves"

DBQ **Document-Based Questions**

25. How does this law pertain to people passing through the empire?

26. How does this statement leave a loophole in the regulation of abuse against slaves?

The Rise of Christianity

▼ Mount of the Beatitudes on the Sea of Galilee in Israel

NATIONAL GEOGRAPHIC **When & Where?**

A.D. 50	A.D. 400	A.D. 750	A.D. 1100
A.D. 30 Jesus preaches in Galilee and Judaea	A.D. 312 Constantine accepts Christianity	A.D. 726 Emperor Leo III removes icons from churches	A.D. 1054 Orthodox and Catholic Churches separate

Chapter Preview

History Online

Chapter Overview Visit jat.glencoe.com for a preview of Chapter 10.

While the Romans built their empire, a group called the Christians spread a new religion called Christianity. Read this chapter to find out how Christianity grew to become one of the major influences on European civilization.

 View the Chapter 10 video in the *World History: Journey Across Time* Video Program.

 ## The First Christians

After the Romans conquered Judah, some Jews opposed Rome peacefully, while others rebelled. During that period, Jesus of Nazareth began preaching a message of love and forgiveness. His life and teachings led to the rise of Christianity.

 ## The Christian Church

In time, Christianity became the Roman Empire's official religion. Early Christians organized the church and collected the New Testament of the Bible.

 ## The Spread of Christian Ideas

Church and government worked closely together in the Byzantine Empire. Christians founded new communities and spread their faith through Europe.

 **Study Organizer**

Sequencing Information *Make this foldable to help you sequence information about the rise of Christianity.*

Step 1 *Fold a piece of paper from top to bottom.*

Step 2 *Then fold back each half to make quarter folds.*

This makes an accordian shape.

Step 3 *Unfold and label the time line as shown.*

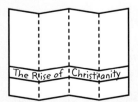

The Rise of Christianity

Step 4 *Fill in important dates as you read like those shown.*

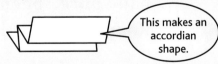

A.D. 30		Jesus begins to preach
A.D. 64	The Rise of Christianity	Romans persecute Christians
A.D. 313		Constantine's conversion
A.D. 726		Emperor Leo III removes icons

Reading and Writing *As you read the chapter, write the important events that occurred in the rise of Christianity.*

339

Chapter 10 Reading Social Studies

Reading Skill
Sequence Clues

1 Learn It!

Looking for Sequence Clues

When we speak, read, or write, we automatically use clues to tell us what happened when. These clues are called sequence words, and they show us the order in which events occur.

Read the following passage about the spread of Christianity. Notice the highlighted sequence words or phrases.

> **After the fall of Rome, the people of Western Europe faced confusion and conflict. As a result, people were looking for order and unity. Christianity helped to meet this need. It spread rapidly into lands that had once been part of the Roman Empire.**
>
> *—from page 361*

Reading Tip

When you have trouble understanding the order in which things occur, create a rough time line to help you keep track of events as you read.

Now read the paragraph again and leave out the highlighted sequence words. Do you see how important they are in helping you understand what you are reading?

2 Practice It!

Finding Clue Words

Read this passage and write down any word or phrase that helps you recognize the sequence of events.

Read to Write ······

Look at the time line that appears at the bottom of page 342. Write a paragraph that uses sequence clues to describe when these events occurred.

Even with all of the hardships, Christianity spread. Over time it even began to draw people from all classes. After A.D. 250, many Romans grew tired of war and feared the end of the empire. They began to admire the faith and courage of the Christians. At the same time, many Christians started to accept the empire.

—*from pages 353–354*

The apostle
Peter preaching ▼

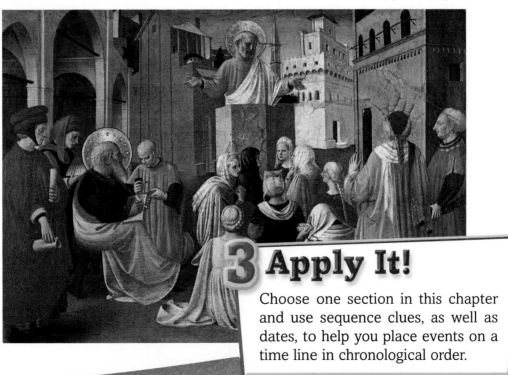

3 Apply It!

Choose one section in this chapter and use sequence clues, as well as dates, to help you place events on a time line in chronological order.

Section 1

The First Christians

Get Ready to Read!

What's the Connection?

You learned that the Romans ruled many areas of the Mediterranean. In one of these areas, Judaea, a new religion, Christianity, began.

Focusing on the Main Ideas

- Roman rule of Judaea led some Jews to oppose Rome peacefully, while others rebelled. *(page 343)*

- Jesus of Nazareth preached of God's love and forgiveness. He was eventually crucified and then reported to have risen from the dead. *(page 344)*

- Jesus' life and a belief in his resurrection led to a new religion called Christianity. *(page 348)*

Locating Places

Jerusalem (juh•ROO•suh•luhm)
Judaea (ju•DEE•uh)
Nazareth (NA•zuh•ruhth)
Galilee (GA•luh•LEE)

Meeting People

Jesus (JEE•zuhs)
Peter
Paul

Building Your Vocabulary

messiah (muh•SY•uh)
disciple (dih•SY•puhl)
parable (PAR•uh•buhl)
resurrection (REH•zuh•REHK•shuhn)
apostle (uh•PAH•suhl)
salvation (sal•VAY•shuhn)

Reading Strategy

Summarizing Information Complete a diagram like the one below showing the purposes of early Christian churches.

Purposes of Churches

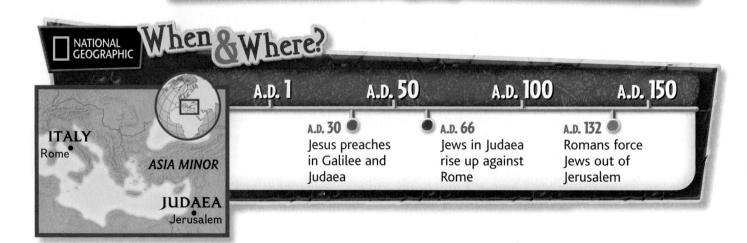

NATIONAL GEOGRAPHIC When & Where?

| A.D. 1 | A.D. 50 | A.D. 100 | A.D. 150 |

A.D. 30 Jesus preaches in Galilee and Judaea

A.D. 66 Jews in Judaea rise up against Rome

A.D. 132 Romans force Jews out of Jerusalem

ITALY
Rome

ASIA MINOR

JUDAEA
Jerusalem

The Jews and the Romans

Main Idea Roman rule of Judaea led some Jews to oppose Rome peacefully, while others rebelled.

Reading Focus Suppose you were separated from your home and could not easily return to it. What effect might this have on you? Read to learn how the Jews were forced to leave their capital city.

As you learned earlier, during the 900s B.C., two great kings, David and Solomon, united the Israelites and created the kingdom of Israel. Its capital was **Jerusalem** (juh•ROO•suh•luhm). This unity did not last long, however. Israel divided into two kingdoms: Israel and Judah. These small kingdoms were later taken over by more powerful neighbors. Israel was destroyed, and its people scattered. But the Jews, the people of Judah, survived.

Roman Rule In 63 B.C. the Romans took over Judah. At first, they ruled through Jewish kings. Then, in A.D. 6, Emperor Augustus turned Judah into a Roman province called **Judaea** (ju•DEE•uh). Instead of a king, a Roman governor called a procurator (PRAH•kyuh•RAY•tuhr) ruled the new province.

The Jews argued among themselves over what to do about the Romans. Some favored working with the Romans. Others opposed Roman rule by closely following Jewish traditions. Still others turned their backs on the Romans. They settled in isolated areas and shared their belongings.

The Jews Rebel Some Jews believed that they should fight the Romans and take back control of their kingdom. These people, called Zealots, convinced many Jews to take up arms against the Romans in A.D. 66. The rebellion was brutally crushed. The Romans destroyed the temple and killed thousands of Jews. A Jewish general named Josephus (joh•SEE•fuhs) fought in the war but later sided with the Romans. He wrote about the horrors of Jerusalem's fall in his work *History of the Jewish War.*

The Jews rebelled again in A.D. 132 and were again defeated. This time the Romans forced all Jews to leave Jerusalem and banned them from ever returning to the city. Saddened by the loss of Jerusalem, many Jews found new homes elsewhere.

By A.D. 700, the Jews had set up communities as far west as Spain and as far east as central Asia. In later centuries, they settled throughout Europe and the Americas. In their scattered communities, the Jews kept their faith alive by studying and following their religious laws.

Reading Check **Explain** Why did many Jews leave Judaea after the A.D. 132 revolt?

These ruins are of the mountaintop Jewish fortress at Masada in Israel. Jewish rebels were defeated by Roman troops here in A.D. 73. What were the Jewish rebels called?

The Life of Jesus

Main Idea Jesus of Nazareth preached of God's love and forgiveness. He was eventually crucified and then reported to have risen from the dead.

Reading Focus If you could give someone advice on how to behave, what would you tell them? Why? Read to learn how Jesus thought people should behave.

During Roman times, many Jews hoped that God would send a **messiah** (muh•SY•uh), or deliverer. This leader would help them win back their freedom. The Israelite prophets had long ago predicted that a messiah would come. Many Jews expected the messiah to be a great king, like David. They thought the messiah would restore the past glories of the Israelite kingdom.

A few decades before the first Jewish revolt against Rome, a Jew named **Jesus** (JEE•zuhs) left his home in **Nazareth** (NA•zuh•ruhth) and began preaching. From about A.D. 30 to A.D. 33, Jesus traveled throughout Judaea and **Galilee** (GA•luh•LEE), the region just north of Judaea, preaching his ideas. Crowds gathered to hear him preach. He soon assembled a small band of 12 close followers called **disciples** (dih•SY•puhlz).

What Did Jesus Teach? According to the Christian Bible, Jesus preached that God was coming soon to rule the world. He urged people to turn from their sins. He also told them that following Jewish religious laws was not as important as having a relationship with God, whom Jesus referred to as his Father.

The main points of Jesus' message are given in a group of sayings known as the Sermon on the Mount. In them, Jesus made it clear that a person had to love and forgive

The Teachings of Jesus

▼ Jesus traveled throughout the regions of Judaea and Galilee, preaching to all who would listen to his religious message. In the Sermon on the Mount, illustrated below, Jesus described God's love and how to be a good person. At right, Jesus is shown as the Good Shepherd, a popular image in early Christian art. *What did Jesus teach about Jewish religious laws?*

from the heart and not just go through the motions of following religious laws. Among Jesus' sayings were "Blessed are the merciful, for they will obtain mercy" and "Blessed are the peacemakers, for they will be called the children of God."

Jesus told his listeners to love and forgive each other because God loves and forgives people. According to Jesus, God's command was simple. He repeated the age-old Jewish teaching: "Love the Lord your God with all your heart and with all your soul and with all your mind and with all your strength." Jesus also stressed another teaching: "Love your neighbor as yourself." Jesus' message of love and forgiveness helped shape the values many people in Europe and America hold today.

To present his message, Jesus often used **parables** (PAR•uh•buhlz). These were stories that used events from everyday life to express spiritual ideas. In the story of the Prodigal (wasteful) Son, Jesus told how a father welcomed back his reckless son with open arms. He forgave his son's mistakes. In another parable, he told of a shepherd who left his flock unguarded to go after one lost sheep. Both stories taught that God forgives mistakes and wants all people to turn away from bad deeds and be saved.

The parable of the Good Samaritan is one of the best known. In this story, a man is beaten by robbers. A priest and another religious leader refuse to help the injured man. However, a Samaritan, a member of a group looked down upon by Jesus' listeners, stops to help the victim. He treats the man's wounds and pays for his stay at an inn. Jesus asked his followers, "Which man do you think truly showed love to his neighbor?"

▼ Jesus used stories, called parables, to describe correct behaviors to his followers. The parables of the Prodigal Son (below) and the Good Samaritan (right) are shown here. *What lesson was taught by the parable of the Prodigal Son?*

Biography

Jesus of Nazareth
c. 6 B.C.–A.D. 30

Much of what we know about Jesus, whose life and teachings established the Christian religion, is based on accounts found in the Bible. According to the Bible, Jesus' birth was guided by God. An angel visited Mary, Jesus' mother, to tell her she was going to have a baby. The angel told Mary her baby would be the Son of God. An angel also visited Joseph, Mary's fiancé, and instructed him to marry her.

Jesus was humbly born in a stable, beside barn animals, in the town of Bethlehem. Mary and Joseph had traveled there to take part in a census ordered by the Romans. Shepherds and wise men, possibly princes from neighboring kingdoms, followed a brightly shining star to honor Jesus in the stable. Christmas is a celebration of Jesus' birth.

The Bible tells very little about the middle years of Jesus' life. He grew up in Nazareth, a small town in Galilee, where he learned the carpenter's trade from Joseph. Later in life, Jesus set out to share his religious teachings. At this point, the Bible provides many stories of Jesus' travels and the miracles he performed. The accounts of Jesus' miracles, such as giving a blind man sight, raising a man from the dead, and calming a storm at sea, brought many followers to his teachings. When Jesus entered Jerusalem the week before his death, he was greeted by cheering crowds. One of Jesus' closest followers, however, betrayed him and turned him over to Roman authorities. Jesus was questioned by Jewish and Roman officials and sentenced to death. Soon afterwards, reports that he had risen from the dead would lead to a new religion—Christianity.

▲ Jesus entering Jerusalem

"I am the light that has come into the world."
—Jesus of Nazareth, John 13:46

◄ An early depiction of Jesus on his throne

Then and Now

What event does Christmas celebrate? What aspects of Christmas today are not related to its traditional meaning?

What Is the Crucifixion? Jesus and his message drew strong responses from people. His followers called attention to instances in which they believed he healed the sick and performed other miracles. They said he was the long-awaited messiah. Other Jews disagreed and said he was a deceiver. Above all, Judaea's Roman rulers feared the effects of Jesus' preaching. A person who could spark such strong reactions might threaten law and order.

About A.D. 33, Jesus went to Jerusalem to celebrate Passover, an important Jewish holiday. There he was greeted by large, cheering crowds. In an event known as the Last Supper, Jesus celebrated the holiday with his 12 disciples. Fearing trouble, leaders in Jerusalem arrested Jesus. Jesus was charged with treason, or disloyalty to the government. As punishment, Jesus was crucified, or hung from a cross until dead. This was Rome's way of punishing political rebels and lower-class criminals.

After Jesus' death, his followers made a startling claim. They announced that Jesus had risen from the dead. Christian tradition states that Mary Magdalene, one of Jesus' followers, was the first to see Jesus alive again. Others, including Jesus' disciples, reported seeing him as well. The disciples also pointed to his empty tomb as proof that Jesus was the messiah. These reports of Jesus' **resurrection** (REH•zuh•REHK•shuhn), or rising from the dead, led to a new religion called Christianity.

Reading Check **Describing** What were the main ideas Jesus taught during his life?

▲ According to the Bible, just before his death, Jesus gathered his disciples together for a meal known as the Last Supper. *Why did the Romans fear Jesus?*

The First Christians

Main Idea Jesus' life and a belief in his resurrection led to a new religion called Christianity.

Reading Focus Have you ever read news stories about people sacrificing their lives to help others? Read to learn about the sacrifice Christians believe Jesus made for everyone.

Jesus' disciples began to spread the message of Jesus and his resurrection. Small groups in the Greek-speaking cities of the eastern Mediterranean accepted this message. Some were Jews, but others were not.

Primary Source · Sermon on the Mount

Jesus encouraged his disciples with the Sermon on the Mount.

"Happy are you when men insult you and persecute you and tell all kinds of evil lies against you because you are my followers. Be happy and glad, for a great reward is kept for you in heaven. This is how the prophets who lived before you were persecuted."

—Matthew 5:11–12

▲ Jesus and his followers

DBQ Document-Based Question

Why does Jesus tell his followers to ignore—even rejoice in—persecution?

Those who accepted Jesus Christ and his teachings became known as Christians. The word *Christ* comes from *Christos,* the Greek word for "messiah."

The early Christians formed churches, or communities for worship and teaching. They met in people's houses, many of which were owned by women. At these gatherings, Christians prayed and studied the Hebrew Bible. They also shared in a ritual meal like the Last Supper to remember Jesus' death and resurrection.

Who Were Peter and Paul? Apostles

(uh•PAH•suhlz), or early Christian leaders who helped set up churches and spread the message of Jesus, played an important role in the growth of Christianity. Perhaps the two most important were **Peter** and **Paul.**

Simon Peter was a Jewish fisher. He had known Jesus while he was alive and had been one of the original 12 people Jesus had called to preach his message. Christian tradition states that he went to Rome after the death of Jesus and helped set up a church there. Today, the leader of Catholic Christians resides in Rome.

Paul of Tarsus was another important Christian leader. He was a well-educated Jew and a Roman citizen. Paul at first hated Christianity and persecuted Christians in Jerusalem. The chief Jewish priest in Jerusalem then sent him to Damascus (duh•MAS•kuhs), a city in Syria, to stop Christians in the city from spreading their ideas.

While on the road to Damascus, Paul had an unusual experience. According to Christian belief, he saw a great light and heard Jesus' voice. Paul became a Christian on the spot. He spent the rest of his life spreading Jesus' message. Paul traveled widely. He founded churches throughout the eastern Mediterranean.

Biography

PAUL OF TARSUS
c. A.D. 10–65

Without the apostle Paul, Christianity might not have become one of the world's most widely accepted religions. It was Paul who spread the word about Jesus to the Gentiles, or non-Jews, and helped Jesus gain acceptance as the messiah.

Paul was a Jew from Tarsus, a major city in Asia Minor. His father was a Roman citizen, and his family followed the laws and rules of the Pharisees—a Jewish group that stressed the need to follow Jewish laws. His parents named their son Saul after the first king of the Jews. The first trade Saul learned was tent making. Around age 10, he was sent to Jerusalem to attend a school under the direction of the famed Pharisee teacher Gamaliel. Saul received a well-rounded education. He learned the language and history of the Romans, Jews, and Greeks.

When Saul was in his twenties, he opposed and persecuted Christians and their newly formed church in Jerusalem. He was on his way to Damascus in Syria to find and arrest Christians there when a vision of Jesus led him to accept Christianity.

Saul began using the Latin name Paul after his conversion to Christianity. He traveled extensively, preaching and writing to Gentiles. He also wrote many important letters, known as epistles, to churches in Rome, Greece, and Asia Minor. These letters are included in the Christian Bible.

Paul convinced many people that if they died as Christians, they would have eternal life. Even though Paul's only meeting with Jesus was supposedly in his vision, Paul visited more places and preached to more people than most of the apostles who had known Jesus in person. Paul worked as a missionary for around 35 years. He was probably killed when the Roman emperor Nero ordered that all Christians be arrested and put to death.

▲ Paul of Tarsus

> "I showed how you should work to help everyone."
> —Paul, Acts 20:35

Then and Now

Can you think of any groups of people in today's world who are persecuted for their beliefs?

▲ A book containing the teachings of Paul

▲ This painting shows the apostle Peter preaching to followers. *What was the role of apostles in the spread of Christianity?*

What Do Christians Believe? From the beginning, Christians taught that Jesus was the Son of God and had come to save people. By accepting Jesus and his teachings, people could gain **salvation** (sal•VAY•shuhn), or be saved from sin and allowed to enter heaven. Like Jesus, after death they would be resurrected and join God in everlasting life.

Because of their faith in Jesus, Christians began to understand God in a new way. Like the Jews, Christians believed in the God of Israel and studied the Hebrew Bible. However, most Christians came to believe that the one God existed in three persons: Father, Son, and Holy Spirit. This idea became known as the Trinity, which comes from a word meaning "three."

 **Identify** Who were Peter and Paul, and why were they important?

Section 1 Review

History Online

Homework Helper Need help with the material in this section? Visit jat.glencoe.com

Reading Summary

Review the **Main Ideas**

- While some Jews opposed Roman rule peacefully, others revolted, leading the Romans to banish Jews from Jerusalem.

- Jesus preached of God's love and forgiveness and gained many followers. After his crucifixion, his followers claimed that he rose from the dead.

- A new religion, Christianity, based on the teachings of Jesus and a belief in his resurrection, spread in the Mediterranean region.

What Did You Learn?

1. What are parables, and why did Jesus use them?

2. What do Christians believe they will gain by accepting Jesus and his teachings?

Critical Thinking

3. **Summarize Information** Draw a diagram like the one below. Add details to identify some of the Christian beliefs taught by Jesus.

Christian Beliefs

4. **Analyze** Why were the Jews looking for a messiah? Did Jesus fulfill most Jews' expectations for a messiah? Explain.

5. **Explain** Why was Jesus put to death?

6. **Expository Writing** Write an essay comparing Christianity to one or more religions that you have already learned about.

7. **Reading** Sequence Clues List five words in this section that serve as sequence clues. Explain how each word provided clues as to when an event occurred.

Section 2

The Christian Church

Get Ready to Read!

What's the Connection?
In the last section, you read about the origins of Christianity. In this section, you will discover how Christianity grew and was organized.

Focusing on the Main Ideas
• Christianity won many followers and eventually became the official religion of the Roman Empire. *(page 352)*

• Early Christians set up a church organization and explained their beliefs. *(page 355)*

Locating Places
Rome

Meeting People
Constantine (KAHN•stuhn•TEEN)
Helena (HEHL•uh•nuh)
Theodosius (THEE•uh•DOH•shuhs)

Building Your Vocabulary
persecute (PURH•sih•KYOOT)
martyr (MAHR•tuhr)
hierarchy (HY•uhr•AHR•kee)
clergy (KLUHR•jee)
laity (LAY•uh•tee)
doctrine (DAHK•truhn)
gospel (GAHS•puhl)
pope

Reading Strategy
Organizing Information Complete a diagram like the one below showing reasons for the growth of Christianity.

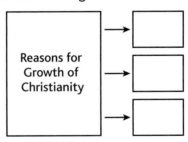

Reasons for Growth of Christianity	→	☐
	→	☐
	→	☐

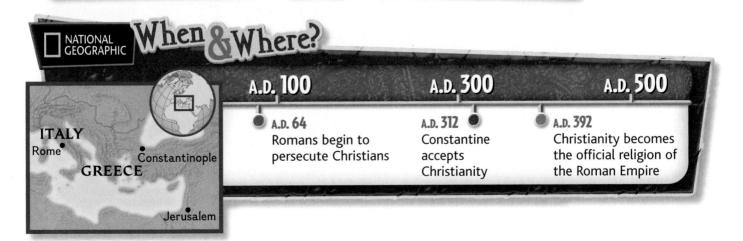

NATIONAL GEOGRAPHIC When & Where?

ITALY
Rome
GREECE
Constantinople
Jerusalem

A.D. **100**   A.D. **300**   A.D. **500**

A.D. **64**
Romans begin to persecute Christians

A.D. **312**
Constantine accepts Christianity

A.D. **392**
Christianity becomes the official religion of the Roman Empire

A Growing Faith

Main Idea Christianity won many followers and eventually became the official religion of the Roman Empire.

Reading Focus Why do you think people like to belong to a community? Read to learn about early Christian communities.

During the 100 years after Jesus' death, Christianity won followers throughout the Roman world. The empire itself helped spread Christian ideas. The peace and order established by **Rome** allowed people to travel in safety. Christians used well-paved Roman roads to carry their message from place to place. Since most of the empire's people spoke either Latin or Greek, Christians could talk with them directly.

Why did Christianity attract followers? First, the Christian message gave meaning to people's lives. Rome's official religion urged people to honor the state and the emperor. Christianity instead reached out to the poor and the powerless who led very hard lives. It offered hope and comfort.

Second, the ideas of Christianity were familiar to many Romans. They already knew about other eastern Mediterranean religions. Like these faiths, Christianity

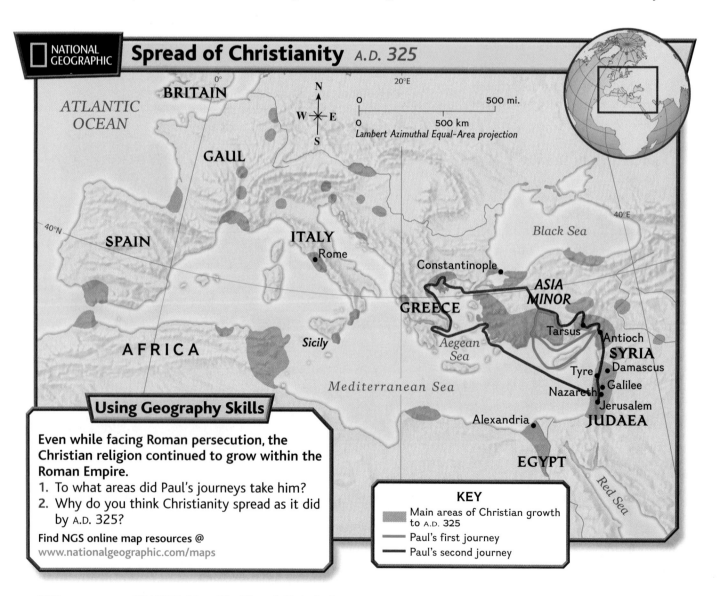

NATIONAL GEOGRAPHIC

Spread of Christianity A.D. 325

ATLANTIC OCEAN
BRITAIN
GAUL
SPAIN
ITALY
Rome
AFRICA
Sicily
40°N
0°
20°E
N W E S
0 _____ 500 mi.
0 _____ 500 km
Lambert Azimuthal Equal-Area projection
Black Sea
40°E
Constantinople
GREECE
ASIA MINOR
Tarsus
Aegean Sea
Mediterranean Sea
Antioch
SYRIA
Tyre • Damascus
Nazareth • Galilee
Jerusalem
JUDAEA
Alexandria
EGYPT
Red Sea

Using Geography Skills

Even while facing Roman persecution, the Christian religion continued to grow within the Roman Empire.
1. To what areas did Paul's journeys take him?
2. Why do you think Christianity spread as it did by A.D. 325?

Find NGS online map resources @
www.nationalgeographic.com/maps

KEY
▨ Main areas of Christian growth to A.D. 325
— Paul's first journey
— Paul's second journey

appealed to the emotions and promised happiness after death.

Finally, Christianity gave people the chance to be part of a caring group. Within their churches, Christians not only worshiped together but helped each other. They took care of the sick, the elderly, widows, and orphans. Many women found that Christianity offered them new roles. They ran churches from their homes, spread Jesus' message, and helped care for those in need.

How Did the Romans Treat Christians?

Over time, Roman officials began to see the Christians as a threat to the government. All people in the empire were usually allowed to worship freely, but the Romans expected everyone to honor the emperor as a god. Christians, like the Jews, refused to do this. They claimed that only God could be worshiped. Christians also refused to serve in the army or hold public office. They criticized Roman festivals and games. As a result, the Romans saw the Christians as traitors who should be punished.

In A.D. 64 the Roman government began to **persecute** (PURH•sih•KYOOT), or mistreat, Christians. At this time, the emperor Nero accused Christians of starting a terrible fire that burned much of Rome. Christianity was made illegal, and many Christians were killed.

Other persecutions followed. During these difficult times, many Christians became **martyrs** (MAHR•tuhrz), people willing to die rather than give up their beliefs. In Rome, because of their beliefs, Christians were forced to bury their dead in catacombs, or underground burial places.

Even with all of the hardships, Christianity spread. Over time it even began to draw people from all classes. After A.D. 250, many Romans grew tired of war

The Way It Was

Focus on Everyday Life

Christian Catacombs Christians believed in resurrection, the idea that the body would one day reunite with the soul. For this reason, they would not allow their dead bodies to be burned, which was the Roman custom. Also, Roman law did not allow bodies to be buried aboveground. Therefore, starting in the A.D. 100s, Christians buried their dead beneath the city of Rome in a series of dark, cold, stench-filled tunnels called catacombs.

Each tunnel was about 8 feet (2.4 m) high and less than 3 feet (1 m) wide. Bodies were stacked in slots along the sides of the tunnels. The catacomb walls were painted with images from the Bible or from Greek or Roman mythology.

More than five million bodies were buried under Roman streets and buildings. Many of the Christians buried there were martyrs who had been killed for their beliefs.

◀ Christian catacombs in Rome

Connecting to the Past
1. Why did Christians bury their dead in catacombs?
2. What skills do you think would be necessary to dig and plan catacombs?

and feared the end of the empire. They began to admire the faith and courage of the Christians. At the same time, many Christians started to accept the empire.

Rome Adopts Christianity In the early A.D. 300s the emperor Diocletian carried out the last great persecution of Christians. Diocletian failed, and Roman officials began to realize that Christianity had grown too strong to be destroyed by force.

Then, in A.D. 312, the Roman emperor **Constantine** (KAHN•stuhn•TEEN) accepted Christianity. According to tradition, Constantine saw a flaming cross in the sky as he was about to go into battle. Written beneath the cross were the Latin words that meant "In this sign you will conquer."

Constantine won the battle and believed that the Christian God had helped him.

In A.D. 313 Constantine issued an order called the Edict of Milan. It gave religious freedom to all people and made Christianity legal. Constantine began giving government support to Christianity. With the help of his mother, **Helena** (HEHL•uh•nuh), he built churches in Rome and Jerusalem. He also let church officials serve in government and excused them from paying taxes.

Constantine's successor, the emperor **Theodosius** (THEE•uh•DOH•shuhs), made Christianity Rome's official religion in A.D. 392. At the same time, he outlawed other religions.

√ **Reading Check** **Explain** Why did the Romans see the Christians as traitors?

Constantine's Conversion

▼ Constantine led his troops to victory at the Battle of the Milvian Bridge after his conversion to Christianity. Constantine's enemies were defeated as a bridge made of boats collapsed under their weight. The *X* and *P* symbols painted on the soldiers' shields represented Greek initials for *Jesus Christ.* **How did Constantine's Edict of Milan support Christianity?**

The Early Church

Main Idea Early Christians set up a church organization and explained their beliefs.

Reading Focus How can good organization make the difference between whether a plan or project fails or succeeds? Read how early Christians organized their churches and chose what to include in the Bible.

In its early years, Christianity was loosely organized. Leaders like Paul traveled from one Christian community to another. They tried to unify the scattered groups. In their teaching, they emphasized that all the individual groups of Christians were part of one body called the church. Early Christians, however, faced a challenge. How were they to unite?

Organizing the Church
The early Christians turned to a surprising model to organize the church—the Roman Empire itself. Like the Roman Empire, the church came to be ruled by a **hierarchy** (HY•uhr•AHR•kee). A hierarchy is an organization with different levels of authority.

The **clergy** (KLUHR•jee) were the leaders of the church. They had different roles from the **laity** (LAY•uh•tee), or regular church members. As the church's organization grew, women were not permitted to serve in the clergy. However, as members of the laity, they continued to care for the sick and needy.

By around A.D. 300, local churches were led by clergy called priests. Several churches formed a diocese (DY•uh•suhs), led by a bishop. A bishop in charge of a city diocese was sometimes also put in charge of an entire region. This made him an archbishop. The five leading archbishops became known as patriarchs (PAY•tree•AHRKS). They led churches in large cities and were in charge of large areas of territory.

The bishops explained Christian beliefs. They also took care of church business. From time to time, bishops met to discuss questions about Christian faith. Decisions they reached at these meetings came to be accepted as **doctrine** (DAHK•truhn), or official church teaching.

What Is the New Testament?
Along with explaining Christian ideas, church leaders preserved a written record of the life of Jesus and put together a group of writings to help guide Christians. Jesus himself left no writings. His followers, however, passed on what they knew about him. By A.D. 300, four accounts of Jesus' life, teachings, and resurrection had become well-known. Christians believed these accounts were written by early followers of Jesus named Matthew, Mark, Luke, and John.

Each work was called a **gospel** (GAHS•puhl), which means "good news." Christians later combined the four gospels with the writings of Paul and other early Christian leaders. Together, these works form the New Testament of the Bible.

◀ Saint Matthew wrote one of the four gospels in the New Testament of the Bible. *What is the subject of the gospels of Matthew, Mark, Luke, and John?*

Other important writings also influenced early Christians. Scholars known as the Church Fathers wrote books to explain church teachings. One leading Church Father was a bishop in North Africa named Augustine. In his writings, Augustine defended Christianity against its opponents. He wrote *The City of God*—one of the first history books written from a Christian viewpoint. He also wrote a work called *Confessions*. It was an account of his personal journey to the Christian faith.

Who Is the Pope?

As the church grew, the bishop of Rome, who was also the patriarch of the West, began to claim power over the other bishops. He believed that he had the authority of Peter, Jesus' leading disciple. Also, his diocese was in Rome, the capital of the empire.

By A.D. 600, the bishop of Rome had gained a special title—**pope**. The title comes from a Latin word meaning "father." Latin-speaking Christians accepted the pope as head of the church. Their churches became known as the Roman Catholic Church. Greek-speaking Christians would not accept the pope's authority over them. You will read in the next section about Christians in the Eastern Roman Empire and their form of Christianity.

✓ **Reading Check** **Identify** What are the gospels, and why are they significant?

Homework Helper Need help with the material in this section? Visit jat.glencoe.com

Section 2 Review

Reading Summary

Review the Main Ideas

- After its followers suffered Roman persecution for several hundred years, Christianity became the official religion of the Roman Empire under Emperor Theodosius.

- As Christianity grew, the church became more united under a hierarchy of leaders. Christian writings were gathered into the New Testament of the Bible.

What Did You Learn?

1. What is a martyr?
2. What writings are included in the New Testament of the Bible?

Critical Thinking

3. **Organizing Information** Draw a chart like the one below. Fill in details on the effects each of the emperors listed had on the acceptance and growth of Christianity.

Roman Emperors		
Diocletian	Constantine	Theodosius

4. **Analyze** Following Jesus' death, why was Christianity able to attract followers?

5. **Analyze** Why do you think the Christian church came to be ruled by a hierarchy?

6. **Conclude** Do you think the Christian religion would have spread so quickly if it had developed in a time other than that of the Roman Empire?

7. **Writing Questions** Write five questions that a reporter who lived at the same time as Constantine might have asked him about Christianity.

Biography

SAINT AUGUSTINE
A.D. 354–430

Augustine was born in North Africa, in what is today the country of Algeria, to upper-class parents. His mother was Christian, but his father was not. His father sent him to the North African city of Carthage to attend good schools. Although he appeared to be an outstanding student, Augustine later said that he made many poor choices during his time at school.

When Augustine finished his education, he returned home to teach grammar. His mother again tried to convince him of the truth of Christianity, but he had joined a group of people who were critical of Christians. According to Augustine's writings, his mother was saddened until a vision promised her that her son would eventually accept Christianity.

Augustine moved to several cities, often teaching rhetoric (the art of speaking). He ended up in Milan, Italy. There he listened to Milan's bishop Ambrose preaching, not because he liked his messages but because he admired the way Ambrose spoke. Slowly, Augustine began to think about the messages of Ambrose's sermons. One day in A.D. 386, Augustine heard a child's voice say to him, "Take up and read." Nearby was a friend's copy of Paul's letters. He began to read the letters and decided that he believed the messages of Christianity. Augustine was soon baptized and founded a monastery—probably the first monastery in his area of North Africa. Later Augustine became a bishop. He recorded his life in A.D. 401 in the book *Confessions*.

▲ St. Augustine

"Even when sad, I remember my times of joy."
–Saint Augustine, *Confessions*

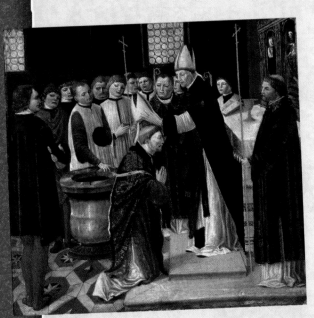

▲ St. Augustine being blessed by the pope

Then and Now

Do research to find out how Christianity has influenced the development of the United States. Provide examples of how it has affected government, society, and the economy.

357

Section 3

The Spread of Christian Ideas

Get Ready to Read!

What's the Connection?
In the last section, you read about the growth of the Christian church. In this section, you will learn how the church underwent a great division and how Christians spread their faith to new lands.

Focusing on the Main Ideas
- Church and government worked closely together in the Byzantine Empire. *(page 359)*
- Christians founded new communities and spread their faith to various parts of Europe. *(page 361)*

Locating Places
Byzantine Empire (BIH•zuhn•TEEN EHM•PYR)
Britain (BRIH•tuhn)
Ireland (EYER•luhnd)

Meeting People
Charlemagne (SHAHR•luh•MAYN)
Basil (BAY•zuhl)
Benedict (BEH•nuh•DIHKT)
Cyril (SIHR•uhl)
Patrick

Building Your Vocabulary
icon (EYE•KAHN)
iconoclast (eye•KAH•nuh•KLAST)
excommunicate (EHK•skuh•MYOO•nuh•KAYT)
schism (SIH•zuhm)
monastery (MAH•nuh•STEHR•ee)
missionary (MIH•shuh•NEHR•ee)

Reading Strategy
Organizing Information Create a diagram to show the reach of Christian missionaries.

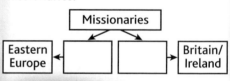

When & Where?

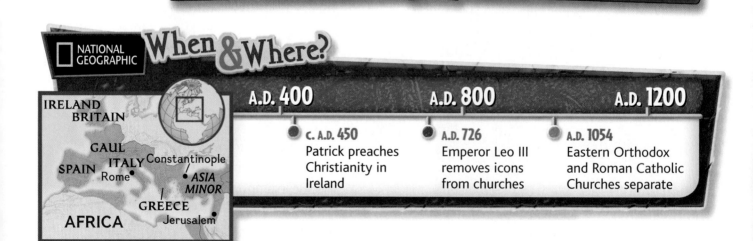

| A.D. 400 | A.D. 800 | A.D. 1200 |

C. A.D. 450 Patrick preaches Christianity in Ireland

A.D. 726 Emperor Leo III removes icons from churches

A.D. 1054 Eastern Orthodox and Roman Catholic Churches separate

The Byzantine Church

Main Idea Church and government worked closely together in the Byzantine Empire.

Reading Focus In our country, religion and government are separated. Read to learn about the relationship between religion and government in the Byzantine Empire.

As you learned earlier, the church of Rome survived the fall of the Western Roman Empire. Its head, the pope, became the strongest leader in Western Europe. Under the pope, the Latin churches of the region became known as the Roman Catholic Church. In the East, however, the Roman Empire continued. It developed into the **Byzantine Empire** (BIH•zuhn•TEEN EHM•PYR). Like Roman Catholics in the West, the Byzantines developed their own form of Christianity. It was based on their Greek heritage and was known as the Eastern Orthodox Church.

Church and State
Church and government worked closely together in the Byzantine Empire. The Byzantines believed their emperor represented Jesus Christ on Earth. The emperor was crowned in a religious ceremony.

The emperor also chose the patriarch of Constantinople, the leading Church official in the Byzantine Empire. In this way, the emperor controlled the Church as well as the government. Byzantines believed that God wanted them to preserve and spread Christianity. All Church and government officials were united in this goal.

History **O**nline

Web Activity Visit jat.glencoe.com and click on *Chapter 10—Student Web Activity* to learn more about the rise of Christianity.

Religious Arguments Byzantines, from the emperor down to the poorest farmer, were very interested in religious matters. In homes and shops, they argued about religious questions. For example, Byzantines loved to discuss the exact relationship between Jesus and God.

In the A.D. 700s, a major dispute divided the Church in the Byzantine Empire. The argument was over the use of **icons** (EYE•KAHNZ). Icons are pictures or images of Jesus, Mary (the mother of Jesus), and the saints, or Christian holy people. Many Byzantines honored icons. They covered the walls of their churches with them. A few important icons were even believed to work miracles.

Some Byzantines, however, wanted an end to the use of icons. They thought that honoring them was a form of idol worship forbidden by God. Supporters of icons,

▼ This gold Byzantine incense burner is in the shape of a church. *What was the Christian church that developed in the Byzantine Empire called?*

▲ This icon on wood shows the archangel Gabriel, who served as a messenger for God according to the Bible. *What reasons were given to support the use of icons?*

Byzantine cross ▶

however, claimed that icons were symbols of God's presence in daily life. These images, they also said, helped explain Christianity to people.

Emperor Leo III did not approve of icons. In A.D. 726 he ordered all icons removed from the churches. Government officials who carried out his orders were known as **iconoclasts** (eye•KAH•nuh•KLASTS), or image breakers. We use this word today to mean someone who attacks traditional beliefs or institutions.

Most Byzantines, many church leaders, and even the pope in Rome opposed the emperor's order. In fact, the dispute over icons damaged ties between the churches of Rome and Constantinople. Over the next 100 years, the argument cooled, and the use of icons became accepted once again. They are still an important part of Eastern Orthodox religious practice.

Conflicts Between Churches Icons were not the only issue that caused bitterness between the churches of Constantinople and Rome. The most serious argument was about how churches were to be run. The pope claimed that he was the head of all Christian churches. The Byzantines did not accept the pope's claim. They believed the patriarch of Constantinople and other bishops were equal to the pope.

Making matters worse was the fact that each church sometimes refused to help the other when outsiders attacked. In the late A.D. 700s, the Byzantine emperor refused to help the pope when Italy was invaded. The pope turned instead to a Germanic people called the Franks for help. The Franks were Roman Catholics and loyal to the pope.

The pope was grateful to the Franks for stopping the invasion. In A.D. 800 he gave the Frankish king, **Charlemagne** (SHAHR•luh•MAYN), the title of emperor. This angered the Byzantines. They believed the leader of the Byzantines was the only true emperor.

This conflict pointed out the differences in how each church felt about relations with the government. In the Byzantine Empire, the emperor was in control, with church leaders respecting his wishes. In the West, however, the pope claimed both spiritual and political power. He often quarreled with kings over church and government affairs.

Finally, after centuries of tension, the pope and the patriarch of Constantinople took a drastic step in their ongoing feud. In A.D. 1054 they **excommunicated** (EHK•skuh•MYOO•nuh•KAY•tuhd) each other. Excommunication means to declare that a person or group no longer belongs to the church. This began a **schism** (SIH•zuhm), or separation, of the two most important branches of Christianity. The split between the Roman Catholic and Eastern Orthodox Churches has lasted to this day.

✓ **Reading Check** **Describe** How did church and government work together in the Byzantine Empire?

Christian Ideas Spread

Main Idea Christians founded new communities and spread their faith to various parts of Europe.

Reading Focus Have you ever tried to get someone to believe something you believe? Read to learn how Christians spread their faith across Europe.

After the fall of Rome, the people of Western Europe faced confusion and conflict. As a result, people were looking for order and unity. Christianity helped to meet this need. It spread rapidly into lands that had once been part of the Roman Empire. It

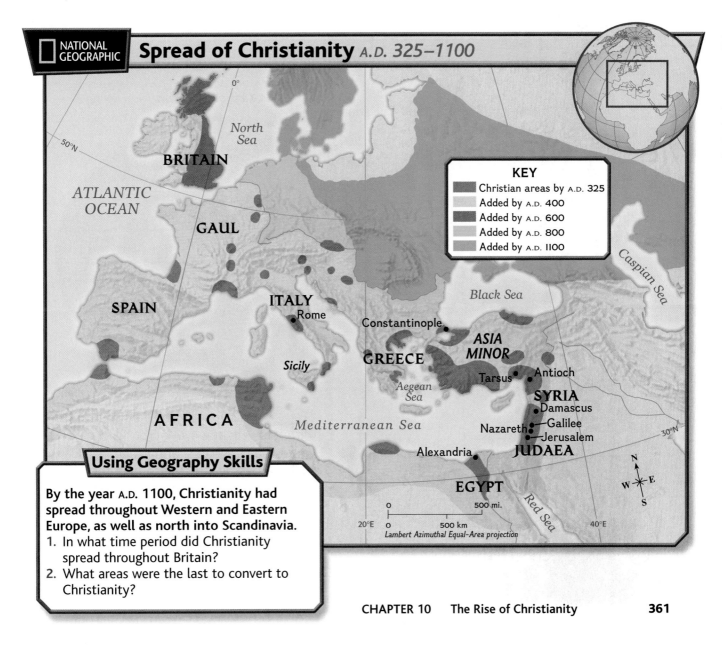

NATIONAL GEOGRAPHIC **Spread of Christianity** A.D. 325–1100

KEY
- Christian areas by A.D. 325
- Added by A.D. 400
- Added by A.D. 600
- Added by A.D. 800
- Added by A.D. 1100

North Sea
BRITAIN
ATLANTIC OCEAN
GAUL
SPAIN
ITALY
Rome
Sicily
AFRICA
Mediterranean Sea
Black Sea
Constantinople
ASIA MINOR
GREECE
Tarsus • Antioch
Aegean Sea
SYRIA
• Damascus
Nazareth • Galilee
• Jerusalem
JUDAEA
Alexandria •
EGYPT
Red Sea
Caspian Sea
50°N
0°
30°N
20°E
40°E

0   500 mi.
0   500 km
Lambert Azimuthal Equal-Area projection

N
W — E
S

Using Geography Skills

By the year A.D. 1100, Christianity had spread throughout Western and Eastern Europe, as well as north into Scandinavia.
1. In what time period did Christianity spread throughout Britain?
2. What areas were the last to convert to Christianity?

also brought new ways of thinking and living to these areas.

What Are Monasteries? During the A.D. 300s, a new kind of religious group was born in the Eastern Roman Empire. Men called monks banded together in religious communities called **monasteries** (MAH•nuh•STEHR•eez). Some monasteries were built near cities, while others arose in isolated areas.

One of the earliest monks was Anthony, who founded a monastery in the deserts of Egypt. Monks tried to live a spiritual life apart from the temptations of the world. Many also tried to do good deeds and be examples of Christian living. Women soon followed the monks' example and formed communities of their own. These women were called nuns, and they lived in convents.

In the early A.D. 400s, Paula, a Roman widow, gave up her wealth and went to Palestine. There she built churches, a hospital, and a convent. Well-educated, Paula helped a scholar named Jerome translate the Bible from Hebrew and Greek into Latin.

Linking Past & Present

Missionaries

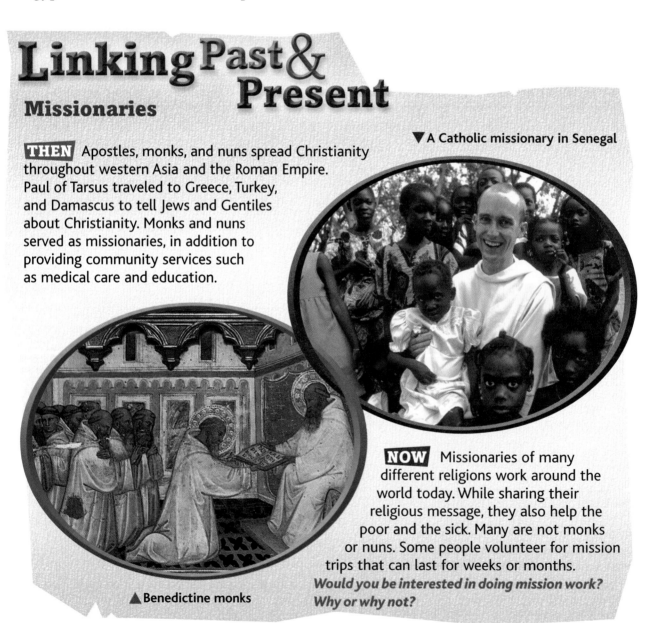

THEN Apostles, monks, and nuns spread Christianity throughout western Asia and the Roman Empire. Paul of Tarsus traveled to Greece, Turkey, and Damascus to tell Jews and Gentiles about Christianity. Monks and nuns served as missionaries, in addition to providing community services such as medical care and education.

▼ A Catholic missionary in Senegal

NOW Missionaries of many different religions work around the world today. While sharing their religious message, they also help the poor and the sick. Many are not monks or nuns. Some people volunteer for mission trips that can last for weeks or months.

Would you be interested in doing mission work? Why or why not?

▲ Benedictine monks

A bishop called **Basil** (BAY•zuhl) drew up a list of rules for monks and nuns to follow. This list, called the Basilian (buh•ZIH•lee•uhn) Rule, became the model for Eastern Orthodox religious life.

In the West, another set of rules was followed. It was written by an Italian monk named **Benedict** (BEH•nuh•DIHKT). Monks who followed the Benedictine Rule gave up their belongings, lived simply, and spent their time in work and prayer. Like Basil's rule in the East, Benedict's rule became the model for monasteries and convents in the West. Basilian and Benedictine communities still exist today.

Monks and nuns began to play important roles in Roman Catholic and Eastern Orthodox life. They ran hospitals and schools and aided the poor. They also helped preserve Greek and Roman writings. One important duty was to serve as **missionaries** (MIH•shuh•NEHR•eez). Missionaries teach their religion to those who do not believe.

Christianity Spreads North

Among the most successful Byzantine missionaries were two brothers, **Cyril** (SIHR•uhl) and Methodius. They carried the Christian message to the Slavs, a people of Eastern Europe.

About A.D. 863, Cyril invented a new alphabet. He wanted to present the Christian message in the Slavic languages. He believed that people would be more interested in Christianity if they could worship and read the Bible in their own languages. The Cyrillic (suh•RIH•lihk) alphabet was based on Greek letters. It is still used today by Russians, Ukrainians, Serbs, and Bulgarians.

Eastern Orthodox missionaries traveled in northern lands that bordered the Byzantine Empire. At the same time, other missionaries from Rome were also busy.

The Cyrillic Alphabet

Cyrillic Letter	Written Name	English Sound
Б	beh	B
Г	gey	G
Ж	zheh	ZH
М	em	M
П	pey	P
С	ess	S
Ф	ef	F
Ч	cheh	CH

Cyril, a Byzantine missionary, developed the Cyrillic alphabet, part of which is shown above. *What peoples still use the Cyrillic alphabet today?*

Christianity Spreads West

In the West, Christian missionaries looked to the islands of **Britain** (BRIH•tuhn) and **Ireland** (EYER•luhnd). In the A.D. 300s, Roman soldiers in Britain were called home to defend the empire against Germanic invaders. When the Romans left, Britain was opened to attack by others.

Starting in the A.D. 400s, tribes from what are today Germany and Denmark invaded Britain. These people were the Angles and the Saxons. These groups united to become the Anglo-Saxons. They built settlements and set up several small kingdoms. The southern part of Britain soon became known as Angleland, or England.

While invading Britain, the Angles and Saxons pushed aside the people already living there. These people were called the Celts (KEHLTS). Some Celts fled to the mountainous regions of Britain. Others went to Ireland.

In the A.D. 400s, a priest named **Patrick** brought Christianity to Ireland. He set up a number of monasteries and churches. Over

the next centuries, Irish monks played an important role in preserving Christian and Roman learning.

The Anglo-Saxon kingdoms of Britain were slower than Ireland to accept the new religion. In A.D. 597 Pope Gregory I sent about 40 monks from Rome to take Christianity to England.

The missionaries converted Ethelbert, the ruler of the English kingdom of Kent. Ethelbert allowed the missionaries to build a church in his capital city of Canterbury. In about 100 years, most of England was Christian. Today, Canterbury is still an important center of Christianity in England.

 **Reading Check** **Analyze** Why were Basil and Benedict important?

◄ Gregory was a monk before he became Pope Gregory I in the late 500s. *How did Gregory impact Christianity in England?*

History Online
Homework Helper Need help with the material in this section? Visit jat.glencoe.com

Section 3 Review

Reading Summary

Review the Main Ideas

- In the Byzantine Empire, Christianity developed into the Eastern Orthodox Church, which in time split with the Roman Catholic Church in the West.

- Eastern Orthodox and Catholic missionaries helped spread Christianity to areas such as Eastern Europe, Ireland, and Britain.

What Did You Learn?

1. What are icons, and why was their use controversial?

2. What roles did monks and nuns play in Roman Catholic and Eastern Orthodox life?

Critical Thinking

3. **Cause and Effect** Draw a diagram to show the causes that led to the schism between the Roman Catholic and Eastern Orthodox Churches.

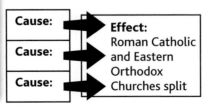

Cause:	
Cause:	**Effect:** Roman Catholic and Eastern Orthodox Churches split
Cause:	

4. **Describe** How did Cyril make the Christian message available to the Slavs?

5. **Explain** What role did the Frankish king Charlemagne play in the schism between the Roman Catholic and Eastern Orthodox Churches?

6. **Analyze** Why do you think the Basilian and Benedictine Rules were put in place for monks?

7. **Expository Writing** Write a newspaper article that describes the spread of Christianity to Ireland and Britain.

Chapter 10 Reading Review

Section 1 — The First Christians

Vocabulary
messiah
disciple
parable
resurrection
apostle
salvation

Focusing on the Main Ideas
- Roman rule of Judaea led some Jews to oppose Rome peacefully, while others rebelled. *(page 343)*
- Jesus of Nazareth preached of God's love and forgiveness. He was eventually crucified and then reported to have risen from the dead. *(page 344)*
- Jesus' life and a belief in his resurrection led to a new religion called Christianity. *(page 348)*

Section 2 — The Christian Church

Vocabulary
persecute
martyr
hierarchy
clergy
laity
doctrine
gospel
pope

Focusing on the Main Ideas
- Christianity won many followers and eventually became the official religion of the Roman Empire. *(page 352)*
- Early Christians set up a church organization and explained their beliefs. *(page 355)*

Saint Matthew ▶

Section 3 — The Spread of Christian Ideas

Vocabulary
icon
iconoclast
excommunicate
schism
monastery
missionary

Focusing on the Main Ideas
- Church and government worked closely together in the Byzantine Empire. *(page 359)*
- Christians founded new communities and spread their faith to various parts of Europe. *(page 361)*

Chapter 10 Assessment and Activities

Review Vocabulary

1. Write a paragraph about the basic beliefs of Christianity using the following words.

   messiah   **salvation**

   resurrection   **gospel**

Write the vocabulary word that completes each sentence. Then write a sentence for each word not chosen.

   a. laity   e. parables
   b. missionaries   f. schism
   c. martyrs   g. apostle
   d. iconoclasts   h. pope

2. Jesus told symbolic stories called ___.
3. The bishop of Rome was called the ___.
4. The ___ in the Christian churches happened in A.D. 1054.
5. Christians who died for their faith were ___.

Review Main Ideas

Section 1 • The First Christians
6. How did Jews react to the Roman rule of Judaea?

7. On what is Christianity based?

Section 2 • The Christian Church
8. How did the Roman Empire eventually recognize Christianity?
9. What did early Christians do to organize their religion?

Section 3 • The Spread of Christian Ideas
10. What was the relationship between the church and the government in the Byzantine Empire?
11. How and where did the Christian religion spread?

Critical Thinking

12. **Analyze** Why do you think Jesus' followers remembered his teachings more when he used parables?
13. **Contrast** How did Jews and Christians differ in their belief about Jesus and his message?
14. **Predict** How would the growth of Christianity have been affected if the emperor Constantine had not become a Christian?

Review Reading Skill — Sequence Clues

Looking for Sequence Clues

Find the words in each of these sentences that help you identify the order in which events occur.

15. At the same time, many Christians started to accept the empire.
16. While on the road to Damascus, Paul had an unusual experience.

17. It is still used today by Russians, Ukrainians, Serbs, and Bulgarians.
18. The southern part of Britain soon became known as Angleland, or England.
19. After Jesus' death, his followers made a startling claim.
20. At first, they ruled through Jewish kings.

To review this skill, see pages 340–341.

Geography Skills

Study the map below and answer the following questions.

21. **Human/Environment Interaction** What geographical feature do you think most helped the spread of Christianity?

22. **Location** By A.D. 325, Christianity had spread to which continents?

23. **Region** Why do you think the cities of Judaea were all important centers of Christianity?

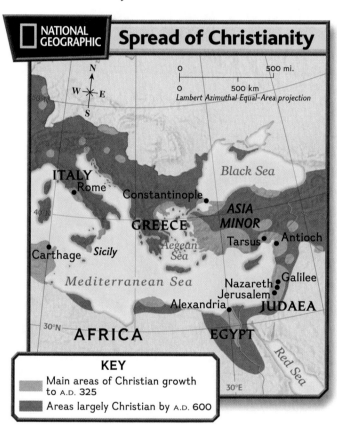

NATIONAL GEOGRAPHIC

Spread of Christianity

0 — 500 mi.
0 — 500 km
Lambert Azimuthal Equal-Area projection

N W E S

Black Sea

ITALY
Rome
Constantinople
ASIA MINOR
GREECE
Tarsus • Antioch
Aegean Sea
Carthage Sicily
Mediterranean Sea
Nazareth • Galilee
Jerusalem
Alexandria JUDAEA
AFRICA EGYPT
Red Sea

KEY
Main areas of Christian growth to A.D. 325
Areas largely Christian by A.D. 600

Read to Write

24. **Creative Writing** Rewrite the parable of the Good Samaritan as if the events took place in the present day. Read your parable to your classmates, and explain any changes in the meaning that occurred as you modernized it.

25. **Using Your FOLDABLES** Use your foldable to write three sentences that summarize the main ideas of this chapter. Share your sentences with the class, and listen to their sentences. Then vote for the one you think best summarizes the chapter.

History Online
Self-Check Quiz To help you prepare for the Chapter Test, visit jat.glencoe.com

Using Technology

26. **Reviewing Media** Use a video or DVD player to view one of the many films made about the life of Jesus or the impact of Christianity on the people of the Roman Empire. Some examples are *Ben Hur, The Robe, The Silver Chalice,* and *The Greatest Story Ever Told.* After you watch the movie, write a review of it. Based on what you have learned about the Roman Empire and Christianity, how accurate is the movie? How does it present Jesus, his early followers, the different Jewish groups in Judaea, and the Romans? Share your review with your classmates.

Linking Past and Present

27. **Recognizing Patterns** Conduct research to find out the number of people worldwide who are Christian, Jewish, Buddhist, Hindu, and Muslim. Also record the countries where people of each religion live. What do you notice about religions in different regions of the world?

Primary Source **Analyze**

Benedict wrote of the importance of keeping busy.

"Idleness [inactivity] is the enemy of the soul. Therefore should the brethren be occupied at stated times in manual labour, and at other fixed hours in sacred reading."

—Benedict, *The Rule*, "Of the Daily Manual Labour"

DBQ Document-Based Questions

28. What does Benedict mean when he says inactivity is "the enemy of the soul"?

29. What do you think probably follows these lines?

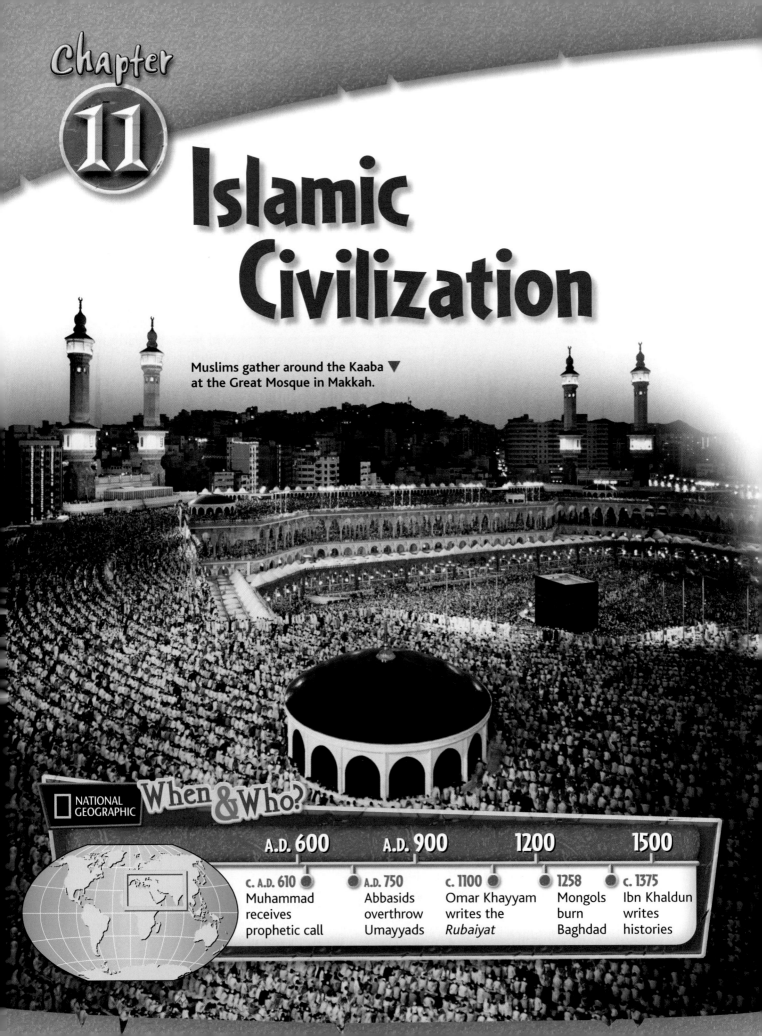

Chapter 11

Islamic Civilization

Muslims gather around the Kaaba ▼
at the Great Mosque in Makkah.

NATIONAL GEOGRAPHIC When & Who?

A.D. 600	A.D. 900	1200	1500
c. A.D. 610 Muhammad receives prophetic call	**A.D. 750** Abbasids overthrow Umayyads	**c. 1100** Omar Khayyam writes the *Rubaiyat*	**1258** Mongols burn Baghdad **c. 1375** Ibn Khaldun writes histories

Chapter Preview

A few hundred years after the beginnings of Christianity, another important religion arose in the Middle East: Islam. Followers of Islam conquered much of the Middle East, northern Africa, and part of Europe. They also made great cultural contributions to the world.

Chapter Overview Visit jat.glencoe.com for a preview of Chapter 11.

 View the Chapter 11 video in the *World History: Journey Across Time* Video Program.

The Rise of Islam

The religion of Islam originated in Arabia. It was based on the teachings of Muhammad.

Islamic Empires

Followers of Islam, called Muslims, conquered or converted people as they spread their faith throughout the Middle East and the Mediterranean.

Muslim Ways of Life

Muslims were skilled traders and builders. They established large cities and made many advances in mathematics, science, and the arts.

Study Organizer

Categorizing Information *Make the following foldable to organize information about the people and places of Islamic civilization.*

Step 1 *Collect two sheets of paper and place them about 1 inch apart.*

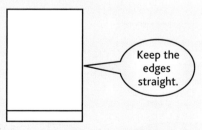

Keep the edges straight.

Step 2 *Fold the bottom edges of the paper to form four tabs.*

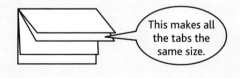

This makes all the tabs the same size.

Step 3 *When all the tabs are the same size, crease the paper to hold the tabs in place and staple the sheets together. Turn the paper and label each tab as shown.*

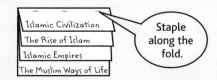

Islamic Civilization
The Rise of Islam
Islamic Empires
The Muslim Ways of Life

Staple along the fold.

Reading and Writing *As you read, use your foldable to write down what you learn about Islamic civilization. Write facts under each appropriate tab.*

Reading Social Studies

1 Learn It!

Main Ideas and Details

Main ideas are the most important ideas in a paragraph, section, or chapter. Supporting details are facts or examples that explain the main idea. Read the following paragraph from Section 3 and notice how the author explains the main idea.

> Several things explain the success of Muslim trade. When Muslim empries expanded, they spread the Arabic language. As a result, Arabic became the language of trade. Muslim rulers also made trade easier by providing merchants with coins.
>
> —*from page 388*

Reading Tip

Often, the first sentence in a paragraph will contain a main idea. Supporting details will come in following sentences.

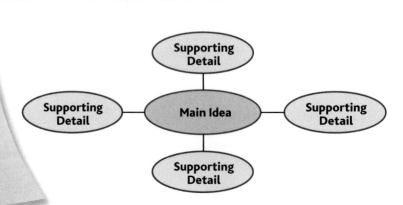

2 Practice It!

Using a Graphic Organizer

Read the following paragraph, and find the main idea and supporting details. Create a graphic organizer like the one that appears at the bottom of page 370.

Read to Write
"The famous Mogul ruler Akbar could not read, yet he set up a large library because he valued education, books, and art." Write a letter to Akbar telling him about your favorite book and why it should be included in his library.

Times were good in India under Akbar. Farmers and artisans produced more food and goods than the Indians needed. As a result, trade increased. Muslim merchants brought paper, gunpowder, and fine porcelain from China to India. In addition, Muslim architects introduced new building styles, such as the arch and dome, to India.

—*from page 386*

3 Apply It!

As you read Chapter 11, create your own graphic organizer to show the main idea and supporting details from at least one paragraph.

Section

1

The Rise of Islam

Get Ready to Read!

What's the Connection?

Previously, you learned about early empires in southwest Asia. During the A.D. 600s, people called Arabs began a new empire in the region. The driving force behind their empire building was the religion of Islam.

Focus on the Main Ideas

- The deserts, coastline, and oases of Arabia helped shape the Arab way of life. *(page 373)*

- The prophet Muhammad brought the message of Islam to the people of Arabia. *(page 374)*

- The Quran provided guidelines for Muslims' lives and the governments of Muslim states. *(page 377)*

Locating Places
Makkah (MAH•kuh)
Kaaba (KAH•buh)
Madinah (mah•DEE•nah)

Meeting People
Bedouin (BEH•duh•wuhn)
Muhammad (moh•HAH•muhd)

Building Your Vocabulary
oasis (oh•AY•suhs)
sheikh (SHAYK)
caravan (KAR•uh•VAN)
Quran (koh•RAHN)

Reading Strategy

Organizing Information Use a diagram like the one below to identify the Five Pillars of faith.

Five Pillars				

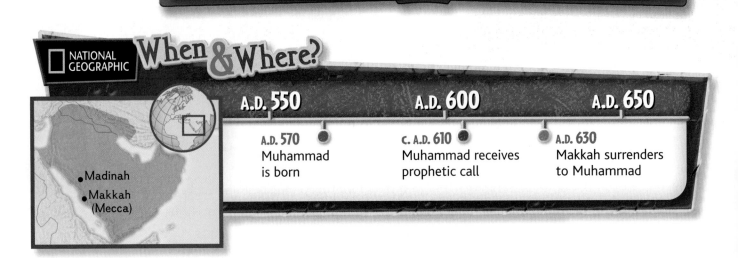

NATIONAL GEOGRAPHIC When & Where?

- Madinah
- Makkah (Mecca)

A.D. 550   A.D. 600   A.D. 650

A.D. 570 Muhammad is born

C. A.D. 610 Muhammad receives prophetic call

A.D. 630 Makkah surrenders to Muhammad

Daily Life in Early Arabia

Main Idea The deserts, coastline, and oases of Arabia helped shape the Arab way of life.

Reading Focus Do you ever think about how rainfall shapes your life? Read on to find out how lack of rain helped shape the Arabs' way of life.

Desert stretches over most of the Arabian peninsula. The heat is intense, and a sandstorm can blind any traveler. Water is found only at **oases** (oh AY seez), green areas fed by underground water. Not all of Arabia is dry, however. In the mountains of the southwest, enough rain falls to support plants such as juniper and olive trees.

To survive, early Arabs organized into tribes who were very loyal to one another. The head of the tribe was called a **sheikh** (SHAYK).

Who Are the Bedouins?
Some Arabs were desert herders. To water and graze their camels, goats, and sheep, they went from oasis to oasis. They were called **Bedouins** (BEH•duh•wuhnz).

Bedouins lived in tents and ate dried fruits and nuts. They drank the milk of their animals. Only rarely would they eat meat. Their animals were much too valuable to be used as food.

Trade and Towns
Many Arabs lived in villages where they farmed or raised animals. These villages were near oases or in the mountain valleys.

Some of the villagers were merchants who transported goods across the desert. To fend off attacks by Bedouins, many traveled in a **caravan,** or group of traveling merchants and animals.

By about A.D. 500, Arabian merchants handled most trade between India and the Mediterranean Sea. As their trade grew, Arab merchants founded towns along the trade routes in Arabia. **Makkah** (MAH•kuh), also known as Mecca, became the largest and richest of them all. It was a crossroads for merchants, and it was also an important religious site. The holiest place in Arabia was in this city.

▼ Today, many Bedouins still roam the desert and live in tents. *Where did Bedouins graze their animals in the desert?*

▲ Bedouin woman making bread

373

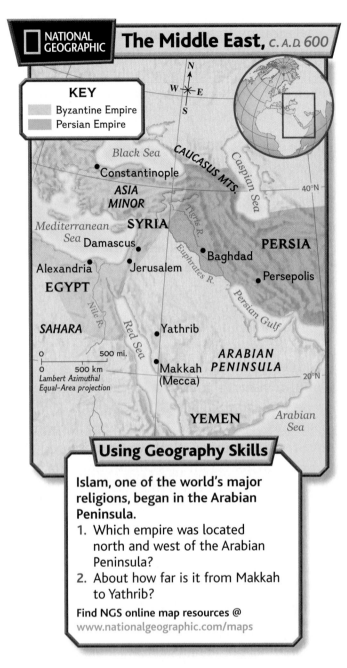

NATIONAL GEOGRAPHIC **The Middle East,** *C. A.D. 600*

KEY
- Byzantine Empire
- Persian Empire

Using Geography Skills

Islam, one of the world's major religions, began in the Arabian Peninsula.

1. Which empire was located north and west of the Arabian Peninsula?
2. About how far is it from Makkah to Yathrib?

Find NGS online map resources @ www.nationalgeographic.com/maps

In the middle of Makkah was the **Kaaba** (KAH buh), a low square building surrounded by statues of gods and goddesses. Arabs believed that the great stone inside the Kaaba was from heaven. Pilgrims, people who travel to a holy place, flocked to Makkah. Arabians worshiped many gods, but the most important was Allah. Allah was considered to be the creator.

✓ **Reading Check** **Analyze** How did geography shape life in Arabia?

Muhammad: Islam's Prophet

Main Idea The prophet Muhammad brought the message of Islam to the people of Arabia.

Reading Focus Have you ever heard someone speak and been moved to tears? The following paragraphs tell about a prophet who moved the Arab people with his words.

Muhammad's Message In A.D. 570 a man named **Muhammad** (moh•HAH•muhd) was born in Makkah. An orphan, he was raised by an uncle. As a teenager, he worked in the trusted job of caravan leader and eventually became a successful merchant. He married and had children.

Despite his success, Muhammad was dissatisfied. He felt that the wealthy town leaders should return to the old ways. He thought they should honor their families, be fair in business, and help the poor.

Muhammad went into the hills to pray. In about A.D. 610, he said he was visited by an angel and told to preach Islam. *Islam* means "surrendering to the will of Allah." *Allah* is the Arabic word for "God."

Inspired, Muhammad returned to Makkah. Everywhere he went, he told people to destroy statues of false gods and to worship only Allah, the one true God.

Muhammad also preached that all people were equal and that the rich should share their goods. In Makkah, where most people lived humbly, this vision of a just society was very powerful. Muhammad was saying that wealth was not as important as leading a good life. When the Day of Judgment arrived, he said God would reward the good people and punish the evildoers.

Opposition to Islam Slowly Muhammad convinced people that his message was true. At first, only his family became

Muslims, or followers of Islam. Soon, however, many of the poor were attracted to his message that goods should be shared.

Wealthy merchants and religious leaders did not like Muhammad's message. They thought he was trying to take away their power. They made his life difficult and beat and tortured his followers.

In A.D. 622 Muhammad and his followers left Makkah. They moved north to a town called Yathrib (YA•thruhb). The journey of Muhammad and his followers to Yathrib became known as the Hijrah (HIH•jruh). The word comes from Arabic and means "breaking off relationships." Later Muslims made the year A.D. 622 the first year of a new Muslim calendar. Yathrib welcomed Muhammad and his followers. Their city was renamed **Madinah** (mah•DEE•nah), which means "the city of the prophet."

Muhammad's Government The people of Madinah accepted Muhammad as God's prophet and their ruler. Muhammad proved to be an able leader. He applied the laws he believed God had given him to all areas of life. He used these laws to settle disputes among the people. Muhammad created an Islamic state—a government that uses its political power to uphold Islam. He required all Muslims to place loyalty to the Islamic state above loyalty to their tribe.

To defend his new government, Muhammad built an army. His soldiers conquered Makkah in A.D. 630, and Muhammad then made it a holy city of Islam. Two years later, Muhammad died. By this time, Islam was spreading to all of Arabia.

✓ **Reading Check** **Explain** Why did Muhammad's message appeal to the poor?

A pilgrimage to Makkah ▶

A Holy Journey

A pilgrimage to the holy city of Makkah often involved a long, difficult journey across deserts and other rough country. Muslim travelers carried palm leaves to show that they were on a pilgrimage. *Where was Muhammad born?*

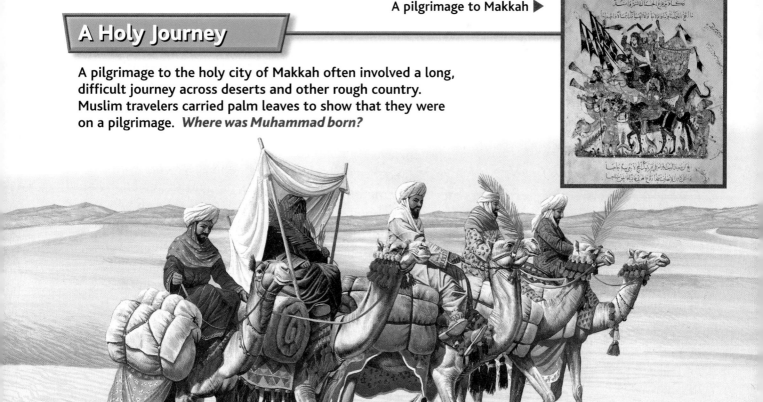

Biography

MUHAMMAD
c. A.D. 570–632

Muhammad experienced great poverty and many hardships early in his life. His father, Abd Allah, died before he was born. His grandfather, Abd al-Muttalib, took care of Muhammad in Makkah for a short time. Abd al-Muttalib felt that Makkah was an unhealthy place to raise a baby, but he could not leave because he was a political leader in the city. So he entrusted Muhammad to a tribe of nomads. They took the baby Muhammad to their home, the desert. When Muhammad was six years old, his mother died. Two years later, when Muhammad was eight, his grandfather also died. Arab custom did not allow minors to inherit anything, so the property and money from Muhammad's father and grandfather could not be passed down to him. To survive, Muhammad needed the protection of Abu Talib, his uncle who now headed the family.

▲ The Mosque of the Prophet in Madinah contains Muhammad's tomb.

Under the care of Abu Talib, Muhammad traveled by camel on trading journeys to Syria. On one of these trips, when he was about twenty-five years old, Muhammad met a wealthy woman named Khadijah. She and Muhammad married and had four daughters. They also had at least two sons who did not live past childhood. Muhammad's marriage to Khadijah made him a wealthy man and a member of Makkah's prosperous merchant class.

However, Muhammad could not forget his early experiences. His childhood had deeply influenced Muhammad and made him a thoughtful person. He often would go up into the hills near Makkah and spend nights in a cave. Alone there, he would reflect on the problems he saw in Makkah and the growing tension between the few people with great wealth and the many people with nothing. It was in these hills that Muhammad claimed an angel told him, "You are the Messenger of God."

▲ The Dome of the Rock in Jerusalem marks the place where Muhammad is believed to have ascended to heaven.

Then and Now

Are any of the problems Muhammad saw in Makkah similar to problems in society we see today? Explain.

Islam's Teachings

Main Idea The Quran provided guidelines for Muslims' lives and the governments of Muslim states.

Reading Focus Do you ever wonder how you should act in certain situations? In the following paragraphs, you will learn where Muslims looked for guidance.

Islam, Judaism, and Christianity have some beliefs in common. Like Jews and Christians, Muslims believe in one God. Muslims believe this one God holds all power and created the universe. They also believe that God determines right and wrong. People are expected to obey God's laws if they want to be blessed in the afterlife.

Jews, Christians, and Muslims also believe that God spoke to people through prophets. For Muslims, early prophets were Abraham, Moses, Jesus, and finally Muhammad. For Christians, Jesus was more than a prophet. He was the son of God and therefore divine. In Islam, Muhammad is seen as a prophet and a very good person but not as divine.

What Is the Quran? Muslims wrote down the messages that Muhammad said he received from Allah. These writings became the **Quran** (koh•RAHN), or holy book of Islam. For Muslims, the Quran is God's written word. For this reason, Muslims strive to follow the Quran.

The Quran instructs Muslims about how they should live. Many of its moral teachings are like those of the Bible. For example, Muslims are told to be honest and to treat others fairly. They are to honor their parents, show kindness to their neighbors, and give generously to the poor. Murder, lying, and stealing are forbidden.

▲ A child studies the Quran

▲ Muslim pilgrims surround the Kaaba in Makkah. *When did Muhammad's soldiers capture the city of Makkah?*

The Five Pillars of Islam

Belief	Muslims must declare that there is no god but Allah and that Muhammad is his prophet.
Prayer	Muslims must pray five times per day facing toward Makkah.
Charity	Muslims must give to the poor.
Fasting	Muslims must not eat from dawn to dusk during the sacred holiday of Ramadan.
Pilgrimage	Muslims must visit Makkah once in their life.

▲ The Five Pillars are acts of worship that all Muslims must carry out. *How many times should Muslims pray each day?*

Many rules in the Quran apply to Muslims' daily life. According to these rules, Muslims should not eat pork, drink liquor, or gamble. The Quran also has rules about marriage, divorce, family life, property rights, and business practices.

Muslims are expected to fulfill the Five Pillars of Islam, or acts of worship. These are shown in the chart at the left.

Scholars of Islam also created a law code that explains how society should be run. This code is taken from the Quran and the Sunna (SUH•nuh). The Sunna is the name given to customs based on Muhammad's words and deeds. Islam's law code covers all areas of daily life. It applies the teachings of the Quran to family life, business, and government.

✓ Reading Check **Evaluate** What role do the Quran and Sunna play in Muslim daily life?

History Online

Homework Helper Need help with the material in this section? Visit jat.glencoe.com

Section 1 Review

Reading Summary

Review the (Main Ideas)

- In the desert of the Arabian Peninsula, the Arab people were mostly herders and traders.

- In the town of Makkah, Muhammad began to preach a new religion, Islam, which soon spread to all of Arabia.

- Muslims believe that Muhammad was Allah's final prophet and that their holy book, the Quran, is Allah's written word.

What Did You Learn?

1. What are oases, and why were they important to Arabs?

2. Name some activities the Quran prohibits.

Critical Thinking

3. **Compare and Contrast** Draw a Venn diagram to compare and contrast Islam, Judaism, and Christianity.

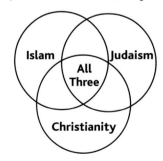

4. **Conclude** Why do you think Muhammad's teachings were popular with poorer people?

5. **Analyze** How did Muhammad link religion and government?

6. **Expository Writing** Suppose you are living in Makkah at the time Muhammad began preaching. Write a short newspaper article that describes Muhammad's teachings and the reactions of people in the city to those teachings.

7. **Reading** **Main Idea** Draw a graphic organizer to show the supporting details for this main idea: *Geography shaped the way that the early Arabs lived.*

Section 2 Islamic Empires

Get Ready to Read!

What's the Connection?
In Section 1, you learned how Islam spread from Madinah to Makkah. In time, Islam's followers brought their beliefs to all of Southwest Asia and parts of Southeast Asia, Africa, and Europe.

Focus on the Main Ideas
- Arabs spread Islam through preaching, conquest, and trade. *(page 380)*
- While Muslims split into two groups, the Arab Empire reached new heights. *(page 382)*
- Turks and Moguls built Muslim empires in Asia, Africa, and Europe. *(page 384)*

Locating Places
Damascus (duh•MAS•kuhs)
Indonesia (IHN•duh•NEE•zhuh)
Timbuktu (TIHM•BUHK•TOO)
Baghdad (BAG•dad)
Delhi (DEH•lee)

Meeting People
Umayyad (oo•MY•uhd)
Sufi (SOO•fee)
Abbasid (uh•BA•suhd)
Suleiman I (SOO•lay•MAHN)
Mogul (MOH•guhl)
Akbar (AK•buhr)

Building Your Vocabulary
caliph (KAY•luhf)
Shiite (SHEE•eyet)
Sunni (SU•nee)
sultan (SUHL•tuhn)

Reading Strategy
Cause and Effect Create a diagram to show why the Arabs were successful conquerors.

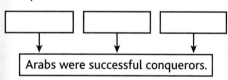

Arabs were successful conquerors.

NATIONAL GEOGRAPHIC When & Where?

Córdoba
Constantinople
Baghdad
Delhi

A.D. 500

A.D. 750 Abbasids overthrow Umayyads

1100

1258 Mongols burn Baghdad

1700

1526 Moguls rule India from Delhi

The Spread of Islam

Main Idea Arabs spread Islam through preaching, conquest, and trade.

Reading Focus When you come up with a new idea, how do you let others know about it? Read on to find out how Arabs spread Islam.

When Muhammad died, his followers chose his successor. He was called a **caliph** (KAY•luhf), which meant successor to the Messenger of God.

The first caliph was Muhammad's father-in-law, Abu Bakr. The first four caliphs ruled from Madinah and were called the Rightly Guided Caliphs. That is because they tried to follow in Muhammad's footsteps. They lived simply, treated others fairly, and also fought hard for Islam. They wanted to spread Allah's message to everyone. Under their rule, the empire expanded to include all of southwest Asia.

Expansion continued under the **Umayyad** (oo•MY•uhd) caliphs, who ruled from A.D. 661 to A.D. 750. They made their capital the city of **Damascus** (duh•MAS•kuhs) in Syria. Now the Arab Empire included North Africa, Spain, and some of India.

The Muslims Build an Empire Just 100 years after Muhammad's death, the Islamic state became a great empire. Why were the Arabs so successful?

Arabs had always been good on horseback and good with the sword, but as Muslims, they also were inspired by their religion. They were fighting to spread

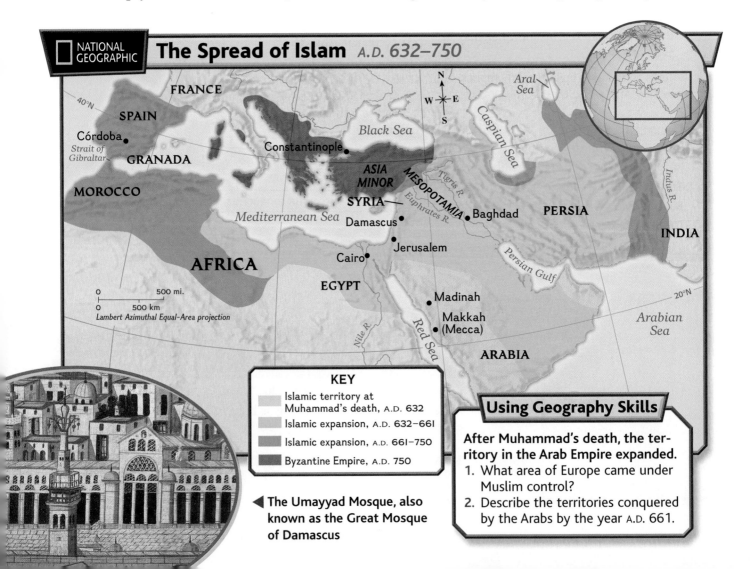

NATIONAL GEOGRAPHIC

The Spread of Islam A.D. 632–750

FRANCE
40°N
SPAIN
Córdoba
Strait of Gibraltar
GRANADA
MOROCCO
Black Sea
Constantinople
Aral Sea
Caspian Sea
ASIA MINOR
MESOPOTAMIA
SYRIA
Tigris R.
Euphrates R.
Baghdad
PERSIA
Indus R.
Mediterranean Sea
Damascus
Jerusalem
Cairo
INDIA
AFRICA
Persian Gulf
EGYPT
Madinah
20°N
Makkah (Mecca)
Arabian Sea
Nile R.
Red Sea
ARABIA

0   500 mi.
0   500 km
Lambert Azimuthal Equal-Area projection

KEY
- Islamic territory at Muhammad's death, A.D. 632
- Islamic expansion, A.D. 632–661
- Islamic expansion, A.D. 661–750
- Byzantine Empire, A.D. 750

◀ The Umayyad Mosque, also known as the Great Mosque of Damascus

Using Geography Skills

After Muhammad's death, the territory in the Arab Empire expanded.
1. What area of Europe came under Muslim control?
2. Describe the territories conquered by the Arabs by the year A.D. 661.

The Rightly Guided Caliphs

	Abu Bakr	Umar	Uthman	Ali
Relationship to Muhammad	father-in-law	friend	son-in-law, member of the Umayyad family	first cousin, son-in-law
Career	merchant	merchant	merchant	soldier, writer
Caliphate	A.D. 632–634	A.D. 634–644	A.D. 644–656	A.D. 656–661
Achievements as Caliph	spread Islam to all of Arabia; restored peace after death of Muhammad; created code of conduct in war; compiled Quran verses	spread Islam to Syria, Egypt, and Persia; redesigned government; paid soldiers; held a census; made taxes more fair; built roads and canals; aided poor	spread Islam into Afghanistan and eastern Mediterranean; organized a navy; improved the government; built more roads, bridges, and canals; distributed text of the Quran	reformed tax collection and other government systems; spent most of caliphate battling Muawiya, the governor of Syria

◄ Islamic glass horse

Understanding Charts

Under the caliphs, Islam spread through the Middle East and into North Africa.
1. Which caliph organized a navy?
2. Compare What achievements did Umar and Ali have in common?

Islam. Muslims believed anyone who died in battle for Islam would go to paradise.

The Arabs were also successful because they let conquered peoples practice their own religion. They called Christians and Jews "People of the Book," meaning that these people, too, believed in one God and had holy writings. Muslims did not treat everyone equally, though. Non-Muslims had to pay a special tax.

When a people are conquered, they tend to adopt the religion and customs of their new rulers. In the Arab Empire, many people became Muslims and learned Arabic. The customs of the conquered countries also influenced the Arabic rulers. Eventually, the term *Arab* meant only that a person spoke Arabic, not that he or she was from Arabia.

Preaching and Trading
Muslims also spread Islam by preaching. A group called **Sufis** (SOO•feez) spent their time praying and teaching Islam. They won many followers throughout the Arab Empire.

Arab merchants also helped to spread Islam. They set up trading posts throughout southeast Asia and taught Islam to the people there. Today, the country of **Indonesia** (IHN•duh•NEE•zhuh) includes more Muslims than any other nation in the world.

Some Arab merchants crossed the Sahara to trade with kingdoms in West Africa. In the 1300s, the west African city of **Timbuktu** (TIHM•BUHK•TOO) became a leading center of Muslim learning.

✓ Reading Check Explain How did Arabs spread the religion of Islam through trade?

Struggles Within Islam

Main Idea While Muslims split into two groups, the Arab Empire reached new heights.

Reading Focus Have you ever belonged to a club whose members could not agree on a leader? Read to find out what happened when Muslims disagreed about who should lead them.

From the moment Muhammad died, Muslims began arguing about who had the right to be caliph. The quarrel over who should succeed Muhammad split the Muslim world into two groups, the Sunnis and the Shiites. This division has remained to the present day. Today most Muslims are Sunnis. Iran and Iraq have the largest populations of Shiites.

How Did Islam Split? Shiites (SHEE•eyets) believed that Ali, Muhammad's son-in-law, should succeed him and that all future caliphs should be Ali's descendants. According to the Shiites, the Umayyad caliphs in Damascus had no right to rule.

Sunnis (SU•nees), who outnumbered Shiites, accepted the Umayyad dynasty as rightful caliphs, though they did not always agree with their policies. Over time, the Shiites and Sunnis developed different religious practices and customs.

Who Were the Abbasids? The **Abbasids** (uh•BA•suhds) were the dynasty that came after the Umayyads. The Umayyads lost power in A.D. 750 because they angered many Muslims, especially in Persia. Persian Muslims felt that Arab Muslims got special treatment. They got the best jobs and paid fewer taxes.

When these Muslims rebelled, people all over the empire joined them. They overthrew the Umayyads, and a new dynasty began. The new caliph was a descendant of Muhammad's uncle. His name was Abu al-Abbas. The new Abbasid dynasty lasted until 1258.

The Abbasids devoted their energies to trade, scholarship, and the arts. They also built a new capital, **Baghdad** (BAG•dad).

Baghdad prospered because it was beside the Tigris River and near the Euphrates River. It was a good location to trade since many people used the rivers to ship goods north and south. As a result, the Arab Empire grew even wealthier.

The Abbasid dynasty is also known for bringing Persian influence into the empire.

Primary Source
Royal Caliphs

Ibn Khaldun recorded historical events and his interpretation of them.

"When one considers what God meant the caliphate to be, nothing more needs [to be said] about it. God made the caliph his substitute to handle the affairs of His servants. He is to make them do the things that are good for them and forbid them to do those that are harmful. He has been directly told so. A person who lacks the power to do a thing is never told to do it."

—Ibn Khaldun,
*The Muqaddimah:
An Introduction to History*

▲ The Great Mosque of Damascus built by the Umayyad caliphs.

DBQ Document-Based Question

According to Khaldun, what is the relationship between God and the caliph?

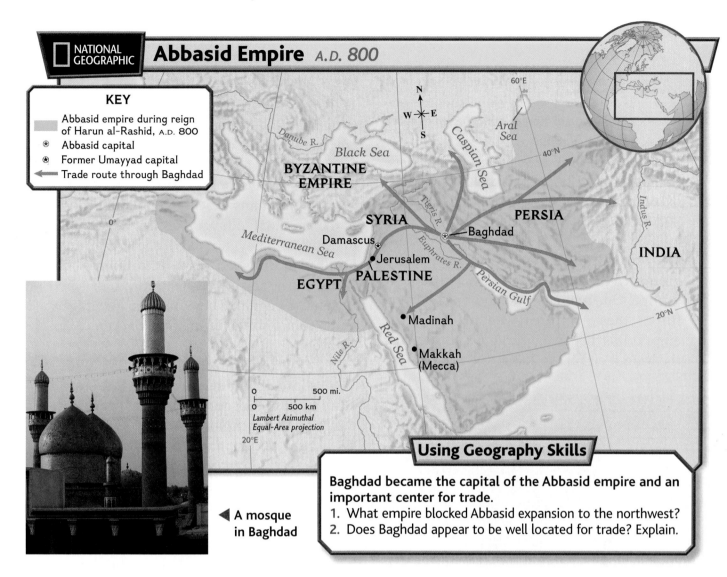

NATIONAL GEOGRAPHIC
Abbasid Empire A.D. 800

KEY

Abbasid empire during reign of Harun al-Rashid, A.D. 800
⊛ Abbasid capital
⊛ Former Umayyad capital
← Trade route through Baghdad

Danube R.
Black Sea
BYZANTINE EMPIRE
Caspian Sea
Aral Sea
SYRIA
PERSIA
Mediterranean Sea
Damascus
Baghdad
Tigris R.
Euphrates R.
INDIA
Indus R.
Jerusalem
PALESTINE
EGYPT
Persian Gulf
Nile R.
Red Sea
Madinah
Makkah (Mecca)

0   500 mi.
0   500 km
Lambert Azimuthal
Equal-Area projection

◀ A mosque in Baghdad

Using Geography Skills

Baghdad became the capital of the Abbasid empire and an important center for trade.
1. What empire blocked Abbasid expansion to the northwest?
2. Does Baghdad appear to be well located for trade? Explain.

Baghdad was very close to Persia, and the Abbasid rulers came to know and love the art and literature of Persia.

The Seljuk Turks Time brought many changes in the 500 years of Abbasid rule. In Egypt and Spain, the Muslims wanted their own caliphs. About the same time, a new people, the Seljuk Turks of central Asia, began moving south into the Arab Empire. The Abbasids were losing control.

The Seljuk Turks were nomads and great warriors. When they first moved into the empire, the Abbasids hired them as soldiers. Soon, however, the Seljuk Turks saw how weak the Abbasids were. They decided to take power for themselves.

First, the Seljuks took over much of what is now Iran and Turkey. Then, in 1055, they boldly took Baghdad itself. The Seljuks were satisfied to rule only the government and army. They let the Abbasid caliph remain as the religious leader. The Seljuk ruler called himself **sultan** (SUHL•tuhn), or "holder of power."

For 200 more years, the empire continued in this way. The Seljuks ruled, but it was still the Abbasid dynasty. Then, in the 1200s, another people swept into the empire. These were the fierce Mongols of central Asia. The Mongols were building their own empire and destroying many of the civilizations they conquered. In 1258 they stormed into Baghdad and burned it to the ground. The Arab Empire had ended.

✓ **Reading Check** **Contrast** What is the difference between Shiite and Sunni Muslims?

Later Muslim Empires

Main Idea Turks and Moguls built Muslim empires in Asia, Africa, and Europe.

Reading Focus How do you react when someone treats you unfairly? Read on to find out how Muslims in Turkey and India treated the people they conquered.

The Arabs built—and lost—the first Muslim empire. Later on, other Muslim groups created empires in Asia, Africa, and Europe. One of the largest and most powerful of these empires was the Ottoman empire that began in Turkey. Another was the Mogul empire in India.

Who Were the Ottomans? In the late 1200s, a group of Turks in the northwest corner of Asia Minor began to build a new empire. The ruler of these Turks was named Osman, and as a result, these Turks became known as the Ottoman Turks.

The Ottomans quickly conquered most of the land that today makes up the country of Turkey. They attacked the Byzantine Empire and pushed north into Europe. In 1453 they seized Constantinople, the Byzantine capital. They changed the city's name to Istanbul and made it the center of their empire.

Ottoman armies also marched south, conquering Syria, Palestine, Egypt, Mesopotamia, and parts of Arabia and North Africa. They used guns and cannons to fight their battles and built a large navy to control the Mediterranean Sea.

Like the Seljuks, the Ottomans called their leader a sultan. The most famous sultan was **Suleiman I** (SOO•lay•MAHN), who ruled in the 1500s. Suleiman was a man of many talents. He was enthusiastic about architecture and built many schools and mosques.

Suleiman was also a brilliant general, who brought Ottoman armies north into Europe. He even threatened the great European capital of Vienna. For all these reasons, Ottomans called him Suleiman the Magnificent.

After his rule, the Ottoman empire began to weaken. Little by little, they lost territory. The empire finally collapsed at the end of World War I.

◀ Muslims pray beneath the large decorated dome of Selimiye Mosque in Edirne, Turkey. Suleiman built this beautiful mosque for his son Selim II. *What were some of the reasons that Suleiman was called "the Magnificent"?*

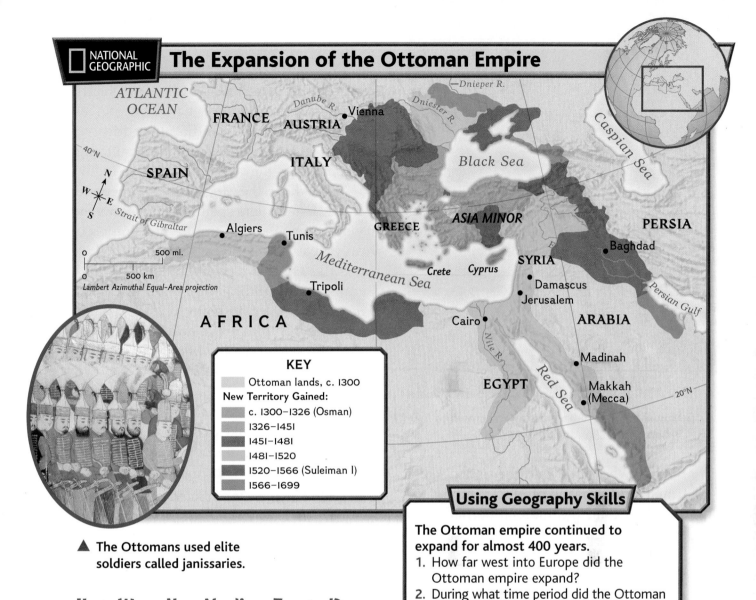

The Expansion of the Ottoman Empire

NATIONAL GEOGRAPHIC

KEY

Ottoman lands, c. 1300
New Territory Gained:
c. 1300–1326 (Osman)
1326–1451
1451–1481
1481–1520
1520–1566 (Suleiman I)
1566–1699

▲ The Ottomans used elite soldiers called janissaries.

Using Geography Skills

The Ottoman empire continued to expand for almost 400 years.
1. How far west into Europe did the Ottoman empire expand?
2. During what time period did the Ottoman empire expand to the Persian Gulf?

How Were Non-Muslims Treated?

The Ottoman empire had many different people, including Turks, Arabs, Greeks, Albanians, Armenians, and Slavs. These groups practiced several religions. While many were Muslims, others were Christians or Jews.

The government made different laws for non-Muslims. They had to pay a special tax, and in return, they were free to practice their religion. They also could run their own affairs. These groups chose leaders to present their views to the sultan.

However, the sultan made some demands on the conquered people. For example, Christian families in Eastern Europe had to send their sons to Istanbul. There the boys became Muslims and trained as soldiers for the sultan.

Who Were the Moguls?

During the 1500s, the **Moguls** (MOH•guhlz) created another Muslim empire in India. These Muslim warriors came from the mountains north of India. The Moguls used guns, cannons, elephants, and horses to conquer territory. In 1526 they made the city of **Delhi** (DEH•lee) the center of their empire.

The greatest Mogul ruler was **Akbar** (AK•buhr). He brought peace and order to the part of India he ruled by treating all his subjects fairly. Most of India's people were Hindu. He allowed them to practice their religion. Both Hindus and Muslims served in Akbar's government.

▲ Mogul emperor Akbar passing the crown to his grandson Shah Jahan

Times were good in India under Akbar. Farmers and artisans produced more food and goods than the Indians needed. As a result, trade increased. Muslim merchants brought paper, gunpowder, and fine porcelain from China to India. In addition, Muslim architects introduced new building styles, such as the arch and dome, to India.

After Akbar, the Mogul empire began to decline. Later rulers spent too much money trying to expand the empire and imposed heavy taxes on the people. Others tried to force the Hindus to convert to Islam and banned the building of Hindu temples. These policies led to many rebellions, and parts of the empire broke away.

At the same time the Moguls began losing power over their subjects, they had to deal with European merchants. The merchants came to India to trade but used their military power to take over Mogul territory. Eventually, the Mogul empire collapsed, and Great Britain took control of most of India.

✓ **Reading Check** **Describe** How did Constantinople change in 1453?

History Online

Homework Helper Need help with the material in this section? Visit jat.glencoe.com

Section 2 Review

Reading Summary

Review the **Main Ideas**

• Arab armies spread Islam as far west as Spain and as far east as India. Muslim traders helped spread the religion to southeast Asia and west Africa.

• Despite splitting into two groups, the Sunni and the Shiite, Muslim power reached its greatest height under the Abbasids.

• In the 1400s and 1500s, two great Muslim empires, the Ottoman and the Mogul, arose.

What Did You Learn?

1. How did the Muslims treat conquered peoples?

2. How far did the Arab Empire spread under the Umayyads?

Critical Thinking

3. **Organizing Information** Draw a chart to organize information about the Ottoman and Mogul empires.

Ottoman Empire	Mogul Empire

4. **Contrast** Describe the differences between the Shiite and Sunni Muslims.

5. **Summarize** Besides conquests by Arab armies, how was Islam spread?

6. **Evaluate** Why was Akbar considered a great ruler?

7. **Persuasive Writing** Which Muslim empire—the Umayyads, the Ottomans, or the Moguls—treated its non-Muslim subjects the most fairly? The least fairly? Write a paragraph to defend your answer.

Get Ready to Read!

What's the Connection?

In Section 2, you learned that many Muslim rulers brought peace and order to their empires. Peace and order helped trade to increase. Trade, in turn, brought great wealth to the Muslim empires.

Focus on the Main Ideas

- While Muslim traders enjoyed great success and cities grew, most Muslims lived in villages in the country. *(page 388)*

- Muslims made valuable contributions in math, science, and the arts. *(page 390)*

Locating Places

Granada (gruh•NAH•duh)
Agra (AH•gruh)

Meeting People

Mamun (mah•MOON)
al-Razi (ahl•RAH•zee)
Ibn Sina (ih•buhn   SEE•nuh)
Omar Khayyam
    (OH•MAHR   KY•YAHM)
Ibn Khaldun (IH•buhn   KAL•DOON)

Building Your Vocabulary

mosque (mahsk)
bazaar (buh•ZAHR)
minaret (MIH•nuh•REHT]
crier (CRY•uhr)

Reading Strategy

Organizing Information Create a pyramid to show the social classes in the early Muslim world.

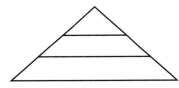

NATIONAL GEOGRAPHIC **When & Who?**

A.D. 800	1100	1400

c. A.D. 900
Al-Razi writes medical texts

c. 1100
Omar Khayyam writes the *Rubaiyat*

c. 1375
Ibn Khaldun writes histories

Trade and Everyday Life

Main Idea While Muslim traders enjoyed great success and cities grew, most Muslims lived in villages in the country.

Reading Focus Have you ever visited a mall or a farm market? These are both places where people gather to sell goods. Read to learn about Muslim traders and their marketplaces.

History Online

Web Activity Visit jat.glencoe.com and click on *Chapter 11—Student Web Activities* to learn more about Islamic civilization.

Muslims were the leading merchants in the Middle East and northern Africa until the 1400s. Their caravans traveled overland from Baghdad to China. Their ships crossed the Indian Ocean to India and Southeast Asia. They carried spices, cloth, glass, and carpets. On their return, they brought rubies, silk, ivory, gold, and slaves.

The Success of Muslim Traders

Several things explain the success of Muslim trade. When Muslim empires expanded, they spread the Arabic language. As a result, Arabic became the language of trade. Muslim rulers also made trade easier by providing merchants with coins.

Muslim merchants kept detailed records of their business deals and the money they made. In time, these practices developed into a new business—banking. Muslims respected traders for their skills and the wealth they created.

What Were Muslim Cities Like?

Trade helped the leading Muslim cities grow. Baghdad, Cairo, and Damascus were located on trade routes that ran from the Mediterranean Sea to central Asia. However, Muslim cities were not only places of trade.

▼ Muslims shop at a textile market.
   What was a bazaar in a Muslim city?

They also became important centers of government, learning, and the arts.

Muslim cities looked very similar. The major buildings were palaces and mosques. **Mosques** (mahsks) are Muslim houses of worship. They also serve as schools and centers of learning.

Another important part of every Muslim city was the **bazaar** (buh•ZAHR), or marketplace. Stalls and shops made up the bazaars. Sellers in the stalls and shops sold goods from Asia. Buyers from all over, including Europe, went from stall to stall to find goods to take home and sell.

Although cities were important, most Muslims lived in villages and farmed the land. Because water was scarce, Muslim farmers used irrigation to bring water to their crops. They grew wheat, rice, beans, and melons in the fields. They raised almonds, blackberries, apricots, figs, and olives in their orchards. Some farmers also raised flowers for use in perfume.

At first, Muslim villagers owned small farms. Later, wealthy landowners took over some of these farms and formed large estates. Farmers and enslaved people worked for the landowners.

Muslim Society
The Muslim people fell into social groups based on power and wealth. At the top were government leaders, landowners, and traders. Below them were artisans, farmers, and workers. The lowest group was made up of enslaved people.

As in other civilizations, slavery was widespread. Because Muslims could not be enslaved, traders brought enslaved people

▲ A Muslim woman weaving a rug

The Way It Was

Focus on Everyday Life

Muslim Carpets and Weavings

Carpets were woven in the Middle East long before the coming of Islam. They became popular in the Islamic world because Muslims used them in their daily worship.

Carpets were often made of sheep's wool or goat hair. Shepherds might knot them by hand, or the carpets might be made on portable looms. Flowers and geometric shapes were popular designs.

The carpets used for the Muslim's daily prayers are called prayer rugs. No matter where Muslims live, they pray five times daily. They kneel down on their prayer rug and pray facing toward Makkah. Prayer rugs are small and can be folded and carried from place to place.

Fine carpets of silk and wool are often hung on the walls of mosques and public buildings. They are considered fine art.

Muslim carpet ▶

Connecting to the Past

1. What animals were needed to make carpets?

2. What is the main reason Muslim carpets have continually been in demand?

from non-Muslim areas. Many of these people were prisoners of war. They often served as servants or soldiers and could buy back their freedom.

Men and women played different roles in the Muslim world. As in other parts of the world, men ran government, society, and business. Women, on the other hand, helped run Muslim families. They also could inherit wealth and own property. Many places had laws requiring women to cover their faces and to wear long robes in public.

✓ **Reading Check** **Explain** How did Muslim rulers give their merchants an advantage?

Muslim Achievements

Main Idea Muslims made valuable contributions in math, science, and the arts.

Reading Focus Did you know that the numbers you use are called Arabic numerals? Read on to find out what other contributions Muslims made.

Arabic was the common language of the Muslim empires. You have already read how Arabic language encouraged trade. It also helped different people in the empires to share knowledge. For example, in A.D. 830 the Abbasid caliph **Mamun** (mah•MOON)

Linking Past & Present

Hijab

THEN The teachings of Muhammad state that women's garments should not attract attention. The female Muslim custom of *hijab*—wearing garments that cover the head and body—was followed only by upper-class women during the first few hundred years of Islam. In the Middle Ages, *hijab* became more common.

▼ Modern Muslim women

NOW *Hijab* today ranges from colorful scarves to black robes. Some women wear *hijab*, and some do not. Many wear *hijab* to follow Muslim tradition. Others think it allows them to be judged for themselves and not their bodies. In certain countries, the government requires women to wear *hijab*. *Why do you think only upper-class women wore hijab in the early centuries of Islam?*

▲ Traditional Muslim women

founded the House of Wisdom in Baghdad. Mamun staffed his center with Christian, Jewish, and Muslim scholars. These scholars exchanged ideas and rewrote Greek, Persian, and Indian works in Arabic.

Scholars in Muslim lands saved much of the learning of the ancient world. Europeans in the West had lost this knowledge after the Western Roman Empire fell. Through Muslim scholars, western Europeans found out about Aristotle and other ancient Greek thinkers.

Mathematics and Science

Muslims made important advances in mathematics. Later, they passed on these discoveries to Europeans. For example, Muslims invented algebra, a type of mathematics still taught in schools today. The Arabs also borrowed the symbols 0 through 9 from Hindu scholars in India. These numbers were later used by Europeans. Today, they are known as "Arabic numerals."

Muslims also made progress in science. Muslim scientists who studied the heavens perfected the Greek astrolabe. Sailors used this tool to study the stars and then determine their location at sea. Muslim scientists used the astrolabe to measure the size and distance around the earth. Based on their measurements, they realized that the earth is round.

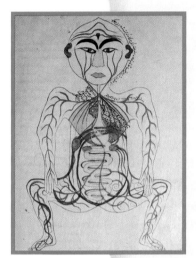

▲ Muslim medical drawing

◀ Muslim astrolabe

Other Muslim scientists experimented with metals and kept records of their work. As a result, the Arabs are considered the founders of chemistry. One of the best-known Muslim chemists was **al-Razi** (ahl•RAH•zee), who lived from A.D. 865 to A.D. 925. Al-Razi developed a system for categorizing substances as animal, mineral, or vegetable. He also wrote books for doctors that helped them to identify diseases.

Arab doctors were the first to discover that blood circulates, or moves to and from the heart. The Persian doctor **Ibn Sina** (ih•buhn SEE•nuh) showed how diseases spread from person to person. As they worked, Muslim doctors published their findings.

Biography

OMAR KHAYYAM
1048–1131
and IBN KHALDUN
1332–1406

Omar Khayyam—who was born in Persia—was a mathematician, astronomer, and philosopher, but he is best known as a poet. Scholars believe that Khayyam wrote only parts of his most famous poem, the *Rubaiyat*, but they are certain that at least 120 verses and the main concepts are his. Stanza XII reads:

> "A Book of Verses underneath the Bough,
> A Jug of Wine, a Loaf of Bread—and Thou
> Beside me singing the Wilderness—
> Oh, Wilderness were Paradise enow [enough]!"
> —Omar Khayyam, *Rubaiyat*

▲ Omar Khayyam

Khayyam wrote books on algebra and music before he was 25 years old. He led an observatory for 18 years and developed a more accurate calendar.

Ibn Khaldun is one of the most famous Arab scholars. He was a historian, geographer, sociologist, and politician. He was born in Tunisia and worked for the rulers of Tunis and Morocco. He also served as ambassador to one of the Spanish kingdoms and as a judge in Cairo, Egypt. He wrote much about social and political change. His best-known work is *Muqaddimah* (Introduction), written in 1375. It is the first volume of his book *Kitab al-Ibar* (universal history). In this book, he tried to develop a scientific way to analyze historical events. He is one of the first historians who studied how geography, economics, and culture affect history.

Then and Now

The *Rubaiyat* is a collection of 4-line verses called quatrains. Find a modern poem that is made up of quatrains.

▲ Ibn Khaldun

392

Muslim Writing The Quran is probably the most famous collection of writings in the Muslim world, but Muslims produced other famous works, as well. One of the most well known is *The Thousand and One Nights*, also called *The Arabian Nights*. It includes tales from India, Persia, and Arabia. One of the stories tells about Aladdin and his magic lamp.

Another Muslim, the Persian poet **Omar Khayyam** (OH•MAHR KY•YAHM), wrote the *Rubaiyat* (ROO•bee•AHT) around 1100. Many consider it one of the finest poems ever written.

In addition to stories and poems, Muslims wrote history. The great Muslim historian **Ibn Khaldun** (IH•buhn KAL•DOON) wrote in 1375 that all civilizations rise, grow, and then fall. He also was one of the first historians to study the effect of geography and climate on people.

Art and Buildings Muslims developed their own form of art based on Islam. Muslims are not allowed to show images of Muhammad or the events of his life in art. They believe that such images might cause people to worship Muhammad instead of Allah. Instead, designs entwined with flowers, leaves, and stars make up most Muslim art. Muslims use these designs to decorate walls, books, rugs, and buildings.

Muslims were known for their beautiful buildings. Mosques filled Muslim cities like Baghdad, Damascus, Cairo, and Istanbul.

Islamic Mosque

In Islamic cities and towns, mosques were centers of religious and daily life. Besides being places of worship, mosques also served as meeting places, schools, and courts. *What was the most striking architectural feature of a mosque?*

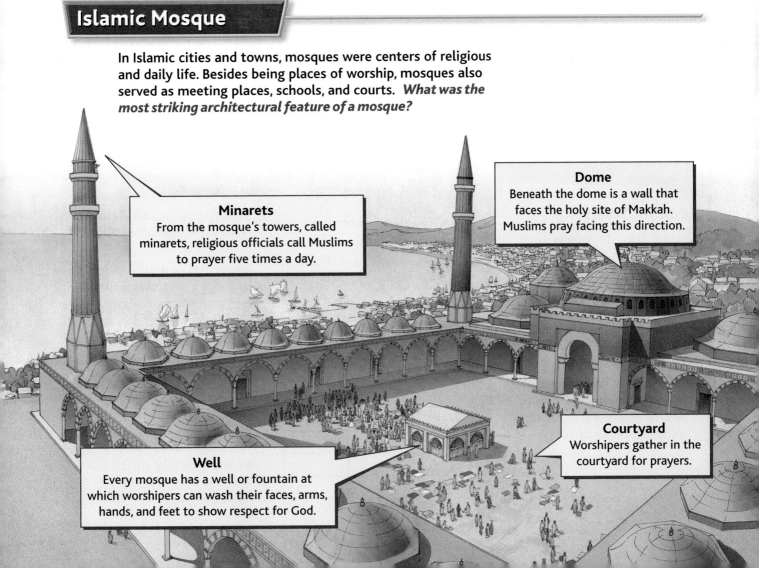

Minarets
From the mosque's towers, called minarets, religious officials call Muslims to prayer five times a day.

Dome
Beneath the dome is a wall that faces the holy site of Makkah. Muslims pray facing this direction.

Well
Every mosque has a well or fountain at which worshipers can wash their faces, arms, hands, and feet to show respect for God.

Courtyard
Worshipers gather in the courtyard for prayers.

▲ The Taj Mahal took more than 20 years to build.
Where is the Taj Mahal located?

Domes top many of the mosques, but a mosque's most striking feature is its **minarets** (MIH•nuh•REHTS). These are towers from which a **crier** (CRY•uhr), or announcer, calls believers to prayer five times a day.

Islamic rulers lived in large brick palaces. These palaces often had courtyards at their center. To cool the courtyards, palace builders added porches, fountains, and pools. To provide protection, they surrounded the palaces with walls. The most famous example of a Muslim palace is the Alhambra (al•HAM•bruh) in **Granada** (gruh•NAH•duh), Spain. It was built in the 1300s.

Another famous Muslim building is the Taj Mahal in **Agra** (AH•gruh), India. The Mogul ruler Shah Jahan built it as a tomb for his wife after she died in 1629. Made of marble and precious stones, the Taj Mahal is one of the world's most beautiful buildings.

Today, the Muslim empires are gone. However, Islam is still a major world religion. About one out of every six persons in the world is a Muslim.

✓ **Reading Check** **Identify** What contributions did Muslims make in math and science?

History **O**nline
Homework Helper Need help with the material in this section? Visit jat.glencoe.com

Section 3 Review

Reading Summary
Review the **Main Ideas**

• There were many Muslim cities such as Baghdad, Cairo, and Damascus, but most Muslims remained farmers in small villages.

• Muslim scholars made important discoveries in fields such as algebra and chemistry, and Muslim writers, artists, and architects also produced important works.

What Did You Learn?

1. Describe the three Muslim social groups.

2. What contributions did Muslims make in the field of medicine?

Critical Thinking

3. **Organizing Information** Draw a chart like the one below. Fill in details about Muslim contributions in the areas of math, science, and the arts.

Math	Science	Arts

4. **Summarize** Describe several factors that made Muslim trade strong.

5. **Analyze** How did the Arabic language and Muslim leaders help preserve and advance the world's knowledge?

6. **Evaluate** Which Muslim contribution do you think had the greatest effect on later civilizations?

7. **Descriptive Writing** Imagine you are living in a Muslim city. Write to a friend describing a bazaar. Describe what a bazaar is and some of the items you might find there.

Section 1 The Rise of Islam

Vocabulary
oasis
sheikh
caravan
Quran

Focusing on the Main Ideas
- The deserts, coastline, and oases of Arabia helped shape the Arab way of life. *(page 373)*
- The prophet Muhammad brought the message of Islam to the people of Arabia. *(page 374)*
- The Quran provided guidelines for Muslims' lives and the governments of Muslim states. *(page 377)*

A child studies ▶ the Quran

Section 2 Islamic Empires

Vocabulary
caliph
Shiite
Sunni
sultan

Focusing on the Main Ideas
- Arabs spread Islam through preaching, conquest, and trade. *(page 380)*
- While Muslims split into two groups, the Arab Empire reached new heights. *(page 382)*
- Turks and Moguls built Muslim empires in Asia, Africa, and Europe. *(page 384)*

Section 3 Muslim Ways of Life

Vocabulary
mosque
bazaar
minaret
crier

Focusing on the Main Ideas
- While Muslim traders enjoyed great success and cities grew, most Muslims lived in villages in the country. *(page 388)*
- Muslims made valuable contributions in math, science, and the arts. *(page 390)*

Review Vocabulary

Write the key term that completes each sentence.

a. caravan   f. minaret

b. caliph   g. sheikh

c. sultan   h. bazaar

d. mosque   i. Sunnis

e. Quran   j. Shiites

1. A crier called Muslims to prayer from the ___ of a mosque.
2. After Muhammad died, his followers chose a ___ to lead them.
3. The most famous ___ was Suleiman.
4. In each Muslim city, a ___ sold goods to local and out-of-town merchants.
5. Arab merchants traveling in a ___ used camels to carry goods across the desert.
6. The Muslim holy book is called the ___.
7. Each tribe of early Arabs was led by a ___.
8. Each ___ was a house of worship and a school.
9. The ___ believed that Muhammad's son-in-law should succeed him.
10. According to the ___, the Umayyad dynasty were rightful caliphs.

Review Main Ideas

Section 1 • The Rise of Islam

11. How did geography affect the early Arabs' way of life?
12. What guidelines did the Quran provide for the governments of Muslim states?

Section 2 • Islamic Empires

13. How did the Arabs spread Islam?
14. Why did the Muslims split into two groups?

Section 3 • Muslim Ways of Life

15. What scientific advances were made by early Muslims?
16. What is significant about Ibn Khaldun's recording of history?

Critical Thinking

17. **Compare** How are Islam, Judaism, and Christianity similar?
18. **Evaluate** Do you think a government that allows people to practice any religion they choose will be stronger than one that does not? Explain.

Review Reading Skill — Main Idea — Main Ideas and Details

19. Read the paragraph below. Create a graphic organizer to show the main idea and supporting details.

> The Muslim people fell into social groups based on power and wealth. At the top were government leaders, landowners, and traders. Below them were artisans, farmers, and workers. The lowest group was made up of enslaved people.

To review this skill, see pages 370–371.

Geography Skills

Study the map below and answer the following questions.

20. **Movement** Why was the Abbasid empire unable to expand to the Black Sea?

21. **Region** What bodies of water could Abbasid merchants use to trade with the outside world?

22. **Place** You learned that the Abbasids changed the capital city from Damascus to Baghdad. Look at the locations of those cities. Which do you think would have been the best location for a capital city? Why?

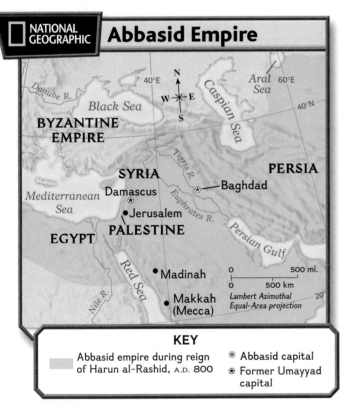

NATIONAL GEOGRAPHIC

Abbasid Empire

KEY
Abbasid empire during reign of Harun al-Rashid, A.D. 800

⊛ Abbasid capital
⊛ Former Umayyad capital

Read to Write

23. **Descriptive Writing** Suppose you are an Arab merchant traveling in the desert with a caravan. Write three diary entries, each describing the events of your day. Each day you choose to describe should focus on a different aspect of the life of a merchant. Share your entries with the class.

24. **Using Your** FOLDABLES Write a poem or short story using the facts from your completed foldable.

Using Technology

25. **Exploring Language** Use the Internet and your local library to find English words that have their origins in the Arabic language. Create a chart using your computer showing English words and their Arabic roots.

Linking Past and Present

26. **Evaluating Impact** Which Islamic invention or development do you think has the greatest effect on the world today? Explain your choice.

Building Citizenship Skills

27. **Analyzing Documents** Do research to find out how the United States Constitution protects religious freedoms. Do you think the way Muslim empires treated religion would be allowed under the U.S. Constitution? Explain.

Primary Source

Analyze

In the first stanza of the *Rubaiyat,* Omar Khayyam welcomes the morning.

"Wake! for the sun, the shepherd of the sky,
Has penned [confined] the stars within their fold on high,
And, shaking darkness from his mighty limbs,
Scatters the daylight from his burning eye."

—*Rubáiyát of Omar Khayyám:
A Paraphrase From
Several Literal Translations,
by Richard Le Gallienne*

DBQ Document-Based Questions

28. What has been penned up by the sun?

29. *Personification* is when a writer gives human qualities to something that is not human. How does Khayyam personify the sun in this stanza?

Comparing New Empires and Faiths

Compare ancient Rome, early Christianity, and early Islam by reviewing the information below. Can you see how the peoples of these civilizations had lives that were very much like yours?

	Ancient Rome Chapters 8 & 9	**Rise of Christianity** Chapter 10	**Islamic Civilization** Chapter 11
Where did these civilizations develop?	• Began on Italian peninsula • Won control of Mediterranean world	• Began in Palestine • Spread throughout the Roman Empire	• Began in Arabia • Arab Empire stretched from North Africa to central Asia
Who were some important people in these civilizations?	• Cincinnatus c. 519–438 B.C. • Augustus, ruled 27 B.C.–A.D. 14 • Theodora c. A.D. 500–548	• Jesus c. 6 B.C.–A.D. 30 • Helena c. A.D. 248–328 • Augustine A.D. 354–430	• Muhammad c. A.D. 570–632 • Omar Khayyam A.D. 1048–1131 • Suleiman I, ruled A.D. 1520–1566
Where did most of the people live?	• Farming villages • Major cities included Rome and Alexandria	• Ports and cities of Mediterranean area	• Desert oases • Farming villages • Major cities included Makkah and Baghdad

	Ancient Rome Chapters 8 & 9	**Rise of Christianity** Chapter 10	**Islamic Civilization** Chapter 11
What were these people's beliefs?	• Belief in many gods and goddesses • Emperors honored as gods • Many local religions	• Belief in one God and Jesus as Son of God and the Savior • Major groups: Eastern Orthodox and Roman Catholic	• Belief in one God (Allah) • Muhammad is final prophet • Major groups: Sunni and Shiite
What was their government like?	• Rome developed from a republic into an empire • An emperor was the chief leader • Army played role in government	• Ranked order of priests, bishops, and archbishops • Bishop of Rome became head of the Roman Catholic Church	• Muhammad founds Islamic state • After Muhammad, leaders called caliphs held religious and political power
What was their language and writing like?	• Latin was official language; Greek spoken in empire's eastern part • Many local languages	• New Testament of Bible written in Greek • Latin became language of Roman Catholic Church	• Quran written in Arabic • Arabic was Arab Empire's official language • Persian and Turkish also spoken
What contributions did they make?	• Introduced ideas about law and government • Developed new styles of building	• Christianity became a world religion • Shaped beliefs and values of Western civilization	• Islam became a world religion • Developed ideas in medicine and mathematics
How do these changes affect me? *Can you add any?*	• Latin contributed many words to English language • Rome's idea of a republic followed by governments today	• Christianity is major religion of the West today • Birth date of Jesus is starting date for Western calendar	• Islam is a major religion today • Developed algebra • Developed game of chess

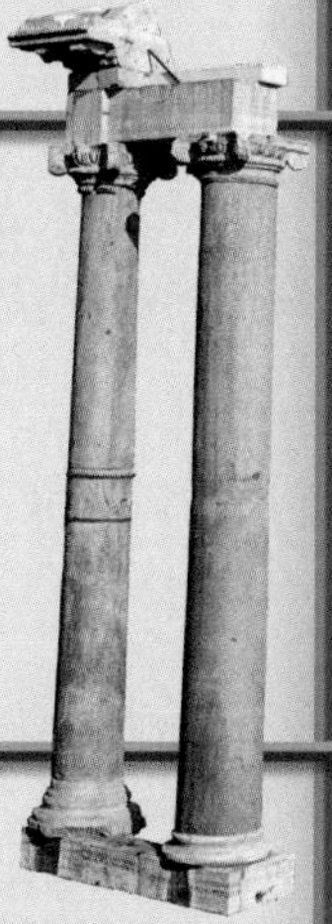

Unit 4

The Middle Ages

Why It's Important

Each civilization that you will study in this unit made important contributions to history.

- The Chinese first produced gunpowder, the compass, and printed books.
- Africans south of the Sahara developed new forms of music and dance.
- The Japanese developed martial arts, such as judo and karate.
- The Europeans took the first steps toward representative government.

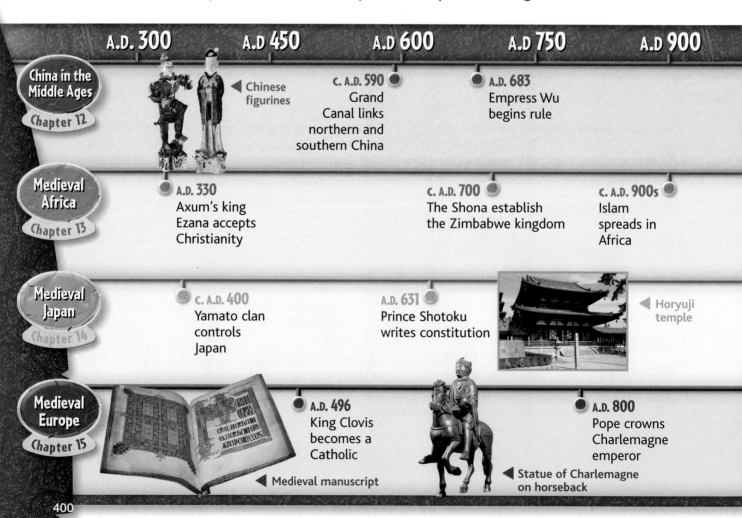

	A.D. 300	A.D 450	A.D 600	A.D 750	A.D 900
China in the Middle Ages Chapter 12		◄ Chinese figurines	C. A.D. 590 Grand Canal links northern and southern China	A.D. 683 Empress Wu begins rule	
Medieval Africa Chapter 13	A.D. 330 Axum's king Ezana accepts Christianity		C. A.D. 700 The Shona establish the Zimbabwe kingdom		C. A.D. 900s Islam spreads in Africa
Medieval Japan Chapter 14	C. A.D. 400 Yamato clan controls Japan		A.D. 631 Prince Shotoku writes constitution	◄ Horyuji temple	
Medieval Europe Chapter 15		A.D. 496 King Clovis becomes a Catholic		A.D. 800 Pope crowns Charlemagne emperor	

◄ Medieval manuscript

◄ Statue of Charlemagne on horseback

Where in the World?

NATIONAL GEOGRAPHIC

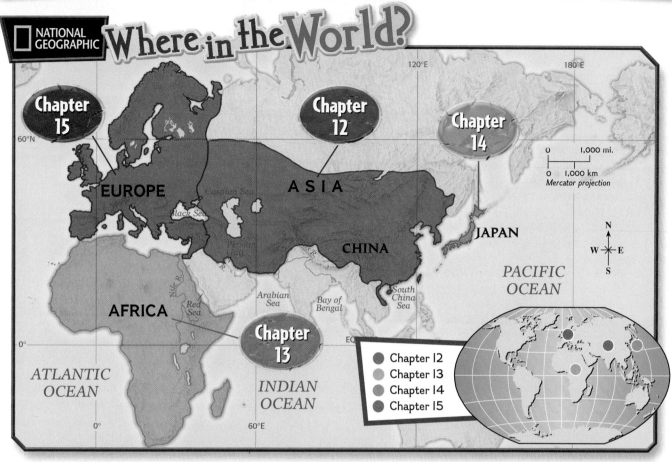

Chapter 15

Chapter 12

Chapter 14

EUROPE

ASIA

JAPAN

PACIFIC
OCEAN

CHINA

AFRICA

Chapter 13

Caspian Sea

Black Sea

Persian Gulf

Nile R.

Red Sea

Arabian Sea

Bay of Bengal

South China Sea

ATLANTIC
OCEAN

INDIAN
OCEAN

60°N

120°E

180°E

60°E

0°

0°

0   1,000 mi.
0   1,000 km
Mercator projection

N W E S

- ● Chapter 12
- ● Chapter 13
- ● Chapter 14
- ● Chapter 15

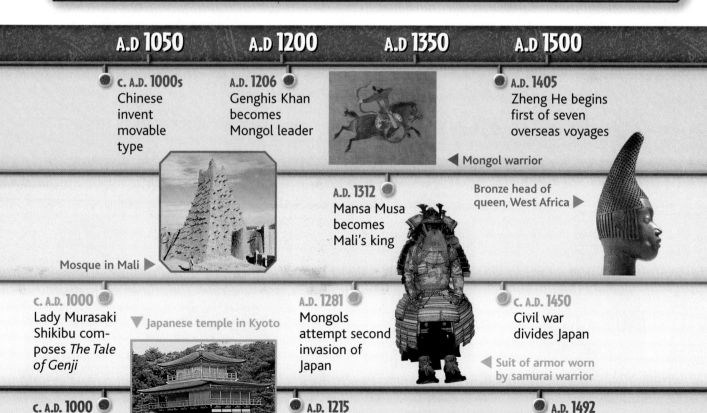

A.D 1050   **A.D 1200**   **A.D 1350**   **A.D 1500**

C. A.D. 1000s
Chinese invent movable type

A.D. 1206
Genghis Khan becomes Mongol leader

A.D. 1405
Zheng He begins first of seven overseas voyages

◄ Mongol warrior

A.D. 1312
Mansa Musa becomes Mali's king

Bronze head of queen, West Africa ►

Mosque in Mali ►

C. A.D. 1000
Lady Murasaki Shikibu composes *The Tale of Genji*

▼ Japanese temple in Kyoto

A.D. 1281
Mongols attempt second invasion of Japan

C. A.D. 1450
Civil war divides Japan

◄ Suit of armor worn by samurai warrior

C. A.D. 1000
Vikings reach North America

A.D. 1215
England's King John signs Magna Carta

A.D. 1492
Ferdinand and Isabella of Spain defeat Moors

◄ Medieval woman spinning wool

Unit 4

Places to Locate

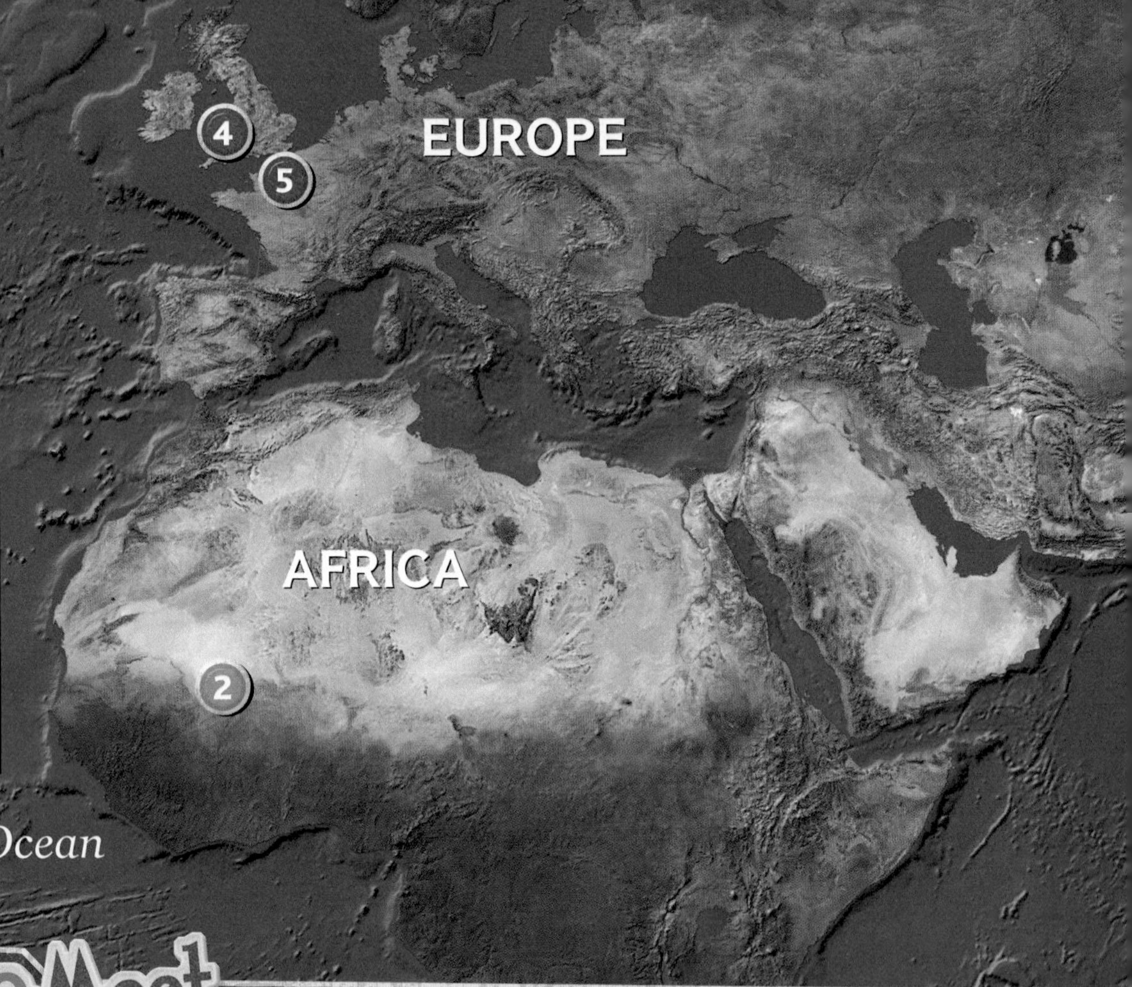

1 Buddha statue

See China in the Middle Ages
Chapter 12

2 Djenne mosque

See Medieval Africa
Chapter 13

EUROPE

4

5

AFRICA

2

Atlantic Ocean

People to Meet

Prince Shotoku

A.D. 573–621
Japanese leader
Chapter 14, p. 489

Charlemagne

A.D. 742–814
Holy Roman emperor
Chapter 15, p. 517

Murasaki Shikibu

C. A.D. 973–1025
Japanese writer
Chapter 14, p. 502

Genghis Kahn

C. A.D. 1167–1227
Mongol conqueror
Chapter 12, p. 427

ASIA

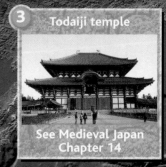

3 Todaiji temple

See Medieval Japan
Chapter 14

4 Caerphilly Castle

See Medieval Europe
Chapter 15

5 Mont St. Michel

See Medieval Europe
Chapter 15

① ③

*Pacific
Ocean*

**Thomas
Aquinas**

A.D. 1225–1274
Christian thinker
Chapter 15, p. 551

Mansa Musa

Ruled A.D. 1312–1337
King of Mali
Chapter 13, p. 466

Zheng He

A.D. 1371–1433
Chinese admiral
Chapter 12, p. 434

Joan Of Arc

A.D. 1412–1431
French heroine
Chapter 15, p. 556

China in the Middle Ages

▼ Imperial Palace at the Forbidden City

NATIONAL GEOGRAPHIC *When & Who?*

A.D. 600	A.D. 900	1200	1500
A.D. 581 Wendi founds Sui dynasty	A.D. 868 Chinese print world's first book	1206 Genghis Khan unites the Mongols	1405 Zheng He begins overseas voyage

Chapter Preview

Like the Arabs, the Chinese were interested in science and technology. Read this chapter to learn about Chinese inventions and how they influence your life today.

History Online
Chapter Overview Visit jat.glencoe.com for a preview of Chapter 12.

 View the Chapter 12 video in the *World History: Journey Across Time* **Video Program.**

Section 1 China Reunites

During the Middle Ages, Chinese rulers brought peace, order, and growth to China. Buddhism became a major religion in China, but the Chinese government supported Confucian ideas.

Section 2 Chinese Society

Farming and trade brought wealth to China. The Chinese developed new technology and enjoyed a golden age of art and writing.

Section 3 The Mongols in China

Led by Genghis Khan, the Mongols built a vast empire. Under his son, Kublai Khan, they went on to conquer China as well.

Section 4 The Ming Dynasty

China's Ming rulers strengthened government and brought peace and prosperity. They supported trading voyages to other parts of Asia and to East Africa.

Categorizing Information *Make this foldable to help you organize your notes about China in the Middle Ages.*

Step 1 *Fold a sheet of paper in half from side to side, leaving ½ inch tab along the side.*

Leave ½ inch tab here.

Step 2 *Turn the paper and fold it into fourths.*

Fold in half, then fold in half again.

Reading and Writing *As you read the chapter, identify the main ideas in the chapter. Write these under the appropriate tab.*

Step 3 *Unfold and cut along the top three fold lines.*

This makes four tabs.

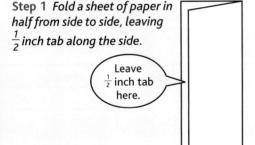

Step 4 *Label as shown.*

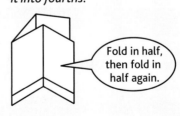

China Reunites | Chinese Society | The Mongols in China | The Ming Dynasty

China in the Middle Ages

Reading Social Studies

1 Learn It!

Reading Between the Lines

To infer means to evaluate information and arrive at a conclusion. When you make inferences, you "read between the lines," or draw conclusions that are not stated directly in the text. We naturally make inferences about things we read, see, and hear every day.

Read this paragraph from Section 3.

> Genghis Khan gathered an army of more than 100,000 warriors. He placed his soldiers into well-trained groups. Commanding them were officers chosen for their abilities, not for their family ties. These changes made the Mongols the most skilled fighting force in the world at that time.
>
> —from page 425

Reading Tip

Sometimes you make inferences by asking yourself questions or making predictions about what is going to come next.

Use this Think-Through chart to help you make inferences.

Text	Question	Inference
Genghis Khan	Who was he?	A powerful leader?
The army had 100,000 warriors	Why did he need so many warriors?	To take over another country or to defend his own?
Officers not chosen for family ties	Why did Genghis Khan want officers without strong family ties?	So they would not worry about their families to better concentrate on battle?
Mongols	Who were they?	Genghis Khan's countrymen? People from Mongolia?

2 Practice It!

Making Inferences

Read the next paragraph, also about Genghis Khan's warriors, and pay attention to highlighted words as you make inferences.

> Genghis Khan began building his empire by conquering other people on the steppes. These victories brought him wealth and new soldiers to fill the army. Soon the Mongols were strong enough to attack major civilizations. In 1211 Mongol forces turned east and invaded China. Within three years, they had taken all of northern China. They then moved west and struck at the cities and kingdoms that controlled parts of the Silk Road.
>
> —from pages 425–426

Read to Write

Read the text under the heading **Scholar-Officials** in Section 1, page 414. Pay attention to the paragraph about how important it was for students to pass tests. Write about any experiences with tests you have had to help you understand the fears and hopes of Chinese students during the Middle Ages.

Create your own Think-Through Chart to help you make further inferences about Genghis Khan's army. You might want to use the highlighted words in your first column and label it **Text.** Your second and third columns can be labeled **Questions** and **Inference.** Read the rest of page 426 to see if your inferences were correct.

3 Apply It!

We also make inferences about other types of text, such as poetry. Read the poems on pages 420–421, and create a Think-Through chart to help understand the poems.

China Reunites

Get Ready to Read!

What's the Connection?
Earlier you read that the Han dynasty of China collapsed and China plunged into civil war. As you will read, China eventually reunited. The new dynasties took Chinese civilization to even higher levels.

Focusing on the Main Ideas
- The Sui and Tang dynasties reunited and rebuilt China after years of war. *(page 409)*

- Buddhism became popular in China and spread to Korea and Japan. *(page 412)*

- The Tang dynasty returned to the ideas of Confucius and created a new class of scholar-officials. *(page 413)*

Locating Places
Korea (kuh•REE•uh)
Japan (juh•PAN)

Meeting People
Wendi (WHEHN•DEE)
Empress Wu (WOO)

Building Your Vocabulary
warlord
economy (ih•KAH•nuh•mee)
reform
monastery (MAH•nuh•STEHR•ee)

Reading Strategy
Categorizing Information Complete a table like the one below to show the time periods, the most important rulers, and the reasons for the decline of the Sui and Tang dynasties.

	Sui	Tang
Time Period		
Important Rulers		
Reasons for Decline		

NATIONAL GEOGRAPHIC **When & Where?**

Changan
Hangzhou

A.D. 500   A.D. 900   1300

A.D. 581 Wendi founds Sui dynasty

A.D. 907 Tang dynasty falls

1279 Mongols end Song rule

Rebuilding China's Empire

Main Idea The Sui and Tang dynasties reunited and rebuilt China after years of war.

Reading Focus Have you ever thought about how the economy in your town or city works? How do goods get to your local stores? Who makes sure roads are paved? Read to learn how China dealt with these issues.

Earlier you read that China's Han empire ended in A.D. 220. For the next 300 years, China had no central government. It broke into 17 kingdoms. War and poverty were everywhere. Chinese **warlords**—military leaders who run a government—fought with each other while nomads conquered parts of northern China.

While China was absorbed in its own problems, it lost control of some of the groups it had conquered. One of these groups was the people of **Korea** (kuh•REE•uh). They lived on the Korean Peninsula to the northeast of China. The Koreans decided to end Chinese rule of their country. They broke away and built their own separate civilization.

The Sui Dynasty Reunites China
China finally reunited in A.D. 581. In that year, a general who called himself **Wendi** (WHEHN•DEE) declared himself emperor. Wendi won battle after battle and finally reunited China. He then founded a new dynasty called the Sui (SWEE).

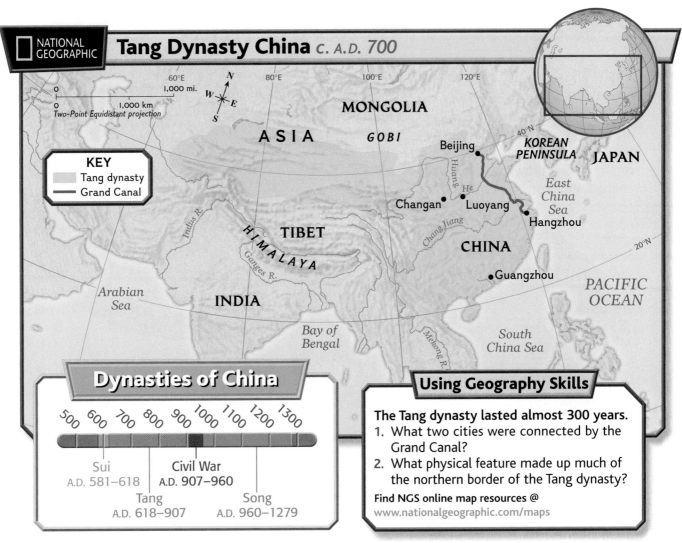

NATIONAL GEOGRAPHIC

Tang Dynasty China C. A.D. 700

KEY
Tang dynasty
Grand Canal

0   1,000 mi.
0   1,000 km
Two-Point Equidistant projection

MONGOLIA
ASIA
GOBI
Beijing
KOREAN PENINSULA
JAPAN
Huang He
Changan • • Luoyang
East China Sea
Hangzhou
TIBET
HIMALAYA
Indus R.
Ganges R.
Chang Jiang
CHINA
Arabian Sea
INDIA
Guangzhou
PACIFIC OCEAN
Bay of Bengal
Mekong R.
South China Sea

Dynasties of China

500 600 700 800 900 1000 1100 1200 1300

Sui
A.D. 581–618

Civil War
A.D. 907–960

Tang
A.D. 618–907

Song
A.D. 960–1279

Using Geography Skills

The Tang dynasty lasted almost 300 years.
1. What two cities were connected by the Grand Canal?
2. What physical feature made up much of the northern border of the Tang dynasty?

Find NGS online map resources @ www.nationalgeographic.com/maps

After Wendi died, his son Yangdi (YAHNG•DEE) took the Chinese throne. Yangdi wanted to expand China's territory. He sent an army to fight the neighboring Koreans, but the Chinese were badly defeated. At home, Yangdi took on many ambitious building projects. For example, the Great Wall had fallen into ruins, and Yangdi had it rebuilt.

Yangdi's greatest effort went into building the Grand Canal. This system of waterways linked the Chang Jiang (Yangtze River) and Huang He (Yellow River). The Grand

History Online

Web Activity Visit jat.glencoe.com and click on *Chapter 12—Student Web Activity* to learn more about China.

Canal became an important route for shipping products between northern and southern China. It helped unite China's economy. An **economy** (ih•KAH•nuh•mee) is an organized way in which people produce, sell, and buy things.

Linking Past & Present

Grand Canal and Three Gorges Dam Project

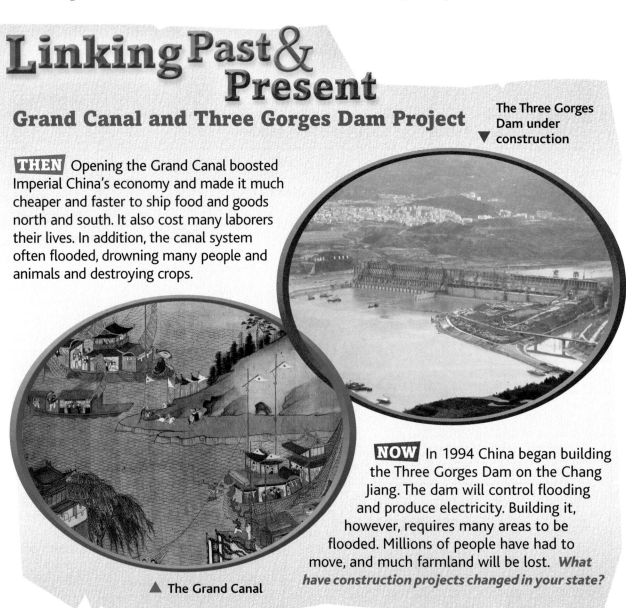

The Three Gorges Dam under ▼ construction

THEN Opening the Grand Canal boosted Imperial China's economy and made it much cheaper and faster to ship food and goods north and south. It also cost many laborers their lives. In addition, the canal system often flooded, drowning many people and animals and destroying crops.

NOW In 1994 China began building the Three Gorges Dam on the Chang Jiang. The dam will control flooding and produce electricity. Building it, however, requires many areas to be flooded. Millions of people have had to move, and much farmland will be lost. *What have construction projects changed in your state?*

▲ The Grand Canal

Yangdi rebuilt China, but he did it by placing hardships on the Chinese people. Farmers were forced to work on the Great Wall and the Grand Canal. They also had to pay high taxes to the government for these projects. Finally, the farmers became so angry that they revolted. The army took control and killed Yangdi. With Yangdi gone, the Sui dynasty came to an end.

The Tang Dynasty In A.D. 618 one of Yangdi's generals took over China. He made himself emperor and set up a new dynasty called the Tang (TAHNG). Unlike the short-lived Sui, the Tang dynasty was in power for about 300 years—from A.D. 618 to A.D. 907. The Tang capital at Changan became a magnificent city, with about one million people living there.

Tang rulers worked to strengthen China's government. They carried out a number of **reforms,** or changes that brought improvements. The most powerful Tang emperor was named Taizong (TY•ZAWNG). He restored the civil service exam system. Government officials were once again hired based on how well they did on exams rather than on their family connections. Taizong also gave land to farmers and brought order to the countryside.

During the late A.D. 600s, a woman named Wu ruled China as empress. She was the only woman in Chinese history to rule the country on her own. A forceful leader, **Empress Wu** (WOO) added more officials to the government. She also strengthened China's military forces.

Under the Tang, China regained much of its power in Asia and expanded the areas under its control. Tang armies pushed west into central Asia, invaded Tibet, and took control of the Silk Road. They marched into Korea and forced the Korean kingdoms to

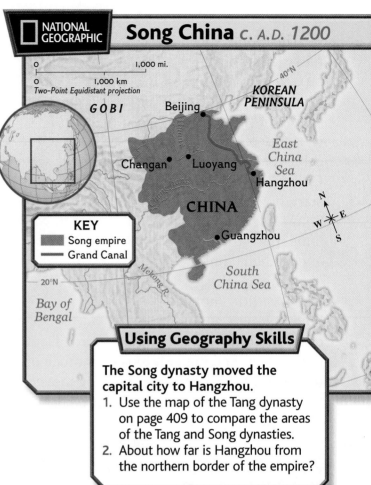

Song China C. A.D. 1200

0 ___ 1,000 mi.
0 ___ 1,000 km
Two-Point Equidistant projection

GOBI

Beijing

KOREAN PENINSULA

Changan Luoyang

East China Sea

Hangzhou

CHINA

KEY
◼ Song empire
— Grand Canal

Guangzhou

Mekong R.

South China Sea

Bay of Bengal

20°N

40°N

Using Geography Skills

The Song dynasty moved the capital city to Hangzhou.
1. Use the map of the Tang dynasty on page 409 to compare the areas of the Tang and Song dynasties.
2. About how far is Hangzhou from the northern border of the empire?

pay tribute, a special kind of tax that one country pays to another to be left alone. The Tang also moved south and took control of northern Vietnam.

By the mid-A.D. 700s, however, the Tang dynasty began to have problems. A new group of nomads—the Turks that you read about earlier—drove the Tang armies out of central Asia and took control of the Silk Road. This damaged China's economy. Revolts in Tibet and among Chinese farmers at home further weakened the Tang. In A.D. 907 all of this disorder brought down the Tang dynasty.

The Song Dynasty For about 50 years after the fall of the Tang, military leaders ruled China. Then, in A.D. 960, one of the generals declared himself emperor and set up the Song (SOONG) dynasty.

The Song dynasty ruled from A.D. 960 to 1279. This period was a time of prosperity and cultural achievement for China. From the start, however, the Song faced problems that threatened their hold on China. Song rulers did not have enough soldiers to control their large empire. Tibet broke away, and nomads took over much of northern China. For safety, the Song moved their capital farther south to the city of Hangzhou (HAHNG•JOH). Hangzhou was on the coast near the Chang Jiang delta.

▲ Statue of the Buddha, carved about A.D. 460 in the Yun-Kang caves in China.

✓ **Reading Check** **Explain** How did Wendi unite China?

Buddhism Spreads to China

Main Idea Buddhism became popular in China and spread to Korea and Japan.

Reading Focus Where do you turn when you are having problems? Read to learn why many Chinese turned to Buddhism when China was in trouble.

Earlier you learned that traders and missionaries from India brought Buddhism to China in about A.D. 150. At the time, the Han dynasty was already weak. Soon afterward, China collapsed into civil war. People everywhere were dying from war and a lack of food and shelter. It was a time of great suffering. Because Buddhism taught that people could escape their suffering, many Chinese seeking peace and comfort became Buddhists.

Chinese Buddhism Early Tang rulers were not Buddhists, but they allowed Buddhism to be practiced in China. They even

City Life in Tang China

Under the Tang, China grew and was prosperous. Tang cities could be large, with many activities occurring within the city's walls. A city contained many shops and temples. The homes of rich families often had two or three floors. *When did the Tang rule China?*

Musicians and dancers

Farmers selling goods

Civil service examinations

Print shop

Making pottery

supported the building of Buddhist temples. Many Chinese Buddhists became monks and nuns. They lived in places called **monasteries** (MAH•nuh•STEHR•eez), where they meditated and worshiped.

Buddhist temples and monasteries provided services for people. They ran schools and provided rooms and food for travelers. Buddhist monks served as bankers and provided medical care.

Not all Chinese people liked Buddhism, however. Many thought that it was wrong for the Buddhist temples and monasteries to accept donations. Others believed that monks and nuns weakened respect for family life because they were not allowed to marry.

In the early A.D. 800s, Tang officials feared Buddhism's growing power. They saw Buddhism as an enemy of China's traditions. In A.D. 845 the Tang had many Buddhist monasteries and temples destroyed. Buddhism in China never fully recovered.

Chinese Buddhism Spreads East
As you read earlier, Korea broke free of China when the Han dynasty fell in A.D. 220. For several hundred years after, Korea was divided into three independent kingdoms.

In the A.D. 300s, Chinese Buddhists brought their religion to Korea. About A.D. 660, the Koreans united to form one country. After that, with government support, Buddhism grew even stronger in Korea.

Buddhism later spread to the nearby islands of **Japan** (juh•PAN). According to legend, one of Korea's kings wrote to Japan's emperor. The letter contained a statue of the Buddha and Buddhist writings. "This religion is the most excellent of all teachings," the king wrote. As time passed, Buddhism won many followers in Japan as well.

✓ Reading Check **Explain** Why did some Chinese people dislike Buddhism?

New Confucian Ideas

Main Idea The Tang dynasty returned to the ideas of Confucius and created a new class of scholar-officials.

Reading Focus Have you ever seen someone get a reward that he or she did not earn? Read to learn how China's rulers tried to avoid this problem when hiring government officials.

You have already read about Confucius and his teachings. Confucius and his followers believed that a good government depended on having wise leaders. The civil service examinations introduced by Han

Primary Source Defending Confucianism

Han Yü (A.D. 768 to A.D. 824) encouraged the Chinese people to remain faithful to Confucianism.

"What were the teachings of our ancient kings? Universal love is called humanity. To practice this in the proper manner is called righteousness. To proceed according to these is called the Way.... They offered sacrifices to Heaven and the gods came to receive them.... What Way is this? I say: This is what I call the Way, and not what the Taoists [Daoists] and the Buddhists called the Way...."

—Han Yü, *Yüan-tao* (Inquiry on The Way)

▲ Han Yü

DBQ **Document-Based Question**

Why does Han Yü think Confucianism should be followed?

The Way It Was

Focus on Everyday Life

Civil Service Exams

Proficiency tests and final exams today take a lot of preparation, but they are not as difficult as China's civil service examinations given during the Tang dynasty. Men of almost all ranks tried to pass the exams so they could hold government jobs and become wealthy. Thousands attempted the tests, but only a few hundred people qualified for the important positions.

Chinese boys began preparing for the exams in primary school. After many years of learning to read and write more than 400,000 words and sayings, the boys—now men in their twenties or early thirties—would take the first of three levels of exams. Students traveled to huge testing sites to take the tests. Food and beds were not provided, so they had to bring their own. Many men became sick or insane because of the stress of the tests and the poor conditions under which they were tested.

▲ Students taking civil service exams

Connecting to the Past

1. How old were the Chinese when they took the tests?
2. Why do you think taking the tests was so stressful for these men?

rulers were a product of Confucian ideas. They were supposed to recruit talented government officials.

After the fall of the Han dynasty, no national government existed to give civil service examinations. Confucianism lost much support, and Buddhism with its spiritual message won many followers. Tang and Song rulers, however, brought Confucianism back into favor.

What Is Neo-Confucianism?

The Tang dynasty gave its support to a new kind of Confucianism called neo-Confucianism. This new Confucianism was created, in part, to reduce Buddhism's popularity. It taught that life in this world was just as important as the afterlife. Followers were expected to take part in life and help others.

Although it criticized Buddhist ideas, this new form of Confucianism also picked up some Buddhist and Daoist beliefs. For many Chinese, Confucianism became more than a system of rules for being good. It became a religion with beliefs about the spiritual world. Confucian thinkers taught that if people followed Confucius's teachings, they would find peace of mind and live in harmony with nature.

The Song dynasty, which followed the Tang, also supported neo-Confucianism. The Song even adopted it as their official philosophy, or belief system.

Scholar-Officials

Neo-Confucianism also became a way to strengthen the government. Both Tang and Song rulers used civil service examinations to hire officials. In doing so, they based the bureaucracy on a merit system. Under a merit system, people are accepted for what they can do and not on their riches or personal contacts.

The examinations tested job seekers on their knowledge of Confucian writings. To pass, it was necessary to write with style as well as understanding. The tests were supposed to be fair, but only men were allowed to take the tests. Also, only rich people had the money that was needed to help their sons study for the tests.

Passing the tests was very difficult. However, parents did all they could to prepare their sons. At the age of four, boys started learning to write the characters of the Chinese language. Later, students had to memorize all of Confucius's writings. If a student recited the passages poorly, he could expect to be hit by his teacher.

After many years of study, the boys took their examinations. Despite all the preparation, only one in five passed. Those who failed usually found jobs helping officials or teaching others. However, they would never be given a government job.

▲ Chinese scholar-officials on horseback

Over the years, the examination system created a new wealthy class in China. This group was made up of scholar-officials. Strict rules set the scholar-officials apart from society. One rule was that they could not do physical work. Students preparing for the tests were taught never to use their hands except for painting or writing.

✓ **Reading Check** **Describe** How did Confucianism change in China?

History **O**nline
Homework Helper Need help with the material in this section? Visit jat.glencoe.com

Section ① Review

Reading Summary

Review the Main Ideas

- While the Sui dynasty was short-lived, the Tang and Song dynasties lasted for hundreds of years and returned power and prosperity to China.

- Buddhism became popular in China and also spread to Korea and Japan.

- A new kind of Confucianism developed in China during the Tang and Song dynasties, and the government used civil service tests to improve itself.

What Did You Learn?

1. What made Buddhism so popular in China?

2. How was neo-Confucianism a response to Buddhism's popularity, and what did it teach?

Critical Thinking

3. **Compare and Contrast** Create a diagram to show how the reigns of Wendi and Yangdi were similar and how they were different.

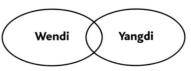

Wendi   Yangdi

4. **Cause and Effect** What events led to the fall of the Tang dynasty?

5. **Sequencing Information** Describe the history of Buddhism during the Tang dynasty.

6. **Analyze** Why had Confucianism fallen out of favor in China before the Tang and Song dynasties?

7. **Drawing Conclusions** Do you think China's civil service system truly brought the most talented individuals into the government? How would you make the system fairer?

Chinese Society

Get Ready to Read!

What's the Connection?

In the last section, you learned about the rise and fall of the Sui, Tang, and Song dynasties. During those dynasties, China's economy began to grow again. Chinese inventors developed many new technologies, and Chinese artists and writers produced new works that are still admired today.

Focusing on the Main Ideas

- The Tang dynasty strengthened China's economy by supporting farming and trade. *(page 417)*

- The Chinese developed new technologies, such as steelmaking and printing. *(page 418)*

- During the Tang and the Song dynasties, China enjoyed a golden age of art and literature. *(page 420)*

Locating Places

Changan (CHAHNG•AHN)

Meeting People

Li Bo (LEE   BOH)
Duo Fu (DWAW   FOO)

Building Your Vocabulary

porcelain (POHR•suh•luhn)
calligraphy (kuh•LIH•gruh•fee)

Reading Strategy

Organizing Information Complete a chart like the one below describing the new technologies developed in China during the Middle Ages.

New Technologies

NATIONAL GEOGRAPHIC When & Where?

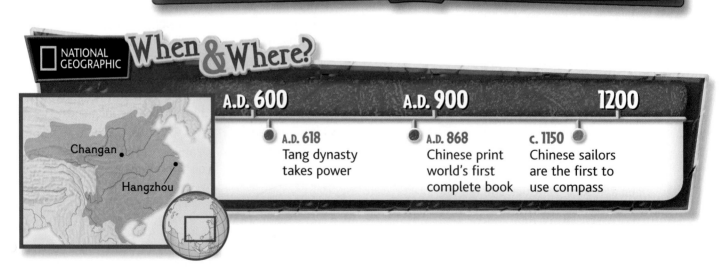

A.D. 600	A.D. 900	1200
A.D. 618 Tang dynasty takes power	A.D. 868 Chinese print world's first complete book	c. 1150 Chinese sailors are the first to use compass

Changan

Hangzhou

A Growing Economy

Main Idea The Tang dynasty strengthened China's economy by supporting farming and trade.

Reading Focus Do you know anyone who drinks tea or wears silk clothing? Both of these goods were first produced in China. Read to learn how farming changed under the Tang dynasty.

When the Han dynasty in China collapsed in the A.D. 200s, it was a disaster for China's economy. As fighting began, cities were damaged and farms were burned. Artisans made fewer goods, farmers grew fewer crops, and merchants had less to trade. Under the Tang dynasty, these problems were solved.

Why Did Farming Improve?
When the Tang rulers took power in A.D. 618, they brought peace to the countryside and gave more land to farmers. As a result, farmers were able to make many advances. They improved irrigation and introduced new ways of growing their crops. Farmers also developed new kinds of rice, which grew well in poor soil, produced more per acre, grew faster, and were resistant to disease.

These changes helped farmers grow more and more rice. China's farmers also began to grow tea, which became a popular drink. They made improvements in other crops as well. With more food available, the number of people in China greatly increased. At the same time, more people moved southward, where rice grew abundantly in the Chang Jiang valley.

China's Trade Grows
Tang rulers also had roads and waterways built. These changes made travel within and outside of China much easier. Chinese merchants were able to increase trade with people in other parts of Asia. The Silk Road, now under Tang control, once again bustled with activity.

▲ A worker holds a tray of silkworms eating mulberry leaves. Eventually the worms will spin cocoons. Workers then collect and unravel the cocoons to make silk thread. *Why do you think silk is still expensive today?*

▼ Silk, shown here being harvested, remained an important trade item for the Chinese. *How did Tang rulers help increase trade?*

One of the items traded by the Chinese was silk fabric. This product gave the road its name and was popular in markets to the west of China. In addition, China traded tea, steel, paper, and porcelain. **Porcelain** (POHR•suh•luhn) is made of fine clay and baked at high temperatures. In return, other countries sent China products such as gold, silver, precious stones, and fine woods.

Other trade routes were also established. Roads linked China to central Asia, India, and southwest Asia. In addition, the Tang opened new ports along China's coast to boost trade.

✓ **Reading Check** **Cause and Effect** How did the new kinds of rice developed in China help its population grow?

New Technology

Main Idea The Chinese developed new technologies, such as steelmaking and printing.

Reading Focus This book is made of paper with letters printed on the paper by a machine. Read to learn how printing was first invented in China during the Tang dynasty.

During the Tang and Song dynasties, new inventions changed China's society. In time, these discoveries spread to other parts of the world.

China Discovers Coal and Steel For most of China's history, people burned wood to heat their homes and cook their food. By

Changan's Royal Palace

The Tang capital city of Changan may have had a population of one million people at its peak. The city had large blocks that included houses, businesses, and temples set along straight streets. Its layout inspired the design of many later cities. The area containing the royal palace, shown below, was bordered by parklands. *What improvements to agriculture allowed China's population to grow during the Tang dynasty?*

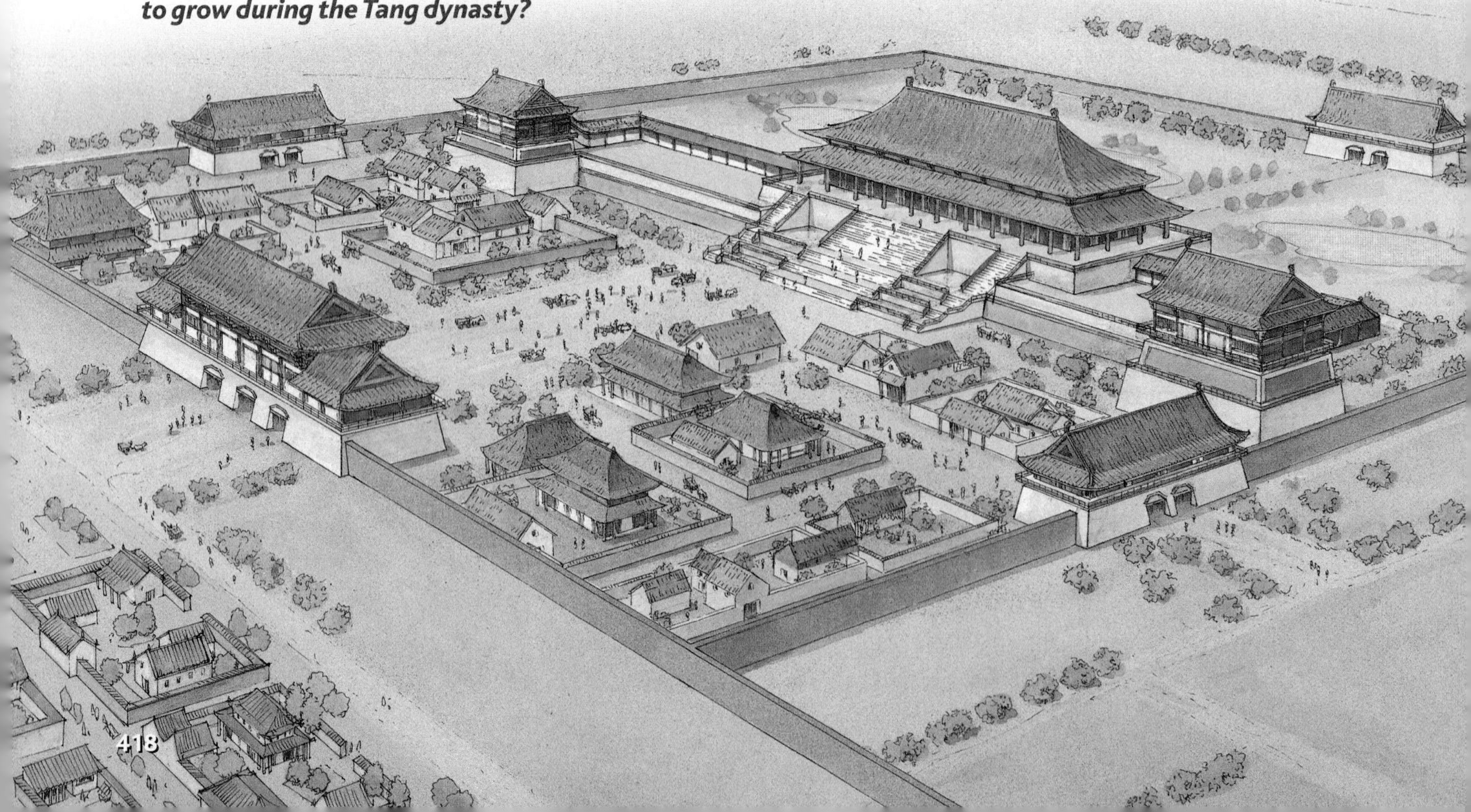

the time of the Tang dynasty, wood was becoming scarce in China. However, the Chinese had discovered that coal could be used to heat things, and soon a coal-mining industry developed.

The Chinese used coal to heat furnaces to high temperatures, which led to another discovery. When iron was produced in hot furnaces heated by coal, the molten iron mixed with carbon from the coal. This created a new, stronger metal known today as steel.

The Chinese used steel to make many things. They made armor, swords, and helmets for their army, but they also made stoves, farm tools, drills, steel chain, and even steel nails and sewing needles.

The Printing Process

Another Chinese invention was a method for printing books. Before printing, books had to be copied by hand. As a result, few books were made, and they were very expensive. The Chinese began printing in the A.D. 600s. They used blocks of wood on which they cut the characters of an entire page. Ink was placed over the wooden block. Then paper was laid on the block to make a print. Cutting the block took a long time. When they were completed, however, the woodblocks could be used again and again to make many copies.

The Chinese soon began printing books. The earliest known printed book dates from about A.D. 868. It is a Buddhist book called the *Diamond Sutra*. The invention of printing was very important. It helped to spread ideas more rapidly.

In the A.D. 1000s, a Chinese printer named Pi Sheng (BEE SHUHNG) invented movable type for printing. With movable type, each character is a separate piece. The pieces can be moved around to make sentences and used again and again. Pi Sheng made his pieces from clay and put them together to produce book pages. However,

The Way It Was

Science and Inventions

Printing When the Chinese invented movable type, they improved the art of printing. A Chinese author described the work of Pi Sheng:

"He took sticky clay and cut in it characters as thin as the edge of a copper coin. Each character formed as it were a single type. He baked them in the fire to make them hard. He had previously prepared an iron plate and he had covered this plate with a mixture of pine resin, wax, and paper ashes. When he wished to print, he took an iron frame and set it on the iron plate. In this he placed the type, set close together. When the frame was full, the whole made one solid block of type."

—Shên Kua, *Dream Pool Jottings*

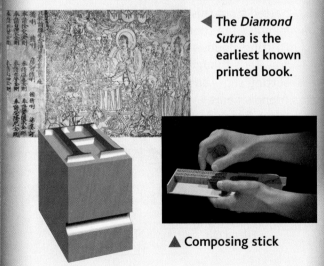

◄ The *Diamond Sutra* is the earliest known printed book.

▲ Composing stick

▲ Movable type block

Connecting to the Past
1. Why do you think Pi Sheng used clay to make his characters?
2. In what instance would woodblock printing have been a better method to use than movable type?

because written Chinese has so many characters, woodblock printing was easier and quicker than using movable type.

Other Chinese Inventions The Chinese made gunpowder for use in explosives. One weapon was the fire lance, an ancestor of the gun. It used gunpowder and helped make the Chinese army a strong force. The Chinese also used gunpowder to make fireworks.

The Chinese also built large ships with rudders and sails. About 1150, Chinese sailors began using the compass to help them find their way. This let ships sail farther from land.

✓**Reading Check** Analyze Why was the invention of printing so important?

Primary Source

Li Bo

In the following poem, Li Bo writes about parting from a friend.

"Green hills sloping from the northern wall, white water rounding the eastern city: once parted from this place the lone weed tumbles ten thousand miles.
Drifting clouds—a traveler's thoughts; setting sun—an old friend's heart.
Wave hands and let us take leave now, *hsiao-hsiao* our hesitant horses neighing."

—Li Bo,
"Seeing a Friend Off"

▲ Li Bo

DBQ Document-Based Question

How are drifting clouds like a traveler's thoughts?

Art and Literature

Main Idea During the Tang and the Song dynasties, China enjoyed a golden age of art and literature.

Reading Focus If you were to choose one poem to read to the class, which poem would it be? Below, you will read a poem that is a Chinese favorite.

The Tang and Song eras were a golden age for Chinese culture. The invention of printing helped to spread Chinese ideas and artwork. Chinese rulers actively supported art and literature, and invited artists and poets to live and work in the capital city of **Changan** (CHAHNG•AHN).

What Was Tang Poetry Like? Chinese writers best expressed themselves in poems. In fact, the Tang dynasty is viewed as the great age of poetry in China. Some Tang poems celebrated the beauty of nature, the thrill of seasons changing, and the joy of having a good friend. Other Tang poems expressed sadness for the shortness of life and mourned the cruelty of friends parting.

Li Bo (LEE BOH) was one of the most popular poets of the Tang era. His poems often centered on nature. The poem below by Li Bo is probably the best-known poem in China. For centuries, Chinese schoolchildren have had to memorize it. Its title is "Still Night Thoughts."

❝Moonlight in front of my bed—
 I took it for frost on the ground!
 I lift my eyes to watch the
  mountain moon,
 lower them and dream of home.❞

—Li Bo,
 "Still Night Thoughts"

Another favorite poet of that time was **Duo Fu** (DWAW FOO). He was a poor civil servant who had a hard life. Civil war swept

▲ This Chinese landscape was painted in the 1100s. *How were Daoist beliefs depicted in landscapes painted during the Song dynasty?*

▼ Chinese calligraphy

▲ Ink and watercolor drawing on silk

China, and food was hard to find. Duo Fu nearly died of starvation. His problems opened his eyes to the sufferings of the common people.

As a result, Duo Fu's poems often were very serious. They frequently dealt with issues such as social injustice and the problems of the poor. Duo Fu wrote the poem below after a rebellion left the capital city in ruins. It is called "Spring Landscape."

> 66 Rivers and mountains survive
>   broken countries.
>   Spring returns. The city grows
>   lush again.
>   Blossoms scatter tears thinking of
>   us, and this
>   Separation in a bird's cry startles
>   the heart.
>
>   Beacon-fires have burned
>   through three months.
>   By now, letters are worth ten
>   thousand in gold.
>
> 99
>
> —Duo Fu,
>   "Spring Landscape"

Painting in Song China
The painting of landscapes became widespread during the Song dynasty. However, Chinese artists did not try to make exact pictures of the landscapes they were painting. Instead, they wished to portray the "idea" of the mountains, lakes, and other features of their landscapes. Also, empty spaces were left in the paintings on purpose. This is because of the Daoist belief that a person cannot know the whole truth about something.

Daoist beliefs also can be seen in the way people are portrayed. They are tiny figures, fishing in small boats or wandering up a hillside trail. In other words, the people are living in, but not controlling, nature. They are only a part of the harmony of the natural setting.

Chinese painters often wrote poetry on their works. They used a brush and ink to write beautiful characters called **calligraphy** (kuh•LIH•gruh•fee).

Chinese Porcelain
During the Tang period, Chinese artisans perfected the making of porcelain. Because porcelain later came from

◀ Ceramic figures from Tang dynasty tomb

These porcelain figures from the ▶ Tang dynasty show travelers on horseback. *What is porcelain sometimes called today?*

▲ Tang dynasty bottle

China to the West, people today sometimes call porcelain by the name "china."

Porcelain can be made into plates, cups, figurines, and vases. In A.D. 851 an Arab traveler described the quality of Tang porcelain: "There is in China a very fine clay from which are made vases. . . . Water in these vases is visible through them, and yet they are made of clay."

The technology for making porcelain spread to other parts of the world. It finally reached Europe in the 1700s.

✓ **Reading Check** **Identify** What did Duo Fu often write about?

History Online

Homework Helper Need help with the material in this section? Visit jat.glencoe.com

Section 2 Review

Reading Summary

Review the Main Ideas

- During the Tang dynasty, both farming and trade flourished, and the empire grew much larger than ever before.

- Many important inventions were developed in China during the Tang and Song dynasties, including steel, printing, and gunpowder.

- Chinese literature and arts, including poetry, landscape painting, and porcelain making, reached new heights during the Tang and Song dynasties.

What Did You Learn?

1. What products were traded by China along the Silk Road?

2. What were some of the subjects of Tang poetry?

Critical Thinking

3. **Organizing Information** Draw a chart to describe the new technologies developed in China.

Metalworking	
Printing	
Weapons	
Sailing	

4. **Summarize** Describe the changes to Chinese agriculture during the Tang dynasty.

5. **Contrast** How do the two forms of printing invented by the Chinese differ?

6. **Evaluate** Which invention of the Tang and Song dynasties do you think has been most important? Explain.

7. **Creative Writing** Read the poem "Still Night Thoughts" by Li Bo again. Then write a short, four-stanza poem similar to Li Bo's about the view from your bedroom or kitchen window.

Section 3

The Mongols in China

Get Ready to Read!

What's the Connection?
As a complex culture developed in China, a northern enemy waited to attack.

Focusing on the Main Ideas
- Genghis Khan and his sons built the Mongol Empire, which stretched from the Pacific Ocean to Eastern Europe. *(page 424)*

- The Mongols conquered China and created a new dynasty that tried to conquer Japan and began trading with the rest of Asia. *(page 428)*

Locating Places
Mongolia (mahn•GOH•lee•uh)
Gobi (GOH•bee)
Karakorum (KAHR•uh•KOHR•uhm)
Khanbaliq (KAHN•buh•LEEK)
Beijing (BAY•JIHNG)

Meeting People
Genghis Khan
  (GEHNG•guhs   KAHN)
Kublai Khan (KOO•BLUH   KAHN)
Marco Polo
  (MAHR•koh   POH•loh)

Building Your Vocabulary
tribe
steppe (STEHP)
terror (TEHR•uhr)

Reading Strategy
Organizing Information Use a diagram like the one below to show the accomplishments of Genghis Khan's reign.

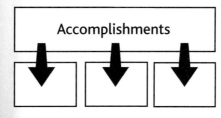

When & Where?

NATIONAL GEOGRAPHIC

Karakorum
Baghdad   Khanbaliq
                (Beijing)

1206 Genghis Khan unites Mongols

1271 Kublai Khan becomes China's emperor

1368 Yuan (Mongol) dynasty falls

1200   1300   1400

The Mongols

Main Idea Genghis Khan and his sons built the Mongol Empire, which stretched from the Pacific Ocean to Eastern Europe.

Reading Focus Have you ever had the chance to ride a horse? For thousands of years, the horse was the most important form of transportation in the world. Read to learn how one people used their skills as horse riders to build a vast empire.

The Mongols lived in an area north of China called **Mongolia** (mahn•GOH•lee•uh). They were made up of **tribes,** or groups of related families, loosely joined together. The Mongols raised cattle, goats, sheep, and horses. They followed their herds as the animals grazed Mongolia's great **steppes** (STEHPS). Steppes are wide rolling grassy plains that stretch from the Black Sea to northern China.

From an early period in their history, the Mongols were known for two things. One was their ability to ride horses well. Mongols practically lived on horseback, learning to ride at age four or five.

The other skill for which the Mongols were known was the ability to wage war. They could fire arrows at enemies from a distance while charging at them. Then they would attack with spears and swords.

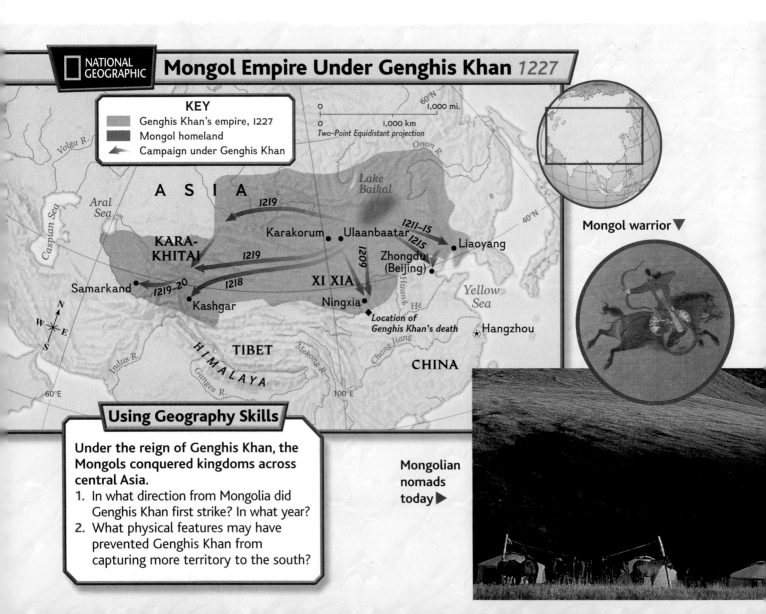

NATIONAL GEOGRAPHIC

Mongol Empire Under Genghis Khan 1227

KEY
- Genghis Khan's empire, 1227
- Mongol homeland
- Campaign under Genghis Khan

0   1,000 mi.
0   1,000 km
Two-Point Equidistant projection

Volga R.

A S I A

Aral Sea

Caspian Sea

KARA-KHITAI

Samarkand

Kashgar

1219

1219

1218

1219-20

Karakorum   Ulaanbaatar

XI XIA

Ningxia

Lake Baikal

Onon R.

1211-15

1215

1209

Zhongdu (Beijing)

Liaoyang

Huang He

Yellow Sea

◆ Location of Genghis Khan's death

Hangzhou

TIBET

H I M A L A Y A

Indus R.

Ganges R.

Mekong R.

Chang Jiang

CHINA

60°E

100°E

60°N

40°N

N E S W

Mongol warrior ▼

Using Geography Skills

Under the reign of Genghis Khan, the Mongols conquered kingdoms across central Asia.

1. In what direction from Mongolia did Genghis Khan first strike? In what year?
2. What physical features may have prevented Genghis Khan from capturing more territory to the south?

Mongolian nomads today ▶

Who Was Genghis Khan? The man who would unite the Mongols was born in the 1160s. He was named Temujin (teh•MOO•juhn), which means "blacksmith." Temujin showed his leadership skills early. He was still a young man when he began to unite the Mongol tribes.

In 1206 a meeting of Mongol leaders took place somewhere in the **Gobi** (GOH•bee), a vast desert that covers parts of Mongolia and China. At that meeting, Temujin was elected **Genghis Khan** (GEHNG•guhs KAHN), which means "strong ruler." Genghis Khan brought together Mongol laws in a new code. He also created a group of tribal chiefs to help him plan military campaigns. From the time of his election until the end of his life, Genghis Khan fought to conquer the lands beyond Mongolia.

Genghis Khan gathered an army of more than 100,000 warriors. He placed his soldiers into well-trained groups. Commanding them were officers chosen for their abilities, not for their family ties. These changes made the Mongols the most skilled fighting force in the world at that time.

Genghis Khan began building his empire by conquering other people on the steppes. These victories brought him wealth and new soldiers to fill the army.

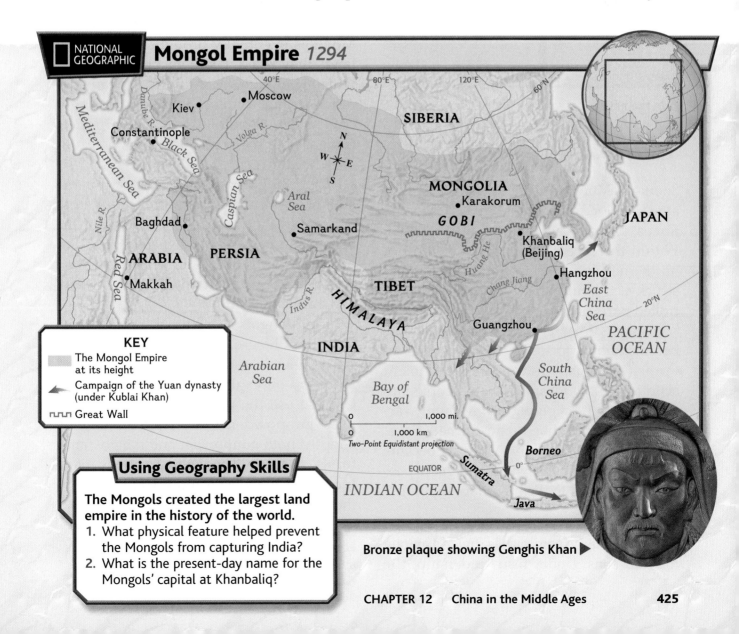

NATIONAL GEOGRAPHIC

Mongol Empire 1294

KEY

The Mongol Empire at its height

Campaign of the Yuan dynasty (under Kublai Khan)

Great Wall

0   1,000 mi.
0   1,000 km
Two-Point Equidistant projection

Using Geography Skills

The Mongols created the largest land empire in the history of the world.
1. What physical feature helped prevent the Mongols from capturing India?
2. What is the present-day name for the Mongols' capital at Khanbaliq?

Bronze plaque showing Genghis Khan ▶

▲ In the battle scene shown here, Mongol troops storm across the Chang Jiang on a bridge made of boats. *After conquering northern China, what areas did the Mongols attack?*

Soon the Mongols were strong enough to attack major civilizations. In 1211 Mongol forces turned east and invaded China. Within three years, they had taken all of northern China. They then moved west and struck at the cities and kingdoms that controlled parts of the Silk Road.

Genghis Khan and his Mongol warriors became known for their cruelty and use of **terror** (TEHR•uhr). Terror refers to violent actions that are meant to scare people into surrendering, or giving up. Mongol warriors attacked, robbed, and burned cities. Within a short time, the Mongols became known for their fierce ways, and many people surrendered to them without fighting.

The Mongol Empire
Genghis Khan died in 1227. His large empire was divided among his four sons. Under their leadership, the empire continued to expand. The Mongols swept into parts of eastern and central Europe. They also conquered much of southwest Asia. In 1258 the famous Muslim city of Baghdad fell to the Mongols. Mongol armies then pushed through Syria and Palestine to Egypt. They were finally stopped by the Muslim rulers of Egypt in 1260.

The Mongols united all of these different territories under their rule. Their empire reached from the Pacific Ocean in the east to Eastern Europe in the west and from Siberia in the north to the Himalaya in the south. It was the largest land empire the world had ever known.

Despite widespread destruction, the Mongols eventually brought peace to the lands they ruled. Peace encouraged trade, which helped the Mongols. Many of Asia's trade routes now lay in Mongol hands. The Mongols taxed the products traded over these roads and, as a result, grew wealthy.

The Mongols felt great respect for the advanced cultures they conquered. Sometimes they even adopted some of the beliefs and customs they encountered. For example, the Mongols in southwest Asia accepted Islam and adopted Arab, Persian, and Turkish ways.

The Mongols also learned many things from the Chinese. As they battled Chinese troops, they learned about gunpowder and its use as an explosive. They also saw the Chinese use the fire lance, a weapon that used gunpowder. Quickly, the Mongols adopted both gunpowder and the fire lance for use in battle. These new weapons made Mongol armies even more frightening to their enemies.

✔ **Reading Check** **Analyze** What military and economic reasons explain why the Mongols were able to build an empire so quickly?

Biography

GENGHIS KHAN
c. A.D. 1167–1227

Mongol Leader

Was Genghis Khan a ruthless warrior who enjoyed causing death and destruction, or was he a skilled leader who improved the lives of those in his empire, or both? Genghis Khan built a huge empire across Asia using loyal, strong, and well-trained warriors. His men killed hundreds of thousands on the quest. Although the wars he and his sons fought were brutal and bloody, they eventually brought peace and prosperity to most of Asia.

Genghis Khan was named Temujin by his father, the Mongol chief Yisugei. Folklore says Temujin had a large blood clot in his right hand, which meant he was destined to become a great warrior. Temujin grew up in his father's camp along the Onon River in Mongolia.

Temujin's father arranged a marriage for his nine-year-old son. His wife came from another tribe, and the marriage helped bring wealth to his family. Borte, his wife at age ten, was beautiful. Temujin and Borte, had four sons when they both became older.

Years later, when his father was killed by the Tartars and his loyal warriors left the tribe, Temujin lost his wealth. His poverty and the disloyalty of his father's soldiers angered him so much that he decided to become a great warrior. Over time, Temujin became Ghengis Khan. When he died after falling from a horse, his son Ogodei was picked to succeed him.

▲ Genghis Khan

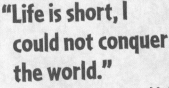

"Life is short, I could not conquer the world."
—attributed to Genghis Khan

▲ Genghis Khan's camp

Then and Now

In Mongolia today, Genghis Khan is considered a national hero. What do you think? Was Genghis Khan a villain or a hero?

Mongol Rule in China

Main Idea The Mongols conquered China and created a new dynasty that tried to conquer Japan and began trading with the rest of Asia.

Reading Focus What does it mean to be tolerant? Read to find out how the Mongols used tolerance to rule the Chinese.

In 1260 the Mongols named Genghis Khan's grandson, Kublai, to be the new khan, or ruler. **Kublai Khan** (KOO•BLUH KAHN) continued the Mongol conquest of China that his father had begun. In 1264 Kublai moved his capital from **Karakorum** in Mongolia to **Khanbaliq** in northern China. Today the modern city of **Beijing** (BAY•JIHNG) stands on the site of the Mongols' Chinese capital.

What Did the Mongols Do in China?

In 1271 Kublai Khan decided to become China's next emperor. Within 10 years, the Mongols had conquered southern China and put an end to the Song dynasty. Kublai Khan started the Yuan (YOO•AHN) dynasty. *Yuan* means "beginning," and its name showed that the Mongols wanted to rule China for a long time. But the Yuan dynasty would last only about 100 years. Kublai would rule for 30 of those years.

Kublai Khan gave Mongol leaders the top jobs in China's government, but he knew he needed Chinese scholar-officials to run the government. So he let many of the Chinese keep their government jobs.

The Mongols were different from the Chinese in many ways. They had their own language, laws, and customs. This kept them separate from Chinese society. The Mongols were rulers at the top of Chinese society, but they did not mix with the Chinese people.

Like many Chinese, the Mongols were Buddhists. They were tolerant, however, of other religions. For example, Kublai Khan invited Christians, Muslims, and Hindus from outside China to practice their faiths and to win converts.

Under Mongol rule, China reached the height of its wealth and power. Its splendor drew foreigners who came to China over the Silk Road. Khanbaliq, the capital, became known for it wide streets, beautiful palaces, and fine homes.

One of the most famous European travelers to reach China was **Marco Polo** (MAHR•koh POH•loh). He came from the city of Venice in Italy. Kublai Khan was

Primary Source: Kublai Khan's Park

Marco Polo recorded a description of the luxury in which Kublai Khan lived.

"[The palace wall] encloses and encircles fully sixteen miles of parkland well watered with springs and streams . . . Into this park there is no entry except by way of the palace. Here the Great Khan keeps game animals of all sorts . . . to provide food for the gerfalcons [large, arctic falcons] and other falcons which he has in here in mew [an enclosure]."

—Marco Polo, "Kublai Khan's Park, c. 1275"

▲ Kublai Khan presents golden tablets to Marco Polo

DBQ Document-Based Question

Why did Kublai Khan keep game animals—ones hunted for sport or food—in his park?

fascinated by Marco Polo's stories about his travels. For about 16 years, Kublai sent Polo on many fact-finding trips. When Polo finally returned to Europe, he wrote a book about his adventures. His accounts of the wonders of China amazed Europeans.

Trade and Conquest The Mongols ruled a large empire that stretched from China to eastern Europe. As a result, China prospered from increased trade with other areas. Goods such as silver, spices, carpets, and cotton flowed in from Europe and other parts of Asia. In return, China shipped out tea, silk, and porcelain. Europeans and Muslims also brought Chinese discoveries, such as steel, gunpowder, and the compass, back to their homelands.

The Mongols enlarged China's empire and conquered Vietnam and northern Korea. The rulers of Korea, called the Koryo, remained in power because they accepted

▲ This drawing from a historic map shows Marco Polo's journey along the Silk Road. *From what European city did Marco Polo travel?*

Mongol control. The Mongols forced thousands of Koreans to build warships. These ships were used by the Mongols to invade Japan. You will read about the Mongol invasions of Japan in a later chapter.

✓ **Reading Check** **Identify** Who founded the Yuan dynasty?

History **O**nline

Homework Helper Need help with the material in this section? Visit jat.glencoe.com

Section 3 Review

Reading Summary

Review the

- Under leaders such as Genghis Khan and his sons, the Mongol Empire expanded until it stretched from the Pacific Ocean to Eastern Europe, and from Siberia south to the Himalaya.

- Kublai Khan conquered China, which led to increased trade between China and other parts of the world.

What Did You Learn?

1. Who was Marco Polo?
2. What areas did the Mongols conquer?

Critical Thinking

3. **Sequencing Information** Draw a time line like the one below. Fill in details to show the Mongols' rise to power in China.

1160s				**1281**
Temujin				**Mongols**
born				**conquer**
				China

4. **Analyze** How did the Mongols use terror in their conquests?

5. **Summarize** How did the Mongols benefit from their contact with the Chinese?

6. **Descriptive Writing** Imagine you are Marco Polo visiting Kublai Khan in Khanbaliq. Write a journal entry describing some of the things you are learning about the Mongol Empire under Kublai Khan.

Section 4

The Ming Dynasty

Get Ready to Read!

What's the Connection?

In Section 3, you read about the Mongol conquest. Eventually, the Chinese drove the Mongols out, and a new dynasty arose.

Focusing on the Main Ideas

- Ming rulers strengthened China's government and brought back peace and prosperity. *(page 431)*

- During the Ming dynasty, China sent a fleet to explore Asia and East Africa. *(page 433)*

Locating Places

Nanjing (NAHN•JIHNG)
Portugal (POHR•chih•guhl)

Meeting People

Zhu Yuanzhang
   (JOO   YOO•AHN•JAHNG)
Yong Le (YUNG   LEE)
Zheng He (JUNG   HUH)

Building Your Vocabulary

treason (TREE•zuhn)
census (SEHN•suhs)
novel (NAH•vuhl)
barbarian (bahr•BEHR•ee•uhn)

Reading Strategy

Cause and Effect Use a chart like the one below to show cause-and-effect links in China's early trade voyages.

Cause
Zheng He traveled to parts of Asia and Africa.

↓

↓

↓

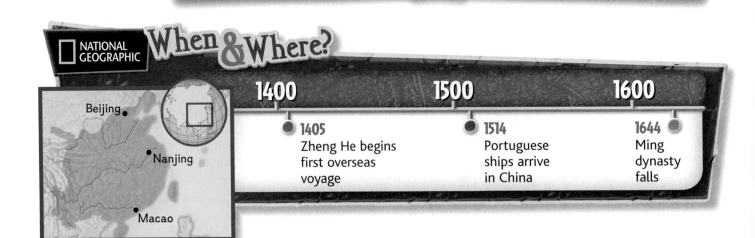

NATIONAL GEOGRAPHIC When & Where?

Beijing
Nanjing
Macao

1400   **1500**   **1600**

1405
Zheng He begins first overseas voyage

1514
Portuguese ships arrive in China

1644
Ming dynasty falls

The Rise of the Ming

Main Idea Ming rulers strengthened China's government and brought back peace and prosperity.

Reading Focus Think about all the different things the government does for people. Imagine if you were running the government and had to rebuild the country after a war. What would you do? Read to learn how the Ming rulers in China rebuilt their country after the Mongols left.

Kublai Khan died in 1294. A series of weak rulers followed him, and Mongol power began to decline. During the 1300s, problems mounted for the Yuan dynasty. Mongol groups in Mongolia to the north broke away. At the same time, many Chinese resented Mongol controls and wanted their own dynasty.

How Did the Ming Dynasty Begin? A series of rebellions finally drove out the Mongols. In 1368 a rebel leader named **Zhu Yuanzhang** (JOO YOO•AHN•JAHNG) became emperor. Zhu reunited the country and set up his capital at **Nanjing** (NAHN•JIHNG) in southern China. There, he founded the Ming, or "Brilliant," dynasty.

As emperor, Zhu took the name Hong Wu, or the "Military Emperor." He brought back order, but he also proved to be a cruel leader. Hong Wu trusted no one and killed officials he suspected of **treason** (TREE•zuhn), or disloyalty to the government. Hong Wu ruled China for 30 years. When he died in 1398, his son became emperor and took the name of **Yong Le** (YUNG LEE).

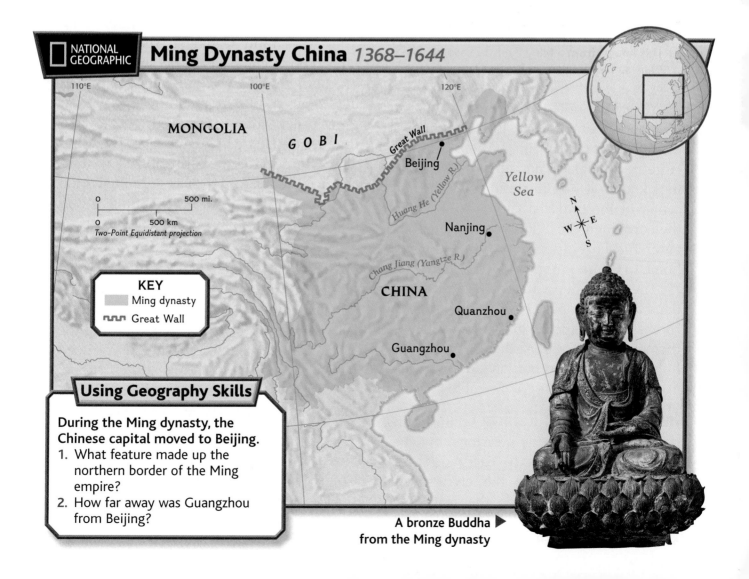

NATIONAL GEOGRAPHIC
Ming Dynasty China *1368–1644*

MONGOLIA

GOBI

Great Wall

Beijing

Huang He (Yellow R.)

Yellow Sea

Nanjing

Chang Jiang (Yangtze R.)

CHINA

Quanzhou

Guangzhou

500 mi.

500 km

Two-Point Equidistant projection

KEY
Ming dynasty
Great Wall

Using Geography Skills

During the Ming dynasty, the Chinese capital moved to Beijing.
1. What feature made up the northern border of the Ming empire?
2. How far away was Guangzhou from Beijing?

A bronze Buddha ▶
from the Ming dynasty

▲ This image, from a Ming dynasty vase, shows Chinese farmworkers collecting tea.

Yong Le worked hard to show that he was a powerful emperor. In 1421 he moved the capital north to Beijing. There, he built a large area of palaces and government buildings known as the Imperial City. The very center of the Imperial City was known as the Forbidden City. Only top officials could enter the Forbidden City because it was home to China's emperors.

The Forbidden City had beautiful gardens and many palaces with thousands of rooms. The emperor and his court lived there in luxury for more than 500 years. The buildings of the Forbidden City still exist. You can visit them if you travel to China.

How Did the Ming Reform China? Ming
emperors made all the decisions, but they still needed officials to carry out their orders. They restored the civil service examinations and made the tests even harder. From time to time, Ming officials carried out a **census** (SEHN•suhs), or a count of the number of people. This helped them collect taxes more accurately.

With the strong government of the early Ming emperors providing peace and security, China's economy began to grow. Hong Wu ordered many of the canals and farms destroyed by the Mongols to be rebuilt and ordered people to move to the new farms. He also ordered new forests to be planted and new roads to be paved.

Agriculture thrived as farmers worked on the new lands and grew more crops. Ming rulers repaired and expanded the Grand Canal so that rice and other goods could again be shipped from southern to northern China. They imported new types of rice from southeast Asia that grew faster. This helped feed the growing number of people living in cities. The Ming also supported the silk industry and encouraged farmers to start growing cotton and weaving cloth. For the first time, cotton became the cloth worn by most Chinese.

Chinese Culture Chinese culture also advanced under the Ming. As merchants and artisans grew wealthier, they wanted to learn more and be entertained. During the Ming period, Chinese writers produced many **novels** (NAH•vuhls), or long fictional stories. The Chinese also enjoyed seeing dramas on stage. These works combined spoken words and songs with dances, costumes, and symbolic gestures.

✓ Reading Check **Identify** What was the Forbidden City?

China Explores the World

Main Idea During the Ming dynasty, China sent a fleet to explore Asia and East Africa.

Reading Focus You probably have heard of Christopher Columbus and his trip to America. Imagine if China had sent ships to America first. Read to learn about Chinese explorations of Asia and East Africa.

Early Ming emperors were curious about the world outside of China. They also wanted to increase China's influence abroad. To reach these goals, Ming emperors built a large fleet of ships. The new ships usually traveled along China's coast. However, they could also sail in the open sea.

Who Was Zheng He? From 1405 to 1431, Emperor Yong Le sent the fleet on seven overseas voyages. The emperor wanted to trade with other kingdoms, show off China's power, and demand that weaker kingdoms pay tribute to China.

The leader of these journeys was a Chinese Muslim and court official named **Zheng He** (JUNG HUH). Zheng He's voyages were quite impressive. His first fleet had 62 large ships, 250 smaller ships, and almost 28,000 men. The largest ship was over 440 feet (134 m) long. That made it more than *five times* as long as the *Santa Maria* that Christopher Columbus sailed almost 90 years later!

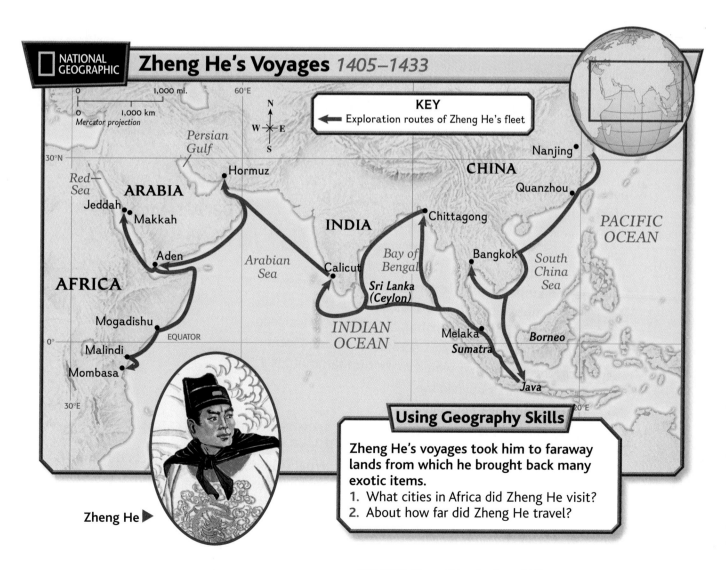

NATIONAL GEOGRAPHIC

Zheng He's Voyages *1405–1433*

KEY
← Exploration routes of Zheng He's fleet

0 — 1,000 mi.
0 — 1,000 km
Mercator projection

Persian Gulf · Hormuz · Red Sea · ARABIA · Jeddah · Makkah · Aden · AFRICA · Mogadishu · EQUATOR · Malindi · Mombasa · Arabian Sea · INDIA · Calicut · Sri Lanka (Ceylon) · INDIAN OCEAN · Bay of Bengal · Chittagong · CHINA · Nanjing · Quanzhou · Bangkok · South China Sea · PACIFIC OCEAN · Melaka · Sumatra · Borneo · Java

Zheng He ▶

Using Geography Skills

Zheng He's voyages took him to faraway lands from which he brought back many exotic items.
1. What cities in Africa did Zheng He visit?
2. About how far did Zheng He travel?

Biography

ZHENG HE
1371–1433

Zheng He ▶

Chinese Navigator

The famous Chinese navigator Zheng He was born in Kunyang in southwest China in 1371. His birth name was Ma He, and he was from a poor Chinese Muslim family. Scholars say that his father and grandfather were honored hajjis—people who successfully made the pilgrimage to Makkah in Arabia. Little did Ma He know that his life would also involve travel. His seven missions across the oceans earned him heroic honors.

His father died when Ma He was little. As a child, Ma He was taken prisoner by the Chinese army. To overcome his sad life, Ma He turned to education. He learned different languages, including Arabic, and studied philosophy and geography. With his language skills and knowledge of the outside world, 10-year-old Ma He became a valuable imperial aide to Chinese officials.

By age 12, he was an assistant to a young prince named Zhu Di. Ma He accompanied the prince on several military missions. The prince, who later became the Emperor Yong Le, became a friend of Ma He. The emperor changed Ma He's name to the honored surname Zheng. Soon after, Zheng He was assigned to lead a fleet of Chinese ships across the Indian Ocean, beginning the career that would make him famous. He's voyages to new lands opened the door for trade among China, India, and Africa. Many of the Chinese moved abroad to sell Chinese goods. Those who learned and spoke more than one language, like Zheng He, prospered.

> **"We have set eyes on barbarian regions far away."**
>
> –Zheng He, as quoted in *Chinese Portraits*

Then and Now

What "Made in China" products do you use on a daily basis? Do research to find out what percentage of goods imported to the United States are from China.

Where Did Zheng He Travel? Zheng He took his first fleet to southeast Asia. In later voyages, he reached India, sailed up the Persian Gulf to Arabia, and even landed in East Africa. In these areas, Zheng He traded Chinese goods, such as silk, paper, and porcelain. He brought back silver, spices, wood, and other goods. From Africa, Zheng He returned home with giraffes and other animals for the emperor's zoo.

As a result of Zheng He's voyages, Chinese merchants settled in Southeast Asia and India. There, they not only traded goods but also spread Chinese culture. Chinese merchants at home and abroad grew rich from the trade of the voyages and added to China's wealth.

Despite these benefits, Chinese officials complained that the trips cost too much. They also said that trips were bad for China's way of life because they brought in new ideas from the outside world and helped merchants become rich.

Confucius had taught that people should place loyalty to society ahead of their own desires. To the officials, China's merchants were disobeying this teaching by working to gain money for themselves.

After Zheng He's death, the Confucian officials persuaded the emperor to stop the voyages. The boats were dismantled, and no more ships capable of long distance ocean travel were allowed to be built. As a result, China's trade with other countries sharply declined. Within 50 years, the ship-building technology was forgotten.

The Europeans Arrive in China Chinese officials were not able to cut off all of China's contacts with the outside world. In 1514 a fleet from the European country of **Portugal** (POHR•chih•guhl) arrived off the coast of China. It was the first time Europeans had ever sailed to China and the first direct

▲ Italian missionary Matteo Ricci (left) was one of the most famous Europeans to visit China. He helped in the development of math and science in China during the late 1500s.

contact between China and Europe since the journeys of Marco Polo.

The Portuguese wanted China to trade with their country. They also wanted to convince the Chinese to become Christians. At the time, the Ming government was not impressed by the Portuguese. China was at the height of its power and did not feel threatened by outsiders. The Chinese thought the Europeans were **barbarians** (bahr•BEHR•ee•uhns), or uncivilized people.

At first, the Chinese refused to trade with the Portuguese, but by 1600, they had allowed Portugal to set up a trading post at the port of Macao (muh•KOW) in southern China. Goods were carried on European ships between Macao and Japan. Still, trade between China and Europe remained limited.

Despite restrictions, ideas from Europe did reach China. Christian missionaries traveled to China on European ships. Many of these missionaries were Jesuits, a special group of Roman Catholic priests. They

▲ This porcelain bowl is from the Ming dynasty.
Where in China did the Portuguese set up a trading post?

were highly educated, and their scientific knowledge impressed the Chinese. To get China to accept European ideas, the Jesuits brought with them clocks, eyeglasses, and scientific instruments. Although they tried, the Jesuits did not convince many Chinese to become Christians.

Why Did the Ming Dynasty Fall? After a long era of prosperity and growth, the Ming dynasty began to decline. Ming emperors had gathered too much power into their own hands. With the emperor having so much control, officials had little desire to make improvements. As time passed, Ming rulers themselves became weak. Greedy officials who lived in luxury took over the country. They placed heavy taxes on the peasants, who began to revolt.

As law and order disappeared, a people called the Manchus attacked China's northern border. The Manchus lived to the northeast of the Great Wall in an area known today as Manchuria. The Manchus defeated Chinese armies and captured Beijing. In 1644 they set up a new dynasty.

 **Reading Check** **Cause and Effect** What caused the Ming dynasty to decline and fall?

History Online
Homework Helper Need help with the material in this section? Visit jat.glencoe.com

Section 4 Review

Reading Summary
Review the Main Ideas

- The Ming dynasty rebuilt and reformed China after the Mongols were driven out. Their dynasty restored peace and prosperity to China.

- During the Ming dynasty, China's contacts with the outside world increased as Zheng He led fleets to faraway lands and European ships began arriving in China.

What Did You Learn?

1. What was the purpose of the Forbidden City and where was it located?

2. How did the Chinese react to the arrival of Portuguese traders in 1514?

Critical Thinking

3. **Organizing Information** Draw a diagram like the one below. Fill in details about the achievements of the Ming dynasty.

Ming Dynasty Achievements

4. **Cause and Effect** Why did Ming rulers repair and expand the Grand Canal?

5. **Summarize** Why did the Emperor Yong Le send Zheng He on his voyages? How did Zheng He's voyages benefit China?

6. **Persuasive Writing** Imagine you are living in China at the time of Zheng He's voyages. Write a newspaper editorial either for or against the voyages. Describe why you think the voyages are aiding or hurting the country as a whole.

7. **Predict** What do you think happened after China tried to limit trade?

Section 1 China Reunites

Vocabulary
warlord
economy
reform
monastery

Focusing on the Main Ideas

• The Sui and Tang dynasties reunited and rebuilt China after years of war. *(page 409)*

• Buddhism became popular in China and spread to Korea and Japan. *(page 412)*

• The Tang dynasty returned to the ideas of Confucius and created a new class of scholar-officials. *(page 413)*

Section 2 Chinese Society

Vocabulary
porcelain
calligraphy

Focusing on the Main Ideas

• The Tang dynasty strengthened China's economy by supporting farming and trade. *(page 417)*

• The Chinese developed new technologies, such as steelmaking and printing. *(page 418)*

• During the Tang and the Song dynasties, China enjoyed a golden age of art and literature. *(page 420)*

▲ Porcelain figures from the Tang dynasty

Section 3 The Mongols in China

Vocabulary
tribe
steppe
terror

Focusing on the Main Ideas

• Genghis Khan and his sons built the Mongol Empire, which stretched from the Pacific Ocean to Eastern Europe. *(page 424)*

• The Mongols conquered China and created a new dynasty that tried to conquer Japan and began trading with the rest of Asia. *(page 428)*

Section 4 The Ming Dynasty

Vocabulary
treason
census
novel
barbarian

Focusing on the Main Ideas

• Ming rulers strengthened China's government and brought back peace and prosperity. *(page 431)*

• During the Ming dynasty, China sent a fleet to explore Asia and East Africa. *(page 433)*

Review Vocabulary

Match the word in the first column with its definition in the second column.

___ 1. treason   **a.** groups of related families loosely joined together

___ 2. warlord   **b.** change that brings improvement

___ 3. terror   **c.** disloyalty to the government

___ 4. economy   **d.** military leader who also runs a government

___ 5. reform   **e.** a count of the number of people

___ 6. steppe   **f.** violent actions meant to scare others

___ 7. tribe   **g.** organized way to buy, sell, and produce

___ 8. census   **h.** wide grassy plain

Review Main Ideas

Section 1 • China Reunites
9. What did the Sui and Tang dynasties do to improve China?
10. How did the Tang rulers change China?

Section 2 • Chinese Society
11. How did Tang rulers strengthen China's economy?
12. What kind of technologies did the Chinese develop?

Section 3 • The Mongols in China
13. Why were the Mongols able to build a huge empire?
14. How did the Mongols rule China?

Section 4 • The Ming Dynasty
15. How did the Ming rulers affect China?
16. Why did the Portuguese want to explore Africa and Asia?

Critical Thinking

17. **Analyze** How did civil service exams help China develop a strong government?
18. **Explain** How did Confucianism change during the Tang dynasty?
19. **Predict** How do you think China would be different today if Tang rulers had not cracked down on Buddhism in A.D. 845?
20. **Hypothesize** The Mongols conquered a vast amount of land, but their Yuan dynasty lasted only about 100 years. Create a hypothesis that might explain this situation.

Review Reading Skill Inferences — Reading Between the Lines

21. Poet Duo Fu's poem "Spring Landscape," on page 421, described what it was like in the capital after a rebellion left the city in ruins. One of the lines from his poem appears here. What can you infer from this line of poetry?

"By now, letters are worth ten thousand in gold."

To review this skill, see pages 406–407.

Geography Skills

Study the map below and answer the following questions.

22. **Location** What was the length of the Grand Canal?
23. **Human/Environment Interaction** What part of Asia did the Tang control that helped China's trade?
24. **Region** What geographic features do you think helped the Tang dynasty expand?

History Online

Self-Check Quiz To help you prepare for the Chapter Test, visit jat.glencoe.com

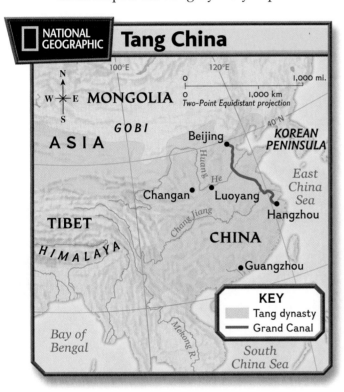

NATIONAL GEOGRAPHIC

Tang China

MONGOLIA

GOBI

ASIA

Beijing

KOREAN PENINSULA

Changan · Luoyang

Huang He

Chang Jiang

East China Sea

Hangzhou

TIBET

HIMALAYA

CHINA

· Guangzhou

Bay of Bengal

Mekong R.

South China Sea

100°E   120°E

40°N

1,000 mi.

1,000 km
Two-Point Equidistant projection

KEY
- Tang dynasty
- Grand Canal

Read to Write

25. **Persuasive Writing** Imagine you are a Portuguese merchant. You have just traveled to China to persuade the Chinese people to trade with your country. Work with a small group to create a script detailing the dialogue that would take place between the Portuguese merchant and a representative of the Chinese government. (Suppose someone is acting as a translator, but do not incorporate the translator into your dialogue.)

26. **Using Your FOLDABLES** On your foldable, add details to the main headings in Section 2. Think about how the changes and arts described there might have had an impact on people's lives. Then write three journal

entries that tell how these things have affected your family's life in China in the Middle Ages. Illustrate your entries.

Using Technology

27. **Building a Database** Use the Internet to gather more information about Genghis Khan. Use the information to create a database for your classmates. Include text, images, and perhaps a time line. Your database should contain information about Genghis Khan as a person and as a ruler.

Linking Past and Present

28. **Expository Writing** Write a short report that describes similarities and differences between the Imperial City of the Ming dynasty and the United States capital, Washington, D.C.

Primary Source Analyze

John of Plano Carpini, a friar, explained why the Mongols were such skilled warriors.

"Their children begin as soon as they are two or three years old to ride and manage horses and to gallop on them, and they are given bows to suit their stature [size] and are taught to shoot; they are extremely agile [move quickly and easily] and also intrepid [fearless]."

—John of Plano Carpini, *History of the Mongols*

DBQ Document-Based Questions

29. Why did each Mongol warrior shoot so well with a bow and arrows?
30. What other qualities made the Mongols excellent warriors?

Medieval Africa

Islamic mosque and marketplace in Djenne, Mali ▼

NATIONAL GEOGRAPHIC **When & Where?**

A.D. 300	A.D. 700	1100	1500
c. A.D. 300 Axum conquers Kush	c. A.D. 750 Arab Muslim traders settle in East Africa	1324 Mansa Musa travels to Makkah	c. 1441 First enslaved Africans arrive in Europe

Chapter Preview

While China enjoyed an artistic golden age, kingdoms in Africa grew rich from trading salt and gold. This chapter will tell you about an African ruler who led a great caravan on a long journey from North Africa to the Arabian Peninsula.

 View the Chapter 13 video in the *World History: Journey Across Time* Video Program.

History Online

Chapter Overview Visit jat.glencoe.com for a preview of Chapter 13.

 ## The Rise of African Civilizations

Africa's geography influenced the rise of its civilizations. The growth of trade led to the exchange of goods and ideas.

 ## Africa's Government and Religion

African rulers developed different forms of government. Traditional religions, Christianity, and Islam shaped early African culture.

 ## African Society and Culture

The family was the foundation of African society. A growing slave trade, however, would disrupt African society.

 ## FOLDABLES™ Study Organizer

Categorizing Information *Make this foldable to help you organize your notes about medieval Africa.*

Step 1 *Draw a map of Africa on one side of a sheet of paper.*

Step 2 *Fold the sheet of paper into thirds from top to bottom.*

Step 3 *Unfold, turn the paper over (to the clean side), and label as shown.*

The Rise of African Civilizations

Africa's Government and Religion

African Society and Culture

Reading and Writing *As you read about the civilizations of Africa, write down three main questions under each heading. Then write an answer to each question.*

Chapter 13

Reading Social Studies

Reading Skill

Compare and Contrast

1 Learn It!

Making Comparisons

One way authors help you to understand information is by organizing material so that you can see how people, places, things, or events compare (are alike) or contrast (are different). Read the following passage:

The contrasts (differences) are highlighted in blue.

First, look at what is being compared or contrasted. In this case, it is the religions of two groups of people from Africa, highlighted in pink.

Some groups, like the Nanti in East Africa, thought people could talk directly with their god. Others, like the Igbo, thought their creator could only be spoken to through less powerful gods and goddesses who worked for him.

Even though Africans practiced their religion differently in different places, their beliefs served similar purposes. They provided rules for living and helped people stay in touch with their history.

—from page 463

The comparisons (similarities) are highlighted in green.

Reading Tip

As you read, look for words that signal the use of comparisons, such as like, similar, or different.

2 Practice It!

Create a Venn Diagram

A Venn diagram can help you to compare and contrast information. Differences are listed in the outside parts of each circle. Similarities are listed in the portion of the two circles that overlap. Read the paragraphs below. Then create a Venn diagram to compare and contrast the roles of European and African women as stated in the paragraphs.

Differences Similarities Differences

Read to Write
You will read about the rise and fall of many wealthy kingdoms in Africa during the Middle Ages. Choose one of the kingdoms and do research to find out what modern African nation occupies that same area today. Write a report to compare and contrast the modern nation and the early African kingdom.

As in most medieval societies, women in Africa acted mostly as wives and mothers. Men had more rights and controlled much of what women did. Visitors to Africa, however, saw exceptions. European explorers were amazed to learn that women served as soldiers in some African kingdoms.

African women also won fame as rulers. In the A.D. 600s, Queen Dahia al-Kahina led the fight against the Muslim invasion of her kingdom, which was located about where Mauritania is today. Another woman ruler was Queen Nzinga, who ruled lands in what are now Angola and Congo. She spent almost 40 years battling Portuguese slave traders.

—from page 470

3 Apply It!

As you read each section, make Venn diagrams to help you compare and contrast important details.

The Rise of African Civilizations

Get Ready to Read!

What's the Connection?

Egypt and Kush were Africa's first great civilizations. In this section, you will learn about African civilizations that developed later.

Focusing on the Main Ideas

- Africa has a vast and varied landscape. *(page 445)*

- West African empires grew rich from trade. *(page 447)*

- Africa's rain forests blocked invaders and provided resources. *(page 450)*

- East African kingdoms and states became centers for trade and new ideas. *(page 451)*

Locating Places

Ghana (GAH•nuh)
Mali (MAH•lee)
Timbuktu (TIHM•BUHK•TOO)
Songhai (SAWNG•HY)
Axum (AHK•SOOM)

Meeting People

Sundiata Keita
  (sun•dee•AH•tuh   KY•tuh)
Mansa Musa
  (MAHN•sah   moo•SAH)
Sunni Ali (sun•EE   ah•LEE)

Building Your Vocabulary

plateau (pla•TOH)
griot (GREE•OH)
dhow (DOW)

Reading Strategy

Summarizing Information
Create diagrams describing the accomplishments of each medieval African civilization.

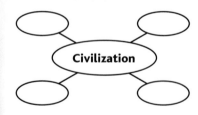

NATIONAL GEOGRAPHIC When & Where?

A.D. 300	A.D. 900	1500
c. A.D. 300 Axum conquers Kush	c. A.D. 750 Arab Muslim traders settle in East Africa	1468 Sunni Ali captures Timbuktu

Timbuktu
Kilwa
Great Zimbabwe

Africa's Geography

Main Idea Africa has a vast and varied landscape.

Reading Focus How can geography discourage people from exploring another place? Read to learn about the geographic features that made it difficult for people to travel across parts of Africa.

In 1906 a teacher named Hans Vischer explored what he called the "death road," a trade route connecting western Africa to the coast of the Mediterranean Sea. No European or American had ever risked the journey before. The "death road" crossed more than 1,500 miles (2,414 km) of the Sahara, the world's largest desert. To get lost meant certain death.

Only nomads living in the region knew the way, but Vischer hoped to map the route. Like the desert nomads, his life depended upon finding oases. Upon his return, Vischer amazed people with stories of the Sahara. He told of swirling winds and shifting sand dunes.

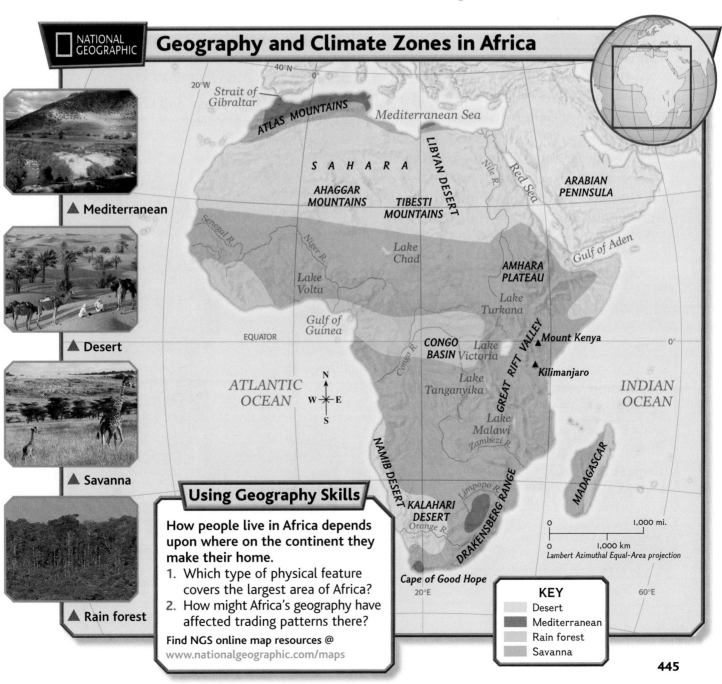

NATIONAL GEOGRAPHIC
Geography and Climate Zones in Africa

▲ Mediterranean

▲ Desert

▲ Savanna

▲ Rain forest

40°N
20°W
Strait of Gibraltar
ATLAS MOUNTAINS
Mediterranean Sea
SAHARA
LIBYAN DESERT
Nile R.
Red Sea
ARABIAN PENINSULA
AHAGGAR MOUNTAINS
TIBESTI MOUNTAINS
Senegal R.
Niger R.
Lake Chad
Gulf of Aden
Lake Volta
AMHARA PLATEAU
Lake Turkana
EQUATOR
Gulf of Guinea
Congo R.
CONGO BASIN
Lake Victoria
Mount Kenya
GREAT RIFT VALLEY
Kilimanjaro
0°
ATLANTIC OCEAN
N
W—E
S
Lake Tanganyika
INDIAN OCEAN
Lake Malawi
Zambezi R.
MADAGASCAR
NAMIB DESERT
KALAHARI DESERT
Orange R.
Limpopo R.
DRAKENSBERG RANGE
Cape of Good Hope
20°E
60°E

0   1,000 mi.
0   1,000 km
Lambert Azimuthal Equal-Area projection

KEY
Desert
Mediterranean
Rain forest
Savanna

Using Geography Skills

How people live in Africa depends upon where on the continent they make their home.

1. Which type of physical feature covers the largest area of Africa?
2. How might Africa's geography have affected trading patterns there?

Find NGS online map resources @
www.nationalgeographic.com/maps

A Vast and Diverse Continent Africa is the world's second-largest continent. The United States fits into Africa three times, with room to spare. The Equator slices through the middle of the continent. Hot, steamy rain forests stretch along each side of it. Yet the rain forests cover only 10 percent of the land.

Most of Africa lies in the tropics. Here dry, sweeping grasslands reach for thousands of miles. Most of the tropical grasslands, known as savannas, have high temperatures and uneven rains. These wide-open grasslands are perfect for raising herds of animals. For much of Africa's history, the people of the savanna were hunters and herders.

North and south of the savannas are the deserts—the Sahara to the north and the Kalahari to the southwest. For many years, these unmapped seas of sand blocked travel. People had to follow the coastline if they wanted to get past the deserts. Areas of mild climate, good for growing crops, are found along the Mediterranean Sea in northwest Africa and in the south.

The African Plateau Almost all of Africa, except the coastal plains, rests on a **plateau** (pla•TOH)—an area of high flat land. Rivers spill off the plateau in crashing waterfalls and rapids, cutting off inland water routes. Although the Nile River is Africa's longest river, the Congo River winds 2,700 miles (4,345 km) through Africa, near the Equator.

In the east, movements of the earth's crust millions of years ago cracked the continent, and parts of the plateau's surface dropped. This formed the Great Rift Valley, where some of the earliest human fossils have been unearthed. The valley extends through eastern Africa from present-day Mozambique to the Red Sea.

✓ **Reading Check** **Cause and Effect** What caused the Great Rift Valley?

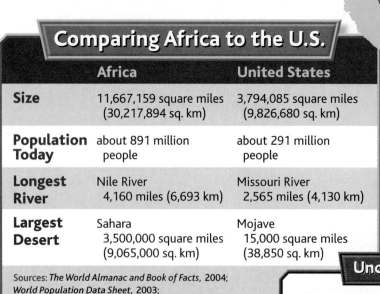

UNITED STATES

AFRICA

Comparing Africa to the U.S.

	Africa	United States
Size	11,667,159 square miles (30,217,894 sq. km)	3,794,085 square miles (9,826,680 sq. km)
Population Today	about 891 million people	about 291 million people
Longest River	Nile River 4,160 miles (6,693 km)	Missouri River 2,565 miles (4,130 km)
Largest Desert	Sahara 3,500,000 square miles (9,065,000 sq. km)	Mojave 15,000 square miles (38,850 sq. km)

Sources: *The World Almanac and Book of Facts,* 2004; *World Population Data Sheet,* 2003; *The New Encyclopaedia Britannica,* 1990

Understanding Charts

Africa has a land area roughly three times that of the United States.
1. How does the size of the Sahara compare to the size of the United States?
2. How does the population of Africa compare to that of the United States?

West African Empires

Main Idea West African empires grew rich from trade.

Reading Focus What would you rather have—a pound of gold or a pound of salt? Both of these goods were important to West Africans and helped them build large trading empires.

Stories of golden lands south of the Sahara seemed hard to believe. There's a country, claimed one story, "where gold grows like plants in the same way as carrots do, and is plucked at sunset."

The Berbers who told the tales had seen the gold with their own eyes. The Berbers, the first known people to settle in North Africa, crossed the Sahara to trade with people in western Africa. They began making the trip about 400 B.C.

For hundreds of years, Berber traders carried goods on horses and donkeys, which often died in the hot Sahara. When the Romans conquered North Africa, they introduced camels from central Asia. Camels, nicknamed "ships of the desert," revolutionized trade. Their broad feet did not sink in the sand, and their humps stored fat for food. In addition, they could travel many days without water.

Traders grouped hundreds, maybe even thousands, of camels together to form caravans. They traded salt and cloth from North Africa and the Sahara for gold and ivory from western Africa. The trade led to the growth of cities in western Africa. Eventually, rulers of these cities began to build a series of empires. During the Middle Ages, these African empires were bigger than most European kingdoms in wealth and size. The first empire to develop was Ghana.

▲ While many of the caravans that crossed the desert going to and from West Africa included about 1,000 camels, some caravans may have had as many as 12,000 camels. *What were some of the items traded by caravans?*

Rise of Ghana Ghana (GAH•nuh) rose to power in the A.D. 400s. It was a "crossroads of trade," a place where trade routes come together. Trade routes reached across the Sahara into North Africa and down the Niger River (NY•juhr) to kingdoms in the rain forest. Some extended all the way to Africa's northeastern coast.

For traders to meet, they had to pass through Ghana. Passage came at a price—a tax paid to Ghana's rulers. These taxes made Ghana rich. Why did traders pay the taxes? First, Ghana knew how to make iron weapons. Like ancient Kush, it used these weapons to conquer its neighbors. Although Ghana owned no gold mines, it controlled the people who did. Second, Ghana built a huge army. "When the king of Ghana calls up his army," said one trader, "he can put 200,000 men in the field."

Third, people wanted the trade items, especially salt and gold, at almost any price. West Africans needed salt to flavor and pre-serve food, and their bodies needed salt to stay healthy. They paid taxes to get salt from Berber mines in the Sahara. In turn, the Berbers paid taxes to get gold to sell at a huge profit in Europe.

Rise of Mali Ghana did not last forever, however. The discovery of new gold mines outside Ghana's control reduced the taxes it collected. In addition, heavy farming robbed the soil of minerals and made it harder to grow enough crops to feed people. Constant fighting also hurt Ghana. Ghana's rulers had accepted the religion of Islam, but they fought with North African Muslims who wanted to build empires of their own.

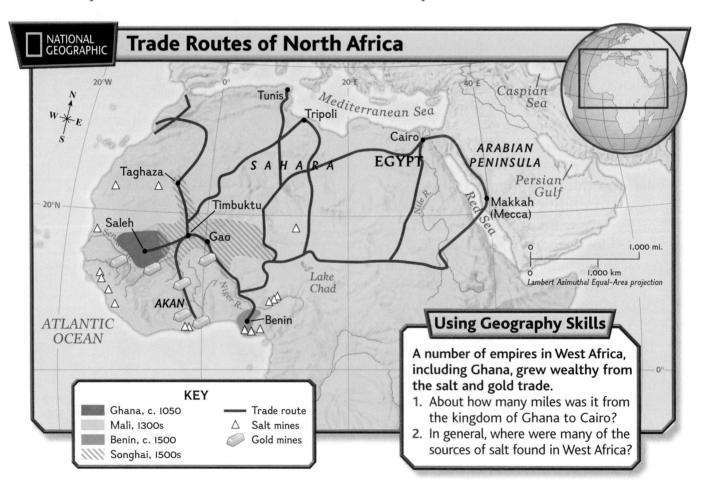

NATIONAL GEOGRAPHIC

Trade Routes of North Africa

KEY

Ghana, c. 1050
Mali, 1300s
Benin, c. 1500
Songhai, 1500s

Trade route
△ Salt mines
Gold mines

Using Geography Skills

A number of empires in West Africa, including Ghana, grew wealthy from the salt and gold trade.
1. About how many miles was it from the kingdom of Ghana to Cairo?
2. In general, where were many of the sources of salt found in West Africa?

After Ghana fell in the 1200s, the king-dom of **Mali** (MAH•lee) replaced it,. West African **griots** (GREE•ohz), or storytellers, give credit to a great warrior-king named **Sundiata Keita** (sun•dee•AH•tuh KY•tuh)—the "Lion Prince." Sundiata, who ruled from 1230 to 1255, seized the capital of Ghana in 1240. He then won control of lands from the Atlantic coast to the trading city of **Timbuktu** (TIHM•BUHK•TOO) and beyond. His conquests put Mali in control of the gold-mining areas, allowing him to rebuild the gold and salt trade.

Rise of Songhai
Mali began a slow decline after the death of its last strong king, **Mansa Musa** (MAHN•sah moo•SAH), in 1332. The kings who followed failed to stop Berber conquerors, who for a time even ruled Timbuktu.

In 1468 **Sunni Ali** (sun•EE ah•LEE), the leader of **Songhai** (SAWNG•HY), stormed into Timbuktu and drove out the Berbers. He then began a campaign of conquest. Sunni Ali used Songhai's location along the Niger River to his advantage. He ordered a fleet of war canoes to seize control of the river trade. His armies then swept west-ward into the Sahara, where they took over Berber salt mines. By the time of his death in 1492, Sunni Ali had built the largest empire in West Africa.

The empire lasted almost 100 more years. In 1591, however, a small army from the Arab kingdom of Morocco crossed the Sahara. Soldiers with cannons, guns, and gunpowder eas-ily cut down Songhai soldiers armed with swords, spears, and bows and arrows. Within months, Songhai's empire was gone.

Reading Check **Analyze** Why did West Africa become the center of three large trade empires?

The Way It Was

Focus on Everyday Life

Africa's Salt Mines Salt mining began in the Sahara in the Middle Ages. Ancient miners worked underground and in sand dunes to extract solid blocks of salt. The salt trade became a successful business for the African people. In ancient times, salt was so desirable that it was traded ounce for ounce for gold.

There are many salt deposits in western Africa because part of the desert was once a shallow sea made up of salt water. When the sea dried up, salt was left behind.

People need a small amount of salt to stay healthy. It is lost when people and animals sweat, so people need some in their food. In ancient times, before refrigerators or canned foods were invented, salt was used to keep foods from going bad. It also was used to add flavor to food.

◀ African salt mine today

Connecting to the Past
1. How do salt deposits form?
2. Why do you think salt was so valuable that it was traded ounce for ounce for gold?

Kingdoms of the Rain Forest

Main Idea Africa's rain forests blocked invaders and provided resources.

Reading Focus What does your state make that people in other places want to buy? Africa's rain forest kingdoms had something the savanna kingdoms wanted. It was not gold or salt, but something just as valuable—food.

Ghana, Mali, and Songhai ruled the wide-open savannas. However, the dense rain forests along the Equator kept them from expanding to the southern coast. People living in the rain forests built their own kingdoms and empires. They included Benin, which arose in the Niger delta, and Kongo, which formed in the Congo River basin.

Griots who live in the Niger delta still tell stories about King Ewuare (eh•WOO•ah•ray), who founded the empire of Benin around 1440. In describing his ancestor's accomplishments, one storyteller boasted:

❝ He fought against and captured 201 towns and villages. . . . He took their . . . rulers captive and caused the people to pay tribute to him. ❞

—J.V. Egharevba,
A Short History of Benin

Farmers in the rain forest kingdoms enjoyed many natural advantages, including farmable soil and a warm, wet climate. In cleared-out areas of the forest, they often produced a surplus, or extra supply, of foods like bananas, yams, or rice.

The Kingdom of Benin

◀ Bronze statue of queen from Benin

Statue of horn player ▶ from Benin

▲ This bronze casting honored the king of Benin. *Around when was the kingdom of Benin founded?*

Food surpluses supported rulers and a class of artisans. Kongo weavers, for example, wove fabrics from bark and plant fibers that looked to Europeans like velvet. In Benin, artists excelled at sculpting and carving metal, wood, and ivory.

Rain forest kingdoms that bordered on the dry savannas traded surplus food and crafts for copper, salt, and leather goods from the savannas. Later, when the Europeans arrived, traders from Benin and Kongo met ships along the coast. They traded, among other things, captives taken in war.

✓ Reading Check **Describe** What advantages did farmers in the rain forests have over farmers in other parts of Africa?

East Africa

Main Idea East African kingdoms and states became centers for trade and new ideas.

Reading Focus Have you ever met someone who used to live somewhere far away? Did their ideas help you to think about the world differently? Read to learn how new ideas arrived along the coast of East Africa.

People today in the East African country of Ethiopia trace their history back to 1005 B.C. In that year, Queen Makeda rose to the throne of a great empire called Saba or Sheba. According to the *Glory of Kings*, Ethiopia's oldest written history, Makeda traveled to meet with King Solomon, ruler

African Trading Empires A.D. 100–1600

	Axum	Ghana	Mali	Songhai	Zimbabwe
Location	East Africa	West Africa	West Africa	West Africa	SE Africa
	AXUM Adulis	GHANA Saleh	MALI Timbuktu	SONGHAI Gao	ZIMBABWE Great Zimbabwe
Time Period	c. 100–1400	c. 400–1200	c. 1200–1450	c. 1000–1600	c. 700–1450
Goods Traded	ivory, frankincense, myrrh, slaves	iron products, animal products, salt, gold	salt, gold	salt, gold	gold, copper, ivory
Key Facts	King Ezana converted to Christianity; made it official religion.	Taxes from traders passing through made Ghana rich.	King Mansa Musa built mosques and libraries.	Songhai gained control of West African trade by conquering Timbuktu and mastering trade by river.	Kings Mutota and Matope built the region's biggest empire.

Understanding Charts

Large trading kingdoms developed in several areas of Africa.
1. Which kingdom developed earliest?
2. Generalize What were some of the common trade items of the West African empires?

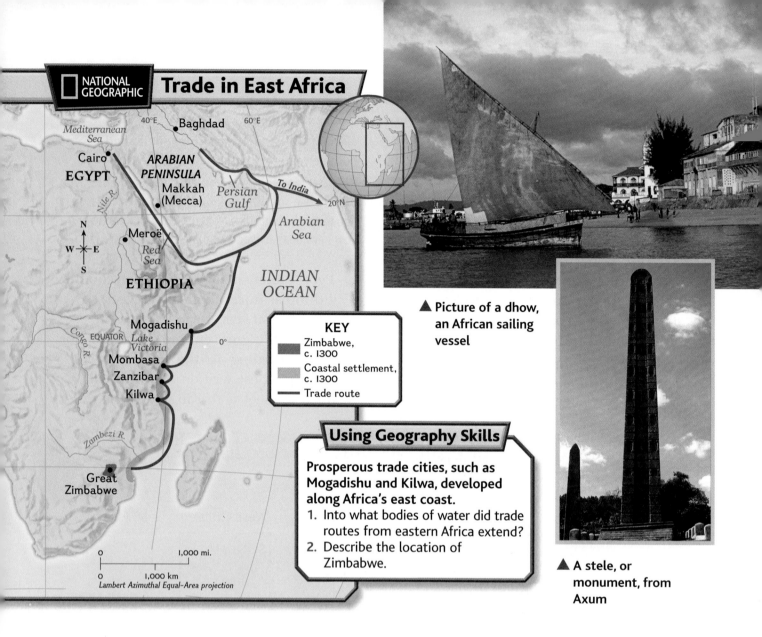

Mediterranean Sea

40°E Baghdad 60°E

Cairo

EGYPT

ARABIAN PENINSULA

Makkah (Mecca)

Persian Gulf

To India

20°N

Arabian Sea

Nile R.

Meroë

Red Sea

ETHIOPIA

INDIAN OCEAN

Congo R.

EQUATOR

Mogadishu

Lake Victoria

0°

Mombasa

Zanzibar

Kilwa

Zambezi R.

Great Zimbabwe

KEY

Zimbabwe, c. 1300

Coastal settlement, c. 1300

Trade route

0   1,000 mi.

0   1,000 km
Lambert Azimuthal Equal-Area projection

▲ Picture of a dhow, an African sailing vessel

Using Geography Skills

Prosperous trade cities, such as Mogadishu and Kilwa, developed along Africa's east coast.
1. Into what bodies of water did trade routes from eastern Africa extend?
2. Describe the location of Zimbabwe.

▲ A stele, or monument, from Axum

of the Israelites. On her return, Makeda introduced ancient Israel's religion to her empire. Over time, eastern Africa would feel the impact of two other religions— Christianity and Islam.

The Rise of Axum Like other empires, Saba declined. However, Ethiopia, known in ancient times as Abyssinia, did not. Its power was centered in a city-state called **Axum** (AHK•SOOM). Axum owed its strength to its location on the Red Sea. Goods from Africa flowed into Axum, which served as a trading center for the ancient Mediterranean and East Asian worlds.

Axum fought neighboring Kush for control of trade routes to inland Africa. Around

A.D. 300, King Ezana of Axum sent his armies against Kush and defeated it. A few years later, Ezana helped to bring a new religion to Africa when he converted to Christianity. In A.D. 334 he made it the official religion of Axum. Within a few hundred years, another religion—Islam— brought many changes to Axum and other trading states along Africa's eastern coast.

Coastal City-States Arab traders from the Arabian Peninsula had been coming to eastern Africa long before the rise of Islam in the early A.D. 600s. They invented a wind-catching, triangular sail that let them sail to Africa. The sails powered sailboats called **dhows** (DOWZ).

In the A.D. 700s, many Arab Muslim traders settled in East African city-states. Here Africans and Arab Muslims shared goods and ideas. By the 1300s, a string of trading ports extended down the East African coast. They included Mogadishu (MAH•guh•DIH•shoo), Kilwa, Mombasa, and Zanzibar. These ports became major links in an Indian Ocean trading network. They traded with places as far away as China.

Great Zimbabwe Another great trading center known as Zimbabwe (zihm•BAH•bway) arose inland in southeastern Africa. Founded around A.D. 700 by the Shona people, Zimbabwe supplied gold, copper, and ivory to the East African coast. From there, African goods were shipped to Arabia, Persia, India, and China.

▲ Some of the walls of Great Zimbabwe still exist. *What trade goods from the interior of Africa passed through Zimbabwe?*

During the 1400s, two kings—Mutota and his son Matope—made Zimbabwe into a large empire. It stretched from south of the Zambezi River to the Indian Ocean. Evidence of Zimbabwe's power can still be seen at Great Zimbabwe, the empire's capital. Here more than 300 huge stone buildings stand—silent reminders of Zimbabwe's past greatness.

✓ **Reading Check** **Explain** How did new technology help East Africa's trade?

History Online

Homework Helper Need help with the material in this section? Visit jat.glencoe.com

Section 1 Review

Reading Summary

Review the Main Ideas

- The continent of Africa has varied landscapes, including rain forests, grasslands, and deserts.

- Beginning in about A.D. 300, a succession of kingdoms, including Ghana, Mali, and Songhai, arose in West Africa.

- Rain forest kingdoms, including Benin and Kongo, traded with the surrounding savanna kingdoms.

- In East Africa, trade with the Arab world helped kingdoms and port cities grow.

What Did You Learn?

1. What items were traded in the kingdoms of West Africa?

Critical Thinking

2. **Organizing Information** Draw a chart like the one below. For each region, write names of the kingdoms and/or city-states that developed there.

West Africa	African Rain Forests	East Africa

3. **Analyze** What city-states grew as trading ports in East Africa, and why were they successful?

4. **Compare and Contrast** Which African kingdoms developed away from the coast? How did their economies compare to other African kingdoms?

5. **Reading** **Compare and Contrast** Create a Venn diagram that shows the similarities and differences of two African kingdoms.

WORLD LITERATURE

SUNDIATA
THE HUNGERING LION

Retold by Kenny Mann

Before You Read

The Scene: This story takes place in Mali on the continent of Africa in the 1100s.

The Characters: Balla Fasseke is the griot who tells the story of Sundiata. Sundiata is the Lion King of Mali. Sogolon and Maghan Kon Fatta are Sundiata's parents. Sassouma is the first wife of Maghan Kon Fatta. Sumanguru is a rival king.

The Plot: The Lion King of Mali, Sundiata, is denied the throne. Sundiata has to prove that he is the rightful king.

Vocabulary Preview

guardian: one who takes care of another person

infirmity: weakness

brewed: prepared by boiling

smiths: metalworkers

multitude: a great number of people

exile: period of time away from one's country

lance: a steel-tipped spear

Have you ever known someone who overcame obstacles to achieve great things? In this story, a young leader must learn to speak and walk in order to take control of his kingdom.

As You Read

Keep in mind that this story is a mixture of fact and legend. However, a king named Sundiata did conquer new lands and expand trade while he ruled the kingdom of Mali.

O people, hear my story! I am Balla Fasseke (bah•lah   fah•SEE•kay) of Mali. I am a *griot.*[1] I am the guardian of the word. In my mind rest the stories of my people and the history of our land. O hear me and remember, for I speak the truth.

Long, long ago, the last king of Ghana fell to the sword of Sumanguru, the Sosso king; Sumanguru, the cruel warrior and mighty sorcerer; Sumanguru, who was to meet his fate at the hands of Sundiata, the Lion King of Mali.

I am Sundiata's *griot.* O hear me, for I speak the truth!

Sundiata was born of Sogolon, who married Maghan Kon Fatta, the ruler of Mali, whose totem[2] was the lion. Sogolon was brought to the king as a maiden, disfigured by a hunchback and ill looks. But she was said to possess the mighty spirit of a buffalo, strong and courageous. Her coming had been foretold to the king, and he took Sogolon as his wife and came to love her.

When Sundiata was born, the king rejoiced. The great royal drums carried the news all over the kingdom. But his first wife, Sassouma, was jealous. Her son should inherit the throne! What need had her husband of another son? She vowed that Sundiata would never become king.

---

[1]**griot:** storyteller
[2]**totem:** animal or plant serving as the symbol of a family or clan

In time, Sassouma saw that she had nothing to fear, for Sundiata was stricken by a strange infirmity. He could neither speak nor walk! How great was Sogolon's sorrow! For seven long years, she tried to cure her son. She consulted with all the wise men of the kingdom and brewed herbs and potions, but to no avail.[3] And Sundiata's father, King Maghan Kon Fatta, despaired. But his *griot,* who was my father, advised the king. "The young seed must endure the storm," he said. "And from this small seed shall spring a great tree."

One day, when the king felt death approach, he called the child to him. "I shall give you the gift each king gives to his heir," he said. And on that day, my people, the king gave me—Balla Fasseke—to Sundiata to be his *griot,* as my father had been the king's *griot,* and his father before that. And on that day, for the first time in his life, Sundiata spoke. "Balla, you shall be my *griot,*" he said. And the king knew that his son—the son of the lion and the buffalo—was worthy to be king.

But when Maghan Kon Fatta died, the councilors ignored his wishes. It was the son of Sassouma who ascended the throne, and not Sundiata, the rightful heir. And Sassouma persecuted Sogolon and her son with evil hatred and banished them to a dark corner of the palace. Oh, how Sogolon's tears flowed in her unhappiness! When Sundiata saw his mother's despair, he looked at her calmly and said, "Today I will walk." Then he sent me, Balla Fasseke, to the royal forges.[4] "Tell the smiths to make me the sturdiest iron rod possible," he ordered.

---

[3]**avail:** benefit
[4]**forges:** furnaces where metal is heated and shaped

Six men were needed to carry the iron rod to Sogolon's house. They threw it on the ground before Sundiata. A huge multitude of people had gathered to see if Sundiata would walk. "Arise, young lion!" I commanded. "Roar, and may the land know that from henceforth, it has a master!"

Sundiata gripped the rod with his two hands and held it upright in the ground. Beads of sweat poured from his face. A deathly silence gripped the people. All at once, with a mighty thrust, Sundiata stood upright. The crowd gasped. The iron rod was bent like a bow. And Sogolon, who had been dumb with amazement, suddenly burst into song:

> Oh day, oh beautiful day,
> Oh day, day of joy,
> Allah Almighty, this is the finest
> day you have created,
> My son is going to walk!
> Hear me, people, for I speak the truth!

Sundiata threw away the rod, and his first steps were those of a giant.

From that day on, Sundiata grew in strength. He became a fine hunter and was much loved by all the people. But Sassouma, whose son was now king, feared Sundiata's growing power. Her plots to kill him failed. And she knew that I would perform any deed to bring Sundiata to the throne. So, to separate us, Sassouma sent me far away to the court of the demon king, Sumanguru. And there I remained for several years. I pretended allegiance to Sumanguru, but always I waited for the day when I would sing the praises of Sundiata once more.

457

Sogolon fled the palace and took Sundiata far from Sassouma's hatred. For seven years they lived in exile, finding food and shelter wherever they could. At last, they came to the city of Mema. Here they met with good luck, for the king of Mema took a liking to Sundiata and treated him like a son. He admired Sundiata's courage and leadership. This king decided to make the young boy his heir and teach him the arts of government and war. And thus, Sundiata grew to manhood.

One day, messengers came running to Sundiata. "Sumanguru has invaded Mali!" they cried. "The king and his mother, Sassouma, have fled. Only you can save our people. Return, young lion, and reclaim your throne!"

This, O people, was the moment of Sundiata's destiny. The king of Mema gave him half his forces. And as Sundiata rode at their head, more and more men joined him until a great army thundered across the plains. And from far-distant Mali, Sumanguru, too, raced to meet his destiny. And I, O my people, I followed, for I knew that soon I would be reunited with Sundiata, my Lion King.

And so it was. Sundiata led his army from Mema, and Sumanguru came from Mali. The two great armies met in battle on the plains of Kirina. I took my chance and escaped at last from Sumanguru. Through the thick clouds of dust and the battle cries of the warriors, I galloped to Sundiata's side. Oh, how great was our joy!

My years with Sumanguru had not been in vain, O my people, for I had learned that Sumanguru feared the magic power of a white rooster. He believed that one touch of the rooster's spur[5] would defeat him forever. And this very spur I had fastened to an arrow, which I gave to my lord, Sundiata.

---

[5]**spur:** a sharp spine on the leg of some birds, especially roosters

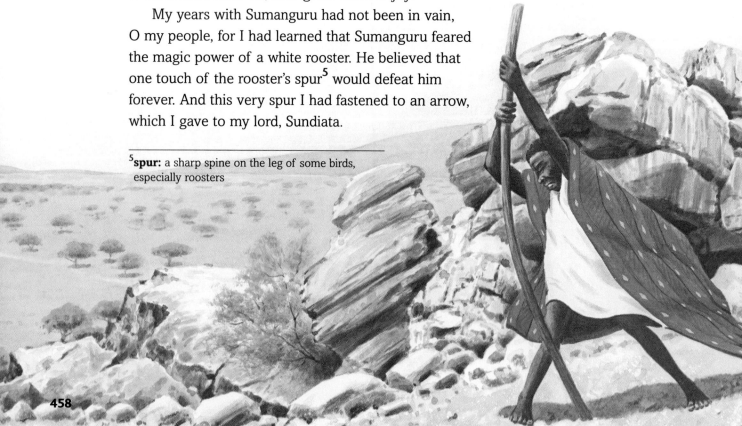

With deadly aim, Sundiata sent the arrow speeding across the battlefield toward Sumanguru. True as a hawk in flight, it met its mark, grazing the sorcerer's shoulder. With a great scream of fear, Sumanguru turned on his horse and fled.

Far away he rode, to the caves of Mount Koulikoro. There we saw Sumanguru, the demon king, fall to his knees and turn to stone. His soldiers, discouraged by his flight, ceased to fight and were defeated.

And so Sundiata returned to Mali to reclaim his throne, and I, Balla Fasseke, went with him to sing of his glory. There waited the twelve kings who had helped Sundiata in exile. Each thrust his lance into the earth before Sundiata. "We shall be united!" they proclaimed. "You have restored peace to our lands. We give you our kingdoms to rule in your great wisdom!" The drums beat out the news. The warriors danced in a joyous frenzy. And the crowd sent a mighty cry to the heavens: "Wassa, Wassa, Ayé!"

And thus did I bear witness to the birth of the great kingdom of Mali. And thus did I see Sundiata become its first emperor.

So listen, O my people, and remember, for I speak the truth. May you live to tell this story to your children, that the name of Sundiata— the Lion King—shall live forever.

Responding to the Reading

1. Why did the king give Sundiata a griot?

2. Foreshadowing is when a storyteller gives you hints of something to come later. This story contains many suggestions that foreshadow Sundiata's successful reign as king. Identify three such hints in the first six paragraphs.

3. **Predict** How might the story be different if Balla Fasseke had not been sent to the court of Sumanguru?

4. **Analyze** Why do you think Sundiata did not walk after receiving his mother's treatments but *did* walk when his half-brother was made king?

5. **Reading** **Read to Write** Suppose you are Sundiata's father. Write a brief speech stating your reasons for choosing Sundiata to be the next king.

Section 2

Africa's Government and Religion

Get Ready to Read!

What's the Connection?

In Section 1, you read about some of the kingdoms and empires that developed in Africa. To hold their kingdoms and empires together, Africans had to create their own governments. One unifying force was the religion of Islam, but many Africans continued to practice their traditional religious beliefs as well.

Focusing on the Main Ideas

- The growth of West African empires led to the growth of centralized governments ruled by kings. *(page 461)*

- Traditional African religions shared certain beliefs and provided a guide for living together. *(page 463)*

- Islam played an important role in medieval Africa, but long-held African beliefs and customs still remained strong. *(page 464)*

Locating Places
Makkah (MAH•kuh)

Meeting People
Olaudah Equiano (oh•LOW•duh EHK•wee•AHN•oh)
Ibn Battuta (IH•buhn bat•TOO•tah)
Askia Muhammad (ahs•KEE•uh moh•HAH•muhd)

Building Your Vocabulary
clan (KLAN)
sultan (SUHL•tuhn)
Swahili (swah•HEE•lee)

Reading Strategy
Organizing Information Use a diagram to show the components of Swahili culture and language.

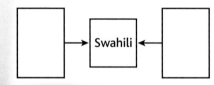

NATIONAL GEOGRAPHIC **When & Where?**

1300	1400	1500
1324 Mansa Musa travels to Makkah	**1352** Ibn Battuta arrives in West Africa	**1492** Sunni Ali dies

Timbuktu
Mogadishu

Government and Society

Main Idea The growth of West African empires led to the growth of centralized governments ruled by kings.

Reading Focus What makes a system of government effective? Read to learn how African rulers governed their empires.

The loud thumping of drums called the citizens of Ghana to a meeting with the king. Anybody with a complaint could speak. In the royal courtyard, the king sat in an open silk tent. He wore a cap of gold and a jewel-covered robe. Royal officials surrounded him. Guard dogs with gold and silver collars stood watch. Before talking to the king, subjects poured dust over their heads or fell to the ground. Bowing, they stated their business and waited for the king's reply.

Ruler and Subject This, said Arab travelers, was how government worked in West Africa. Kings settled arguments, managed trade, and protected the empire. But they expected complete obedience in return.

With the growth of empires, Africans invented new ways to govern themselves. The most successful states, like Ghana, formed some type of central authority. Power usually rested with a king—or, in a few cases, a queen.

Both rulers and people benefited. Merchants received favors from the kings, and the kings received taxes from the merchants. Local rulers kept some power, and the kings in turn received their loyalty. This allowed kingdoms to grow richer and to extend their control over a larger area. The system also helped keep the peace.

Ghana's Government The kings of Ghana relied on help from a council of ministers, or group of close advisers. As the empire

▼ The carving below shows a king of Benin on his throne. The ivory armband (lower left) was worn by the king during ceremonies. *Why did African kings allow local rulers to keep some power?*

grew, rulers divided it into provinces. Lesser kings, often conquered leaders, governed each of these areas. Beneath them, district chiefs oversaw smaller districts. Each district usually included a chief's **clan** (KLAN)—a group of people descended from the same ancestor.

Kings held tightly to their power. They insisted that local rulers send their sons to the royal court. They rode through the countryside seeking reports of injustice or rebellion. Most important, they controlled trade.

Nobody could trade without the king's permission. Also, nobody could own gold nuggets except the king. People traded only in gold dust. "If kings did otherwise," said one Arab traveler, "gold would become so abundant as practically to lose its value."

Ghana Profits From Trade

Al Bekri described the way Ghana taxed merchants to increase its own wealth.

"The king [of Ghana] exacts the right of one *dinar* of gold on each donkey-load of salt that enters his country, and two *dinars* of gold on each load of salt that goes out. A load of copper carries a duty of five *mitqals* and a load of merchandise ten *mitqals*. The best gold in the country comes from Ghiaru, a town situated eighteen days' journey from the capital [Kumbi]."

— Abdullah Abu-Ubayd al Bekri, "Ghana in 1067"

▲ Ghana's wealth came from trade caravans.

DBQ Document-Based Question

Which do you think has more worth, a dinar or a mitqal? Why?

One thing about Ghana's government, however, confused outsiders. "It is their custom," exclaimed an Arab writer, "that the kingdom is inherited only by the son of the king's sister." In Arab states, property passed through a man's sons, not the sons of his sister. In Ghana, the throne went to the king's nephew.

Mali's Government

Mali followed the example of Ghana, but on a larger scale. It had more territory, more people, and more trade, so royal officials had more responsibilites. One supervised fishing on the Niger. Another looked after the empire's forests. A third oversaw farming, and a fourth managed money.

Kings divided the empire into provinces, like Ghana. However, Sundiata, the founder of Mali, put his generals in charge of them. People accepted it because the generals protected them from invaders. Also, the generals often came from the provinces they ruled.

Mali's other great king, Mansa Musa, rewarded citizens with gold, land, and horses to keep them loyal. He granted military heroes the "National Honor of the Trousers." As one Arab said:

> 66 Whenever a hero adds to the lists of his exploits, the king gives him a pair of wide trousers. . . . [T]he greater the number of the knight's [soldier's] exploits, the bigger the size of his trousers. 99
>
> —Al-Dukhari, as quoted in *Topics in West African History*

Because only the king and royal family could wear sewn clothes, this was a big honor indeed. Most people wore only wrapped clothes.

Songhai's Government

Songhai built on the traditions of Ghana and Mali. Its founder, Sunni Ali, divided his empire into provinces. However, he never finished setting up his empire. Sunni continually moved, fighting one battle or another.

In 1492 Sunni Ali died mysteriously on a return trip home. Some say he drowned while crossing a stream. Others say his enemies killed him. The next year, a Songhai general named Muhammad Ture seized control of the government. Unlike Sunni Ali, Muhammad Ture was a loyal Muslim. His religious ideas affected Songhai's government.

✓ Reading Check **Contrast** How was Mali ruled differently from Ghana?

Traditional African Religions

Main Idea Traditional African religions shared certain beliefs and provided a guide for living together.

Reading Focus What questions do most religions try to answer? As you read this section, look for questions answered by traditional African religions.

For centuries, Europeans believed Africans did not have a religion. **Olaudah Equiano** (oh•LOW•duh EHK•wee•AHN•oh), a member of the Igbo, disagreed. The Igbo, he wrote, "believe that there is one Creator of all things, and that he . . . governs events, especially our deaths and captivity."

Most African groups shared the Igbo belief in one supreme god. They understood the Christian and Muslim idea of a single god, but many wanted to continue their own religious practices.

These practices varied from place to place. Some groups, like the Nanti in East Africa, thought people could talk directly with their god. Others, like the Igbo, thought their creator could only be spoken to through less powerful gods and goddesses who worked for him.

Even though Africans practiced their religion differently in different places, their beliefs served similar purposes. They provided rules for living and helped people stay in touch with their history.

When relatives died, many Africans believed their spirits stayed with the community. They believed these spirits could talk to the supreme god or help solve problems. As a result, many Africans honored their ancestors.

Reading Check **Explain** What was the role of ancestors in African religion?

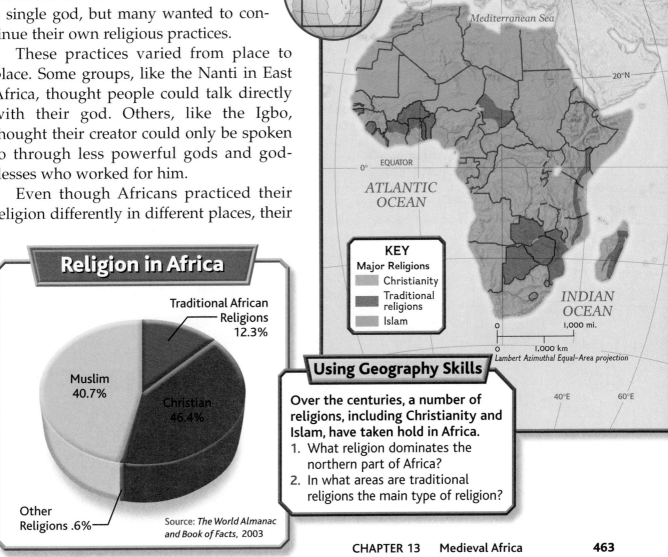

Religion in Africa

Traditional African Religions 12.3%

Muslim 40.7%

Christian 46.4%

Other Religions .6%

Source: *The World Almanac and Book of Facts*, 2003

NATIONAL GEOGRAPHIC
African Religions Today

Mediterranean Sea

ATLANTIC OCEAN

EQUATOR

INDIAN OCEAN

KEY
Major Religions
- Christianity
- Traditional religions
- Islam

0 1,000 mi.
0 1,000 km
Lambert Azimuthal Equal-Area projection

Using Geography Skills

Over the centuries, a number of religions, including Christianity and Islam, have taken hold in Africa.
1. What religion dominates the northern part of Africa?
2. In what areas are traditional religions the main type of religion?

Islam in Africa

Main Idea Islam played an important role in medieval Africa, but long-held African beliefs and customs still remained strong.

Reading Focus Have you ever changed your ideas because someone you respect has different ideas than you do? Learn how African rulers helped spread Islam and how Arabs and Africans influenced each other.

Ibn Battuta (IH•buhn bat•TOO•tah), a young Arab lawyer from Morocco, set out in 1325 to see the Muslim world. Since the A.D. 600s, the religion of Islam had spread from the Arabian Peninsula to Africa and elsewhere.

Ibn Battuta traveled throughout the lands of Islam for almost 30 years. He covered a distance of more than 73,000 miles (117,482 km). When Ibn Battuta arrived in West Africa in 1352, Islam had been practiced there for hundreds of years. Yet he soon realized that not all people in West Africa accepted Islam. Many people in the countryside still followed traditional African religions. Islam was popular in the cities where rulers and traders accepted it by choice or because it helped them trade with Muslim Arabs.

Some Muslims complained that Sundiata Keita and Sunni Ali—western Africa's two great empire builders—did not do enough to win people over to Islam. The two leaders were more concerned about stopping rebellions than spreading religion.

Ibn Battuta found things in West Africa that surprised him. He was amazed that women did not cover their faces with a veil,

The City of Djenne

Like Timbuktu, the city of Djenne became a center for both trade and Islam. Traders from the deserts to the north and the rain forests to the south met at Djenne, located on the Bani River. The first Great Mosque at Djenne was probably built in the 1200s.
Did all of the people in West Africa accept Islam? Explain.

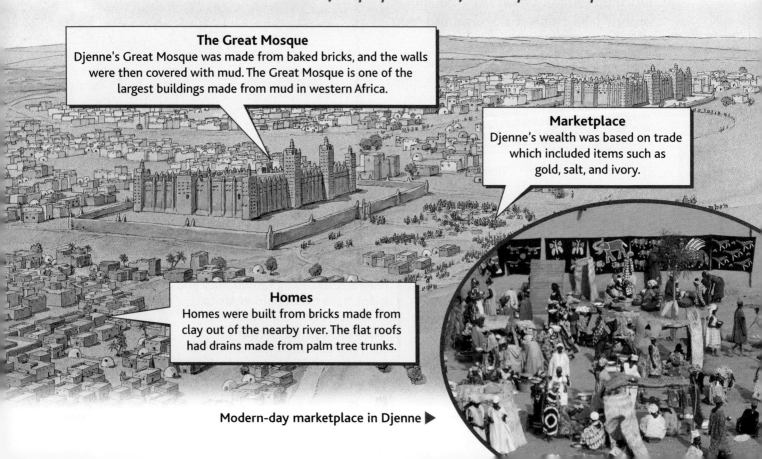

The Great Mosque
Djenne's Great Mosque was made from baked bricks, and the walls were then covered with mud. The Great Mosque is one of the largest buildings made from mud in western Africa.

Marketplace
Djenne's wealth was based on trade which included items such as gold, salt, and ivory.

Homes
Homes were built from bricks made from clay out of the nearby river. The flat roofs had drains made from palm tree trunks.

Modern-day marketplace in Djenne ▶

as was the Muslim custom. However, he did find that West Africans studied the Quran, the Muslim holy book. "They zealously [eagerly] learn the Quran by heart," he wrote.

Mali and Mansa Musa Much of what pleased Ibn Battuta was the work of Mansa Musa. Mansa Musa had allowed different religions but had worked to make Islam stronger. He used the wealth of Mali to build more mosques, or Muslim places of worship. He also set up libraries at Timbuktu, which collected books from all over the Muslim world.

In 1324 Mansa Musa made Mali known to other parts of the world when he set out on a long journey to the city of **Makkah** (MAH•kuh), also known as Mecca. As you read in the chapter on Islam, all Muslims are supposed to make a pilgrimage to the Muslim holy city of Makkah. When Mansa Musa set out on his trip, however, he made sure everybody knew he was the leader of a great empire.

Mansa Musa's caravan had thousands of people, including enslaved people, and 100 pack camels. Each camel carried gold. While in Makkah, Mansa Musa convinced some of Islam's finest architects, teachers, and writers to return with him to Mali. There they helped spread Islam in West Africa.

Songhai and Askia Muhammad Sunni Ali practiced the traditional religion of the Songhai people. However, he declared himself a Muslim to keep the support of townspeople. After Sunni Ali died, his son refused to follow his father's example.

As you read earlier, Muhammad Ture, one of Sunni Ali's generals, saw a chance to take over the government. With the support of Muslim townspeople, he declared himself king. In a bloody war, he drove Sunni Ali's family from Songhai. He then took the name Askia, a rank in the Songhai army.

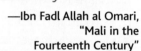 The Sultan of Mali

The sultan in this passage is Mansa Musa. He is described by an Arab scholar named Ibn Fadl Allah al Omari.

▲ Mansa Musa

"The sultan of this kingdom presides in his palace on a great balcony called *bembe* where he has a great seat of ebony that is like a throne fit for a large and tall person: on either side it is flanked by elephant tusks turned towards each other. His arms [weapons] stand near him, being all of gold, saber, lance, quiver, bow and arrows. He wears wide trousers made of about twenty pieces [of stuff] of a kind which he alone may wear."

—Ibn Fadl Allah al Omari, "Mali in the Fourteenth Century"

DBQ Document-Based Questions

What impression did Mansa Musa want to make on newcomers to his kingdom? How do you know?

Under **Askia Muhammad** (ahs•KEE•uh moh•HAH•muhd), Songhai built the largest empire in medieval West Africa. He kept local courts in place but told them to honor Muslim laws. He also made Timbuktu an important center of Islamic culture and set up some 150 schools to teach the Quran.

Web Activity Visit jat.glencoe.com and click on *Chapter 13—Student Web Activity* to learn more about medieval Africa.

Biography

MANSA MUSA
Ruled 1312–1337

Mansa Musa ruled the West African empire of Mali with great skill and organization. Under Mansa Musa's guidance, Mali became a great center of education, commerce, and the arts. Mali was one of the largest empires in the world at the time. In fact, the kingdom was so vast that Mansa Musa once bragged it would take a year to travel from the northern border to the southern border.

Despite Mali's enormous size and wealth, the kingdom was not well-known outside the continent of Africa. Mansa Musa's pilgrimage to Makkah in 1324, however, announced Mali's riches and achievements to the world. Traveling on horseback, Mansa Musa was joined by many people, including 8,000 enslaved people, 100 camels to carry baggage, and 24,000 pounds of gold. Each person carried a staff of gold. According to Egyptian historians and the accounts of observers, Mansa Musa spent so much gold in Cairo, Egypt, that the value of gold dropped in Cairo and did not recover for more than 12 years.

Mansa Musa's famous pilgrimage to Makkah brought attention to his kingdom. Mali was included on world maps as early as 1339. Many European nations and kingdoms in North Africa and the Middle East wished to establish trade connections with Mali and gain some of its wealth. Mali's territory and trade connections expanded even further with the capture of the cities Gao and Timbuktu, which also flourished under Mansa Musa's rule.

▲ Mansa Musa

▲ A village in Mali today

Then and Now

Mali was unnoticed by the rest of the world until Mansa Musa's pilgrimage. Is it possible for a present-day country to go unnoticed? Why or why not?

The empire survived family disputes. But, as you have read, it did not survive the guns of Moroccan invaders. The invasion in 1591 shattered the empire.

Islam in East Africa In 1331 Ibn Battuta visited Mogadishu, a trading port on the East African coast. Its **sultan** (SUHL•tuhn), or leader, said in perfect Arabic, "You have honored our country by coming." A moment later, Ibn Battuta heard the sultan speak in **Swahili** (swah•HEE•lee).

The word *Swahili* comes from an Arabic word meaning "people of the coast." By 1331, however, it had come to mean two things: the unique culture of East Africa's coast and the language spoken there.

The Swahili culture and language, which exist in East Africa today, blended African and Muslim influences. African influences came from the cultures of Africa's interior. Muslim influences came from Arab and Persian settlers.

When Europeans from Portugal arrived on the coast in the early 1500s, they tried to destroy the Swahili culture. The Swahili responded by halting inland trade. In the end, the Swahili culture outlived European rule.

Islam's Impact on Africa Islam had a far-reaching impact on northern and eastern Africa. Africans who accepted Islam also adopted Islamic laws and ideas about right and wrong. Sometimes these changes were opposed by people who favored traditional African ways.

Islam also advanced learning. Muslim schools drew students from many parts of Africa and introduced the Arabic language to many Africans. Islam also influenced African art and buildings. Muslim architects built beautiful mosques and palaces in Timbuktu and other cities.

✓ **Reading Check** **Explain** How did Askia Muhammad gain control of Songhai?

History Online
Homework Helper Need help with the material in this section? Visit jat.glencoe.com

Section 2 Review

Reading Summary

Review the Main Ideas

- The empires of West Africa were ruled by kings, who closely controlled trade and divided their lands among lesser chiefs to aid in governing.

- Many African religions believed in a single creator and honored the spirits of ancestors.

- Islam became the dominant religion in the kingdoms of West and East Africa.

What Did You Learn?

1. How did the kings of Ghana hold tightly to their power?

2. How did Mansa Musa attempt to strengthen Islam in Mali?

Critical Thinking

3. **Cause and Effect** Draw a diagram to show the effects of Islam on West and East Africa.

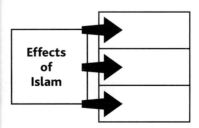

4. **Analyze** How did having the central authority rest with a single person benefit the king, individuals, and the kingdom? How is this model of a government reflected in modern government?

5. **Expository Writing** Imagine you were a witness to Mansa Musa's pilgrimage to Makkah. Write a newspaper article describing the pilgrimage.

6. **Reading** Compare and Contrast Draw a Venn diagram to compare the leadership of Mansa Musa and Askia Muhammad.

African Society and Culture

Get Ready to Read!

What's the Connection?

By the time Europeans came to Africa, people all over the continent had developed complex cultures. For most Africans, life centered on farming villages, like the ones you will read about in this section. Here the family formed the basis of society.

Focusing on the Main Ideas

• The Bantu migrations helped shape many cultures in Africa south of the Sahara. *(page 469)*

• The African slave trade changed greatly when Muslims and Europeans began taking captives from the continent. *(page 472)*

• Enslaved Africans developed rich cultures that influenced many other cultures, including our own. *(page 474)*

Locating Places
Benue River (BAYN•way)

Meeting People
Dahia al-Kahina
  (dah•HEE•ah ahl•kah•HEE•nah)
Nzinga (ehn•ZIHN•gah)

Building Your Vocabulary
extended family
matrilineal (MA•truh•LIH•nee•uhl)
oral history

Reading Strategy
Compare and Contrast Create a Venn diagram like the one below showing the similarities and differences between the enslavement of Africans in Africa and the enslavement of Africans in Europe.

Enslavement in Africa ⃝⃝ Enslavement in Europe

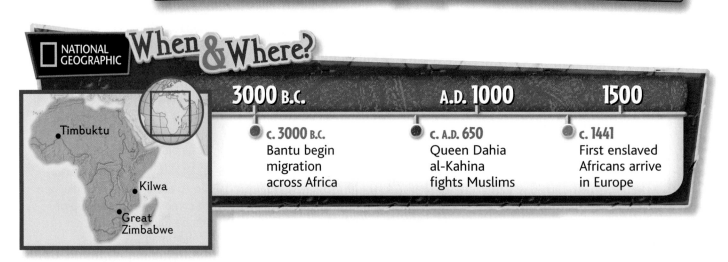

When & Where?

3000 B.C.	A.D. 1000	1500
c. 3000 B.C. Bantu begin migration across Africa	c. A.D. 650 Queen Dahia al-Kahina fights Muslims	c. 1441 First enslaved Africans arrive in Europe

Timbuktu
Kilwa
Great Zimbabwe

Life in Medieval Africa

Main Idea The Bantu migrations helped shape many cultures in Africa south of the Sahara.

Reading Focus Have you ever noticed that even though people are different, they all have some things in common? Read to learn why people in different regions of Africa have similar traditions and cultures.

Around 3000 B.C., fishing groups along the **Benue River** (BAYN•way) in present-day eastern Nigeria packed belongings in their canoes and moved south. The wanderers called themselves *Bantu,* meaning "the people."

The Bantu traveled slowly and by different routes. At least some paddled down the Congo River—a waterway twisting 2,700 miles (4,345 km) through the rain forests. Many settled, for a time, in the grasslands of central Africa. From there, they fanned out over much of the land south of the Sahara. By A.D. 400, Bantu peoples had settled most of Africa.

Historians are not sure why the Bantu left their homeland. Perhaps the land became too crowded. Maybe farmers wore out the soil. Or the Bantu may have just drifted, the way pioneers sometimes do.

Wherever they went, the Bantu took their culture with them. They spread skills such as pottery making, mining, and ironworking. They also spread their language. Today more than 120 million Africans speak hundreds of Bantu languages, including Swahili.

The Bantu migrations, or movements of a large number of people, are the reason people all across Africa share some common ideas and traditions. The Bantu, for example, believed in one supreme creator and a spirit world where ancestors live. As you read in the last section, this was a common belief in many places in Africa.

Importance of Family The family formed the basis of African society. People often lived in **extended families,** or families made up of several generations. They included anywhere from ten to hundreds of members.

Many villages, especially Bantu villages, were **matrilineal** (MA•truh•LIH•nee•uhl). They traced their descent through mothers rather than fathers. When a woman married, however, she joined her husband's family. To make up for the loss, her family received gifts—cloth, metal tools, cattle, or goats—from the husband's family.

All families valued children greatly. They saw them as a link between the past and the future. Some people, like the Yoruba of what is today Nigeria, believed

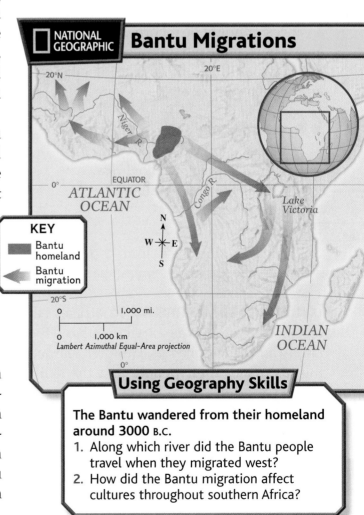

NATIONAL GEOGRAPHIC Bantu Migrations

KEY
- Bantu homeland
- Bantu migration

Using Geography Skills

The Bantu wandered from their homeland around 3000 B.C.
1. Along which river did the Bantu people travel when they migrated west?
2. How did the Bantu migration affect cultures throughout southern Africa?

▲ **This panel shows a family from the Congo at work.**
What was an extended family in Bantu society?

an ancestor might be reborn in a child. They also knew children guaranteed that the family would live on. In praising children, one Yoruba poet wrote:

66 A child is like a rare bird.
A child is precious like coral.
A child is precious like brass.
You cannot buy a child on
the market.

. . . .

One's child is one's child. 99

—Yoruba, "Praise of a Child"

Education and Community
In Africa's villages, education was carried out by the family and other villagers. Children learned the history of their people and the skills needed as adults.

In West Africa, griots, or storytellers, helped in schooling. They kept alive an **oral history**—the stories passed down from generation to generation. Many stories included a lesson about living. Lessons also were given through short proverbs.

One Bantu proverb stated: "A good deed will make a good neighbor." Grandparents and other older people also kept oral histories alive.

Role of Women
As in most medieval societies, women in Africa acted mostly as wives and mothers. Men had more rights and controlled much of what women did. Visitors to Africa, however, saw exceptions. European explorers were amazed to learn that women served as soldiers in some African kingdoms.

African women also won fame as rulers. In the A.D. 600s, Queen **Dahia al-Kahina** (dah•HEE•uh ahl•kah•HEE•nah) led the fight against the Muslim invasion of her kingdom, which was located about where Mauritania is today. Another woman ruler was Queen **Nzinga** (ehn•ZIHN•gah), who ruled lands in what are now Angola and Congo. She spent almost 40 years battling Portuguese slave traders.

✓ Reading Check **Explain** How were Bantu families organized?

Biography

QUEEN NZINGA
c. 1582–1663

Angolan Warrior-Leader

It was rare in the 1600s for women to take active roles in politics and war, but one African woman—Queen Nzinga of Matamba—was known for her military leadership and political skills. Nzinga was the daughter of the king of the Ndongo people. The Ndongo lived in southwest Africa in what is today called Angola. Nzinga quickly learned archery and hunting. She was intelligent and a natural athlete. Nzinga's father failed to notice his daughter. He was too busy defending the kingdom from the Portuguese, who wanted to buy enslaved Africans and ship them overseas.

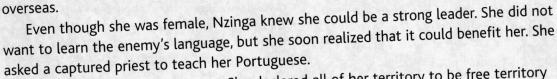

▲ Enslaved Africans in a ship's hold being taken to America.

Even though she was female, Nzinga knew she could be a strong leader. She did not want to learn the enemy's language, but she soon realized that it could benefit her. She asked a captured priest to teach her Portuguese.

In 1623 Nzinga became queen. She declared all of her territory to be free territory and promised that all enslaved Africans who made it to the kingdom would be free. For nearly 30 years, she led her people in battles against the Portuguese. She allied with other African kingdoms to seal the trade routes used to ship enslaved Africans out of the country. In 1662 she negotiated a peace agreement with the Portuguese. She died the next year at age 81.

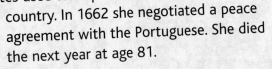

◀ The Portuguese built Elmire Castle on the coast of Ghana to hold enslaved Africans before shipping them overseas.

Then and Now

Do research to find the name of a modern female leader. Compare her leadership skills to those of Queen Nzinga.

Slavery

Reading Focus You know that there was a time in American history when people of African ancestry were enslaved. Read to learn about slavery in African society and the beginning of the European slave trade.

In 1441 a Portuguese sea captain sailed down Africa's western coast. His goal was to bring the first African captives back to Portugal. During the voyage, the captain and his nine sailors seized 12 Africans—men, women, and boys. The ship then sailed back to Portugal. These captives represented only a small portion of a slave trade that would grow into the millions.

Slavery Within Africa

Europeans did not invent slavery. For a long time, it had existed throughout the world. In Africa, Bantu chiefs raided nearby villages for captives. These captives became laborers or were freed for a payment.

Africans also enslaved criminals or enemies taken in war. These enslaved Africans became part of the Saharan trade. However, as long as Africans stayed in Africa, hope of escape still existed. Enslaved Africans might also win their freedom through hard work or by marrying a free person.

The trade in humans also grew as the trade with Muslim merchants increased. The Quran forbade enslavement of Muslims. Muslims, however, could enslave non-Muslims. Arab traders, therefore, began to trade horses, cotton, and other goods for enslaved, non-Muslim Africans.

When Europeans arrived in West Africa, a new market for enslaved Africans opened. Africans armed with European guns began raiding villages to seize captives to sell.

▲ On a slave ship, enslaved people were transported in the dark, crowded spaces of the ship's cargo deck. *Why were enslaved Africans used on Portuguese plantations?*

The European Slave Trade

In 1444 a Portuguese ship docked at a port in Portugal. Sailors unloaded the cargo—235 enslaved Africans. Tears ran down the faces of some. Others cried for help. A Portuguese official described the scene:

66 **But to increase their sufferings still more, . . . was it needful to part fathers from sons, husbands from wives, brothers from brothers.** 99

—Gomes Eannes de Zurara, as quoted in *The Slave Trade*

Barely three years had passed since the arrival of the first African captives in Portugal. Some merchants who had hoped to sell gold brought from Africa now sold humans instead. At first, most enslaved Africans stayed in Portugal, working as laborers. This changed when the Portuguese settled the Atlantic islands of Madeira, the Azores, and Cape Verde. There the climate was perfect for growing cotton, grapes, and sugarcane on plantations, or huge farms.

Harvesting sugarcane was hard labor. Planters could not pay high wages to get workers, so they used enslaved Africans instead. Many Africans had farming skills and the ability to make tools. Enslaved people were not paid and could be fed and kept cheaply. By 1500, Portugal was the world's leading supplier of sugar.

The rest of Europe followed Portugal's example. In the late 1400s, Europeans arrived in the Americas. They set up sugar plantations and brought enslaved Africans across the Atlantic Ocean to work the fields. They also used enslaved people to grow tobacco, rice, and cotton.

✓ **Reading Check** **Analyze** How did exploration change the African slave trade?

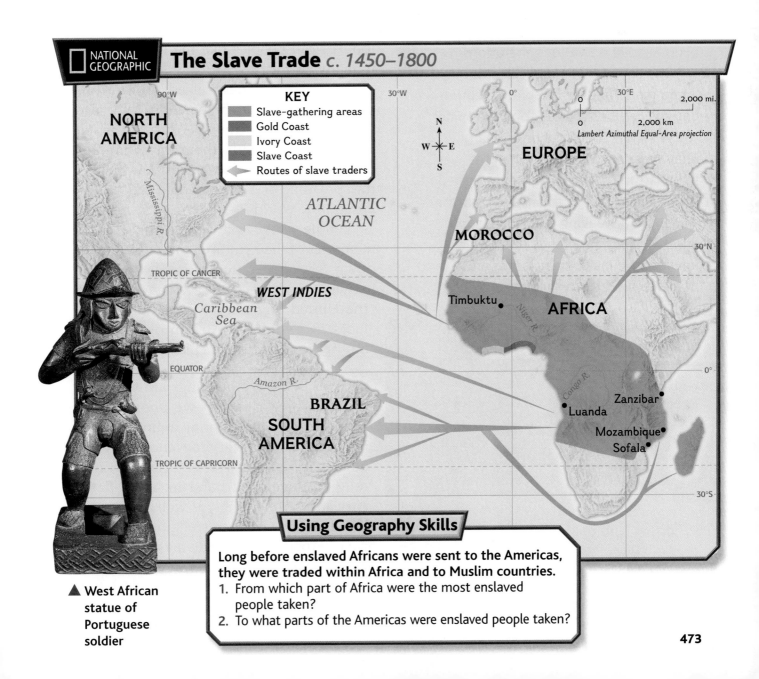

NATIONAL GEOGRAPHIC — The Slave Trade c. 1450–1800

KEY
- Slave-gathering areas
- Gold Coast
- Ivory Coast
- Slave Coast
- → Routes of slave traders

2,000 mi.
2,000 km
Lambert Azimuthal Equal-Area projection

NORTH AMERICA

ATLANTIC OCEAN

TROPIC OF CANCER

WEST INDIES

Caribbean Sea

EQUATOR

Amazon R.

BRAZIL
SOUTH AMERICA

TROPIC OF CAPRICORN

Mississippi R.

EUROPE

MOROCCO

30°N

Timbuktu

Niger R.

AFRICA

Congo R.

Luanda

Zanzibar

Mozambique

Sofala

0°

30°S

90°W   30°W   0°   30°E

▲ West African statue of Portuguese soldier

Using Geography Skills

Long before enslaved Africans were sent to the Americas, they were traded within Africa and to Muslim countries.
1. From which part of Africa were the most enslaved people taken?
2. To what parts of the Americas were enslaved people taken?

473

The Way It Was

Focus on Everyday Life

***Kente* Cloth** *Kente* is the name of a colorful woven cloth. Its name comes from a word that means "basket." The first weavers were mostly men. They used fibers to make cloth that looked like the patterns in baskets. Strips were sewn together to make colorful patterns. *Kente* was worn by tribal chiefs and is still popular today. This African folktale about *kente* cloth has been handed down for generations:

One day two friends walked through a rain forest and saw a spider creating designs in its web. They took the spider web to show their friends and family. They were greatly upset when the web fell apart in their hands. They returned the next day to watch and learn as the spider did a weaving dance and spun another web. The friends took their newfound skills to their looms and made colorful cloth they called *kente*.

African women ▶ wearing *kente* cloth

Connecting to the Past
1. Why does the legend suggest that Africans learned to weave *kente* cloth from a spider?
2. Why do you think the first *kente* cloth weavers were mostly men?

African Culture

Main Idea Enslaved Africans developed rich cultures that influenced many other cultures, including our own.

Reading Focus Do you have any traditions that have been in your family for a long time? Read to learn how Africans took their culture with them when they were enslaved and sent overseas.

"We are almost a nation of dancers, musicians, and poets," declared Olaudah Equiano in describing the Igbo people of West Africa. He might have added artists, weavers, woodcarvers, and metalworkers too. African peoples like the Igbo excelled in many art forms.

When slave traders seized Africans like Equiano from their homelands, they also uprooted their cultures. Africans carried these cultures with them in what has become known as the African Diaspora—the spreading of African people and culture around the world.

People of African descent held on to memories of their cultures and passed them down from generation to generation. The heritage of Africa can be seen and heard in the United States today—not just in the faces and voices of African descendants but in their gifts to our culture.

African Art Cave paintings are the earliest form of African art we know about. They show people hunting animals, dancing, and doing everyday chores. As in other parts of the world, African art and religion developed hand in hand. Early African cave paintings, as well as later art, almost always had some religious meaning or use. Woodcarvers made masks and statues, for example, to celebrate African religious beliefs. Each carved piece of wood captured some part of the spiritual world.

African works of art also told stories and served practical purposes. Artists working in wood, ivory, or bronze showed the faces of important leaders, everyday people, and, later, European explorers and traders. Weavers designed cloth similar to cloth still worn today. You may have seen the brightly colored kente cloth of West Africa. Many people wear it today.

Music and Dance Music played a part in almost all aspects of African life. People used it to express their religious feelings or to get through an everyday task, like planting a field.

In many African songs, a singer calls out a line, then other singers repeat it back. Musical instruments, such as drums, whistles, horns, flutes, or banjos, were used to keep the beat.

Africans believed dance allowed the spirits to express themselves. So they used it to celebrate important events such as birth and death. Nearly everybody danced. Lines of men and women swayed and clapped their hands. Individual dancers

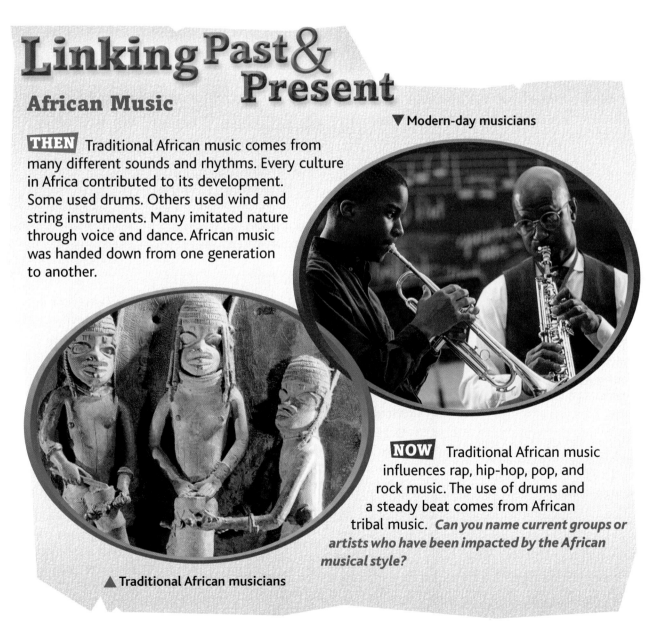

Linking Past & Present

African Music

THEN Traditional African music comes from many different sounds and rhythms. Every culture in Africa contributed to its development. Some used drums. Others used wind and string instruments. Many imitated nature through voice and dance. African music was handed down from one generation to another.

▼ Modern-day musicians

NOW Traditional African music influences rap, hip-hop, pop, and rock music. The use of drums and a steady beat comes from African tribal music. *Can you name current groups or artists who have been impacted by the African musical style?*

▲ Traditional African musicians

◀ Griots still share the stories and lessons of their ancestors. **What were traditional African stories often about?**

leaped and twirled. In the background, drummers sounded out the rhythm.

Enslaved Africans some times relied on music to remind them of their homeland. Songs of hardship eventually developed into a type of music that we know today as the blues. Songs of religious faith and hopes for freedom grew into spirituals or gospel songs. Over time, other forms of African-based music developed, such as ragtime, jazz, rock and roll, and, more recently, rap.

Storytelling Africans also kept alive their storytelling tradition. A few enslaved Africans escaped and were able to record their stories. Others retold their stories aloud. Those who heard the stories repeated them. They also retold tales taught by griots in the African homeland. Popular stories often told how small animals, such as turtles and rabbits, outsmarted larger ones.

In more recent times, some African Americans have renewed ties with their past by taking African names or giving them to their children. This also helps keep alive African history and culture.

✓ **Reading Check** **Explain** Why did Africans use dance to celebrate important events?

History Online

Homework Helper Need help with the material in this section? Visit jat.glencoe.com

Section 3 Review

Reading Summary

Review the Main Ideas

• Many Africans south of the Sahara lived in small villages. Family was very important, and women had fewer rights than men.

• Africans had kept slaves long before they began to trade enslaved persons to Muslims and Europeans.

• As enslaved Africans were taken to new areas, African culture, including art, music, and story-telling, spread around the world.

What Did You Learn?

1. What was the African Diaspora?

2. What is the earliest form of African art known? Describe some of the subjects portrayed in the art.

Critical Thinking

3. **Organizing Information** Draw a diagram like the one below. Fill in details about African music and dance.

African Music and Dance

4. **Compare** How were African art and religion related?

5. **Identify** What was Queen Dahia al-Kahina's greatest accomplishment?

6. **Infer** Why do you think some Africans liked tales in which small animals outsmarted larger animals?

7. **Persuasive Writing** Portuguese plantation owners relied on slave labor to help them grow sugarcane. Suppose you had a family member who was enslaved on a plantation. Write a letter to the plantation owner explaining why this practice is unacceptable.

Section 1 The Rise of African Civilizations

Vocabulary
plateau
griot
dhow

Focusing on the Main Ideas
- Africa has a vast and varied landscape. *(page 445)*
- West African empires grew rich from trade. *(page 447)*
- Africa's rain forests blocked invaders and provided resources. *(page 450)*
- East African kingdoms and states became centers for trade and new ideas. *(page 451)*

Section 2 Africa's Government and Religion

Vocabulary
clan
sultan
Swahili

Focusing on the Main Ideas
- The growth of West African empires led to the growth of centralized governments ruled by kings. *(page 461)*
- Traditional African religions shared certain beliefs and provided a guide for living together. *(page 463)*
- Islam played an important role in medieval Africa, but long-held African beliefs and customs still remained strong. *(page 464)*

Section 3 African Society and Culture

Vocabulary
extended family
matrilineal
oral history

Focusing on the Main Ideas
- The Bantu migrations helped shape many cultures in Africa south of the Sahara. *(page 469)*
- The African slave trade changed greatly when Muslims and Europeans began taking captives from the continent. *(page 472)*
- Enslaved Africans developed rich cultures that influenced many other cultures, including our own. *(page 474)*

▲ Family life in the Congo

Review Vocabulary

Write *True* for each true statement. Replace the word in italics to make false statements true.

___ 1. Wooden boats known as *griots* were powered by triangular sails.

___ 2. An area of high, flat land is a *plateau.*

___ 3. Each district in Ghana usually included a chief's *clan.*

___ 4. African *dhows* are storytellers.

___ 5. *Matrilineal* societies trace their descent through mothers.

___ 6. *Swahili* culture and language exist in Africa today.

Review Main Ideas

Section 1 • The Rise of African Civilizations

7. What were the advantages of living in Africa's rain forests?

8. Why were East African kingdoms and states important?

Section 2 • Africa's Government and Religion

9. How were West African empires governed?

10. Describe the religious beliefs of medieval Africans.

Section 3 • African Society and Culture

11. What was the result of the Bantu migrations?

12. How did slavery in medieval Africa change?

Critical Thinking

13. **Predict** What do you think would have happened in Ghana if the people had been allowed to trade with gold nuggets instead of gold dust?

14. **Explain** What caused the decline of Ghana and Songhai?

15. **Analyze** Why do you think the Bantu language changed as people moved into different parts of Africa?

Review

Reading Skill Compare and Contrast **Making Comparisons**

16. Read the paragraph below, then create a Venn diagram that shows similarities and differences between the continents of Africa and North America.

> Africa is the world's second-largest continent. The United States fits into Africa three times, with room to spare. The Equator slices through the middle of the continent. Hot, steamy rain forests stretch along each side of it. Yet the rain forests cover only 10 percent of the land.

To review this skill, see pages 442–443.

Geography Skills

Study the map below and answer the following questions.

17. **Human/Environment Interaction** What obstacle did the empires in western Africa have to overcome in order to trade with cities in northern Africa?

18. **Location** In which parts of Africa do you think people had the best opportunities to trade by sea?

19. **Movement** How do you think more inland water routes would have changed the cultures of Africa?

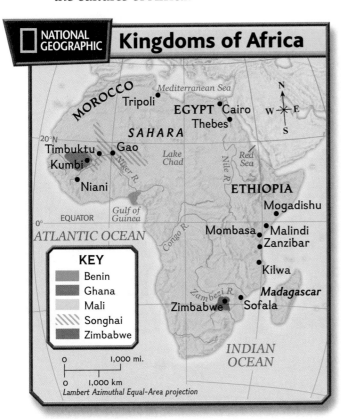

NATIONAL GEOGRAPHIC **Kingdoms of Africa**

KEY
- Benin
- Ghana
- Mali
- Songhai
- Zimbabwe

0   1,000 mi.
0   1,000 km
Lambert Azimuthal Equal-Area projection

Read to Write

20. **Descriptive Writing** Write an essay describing evidence of the African Diaspora in your community, city, or state. Make note of music, dance, literature, art, and other aspects of culture.

21. **Using Your FOLDABLES** Use the answers in your foldable to create a poster that shows what Africa was like in the past. Draw sketches, create maps, find pictures of artifacts, and so on to visually describe the cultures.

Using Technology

22. **Multimedia Presentation** Choose a present-day African country to research. Use the Internet to find information on that country from its early history to the present. Then create a multimedia presentation about that country, including images and a time line of important events in the country's history. Be sure to include aspects of culture, natural resources, and government.

Linking Past and Present

23. **Narrative Writing** Even though people record many things on paper or on a computer, they often tell stories about their lives as oral histories. Ask a family member, neighbor, teacher, or other adult to tell a story that has been passed down in his or her family. Record that oral history in narrative form.

Primary Source Analyze

This report was written by the first engineer ever to see the ruins of Great Zimbabwe.

"The ruins are . . . terraces, which rise up continually from the base to the apex [highest point] of all the hills. . . . The way that the ancients seem to have levelled off the contours of the various hills . . . is very astonishing, as they seem to have been levelled with as much exactitude as we can accomplish with our best mathematical instruments."

—Telford Edwards, as quoted in
The Mystery of the Great Zimbabwe

DBQ **Document-Based Questions**

24. What in particular amazes the engineer about Great Zimbabwe?
25. How do you think the people of Great Zimbabwe accomplished such precision?

Medieval Japan

Kingaku Temple in Kyoto, Japan ▼

NATIONAL GEOGRAPHIC **When & Where?**

A.D. 300	A.D. 700	1100	1500

c. A.D. 300
Yayoi people organize into clans

A.D. 646
Taika reforms strengthen emperor's powers

1192
Rule by shoguns begins

c. 1300s
Noh plays first performed

Chapter Preview

Warriors in Japan, like those in Africa, were known for their fighting skills. Japanese warriors trained their minds and bodies for battle. Read this chapter to find out about their training methods and how they are used today.

History Online

Chapter Overview Visit jat.glencoe.com for a preview of Chapter 14.

 View the Chapter 14 video in the *World History: Journey Across Time* Video Program.

Section 1 Early Japan

Japan's islands and mountains have shaped its history. The Japanese developed their own unique culture but looked to China as a model.

Section 2 Shoguns and Samurai

Japan's emperors lost power to military leaders. Warrior families and their followers fought each other for control of Japan.

Section 3 Life in Medieval Japan

The religions of Shinto and Buddhism shaped Japan's culture. Farmers, artisans, and merchants brought wealth to Japan.

Study Organizer

Categorizing Information *Make this foldable to help you organize information about the history and culture of medieval Japan.*

Step 1 *Mark the midpoint of the side edge of a sheet of paper.*

Draw a mark at the midpoint

Step 2 *Turn the paper and fold in each outside edge to touch at the midpoint. Label as shown.*

Japan

Step 3 *Open and label your foldable as shown.*

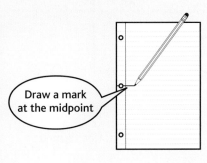

Early Japan | Shoguns and Samurai | Life in Medieval Japan

Reading and Writing *As you read the chapter, organize your notes by writing the main ideas with supporting details under the appropriate tab.*

Chapter 14

Reading Social Studies

Reading Skill

Cause and Effect

1 Learn It!

Identifying Cause and Effect

Learning to identify causes (reasons) and effects (results) will help you understand how and why things happen in history. Read the following passage and think about the result (effect) of Japan having mountains. Then see how the information can be pulled out and placed into a graphic organizer.

Cause

Because of Japan's mountains, only about 20 percent of its land can be farmed. Throughout Japan's history, local armies often fought over the few patches of fertile farmland. Just as in ancient Greece, the ragged terrain forced many Japanese to turn to the sea for a living.

—from page 485

Effects

Reading Tip

Find different ways to organize information as you read. Create graphic organizers that suit your own learning style to help you make sense of what you are reading.

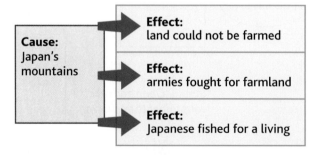

Cause:
Japan's mountains

Effect:
land could not be farmed

Effect:
armies fought for farmland

Effect:
Japanese fished for a living

2 Practice It!
Using Graphic Organizers

Read the following paragraph and either use the graphic organizer below or create your own to show the effects of Yoritomo's ruthless rule.

Read to Write ·······
After reading Section 2, write a paragraph that summarizes the reasons why the power of Japan's emperor declined during the A.D. 800s.

Yoritomo proved to be a ruthless ruler. He killed most of his relatives, fearing that they would try to take power from him. Yoritomo and the shoguns after him appointed high-ranking samurai to serve as advisers and to run the provinces. Bound by an oath of loyalty, these samurai lords ruled Japan's villages, kept the peace, and gathered taxes. They became the leading group in Japanese society.

—*from page 495*

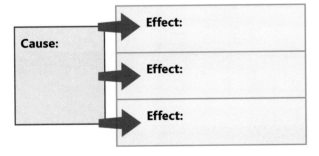

Cause:

Effect:

Effect:

Effect:

3 Apply It!

As you read Chapter 14, be aware of causes and effects in Japanese history. Find at least five causes and their effects, and create graphic organizers to record them.

Section 1

Early Japan

Get Ready to Read!

What's the Connection?
During the Middle Ages, another civilization developed in East Asia. It arose on the islands of Japan off the coast of the Korean Peninsula.

Focusing on the Main Ideas
- Japan's mountains and islands isolated Japan and shaped its society. *(page 485)*
- Japan was settled by people who came from northeast Asia. They were organized into clans and ruled by warriors. *(page 486)*
- Prince Shotoku created Japan's first constitution and borrowed many ideas from China. *(page 488)*
- The Japanese religion called Shinto was based on nature spirits. *(page 490)*

Locating Places
Japan (juh•PAN)
Hokkaido (hah•KY•doh)
Honshu (HAHN•shoo)
Shikoku (shih•KOH•koo)
Kyushu (kee•OO•shoo)

Meeting People
Jomon (JOH•mohn)
Yayoi (YAH•yoy)
Jimmu (jeem•mu)
Shotoku (shoh•toh•koo)

Building Your Vocabulary
clan (KLAN)
constitution (KAHN•stuh•TOO•shuhn)
animism (A•nuh•MIH•zuhm)
shrine (SHRYN)

Reading Strategy
Organizing Information Create a diagram to show the basics of the Shinto religion.

Shinto Religion

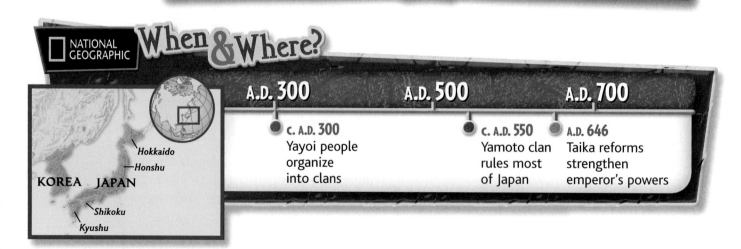

NATIONAL GEOGRAPHIC

When & Where?

KOREA JAPAN
Hokkaido
Honshu
Shikoku
Kyushu

A.D. 300

C. A.D. 300
Yayoi people organize into clans

A.D. 500

C. A.D. 550
Yamoto clan rules most of Japan

A.D. 700

A.D. 646
Taika reforms strengthen emperor's powers

Japan's Geography

Main Idea Japan's mountains and islands isolated Japan and shaped its society.

Reading Focus Have you ever been in a place with no television, radio, or telephone? How would you feel if you did not know what was going on outside your home? Read to learn how Japan's geography isolated the Japanese and shaped their society.

Japan (juh•PAN) is a chain of islands that stretches north to south in the northern Pacific Ocean. Japan's islands number more than 3,000, and many of them are tiny. For centuries, most Japanese have lived on the four largest islands: **Hokkaido** (hah•KY•doh), **Honshu** (HAHN•shoo), **Shikoku** (shih•KOH•koo), and **Kyushu** (kee•OO•shoo).

Like China, much of Japan is covered by mountains. In fact, the islands of Japan are actually the tops of mountains that rise from the floor of the ocean. About 188 of Japan's mountains are volcanoes. Many earthquakes occur in Japan because the islands lie in an area where parts of the earth's surface often shift.

Because of Japan's mountains, only about 20 percent of its land can be farmed. Throughout Japan's history, local armies often fought over the few patches of fertile farmland. Just as in ancient Greece, the rugged terrain forced many Japanese to turn to the sea for a living. Early on, they settled in villages along the coast and fished for food. Fish and seafood are still important in the Japanese diet.

The sea surrounding Japan's islands made it easy for people in ships to travel along the coast and from island to island. It encouraged people to become merchants, traveling from village to village with goods to trade. The vast ocean around Japan's islands, however, kept the Japanese people isolated, or separate, from the rest of Asia. As a result, Japan developed its own fiercely independent society with its own religion, art, literature, and government.

✓ **Reading Check** **Describe** How did Japan's geography shape its society?

▼ Mount Fuji is an important national symbol. *How did the region's mountains affect early settlement in Japan?*

NATIONAL GEOGRAPHIC
Geography of Japan

Hokkaido
40°N
Sea of Japan (East Sea)
Honshu
PACIFIC OCEAN
Yellow Sea
Heian (Kyoto)
Mt. Fuji
Edo (Tokyo)
Kamakura
Nara
Shikoku
Kyushu
130°E   140°E
0   400 mi.
0   400 km   30°N
Lambert Conformal Conic projection

Using Geography Skills

Japan's geography isolated the country and helped form a unique culture.

1. List, from north to south, the four major islands that make up Japan.
2. What body of water separates Japan from mainland Asia?

Find NGS online map resources @ www.nationalgeographic.com/maps

The First Settlers

Main Idea Japan was settled by people who came from northeast Asia. They were organized into clans and ruled by warriors.

Reading Focus Do you have many relatives? Do your relatives all come together to do things? Read to learn how the early Japanese people were organized into groups made up of people who were all related to each other.

Japan's earliest people probably came from northeast Asia between 30,000 and 10,000 B.C. At that time, Japan was joined to the Asian continent by land. These early people hunted animals and gathered wild plants. They used fire and stone tools, and they lived in pits dug into the ground.

Who Were the Jomon?

In about 5000 B.C., these wandering groups began to develop a culture. They made clay pottery, using knotted cords to make designs on the clay's surface. Today, this culture is called **Jomon** (JOH•mohn), which means "cord marks" in the Japanese language. Modern archaeologists have found many pieces of Jomon pottery throughout Japan. Over time, the Jomon people settled in fishing villages along the coast. Fishing became their way of life.

Why Are the Yayoi Important?

The Jomon culture lasted until about 300 B.C. At that time, a new group of people appeared in Japan. Modern archaeologists have named this culture **Yayoi** (YAH•yoy), after the place in Japan where they first dug up its artifacts.

The Yayoi were the ancestors of the Japanese people. They introduced farming to Japan and practiced a number of skills that they may have learned from the Chinese and Koreans. They made pottery on a potter's wheel and grew rice in paddies. A paddy is a rice field that is flooded when rice is planted and drained for the harvest.

The Yayoi also were skilled in metalworking. They made axes, knives, and hoes from iron, and swords, spears, and bells from bronze. Bells were used in religious rituals—a practice that is still common in Japan today.

◄ Female figurine from the Jomon culture (left); Jomon vase (below)

Bronze bell from the ► Yayoi people (right); Yayoi pottery (below)

By A.D. 300, the Yayoi, or the early Japanese, had organized themselves into **clans** (KLANZ). A clan is a group of families related by blood or marriage. Yayoi clans were headed by a small group of warriors. Under the warriors were the rest of the people—farmers, artisans, and servants of the warriors. The clan's warrior chiefs protected the people in return for a share of the rice harvest each year.

The Yayoi buried their chiefs in large mounds known as *kofun.* Made of dirt, these tombs were carefully shaped and surrounded by ditches. They were filled with personal belongings, such as pottery, tools, weapons, and armor. Many of the tombs were as big as Egypt's pyramids. The largest tomb still stands today. It is longer than five football fields and at least eight stories high.

Who Are the Yamato?

Like many other people whose society began in ancient times, the Japanese have myths, or stories that tell how things began. The most important myth explained the creation of Japan. It says that centuries ago, two gods dipped a spear into the sea. When they pulled it out, drops of salty water fell on the water's surface and formed the islands of Japan. The two gods then created the sun goddess, Amaterasu, to rule over Earth. They also created the storm god, Susanowo, as her companion.

Susanowo was sent to Earth. There, his children became the first people of Japan. Amaterasu, however, sent her grandson Ninigi to rule over them. To make sure that everyone would accept his power, she gave Ninigi her mirror, her jewel, and a great sword. These objects became the sacred symbols of leadership in early Japan.

Historians today are not sure of the actual events on which this myth is based. However, they do know that during the

▲ The sun goddess, Amaterasu, emerges from her cave, bringing light into the world. *Which group claimed that they came from Amaterasu?*

A.D. 500s, a clan called the Yamato became strong enough to bring most of Japan under its rule. The other clans still held their lands, but they had to give their loyalty to the Yamato chief.

Yamato chiefs claimed that they came from the sun goddess and, therefore, had a right to rule Japan. Japanese legend states that a Yamato leader named **Jimmu** (jeem•mu) took the title "emperor of heaven." He founded a line of rulers in Japan that has never been broken. Akihito (AH•kee•HEE•toh), who is Japan's emperor today, is one of his descendants.

✓ Reading Check **Identify** What do historians know for sure about the rise of the Yamato?

Prince Shotoku's Reforms

Main Idea Prince Shotoku created Japan's first constitution and borrowed many ideas from China.

Reading Focus When you try something new, are you tempted to use what someone else has done as a model? Read to find out how Shotoku used China as a model for his reforms in Japan.

About A.D. 600, a Yamato prince named **Shotoku** (shoh•TOH•koo) took charge of Japan on behalf of his aunt, the empress Suiko (swee•koh). He wanted to create a strong government, and he looked to China as an example of what to do. You remember that in China, a powerful emperor ruled with the help of trained officials chosen for their abilities.

To reach this goal for Japan, Shotoku created a **constitution** (KAHN•stuh•TOO•shuhn), or a plan of government. Shotoku's constitution gave all power to the emperor, who had to be obeyed by the Japanese people. He also created a bureaucracy and gave the emperor the power to appoint all the officials. The constitution listed rules for working in the government. The rules were taken from the ideas of Confucius.

Shotoku also wanted Japan to learn from China's brilliant civilization. He sent officials and students to China to study. The Japanese not only learned about Buddhist teachings but also absorbed a great deal about Chinese art, medicine, and philosophy.

Shotoku ordered Buddhist temples and monasteries to be built throughout Japan. One of them, called Horyuji (HOHR•yoo•JEE), still stands. It is Japan's oldest temple and the world's oldest surviving wooden building.

After Shotoku, other officials continued to make Japan's government look like China's. In A.D. 646 the Yamato began the Taika, or Great Change. They divided Japan into provinces, or regional districts, all run by officials who reported to the emperor. In addition, all land in Japan came under the emperor's control.

Clan leaders could direct the farmers working the land, but they could not collect taxes anymore. Instead, government officials were to gather part of the farmers' harvest in taxes for the emperor. Together with Shotoku's reforms, this plan created Japan's first strong central government.

Reading Check **Identify** What happened during the Great Change?

Primary Source

Japan's New Constitution

This is part of the constitution created by Shotoku.

"Harmony is to be cherished, and opposition for opposition's sake must be avoided as a matter of principle. . . .

When an imperial command is given, obey it with reverence. The sovereign is likened to heaven, and his subjects are likened to earth. With heaven providing the cover and earth supporting it, the four seasons proceed in orderly fashion, giving sustenance to all that which is in nature. If earth attempts to overtake the functions of heaven, it destroys everything.

Cast away your ravenous desire for food and abandon your covetousness [envy] for material possessions. If a suit is brought before you, render a clear-cut judgement. . . .

Punish that which is evil and encourage that which is good."

—Prince Shotoku,
"The Seventeen Article Constitution"

DBQ **Document-Based Question**

To what are the emperor and his subjects compared?

Biography

PRINCE SHOTOKU
A.D. 573–621

Prince Shotoku was born into the powerful Soga family, as the second son of Emperor Yomei. Shotoku's real name is Umayado, which means "the prince of the stable door." According to legend, Shotoku's mother gave birth to him while she was inspecting the emperor's stables. During Shotoku's childhood, Japan was a society of clans, or large extended families. There was fighting between Shotoku's own Soga family and their rival, the Mononobe family. The Soga and Mononobe clans were Japan's two most powerful families, and each wanted to rule Japan.

Shotoku was a very bright, articulate child. He learned about Buddhism from one of his great uncles. He then studied with two Buddhist priests and became devoted to Buddhism.

At the age of 20, Shotoku became Japan's crown prince. The early teachings of Buddhism strongly influenced his leadership. He introduced political and religious reforms that helped build a strong central government in Japan modeled after China. At the request of his aunt, the empress, Shotoku often spoke about Buddhism and the process of enlightenment.

▲ Statue believed to be of Prince Shotoku

He also wrote the first book of Japanese history.

When Prince Shotoku died, the elderly people of the empire mourned as if they had lost a dear child of their own. A written account describes their words of grief: "The sun and moon have lost their brightness; heaven and earth have crumbled to ruin: henceforward, in whom shall we put our trust?"

▲ The Horyuji temple, built by Prince Shotoku

Then and Now

Think of a recent leader or other public figure whose death caused people to mourn as if they knew that person well. Who is it? Why do you think people identified with that person? Why did the Japanese identify so closely with Shotoku?

What Is Shinto?

◄ Shinto priests

Main Idea The Japanese religion, called Shinto, was based on nature spirits.

Reading Focus Today we know the importance of protecting the environment. Why is nature important to us? Read to learn why the early Japanese thought nature was important.

Like many ancient peoples, the early Japanese believed that all natural things are alive, even the winds, the mountains, and the rivers. They believed that all of these things have their own spirits. This idea is called **animism** (A•nuh•MIH•zuhm). When people needed help, they asked the nature spirits, whom they called *kami*, to help them.

To honor the *kami*, the Japanese worshiped at **shrines** (SHRYNZ), or holy places. There, priests, musicians, and dancers performed rituals for people who asked the gods for a good harvest, a wife or a child, or some other favor.

These early Japanese beliefs developed into the religion of Shinto. The word *Shinto* means "way of the spirits," and many Japanese still follow Shinto today. Followers believe the *kami* will help only if a person is pure. Many things, such as illness, cause spiritual stains that must be cleansed by bathing and other rituals before praying.

✓ **Reading Check** **Explain** How did the Japanese honor the *kami*?

History Online

Homework Helper Need help with the material in this section? Visit jat.glencoe.com

Section 1 Review

Reading Summary

Review the **Main Ideas**

- Japan's mountainous islands contain little land for farming, leading many people to turn to the sea for a living.

- Japan was settled by people from northeast Asia, organized into clans and ruled by warriors.

- While ruling Japan, Prince Shotoku made the emperor a strong ruler and set up a government similar to China's.

- Japan's first religion, Shinto, was based on the idea of nature spirits called *kami*.

What Did You Learn?

1. What skills did the Yayoi practice that they may have learned from the Chinese and Koreans?

2. In the Shinto religion, what do people worship? How are they worshiped?

Critical Thinking

3. **Sequencing Information** Draw a time line like the one below. Fill in dates and information related to events in Japanese history from the Jomon to Shotoku.

    ├──┼──┼──┼──┼──┤
    5000 B.C.   A.D. **646**

4. **Summarize** Describe Japanese society under the Yayoi around A.D. 300.

5. **Analyze** In what ways did Shotoku look to China to improve Japan?

6. **Expository Writing** Imagine you are visiting Japan sometime in the A.D. 300s. Write a letter to a friend describing what you have observed and learned about the Shinto religion.

7. **Reading** Cause and Effect Create a cause-and-effect graphic organizer that shows how geography affected the early development of Japan.

Section 2

Shoguns and Samurai

Get Ready to Read!

What's the Connection?
In the last section, you learned how Japan's leaders looked to China as a model of government. As you have learned, warlords sometimes took over parts of China. As you will read, Japan had similar problems.

Focusing on the Main Ideas
- During the A.D. 700s, Japan built a strong national government at Nara, and Buddhism became a popular religion. *(page 492)*

- Japan's civilian government and the emperor came to be dominated by military rulers known as shoguns. *(page 493)*

- As the shogun's power weakened, Japan broke into warring kingdoms run by rulers known as daimyo. *(page 496)*

Locating Places
Heian (HAY•ahn)
Kamakura (kah•MAH•kuh•RAH)

Meeting People
Minamoto Yoritomo (mee•nah• moh•toh   yoh•ree•toh•moh)
Ashikaga Takauji (ah•shee•kah• gah   tah•kow•jee)

Building Your Vocabulary
samurai (SA•muh•RY)
shogun (SHOH•guhn)
daimyo (DY•mee•OH)
vassal (VA•suhl)
feudalism (FYOO•duhl•IH•zuhm)

Reading Strategy
Showing Relationships Create a diagram to show the relationship between daimyo and samurai.

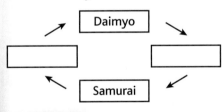

When & Where?

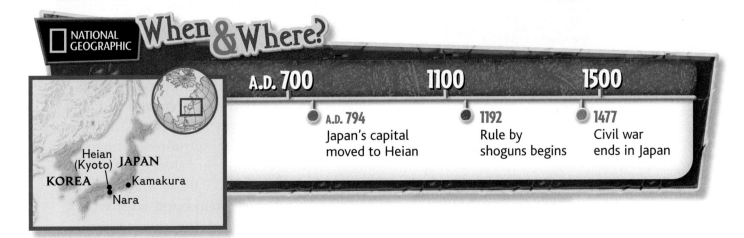

A.D. 700	1100	1500
A.D. 794 Japan's capital moved to Heian	**1192** Rule by shoguns begins	**1477** Civil war ends in Japan

Heian (Kyoto) JAPAN
KOREA
Nara
Kamakura

Nara Japan

Main Idea During the A.D. 700s, Japan built a strong national government at Nara, and Buddhism became a popular religion.

Reading Focus Do you know anyone who was hired for a job because they were friends with the boss or because the boss knew their family? Read to learn how Japan's emperor chose people for government jobs.

In the early A.D. 700s, Japan's emperors built a new capital city called Nara. For the next 100 years, Nara was the center of government and religion in Japan. Because of Nara's importance, the history of Japan during the A.D. 700s is called the Nara Period.

The city of Nara looked much like China's capital of Changan, only smaller. It had broad streets, large public squares, government offices, Buddhist temples, and Shinto shrines. Nobles and their families lived in large, Chinese-style homes. The typical home of a noble had wooden walls, a heavy tile roof, and polished wooden floors. It also included an inner garden.

The Emperor's Government

At Nara, Japanese emperors added to the changes begun by Prince Shotoku. They organized government officials into ranks, or levels of importance from top to bottom. However, unlike China, Japan did not use examinations to hire officials. Instead, the emperor gave the jobs to nobles from powerful families. Once a person was appointed to a job, he could pass on his office to his son or other relatives. For their services, top government officials received estates, or large farms. They also were given farmers to work the land.

The emperor's power came from his control of the land and its crops. To measure Japan's wealth, the government carried out a census. It counted all the people in the country. The census also listed the lands on which people lived and worked. Based on the census results, all people who held land from the emperor had to pay taxes in rice or silk cloth. The men counted in the census had to serve in the army.

Buddhism Spreads in Japan

At the same time that the emperor's government was growing strong, Buddhism became popular in Japan. Buddhism came to Japan from Korea in the A.D. 500s. Japanese government officials and nobles were the first to accept the new religion. Then, during the A.D. 600s and A.D. 700s, Buddhism spread rapidly among the common people. It soon became a major religion in Japan and had an important role in government and society.

As Buddhism became more powerful, nobles who were not Buddhists began to oppose the religion. Soon, those who backed Buddhism and those who opposed it were fighting for control of the government.

▲ Built in the early A.D. 600s, the Horyuji temple in Nara, Japan, is the oldest wooden building in the world.

Inside the ▶
Todaji temple is
Japan's largest
statue of Buddha.
It is made of
copper and gold,
weighs 250 tons,
and is nearly
50 feet tall.

▲ The Todaji temple was first built in A.D. 752
to serve as the head temple for Buddhism in
Japan. It is the world's largest wooden structure.
This reconstruction was built in 1692.

In A.D. 770 a Buddhist monk who served in the government tried to seize the throne and become emperor. He was stopped by the emperor's family and leading nobles.

Frightened by this event, the emperor and his family briefly turned away from Buddhism. Remember how the government in China attacked Buddhist monasteries when they became strong? In Japan, instead of attacking the Buddhists, the emperor simply decided to leave Nara and its many Buddhist monks.

✓ Reading Check Contrast How was the Japanese system of hiring officials different from the Chinese system?

The Rise of the Shogun

Main Idea Japan's civilian government and the emperor came to be dominated by military rulers known as shoguns.

Reading Focus Every leader promises certain things to the people in return for their support. In the United States, what promises do politicians make to win votes? Read to learn how Japan's nobles increased their power by giving land in return for people's support.

In A.D. 794, Emperor Kammu of Japan began building a new capital city called **Heian** (HAY•ahn). This city later became known as Kyoto (kee•OH•toh). Like Nara, Heian was modeled on the Chinese city of Changan. It remained the official capital of Japan for more than 1,000 years.

The Government Weakens During the A.D. 800s, the emperor's power declined. Why did this happen? After a time of strong emperors, a number of weak emperors came to the throne. Many of these emperors were only children, and court officials known as regents had to govern for them. A regent is a person who rules for an emperor who is too young or too sick to rule. When the emperors grew up, however, the regents refused to give up their power.

Most regents came from a clan called the Fujiwara. Under the Fujiwara, Japan's emperors were honored, but they no longer had real power. Instead of ruling, these emperors spent time studying Buddhism or writing poetry in their palace at Heian.

History Online

Web Activity Visit jat.glencoe.com and click on *Chapter 14—Student Web Activity* to learn more about medieval Japan.

As the Fujiwara grew wealthy and powerful in Heian, other powerful nobles gained control of much of the land in the provinces of Japan. This happened because the government gave the nobles lands as a way to pay them for their work. At the same time, new lands were settled as Japan's empire expanded. The nobles who settled farmers on these lands were allowed to keep the lands.

To keep the nobles happy, the government let them stop paying taxes, but it put them in charge of governing the lands under their control. In order to govern their lands, the nobles began collecting more taxes from the peasants working the land.

A samurai's helmet was often individually decorated.

A samurai usually carried two swords. The longer one was called the *katana*, the shorter one was the *wakizashi*.

The *naginata* was a blade mounted on a long handle. It was used against cavalry.

A samurai's armor was made from scales of metal or leather, brightly painted, and laced together with silk or leather.

▲ At first, most samurai fought on horseback. Later samurai were foot soldiers who fought with a variety of weapons. *What was the samurai code of conduct called?*

Who Were the Samurai? To protect their lands and enforce the law, nobles formed private armies. To create their armies, they gave land to warriors who agreed to fight for them. These warriors became known as **samurai** (SA•muh•RY).

In battle, samurai fought on horseback with swords, daggers, and bows and arrows. They wore armor made of leather or steel scales laced together with silk cords. Their helmets had horns or crests, and they wore masks designed to be terrifying.

The word *samurai* means "one who serves." The samurai lived by a strict code of conduct. It was called Bushido, or "the way of the warrior." This code demanded that a samurai be loyal to his master as well as courageous, brave, and honorable. Samurai were not supposed to care for wealth. They regarded merchants as lacking in honor.

Pledged to these principles, a samurai would rather die in battle than betray his lord. He also did not want to suffer the disgrace of being captured in battle. The sense of loyalty that set apart the samurai continued into modern times. During World War II, many Japanese soldiers fought to the death rather than accept defeat or capture. Since that conflict, the Japanese have turned away from the military beliefs of the samurai.

What Is a Shogun? By the early 1100s, the most powerful Japanese families had begun fighting each other using their samurai armies. They fought over land and to gain control over the emperor and his government. In 1180 the Gempei War began. The Gempei War was a civil war between the two most powerful clans: the Taira family and the Minamoto family. In 1185 the Minamoto forces defeated the Taira in a sea battle near the island of Shikoku.

The leader of the Minamoto was a man named **Minamoto Yoritomo** (mee•nah•moh•toh yoh•ree•toh•moh). (In Japanese a person's family name comes first, followed by the personal name.) Yoritomo was the commander of the Minamoto armies. After Yoritomo won the Gempei War, the emperor worried that the Minamoto family would try to replace the Yamato family as the rulers of Japan. He decided it would be better to reward Yoritomo to keep him loyal.

In 1192 the emperor gave Yoritomo the title of **shogun** (SHOH•guhn)—commander of all of the emperor's military forces. This decision created two governments in Japan. The emperor stayed in his palace at Heian with his bureaucracy. He was still officially the head of the country, but he had no power. Meanwhile the shogun set up his own government at his headquarters in **Kamakura** (kah•MAH•kuh•RAH), a small seaside town. This military government was known as a shogunate. Japan's government was run by a series of shoguns for the next 700 years.

Yoritomo proved to be a ruthless ruler. He killed most of his relatives, fearing that they would try to take power from him. Yoritomo and the shoguns after him appointed high-ranking samurai to serve as advisers and to run the provinces. Bound by an oath of loyalty, these samurai lords ruled Japan's villages, kept the peace, and gathered taxes. They became the leading group in Japanese society.

The Mongols Attack In the late 1200s, the Kamakura shogunate faced its greatest test. In 1274 and again in 1281, China's Mongol emperor Kublai Khan sent out ships and

Primary Source

Bushido Code

This passage describes the samurai's Bushido.

"It is further good fortune if . . . [a servant] had wisdom and talent and can use them appropriately. But even a person who is good for nothing . . . will be a reliable retainer [servant] if only he has the determination to think earnestly of [respect and admire] his master. Having only wisdom and talent is the lowest tier [level] of usefulness."

—Yamamoto Tsunetomo,
Hagakure: The Book of the Samurai

◀ Samurai armor

DBQ **Document-Based Question**

How powerful is a samurai's determination to respect and admire his master?

warriors to invade Japan. Both times, the Mongols were defeated because violent Pacific storms smashed many of their ships. The Mongol troops who made it ashore were defeated by the Japanese.

The victorious Japanese named the typhoons *kamikaze* (KAH•mih•KAH•zee), or "divine wind," in honor of the spirits they believed had saved their islands. Much later, during World War II, Japanese pilots deliberately crashed their planes into enemy ships. They were named kamikaze pilots after the typhoons of the 1200s.

Reading Check **Identify** Who was the shogun, and why was he important?

The Way It Was

Focus on Everyday Life

Samurai The path to becoming a samurai was difficult and dangerous. Mothers in samurai families began teaching their sons Bushido at a young age. They taught their sons to place bravery, honor, and loyalty above all else. Each young warrior knew and could recite from memory the brave feats of his samurai ancestors.

For centuries, young samurai lived apart from their families in the castle of their lord or in the barracks of their lord's town. Beginning in the 1800s, samurai schools were built, and boys lived there to continue the educations their mothers had started. From the age of 10, they trained in the martial arts and studied other subjects, such as math and astronomy. By the age of 16, some young men were already promising warriors who distinguished themselves in battle.

Painting of a ▶ samurai hero

Connecting to the Past

1. What lessons was the mother of a samurai responsible for teaching her young son?
2. Do you think soldiers today have a code of conduct similar to Bushido? Explain.

The Daimyo Divide Japan

Main Idea As the shogun's power weakened, Japan broke into warring kingdoms run by rulers known as daimyo.

Reading Focus Have you ever been promised something and then been upset when the promise was broken? Read to learn how Japan's shogun lost power because the samurai felt he had broken his promises.

The Kamakura shogunate ruled Japan until 1333. By that time, many samurai had become resentful. Over the years, as samurai divided their lands among their sons, the piece of land each samurai owned became smaller and smaller. By the 1300s, many samurai felt they no longer owed the shogun loyalty because he had not given them enough land.

In 1331 the emperor rebelled, and many samurai came to his aid. The revolt succeeded, but the emperor was not able to gain control of Japan because he too refused to give more land to the samurai. Instead, a general named **Ashikaga Takauji** (ah•shee•kah•gah   tah•kow•jee) turned against the emperor and made himself shogun in 1333. A new government known as the Ashikaga shogunate began.

The Ashikaga shoguns proved to be weak rulers, and revolts broke out across Japan. The country soon divided into a number of small territories. These areas were headed by powerful military lords known as **daimyo** (DY•mee•OH).

The daimyo pledged loyalty to the emperor and the shogun. However, they ruled their lands as if they were independent kingdoms. To protect their lands, the daimyo created their own local armies made up of samurai warriors, just as other nobles had done in the past.

Many samurai became **vassals** (VA•suhlz) of a daimyo. That is, a samurai gave an oath of loyalty to his daimyo and promised to serve him in times of war. In return, each daimyo gave land to his samurai warriors—more land than they had been given by the shogun. This bond of loyalty between a lord and a vassal is known as **feudalism** (FYOO•duhl•ɪн•zuhm). In the next chapter, you will learn about a similar form of feudalism that arose in Europe during the Middle Ages.

With the breakdown of central government, Japan's warriors fought each other. From 1467 to 1477, the country suffered through the disastrous Onin War. During this conflict, the city of Kyoto (Heian) was almost completely destroyed. Armies passed back and forth through the city, burning temples and palaces.

For 100 years after the Onin War, a series of weak shoguns tried to reunite Japan. Powerful daimyo, however, resisted their

▲ The Takamatsu castle was built in 1590. It sits on the edge of a sea and was once surrounded by moats, gates, and towers for protection.

control. Fighting spread throughout the country. The violence finally brought down the Ashikaga shogunate in 1567. By that time, only a handful of powerful daimyo remained. Each of these daimyo was eager to defeat his rivals and rule all of Japan.

✔ **Reading Check** **Analyze** Why were shoguns unable to regain control of Japan after the Onin War?

History Online

Homework Helper Need help with the material in this section? Visit jat.glencoe.com

Section ❷ Review

Reading Summary

Review the Main Ideas

- During the Nara Period, the emperor's power grew, and Buddhism spread among Japan's common people.

- Over time, the Japanese emperors lost power to nobles and their armies of samurai. Eventually a military ruler, called a shogun, ruled the country.

- In the 1400s and 1500s, the shoguns lost power, and military lords, called daimyo, divided Japan into a number of small territories.

What Did You Learn?

1. What was a shogun? Who was the first shogun, and how did he gain his position of power?

2. What prevented the Mongol conquest of Japan?

Critical Thinking

3. **Organizing Information** Draw a diagram like the one below. Add details about the samurai, such as their weapons, dress, and beliefs.

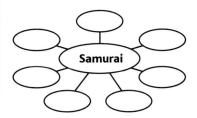

Samurai

4. **Describe** Describe events related to the growth of Buddhism in Japan.

5. **Explain** Why did the power of the Japanese emperors decline during the A.D. 800s?

6. **Analyze** How did the beliefs of the samurai affect Japanese soldiers in World War II?

7. **Expository Writing** Create a constitution, or plan for government, that describes the relationship between the emperor and shogun, the daimyo, and the samurai.

Section 3

Life in Medieval Japan

Get Ready to Read!

What's the Connection?

In the last section, you learned how warriors known as shoguns and samurai came to rule Japan. During that time, the Japanese suffered from many wars. However, Japan's economy continued to grow, and its people produced beautiful art, architecture, and literature.

Focusing on the Main Ideas

• Buddhism and Shinto shaped much of Japan's culture. These religions affected Japanese art, architecture, novels, and plays. *(page 499)*

• Some Japanese nobles, merchants, and artisans grew wealthy during the shogun period, but the lives of women remained restricted in many areas of life. *(page 503)*

Locating Places
Kyoto (kee•OH•toh)

Meeting People
Murasaki Shikibu (MUR•uh•SAH•kee shee•kee•boo)

Building Your Vocabulary
sect (SEHKT)
martial arts (mahr   shuhl)
meditation (MEH•duh•TAY•shuhn)
calligraphy (kuh•LIH•gruh•fee)
tanka (TAHNG•kuh)
guild (GIHLD)

Reading Strategy
Summarizing Information Complete a diagram like the one below describing the role of women in the families of medieval Japan.

Role of Women

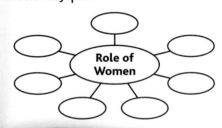

When & Where?

1000	1200	1400
c. 1000 Lady Murasaki Shikibu writes *The Tale of Genji*	**c. 1100s** Zen Buddhism spreads in Japan	**c. 1300s** Noh plays first performed

JAPAN

KOREA • Heian (Kyoto)

Japanese Religion and Culture

Main Idea Buddhism and Shinto shaped much of Japan's culture. These religions affected Japanese art, architecture, novels, and plays.

Reading Focus Have you ever seen paintings, sculptures, and works of literature that have religious subjects or messages? In medieval Japan, the religions of Shinto and Buddhism greatly influenced the arts.

During the Middle Ages, religion was a part of everyday life for the Japanese. Most Japanese came to believe in both Buddhism and Shinto, and worshiped at Shinto shrines and Buddhist temples. To them, each religion met different needs. Shinto was concerned with daily life, while Buddhism prepared people for the life to come. During the Middle Ages, Buddhist ideas inspired many Japanese to build temples, produce paintings, and write poems and plays.

▲ A Zen monk sits beside a Japanese rock garden while meditating. *What is the purpose of meditation?*

Pure Land Buddhism
As you have already learned, Mahayana Buddhism began in India and spread to China and Korea. By the time Buddhism reached Japan, it had developed into many different **sects** (SEHKTS), or smaller religious groups.

One of the most important sects in Japan was Pure Land Buddhism. Pure Land Buddhism was a type of Mahayana Buddhism. It won many followers in Japan because of its message about a happy life after death. Pure Land Buddhists looked to Lord Amida, a buddha of love and mercy. They believed Amida had founded a paradise above the clouds. To get there, all they had to do was have faith in Amida and chant his name.

What Is Zen Buddhism?
Another important Buddhist sect in Japan was Zen. Buddhist monks brought Zen to Japan from China during the 1100s. Zen taught that

people could find inner peace through self-control and a simple way of life.

Followers of Zen learned to control their bodies through **martial arts** (MAHR•shuhl), or sports that involved combat and self-defense. This appealed to the samurai, who trained to fight bravely and fearlessly.

Followers of Zen Buddhism also practiced **meditation** (MEH•duh•TAY•shuhn). In meditation, a person sat cross-legged and motionless for hours, with the mind cleared of all thoughts and desires. Meditation helped people to relax and find inner peace.

Art and Architecture
During the Middle Ages, the Japanese borrowed artistic ideas from China and Korea. Then, they went on to develop their own styles. The arts of Japan revealed the Japanese love of beauty and simplicity.

During the Middle Ages, artisans in Japan made wooden statues, furniture, and

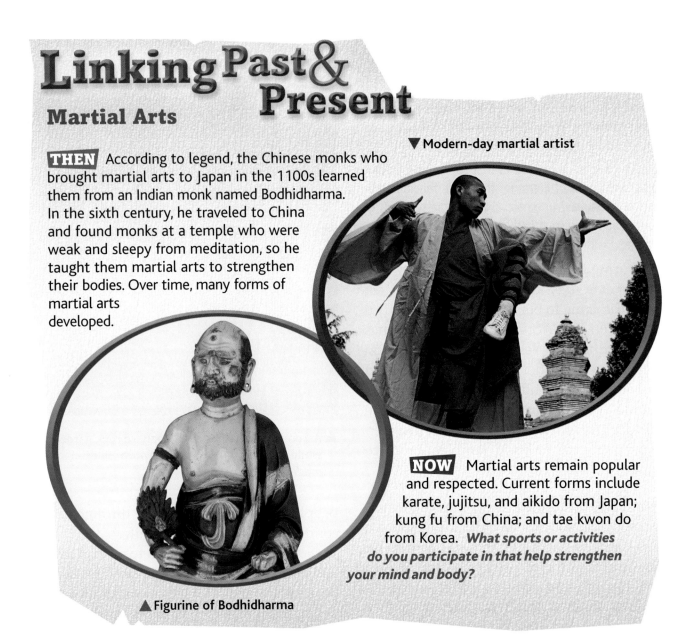

Linking Past & Present

Martial Arts

THEN According to legend, the Chinese monks who brought martial arts to Japan in the 1100s learned them from an Indian monk named Bodhidharma. In the sixth century, he traveled to China and found monks at a temple who were weak and sleepy from meditation, so he taught them martial arts to strengthen their bodies. Over time, many forms of martial arts developed.

▼ Modern-day martial artist

NOW Martial arts remain popular and respected. Current forms include karate, jujitsu, and aikido from Japan; kung fu from China; and tae kwon do from Korea. *What sports or activities do you participate in that help strengthen your mind and body?*

▲ Figurine of Bodhidharma

household items. On many of their works, they used a shiny black and red coating called lacquer. From the Chinese, Japanese artists learned to do landscape painting. Using ink or watercolors, they painted scenes of nature or battles on paper scrolls or on silk. Japanese nobles at the emperor's court learned to fold paper to make decorative objects. This art of folding paper is called origami. They also arranged flowers. Buddhist monks and the samurai turned tea drinking into a beautiful ceremony.

Builders in Japan used Chinese or Japanese styles. Shinto shrines were built in the Japanese style near a sacred rock, tree, or other natural feature that they considered beautiful. Usually a shrine was a wooden building, with a single room and a roof made of rice straw. People entered the shrine through a sacred gate called a torii.

Unlike Shinto shrines, Buddhist temples were built in the Chinese style. They had massive tiled roofs held up by thick, wooden pillars. The temples were richly decorated. They had many statues, paintings, and altars.

Around their buildings, the Japanese created gardens designed to imitate nature in a miniature form. Some of these gardens had carefully placed rocks, raked sand, and a few plants. They were built this way to create a feeling of peace and calmness.

Poems and Plays During the A.D. 500s, the Japanese borrowed China's writing system. They wrote their language in Chinese picture characters that stood for whole words. Because the Japanese and Chinese languages were so different, the Japanese found it difficult to use these characters. Then, in the A.D. 800s, they added symbols that stood for sounds, much like the letters of an alphabet. This addition made reading and writing much easier.

Calligraphy (kuh•LIH•gruh•fee), the art of writing beautifully, was much admired in Japan. Every well-educated person was expected to practice it. A person's handwriting was considered to reveal much about his or her education, social standing, and character.

During the Middle Ages, the Japanese wrote poems, stories, and plays. Japan's oldest form of poetry was the **tanka** (TAHNG•kuh). It was an unrhymed poem of five lines. Tanka poems capture nature's beauty and the joys and sorrows of life. The following tanka was written by an anonymous poet:

66 On autumn nights
the dew is
colder than ever—
in every clump of grasses
the insects weep **99**

—author unknown,
tanka from the *Kokinshū*

Women living in Heian wrote Japan's first great stories around 1000. One woman,

Lady **Murasaki Shikibu** (MUR•uh•SAH•kee shee•kee•boo), wrote *The Tale of Genji.* This work describes the adventures of a Japanese prince. Some people believe the work is the world's first novel, or long fictional story.

About 200 years later, Japan's writers turned out stirring tales about warriors in battle. The greatest collection was *The Tale of Heike.* It describes the fight between the Taira and the Minamoto clans.

The Japanese also created plays. The oldest type of play is called Noh. Created during the 1300s, Noh plays were used to teach Buddhist ideas. Noh plays were performed on a simple, bare stage. The actors wore masks and elaborate robes. They danced, gestured, and chanted poetry to the music of drums and flutes.

✓ **Reading Check** **Analyze** How are martial arts and meditation connected to Zen Buddhism's principle of self-control?

▲ Noh masks like these were often carved from a single piece of wood and were lightweight, so an actor could wear it for several hours. *Why were Noh plays performed?*

Biography

MURASAKI SHIKIBU

c. A.D. 973–1025

Murasaki Shikibu was a great novelist and poet of the Japanese Heian period. She was one of the first modern novelists. Murasaki became famous from writing *The Tale of Genji*, but her work also included a diary and over 120 poems.

Murasaki was born into the Fujiwara clan, a noble family but not a rich family. Her father was a scholar and a governor. In fact, the name Shikibu refers to her father's position at court. Murasaki's mother and older sister died when she was a child. Traditionally, children were raised by the mother and her family, but Murasaki's father decided to raise his daughter himself. He broke another custom by educating his daughter in Chinese language and literature, subjects reserved for boys.

Murasaki married and had a daughter, but her husband died after only a few years of marriage. Around that time, Murasaki began writing *The Tale of Genji* and working as an attendant to Empress Akiko. She based the novel on life at court, which she knew about through her father's job and her own. The last reference to her is in 1014, but many scholars believe that she lived for about a decade after that.

Much about Murasaki's life—and life at the emperor's palace—is revealed in her diary. This excerpt describes the preparations for a celebration honoring the birth of a new prince:

▲ Murasaki Shikibu

> "Even the sight of the lowest menials [servants], chattering to each other as they walked round lighting the fire baskets under the trees by the lake and arranging the food in the garden, seemed to add to the sense of occasion. Torchbearers stood everywhere at attention and the scene was as bright as day."
>
> —Murasaki Shikibu,
> *The Diary of Lady Murasaki*

▲ Scene from
The Tale of Genji

Then and Now

Do you keep a diary? What might you and your classmates record in a diary that would be useful to people a few centuries from now?

Economy and Society

Main Idea Some Japanese nobles, merchants, and artisans grew wealthy during the shogun period, but the lives of women remained restricted in many areas of life.

Reading Focus What determines whether a person is wealthy or poor? Read to find what contributed to the growing wealth of Japan.

Under the shoguns, Japan not only developed its arts but also produced more goods and grew richer. However, only a small number of Japanese benefited from this wealth. This group included the emperor, the nobles at his court, and leading military officials. A small but growing class of merchants and traders also began to prosper. Most Japanese, however, were farmers who remained poor.

Farmers and Artisans Much of Japan's wealth came from the hard work of its farmers. Japanese farmers grew rice, wheat, millet, and barley. Some had their own land, but most lived and worked on the daimyo estates. Despite hardships, life did improve for Japan's farmers during the 1100s. They used better irrigation and planted more crops. As a result, they could send more food to the markets that were developing in the towns.

At the same time, the Japanese were producing more goods. Artisans on the daimyo estates began making weapons, armor, and tools. Merchants sold these items in town markets throughout Japan. New roads made travel and trade much easier. As trade increased, each region focused on making goods that it could best produce. These goods included pottery, paper, textiles, and lacquered ware. All of these new products helped Japan's economy grow.

As the capital, **Kyoto** (kee•OH•toh) became a major center of production and trade. Many artisans and merchants settled there. They formed groups called **guilds** (GIHLDZ) (or *za* in Japanese) to protect and increase their profits. The members of these guilds relied on a wealthy daimyo to protect them from rival artisans. They sold the daimyo goods that he could not get from his country estates.

Japan's wealth also came from increased trade with Korea, China, and Southeast Asia. Japanese merchants exchanged lacquered goods, sword blades, and copper for silk, dyes, pepper, books, and porcelain.

◀ This painting shows Japanese farmers working the land. *What were some crops grown by medieval Japanese farmers?*

The Role of Women During the Middle Ages, a Japanese family included grandparents, parents, and children in the same household. A man headed the family and had total control over family members. A woman was expected to obey her father, husband, and son. In wealthy families, parents arranged the marriages of their children to increase the family's wealth.

In early Japan, about the time of Prince Shotoku, wealthy women enjoyed a high position in society. There were several women rulers, and women could own property. When Japan became a warrior society with samurai and daimyo, upper-class women lost these freedoms.

In farming families, women had a greater say in whom they married. However, they worked long hours in the fields planting or harvesting rice. In addition, they cooked, spun and wove cloth, and cared for their children. In the towns, the wives of artisans and merchants helped with family businesses and ran their homes. The wives of merchants were perhaps the best off.

Despite the lack of freedom, some women managed to contribute to Japan's culture. These talented women gained fame as artists, writers, and even warriors. In *The Tale of the Heike,* one female samurai named Tomoe is described this way:

> 66 **Tomoe was indescribably beautiful; the fairness of her face and the richness of her hair were startling to behold. Even so, she was a fearless rider and a woman skilled with the bow. Once her sword was drawn, even the gods . . . feared to fight against her. Indeed, she was a match for a thousand.** 99

—Heike Monogatori,
The Tale of the Heike

✓ **Reading Check** **Identify** Which groups in Japan benefited from the country's wealth?

History Online
Homework Helper Need help with the material in this section? Visit jat.glencoe.com

Section 3 Review

Reading Summary

Review the Main Ideas

- In medieval Japan, several forms of Buddhism, along with Shinto, were practiced, and the arts, architecture, and literature flourished.

- During the time of the shoguns, Japan's economy grew stronger. In the family, women lost some of their freedoms as Japan became a warrior society.

What Did You Learn?

1. How did the Shinto and Buddhist religions meet different needs in Japan?

2. What were Noh plays, and how were they performed?

Critical Thinking

3. **Organizing Information** Draw a table like the one shown. Add details to show the characteristics of Pure Land Buddhism and Zen Buddhism.

Pure Land Buddhism	Zen Buddhism

4. **Describe** How did guilds benefit artisans and daimyos?

5. **Analyze** Why do you think women lost some of their freedoms when Japan became a warrior society?

6. **Descriptive Writing** Write a brief article for a travel magazine describing the architecture of Shinto shrines and Buddhist temples in Japan during the Middle Ages.

Section 1 Early Japan

Vocabulary
clan
constitution
animism
shrine

Focusing on the Main Ideas
- Japan's mountains and islands isolated Japan and shaped its society. *(page 485)*
- Japan was settled by people who came from northeast Asia. They were organized into clans and ruled by warriors. *(page 486)*
- Prince Shotoku created Japan's first constitution and borrowed many ideas from China. *(page 488)*
- The Japanese religion, called Shinto, was based on nature spirits. *(page 490)*

Section 2 Shoguns and Samurai

Vocabulary
samurai
shogun
daimyo
vassal
feudalism

Focusing on the Main Ideas
- During the A.D. 700s, Japan built a strong national government at Nara, and Buddhism became a popular religion. *(page 492)*
- Japan's civilian government and the emperor came to be dominated by military rulers known as shoguns. *(page 493)*
- As the shogun's power weakened, Japan broke into warring kingdoms run by rulers known as daimyo. *(page 496)*

Section 3 Life in Medieval Japan

Vocabulary
sect
martial arts
meditation
calligraphy
tanka
guild

Focusing on the Main Ideas
- Buddhism and Shinto shaped much of Japan's culture. These religions affected Japanese art, architecture, novels, and plays. *(page 499)*
- Some Japanese nobles, merchants, and artisans grew wealthy during the shogun period, but the lives of women remained restricted in many areas of life. *(page 503)*

Murasaki Shikibu ▶

Chapter 14 Assessment and Activities

Review Vocabulary

Write the key term that completes each sentence.

a. tanka   e. shogun
b. daimyo   f. guilds
c. clans   g. samurai
d. sects   h. meditation

1. The ___ was the military leader of Japan.
2. Many artisans and merchants formed ___ for protection and profit.
3. The Yayoi formed ___ that were headed by a small group of warriors.
4. In ___, a person clears the mind of all thoughts and desires.
5. The ___ is an unrhymed poem of five lines.
6. Each vassal gave an oath of loyalty to his ___.
7. The private armies of Japanese nobles were made up of ___.
8. Buddhism was divided into many different ___.

Review Main Ideas

Section 1 • Early Japan

9. How did geography shape Japanese society?
10. How did Shotoku use Chinese government and culture as a model?

Section 2 • Shoguns and Samurai

11. Describe the roles of shoguns.
12. What happened when the shogun's power weakened?

Section 3 • Life in Medieval Japan

13. Which religions shaped much of Japan's culture?
14. How did the shogun period affect different groups of Japanese people?

Critical Thinking

15. **Analyze** Why do you think the early Japanese people were so independent?
16. **Contrast** How were the Yayoi more advanced than the Jomon?

Review Reading Skill — Cause and Effect — Identifying Cause and Effect

17. Read the paragraph below. Create a graphic organizer that shows the cause and effects described in the passage.

The sea surrounding Japan's islands made it easy for people in ships to travel along the coast and from island to island. It encouraged people to become merchants, traveling from village to village with goods to trade. The vast ocean around Japan's islands, however, kept the Japanese people isolated, or separate, from the rest of Asia. As a result, Japan developed its own fiercely independent society with its own religion, art, literature, and government.

To review this skill, see pages 482–483.

Geography Skills

Study the map below and answer the following questions.

18. **Place** Which of the four major Japanese islands has been home to the country's major cities?

19. **Human/Environment Interaction** How do you think Japan's geography and location have helped it become a center of production and trade?

20. **Location** Identify present-day countries, states, or provinces that are made up largely of islands. How are they similar to and different from the Japanese islands?

NATIONAL GEOGRAPHIC **Geography of Japan**

130°E 140°E
400 mi.
400 km
Lambert Conformal Conic projection
N W E S
Hokkaido
40°N
Honshu
Heian (Kyoto)
Mt. Fuji
Osaka
Edo (Tokyo)
Nara
Shikoku
Kyushu
30°N

Read to Write

21. **Creative Writing** Review this chapter and conduct research to gather information about the Mongols' attack on the Kamakura shogunate. Work with a group to write a script for a short play about the events before, during, and after the invasion. Use historical figures as well as fictional characters. Create a mask for each character, similar to the style of early Japanese masks. Present your play to the class.

22. **Using Your FOLDABLES** Write a poem, series of journal entries, or short story using the main ideas and supporting details from your completed foldable.

Using Technology

23. **Designing a City** When Emperor Kammu built Heian, he modeled it on Changan. If you were to design a city, what current cities and towns would inspire you? Use the Internet and your local library to research different features and layouts of cities. Combine the components you like best into a plan for a new city. Use a computer to make a scale drawing of your city. Then list the borrowed components and the current cities from which you borrowed them.

Linking Past and Present

24. **Analyzing Art** Medieval Japanese art, architecture, and literature reflected the Japanese love of beauty and simplicity. What values are reflected in present-day art?

Primary Source Analyze

Seami, a great actor in Noh plays, explained how acting is mastered.

"As long as an actor is trying to imitate his teacher, he is still without mastery. . . . An actor may be said to be a master when, by means of his artistic powers, he quickly perfects the skills he has won through study and practice, and thus becomes one with the art itself."

—Seami Jūokubushū Hyōshaku, "The Book of the Way of the Highest Flower (Shikadō-Sho)"

DBQ Document-Based Questions

25. What is the first step in learning acting?

26. How does an actor "become one with the art itself"?

Medieval Europe

Caerphilly Castle in
South Wales, United Kingdom ▼

NATIONAL GEOGRAPHIC When & Where?

A.D. 500	A.D. 825	1150	1475
A.D. 496 King Clovis becomes a Catholic	C. A.D. 800 Feudalism begins in Europe	1095 First Crusade begins	1346 Black Death arrives in Europe

Chapter Preview

Between A.D. 500 and 1500, Europe was ruled by warriors much like those in early Japan. Despite constant fighting, Europeans made advances in their culture. European ideas about government and religion still shape our lives today.

History Online
Chapter Overview Visit jat.glencoe.com for a preview of Chapter 15.

View the Chapter 15 video in the *World History: Journey Across Time* Video Program.

The Early Middle Ages

During the Middle Ages, Western Europe built a new civilization based on Christian, Roman, and Germanic ways.

Feudalism

Government weakness and the need for safety led to the rise of feudalism.

Kingdoms and Crusades

As the kingdoms of England and France established parliaments, Russia's rulers laid the foundations for its government.

The Church and Society

Religion in medieval Europe helped to shape European culture.

The Late Middle Ages

Disease and war took the lives of millions of people in the late Middle Ages.

FOLDABLES™
Study Organizer

Sequencing Information *Make this foldable to help you sequence important events that occurred in medieval Europe.*

Step 1 *Fold two sheets of paper in half from top to bottom. Cut each in half.*

Cut along the fold lines.

Step 2 *Turn and fold the four pieces in half from top to bottom.*

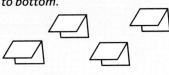

Step 3 *Tape the ends of the pieces together (overlapping the edges slightly) to make an accordion time line.*

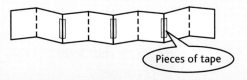

Pieces of tape

Reading and Writing *As you read the chapter, write the important events and dates that occurred in medieval Europe on each section of your time line.*

509

Reading Social Studies

1 Learn It!

Just Ask

Answering questions about what you have read is one way to show what you know, but asking thoughtful questions about the topic can often show even greater understanding. How do you learn to ask great questions?

1. Use question starters such as *who, what, when, where, how,* and *why*.
2. Do more than just read the words on the page—think deeply about the concepts. For example, ask questions such as "What would have happened if . . .?"

Read the following passage from Section 5, and look at the questions that follow.

> Charles, the prince who ruled southern France, wanted to take back the north. In 1429 a French peasant girl named Joan was brought to him. She told him that her favorite saints had urged her to free France. Joan's honesty persuaded Charles to let her go with a French army to Orléans. Joan's faith stirred the soldiers, and they took the city.
>
> —*from page 557*

Reading Tip

Make studying like a game. Create questions and then read to find answers to your own questions.

Here are some questions you might ask about the above paragraph:

- What did Joan say to persuade Charles to let her ride with the army?
- How did Joan's faith stir the soldiers?
- Why did Joan believe saints wanted her to free France?
- What happened to Joan after the French took the city?

2 Practice It!

Ask and Answer

Read this passage about the Black Death.

A terrible plague, known as the Black Death, swept across Europe and Asia. A plague is a disease that spreads quickly and kills many people. Most scientists think the Black Death was bubonic plague—a disease caused by a type of bacteria carried by fleas. These fleas infested black rats, and in the Middle Ages, these rats were everywhere.

—from page 554

Read to Write

Write a *What If* paragraph based on your reading. For example, *what if* Joan had become Queen of France, or *what if* fleas carried the Black Death today? Add lots of details as if you were answering questions others might ask about your *What If* ideas.

Create three questions based on the above paragraph. Remember that not all questions have answers.

3 Apply It!

As you read the chapter, look for answers to section headings that are in the form of questions. For the other sections, turn the headings into questions that you can answer as you read.

The Early Middle Ages

Get Ready to Read!

What's the Connection?

After the fall of Rome came a period called the Middle Ages, or medieval times. It is a fitting name for the period that lies between ancient and modern times.

Focusing on the Main Ideas

- Geography influenced where medieval Europeans settled and what they did. *(page 513)*

- The Franks, Angles, and Saxons of Western Europe built new societies and defended them against Muslims, Magyars, and Vikings. *(page 514)*

- The Catholic Church spread Christianity through Western Europe. *(page 519)*

Locating Places

Aachen (AH•kuhn)
Scandinavia (SKAN•duh•NAY•vee•uh)
Holy Roman Empire

Meeting People

Clovis (KLOH•vuhs)
Charles Martel (mahr•TEHL)
Charlemagne (SHAHR•luh•MAYN)
Otto I (AH•toh)
Gregory the Great

Building Your Vocabulary

fjord (fee•AWRD)
missionary (MIH•shuh•NEHR•ee)
excommunicate
  (EHK•skuh•MYOO•nuh•KAYT)
concordat (kuhn•KAWR•DAT)

Reading Strategy

Organizing Information Create a table to show the major accomplishments of medieval leaders.

Leader	Major Accomplishments

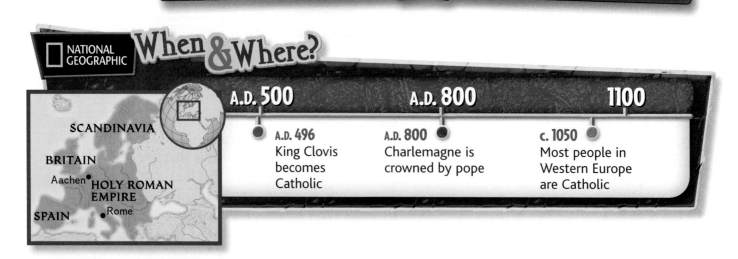

NATIONAL GEOGRAPHIC **When & Where?**

SCANDINAVIA
BRITAIN
Aachen • HOLY ROMAN EMPIRE
SPAIN • Rome

A.D. 500   **A.D. 800**   **1100**

A.D. 496
King Clovis becomes Catholic

A.D. 800
Charlemagne is crowned by pope

c. 1050
Most people in Western Europe are Catholic

The Geography of Europe

Main Idea Geography influenced where medieval Europeans settled and what they did.

Reading Focus If you wanted to go sledding or swimming, where would you go? Your answer will be based partly on geography. Read to learn how geography shaped life in Europe during the Middle Ages.

The Roman Empire had united all the land surrounding the Mediterranean Sea. When the last Roman emperor in the West fell from power in A.D. 476, that unity was lost. Western Europe was divided into many kingdoms as wave after wave of Germanic invaders swept south and west, conquering large areas of Europe.

Now that Rome no longer united people, Europe's geography began to play a more important role in shaping events. Europe is a continent, but it is also a very large peninsula made up of many smaller peninsulas. As a result, most of Europe lies within 300 miles (483 km) of an ocean or sea. This encouraged trade and fishing and helped Europe's economy to grow.

Rivers also played an important role in Europe. The Rhine, Danube, Vistula, Volga, Seine, and Po Rivers made it easy to travel into the interior of Europe and encouraged people to trade.

The seas and rivers provided safety as well as opportunities for trade. The English Channel, for instance, separated Britain and Ireland from the rest of Europe. As a result,

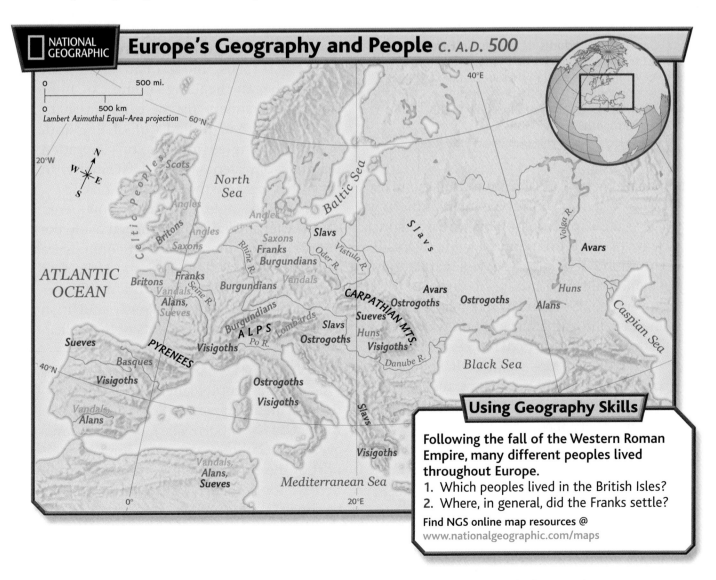

Europe's Geography and People c. A.D. 500

Using Geography Skills

Following the fall of the Western Roman Empire, many different peoples lived throughout Europe.
1. Which peoples lived in the British Isles?
2. Where, in general, did the Franks settle?

Find NGS online map resources @
www.nationalgeographic.com/maps

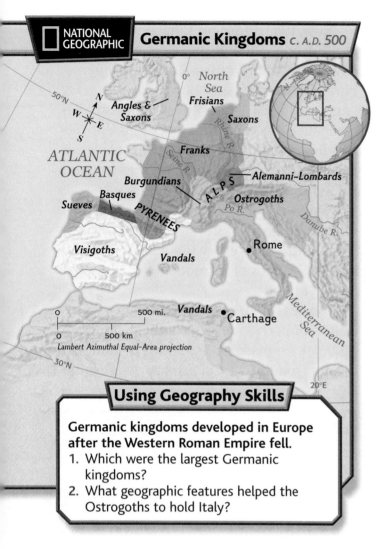

NATIONAL GEOGRAPHIC **Germanic Kingdoms** C. A.D. 500

Using Geography Skills

Germanic kingdoms developed in Europe after the Western Roman Empire fell.
1. Which were the largest Germanic kingdoms?
2. What geographic features helped the Ostrogoths to hold Italy?

The Germanic Kingdoms

Main Idea The Franks, Angles, and Saxons of Western Europe built new societies and defended them against Muslims, Magyars, and Vikings.

Reading Focus Have you ever moved to a new place? What adjustments did you have to make? Read to learn how the Germanic peoples who invaded Europe had to adjust to the lands they occupied.

After Rome fell, Western Europe was divided into many kingdoms. These kingdoms developed different societies based on their locations. The Visigoths in Spain and the Ostrogoths in Italy were close to the center of the old Roman Empire. As a result, they adopted many Roman ways. People farther from Rome held on to more of their Germanic traditions.

In Britain as the empire began to weaken, Roman culture declined quickly. In the A.D. 300s, the Roman legions in Britain began heading home to fight Germanic invaders. By the early A.D 400s, the Romans had pulled out of England. Soon the Angles and Saxons invaded Britain from Denmark and Germany. In time, they became the Anglo-Saxons.

When the Angles and Saxons conquered southeastern Britain, they pushed aside the people living there. These people were called the Celts (KEHLTS). Some Celts fled north and west to the mountains. Others went to Ireland. Scottish, Welsh, and Irish people today are descendants of the Celts.

Who Were the Franks? During the A.D. 400s, a Germanic people called the Franks settled the area that is now France. In A.D. 496 King **Clovis** (KLOH•vuhs) of the Franks became a Catholic. This won him the support of the Romans living in his kingdom. Before long, nearly all of the Franks became Catholic.

people there were sheltered from the many wars fought on Europe's mainland. They were able to develop their own distinct ways of life. Within Europe, wide rivers like the Rhine also kept people separated and enabled different cultures to develop.

Europe also has many mountain ranges. In the east, the Carpathians cut off what is now Ukraine and Russia from southeast Europe. In the middle, the Alps separated Italy from central Europe. To the southwest, the Pyrenees isolated Spain and Portugal. The mountains, like the rivers, made it difficult for one group to rule all of Europe and encouraged the development of independent kingdoms.

Reading Check **Identify** What did Europe's seas and rivers provide for its people?

After Clovis died, his sons divided the kingdom among themselves. Later, their sons divided these kingdoms even further. These kings often fought over land. While they fought, the nobles under them took over many royal duties. The most important of these nobles was called the "mayor of the palace." By A.D. 700, the mayors were giving out land, settling disputes, and fighting their own wars.

Of all the mayors, the most powerful was **Charles Martel** (mahr•TEHL). He wanted to unite all the Frankish nobles under his rule. The Catholic Church wanted to restore the Western Roman Empire and was willing to support rulers who had a chance to reunite Europe. The pope—the head of the Catholic Church—offered his support to Charles Martel.

First, however, Europe had to be kept Christian. In A.D. 711 a Muslim army from North Africa conquered Spain. The Muslim forces wanted to spread Islam across Europe. In A.D. 732 Charles Martel led the Franks against the Muslims. He defeated them at the Battle of Tours. This stopped the Muslim advance into Europe. As a result, Christianity remained Western Europe's major religion.

When Charles Martel died, his son Pepin (PEH•puhn) became mayor of the palace. With the help of the pope and most Frankish nobles, Pepin became the new king of the Franks. When a Germanic group called the Lombards threatened the pope, Pepin took his army into Italy and defeated them. He donated the land he had conquered to the pope. The pope ruled these lands as if he were a king, and they became known as the Papal States.

Who Was Charlemagne?

After Pepin died, his son Charles became king. Like his father, Charles went to the aid of the pope when the Lombards tried to regain their territory. He also invaded Germany and defeated the Saxons living there. He ordered them to convert to Christianity. He then invaded Spain and gained control of the northeastern corner from the Muslims.

By A.D. 800, Charles's kingdom had grown into an empire. It covered much of western and central Europe. Charles's

The Crowning of Charlemagne

In A.D. 800 the pope crowned Charlemagne "Emperor of the Romans," officially creating a new Roman Empire. *How large was Charlemagne's empire in A.D. 800?*

The Frankish Kingdom C. A.D. 500–800

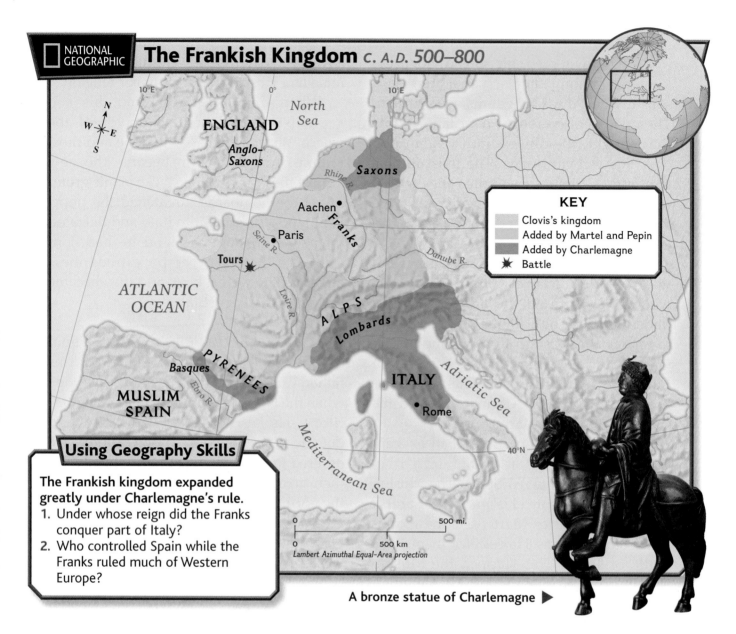

KEY
- Clovis's kingdom
- Added by Martel and Pepin
- Added by Charlemagne
- ✸ Battle

ENGLAND
Anglo-Saxons
North Sea
Saxons
Rhine R.
Aachen •
Franks
• Paris
Seine R.
Tours ✸
Danube R.
ATLANTIC OCEAN
Loire R.
A L P S
Lombards
Basques
PYRENEES
Ebro R.
MUSLIM SPAIN
ITALY
• Rome
Adriatic Sea
Mediterranean Sea
40°N

0   500 mi.
0   500 km
Lambert Azimuthal Equal-Area projection

Using Geography Skills

The Frankish kingdom expanded greatly under Charlemagne's rule.
1. Under whose reign did the Franks conquer part of Italy?
2. Who controlled Spain while the Franks ruled much of Western Europe?

A bronze statue of Charlemagne ▶

conquests earned him the name of **Charlemagne** (SHAHR•luh•MAYNE), or Charles the Great.

The pope was impressed with Charlemagne. On Christmas day in A.D. 800, Charlemagne was worshiping at the church of St. Peter in Rome. After the service, the pope placed a crown on Charlemagne's head and declared him the new Roman emperor. Charlemagne was pleased but also concerned. He did not want people to think the pope had the power to choose who was emperor.

Charlemagne made **Aachen** (AH•kuhn) the capital of his empire. To uphold his

laws, he set up courts throughout the empire. Nobles called counts ran the courts. To keep the counts under control, Charlemagne sent out inspectors called "the lord's messengers" to make sure the counts were obeying orders.

Unlike other earlier Frankish rulers, Charlemagne believed in education. He had tried late in life to learn to write and wanted his people to be educated too. He asked a scholar named Alcuin (AL•kwuhn) to start a school in one of the royal palaces. Alcuin trained the children of government officials. His students studied religion, Latin, music, literature, and arithmetic.

Biography

CHARLEMAGNE
A.D. 742–814

Charles the Great (Charlemagne) became king of the Franks at age 29. He married and divorced many different women and had at least 18 children.

Charlemagne was an intelligent person. He studied many subjects and especially enjoyed astronomy. He could speak many languages, including German, Latin, and Greek. He also could read but had trouble writing. Einhard, the king's historian and scribe, wrote that Charlemagne "used to keep tablets under his pillow in order that at leisure hours he might accustom his hand to form the letters; but as he began these efforts so late in life, they met with ill success."

Charlemagne was disappointed to learn that the Franks were not as educated as the people of Britain and Ireland. In A.D. 782 he arranged for several famous scholars to come to his capital in Aachen and create a school in the royal palace. During his reign, schools opened throughout his empire, and many people were educated.

▲ Charlemagne

▼ The Palatine Chapel at Charlemagne's palace in Aachen

"No one shall . . . be kept back from the right path of justice by . . . fear of the powerful."

–Charlemagne, as quoted in "The World of Charlemagne"

Then and Now

Charlemagne realized the importance of education. He arranged reading and writing lessons for his people. What types of school programs does our government fund?

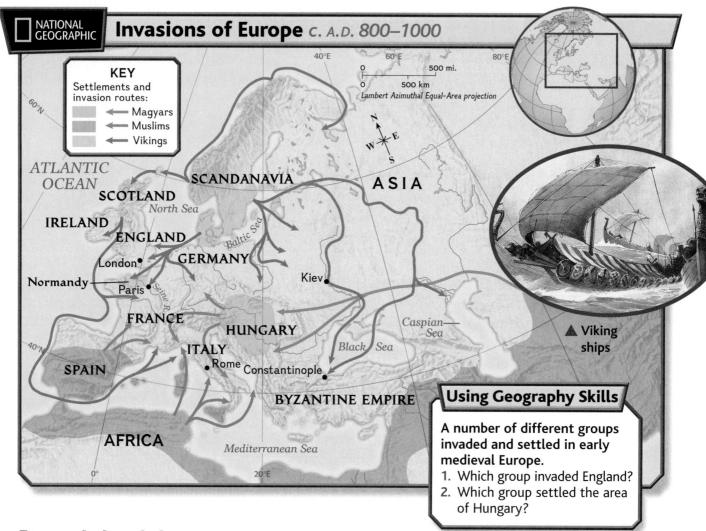

Invasions of Europe C. A.D. 800–1000

KEY
Settlements and invasion routes:
← Magyars
← Muslims
← Vikings

0   500 mi.
0   500 km
Lambert Azimuthal Equal-Area projection

ATLANTIC OCEAN
SCANDANAVIA
ASIA
SCOTLAND
North Sea
IRELAND
ENGLAND
Baltic Sea
London
GERMANY
Normandy
Paris
Seine R.
Kiev
FRANCE
Caspian Sea
HUNGARY
Black Sea
ITALY
Rome
Constantinople
SPAIN
▲ Viking ships
BYZANTINE EMPIRE
AFRICA
Mediterranean Sea

Using Geography Skills

A number of different groups invaded and settled in early medieval Europe.
1. Which group invaded England?
2. Which group settled the area of Hungary?

Europe Is Invaded After Charlemagne died in A.D. 814, his empire did not last long. His son Louis was not a strong leader, and after Louis died, Louis's sons divided the empire into three kingdoms.

These three kingdoms were weakened further by a wave of invaders who swept across Europe in the A.D. 800s and A.D. 900s. From the south came Muslims, who raided France and Italy from Spain and North Africa. From the east came the Magyars, a nomadic people who had settled in Hungary. From **Scandinavia** (SKAN•duh•NAY•vee•uh) came the Vikings, whose raids terrified all of Europe.

Scandinavia is in northern Europe. Norway, Sweden, and Denmark are all part of Scandinavia today. Much of Scandinavia has a long, jagged coastline. It has many **fjords** (fee•AWRDS), or steep-sided valleys that are inlets of the sea. The Viking people lived in villages in the fjords. They were known as the Norsemen, or "north men."

Scandinavia has little farmland. This forced the Vikings to rely on the sea for food and trade. They became skilled sailors and built sturdy boats called longboats. These boats could survive the rough Atlantic and also navigate shallow rivers.

In the A.D. 700s and A.D. 800s, the Vikings began raiding Europe, probably because their population had grown too big to support itself at home. The word *viking* comes from their word for raiding. They robbed villages and churches, carrying off grain, animals, and anything else of value. They even conquered part of western France. This area was named Normandy, after the Norsemen who ruled it.

The Holy Roman Empire

The raids by Muslims, Magyars, and Vikings helped to destroy the Frankish kingdoms. In the A.D. 900s, the eastern Frankish kingdom, which became known as Germany, was divided into many tiny states ruled by counts, dukes, and other nobles. In A.D. 911 a group of these nobles tried to unite Germany by electing a king. The king did not have much power, however, because the nobles wanted to remain independent.

One of the stronger kings of Germany was **Otto I** (AH•toh). He fought the Magyars and sent troops into Italy to protect the pope. To reward Otto for his help, the pope declared him emperor of the Romans in A.D. 962. Otto's territory, which included most of Germany and northern Italy, became known as the **Holy Roman Empire.**

Most of the emperors of the Holy Roman Empire were not very powerful. Two of the strongest ones, Frederick I and Frederick II, tried to unite northern Italy and Germany under a single ruler with a strong central government in the 1100s and 1200s. The popes fought against these plans because they did not want the emperor to control them. They banded together with Italy's cities to resist the emperors' forces. As a result, both Germany and Italy remained divided into small kingdoms until the 1800s.

Reading Check Explain Who were the Vikings, and why did they raid Europe?

The Rise of the Catholic Church

Main Idea The Catholic Church spread Christianity through Western Europe.

Reading Focus Do you have a goal you would devote your life to reaching? Read to learn the goals of the Catholic Church in the early Middle Ages.

Both religion and geography played an important role in shaping life in Europe. By the time the Western Roman Empire collapsed, Christianity had become the official religion of Rome. After the Roman government fell apart, the Roman Catholic Church began to play an important role in the growth of a new civilization in Western Europe.

Why Were Monks Important?

At the time Rome fell, much of northwest Europe was not yet Christian. One exception was Ireland. In the A.D. 400s, a priest named Patrick traveled to Ireland, where he spread the Christian message and set up churches and monasteries. For several hundred years,

▲ Pope Gregory I helped spread Christianity in a number of ways. Here he is shown teaching boys the songs that became known as Gregorian chants. *Which area of northwest Europe had accepted Christianity before the fall of the Western Roman Empire?*

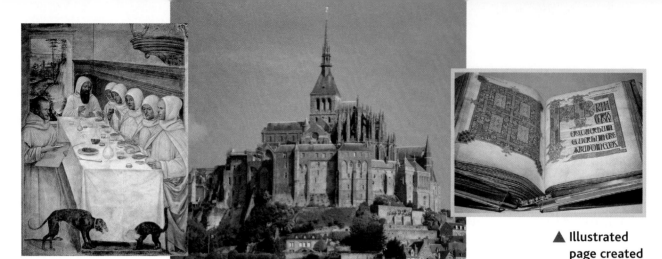

▲ Monks eating together in a monastery

▲ The monastery at Mont St. Michel in France is a beautiful work of architecture that took several hundred years to complete. *How did monasteries help local people in Europe?*

▲ Illustrated page created by monks

Irish monks played an important role in preserving Roman learning and passing it on to the people of Europe.

Patrick's success inspired others, including Pope Gregory I, or **Gregory the Great.** Gregory I was pope from A.D. 590 to A.D. 604. He wanted all of Europe to become Christian, and he asked monks to become **missionaries** (MIH•shuh•NEHR•eez)—people who are sent out to teach their religion.

In A.D. 597 Gregory sent 40 monks to southern Britain to teach Christianity. The monks converted Ethelbert, ruler of the kingdom of Kent. Ethelbert allowed the missionaries to build a church in his capital city of Canterbury. Meanwhile, Irish monks brought Christianity to northern Britain. By A.D. 800, monks were spreading Christianity throughout Europe. As a result, most people in Western Europe had become Catholics by 1050.

Monasteries played an important role in medieval Europe. Monks schooled people, provided food and rest to travelers, and offered hospital care for the sick. They taught carpentry and weaving and developed better methods of farming. They also helped to preserve knowledge.

Many monasteries had scriptoria, or writing rooms, where monks made copies of important works. The monks copied Christian writings, including the Bible, as well as works of Roman and Greek writers.

Over time, monasteries began to play a role in Europe's politics. Monks took a vow of poverty, wore simple clothes, and ate simple food, but their monasteries could make money. Each monastery produced goods and owned land, and over time many of them became wealthy. The leader of a monastery is called an abbot (A•buht), and many abbots became involved in politics. They served as advisers to kings and acted as rulers of the lands near their monasteries.

Why Is Gregory VII Important? The growing role of abbots and other Church leaders in Europe's politics caused many arguments over who was in charge. Kings wanted Church leaders to obey them, while the pope claimed he could crown kings.

In 1073 Gregory VII was elected pope. He wanted to stop nobles and kings from interfering in Church affairs. He issued a decree, or order, forbidding kings from appointing high-ranking Church officials.

The pope's decree angered Henry IV, the Holy Roman emperor. For many years, the Holy Roman emperor had appointed bishops in Germany. Without them, Henry IV risked losing power to the nobles.

Henry refused to obey Gregory. He declared that Gregory was no longer pope. Gregory then stated that Henry was no longer emperor. He **excommunicated** (EHK•skuh•MYOO•nuh•KAY•tuhd) Henry. This means to exclude a person from church membership. Catholics believed that if they were excommunicated, they could not go to heaven.

When the German nobles defended the pope, Henry backed down. He traveled to Italy and stood barefoot in the snow outside the pope's castle asking to be forgiven. Gregory forgave Henry, but the German nobles still chose a new king. When Gregory accepted the new king as emperor, Henry went to war. He captured Rome and named a new pope. Gregory's allies drove out Henry's forces, but the dispute was not resolved.

In 1122 a new pope and the German king finally agreed that only the pope could choose bishops, but only the emperor could give them jobs in the government. This deal, called the Concordat of Worms, was signed in the city of Worms. A **concordat** (kuhn•KAWR•DAT) is an agreement between the pope and the ruler of a country.

By the time Innocent III became pope in 1198, the Catholic Church was at the height of its power. Innocent was able to control kings. If a ruler did not obey, Innocent would excommunicate him or issue an interdict (IHN•tuhr•DIHKT) against the ruler's people. An interdict forbids priests from providing Christian rituals to a group of people. The pope hoped that by using an interdict, local people would pressure their ruler to obey.

✔**Reading Check** **Contrast** How did Gregory VII and Henry IV disagree?

History **O**nline

Homework Helper Need help with the material in this section? Visit jat.glencoe.com

Section ① Review

Reading Summary

Review the (Main Ideas)

• During the Middle Ages, Europe's geography affected where people lived, their ways of life, and their relations with other people.

• The Angles and Saxons invaded Britain, the Franks created an empire in Western Europe, and the Saxons created a German kingdom that became the Holy Roman Empire.

• Monks helped spread Christianity throughout Europe, and the Catholic Church became strong in the early Middle Ages.

What Did You Learn?

1. What happened at the Battle of Tours, and why is the battle significant?

2. Why were monasteries important to medieval Europe?

Critical Thinking

3. **Summarizing Information** Draw a diagram like the one below. Use it to describe the role of monks in medieval Europe.

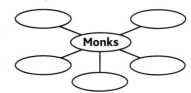

Monks

4. **Analyze** How did Charlemagne demonstrate his support for education?

5. **Describe** Imagine you live in central Europe in medieval times. Prepare a poster that describes the Vikings and the dangers they pose to your town.

6. **Reading** **Asking Questions** Henry IV "stood barefoot in the snow" to gain the pope's forgiveness. If you were asked to interview Henry IV about this experience, what three questions would you ask?

Section 2

Feudalism

Get Ready to Read!

What's the Connection?

In the last section, you read how the Vikings spread fear and destruction throughout Europe. During the Middle Ages, villagers and townspeople looked to nobles to protect them.

Focusing on the Main Ideas

- Feudalism developed in Europe in the Middle Ages. It was based on landowning, loyalty, and the power of armored knights on horseback. *(page 523)*

- Knights followed a code of chivalry and lived in castles, while peasants lived in simple houses and worked hard all year long. *(page 526)*

- Increased trade led to the growth of towns and cities and the rise of guilds and city governments. *(page 528)*

Locating Places

Venice (VEH•nuhs)

Flanders (FLAN•duhrz)

Building Your Vocabulary

feudalism (FYOO•duhl•IH•zuhm)

vassal (VA•suhl)

fief (FEEF)

knight (NYT)

serf (SUHRF)

guild (GIHLD)

Reading Strategy

Compare and Contrast Complete a Venn diagram like the one below showing the similarities and differences between serfs and slaves.

Serfs   Slaves

When & Where?

NATIONAL GEOGRAPHIC

A.D. 800   1000   1200

c. A.D. 800s
Feudalism
begins in Europe

c. 1100
Flanders and
Italy trade
goods regularly

c. 1200
Guilds are
widespread
in Europe

SCANDINAVIA
ENGLAND
Bruges• HOLY ROMAN
FRANCE EMPIRE
SPAIN   •Venice
                •Rome
        ITALY

What Is Feudalism?

Main Idea Feudalism developed in Europe in the Middle Ages. It was based on landowning, loyalty, and the power of armored knights on horseback.

Reading Focus What would it be like to live in a country where the government has fallen apart? Read to learn how the fall of Charlemagne's government changed life for people in the Middle Ages.

When Charlemagne's grandfather, Charles Martel, needed an army to fight the Muslims invading France, he began giving estates—large farms—to nobles willing to fight for him. The nobles used the income from the estates to pay for their horses and weapons. Although Charles Martel did not realize it, he was using a new way of organizing society that would eventually spread across most of Europe.

When Charlemagne's empire collapsed, Western Europe lost its last strong central government. Landowning nobles became more and more powerful. They gained the right to collect taxes and to enforce laws on their estates. When invaders spread ruin throughout Europe, the peasants, or farmers, could not rely on kings. Instead, they looked to nobles for protection.

During the A.D. 800s, this shift of power from kings to nobles led to a new system known as **feudalism** (FYOO•duhl•IH•zuhm). Under feudalism, landowning nobles governed and protected the people in return for services, such as fighting in a noble's army or farming the land. By A.D. 1000, the kingdoms of Europe were divided into thousands of feudal territories. Some of these territories were large, but most were very small, smaller even than the city-states of Greece and Sumeria. At the center of each, however, was not a city but a noble's castle, or fortress.

The Role of Vassals and Knights

Feudalism was based on ties of loyalty and duty among nobles. Nobles were both lords and vassals. A **vassal** (VA•suhl) was a noble who served a lord of higher rank. In return, the lord protected the vassal.

The tie between a lord and his vassal was made known in a public ceremony. The vassal put his hands together and placed them between the hands of his lord. Then the vassal swore "to keep faith and loyalty to you against all others."

Kings and queens

Lords and ladies

Knights

Peasants and serfs

▲ Under feudalism each level of society had duties to the groups above and below it. *Which group in the diagram served as vassals to the lords and ladies?*

A vassal showed his loyalty by serving in his lord's army. In return for the vassal's military service, a lord granted his vassal land. The land granted to a vassal was known as a **fief** (FEEF). Vassals governed the people who lived on their fiefs.

These vassals were **knights** (NYTS), or warriors in armor who fought on horseback. Up until the A.D. 700s, nobles in Western Europe mostly fought on foot. They wore coats of mail—armor made from metal links—and carried swords and shields. In the A.D. 700s, a new invention, the stirrup, made it possible for an armored man to sit on a horse and charge while holding a lance, a long heavy spear. Knights would charge enemies, spearing them with their lances. From the A.D. 700s to the 1200s, armored knights on horseback were the most powerful soldiers in Europe.

Europe was not the only place with a feudal society. As you remember from an earlier chapter, Japan had a similar system between A.D. 800 and 1500. Powerful nobles owed only a loose loyalty to the Japanese emperor. The nobles in turn relied on samurai. Like knights, the samurai owed loyalty to their lords and provided military service for them. Also like knights in Europe, the samurai wore armor and fought on horseback.

What Was the Manorial System? The fiefs of the Middle Ages were called manors. The lords ruled the manor, and peasants worked the land. Some peasants were freemen, who paid the noble for the right to farm the land. They had rights under the law and could move whenever and wherever they wished.

Most peasants, however, were **serfs** (SUHRFS). Serfs could not leave the manor, own property, or marry without the lord's approval. Lords even had the right to try

A Medieval Manor

A medieval manor usually consisted of the lord's manor house or castle, the surrounding fields, and a peasant village. While minor knights or nobles would own only one manor, more powerful lords might own several. A powerful lord would spend time at each of his manors during the year. *What duty did lords have to their serfs?*

Fields
In the spring, serfs planted crops such as summer wheat, barley, oats, peas, and beans. Crops planted in the fall included winter wheat and rye. Women often helped in the fields.

serfs in their own court. Serfs were not enslaved, however. Lords could not sell the serfs or take away the land given to serfs to support themselves. Lords also had a duty to protect their serfs, providing them the safety they needed to grow crops.

Serfs worked long hours on the lord's land and performed services for the lord. They spent three days working for the lord and the rest of the week growing food for themselves. They also had to give a portion of their own crops to the lord and pay him for the use of the village's mill, bread oven, and winepress.

It was not easy for serfs to gain their freedom. One way was to run away to the towns. If a serf remained in a town for more than a year, he or she was considered free. By the end of the Middle Ages, serfs in many kingdoms were also allowed to buy their freedom.

How Did Farming Improve? During the Middle Ages, Europeans invented new technology that helped increase the amount of crops they could grow. Perhaps the most important was a heavy wheeled plow with an iron blade. It easily turned over Western Europe's dense clay soils.

Another important invention was the horse collar. The horse collar made it possible for a horse to pull a plow. Horses could pull plows much faster than oxen, allowing peasants to plant more crops and produce more food.

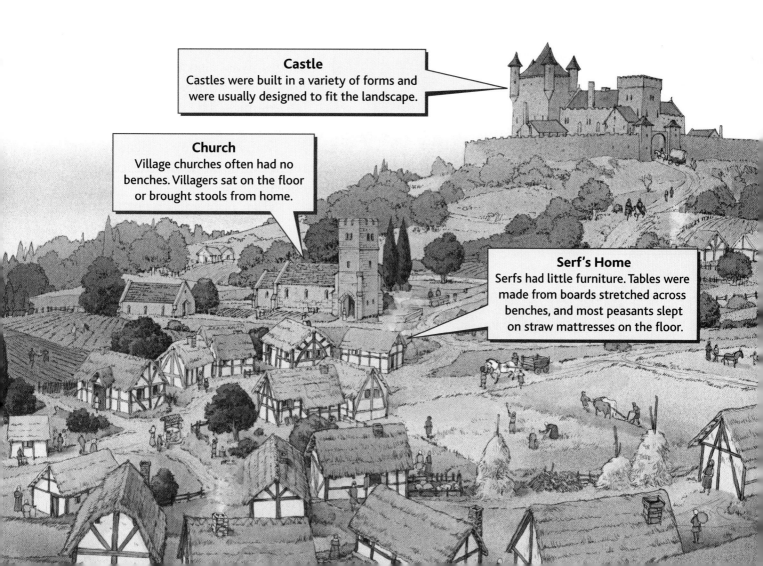

Castle
Castles were built in a variety of forms and were usually designed to fit the landscape.

Church
Village churches often had no benches. Villagers sat on the floor or brought stools from home.

Serf's Home
Serfs had little furniture. Tables were made from boards stretched across benches, and most peasants slept on straw mattresses on the floor.

Europeans also found new ways to harness water and wind power. Europe's many rivers powered water mills that ground grain into flour. Where rivers were not available, windmills were used for grinding grains, pumping water, and cutting wood.

Peasants also learned to grow more food by rotating crops on three fields instead of two. The rotation kept soil fertile. One field was planted in fall and another in spring. The third field was left unplanted. The three-field system meant that only one-third, rather than one-half, of the land was unused at any time. As a result, more crops could be grown.

Reading Check **Explain** How could a noble be both a lord and a vassal?

▲ Nobles celebrated special occasions with large feasts, which included many courses of meats, fruits, and vegetables. *What were the wife's duties when a nobleman went off to war?*

Life in Feudal Europe

Main Idea Knights followed a code of chivalry and lived in castles, while peasants lived in simple houses and worked hard all year long.

Reading Focus Have you heard the phrase "knight in shining armor"? Read to learn why these words apply to how a knight acts as well as how he dresses.

During the Middle Ages, nobles were the most powerful people in Europe. Great lords had much more wealth and land than ordinary knights. However, their belief in the feudal system united lords and knights in defending their society.

How Did Nobles Live? Knights followed certain rules called the code of chivalry (SHIH•vuhl•ree). A knight was expected to obey his lord, to be brave, to show respect to women of noble birth, to honor the church, and to help people. A knight was also expected to be honest and to fight fairly against his enemies. The code of chivalry became the guide to good behavior. Many of today's ideas about manners come from the code of chivalry.

When noblemen went to war, their wives or daughters ran the manors. This was no small job because manors had many officials and servants. Keeping track of the household's accounts took considerable skill. The lady of a manor also had to oversee the storing of food and other supplies needed to run the household.

The center of the manor was a castle. At first, castles were built of wood. Later, they were built of stone. A castle had two basic parts. One was a human-made or

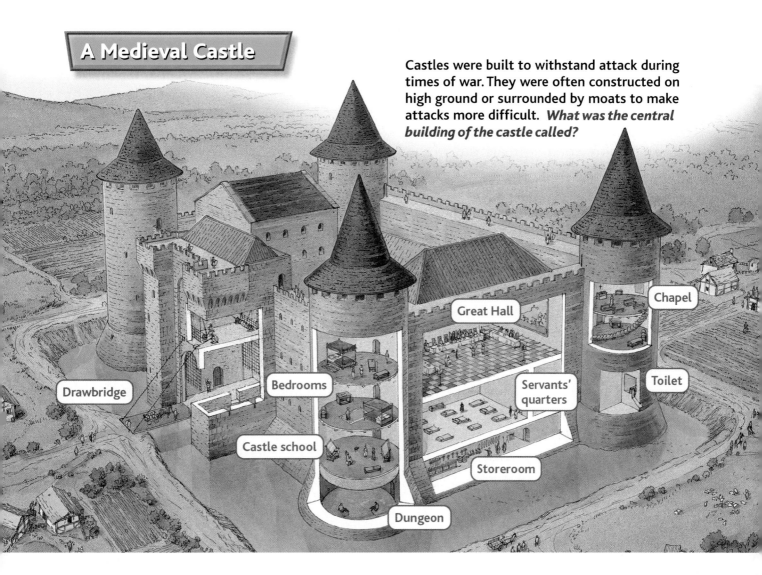

Castles were built to withstand attack during times of war. They were often constructed on high ground or surrounded by moats to make attacks more difficult. *What was the central building of the castle called?*

Great Hall

Chapel

Drawbridge

Bedrooms

Servants' quarters

Toilet

Castle school

Storeroom

Dungeon

naturally steep-sided hill called a motte (MAHT). The bailey was an open space next to the motte. High stone walls encircled the motte and bailey. The keep, or central building of the castle, was built on the motte.

The keep had a number of stories. The basement housed storerooms for tools and food. On the ground floor were kitchens and stables, and above the ground floor was a great hall. Here the people of the household ate and sometimes slept, and the lord of the castle held court and received visitors. Smaller rooms opened off the great hall. They included chapels, toilets, and bedrooms with huge curtained beds.

In the later Middle Ages, nobles owned more jewelry, better clothes, and exotic spices. They also built more elaborate castles with thicker walls, more towers, finer furniture, and richer decoration.

What Was Peasant Life Like? The homes of peasants were much simpler. They lived in wood-frame cottages plastered with clay. Their roofs were thatched with straw. The houses of poorer peasants had a single room. Better cottages had a main room for cooking and eating and another room for sleeping.

Peasants worked year-round. They harvested grain in August and September. In October they prepared the ground for winter crops. In November they slaughtered livestock and salted the meat to keep it for winter. In February and March, they plowed the land for planting oats, barley, peas, and beans. In early summer they weeded the fields, sheared the sheep, and tended small vegetable gardens.

Peasants took a break from work and went to church on Catholic feast days. They celebrated more than 50 feast days each year. The most important were Christmas and Easter. On feast days and at Sunday worship, the village priest taught them the basic beliefs of Christianity.

Peasant women worked in the fields and raised children at the same time. They also gathered and prepared their family's food. Each day they mixed bread dough and baked it in community ovens. Bread was a basic staple of the medieval diet. Peasant bread was dark and heavy. Peasants ate it with vegetables, milk, nuts, and fruits. Sometimes they added eggs or meat, and they often had ale to drink.

Reading Check **Identify** What was the code of chivalry?

Trade and Cities

Main Idea Increased trade led to the growth of towns and cities and the rise of guilds and city governments.

Reading Focus What effect would a new shopping mall have on your community? Read to learn how the growth of trade and the rise of cities changed the way people lived and worked in medieval Europe.

When the Roman Empire collapsed, almost all trade in Western Europe came to an end. Bridges and roads fell into disrepair. Law and order vanished. Money was no longer used. Most people spent their entire lives in the tiny villages where they were born and knew almost nothing about the rest of the world.

By 1100, feudalism had made Europe safer, and new technology enabled people to produce more food and goods. Nobles

Medieval City Life

◄ This scene shows a market in a medieval town. *Which area became the center of trade for northern Europe?*

A mayor of London from the early 1200s ▶

repaired bridges and roads, arrested bandits, and enforced the law. As a result, trade resumed.

As trade increased, towns grew larger, and several cities became wealthy from trade. For example, the city of **Venice** (VEH•nuhs) in Italy built a fleet of trading ships. It became a major trading center by A.D. 1000. Venice and other Italian cities began trading with the Byzantine Empire and soon became the center of trade in the Mediterranean.

Meanwhile, towns in **Flanders** (FLAN•duhrz)—which today is part of Belgium—became the center of trade for northern Europe. This area was known for its woolen cloth. Merchants from England, Scandinavia, France, and the Holy Roman Empire met there to trade their goods for wool. Flemish towns such as Bruges and Ghent became centers for making and trading cloth.

By 1100, Flanders and Italy were exchanging goods regularly. To encourage

History Online

Web Activity Visit jat.glencoe.com and click on *Chapter 15—Student Web Activity* to learn more about the Middle Ages.

this trade, the counts of Champagne in northern France began holding trade fairs. Northern European merchants exchanged furs, tin, honey, and wool for cloth and swords from northern Italy and silks, sugar, and spices from Asia.

During the early Middle Ages, people bartered, or traded goods for other goods. As trade increased, demand for gold and silver coins rose. Slowly, people began using money again to pay for goods. Merchants set up trading companies and banks to manage the sale of goods and the use of money.

▲ This illustration from a medieval book shows glassblowers at work. *What were some of the items exchanged at trade fairs?*

▼ A stained glass window showing the arms, or symbol, of a blacksmiths' group

How Were Cities Governed? Towns were often located on land owned by lords. This meant the towns were under their control. However, townspeople needed freedom to trade. They wanted to make their own laws and were willing to pay for the right to make them. In exchange for paying taxes, people in towns were granted certain basic rights by their lords. These included the right to buy and sell property and the freedom from having to serve in the army.

Over time, medieval towns set up their own governments. Only males who had been born in the city or who had lived there for a certain length of time were citizens. In many cities, these citizens elected the members of a city council. The council served as judges, city officials, and lawmakers. Candidates from the wealthiest and most powerful families were usually able to control the elections so that only they were elected.

Crafts and Guilds

Trade encouraged manufacturing. People produced cloth, metalwork, shoes, and other goods right in their houses. Over time, these craftspeople organized **guilds** (GIHLDZ), or business groups. By 1200, tanners, carpenters, bakers, and almost every other type of craftspeople had guilds. The rise of towns and guilds created a new middle class in medieval Europe. People in the middle class were not lords, vassals, or serfs. They did not own land, but they did have some wealth and freedom.

Craft guilds set standards for quality in products. They decided how goods were to be made and set the prices at which the finished goods were sold. Guilds also decided who could join a trade and the steps they had to follow to do so.

A person could become an apprentice around the age of 10. An apprentice learned a trade from a master craftsperson who provided room and board but no wages. After five to seven years of service, the apprentice became a journeyman and worked for wages. To become a master, a journeyman had to produce a masterpiece—an outstanding example of the craft.

What Was City Life Like?

Medieval cities had narrow, winding streets. Houses were crowded against one another, and the

▼ A street in France dating back to medieval times

▲ Medieval streets were narrow and often contained wastewater and garbage. *Why was fire a major threat in medieval cities?*

second and third stories were built out over the streets. Candles and fireplaces were used for light and heat, and the houses were built mostly of wood. As a result, medieval cities could be destroyed rapidly once a fire started.

The cities were often dirty and smelly. Wood fires in people's homes and shops filled the air with ashes and smoke. Brewers, dyers, and poor people who could not afford wood burned cheap coal, polluting the air even more. Butchers and tanners dumped blood and other animal wastes into the rivers. Because of the pollution, cities did not use the rivers for drinking water but used wells instead.

City women ran their households, prepared meals, raised their children, and managed the family's money. Often they

▲ This painting shows a medieval woman spinning wool as her husband warms himself by the fire. *What were some responsibilities of women in medieval cities?*

helped their husbands in their trades. Some women developed their own trades to earn extra money. Sometimes when a master craftsperson died, his widow carried on his trade. As a result, women in medieval towns could lead independent lives. In fact, many women became brewers, weavers, and hatmakers.

Reading Check **Analyze** In what ways do you think the shift from a barter system to a money system changed medieval Europe?

Section 2 Review

History Online
Homework Helper Need help with the material in this section? Visit jat.glencoe.com

Reading Summary

Review the Main Ideas

- Under the system known as feudalism, Europe was divided into thousands of territories owned by nobles with the lands worked by serfs.

- During the Middle Ages, nobles lived in large castles, while serfs lived in small wood cottages.

- As medieval trade increased, towns grew and craftspeople organized guilds.

What Did You Learn?

1. What was a vassal?

2. Describe the system of crop rotation used in the later Middle Ages, and explain how it increased the amount of food being grown.

Critical Thinking

3. **Compare and Contrast** Draw a chart to compare the duties and obligations of lords, knights, and serfs.

Lords	Knights	Serfs

4. **Summarize** Explain the shift of power from kings to nobles during the Middle Ages.

5. **Cause and Effect** How did an increase in trade lead to the growth of towns and cities?

6. **Conclude** What were guilds, and why were they important?

7. **Creative Writing** Write a For Sale advertisement for a medieval castle. Describe the castle's rooms and surroundings, including the manor and its residents.

You Decide...

Feudalism: Good or Bad?

Feudalism was the major social and political system in medieval Europe. It developed as power passed from kings to local lords.

A Good System?

Feudalism brought together two powerful groups: lords and vassals. The lords gave vassals land in return for military and other services. Feudalism was a help to Western Europeans for the following reasons:

- Feudalism helped protect communities from the violence and warfare that broke out after the fall of Rome and the collapse of strong central government in Western Europe. Feudalism secured Western Europe's society and kept out powerful invaders.

- Feudalism helped restore trade. Lords repaired bridges and roads. Their knights arrested bandits, enforced the law, and made it safe to travel on roads.

- Feudalism benefited lords, vassals, and peasants. Lords gained a dependable fighting force in their vassals. Vassals received land for their military service. Peasants were protected by their lords. The lord also built mills to grind grain and blacksmith shops and woodworking shops to make tools.

- Feudal ceremonies, oaths, and contracts required lords and vassals to be faithful and to carry out their duties to each other. These kinds of agreements and rituals later helped shape the development of Western governments.

- Feudalism did not allow one person or organization to become too powerful. Power was shared among

◀ **Serfs working the land**

◀ Landowning nobles often served as knights.

many people and groups. This was the first step to European ideas about limited government, constitutions, and civil rights.

A Bad System?

Feudalism did not always work as well in real life as it it did in theory, and it caused many problems for society.

- Feudalism provided some unity and security in local areas, but it often did not have the strength to unite larger regions or countries. Small feudal governments could not afford big projects, such as building aqueducts, sewers, or fleets of ships, that might benefit society.

- Because there was no strong central government to enforce laws fairly, it was easy to use force, violence, and lies to get one's way. This led to many wars among lords. Feudalism protected Western Europe from outside invaders, but it did not bring peace to a region.

- Lords or vassals often placed their personal interests over the interests of the areas they ruled. Feudal lords had complete power in their local areas and could make harsh demands on their vassals and peasants.

- Feudalism did not treat people equally or let them move up in society. A person born a serf was supposed to remain a serf, just as a person born a lord received special treatment without earning it.

- Most peasants were serfs. They were not allowed to leave their lord's lands. Serfs had to work three or four days each week as a payment to the lords or vassals for allowing them to farm for themselves on other days. The serfs were restricted in movement and even daily activities because they could not leave the land without permission.

You Be the Historian

Checking for Understanding

1. Do you think feudalism helped or hurt Western Europe's development?

2. Is there any way feudal lords could have worked their lands without using serfs?

3. Imagine what your life would have been if you were born into a feudal society. Write at least three brief diary entries. Describe your daily life as a lord, vassal, or serf and your relationship with the other two groups. Your entries should show feudalism as either a good or bad system.

Section 3

Kingdoms and Crusades

Get Ready to Read!

What's the Connection?
In the last section, you read about how Western Europeans lived during the Middle Ages. This section describes the political changes that took place while people went about their daily lives.

Focusing on the (Main Ideas)
- England developed a system in which the king's power was limited by Parliament. *(page 535)*

- French kings called the Capetians conquered lands held by the English in western France and set up France's first parliament. *(page 538)*

- After the Mongols destroyed the Kievan state, the rulers of Moscow built a new Russian state headed by a czar. *(page 539)*

- European crusaders captured Jerusalem but were later driven out by the Muslims. *(page 541)*

Locating Places
Normandy (NAWR•muhn•dee)
Kiev (KEE•EHF)
Moscow (MAHS•koh)

Meeting People
William the Conqueror
King John
Philip II (FIH•luhp)
Saladin (SA•luh•DEEN)

Building Your Vocabulary
grand jury
trial jury
clergy (KLUHR•jee)

Reading Strategy
Cause and Effect Complete a diagram to show the causes and effects of the Crusades.

Causes	Effects
➡	
➡	

NATIONAL GEOGRAPHIC When & Where?

ENGLAND
Moscow
HOLY RUSSIA
ROMAN
FRANCE EMPIRE Kiev
Clermont
Rome
SPAIN

PALESTINE
Jerusalem

A.D. 900 | **1150** | **1400**

c. A.D. 871
Alfred becomes England's king

1095
Pope Urban II calls the First Crusade

1480
Ivan the Great ends Mongol rule

England in the Middle Ages

Main Idea England developed a system in which the king's power was limited by Parliament.

Reading Focus Do you know anyone who has had to go to court or has served on a jury? Read to learn how these institutions began in medieval England.

In section one, you learned that Germanic peoples called the Angles and Saxons invaded Britain in the early A.D. 400s. They took over much of the country from the Celts and set up many small kingdoms. In the late A.D. 800s, Vikings attacked Britain. King Alfred of Wessex, later known as Alfred the Great, united the Anglo-Saxon kingdoms and drove away the Vikings. Alfred's united kingdom became known as "Angleland," or England.

Alfred ruled England from A.D. 871 to A.D. 899. He founded schools and hired scholars to rewrite Latin books in the Anglo-Saxon language. However, the Anglo-Saxon kings who came after him were weak rulers.

Who Was William the Conqueror?
In the A.D. 900s, the Vikings conquered part of western France across the English Channel from England. This region came to be called **Normandy** (NAWR•muhn•dee), after the Vikings, or Norsemen, who ruled it. By the middle of the A.D. 1000s, Normandy was ruled by William, a descendant of the Viking ruler who had conquered Normandy. William was also a cousin of King Edward of England.

When Edward died, a noble named Harold Godwinson claimed England's throne. However, William believed that he, not Harold, should be king of England. In 1066, William and his army of knights landed in England. They defeated Harold and his foot soldiers at the Battle of Hastings. William was then crowned king of England and became known as **William the Conqueror.**

▼ This painting of the Battle of Hastings shows Norman knights on horseback led by William the Conqueror attacking the English foot soldiers. *What area did William rule before he attacked England?*

At first the Anglo-Saxons resisted William's rule. He had to find a way to stop Anglo-Saxon revolts and to control his own soldiers. He did so by giving land to his Norman knights. Then he made them swear loyalty to him as ruler of England.

William wanted to know all about his new kingdom. So he took the first census in Europe since Roman times. This census was known as the Domesday Book. It counted people, manors, and farm animals.

The Normans who ruled England brought Europe's customs to England.

Under William's rule, officials and nobles spoke French. Ordinary Anglo-Saxons still spoke their own language, which later became English. They also learned new skills from Norman weavers and other artisans. The Normans, in turn, kept many of the Anglo-Saxons' government practices. For example, they depended on local officials, called sheriffs, to keep order. As more and more Normans and Anglo-Saxons married, their ways of doing things merged into a new English culture.

Linking Past & Present

The Jury System

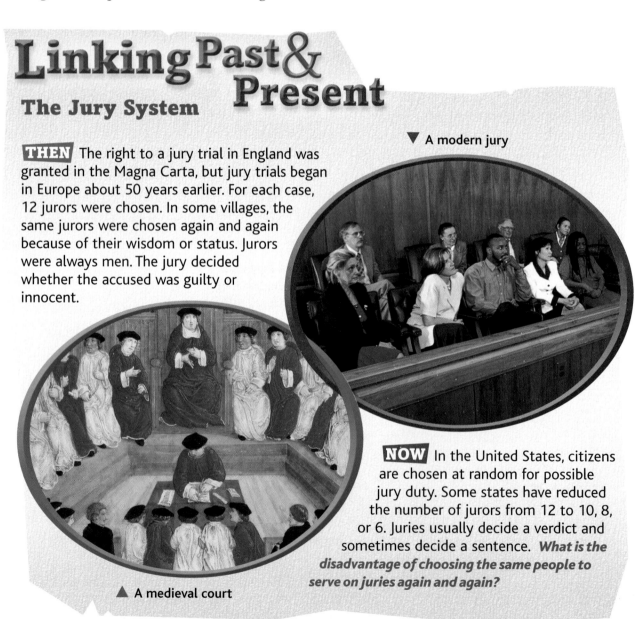

THEN The right to a jury trial in England was granted in the Magna Carta, but jury trials began in Europe about 50 years earlier. For each case, 12 jurors were chosen. In some villages, the same jurors were chosen again and again because of their wisdom or status. Jurors were always men. The jury decided whether the accused was guilty or innocent.

▼ A modern jury

NOW In the United States, citizens are chosen at random for possible jury duty. Some states have reduced the number of jurors from 12 to 10, 8, or 6. Juries usually decide a verdict and sometimes decide a sentence. *What is the disadvantage of choosing the same people to serve on juries again and again?*

▲ A medieval court

Henry II and the Common Law The power of the English king increased under Henry II. Henry ruled England from 1154 to 1189. Henry used the law courts to increase his power. He set up a central court with trained lawyers and judges. Then he appointed circuit judges, who traveled across the country hearing cases. He also established a body of common law, or law that was the same throughout the whole kingdom.

Henry set up juries to handle arguments over land. In time, two kinds of juries developed. The **grand jury** decided whether people should be accused of a crime. The **trial jury** decided whether an accused person was innocent or guilty.

What Was the Magna Carta?

Henry's son John became king of England in 1199. **King John** raised taxes in England and punished his enemies without trials. Many English nobles resented the king's power. They refused to obey him unless he agreed to guarantee certain rights.

The nobles met with King John at a meadow called Runnymede in 1215. There they forced John to sign a document of rights called the Magna Carta, or the Great Charter. The Magna Carta took away some of the king's powers. He could no longer collect taxes unless a group called the Great Council agreed. Freemen accused of crimes had the right to fair trials by their peers, or equals. The Magna Carta also stated that the king and vassals both had certain rights and duties. The Magna Carta was important because it helped to establish the idea that people have rights and that the power of the government should be limited.

In the 1200s, another English king, Edward I, called for a meeting of people from different parts of England. Their

job was to advise him and help him make laws. This gathering, called the Parliament, was an important step toward representative government. At first, Parliaments were made up of two knights from every county, two people from every town, and all high-ranking nobles and church officials. Later, Parliament divided into two houses. High-ranking nobles and church officials met as the House of Lords. Knights and townspeople met as the House of Commons.

Reading Check **Explain** How did the Magna Carta affect the king's power?

The Kingdom of France

Main Idea French kings called the Capetians conquered lands held by the English in western France and set up France's first parliament.

Reading Focus Has a poll ever been taken in your class? Read to find out how one French king found out what his people were thinking.

In A.D. 843 Charlemagne's empire was divided into three parts. The western part eventually became the kingdom of France. In A.D. 987 Frankish nobles chose Hugh Capet to be their king. Hugh was the first of the Capetian (kuh•PEE•shuhn) kings of France. The Capetians controlled the area around Paris (PAR•uhs), the capital. Many French nobles had more power than the kings did. This began to change when **Philip II** (FIH•luhp) became king of France.

Philip ruled from 1180 to 1223. When he took the throne, England's king ruled parts of western France. Philip went to war against England and conquered most of these territories. As a result, French kings gained more land and became more powerful.

Philip IV, called Philip the Fair, ruled from 1285 to 1314. In 1302 he met with representatives from the three estates, or classes, of French society. The first estate was the **clergy** (KLUHR•jee), or people who had been ordained as priests. Nobles made up the second estate, and townspeople and peasants were the third estate. This meeting began the Estates-General, France's first parliament. It was the first step in France toward representative government.

✓ Reading Check **Describe** How did King Philip II bring power back to French kings?

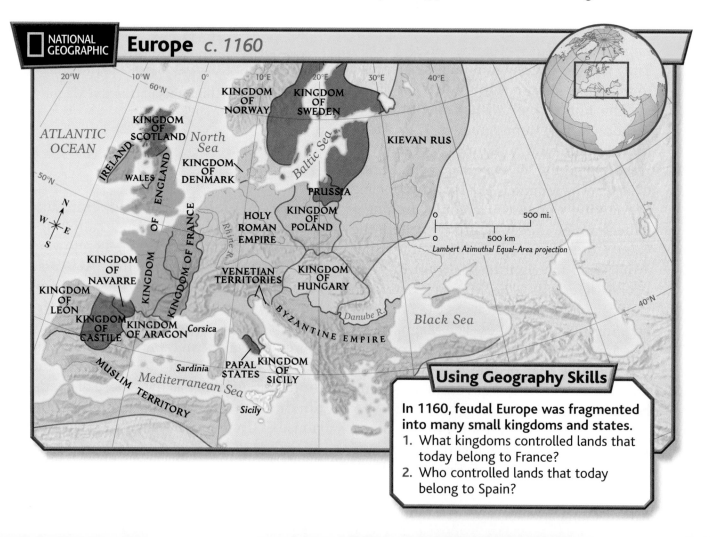

NATIONAL GEOGRAPHIC

Europe c. 1160

Using Geography Skills

In 1160, feudal Europe was fragmented into many small kingdoms and states.
1. What kingdoms controlled lands that today belong to France?
2. Who controlled lands that today belong to Spain?

Eastern Europe and Russia

Main Idea After the Mongols destroyed the Kievan state, the rulers of Moscow built a new Russian state headed by a czar.

Reading Focus Why do you think some of the cities in your state grew large while others stayed small? Read to learn how the cities of Kiev and Moscow grew to become the centers of large Slavic states.

About A.D. 500, a people called the Slavs organized villages in Eastern Europe. Each village was made up of families related to each other. The villagers shared their land, animals, tools, and seeds. Each family built its house partly underground. This kept the family warm during the cold winters.

In time, the Slavs divided into three major groups: the southern, western, and eastern Slavs. The southern Slavs became the Croats, Serbs, and Bulgarians. The western Slavs became the Poles, Czechs, and Slovaks. The eastern Slavs became the Ukrainians (yoo•KRAY•nee•uhnz), Belorussians (BEH•loh•RUH•shuhnz), and Russians (RUH•shuhnz).

By A.D. 600, the eastern Slavs controlled the land between the Carpathian Mountains and the Volga River. In the early Middle Ages, the eastern Slavs created farmland by chopping down the forests and then burning the trees to fertilize the soil. They planted barley, rye, and flax.

What Was the Kievan Rus?
In the late A.D. 700s, Vikings began moving into the Slavs' territory from the north. Over time, the Vikings became rulers of the Slavs. The Slavs called their Viking rulers the Rus. Over time, the Vikings and Slavs intermarried and blended into one people.

Around A.D. 900, a Viking leader named Oleg created a Rus state around the city of **Kiev** (KEE•EHF). Called the Kievan Rus, this state was really a group of small territories.

Primary Source — Ibn Fadlan Describes the Rus

In A.D. 921, the Muslim official Ibn Fadlan encountered the Rus while visiting a settlement on the Volga River.

▲ Statue of a Rus leader

"I have seen the Rūs as they came on their merchant journeys and encamped by the [Volga River]. I have never seen more perfect physical specimens, tall as date palms, blonde and ruddy; they wear neither [coats] nor caftans [long shirts], but the men wear a garment which covers one side of the body and leaves a hand free.... They build big houses of wood on the [Volga] shore, each holding ten to twenty persons more or less."

—Ibn Fadlān, *Risāla*

DBQ Document-Based Question

Of what occupation are the Rus that Ibn Fadlan describes?

The main ruler was the Grand Duke of Kiev. Local princes, rich merchants, and landowning nobles called boyars (boh•YAHRZ) helped him govern.

The rulers who came after Oleg increased the size of the Kievan Rus. In time, it reached from the Baltic Sea in the north to the Black Sea in the south. It stretched from the Danube River in the west to the Volga River in the east.

The growth of the Kievan Rus attracted missionaries from the Byzantine Empire. One Rus ruler, Vladimir, married the Byzantine emperor's sister. He became an Eastern Orthodox Christian and declared his people Eastern Orthodox.

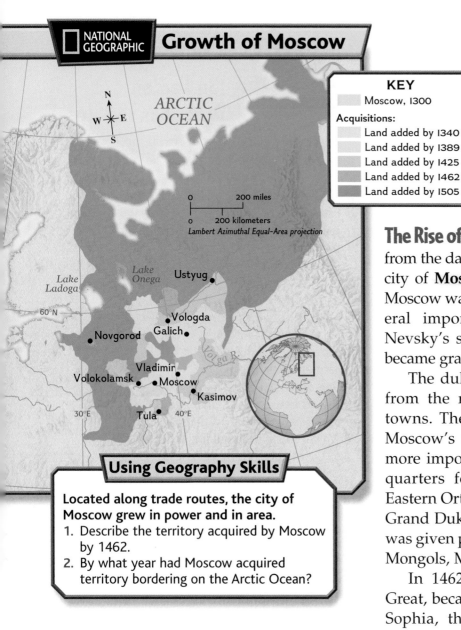

NATIONAL GEOGRAPHIC Growth of Moscow

KEY

Moscow, 1300

Acquisitions:

Land added by 1340

Land added by 1389

Land added by 1425

Land added by 1462

Land added by 1505

Using Geography Skills

Located along trade routes, the city of Moscow grew in power and in area.

1. Describe the territory acquired by Moscow by 1462.
2. By what year had Moscow acquired territory bordering on the Arctic Ocean?

Kiev Falls to the Mongols

About 1240, the Mongols swept into the Kievan Rus. The Slavs called the Mongols "Tatars" because one of the Mongol tribes was the Tata people. The Mongols destroyed nearly all the major cities and killed many people.

The only major city of the Kievan Rus that was spared was the northern city of Novgorod. Nonetheless, Novgorod's rulers as well as other Russian rulers, had to pay tribute to the khan, the Mongol leader, and accept the Mongols as their rulers.

Although Novgorod had been spared by the Mongols, it faced attacks from the west by Germans and Swedes. Led by Alexander Nevsky, the Slavs of Novgorod defeated the Swedes and Germans. For his help in defending lands controlled by the Mongols, the Mongol khan rewarded Nevsky with the title of grand duke.

The Rise of Moscow

As the Slavs recovered from the damage caused by the Mongols, the city of **Moscow** (MAHS•koh) began to grow. Moscow was located at the crossroads of several important trade routes. Alexander Nevsky's son Daniel and his descendants became grand dukes of Moscow.

The dukes of Moscow married women from the ruling families in other Slavic towns. They also fought wars to expand Moscow's territory. Moscow became even more important when it became the headquarters for the Russian branch of the Eastern Orthodox Church. When Ivan I, the Grand Duke of Moscow from 1328 to 1341, was given permission to collect taxes for the Mongols, Moscow grew even greater.

In 1462 Ivan III, known as Ivan the Great, became the grand duke. He married Sophia, the niece of the last Byzantine emperor. Afterward, Ivan began living in the style of an emperor. He had architects build fine palaces and large cathedrals in the Kremlin—the fortress at the center of Moscow. He even began calling himself czar. Czar was a shortened version of Caesar. In Russian, czar means emperor.

Ivan IV lived up to his title. In 1480 he finally ended Mongol rule over Moscow's territory. Then he expanded his territory to the north and west. When Ivan IV died in 1505, the Russians were well on the way toward building a vast empire.

✓ **Reading Check** **Cause and Effect** Why was Alexander Nevsky important?

The Crusades

Main Idea European crusaders captured Jerusalem but were later driven out by the Muslims.

Reading Focus Have you ever put all your energy into making something important happen? Read to learn why Europeans thought capturing the city of Jerusalem was important.

During the Middle Ages, the Byzantine Empire in the East came under attack. In 1071 an army of Muslim Turks defeated the Byzantines and seized control of most of the Byzantine lands in Asia Minor.

The Byzantine emperor did not have enough money or troops to drive out the Turks. In desperation, he asked the pope to help him defend his Christian empire against the Muslim invaders.

In 1095 Pope Urban II spoke before a large crowd in eastern France. He asked Europe's lords to launch a crusade, or holy war, against the Muslim Turks. He urged them to capture Jerusalem and free the Holy Land where Jesus had lived from the Muslims. The pope explained why the crusade was needed:

66 Jerusalem is the navel [center] of the world. . . . This is the land which the Redeemer [Jesus] of mankind illuminated by his coming. . . . This royal city, situated in the middle of the world, is now held captive by his enemies. . . . It looks and hopes for freedom; it begs unceasingly that you will come to its aid. 99

—Pope Urban II,
as quoted in *The Discoverers*

As the pope spoke, the excited crowd cried out, "It is the will of God, it is the will of God." The Crusades had begun.

Early Victories

Several thousand soldiers on horseback and as many as ten thousand on foot headed east. Many of them wore a red cross on their clothes as a sign of their obedience to the pope's call.

In 1098 the First Crusade captured Antioch in Syria. From there, the crusaders entered Palestine, reaching Jerusalem in 1099. After a bloody fight, they stormed the city, killing Muslims, Jews, and Christians alike.

In the painting above, Pope Urban II calls for a crusade against the Muslims. At right, the crusaders attack Jerusalem with siege towers and catapults. *What was the pope's goal for the crusade?*

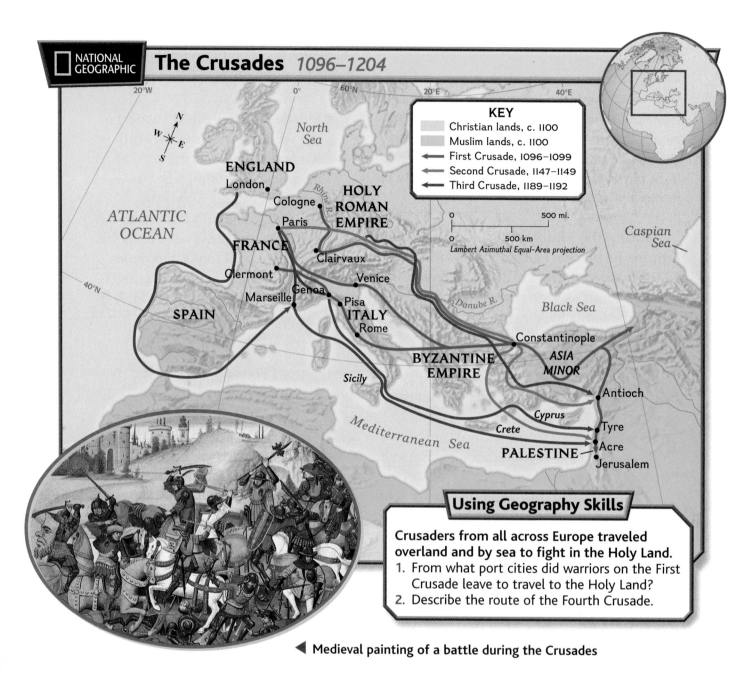

The Crusades 1096–1204

KEY
Christian lands, c. 1100
Muslim lands, c. 1100
→ First Crusade, 1096–1099
→ Second Crusade, 1147–1149
→ Third Crusade, 1189–1192

0   500 mi.
0   500 km
Lambert Azimuthal Equal-Area projection

North Sea

ENGLAND
London
Cologne
Paris
HOLY ROMAN EMPIRE
ATLANTIC OCEAN
FRANCE
Clairvaux
Clermont
Venice
Marseille
Genoa
Pisa
ITALY
Rome
SPAIN
Rhine R.
Danube R.
Caspian Sea
Black Sea
Constantinople
ASIA MINOR
BYZANTINE EMPIRE
Sicily
Antioch
Cyprus
Tyre
Crete
Acre
PALESTINE
Jerusalem
Mediterranean Sea

Using Geography Skills

Crusaders from all across Europe traveled overland and by sea to fight in the Holy Land.
1. From what port cities did warriors on the First Crusade leave to travel to the Holy Land?
2. Describe the route of the Fourth Crusade.

◀ Medieval painting of a battle during the Crusades

Having driven the Muslims from the region, the crusaders created four states: the Kingdom of Jerusalem in Palestine, the country of Edessa and the principality of Antioch in Asia Minor, and the country of Tripoli where Lebanon is located today. These four states were surrounded by Muslims and depended on the Italian cities of Genoa, Pisa, and Venice for supplies.

The Muslims fought back, however, and in 1144 they captured Edessa. In response, European rulers sent another crusade to regain the lost lands. This Second Crusade, however, was a total failure.

In 1174 a Muslim named **Saladin** (SA•luh•DEEN) became ruler of Egypt. He united Muslims and declared war against the Christian states the crusaders had built. Saladin proved to be a brilliant commander. He defeated the Christians and captured Jerusalem in 1187.

The fall of Jerusalem led to the Third Crusade. Emperor Frederick of the Holy Roman Empire, King Richard I of England, (known as Richard the Lion-Hearted), and King Philip II of France gathered their armies and headed east to fight Saladin.

The Third Crusade had many problems. Frederick drowned crossing a river. The English and French arrived by sea and captured a coastal city but were unable to push inland. After Philip went home, Richard secured a small territory along the coast. He then agreed to a truce after Saladin promised that Christian pilgrims could travel to Jerusalem in safety.

Around 1200, Pope Innocent III called for a Fourth Crusade. Merchants from Venice used the crusade to weaken their trading rival, the Byzantine Empire. They convinced the crusaders to attack Constantinople, the Byzantine capital. For three days, the crusaders burned and looted the city. The attack shocked Western Europeans and weakened the Byzantines.

Six more crusades were launched over the next 60 years, but they achieved very little. Gradually, the Muslims conquered all of the territory they had lost to the First Crusade. In 1291, a bit more than 200 years after the First Crusade had set out, the last Christian city fell to Muslim forces.

The Crusades affected Europe in two ways. They increased trade between Europe and the Middle East, and they helped break down feudalism. Nobles who joined the Crusades sold their lands and freed their serfs. This reduced their power and helped kings build stronger central governments. Kings also began taxing the new trade with the Middle East. These taxes helped them build stronger kingdoms in Western Europe.

✓ **Reading Check** **Compare and Contrast** What did the First Crusade accomplish? What did the Third Crusade accomplish?

Section 3 Review

History Online
Homework Helper Need help with the material in this section? Visit jat.glencoe.com

Reading Summary

Review the Main Ideas

- The English king granted rights to his people in the Magna Carta and established a parliament.

- French kings regained French territories from the English and, like the English, created a parliament.

- Russia had its beginnings in the territories of the Kievan Rus and Moscow.

- West Europeans launched crusades to capture Jerusalem and Palestine from the Muslims.

What Did You Learn?

1. What is the significance of the Battle of Hastings?

2. What groups developed from the three major divisions of Slavs in Eastern Europe?

Critical Thinking

3. **Organizing Information** Draw a chart to list the kings of England and France and their achievements.

King/Country	Achievements

4. **Evaluate** What was the importance of the Magna Carta?

5. **Summarize** Describe the development of England's Parliament, and discuss its role in changing government.

6. **Explain** Why did cities such as Venice flourish as a result of the Crusades?

7. **Expository Writing** Write an essay describing how the Crusades affected feudalism.

Section 4

The Church and Society

Get Ready to Read!

What's the Connection?

Kings and popes had a powerful effect on the lives of medieval people, as did religion. In this section, you will learn how religion in medieval Europe shaped its culture.

Focusing on the **Main Ideas**

- The Catholic Church played an important role in medieval Europe and used its power to uphold its teachings. *(page 545)*

- Church and government leaders supported learning and the arts in medieval Europe. *(page 549)*

Locating Places

Bologna (buh•LOH•nyuh)

Meeting People

Francis of Assisi
(FRAN•suhs uhv uh•SIHS•ee)

Thomas Aquinas
(TAH•muhs uh•KWY•nuhs)

Building Your Vocabulary

mass
heresy (HEHR•uh•see)
anti-Semitism
(AN•tih•SEH•muh•TIH•zuhm)
theology (thee•AH•luh•jee)
scholasticism
(skuh•LAS•tuh•SIH•zuhm)
vernacular (vuhr•NA•kyuh•luhr)

Reading Strategy

Organizing Information Complete a Venn diagram to show the similarities and differences between Romanesque and Gothic cathedrals.

Romanesque Cathedrals   Gothic Cathedrals

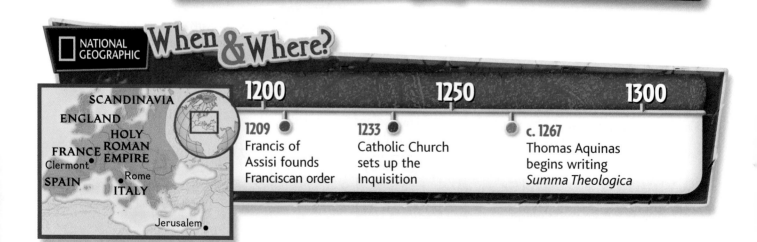

NATIONAL GEOGRAPHIC **When & Where?**

| 1200 | 1250 | 1300 |

1209
Francis of Assisi founds Franciscan order

1233
Catholic Church sets up the Inquisition

c. 1267
Thomas Aquinas begins writing *Summa Theologica*

SCANDINAVIA
ENGLAND
HOLY ROMAN EMPIRE
FRANCE
Clermont
SPAIN
Rome
ITALY
Jerusalem

Religion and Society

Main Idea The Catholic Church played an important role in medieval Europe and used its power to uphold its teachings.

Reading Focus Have you ever noticed how many things in society have been influenced by religion? What examples can you give? Read to learn about the important role religion played in the lives of people living in the Middle Ages.

Between 1050 and 1150, a strong wave of religious feeling swept across Western Europe. As a result, more monasteries were built, and new religious orders, or groups of priests, monks, and nuns, were started.

New Religious Orders

The Cistercian (sihs•TUHR•shuhn) order was founded in 1098. Cistercian monks farmed the land as well as worshiped and prayed. They developed many new farming techniques that helped Europeans grow more crops.

The most famous Cistercian monk was Bernard of Clairvaux (klar•VOH). Bernard helped promote the Second Crusade. He also advised the pope and defended the poor against the rich.

Many women entered convents between A.D. 1000 and 1200. Most of them were from noble families. They included widows and women unable or unwilling to marry. Women who were scholars found convents ideal places for study and writing.

Most educated women in medieval Europe were nuns. One famous woman was Hildegard of Bingen (HIHL•duh•GAHRD uhv BIHNG•uhn). She headed a convent in Germany and composed music for the Church. Her work is remarkable because at that time, men wrote most church music.

▲ This religious painting from the wall of a church in Italy depicts the pope and other Christian leaders, a number of saints, and Jesus ruling over all.
How did Cistercian monks aid European society?

545

The Franciscan Way of Life

Francis of Assisi recorded instructions for living in the Franciscan order. This passage is about the nature of love.

"Blessed that friar who loves his brother as much when he is sick and can be of no use to him as when he is well and can be of use to him. Blessed that friar who loves and respects his brother as much when he is absent as when he is present and who would not say anything behind his back that he could not say charitably [nicely] to his face."

—Francis of Assisi, as quoted in "Admonitions"

Francis of Assisi ▶

DBQ Document-Based Question

Does Francis of Assisi think that love for another person should be constant, or changing? How do you know?

Until the 1200s, most people in religious orders stayed in their monasteries separate from the world. They lived a simple life of prayer and hard work. In the 1200s, several new religious orders were created. The men in these religious orders were called friars. *Friar* comes from a Latin word for "brother."

Friars were different from monks. They did not stay in their monasteries. Instead, they went out into the world to preach. Friars lived by begging. They could not own property or keep any personal wealth.

The first order of friars was founded by **Francis of Assisi** (FRAN•suhs uhv uh•SIHS•ee) in 1209. These friars became known as Franciscans. They lived in towns and taught Christianity to the people. In addition, the Franciscans helped the poor and served as missionaries.

A Spanish priest named Dominic de Guzmán founded another group of friars called the Dominicans. The Dominicans' goal was to defend Church teachings. Dominican friars spent years in study so they could preach to well-educated people.

The Role of Religion Throughout medieval Western Europe, daily life revolved around the Catholic Church. Priests ran schools and hospitals. They also recorded births, performed weddings, and conducted burials. On Sundays and holy days, people went to **mass**—or the Catholic worship service.

During mass, medieval Christians took part in Church rituals called sacraments. The most important sacrament was communion, in which people took bread and wine to remind them of Jesus' death on the cross for their sins. Only clergy could give people the sacraments.

Many Christians also prayed to saints. Saints were holy men and women who had died and were believed to be in heaven. Their presence before God enabled the saints to ask favors for people who prayed to them.

Of all the saints, Mary, the mother of Jesus, was the most honored. Many churches were named for her. Several French churches carried the name *Notre Dame*, or "Our Lady," in honor of Mary.

Some people tried to make a connection to the saints by touching relics. Relics were usually bones or personal belongings of saints. People believed that relics had special powers, such as the ability to heal the sick.

Medieval Christians also believed that God blessed pilgrims, or religious travelers who journeyed to holy places. The holiest place was Jerusalem in the Middle East.

What Was the Inquisition?

The Catholic Church was very powerful in medieval society, and most of its leaders wanted everyone to accept the Church's teachings. Church leaders feared that if people stopped believing Church teachings, it would weaken the Church and endanger people's chances of getting into heaven.

Using its power, the Church tried to put an end to **heresy** (HEHR•uh•see), or religious beliefs that conflict with Church teachings. At first, it tried to stop the spread of heresy by sending friars like the Dominicans to preach the Church's message. Then, in 1233, the pope established a court called the Inquisition (IHN•kwuh•ZIH•shuhn), or Church court. To Church leaders,

heresy was a crime against God. The Inquisition's job was to try heretics, or people suspected of heresy.

People brought before the Inquisition were urged to confess their heresy and to ask forgiveness. When they confessed, the Inquisition punished them and then allowed them to return to the Church. People who refused to confess could be tortured until they admitted their heresy. Those who did not confess were considered guilty. The Inquisition turned them over to political leaders, who could execute them.

How Were the Jews Treated?

Church leaders persecuted Jews as actively as they punished heretics. Many Europeans hated Jews for refusing to become Christians. Others hated them because many Jews were moneylenders who charged interest. At that time, Christians believed charging interest was a sin.

▲ This painting shows an accused heretic being questioned by the Inquisition. *What happened to people who refused to confess to the Inquisition?*

Jewish Expulsions c. 1100–1500

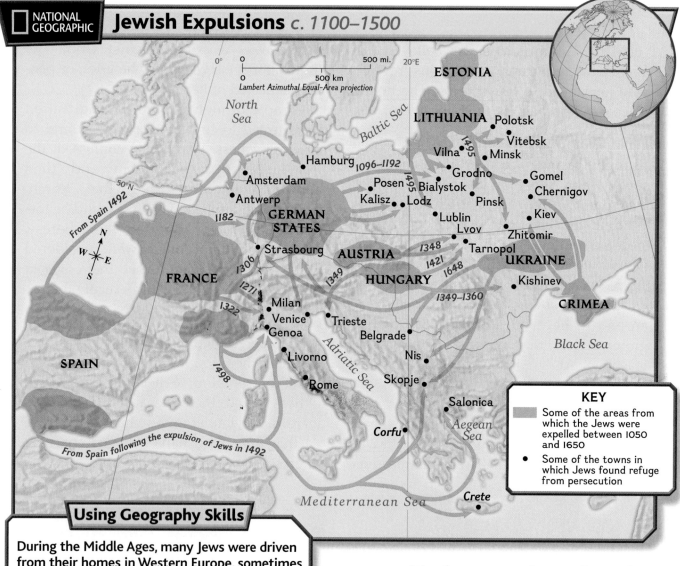

KEY

■ Some of the areas from which the Jews were expelled between 1050 and 1650

● Some of the towns in which Jews found refuge from persecution

Using Geography Skills

During the Middle Ages, many Jews were driven from their homes in Western Europe, sometimes from areas where their families had lived for generations.

1. From where did many of the Jews who moved to Eastern Europe come?
2. Where did many of the Jews expelled from Spain settle?

When disease or economic problems hurt society, people blamed the Jews. Jews became scapegoats—people who are blamed for other people's troubles. Hatred of Jews is known as **anti-Semitism** (AN•tih•SEH•muh•TIH•zuhm).

Anti-Semitism in the Middle Ages took horrible forms. Christian mobs attacked and killed thousands of Jews. Governments made Jews wear special badges or clothing. In some places, Jews had to live in separate communities known as ghettos. Jews also lost the right to own land and to practice certain trades. This was why many of them had to become peddlers and moneylenders, jobs that Christians despised.

Beginning in the 1100s, European rulers began driving out their Jewish subjects. England expelled Jews in 1290. France expelled groups of Jews several times. Some German cities also forced Jews to leave. Many of these Jews settled in Poland and other Eastern European countries. Over the years, the Jews of Eastern Europe established thriving communities based on their religious traditions.

Reading Check Contrast How did the main goal of the Franciscans differ from the main goal of the Dominicans?

Medieval Culture

Main Idea Church and government leaders supported learning and the arts in medieval Europe.

Reading Focus What are the most important parts of American culture today? Read to learn about the kinds of things that made up the culture of medieval Europe.

As strong governments arose, people in medieval Europe felt safer. As a result, trade, banking, and businesses prospered. A good economy meant more money to support learning and the arts and to pay for new churches and other buildings.

Medieval Art and Architecture Europe experienced a building boom in the A.D. 1000s and 1100s. Architecture is one way a society shows what is important to its culture. In the Middle Ages, religion was an important part of life and society. As a result, Church leaders and wealthy merchants and nobles paid to build large new churches called cathedrals. The new cathedrals were built in either the Romanesque (ROH•muh•NEHSK) style or the Gothic style.

Romanesque churches were rectangular buildings with long, rounded roofs called barrel vaults. These roofs needed huge pillars and thick walls to hold them up. Windows let in little light because they were small and set back in the thick walls.

Gothic cathedrals had ribbed vaults and pointed arches instead of rounded barrel vaults. This allowed Gothic churches to be taller than Romanesque churches. Gothic churches also used flying buttresses. These stone supports were built onto the cathedral's outside walls. They made it possible to build churches with thinner walls and large stained glass windows.

Medieval Church Architecture

Early Christian churches (above) were often rectangular with flat roofs, like some Roman buildings. Romanesque churches (top right) had rounded barrel vault ceilings, eliminating the flat roof. Gothic cathedrals, such as St. Etienne in Bourges (right), used flying buttresses on the exterior to hold up the tall ceiling inside. **Who paid for cathedrals to be built?**

▲ This medieval art shows students in a university classroom. *What were some of the subjects studied in medieval universities?*

Stained glass windows were picture Bibles for Christians who could not read. The pieces of stained glass often formed scenes from Jesus' life and teachings. They also let in sunlight, which came to symbolize the divine light of God.

The First Universities

Two of the first European universities were in **Bologna** (buh•LOH•nyuh), Italy, and Paris, France. Masters, or teachers, were also teaching at Oxford, England by 1096. Oxford University was founded in 1231.

Universities were created to educate and train scholars. They were like the guilds that trained craftspeople. In fact, *university* comes from the Latin word for "guild." In medieval universities, students studied grammar, logic, arithmetic, geometry, music, and astronomy. Students did not have books because books were rare before the European printing press was created in the 1400s.

University students studied their subjects for four to six years. Then a committee of teachers gave them an oral exam. If the students passed, they were given their degree.

After obtaining a basic degree, a student could go on to earn a doctor's degree in law, medicine, or **theology** (thee•AH•luh•jee)— the study of religion and God. Earning a doctor's degree could take 10 years or more.

Who Was Thomas Aquinas?

Beginning in the 1100s, a new way of thinking called **scholasticism** (skuh•LAS•tuh•SIH•zuhm) began to change the study of theology. Followers used reason to explore questions of faith. A Dominican friar and priest named **Thomas Aquinas** (TAH•muhs uh•KWY•nuhs) was scholasticism's greatest champion. He is best known for combining Church teachings with the ideas of Aristotle.

Europeans had forgotten about Aristotle after Rome fell and his works had been lost. In the 1100s, however, Muslim and Jewish scholars reintroduced Aristotle to Europe using copies of his books that had been preserved in Muslim libraries. Aristotle's ideas upset many Christian thinkers because he used reason, not faith, to arrive at his conclusions about the meaning of life.

In the 1200s, Thomas Aquinas wrote several works explaining that Aristotle would have agreed with many Christian teachings. About 1267, Aquinas began writing *Summa Theologica,* or a summary of knowledge on theology. In this book, Aquinas asked hard questions such as "Does God exist?"

Aquinas wrote about government as well as theology, with an emphasis on the idea of natural law. People who believe in natural law think that there are some laws that are part of human nature. These laws do not have to be made by governments.

Aquinas claimed that natural law gave people certain rights that the government should not take away. These included the right to live, to learn, to worship, and to reproduce. Aquinas's writings on natural law have influenced governments to the present day. Our belief that people have rights can partly be traced to the ideas of Thomas Aquinas.

Biography

THOMAS AQUINAS
1225–1274

▲ Thomas Aquinas

Thomas Aquinas was born in 1225 in his family's castle between Rome and Naples, Italy. His parents, Countess Theodora and Count Landulf of Aquino, were from noble families. At age five, Aquinas began school at Monte Cassino, a Benedictine monastery where his uncle was the abbot. Monastic schools required students to learn many subjects, including grammar, speech, mathematics, science, and music. When he was older, Aquinas studied at the University of Naples.

Aquinas joined the Dominican friars around 1244, against the wishes of his family. As a new Dominican, he studied in Paris under Albertus Magnus (Albert the Great). Both Aquinas and Albertus greatly admired the ideas of Aristotle.

Aquinas spent the next few decades studying, teaching, and writing. He lived in Paris, Rome, and other cities in France and Italy and taught theology. He wrote about the Bible, groups within the Church, and the ideas of philosophers. *Summa Theologica* best explains how Aquinas combines Aristotle's ideas with those of the Church. He began writing his *Summa Theologica* around 1267 and worked on it until his death.

In 1274 the pope asked Aquinas to travel to France to attend the Council of Lyons. Even though he was not in good health, he set out for the French city. He became very sick along the way. Aquinas wanted to live out his last days in a monastery, so he was taken to a Cistercian abbey in the town of Fossanova, where he died on March 7, 1274.

Aquinas's ideas were respected during his lifetime, and as time passed they became even more important. His writings influenced governments and the Roman Catholic Church. He was made a saint in 1323.

> **"The happy man in this life needs friends."**
> –St. Thomas Aquinas,
> *Summa Theologiae*

Then and Now

The writings of Thomas Aquinas influenced governments and religions for a long time after his death. Which present-day writers or leaders do you think have ideas that will influence people for centuries to come?

▲ Monte Cassino monastery

Medieval Literature During the Middle Ages, educated people throughout Europe generally spoke or wrote in Latin. The Church used Latin in its worship and daily affairs. University teachers taught in Latin, and serious authors wrote in that language.

In addition to Latin, each region had its own local language that people used every day. This everyday language is called the **vernacular** (vuhr•NA•kyuh•luhr). The vernacular included early versions of Spanish, French, English, Italian, and German.

During the 1100s, new literature was written in the vernacular. Educated people enjoyed vernacular literature, especially troubadour (TROO•buh•DOHR) poetry. These poems were about love, often the love of a knight for a lady.

Another type of vernacular literature was the heroic epic. In heroic epics, bold knights fight for kings and lords. Women seldom appear in this literature. An early example of a heroic epic is the *Song of Roland*, written in French about 1100.

In the *Song of Roland*, a brave knight named Roland fights for Charlemagne against the Muslims. Roland sounds his horn for Charlemagne to help him, but it is too late:

> **The Count Rollanz [Roland], with sorrow and with pangs,**
> **And with great pain sounded his olifant [horn]:**
> **Out of his mouth the clear blood leaped and ran,**
> **About his brain the very temples cracked.**
> **Loud is its voice, that horn he holds in hand;**
> **Charlès [Charlemagne] hath heard, where in the pass he stands,**
> **And Neimès [a commander] hears, and listen all the Franks.**

—*Song of Roland*

Reading Check **Explain** What is natural law?

History Online
Homework Helper Need help with the material in this section? Visit jat.glencoe.com

Section 4 Review

Reading Summary

Review the Main Ideas

- In the Middle Ages, new religious orders developed to spread Christianity. Nonbelievers and people of other faiths were mistreated.

- In medieval Europe, a number of universities opened, large Christian churches known as cathedrals were built, and European languages developed.

What Did You Learn?

1. What is theology?

2. What is vernacular language, and what were common vernacular languages in medieval times?

Critical Thinking

3. **Compare and Contrast** Draw a Venn diagram like the one below. Use it to describe the similarities and differences between Cistercians, Franciscans, and Dominicans.

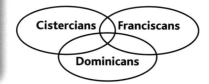

Cistercians / Franciscans / Dominicans

4. **Summarize** How did the Inquisition treat the people brought before it?

5. **Analyze** How did Christian beliefs result in a resettlement of Jews? Where did many Jews settle in the Middle Ages?

6. **Explain** What were Thomas Aquinas's beliefs related to government?

7. **Persuasive Writing** Write a letter to a medieval university telling them why you would like to become a student there. Be sure to discuss the subjects you would like to study.

Section 5

The Late Middle Ages

Get Ready to Read!

What's the Connection?
In previous sections, you learned about the politics, religion, and culture of much of medieval Europe. In this section, you will find out about the disasters and conflicts of the late Middle Ages.

Focusing on the Main Ideas
- A terrible plague, known as the Black Death, swept through Europe in the 1300s, killing millions. *(page 554)*
- Western Europe was devastated by war in the 1300s and 1400s as England and France fought each other, and Spain and Portugal fought against the Muslims. *(page 557)*

Locating Places
Crécy (kray•SEE)
Orléans (AWR•lay•AHN)

Meeting People
Joan of Arc
Isabella of Castile
Ferdinand of Aragon

Building Your Vocabulary
plague (PLAYG)
Reconquista (RAY•kohn•KEES•tuh)

Reading Strategy
Summarizing Information Complete a table like the one below showing the path of the Black Death in Europe and Asia.

Time Period	Affected Areas
1330s	
1340s	
1350s	

NATIONAL GEOGRAPHIC **When & Where?**

London
Paris
Orléans
Granada
SICILY

1300

1400

1500

1346
The Black Death arrives in Europe

1429
Joan of Arc inspires the French

1492
The Spanish defeat the Muslims and expel the Jews

The Black Death

Main Idea A terrible plague, known as the Black Death, swept through Europe in the 1300s, killing millions.

Reading Focus Have you ever been given a shot to prevent the flu or to protect you from another disease? Read to learn what happened in Europe before modern medicine could control contagious diseases.

The Middle Ages in Europe reached a high point during the 1200s. In the 1300s, however, disaster struck. A terrible **plague** (PLAYG), known as the Black Death, swept across Europe and Asia. A plague is a disease that spreads quickly and kills many people. Most scientists think the Black Death was bubonic plague—a disease caused by a type of bacteria carried by fleas. These fleas infested black rats, and in the Middle Ages, these rats were everywhere.

The Black Death probably began somewhere in the Gobi, a desert in central Asia. It had been around for centuries, but in the 1300s, it began to spread farther and more quickly than ever before. Scientists are still not sure why this happened.

Historians believe the Mongol Empire was partly responsible for the plague spreading so fast. The empire covered all the land from Eastern Europe through central Asia to China. The Mongols opened up trade between China, India, the Middle East, and Europe. They encouraged the use of the Silk Road and other trade routes.

By the early 1300s, more goods were being shipped across central Asia than ever before. This made it possible for the Black Death to spread rapidly, as caravans infested with rats carried it from city to city.

The first outbreak took place in China in 1331. It erupted there again in 1353. The

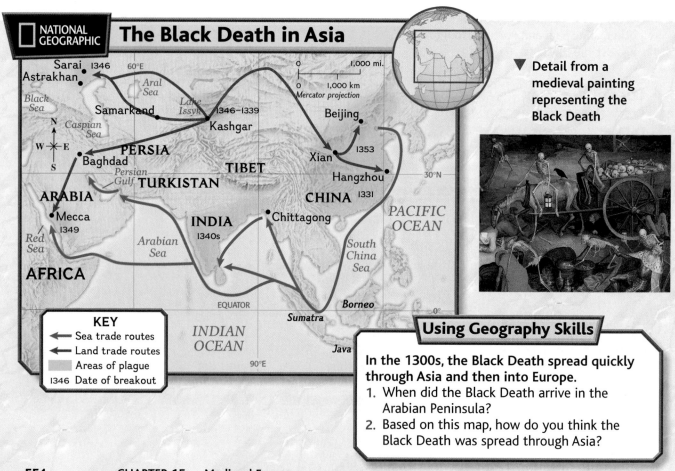

NATIONAL GEOGRAPHIC
The Black Death in Asia

Sarai 1346
Astrakhan
Black Sea
Aral Sea
Samarkand
Lake Issyk
Kashgar 1346–1339
Beijing
Caspian Sea
PERSIA
Baghdad
Persian Gulf
TURKISTAN
TIBET
Xian 1353
Hangzhou
CHINA 1331
ARABIA
Mecca
1349
Red Sea
Arabian Sea
INDIA
1340s
Chittagong
PACIFIC OCEAN
AFRICA
South China Sea
EQUATOR
Borneo
Sumatra
INDIAN OCEAN
Java
60°E
30°N
0°
90°E

0   1,000 mi.
0   1,000 km
Mercator projection

KEY
⟵ Sea trade routes
⟵ Land trade routes
▢ Areas of plague
1346 Date of breakout

▼ Detail from a medieval painting representing the Black Death

Using Geography Skills

In the 1300s, the Black Death spread quickly through Asia and then into Europe.
1. When did the Black Death arrive in the Arabian Peninsula?
2. Based on this map, how do you think the Black Death was spread through Asia?

disease killed between 40 and 60 million people, cutting China's population nearly in half. The disease appeared in India in the 1340s and reached Makkah, deep inside Muslim lands, in 1349. In the meantime, it also spread to Europe.

The Black Death appeared in Europe in 1346 at the city of Caffa on the Black Sea. The city had been under attack by Mongols when the plague erupted. The Mongols, with their troops dying, called off the attack. In anger they also threw bodies of infected soldiers into the city.

Caffa was a trade colony controlled by Italian merchants from the city of Genoa. Their ships carried the plague to Sicily in October 1347. From there it spread into Europe. By the end of 1349, it had spread through France and Germany and had arrived in England. By 1351, it had reached Scandinavia, Eastern Europe, and Russia.

As many as 38 million Europeans—nearly one out of every two people—died of the Black Death between 1347 and 1351.

The death of so many people in the 1300s turned Europe's economy upside down. Trade declined and wages rose sharply because workers were few and in demand. At the same time, fewer people meant less demand for food, and food prices fell.

Landlords found they had to pay workers more and charge lower rents. Some peasants bargained with their lords to pay rent instead of owing services. This meant that they were no longer serfs. In this way, the plague, like the Crusades, helped to weaken the feudal system and change European society.

✓ Reading Check Identify How many Europeans died of the plague between 1347 and 1351?

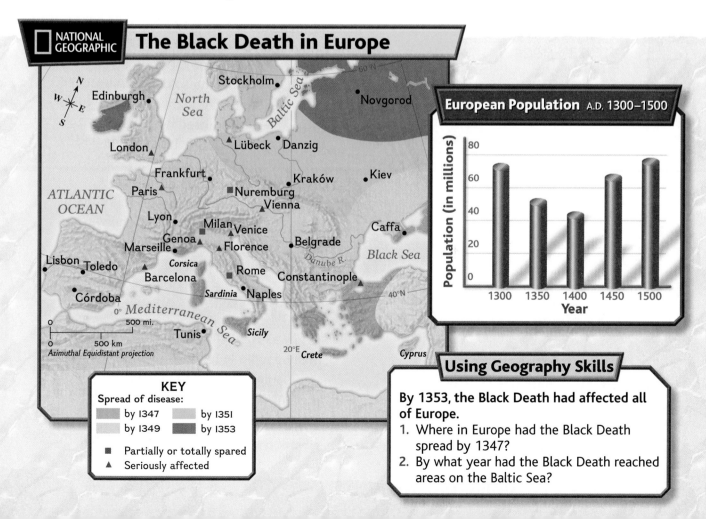

The Black Death in Europe

NATIONAL GEOGRAPHIC

European Population A.D. 1300–1500

KEY
Spread of disease:
- by 1347
- by 1349
- by 1351
- by 1353
- ■ Partially or totally spared
- ▲ Seriously affected

Using Geography Skills

By 1353, the Black Death had affected all of Europe.
1. Where in Europe had the Black Death spread by 1347?
2. By what year had the Black Death reached areas on the Baltic Sea?

Biography

JOAN OF ARC
1412–1431

Jeanne d'Arc—better known as Joan of Arc—was born January 6, 1412, in the village of Domremy in eastern France. Joan was the youngest of five children. When she was 13, she began having visions of saints telling her to attend church and to be a good person. As time passed, the voices began telling her to speak with Charles VII about her ability to help France. After three attempts, she was finally allowed to see the leader. Charles spoke with Joan and had her questioned by doctors and priests. All of them believed Joan was a good person and was telling the truth.

Joan was sent with the French army to the city of Orléans, which was surrounded by the English. Everywhere she went, Joan carried a banner with religious pictures on it. Even though she did not have a weapon, she rode at the front of the troops, giving them directions and encouragement. The troops came to believe God was on their side. Inspired by Joan, they fought harder and better than ever before. They defeated the English at Orléans and began driving them out of France.

In 1430 Joan said the saints revealed to her that she would soon be captured. In late May, she was seized by the English and charged with heresy and improper dress—for the soldier's uniform she wore as army commander. Joan was found guilty and told that if she admitted her crimes, she would not be executed. She insisted she had done nothing wrong and was executed on May 30, 1431. Almost two decades later, an investigation into the matter found Joan innocent of all charges. In 1920 she was made a saint by the Roman Catholic Church.

> "Courage! Do not fall back."
> –Joan of Arc

◄ Joan of Arc on horseback

Then and Now

Joan was tried and found guilty, even though many people felt she was innocent. She was also denied many rights during her trial. What prevents this from happening today in the United States?

A Troubled Continent

Main Idea Western Europe was devastated by war in the 1300s and 1400s as England and France fought each other, and Spain and Portugal fought against the Muslims.

Reading Focus Have you ever had a hero you looked up to? Read to learn what happened when a young peasant girl became a hero to the French people.

The plague was not Europe's only problem in the late Middle Ages. The English and French went to war with each other, while the Spanish and Portuguese fought to drive out the Muslims who had conquered them centuries before.

The Hundred Years' War

In Section 3, you learned that William of Normandy became king of England in 1066, although he still ruled Normandy. French kings wanted to drive the English out of Normandy. English kings claimed a right to the land, and in 1337 the English king Edward III declared himself king of France. This angered the French even more. War began, and it lasted for over 100 years.

The first major battle of the Hundred Years' War took place at **Crécy** (kray•SEE) after Edward invaded France. English archers defeated the French army and forced the French king to give up some of his kingdom.

Under a new king, however, the French slowly won back their land. Then in 1415 Henry V of England went on the attack. England's archers again won the battle and left the English in control of northern France.

Who Was Joan of Arc?

Charles, the prince who ruled southern France, wanted to take back the north. In 1429 a French peasant girl named Joan was brought to him. She told him that her favorite saints had urged her to free France. Joan's honesty persuaded Charles to let her go with a French army to

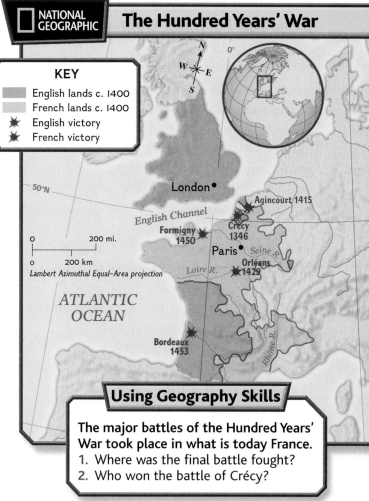

KEY
- English lands c. 1400
- French lands c. 1400
- ✴ English victory
- ✴ French victory

London
Agincourt 1415
English Channel
Crécy 1346
Formigny 1450
Paris   Seine R.
Orléans 1429
Loire R.
ATLANTIC OCEAN
Bordeaux 1453
Rhône R.

0 200 mi.
0 200 km
Lambert Azimuthal Equal-Area projection

50°N

Using Geography Skills

The major battles of the Hundred Years' War took place in what is today France.
1. Where was the final battle fought?
2. Who won the battle of Crécy?

Orléans (AWR•lay•AHN). Joan's faith stirred the soldiers, and they took the city.

Shortly after, with Joan at his side, Charles was declared king. A few months later, however, the English captured Joan. They handed her over to the Inquisition, which had her burned at the stake. She later became known as **Joan of Arc.**

The French finally defeated the English in 1453. The king had spent almost all of his money, but the war strengthened French feelings for their country. French kings used that spirit to develop a strong government.

The Hundred Years' War also took a toll on the English and their economy. In addition, a civil war known as the Wars of the Roses, broke out among the nobles over who should be king. The winner, Henry Tudor, became King Henry VII.

Spain and Portugal Fight the Muslims

During the Middle Ages, Muslims ruled most of Spain and Portugal. These two lands make up the Iberian Peninsula. Most of the peninsula's people, however, were Christians. Some were also Jews.

The Muslims developed a rich culture in Spain and Portugal. They built beautiful mosques and palaces, such as the Alhambra in the southern kingdom of Granada. They also founded schools where Muslims, Jews, and Christians studied together. Most Christians, however, opposed Muslim rule. Their struggle to take back the Iberian Peninsula was called the *Reconquista* (RAY•kohn•KEES•tuh), or "reconquest."

By the 1200s, the Christians had set up three kingdoms: Portugal in the west, Castile in the center, and Aragon on the Mediterranean coast. Over the next 200 years, the Muslims slowly lost ground, until all that remained was Granada in the south.

In 1469 Princess **Isabella of Castile** married Prince **Ferdinand of Aragon.** Within 10 years, they became king and queen and joined their lands into one country called Spain. Ferdinand and Isabella wanted all of Spain to be Catholic. They turned first to the Jews. To escape persecution, some Jews became Christians. Ferdinand and Isabella, however, believed many still secretly practiced Judaism. So they set up the Spanish Inquisition.

The Spanish Inquisition tried and tortured thousands of people charged with heresy. In 1492 Ferdinand and Isabella told Jews to convert or leave Spain. Most left the country.

Next the king and queen turned to the Muslims. In 1492 Spain's armies conquered Granada. Ten years later, Muslims had to convert or leave. Most left Spain for North Africa.

✓ **Reading Check** **Cause and Effect** What caused the Hundred Years' War?

History Online

Homework Helper Need help with the material in this section? Visit jat.glencoe.com

Section 5 Review

Reading Summary

Review the Main Ideas

- A plague, known as the Black Death, killed millions of people in Europe and Asia and greatly changed Europe's economy and society.

- Wars between England and France weakened those countries' economies, and Spain became a united Catholic country.

What Did You Learn?

1. How was the Black Death spread?

2. Who was Joan of Arc, and what role did she play in the Hundred Years' War?

Critical Thinking

3. **Understanding Cause and Effect** Draw a diagram like the one below. Fill in some of the effects of the Black Death on Europe.

4. **Analyze** How did the Hundred Years' War affect the countries involved?

5. **Summarize** Describe the history of Spain and Portugal during the Middle Ages.

6. **Conclude** Do you think the removal of the Jews and Muslims from Spain was a wise policy? Explain your answer.

7. **Reading** **Asking Questions** Write three question that Charles might have asked Joan of Arc to determine if he would support her efforts.

Chapter 15 Reading Review

Section 1   The Early Middle Ages

Vocabulary
fjord
missionary
excommunicate
concordat

Focusing on the Main Ideas
- Geography influenced where medieval Europeans settled and what they did. *(page 513)*
- The Franks, Angles, and Saxons of Western Europe built new societies and defended them against Muslims, Magyars, and Vikings. *(page 514)*
- The Catholic Church spread Christianity through Western Europe. *(page 519)*

Section 2   Feudalism

Vocabulary
feudalism
vassal
fief
knight
serf
guild

Focusing on the Main Ideas
- Feudalism developed in Europe in the Middle Ages. It was based on landowning, loyalty, and the power of armored knights on horseback. *(page 523)*
- Knights followed a code of chivalry and lived in castles, while peasants lived in simple houses and worked hard all year long. *(page 526)*
- Increased trade led to the growth of towns and cities and the rise of guilds and city governments. *(page 528)*

Section 3   Kingdoms and Crusades

Vocabulary
grand jury
trial jury
clergy

Focusing on the Main Ideas
- England developed a system in which the king's power was limited by Parliament. *(page 535)*
- French kings called the Capetians conquered lands held by the English in western France and set up France's first parliament. *(page 538)*
- After the Mongols destroyed the Kievan state, the rulers of Moscow built a new Russian state headed by a czar. *(page 539)*
- European crusaders captured Jerusalem but were later driven out by the Muslims. *(page 541)*

Section 4   The Church and Society

Vocabulary
mass
heresy
anti-Semitism
theology
scholasticism
vernacular

Focusing on the Main Ideas
- The Catholic Church played an important role in medieval Europe and used its power to uphold its teachings. *(page 545)*
- Church and government leaders supported learning and the arts in medieval Europe. *(page 549)*

Section 5   The Late Middle Ages

Vocabulary
plague
Reconquista

Focusing on the Main Ideas
- A terrible plague, known as the Black Death, swept through Europe in the 1300s, killing millions. *(page 554)*
- Western Europe was devastated by war in the 1300s and 1400s as England and France fought each other, and Spain and Portugal fought against the Muslims. *(page 557)*

559

Review Vocabulary

Match the word in the first column with its definition in the second column.

____ 1. fief   a. worked their own land and a lord's land

____ 2. serf   b. the study of religion and God

____ 3. concordat   c. people ordained as priests

____ 4. clergy   d. land granted to a vassal

____ 5. heresy   e. agreement between the pope and the ruler of a country

____ 6. theology   f. a belief different from Church teachings

Review Main Ideas

Section 1 • The Early Middle Ages

7. Which peoples invaded Europe in the Middle Ages?

8. How did the Catholic Church affect medieval Europe?

Section 2 • Feudalism

9. What was the basis for wealth and power in medieval Europe?

10. What was the result of increased trade?

Section 3 • Kingdoms and Crusades

11. What changes in England and France were steps toward representative government?

12. Which groups were at war with each other in the Crusades? For what were they fighting?

Section 4 • The Church and Society

13. How did the Catholic Church use its power to uphold its teachings?

14. Why did learning and the arts flourish in medieval Europe?

Section 5 • The Late Middle Ages

15. What was the Black Death, and how did it change Europe?

16. Which European nations were at war during the 1300s and 1400s?

Critical Thinking

17. **Cause and Effect** What improvements in farming led to an increase in the production of food?

18. **Compare** What did Alfred the Great and William the Conqueror succeed in doing?

Review

Reading Skill | Questioning — Just Ask

19. Read the passage from page 525. Write six questions that you might ask about it. Use a different question starter for each question: *who, what, when, where, how,* and *why.*

> During the Middle Ages, Europeans invented new technology that helped increase the amount of crops they could grow. Perhaps the most important was a heavy wheeled plow with an iron blade. It easily turned over Western Europe's dense clay soils.

To review this skill, see pages 510–511.

Geography Skills

Study the map below and answer the following questions.

20. **Place** On which river was the battle of Orléans fought?

21. **Interaction** Which rival do you think had an advantage at the point shown on the map? Consider the battles, amount of land held, natural advantages, and so on.

22. **Location** Why were most battle sites near the English Channel?

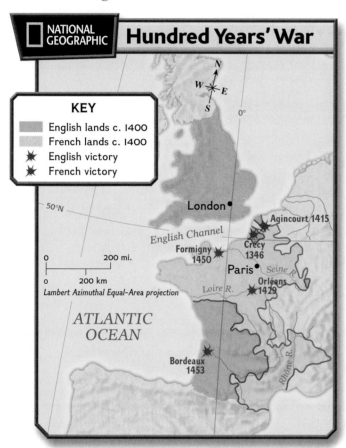

NATIONAL GEOGRAPHIC

Hundred Years' War

KEY
- English lands c. 1400
- French lands c. 1400
- ✳ English victory
- ✳ French victory

London
Agincourt 1415
English Channel
Formigny 1450
Crécy 1346
Paris
Orléans 1429
Seine R.
Loire R.
Bordeaux 1453
Rhône R.

ATLANTIC OCEAN

50°N
0°

0 200 mi.
0 200 km
Lambert Azimuthal Equal-Area projection

Read to Write

23. **Script Writing** Suppose you are living in a small medieval town. Suddenly, the people of your town begin dying from the plague. You and your family have to decide whether to stay in the town or leave. Write a dialogue between you, family members, and perhaps some neighbors. The dialogue should give the advantages and disadvantages of both actions and should show the family reaching a decision about what to do.

History Online

Self-Check Quiz To help prepare for the Chapter Test, visit jat.glencoe.com

24. **Using Your FOLDABLES** Discuss as a class why the events of medieval Europe occurred. Then choose one major event from your foldable, and write a paragraph that predicts how history would have been different if that event had not occurred.

Using Technology

25. **Modeling** Do research to find out more about the parts of a manor and its general layout. (For example, you know that the castle of the lord and lady was at the center of the manor.) Then work with your classmates to create a computer drawing or model of a manor.

Linking Past and Present

26. **Comparing** Describe how present-day universities compare to medieval ones, such as those in Bologna, Paris, and Oxford. In your description, explain what it would be like to have to learn without the use of books.

Primary Source Analyze

King Louis IX asked the following of his vassals.

"All vassals of the king are bound to appear before him when he shall summon them, and to serve him at their own expense for forty days and forty nights, with as many knights as each one owes."

—King Louis IX, "Legal Rules for Military Service"

DBQ Document-Based Questions

27. Did knights directly serve the king and appear when he called them?

28. What do you think happened if the king needed the vassals and knights for more than 40 days and nights?

Comparing Medieval Civilizations

Compare civilizations of the Middle Ages by reviewing the information below. Can you see how the peoples of these civilizations had lives that were very much like yours?

Where in the World?

- Chapter 12
- Chapter 13
- Chapter 14
- Chapter 15

NATIONAL GEOGRAPHIC

	China in the Middle Ages Chapter 12	Medieval Africa Chapter 13	Medieval Japan Chapter 14	Medieval Europe Chapter 15
Where did these civilizations develop?	• Mainland of East Asia	• West Africa; Southern Africa; East Africa	• Islands off coast of East Asia	• Northwestern Europe and Mediterranean area
Who were some important people in these civilizations?	• Taizong, ruled A.D. 627–649 • Empress Wu, ruled A.D. 684–705 • Kublai Khan, ruled A.D. 1271–1294 • Zheng He, A.D. 1371–1433	• Ibn Battuta, A.D. 1307–1377 • Mansa Musa, ruled A.D. 1312–1337 • Sunni Ali, ruled A.D. 1464–1492 • Queen Nzinga, ruled C. A.D. 1623–1663	• Prince Shotoku, A.D. 574–622 • Murasaki Shikibu, C. A.D. 973–1025 • Miramoto Yoritomo, A.D. 1147–1199 • Ashikaga Takauji, A.D. 1305–1358	• Charlemagne, ruled A.D. 768–814 • William the Conqueror, ruled A.D. 1066–1087 • Thomas Aquinas, A.D. 1225–1274 • Joan of Arc, A.D. 1412–1431
Where did most of the people live?	• Farming villages and towns along major rivers	• Farming villages; trading centers, such as Timbuktu and Kilwa	• Fishing and farming villages in coastal plains area	• Farming villages on estates located on plains; trading centers in Italy and Flanders

	China in the Middle Ages **Chapter 12**	Medieval Africa **Chapter 13**	Medieval Japan **Chapter 14**	Medieval Europe **Chapter 15**
What were these people's beliefs?	• Confucianism, Daoism, Buddhism 	• Traditional African religions, Christianity, Islam	• Shintoism, Buddhism 	• Roman Catholic with small numbers of Jews and Muslims
What was their government like?	• Emperors ruled with the help of scholar-officials selected by exams	• Ruled by kings, close advisers, and local officials 	• Emperors ruled in name but power held by military leaders 	• Feudal territories united into kingdoms
What was their language and writing like?	• Chinese: symbols standing for objects are combined to represent ideas 	• Many languages and different writing systems, but much knowledge passed on by oral history	• Japanese: Chinese characters standing for ideas as well as symbols representing sounds	• Many languages derived from Latin and Germanic 
What contributions did they make?	• Civil service based on merit; invented moveable type, gunpowder, and the compass	• Produced tradition of storytelling, dance, music, and sculpture	• Developed ideas based on harmony with nature; produced martial arts 	• Developed universities and representative government
How do these changes affect me? *Can you add any?*	• The Chinese invented fire-works, the compass, and printed books	• Early Africans passed on musical traditions that led to jazz, rap, gospel, reggae	• Japanese warriors developed martial arts, such as judo and karate	• Medieval Europeans passed on Christian ideas and a system of banking

Unit 5

A Changing World

Why It's Important

Each civilization that you will study in this unit made important contributions to history.

- Native Americans built a network of trade routes.
- Renaissance and Reformation Europeans affirmed the importance of the human individual.
- People in early modern Europe and America developed ideas about freedom and democracy.

A.D. 1400	A.D. 1450	A.D. 1500	A.D. 1550

The Americas
Chapter 16

C. A.D. 1400
Aztec Empire reaches its height

A.D. 1533
Spanish forces defeat the Inca in Peru

Mask of an Aztec god ▶

Renaissance and Reformation
Chapter 17

C. A.D. 1440
Johannes Gutenberg uses movable type in printing press

◀ Page from Gutenberg Bible

A.D. 1508
Michelangelo paints Sistine Chapel in Rome

Statue of ▶ David by Michelangelo

A.D. 1555
Peace of Augsburg divides Germany into Catholic and Protestant states

Enlightenment and Revolution
Chapter 18

A.D. 1488
Bartholomeu Dias of Portugal sails around southern tip of Africa

◀ Early compass

A.D. 1518
First enslaved Africans brought to Americas

A.D. 1543
Copernicus presents a new view of the universe

◀ Ferdinand Magellan

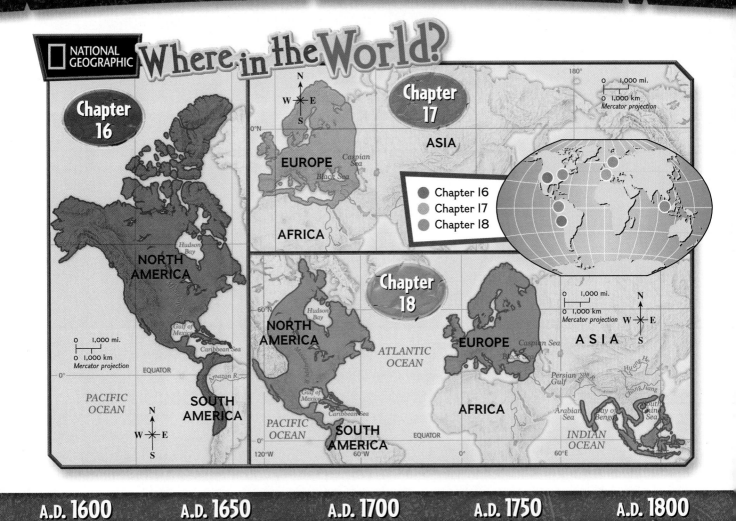

NATIONAL GEOGRAPHIC — Where in the World?

Chapter 16

NORTH AMERICA

Hudson Bay

Gulf of Mexico

Caribbean Sea

Amazon R.

PACIFIC OCEAN

SOUTH AMERICA

EQUATOR

0°

0 1,000 mi.
0 1,000 km
Mercator projection

N W E S

Chapter 17

ASIA

EUROPE

Caspian Sea

Black Sea

AFRICA

0°N

N W E S

180°

0 1,000 mi.
0 1,000 km
Mercator projection

- Chapter 16
- Chapter 17
- Chapter 18

Chapter 18

NORTH AMERICA

Hudson Bay

Mississippi R.

Gulf of Mexico

Caribbean Sea

ATLANTIC OCEAN

PACIFIC OCEAN

SOUTH AMERICA

EUROPE

Caspian Sea

Black Sea

AFRICA

ASIA

Persian Gulf

Arabian Sea

Bay of Bengal

South China Sea

Huang He

Chang Jiang

INDIAN OCEAN

EQUATOR

60°N

120°W   60°W   0°   60°E

0 1,000 mi.
0 1,000 km
Mercator projection

N W E S

Timeline

A.D. 1600   A.D. 1650   A.D. 1700   A.D. 1750   A.D. 1800

C. A.D. 1570
Eastern Woodland peoples form Iroquois League

A.D. 1769
Spaniards found mission at San Diego

A.D. 1839
Scientists uncover Mayan city of Copan

◀ Native American warrior shirt

A.D. 1598
King Henry IV introduces religious toleration in France

A.D. 1608
First checks are used to replace cash in the Netherlands

A.D. 1648
Thirty Years' War ends

◀ Queen Elizabeth I of England

A.D. 1690
John Locke develops theory of government

A.D. 1702
First daily newspaper published in London

A.D. 1776
American Revolution begins

◀ World map, 1630

George Washington ▶

Unit 5

Places to Locate

Machu Picchu

See The Americas
Chapter 16

Tikal

See The Americas
Chapter 16

NORTH AMERICA

SOUTH AMERICA

Atlantic Ocean

Pacific Ocean

People to Meet

Pachacuti

Ruled A.D. 1438–1471
Inca ruler
Chapter 16, page 589

Leonardo da Vinci

A.D. 1452–1519
Italian artist and scientist
Chapter 17, page 622

Martin Luther

A.D. 1483–1546
German Protestant leader
Chapter 17, page 638

Hernán Cortés

A.D. 1485–1547
Spanish conqueror
Chapter 16, page 598

ASIA

EUROPE

AFRICA

Indian Ocean

3 Sistine Chapel

See Renaissance and Reformation Chapter 17

4 Wittenberg

See Enlightenment and Revolution Chapter 18

5 Versailles

See Enlightenment and Revolution Chapter 18

Catherine de' Medici

A.D. 1519–1589
French queen
Chapter 17, page 647

Elizabeth I

Ruled A.D. 1558–1603
English queen
Chapter 18, page 665

John Locke

A.D. 1632–1704
English political thinker
Chapter 18, page 683

Isaac Newton

A.D. 1642–1727
English mathematician
Chapter 18, page 677

Chapter 16

The Americas

▼ The ruins of Machu Picchu near Cuzco, Peru

NATIONAL GEOGRAPHIC **When & Where?**

c. 1500 B.C.	A.D. 500	A.D. 1000	A.D. 1500
c. 1200 B.C. Olmec build an empire in Mexico	**A.D. 500** Mayan cities flourish in Mesoamerica	**c. A.D. 1250** Aztec arrive in central Mexico	**A.D. 1492** Columbus reaches the Americas

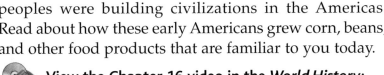

Chapter Preview

During Europe's medieval age, many different peoples were building civilizations in the Americas. Read about how these early Americans grew corn, beans, and other food products that are familiar to you today.

 View the Chapter 16 video in the *World History: Journey Across Time* Video Program.

Section 1 — The First Americans

The first people in the Americas arrived thousands of years ago. Farming led to the growth of civilizations in what is now Mexico, Central America, and Peru.

Section 2 — Life in the Americas

The Maya, Aztec, and many other Native American cultures developed in North and South America.

Section 3 — The Fall of the Aztec and Inca Empires

Spanish explorers and soldiers were drawn to the riches of Native American civilizations. Using horses and guns, they defeated the Aztec and Inca Empires in the early A.D. 1500s.

FOLDABLES™ Study Organizer

Organizing Information *Make this foldable to help you organize information about the history and culture of the Americas.*

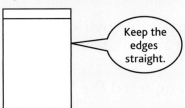

Step 1 *Collect two sheets of paper and place them about 1 inch apart.*

Keep the edges straight.

Step 2 *Fold up the bottom edges of the paper to form four tabs.*

This makes all the tabs the same size.

Step 3 *When all the tabs are the same size, crease the paper to hold the tabs in place and staple the sheets together. Label each tab as shown.*

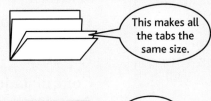

The Americas
The First Americans
Life in the Americas
The Aztec and Inca

Staple along the fold.

Reading and Writing
As you read the chapter, write the main ideas presented in each of the three sections under the tabs of your foldable. Note details that support the main ideas.

Reading Skill

Summarizing

1 Learn It!

Summarizing Information

Summarizing what you have read, either orally or in writing, is a good way to increase your understanding of the text. Read the information about Christopher Columbus on pages 594–595, **Columbus Arrives in America** and **Columbus Returns.** With a partner, summarize the main points. One person should summarize what he or she read while the other listens. Then the second person should resummarize, adding details that the partner may have left out.

Reading Tip

As you read, place sticky notes at the tops of pages as a reminder to return to sections that you may need to reread.

When you are finished, look at the following list to see if you included all the important details.

- Columbus first arrived in the Americas in 1492.

- He believed he had reached Asia but actually landed on an island in the Caribbean Sea.

- He took home many exotic treasures to impress the Spanish rulers.

- He returned the next year with soldiers.

- He landed on Hispaniola, which is present-day Haiti and the Dominican Republic.

- Conquistadors conquered the Native Americans.

- Spain gained a foothold in the Americas.

② Practice It!
Retelling

Read the description of how **Spain Conquers Mexico** on pages 595–596. Before you begin, read the first paragraph about Cortés aloud:

> The voyages of Christopher Columbus, who sailed to the Americas four times, inspired many poor nobles to go to America to seek their fortunes. Many came from the part of Spain known as the Extremadura. Its poor soil, blistering hot summers, and icy winters held little chance for wealth. One of these nobles was 19-year-old Hernán Cortés.
>
> —*from pages 595–596*

With a partner, summarize the story of Cortés and how he destroyed the Aztec capital. As you are retelling, you may want to refer back to the text, reading aloud words in quotation marks or italics to provide an authentic voice to your story. Listen carefully so that you can add details that your partner may have left out.

Read to Write

Choose one of the historical figures from Chapter 16 and expand his or her story with details from your own imagination. Add quotes, descriptions, and events that you think might have happened to create a richer, although fictionalized, narrative.

③ Apply It!

As you read this chapter, practice summarizing. Stop after each section and write a brief summary of the major points in that section.

Get Ready to Read!

What's the Connection?
While Western Europe rebuilt itself after the fall of Rome, diverse cultures thrived in the Americas.

Focusing on the Main Ideas
• It is believed that the first people in the Americas came from Asia during the Ice Age. *(page 573)*

• The invention of farming led to the rise of civilizations in the Americas. *(page 574)*

• Early people in the northern part of the Americas built complex cultures based on farming and trade. *(page 578)*

Locating Places
Mesoamerica
   (MEH•zoh•uh•MEHR•ih•kuh)
Teotihuacán
   (TAY•oh•TEE•wuh•KAHN)
Cuzco (KOOS•koh)
Cahokia (kuh•HOH•kee•uh)

Meeting People
Olmec (OHL•mehk)
Maya (MY•uh)
Toltec (TOHL•TEHK)
Moche (MOH•cheh)
Inca (IHNG•kuh)
Hohokam (HOH•hoh•KAHM)
Anasazi (AH•nuh•SAH•zee)

Building Your Vocabulary
glacier (GLAY•shuhr)
monopoly (muh•NAH•puh•lee)

Reading Strategy
Summarizing Information Create a chart to show the characteristics of the Olmec and Moche.

	Location	Dates	Lifestyle
Olmec			
Moche			

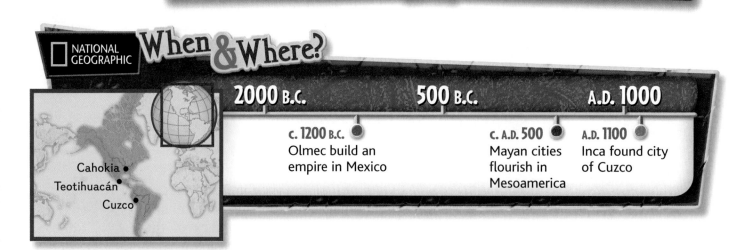

NATIONAL GEOGRAPHIC When & Where?

2000 B.C.	500 B.C.	A.D. 1000
c. 1200 B.C. Olmec build an empire in Mexico	**c. A.D. 500** Mayan cities flourish in Mesoamerica	**A.D. 1100** Inca found city of Cuzco

Cahokia •
Teotihuacán •
Cuzco •

Pathway to the Americas

Main Idea It is believed that the first people in the Americas came from Asia during the Ice Age.

Reading Focus When and how did the first people travel to the Americas? Nobody knows for sure. The story of their arrival remains one of history's mysteries.

We know people came to America a long time ago, but how did they get here? Today, America is not connected by land to the rest of the world, but in the past it was. Scientists have studied the earth's geography during the Ice Age—a period when temperatures dropped sharply. At that time, much of the earth's water froze into huge sheets of ice, or **glaciers** (GLAY•shuhrz).

As the ice froze and the seas fell, an area of dry land was exposed between Asia and Alaska. Scientists call this land bridge Beringia (buh•RIHN•jee•uh), after Vitus Bering, a famous European explorer. They think that people in Asia followed the animals they were hunting across this land bridge into the Americas. By testing the age of bones and tools at ancient campsites, scientists estimate that the first people arrived between 15,000 to 40,000 years ago.

When the Ice Age ended about 10,000 years ago, the glaciers melted and released water back into the seas. The land bridge to America disappeared beneath the waves.

Hunting and Gathering Hunters in the Americas were constantly on the move in search of food. They fished and gathered nuts, fruits, or roots. They also hunted massive prey, such as the woolly mammoth, antelope, caribou, and bison.

It took several hunters to kill a woolly mammoth, which could weigh as much as 9 tons. These big animals provided meat, hides for clothing, and bones for tools.

As the Ice Age ended, some animals became extinct, or disappeared from the earth. The warm weather, however, opened new opportunities to early Americans.

Reading Check **Explain** Why is there no longer a land bridge between Asia and America?

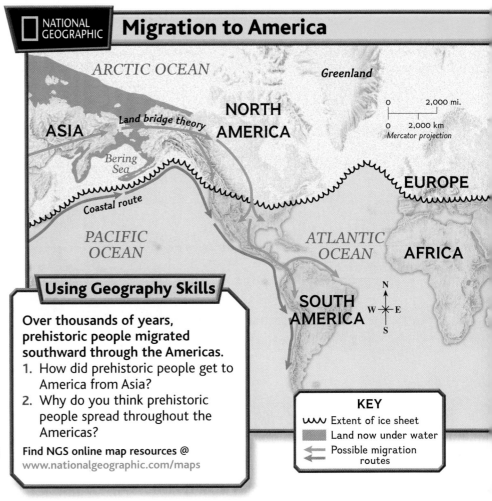

NATIONAL GEOGRAPHIC

Migration to America

ARCTIC OCEAN
Greenland
ASIA
Land bridge theory
NORTH AMERICA
Bering Sea
EUROPE
Coastal route
PACIFIC OCEAN
ATLANTIC OCEAN
AFRICA
SOUTH AMERICA

0   2,000 mi.
0   2,000 km
Mercator projection

Using Geography Skills

Over thousands of years, prehistoric people migrated southward through the Americas.

1. How did prehistoric people get to America from Asia?
2. Why do you think prehistoric people spread throughout the Americas?

Find NGS online map resources @ www.nationalgeographic.com/maps

KEY
ᔕᔕᔕ Extent of ice sheet
▧ Land now under water
← Possible migration routes

◀ Stone arrowhead

First American Civilizations

Main Idea The invention of farming led to the rise of civilizations in the Americas.

Reading Focus What would our lives be like if people had never learned to farm? Read to learn how farming made civilization possible in Mexico, Central America, and South America.

The first Americans were hunter-gatherers, but as the Ice Age ended and the climate warmed, people in America made an amazing discovery. They learned that seeds could be planted and they would grow into crops that people could eat.

Farming began in **Mesoamerica** (MEH•zoh•uh•MEHR•ih•kuh) 9,000 to 10,000 years ago. *Meso* comes from the Greek word for "middle." This region includes lands stretching from the Valley of Mexico to Costa Rica in Central America.

The region's geography was ideal for farming. Much of the area had a rich, volcanic soil and a mild climate. Rains fell in the spring, helping seeds to sprout. They decreased in the summer, allowing crops to ripen for harvest. Then, in the autumn, the rains returned, soaking the soil for the next year's crop.

The first crops grown in the Americas included pumpkins, peppers, squash, gourds, and beans. It took longer to develop corn, which grew as a wild grass. Early plants produced a single, one-inch cob. After hundreds of years, the early Americans finally learned how to cross corn

Hunting the Woolly Mammoth

Working in groups, hunters could bring down large prey, such as a woolly mammoth. *Why do you think early hunters preferred to hunt large animals such as mammoths instead of smaller animals?*

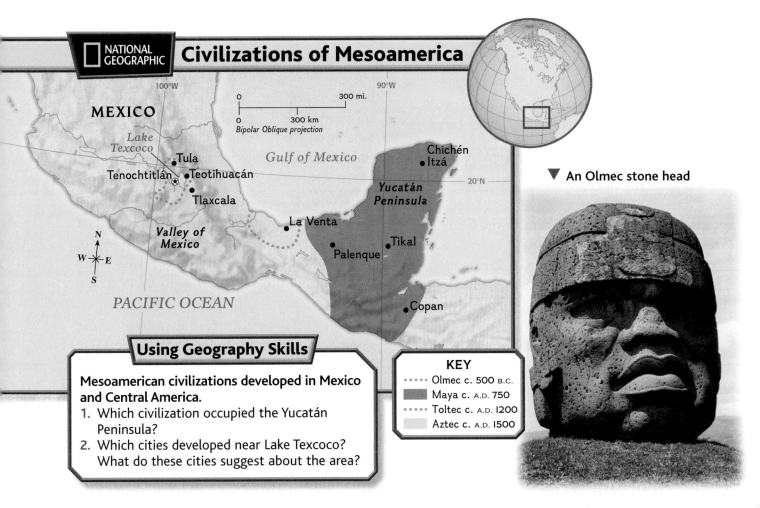

MEXICO

Lake Texcoco

100°W

Tula

Tenochtitlán ⊛ Teotihuacán

Tlaxcala

Valley of Mexico

0 — 300 mi.
0 — 300 km
Bipolar Oblique projection

Gulf of Mexico

90°W

Chichén Itzá

Yucatán Peninsula

20°N

La Venta

Tikal

Palenque

N
W E
S

PACIFIC OCEAN

Copan

▼ An Olmec stone head

Using Geography Skills

Mesoamerican civilizations developed in Mexico and Central America.
1. Which civilization occupied the Yucatán Peninsula?
2. Which cities developed near Lake Texcoco? What do these cities suggest about the area?

KEY
- Olmec c. 500 B.C.
- Maya c. A.D. 750
- Toltec c. A.D. 1200
- Aztec c. A.D. 1500

with other grasses to get bigger cobs and more cobs per plant. With this discovery, corn, also known as maize, became the most important food in the Americas.

Mesoamerican Civilizations Growing corn and other crops allowed the Mesoamericans to stop wandering in search of food. As a result, they formed more complex societies. Starting around 1500 B.C., the first of several ancient civilizations appeared.

Near present-day Vera Cruz, Mexico, a people called the **Olmec** (OHL•mehk) built a far-reaching trading empire. It started around 1200 B.C. and lasted about 800 years.

The Olmec enjoyed rich farming resources, but they lacked other raw materials. They traded salt and beans with inland peoples to get jade for jewelry and obsidian, or volcanic glass, to make sharp-edged knives. They used other trade goods, such as hematite, a shiny volcanic stone, to

make polished mirrors and basalt for carving gigantic stone heads.

The Olmec used the region's many rivers as highways for trade, but eventually, the inland peoples seized control of the trade. One of these groups built the first planned city in the Americas. It became known as **Teotihuacán** (TAY•oh•TEE•wuh•KAHN), or "Place of the Gods." The city reached its height around A.D. 400. It had a population of between 120,000 to 200,000 people.

As Teotihuacán's power spread, a people called the **Maya** (MY•uh) built another civilization in the steamy rain forests of the Yucatán Peninsula (YOO•kuh•TAN). They, too, traded throughout Mesoamerica. The Maya used their central location to reach into what is now southern Mexico and Central America. Mayan traders in sea-going canoes paddled along the coast, perhaps reaching as far as the present-day United States.

What Happened to the Maya? Teotihuacán and Mayan cities hit their peaks in the A.D. 400s and A.D. 500s. Then, around A.D. 600, Teotihuacán started to decline. No one is sure why this happened. Some experts say overpopulation drained the city of food and resources. Others blame a long drought, or period without rain. Still others say that the poor people rebelled against their rich rulers. Whatever the reason, by A.D. 750, the city had been destroyed.

The Mayan civilization lasted about 200 years longer. But it also came to a mysterious end. The Maya abandoned their cities, and by the A.D. 900s, the cities lay deserted, hidden in a thick tangle of vines.

As the Maya left their cities, a people called the **Toltec** (TOHL•TEHK) seized what is now northern Mexico. These warrior nomads built the city of Tula northwest of present-day Mexico City. From Tula, they conquered lands all the way to the Yucatán Peninsula.

Toltec rulers tightly controlled trade. They held a **monopoly** (muh•NAH•puh•lee), or sole right, to the trade in obsidian. As a result, the Toltec kept other people from making weapons to challenge them.

◀ Figure of Mayan leader

▼ This pyramid was in the Mayan city of Tikal, which was located in present-day Guatemala. *What caused the downfall of the Mayan civilization?*

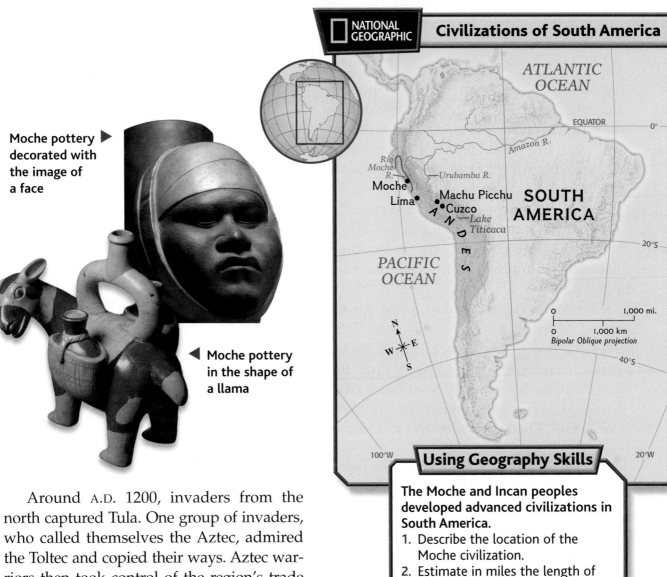

Moche pottery ▶ decorated with the image of a face

◀ Moche pottery in the shape of a llama

ATLANTIC OCEAN

EQUATOR

Amazon R.

Río Moche R.

Urubamba R.

Moche

Lima

Machu Picchu

Cuzco

Lake Titicaca

SOUTH AMERICA

PACIFIC OCEAN

ANDES

0°

20°S

40°S

0   1,000 mi.

0   1,000 km
Bipolar Oblique projection

N E S W

100°W   20°W

Using Geography Skills

The Moche and Incan peoples developed advanced civilizations in South America.
1. Describe the location of the Moche civilization.
2. Estimate in miles the length of the Inca Empire.

Around A.D. 1200, invaders from the north captured Tula. One group of invaders, who called themselves the Aztec, admired the Toltec and copied their ways. Aztec warriors then took control of the region's trade and built a huge empire. When Europeans arrived in the A.D. 1500s, the Aztec ruled about five million people.

The Moche and Inca South of Mesoamerica, other civilizations developed along the west coast of South America. The **Moche** (MOH• cheh) people were located in the dry coastal desert of what is now Peru.

The Moche ruled from about A.D. 100 to A.D. 700. They dug canals that carried water from rivers in the Andes mountain ranges to their desert homeland. Because of this irrigation, the desert bloomed with crops.

The Moche suffered no shortage of food. They ate corn, squash, beans, and peanuts. They also hunted llamas and guinea pigs and fished in the nearby Pacific Ocean.

This wealth of food freed the Moche to do other things. Moche engineers designed huge pyramids, such as the Pyramid of the Sun. Moche traders exchanged goods with people as far away as the rain forests of the Amazon River valley. These goods included pottery, cloth, and jewelry.

The Moche did not have a written language. Instead, their culture's story is told

History Online

Web Activity Visit jat.glencoe.com and click on *Chapter 16—Student Web Activity* to learn more about civilizations in the Americas.

through artwork. Pottery often showed animals important to the Moche, such as the llama. The llama served as a pack animal, carrying goods for long distances. It also provided meat for food and wool for weaving.

For all their achievements, however, the Moche never expanded much beyond their homeland. The work of empire building belonged to another people called the **Inca** (IHNG•kuh).

The Incan homeland lay in the Andes mountain ranges of present-day Peru. They chose to live in high river valleys, often above 10,000 feet (3,048 m). Over time, the Inca built the biggest empire in the ancient Americas. It centered around the capital of **Cuzco** (KOOS•koh), founded in A.D. 1100.

✓ **Reading Check** **Explain** How did the Toltec keep other people from challenging them?

Civilizations in North America

Main Idea Early people in the northern part of the Americas built complex cultures based on farming and trade.

Reading Focus Would you be surprised to learn that early North Americans built large cities? Read to learn about the complex civilizations that developed in the American Southwest, then in the Mississippi River valley.

North of Mesoamerica, Native Americans developed their own ways of living. Still, they had learned something important from their Mesoamerican neighbors. They learned how to farm.

Farming in what would someday be the United States began in the American Southwest. It also spread from Mesoamerica along the coast and up the Mississippi, Missouri, and Ohio Rivers. As farming developed, so did new civilizations.

The Way It Was

Focus on Everyday Life

Anasazi Cliff Dwellings From far away they look like sand castles tightly stacked into the side of a canyon wall. Up close they are life-sized, ancient cliff homes. The two cowboys who discovered them in A.D. 1888 called them the "magnificent city." They found them while crossing a snowy flat-topped mountain in southwestern Colorado. The men had stumbled upon the homes of the Anasazi—an ancient people who once lived in the Southwest.

The Anasazi built nearly 600 cliff dwellings in the area now protected within Mesa Verde National Park. They began building villages under overhanging

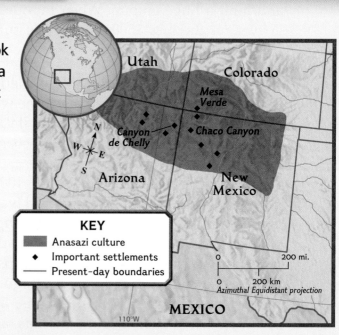

The Hohokam and Anasazi News of farming traveled north along with Mesoamerican traders. But it took a long time for nomads in the scorching deserts of the Southwest to try farming.

Finally, around A.D. 300, a people called the **Hohokam** (HOH•hoh•KAHM) planted gardens on lands between the Salt and Gila Rivers. They dug more than 500 miles (805 km) of canals to carry river waters to their fields. They grew corn, cotton, beans, and squash. They also made pottery, turquoise pendants, and the world's first etchings by using cactus juice to eat through the surface of shells.

The Hohokam thrived for about 1,000 years. In the mid-A.D. 1300s, they mysteriously fled. Perhaps a long drought drove them away, or floods from heavy rains destroyed their canals. No one is sure.

Around A.D. 600, as the Hohokam planted fields near rivers, the **Anasazi** (AH•nuh•SAH•zee) moved into the region's canyons and cliffs. They also took up farming. However, they did not rely only on rivers for irrigation. They collected water that ran off cliffs during heavy rains and channeled it to their fields.

Anasazi culture reached its height at Chaco Canyon, an area in present-day New Mexico. The people there controlled the trade in turquoise. They used it like money, to buy goods from many different regions including Mesoamerica.

The Anasazi lived in huge apartment-like houses carved into cliffs. The cliff houses had hundreds of rooms and held thousands of people. Spanish explorers later called these buildings *pueblos*—the Spanish word for "village." The Anasazi

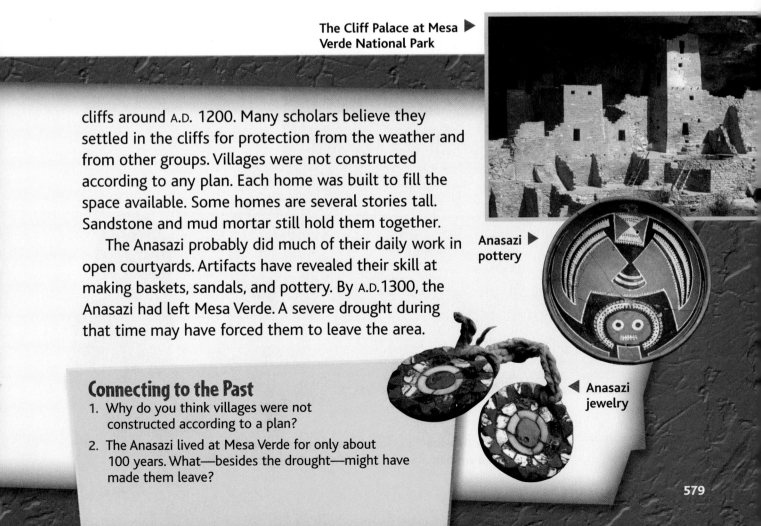

The Cliff Palace at Mesa Verde National Park ▶

cliffs around A.D. 1200. Many scholars believe they settled in the cliffs for protection from the weather and from other groups. Villages were not constructed according to any plan. Each home was built to fill the space available. Some homes are several stories tall. Sandstone and mud mortar still hold them together.

The Anasazi probably did much of their daily work in open courtyards. Artifacts have revealed their skill at making baskets, sandals, and pottery. By A.D. 1300, the Anasazi had left Mesa Verde. A severe drought during that time may have forced them to leave the area.

Anasazi ▶
pottery

◀ Anasazi
jewelry

Connecting to the Past
1. Why do you think villages were not constructed according to a plan?
2. The Anasazi lived at Mesa Verde for only about 100 years. What—besides the drought—might have made them leave?

prospered until a 50-year drought occurred in the early A.D. 1000s. Like the Hohokam, they also drifted away.

Who Were the Mound Builders?
Far to the east, across the Mississippi River, another civilization was taking shape. It started around 1000 B.C. and lasted until about A.D. 400. Its founders built huge mounds made of earth, some in the shape of animals. Such earthworks gave these people their name—"Mound Builders."

Two groups formed the mound-building culture—first the Adena, then the Hopewell. Together they settled on lands stretching from the Great Lakes to the Gulf of Mexico.

Although the Mound Builders lived mostly as hunters and gatherers, they experimented with farming. Scientists think they tamed many wild plants, including sunflowers, gourds, and barley. It is likely that women planted the first seeds. Women probably knew the most about plants because they gathered wild foods while the men hunted.

Corn was first brought to the region around A.D. 100, probably carried there by traders. These traders traveled near and far to find raw materials for weapons, jewelry, and fine carvings. Many of these objects were placed in huge burial mounds to honor the dead.

The Mississippians
The mound-building culture changed when the Hopewell mysteriously declined and a new people known as the Mississippians emerged. The Mississippians were named for their location in the Mississippi River valley. Their lands reached from present-day Ohio, Indiana, and Illinois, south to the Gulf of Mexico.

◀ The Great Serpent Mound in southern Ohio is an example of the earthen mounds built by the Adena culture. *Besides the Adena, what other group made up the mound-building culture?*

These two-foot-high marble statues of a man ▶ and a woman are from a mound in Georgia.

A Cahokia mound in Illinois ▶

The Mississippians found that plants grew well in the rich floodplains along the river. They harvested enough crops to become full-time farmers. The most common crops included corn, squash, and beans.

As in Mesoamerica, large-scale farming led to the rise of cities. Some contained 10,000 or more people. The largest city, **Cahokia** (kuh•HOH•kee•uh), may have had 30,000 people. The remains of this city can still be seen in southwestern Illinois.

The Mississippians built a different kind of mound. Their mounds were pyramid shaped but with flat tops. The base of the biggest one covered 16 acres (6.5 ha), more than the base of the Great Pyramid of Egypt.

The finished mound, known today as Monks Mound, rose more than 100 feet (30 m) high. From the mound's summit, rulers gazed down at dozens of smaller mounds. The flat tops of the mounds held temples, homes for the rich, and burial places.

In the early A.D. 1300s, the Mississippian civilization collapsed, and the cities were abandoned. Perhaps other Native Americans attacked them, or the city may have become too big to feed itself.

✓ **Reading Check** **Identify** How was turquoise used by the Anasazi of Chaco Canyon?

Section 1 Review

History Online

Homework Helper Need help with the material in this section? Visit jat.glencoe.com

Reading Summary

Review the  **Main Ideas**

- The first Americans were most likely hunter-gatherers who came from Asia across a land bridge.

- A number of civilizations developed in the Americas, including the Olmec, Maya, and Toltec in Central America and Mexico, and the Moche and Inca in South America. All were dependent on farming.

- In North America, farming civilizations arose in the Southwest and then in the Ohio and Mississippi River valleys.

What Did You Learn?

1. Why was Mesoamerica's geography ideal for farming?

2. How did the first Americans develop corn?

Critical Thinking

3. **Summarizing Information** Draw a chart like the one below. Add details about the early peoples of North America.

Native Americans
Southwest
East/Mississippi River Valley

4. **Summarize** How and when did the first people come to the Americas, and how did they live once they were here?

5. **Geography** How did geography shape the development of the Anasazi civilization?

6. **Expository Writing** Write a short essay comparing the civilizations that developed in Mesoamerica to those that developed in South America.

7. **Reading Summarizing Information** Write a paragraph that summarizes how farming led to the development of civilizations.

Section 2

Life in the Americas

Get Ready to Read!

What's the Connection?

In Section 1, you read about the rise of the first civilizations in the Americas. The first Americans had to use whatever natural resources the land had to offer. As a result, they developed many different cultures suited to where they lived.

Focusing on the Main Ideas

- The Maya adjusted to life in the tropical rain forest and built a culture based on their religious beliefs. *(page 583)*

- The Aztec moved into the Valley of Mexico, where they created an empire based on conquest and war. *(page 585)*

- To unite their huge empire, Incan rulers set up a highly organized government and society. *(page 588)*

- The geography in lands north of present-day Mexico shaped the developement of many different Native American cultures. *(page 590)*

Locating Places
Petén (peh•TEHN)
Tenochtitlán
(tay•NAWCH•teet•LAHN)

Meeting People
Pachacuti (PAH•chah•KOO•tee)
Iroquois (IHR•uh•KWOY)

Building Your Vocabulary
quipu (KEE•poo)
igloo
adobe (uh•DOH•bee)
confederation
(kuhn•FEH•duh•RAY•shuhn)

Reading Strategy
Organizing Information Use a pyramid to show the Inca's social classes.

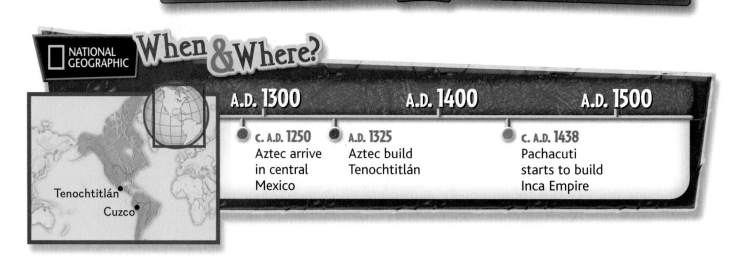

NATIONAL GEOGRAPHIC When & Where?

A.D. 1300   A.D. 1400   A.D. 1500

c. A.D. 1250
Aztec arrive in central Mexico

A.D. 1325
Aztec build Tenochtitlán

c. A.D. 1438
Pachacuti starts to build Inca Empire

Tenochtitlán
Cuzco

The Mayan People

Main Idea The Maya adjusted to life in the tropical rain forest and built a culture based on their religious beliefs.

Reading Focus What would it be like to live in a jungle? What resources would be easy to find? Read to learn how the Maya adapted to life in the jungles of Mesoamerica.

In A.D. 1839 an American lawyer named John Lloyd Stevens and an English artist named Frederick Catherwood slashed their way into the tangled Yucatán rain forest. There they made an amazing discovery. They found the vine-covered ruins of an ancient city.

Stevens and Catherwood soon learned that the people who had built the city were called the Maya, and that they were the ancestors of the millions of Maya who still live in present-day Mexico, Guatemala, Honduras, El Salvador, and Belize.

Mayan City-States At first glance, it looked like the Maya had settled in one of the worst spots on Earth. They picked the **Petén** (peh•TEHN), the Mayan word for "flat region." Located in present-day Guatemala, the Petén's dense forests nearly blocked out the sun. Stinging insects filled the air. Poisonous snakes slithered on the ground, and monkeys and parrots screeched in the treetops. Even so, the ancient Maya thrived.

The Maya saw what others missed. Swamps and sinkholes gave them a year-round source of water. The sinkholes—areas where the earth has collapsed—connected the Maya with a huge system of underground rivers and streams. They served as Mayan wells.

Even with a ready water supply, only an organized culture could have succeeded in building cities and fields in the Petén. The effort required cooperation among many people, which could only be accomplished by having an organized government.

▲ This Mayan wall painting shows musicians celebrating a royal birth.
Where did the Maya first settle?

The Way It Was

Sports & Contests

Mayan Ball Game Mayan cities had many ball courts. In a Mayan ball game, teams of two or three players tried to drive a hard rubber ball through a decorated stone ring. Players wore helmets, gloves, and knee and hip guards made of animal hide to protect themselves against the hard rubber balls. They were not allowed to use their hands or feet to throw or bat the ball. They had to use their hips to drive the ball through the stone rings.

Because the stone rings were placed 27 feet (8 m) above the ground on a large rectangular field, players had to have incredible skill to score a goal. Making a goal was so rare that when a player scored, crowds rewarded the hero with clothing and jewelry.

Scholars think that a Mayan ball game was more than a sport or contest. It had a religious and symbolic meaning— as well as deadly results. The losing team was sacrificed to the gods in a ceremony after the game.

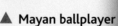

▲ Mayan ballplayer

Connecting to the Past

1. How did a player score in a Mayan ball game?
2. Why was losing especially painful for a team?

The Maya set up city-states. Within each city-state, rulers supplied the leadership— and military force—for great building projects. Leadership passed from one king to the next, and the city-states often fought with each other.

Life in the Mayan Cities The rulers of Mayan city-states said they were descended from the sun. They claimed the right to rule as god-kings and expected every person to serve them. Service included building huge monuments to honor them.

As god-kings, Mayan rulers taught their subjects how to please the gods. One way was human sacrifice. The Maya believed that the gods gave their life-giving fluid, rain, to keep humans strong. So humans kept the gods strong by giving their own life-giving fluid, blood.

When the Maya marched into battle, they wanted captives more than they wanted land. During times of drought, Mayan priests offered the captives to Chac, the god of rain and sunlight. The Maya believed Chac lived in the waters below the sinkholes. Captives were often thrown into these watery pits to earn the god's favor.

The Maya believed that the gods controlled everything that happened on Earth. As a result, religion was at the core of Mayan life. A huge pyramid with a temple at the top towered over every city. Priests, who claimed to know what the gods wanted, set up a strict class system in which everyone had a place.

Royal Mayan women often married into royal families in distant Mayan city-states. This practice strengthened trade. It also helped form alliances—political agreements between people or states to work together.

▲ Statue of a Mayan god

Women played a large role in the Mayan city-states. In one Mayan carving, a woman wears a war headdress and rides atop a platform carried by soldiers. In the city-state of Calakmul, at least two women served as all-powerful queens. One of them may have helped to found the city.

Mayan Science and Writing Both queens and kings turned to Mayan priests for advice. The priests thought gods revealed their plans through movements of the sun, moon, and stars, so they studied the heavens closely.

The Maya also needed to know when to plant their crops. By watching the sky, the priests learned about astronomy. They developed a 365-day calendar to keep track of heavenly movements. They used it to predict eclipses and to schedule religious festivals, plantings, and harvests. To chart the passage of time, the Maya developed a system of mathematics. They invented a method of counting based on 20.

The Maya also invented a written language to record numbers and dates. Like the Egyptians, the Maya used a system of hieroglyphics. Symbols represented sounds, words, or ideas. Only nobles could read them, however. After the collapse of the Mayan civilization, nobody could read them at all. Only in recent times have scholars begun to unlock the stories told by the hieroglyphics.

Reading Check **Identify** What was the main advantage of living in a tropical rain forest?

The Aztec

Main Idea The Aztec moved into the Valley of Mexico, where they created an empire based on conquest and war.

Reading Focus Why do you think some countries try to conquer other countries? Read to learn why the Aztec people conquered their neighbors and built an empire.

The warlike Aztec nomads who arrived in the Valley of Mexico about A.D. 1250 were anything but welcome. One king was sure he knew a way to get rid of them. He granted the Aztec a patch of snake-filled land. He expected the deadly serpents to destroy them. Instead, the Aztec feasted on roasted snakes and eventually built their own kingdom.

The Aztec Government The Aztec clearly knew how to survive. They had wandered for hundreds of years in search of a home that

An Aztec Warrior

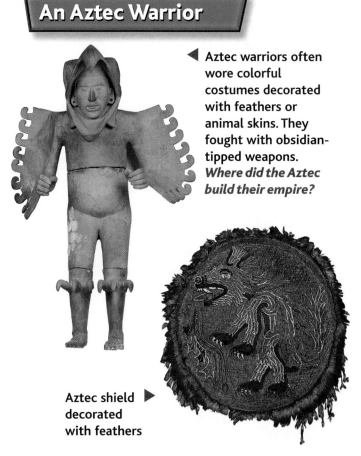

◀ Aztec warriors often wore colorful costumes decorated with feathers or animal skins. They fought with obsidian-tipped weapons. *Where did the Aztec build their empire?*

Aztec shield ▶ decorated with feathers

they believed their sun god—the feathered serpent Quetzalcoatl (KWEHT•suhl•kuh•WAH•tuhl)—had promised them. According to legend, the Aztec would know they had found this place when an eagle "screams and spreads its wings, and eats . . . the serpent."

According to Aztec legend, they found their homeland after they sacrificed a local princess to one of their gods. The princess's father vowed to wipe out the Aztec, who only numbered several hundred. The Aztec went on the run. In A.D. 1325, they took shelter on a soggy, swampy island in Lake Texcoco (tehs•KOH•koh). There an eagle greeted them from its perch on a prickly pear cactus. It tore apart a snake dangling from its beak. Then it spread its wings and screamed in triumph. Filled with wonder at this sight, the Aztec believed that they had reached the end of their journey.

Priests, speaking for the gods, told the Aztec what to do next: build a great city. Workers toiled day and night. They dug soil from the lake bottom to build bridges to the mainland. They built floating gardens, piling soil on rafts anchored to the lake bottom.

The Aztec called their new city **Tenochtitlán** (tay•NAWCH•teet•LAHN), which means "place of the prickly pear cactus." As the city rose from the marshes, the Aztec dreamed of conquest and wealth. They wanted to collect tribute, or payment for protection, from conquered peoples.

To fulfill their goal, the Aztec turned to strong kings who claimed descent from the gods. A council of warriors, priests, and nobles picked each king from the royal family. Council members usually chose the last king's son, but not always. They looked for a king who would bring glory to the Aztec. They expected a king to prove himself by leading troops into battle.

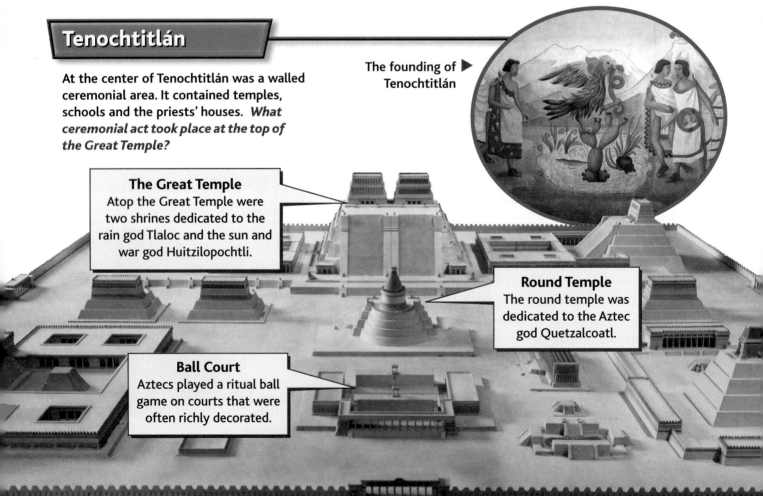

Tenochtitlán

At the center of Tenochtitlán was a walled ceremonial area. It contained temples, schools and the priests' houses. *What ceremonial act took place at the top of the Great Temple?*

The founding of ▶ Tenochtitlán

The Great Temple
Atop the Great Temple were two shrines dedicated to the rain god Tlaloc and the sun and war god Huitzilopochtli.

Round Temple
The round temple was dedicated to the Aztec god Quetzalcoatl.

Ball Court
Aztecs played a ritual ball game on courts that were often richly decorated.

Aztec Daily Life

Aztec homes were simple and built for usefulness rather than beauty. *How do you think the Aztec used each of the household items shown here?*

▲ Aztec bowl and loom

► Aztec grinding stone

▲ Painting of Aztec home

Life in the Aztec Empire

The king, or emperor, was at the top of Aztec society. The rest of the population fell into four classes: nobles, commoners, unskilled laborers, and enslaved people. Commoners formed the largest group, working as farmers, artisans, or traders. They could join the noble class by performing one act of bravery in war. They, or their children if the soldier died, received land and the rank of noble.

In serving their gods, the Aztec saw death as honorable. Those worthy of an afterlife included soldiers who died in battle, captives who gave their lives in sacrifice, and women who died in childbirth. Others went to the "Land of the Dead," the lowest level in the underworld.

From an early age, children learned about the glories of war and their duties as an Aztec. When a baby boy came into the world, the midwife, or woman who helped with the birth, cried: "You must understand that your home is not here where you have been born, for you are a warrior!"

A baby girl heard different words. As she drew her first breath, the midwife declared: "As the heart stays in the body, so you must stay in the house." Although women stayed at home, those who gave birth were honored as heroes by Aztec society.

Nearly everything the Aztec did grew out of a promise. Speaking through priests, the god Huitzilopochtli (wee•tsee•loh•POHKT•lee) vowed: "We shall conquer all the people in the universe."

This promise inspired the Aztec to honor the god with a huge pyramid in the center of Tenochtitlán. Known as the Great Temple, it rose 135 feet (41 m) high and had more than 100 steps. Thousands of victims were taken to the top, where they were sacrificed to the gods.

✓ Reading Check **Describe** How could commoners move into the noble class?

Life in the Inca Empire

Main Idea To unite their huge empire, Incan rulers set up a highly organized government and society.

Reading Focus Have you ever tried to organize a large number of people? It is not easy to get everyone to work together. Read how the Inca organized their society and developed ways to hold their empire together.

The ancient Inca blamed earthquakes on the god Pachacamac, "Lord of the earth." Whenever Pachacamac lost his temper, the earth shook. Pachacamac was the highest Incan god. It is not surprising that the greatest Incan leader took the name **Pachacuti** (PAH•chah•KOO•tee), which means "Earthshaker."

Pachacuti lived up to his name. Starting around A.D. 1438, Pachacuti and his son, Topa Inca, built the largest ancient empire in the Americas. It stretched north to south about 2,500 miles (4,023 km)—about the distance between present-day Los Angeles and New York.

▲ Incan gold mask

Pachacuti created a plan to hold his empire together. He set up a strong central government but let local rulers stay in power. To ensure their loyalty, he took their sons to Cuzco for training.

Pachacuti united the empire in other ways too. He required people to learn Quechua (KEH•chuh•wuh), the language spoken by the Inca. He also designed a system of roads, which covered about 25,000 miles (40,234 km) when finished.

An Organized Society

The Inca believed the sun god Inti protected Cuzco, the Incan capital. The rulers who lived there called themselves "sons of the sun." As such, rulers and their wives, known as Coyas, were at the top of society.

The head priest and commander of the armies were just below the royal couple. Next came regional army leaders. Below them were temple priests, army commanders, and skilled workers—musicians, artisans, and accountants. The bottom level consisted of farmers, herders, and ordinary soldiers.

The Inca further divided society into 12 job categories. Within these, every man, woman, and child over age five had work to do. Young girls, for example, were baby-sitters, while young boys chased birds from gardens.

What Was Incan Culture Like?

The Inca rarely honored their gods with human sacrifice. They turned to sacrifice only in times of trouble, such as during earthquakes, or on special occasions. Priests most often sacrificed children, whom they thought were more pure than adults. The Inca worshiped the sacrificed children as gods.

To please their gods, the Inca built large works of stone. They had no system of writing, no wheels, and no iron tools. Yet they built places like Machu Picchu (MAH•choo PEE•choo), a retreat for Incan kings.

Building large structures required the Inca to develop a way to do mathematical calculations. The Inca used a **quipu** (KEE•poo), a rope with knotted cords of different lengths and colors. Each knot represented a number or item, which was also a way of keeping records.

The Inca were skilled engineers. Workers fit stones so tightly together that a knife could not slip between them. Because the Inca used no mortar, the stone blocks could slide up and down without collapsing whenever an earthquake rocked the earth.

Reading Check **Explain** How did Pachacuti make sure local leaders would be loyal to him?

Biography

PACHACUTI
Ruled 1438–1471

Pachacuti was the son of the eighth Inca king, Viracocha. In 1438 an enemy from the north attacked the capital city, Cuzco. Viracocha fled, but Pachacuti stayed behind to defend the city and defeat the enemy. Because of his victory, Pachacuti became king.

At first, Pachacuti concentrated on expanding the Inca Empire. When he wanted to conquer a kingdom, he first sent messengers to tell the local rulers all the benefits of being part of the Inca Empire and then asked them to join willingly. If they accepted, they were treated with respect and given some rights. If they refused, the Incas attacked with brutal force.

Pachacuti next turned his attention to rebuilding Cuzco. He was the first to use white granite as a building material. No mortar was needed to hold the granite stones together because the sides of each piece were cut accurately and fit closely together.

Pachacuti built an estate for himself called Machu Picchu. It was made of white granite and was located thousands of feet high in the Andes. Recent research suggests that Machu Picchu was used not only as a home for the royal family, but also as a center for celebrations and ceremonial gatherings.

According to legend translated from a sacred text, Pachacuti became very sick when he was an elderly man. He called all of his relatives to his bedside. He divided his possessions among them and then made a speech with instructions for his burial.

▲ Pachacuti

> "I was born as a flower of the field . . ."
>
> –Pachacuti, as quoted in *History of the Incas*

▲ Machu Picchu

Then and Now

How can a nation today get another nation to do something without threatening war?

589

Life in North America

Main Idea The geography in lands north of present-day Mexico shaped the development of many different Native American cultures.

Reading Focus What would your life have in common with people living in a different place but with the same geography? Read to learn how the geography of North America shaped the life of Native Americans living here.

By A.D. 1500, about two million people lived north of Mesoamerica. They spoke around 300 languages and called themselves by thousands of different names.

These Native Americans had inherited the cultures of their ancestors. As early Americans spread out across North America, they adjusted to the varied environments where they settled. They not only survived—they lived well.

The People of the Far North Scientists think the early people who settled the Arctic regions of present-day Canada and Alaska arrived by boat, perhaps around 3000 B.C. This was long after the Ice Age had ended. These people called themselves the Inuit, which means "the people."

The Inuit, like other early Americans, found ways to live in their harsh environment. They built **igloos,** dome-shaped homes, from blocks of ice and snow. They used dogsleds to travel on land and seal-skin kayaks to travel by sea.

Most peoples of the Far North hunted. They ate seals, walruses, and land animals like caribou and polar bears. They especially prized strips of blubber, or fat, from seals and whales. The fat provided oil for lamps, and it also gave the Inuit valuable calories.

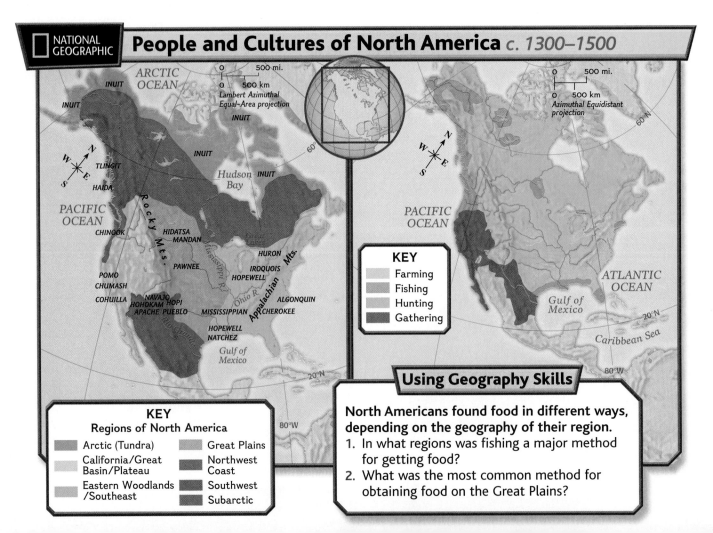

NATIONAL GEOGRAPHIC

People and Cultures of North America c. 1300–1500

KEY
- Farming
- Fishing
- Hunting
- Gathering

KEY
Regions of North America
- Arctic (Tundra)
- California/Great Basin/Plateau
- Eastern Woodlands /Southeast
- Great Plains
- Northwest Coast
- Southwest
- Subarctic

Using Geography Skills

North Americans found food in different ways, depending on the geography of their region.
1. In what regions was fishing a major method for getting food?
2. What was the most common method for obtaining food on the Great Plains?

The carved wooden totem (far right) ▶ was made by Native Americans from the Pacific Northwest. The kachina doll (right) was made by the Hopi people of the Southwest. *Why was the Pacific Northwest region heavily populated?*

Life on the West Coast

The groups that settled along North America's Pacific coast enjoyed a milder climate than the Inuit. In the Pacific Northwest, peoples such as the Tlingit (TLIHNG•kuht), Haida, and Chinook used towering cedar trees to build wooden houses and huge oceangoing canoes. They fished the seas for otters, seals, and whales. Each spring, saltwater salmon clogged the rivers as they swam upstream to lay eggs.

Because of rich food resources, the Pacific Northwest was one of the most heavily populated regions north of Mesoamerica. Only the area that is today California supported more people.

Scientists think California was home to about 500 early American cultures. Each culture specialized in using the natural resources found in California's many environments.

Along the northern coast, people like the Chumash fished. In the southern desert, the Cahuilla harvested dates from palm trees and gathered seeds, roots, and pods. In the central valley, the Pomo gathered acorns and pounded them into flour.

Life in the Southwest

People who settled in the dry deserts of the Southwest lacked the abundant resources of the California peoples. However, early Americans like the Hohokam and Anasazi had taught their descendants important lessons. The Hopi, Acoma, Pueblo, and Zuni knew how to farm the dry land. Like their ancestors, they dug irrigation canals. They built apartment-like homes, using a type of sun-dried mud brick called **adobe** (uh•DOH•bee).

In the A.D. 1500s, two groups of hunters—the Apache and the Navajo—moved into the area. The Apache remained hunters, but over time the Navajo started to farm like their neighbors.

Life on the Great Plains

People on the Great Plains farmed, but it was not easy. Seas of grass covered the lands stretching from the Rocky Mountains to the Mississippi River. The dense grass roots made farming difficult, especially without iron tools. Peoples like the Mandan, Hidatsa, and Pawnee grew gardens in the fertile land along the Missouri, Arkansas, and Red Rivers.

While the women tended gardens, the men hunted the huge herds of buffalo that grazed on the grasslands. They hunted on foot, because at that time there were no horses in America. The buffalo gave them meat for food, bones for tools, and skins for clothing and shelter.

Life in the Eastern Woodlands
Unlike the Plains, dense forests covered lands east of the Mississippi River. Here people combined farming with hunting and fishing. Farming was more widespread in the Southeast Woodlands, where a mild climate led to a long growing season. In the cooler Northeast Woodlands, people relied more on hunting.

All over the Woodlands, groups formed governments. Some, such as the Natchez in present-day Mississippi, set up strict social classes. Others, like the Cherokee in Georgia and North Carolina, had formal codes of law.

In a few cases, Native Americans in the Woodlands set up **confederations** (kuhn•FEH•duh•RAY•shuhnz), or governments that link several groups. The most famous was the league formed by the **Iroquois** (IHR•uh•KWOY). The Iroquois League included five groups: Onondaga, Seneca, Mohawk, Oneida, and Cayuga.

The Iroquois formed the league to end the fighting among themselves. A code of laws, known as the Great Peace, governed the league. Women, who controlled Iroquois land, selected male members to sit on a Grand Council. Together council members worked out their differences and made decisions in complete agreement. The Council helped members unite against other Woodland peoples, such as the powerful Algonquian (al•GAHN•kwee•uhn).

✓ Reading Check **Describe** How did geography shape the lives of the people north of present-day Mexcio?

History **O**nline

Homework Helper Need help with the material in this section? Visit jat.glencoe.com

Section ② Review

What Did You Learn?

Reading Summary

Review the Main Ideas

- In the rain forests of Central America, the Maya developed a civilization divided into city-states.
- A fierce warrior people, the Aztec created a strong empire in central Mexico.
- In the Andes, the Inca created the largest empire in the Americas.
- North America's varied geography led to the development of many diverse Native American groups.

1. How did the Incan leader Pachacuti maintain the great empire he built?

2. Who were the people of the Far North, and what sorts of food did they eat?

Critical Thinking

3. **Compare and Contrast** Draw a Venn diagram like the one shown. Add details to compare Aztec and Incan society.

Aztec Society   Incan Society

4. **Science Link** How and why did the Maya study astronomy?

5. **Summarize** How did the Aztec find and build their capital city?

6. **Drawing Conclusions** Why do you think the Inca required everyone in their society to do a specific job? Do you think this is a good idea for a society? Explain.

7. **Descriptive Writing** Imagine you are an early European explorer in North America. Write a journal entry describing your encounter with a Native American people in one of the regions described in the section.

Section 3

The Fall of the Aztec and Inca Empires

Get Ready to Read!

What's the Connection?

As the 1400s drew to a close, people in the Americas and Europe knew nothing of each other. This changed when Europeans began exploring the world and searching for trade routes to Asia.

Focusing on the Main Ideas

- Christopher Columbus found the Americas while trying to find a sea route to Asia. *(page 594)*
- Spanish conquerors defeated the Aztec with the help of horses, guns, and European disease. *(page 595)*
- The riches of the Aztec Empire led other Spanish conquerors to seek their fortunes in South America. *(page 599)*

Locating Places

Hispaniola (HIHS•puh•NYOH•luh)

Extremadura
(EHK•struh•muh•DUR•uh)

Meeting People

Christopher Columbus

Hernán Cortés
(ehr•NAHN kawr•TEHZ)

Montezuma II (MAHN•tuh•ZOO•muh)

Malintzin (mah•LIHNT•suhn)

Francisco Pizarro
(fran•SIHS•koh puh•ZAHR•oh)

Atahualpa (AH•tuh•WAHL•puh)

Building Your Vocabulary

conquistador
(kahn•KEES•tuh•DAWR)

treason (TREE•zuhn)

Reading Strategy

Cause and Effect Create a diagram to show the reasons Cortés was able to conquer the Aztec.

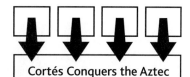

Cortés Conquers the Aztec

NATIONAL GEOGRAPHIC When & Where?

1450		1500		1550

1492 Christopher Columbus reaches the Americas

1521 Cortés defeats Aztec

1533 Francisco Pizarro conquers the Inca

Tenochtitlán
Cuzco

The Spanish Arrive in America

Main Idea Christopher Columbus found the Americas while trying to find a sea route to Asia.

Reading Focus What is the most vivid memory you have of a place you have visited? Read to learn what the Spanish found when they set out to explore the world.

In 1492 the Aztec appeared unbeatable. Around 250,000 people lived in Tenochtitlán, making it the largest city in the Americas—if not the world. In just a few short years, however, people from Europe would destroy their empire.

Columbus Arrives in America As you learned previously, by the 1400s several strong European kingdoms had developed in Western Europe. Those kingdoms knew that money could be made if they could find a way to trade with the countries of East Asia without having to deal with the Muslim kingdoms in between.

One by one, the people of Western Europe took to the sea to find a route to Asia. The first were the Portuguese, who began mapping Africa's eastern coast, hoping to find a way around Africa.

Next were the Spaniards, who decided to finance a trip by an Italian sea captain named **Christopher Columbus.** Columbus convinced Spain's rulers that he could reach Asia by sailing west across the Atlantic Ocean. He had no idea that two continents blocked his way.

Columbus set sail with three ships in August 1492. In October, he landed on an island in the Caribbean Sea. Columbus believed he had arrived in Asia. He traveled farther into the Caribbean and landed on the island of **Hispaniola** (HIHS•puh•NYOH•luh), which is today Haiti and the Dominican Republic. He then returned home carrying colorful parrots, some gold and spices, and several Native American captives. His success astonished and pleased Spain's rulers and convinced them to pay for another trip.

Columbus Returns Columbus set out again in 1493. This time, he came to conquer, bringing soldiers to help him. In the spring of 1494, the Spanish landed on Hispaniola.

▲ In the painting above, Christopher Columbus is depicted landing on the island of San Salvador. *Why did Columbus sail west across the Atlantic?*

The Taino who lived there got their first look at the **conquistadors** (kahn•KEES•tuh•DAWRZ), the soldier-explorers sent to the Americas by Spain. What they saw frightened them. Armor-clad men rode on armor-clad horses. Snarling dogs ran by their sides. In a show of power, the soldiers fired guns that spit out flames and lead balls.

Soldiers claimed the island for Spain. Then they enslaved the Taino and forced them to work for the Spanish. Spain now had a foothold in the Americas.

Reading Check **Identify** Who were the conquistadors?

Spain Conquers Mexico

Main Idea Spanish conquerors defeated the Aztec with the help of horses, guns, and European disease.

Reading Focus Think of decisions that you have already made today. Read to learn how the decisions made by two people–a Spanish conqueror and an Aztec king–changed the course of history.

The voyages of Christopher Columbus, who sailed to the Americas four times, inspired many poor nobles to go to America to seek their fortunes. Many came from the part of Spain known as the

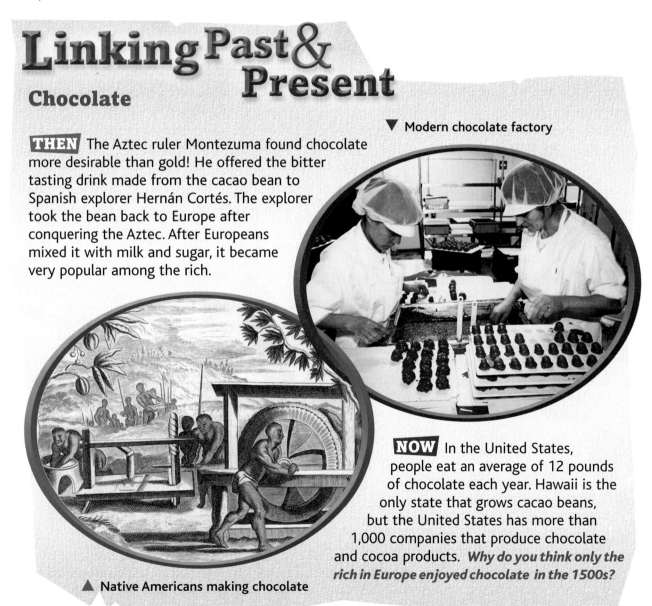

Linking Past & Present

Chocolate

THEN The Aztec ruler Montezuma found chocolate more desirable than gold! He offered the bitter tasting drink made from the cacao bean to Spanish explorer Hernán Cortés. The explorer took the bean back to Europe after conquering the Aztec. After Europeans mixed it with milk and sugar, it became very popular among the rich.

▼ **Modern chocolate factory**

NOW In the United States, people eat an average of 12 pounds of chocolate each year. Hawaii is the only state that grows cacao beans, but the United States has more than 1,000 companies that produce chocolate and cocoa products. *Why do you think only the rich in Europe enjoyed chocolate in the 1500s?*

▲ **Native Americans making chocolate**

Extremadura (EHK•struh•muh•DUR•uh). Its poor soil, blistering hot summers, and icy winters held little chance for wealth. One of these nobles was 19-year-old **Hernán Cortés** (ehr•NAHN kawr•TEHZ).

As a teenager, Cortés had a choice of three jobs: priest, lawyer, or soldier. His parents picked lawyer, but Cortés picked soldier. In 1504 he set out for Hispaniola. In 1511 he took part in the Spanish invasion of Cuba. His courage impressed the Spanish commander, who gave Cortés control over several Native American villages and the goods they produced.

Six years later, smallpox swept across Cuba, killing thousands of Native Americans. The Spanish commander asked Cortés to find new people who could be forced to work for the Spanish. Cortés knew just where to look.

That same year, a ship sent to explore the coast of the Yucatán returned to Cuba. Unlike earlier search parties, the soldiers did not fight with the Maya who lived there. Instead a group of Maya paddled out to greet them. As one soldier recalled:

> **66** They brought gold cast in bars . . . a beautiful gold mask, a figurine [statue] of a man with a half mask of gold, and a crown of gold beads. **99**
>
> —Juan Díaz, as quoted in "Conquest and Aftermath"

Cortés needed to hear no more. He made plans to sail. On February 18, 1519, Cortés set sail for Mexico.

Cortés Invades Mexico

When Cortés arrived, the Aztec emperor was **Montezuma II** (MAHN•tuh•ZOO•muh), also called Moctezuma. Montezuma expected the invaders. In a dream, he looked into a mirror and saw a huge army headed over the mountains. "What shall I do?" cried the emperor. "Where shall I hide?"

The dreaded invasion began in April 1519 when Cortés stepped onto a beach near present-day Veracruz. He came with 550 soldiers, 16 horses, 14 cannons, and a few dogs. How could such a small force conquer a huge warrior empire?

▲ Spanish armor

▲ Spanish sword

▲ Aztec war club

◀ The Aztec's simple weapons were no match for the guns and cannons of the Spanish. *Besides weapons and horses, what else did the Spanish bring that would help them defeat the Aztec?*

First, Cortés knew how to use Spanish horses and guns to shock Native Americans. In a display of power, he forced thousands of Tabascans (tuh•BAS•kuhnz), a people living in Mesoamerica, to surrender. Second, the Tabascans gave Cortés another weapon—a Mayan woman named **Malintzin** (mah•LIHNT•suhn). She spoke both Mayan and Nahuatl (NAH•WAH•tuhl), the language of the Aztec.

Speaking through a Spaniard who knew Mayan, Malintzin described the Aztec Empire to Cortés. She also told Cortés how subjects of the Aztec resented their rulers and would join with him to fight Montezuma. Acting as a translator, she helped Cortés form alliances.

Finally, Cortés had the help of invisible allies—germs that carried diseases, such as measles and smallpox. These diseases would eventually kill more Aztec than the Spanish swords.

Cortés Defeats the Aztec The Spaniards traveled 400 miles (644 km) to reach Tenochtitlán, the Aztec capital. Messengers reported their every move to Montezuma. The Aztec believed in a light-skinned god named Quetzalcoatl. This god, who opposed sacrifice, had sailed away long ago, promising to return someday to reclaim his land. Montezuma was afraid Cortés was the god returning home. As a result, he did not want to attack the Spaniards right away.

As Cortés marched closer, Montezuma decided to ambush the Spanish troops. Cortés learned of the plan and attacked first, killing 6,000 people. In November 1519, the Spaniards marched into Tenochtitlán and took control of the city. To prevent the Aztec from rebelling, Cortés took Montezuma hostage. He then ordered the Aztec to stop sacrificing people.

Primary Source

The Aztec Defeat

This excerpt describes the aftermath of Cortés's victory.

"Broken spears lie in the roads; we have torn our hair in our grief. The houses are roofless now, and their walls are red with blood. . . . We have pounded our hands in despair against the adobe walls, for our inheritance, our city, is lost and dead. The shields of our warriors were its defense, but they could not save it."

—author unknown, from *The Broken Spears*, edited by Miguel Leon-Portilla

▲ Battle scene between Aztec and Spanish soldiers

DBQ Document-Based Question

The Aztec felt that their lost city was their inheritance. What does that mean?

Cortés's orders angered the Aztec, who planned a rebellion. Fighting erupted, and the Spanish killed thousands of Aztec. Montezuma tried to stop the fighting, but he too was killed. Outnumbered, the Spanish fought their way out of the city and took refuge in the nearby hills with their allies.

While Cortés prepared a second attack, smallpox broke out in Tenochtitlán. Greatly weakened, the Aztec were no match for the Spanish and their allies. In June 1521, the Spanish destroyed the Aztec capital.

Reading Check **Explain** Why did the Aztec think they should welcome Cortés?

Biography

MONTEZUMA II
1480–1520
HERNÁN CORTÉS
1485–1547

Montezuma ▶

Although Montezuma II became known as the emperor who let the Spanish capture the Aztec Empire, most of his years as a ruler had been very successful. Montezuma Xocoyotl was the youngest son of Emperor Axacayatl. Aztec leadership was not hereditary, so after Axacayatl's death a man named Ahuitzotl was selected emperor. Montezuma was in his early twenties when he was chosen emperor. He became a popular leader. He led his armies in battle and won over 40 battles against kingdoms south of the Aztec Empire. His one major mistake was in his dealings with the Spanish conquistadors.

Leading the Spanish march into the Aztec Empire in 1519 was a 34-year-old Spaniard named Hernán Cortés. Cortés was born in the province of Extremadura, Spain. At age 19, Cortés left the university and boarded a ship for the Spanish lands in America. He was determined to make his fortune.

In 1511, Spanish troops led by Diego Velázquez conquered Cuba. Cortés took part in the invasion, and his courage impressed Velázquez. He rewarded Cortés by giving him control of several Native American villages. Six years later, smallpox swept across Cuba, killing thousands of Native Americans. Without Native American workers, the farms and mines the Spanish had built in Cuba could not function. Velázquez asked Cortés to lead an expedition to the Yucatán Peninsula to find new peoples who could be forced to work for the Spanish. He was also asked to investigate reports of a wealthy civilization there. On February 18, 1519, Cortés set sail for Mexico.

▲ Hernán Cortés

Several years later, after conquering the Aztec, Cortés took part in one more expedition to Honduras and then served as Governor General of New Spain. He returned to Spain a very wealthy man and died near the city of Seville in 1547.

Then and Now

Because of their encounter in war, the names of Montezuma and Cortés often appear together in history books. What two leaders today do you think will be paired in future history books? Why?

Pizarro Conquers the Inca

Main Idea The riches of the Aztec Empire led other Spanish conquerors to seek their fortunes in South America.

Reading Focus Have you ever done anything because you have seen other people do it and succeed? Read to learn how another conquistador followed the example of Cortés and conquered the Inca.

In 1513 Vasco Núñez de Balboa (VAHS•koh NOON•yays day bal•BOH•uh) led a band of soldiers across the jungle-covered mountains of present-day Panama. Native Americans said that if Balboa traveled south along a western sea, he would find a great empire filled with gold.

Balboa found the sea, known today as the Pacific Ocean. However, he never found the golden empire. A jealous Spanish official in Panama falsely charged him with **treason** (TREE•zuhn), or disloyalty to the government, and ordered him beheaded.

Francisco Pizarro (fran•SIHS•koh puh•ZAHR•oh), who marched with Balboa, took up the search. Pizarro could not write his name, but he knew how to fight. Like Balboa and Cortés, Pizarro came from the harsh Extremadura. Unlike his neighbors, however, he was not of noble birth.

At age 16, Pizarro fled a job herding pigs to fight in Italy. In 1502 he arrived in the Americas. Helping explore Panama, he became a wealthy landowner. But Pizarro longed to find the golden empire.

Pizarro and the Inca By the 1530s, the Inca thought they ruled most of the world. Two threats from the north soon proved they did not. The Inca could do nothing to stop the southward spread of smallpox. They also failed to scare away Pizarro, who led 160 adventurers up the mountains to the Incan homeland.

The Inca tried to ignore him, but Pizarro, now in his 50s, would not leave. He raided Incan storehouses and fired guns at villagers. The Incan emperor, **Atahualpa** (AH•tuh•WAHL•puh), thought Pizarro was crazy or a fool. How could this man stand up to an army of 80,000 Incan warriors?

Atahualpa misjudged Pizarro. The Spaniard had an advantage. The Inca knew little about the Europeans, but Pizarro knew a lot about Native Americans. He had spent more than 30 years fighting Native

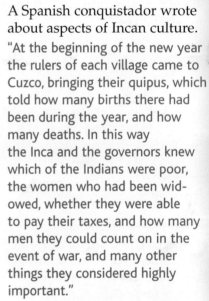

Primary Source — Incan Record Keeping

A Spanish conquistador wrote about aspects of Incan culture.

"At the beginning of the new year the rulers of each village came to Cuzco, bringing their quipus, which told how many births there had been during the year, and how many deaths. In this way the Inca and the governors knew which of the Indians were poor, the women who had been widowed, whether they were able to pay their taxes, and how many men they could count on in the event of war, and many other things they considered highly important."

—Pedro de Cieza de Léon, *The Second Part of the Chronicle of Peru*

▲ Quipu

DBQ Document-Based Question

Quipus were used to calculate records and building plans. How else do you think the Inca might have used quipus?

Americans. Also, his good friend Hernán Cortés gave Pizarro an inside look at the conquest of the Aztec. In late 1532, Pizarro decided on a plan so bold that even Cortés might not have risked it.

Pizarro Defeats the Inca Spanish messengers invited Atahualpa to a meeting. Atahualpa agreed but made the mistake of leaving most of his huge army behind. He believed that his 5,000 bodyguards were enough protection. He also decided, based on Pizarro's small force, that the Inca needed no weapons.

When they met, Pizarro wasted no time in asking the emperor to give up his gods. When Atahualpa laughed at his request, Pizarro ordered an attack. Cannons roared, trumpets blared, and sword-swinging soldiers shrieked battle cries. Pizarro then seized Atahualpa and dragged him off the battlefield.

Atahualpa tried to buy his freedom. He offered to fill his jail cell with gold and a nearby room with silver. Pizarro jumped at the deal. Atahualpa kept his part of the bargain. Pizarro did not. He charged the emperor with many crimes: plotting a rebellion, worshiping false gods, having too many wives, and more. In 1533 a military court found the emperor guilty and sentenced him to death.

To reward Pizarro, the Spanish king made him governor of Peru. Pizarro then chose a new emperor for the Inca, but the emperor had to follow Pizarro's orders. Pizarro's conquest of Peru opened most of South America to Spanish rule. Spain controlled a vast territory covering 375,000 square miles (975,000 sq km) with almost 7 million inhabitants. It was on its way to building the world's first global empire.

✓ **Reading Check** **Explain** How did Pizarro fail to keep his promise to Atahualpa?

History Online

Homework Helper Need help with the material in this section? Visit jat.glencoe.com

Section 3 Review

Reading Summary

Review the Main Ideas

- Searching for a sea route to Asia, Christopher Columbus arrived in the Americas and claimed lands there for Spain.

- With a small army, Spanish conquistador Hernán Cortés conquered Montezuma and the Aztec capital of Tenochtitlán.

- In Peru, a small Spanish force led by Francisco Pizarro captured the Inca Empire.

What Did You Learn?

1. How did Christopher Columbus convince Spanish rulers to pay for a second trip?

2. Why did Cortés sail from Cuba to Mexico in search of the Aztec?

Critical Thinking

3. **Sequencing Information** Draw a time line like the one shown. Fill in events related to Cortés's capture of Tenochtitlán.

1517: Spanish ship brings back gold from Yucatán

4. **Predict** How might the history of the Aztec people be different without the legend of the Aztec god Quetzalcoatl?

5. **Analyze** Why were the Aztec and the Inca so easily defeated by smaller Spanish forces?

6. **Expository Writing** Imagine you are an Aztec or an Inca seeing a Spanish conquistador for the first time. Write a newspaper article describing what you have observed.

Section ① The First Americans

Vocabulary
glacier
monopoly

Focusing on the Main Ideas
- It is believed that the first people in the Americas came from Asia during the Ice Age. *(page 573)*
- The invention of farming led to the rise of civilizations in the Americas. *(page 574)*
- Early people in the northern part of the Americas built complex cultures based on farming and trade. *(page 578)*

Section ② Life in the Americas

Vocabulary
quipu
igloo
adobe
confederation

Focusing on the Main Ideas
- The Maya adjusted to life in the tropical rain forest and built a culture based on their religious beliefs. *(page 583)*
- The Aztec moved into the Valley of Mexico, where they created an empire based on conquest and war. *(page 585)*
- To unite their huge empire, Incan rulers set up a highly organized government and society. *(page 588)*
- The geography in lands north of present-day Mexico shaped the development of many different Native American cultures. *(page 590)*

▲ Mayan ballplayer

Section ③ The Fall of the Aztec and Inca Empires

Vocabulary
conquistador
treason

Focusing on the Main Ideas
- Christopher Columbus found the Americas while trying to find a sea route to Asia. *(page 594)*
- Spanish conquerors defeated the Aztec with the help of horses, guns, and European disease. *(page 595)*
- The riches of the Aztec Empire led other Spanish conquerors to seek their fortunes in South America. *(page 599)*

Review Vocabulary

Match the word in the first column with its definition in the second column.

___ 1. conquistador   a. disloyalty to the government

___ 2. glacier   b. Spanish soldier-explorer

___ 3. adobe   c. sun-dried mud bricks

___ 4. confederation   d. huge sheet of ice

___ 5. treason   e. form of government that links several different groups

Review Main Ideas

Section 1 • The First Americans

6. When did the first people arrive in the Americas? On which continent did they live originally?

7. How did farming lead to the rise and development of civilizations in present-day Mexico, Central America, and Peru?

Section 2 • Life in the Americas

8. Explain the differences between the Maya and Aztec civilizations.

9. How did geography shape the development of the Native American cultures north of present-day Mexico?

Section 3 • The Fall of the Aztec and Inca Empires

10. What was the goal of Christopher Columbus's voyage in 1492?

11. What three factors made it possible for the Spanish to conquer the Aztec and the Inca?

Critical Thinking

12. **Analyze** How do the houses of North American peoples reflect the geography of their regions?

13. **Infer** Why do you think the Mayan civilization came to an end?

14. **Predict** What do you think would have happened if the Inca had taken Pizarro's raids more seriously?

Review Reading Skill — Summarizing

Summarizing Information

Read the paragraph below, then choose the statement that best summarizes its content.

The region's geography was ideal for farming. Much of the area had a rich, volcanic soil and a mild climate. Rains fell in the spring, helping seeds to sprout. They decreased in the summer, allowing crops to ripen for harvest.

15. a. The Ice Age ended as the climate warmed.

b. Rain fell in the spring.

c. Climate and soil made the region ideal for farming.

d. Seeds that are planted grow into crops.

To review this skill, see pages 570–571.

Geography Skills

Study the map below and answer the following questions.

16. **Human/Environment Interaction** Why do you think the Inca built stone walls in parts of Cuzco?

17. **Location** What natural defenses existed around Cuzco?

18. **Movement** What do the roads leading out of Cuzco reveal about the contact between the capital city and the rest of the empire?

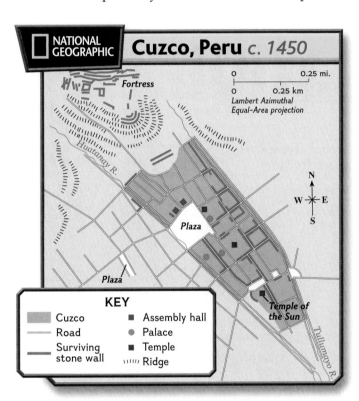

NATIONAL GEOGRAPHIC

Cuzco, Peru c. 1450

Fortress

0   0.25 mi.

0   0.25 km
Lambert Azimuthal
Equal-Area projection

Huatanay R.

Plaza

Plaza

Temple of the Sun

Tullumayo R.

KEY

- ▬ Cuzco
- ─ Road
- ▬ Surviving stone wall
- ■ Assembly hall
- ● Palace
- ■ Temple
- \\\\\ Ridge

Read to Write

19. **Persuasive Writing** Suppose you are a Native American during the Spanish conquests. Write a letter to the conquistadors to persuade them to trade with your culture rather than conquer it. Your letter should state the ways Europeans and Native Americans can learn from each other.

20. **Using Your FOLDABLES** Create an outline map of the Americas on poster board. It should be big enough for the entire class to work together. Label each country and the location of each civilization from your chapter. Then use your foldables to write facts about each civilization on the map.

Using Technology

21. **Preparing a Report** Use the Internet and your library to gather information about the Mound Builders. Note their reasons for mound building and the shapes of mounds. Then prepare an illustrated report on the computer to compare the mounds to other structures of early civilizations.

Linking Past and Present

22. **Evaluating Information** What impact have Native American ways of the past had on present-day life in the Americas?

23. **Building Citizenship Skills** The Iroquois League was an important confederation of the early Americas. Do confederations exist today? Do they serve the same purpose as the Iroquois League?

Primary Source Analyze

Some Europeans, including this Dominican friar, worked to protect the Native Americans by writing about their cultures.

"They [Native American leaders] issued public edicts and personal commands to all nobles and provincial governors, of whom there were many, that all poor, widows and orphans in each province should be provided for from their own royal rents and riches."

—Bartolomé de las Casas, "Apologetic History of the Indies"

DBQ Document-Based Questions

24. What does this tell you about Native American leaders' attitude toward those in need?

25. Do you think the nobles and provincial governors supported this edict? Why or why not?

The Renaissance and Reformation

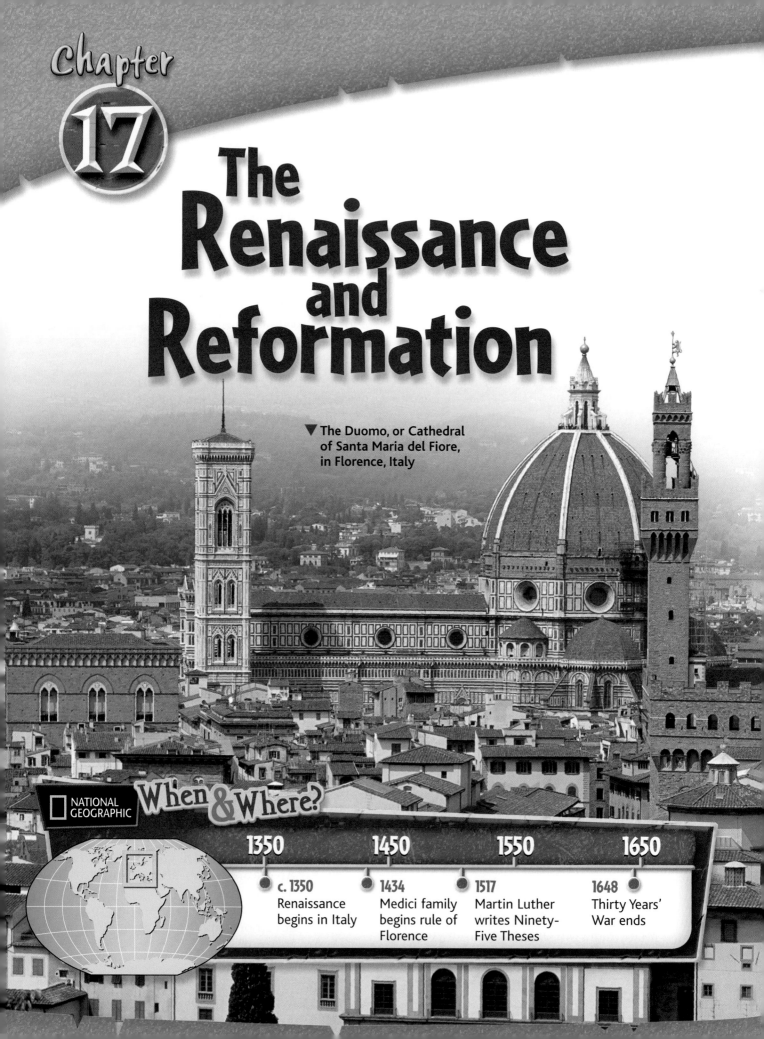

▼ The Duomo, or Cathedral of Santa Maria del Fiore, in Florence, Italy

NATIONAL GEOGRAPHIC When & Where?

1350	1450	1550	1650
c. 1350 Renaissance begins in Italy	1434 Medici family begins rule of Florence	1517 Martin Luther writes Ninety-Five Theses	1648 Thirty Years' War ends

Chapter Preview

New ideas brought the Middle Ages to an end. Read this chapter to find out how advances in the arts and learning and dramatic changes to Christianity led to the beginning of modern times in Europe.

History Online

Chapter Overview Visit jat.glencoe.com for a preview of Chapter 17.

View the Chapter 17 video in the *World History: Journey Across Time* Video Program.

The Renaissance Begins

During the Renaissance, new values and new art developed in wealthy Italian city-states.

New Ideas and Art

Wealthy leaders in Italian city-states supported talented artists and writers, and Renaissance art and ideas spread from Italy to northern Europe.

The Reformation Begins

Martin Luther and other reformers, such as John Calvin, broke from the Catholic Church and began a new Christian movement that came to be called Protestantism.

Catholics and Protestants

While the Catholic Church attempted to carry out reforms, Catholics and Protestants fought bloody religious wars across Europe.

FOLDABLES™
Study Organizer

Compare-Contrast *Make this foldable to help you compare and contrast what you learn about the Renaissance and Reformation.*

Step 1 *Fold a sheet of paper in half from side to side.*

Step 2 *Turn the paper and fold it into thirds.*

Step 3 *Unfold and cut the top layer only along both folds.*

This will make three tabs.

Fold it so the left edge lies about $\frac{1}{2}$ inch from the right edge.

Step 4 *Label as shown.*

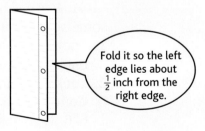

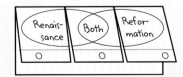

Reading and Writing
As you read the sections on the Renaissance and Reformation, record important concepts and events under the appropriate tabs. Then record ideas similar to both under the middle tab.

Reading
Skill

Analyze and
Clarify

1 Learn It!

Go Beyond the Words

Analyzing a passage means going beyond the definition of the words. It is a way of reading for deep understanding, not just memorizing or studying to pass a test. Read the following paragraph from Section 2.

> Renaissance painters also used new techniques. The most important was perspective, a method that makes a drawing or painting look three-dimensional. Artists had tried to use perspective before, but Renaissance artists perfected it. Using perspective, objects in a scene appear to be at different distances from the viewer. The result is a more realistic image.
>
> —*from page 623*

Reading Tip

When reading, break the text into smaller parts to help you understand the whole.

How can you analyze this passage? Here are some suggestions:

1. Look at the drawing on page 626. Is the drawing realistic as described by the paragraph?
2. Look at another painting or drawing in this book. Compare the perspective to the drawing on page 626. Which is more realistic? Why?
3. With a partner, sketch a view of your classroom. Exchange sketches and see if you can tell where your partner was standing when he or she made the sketch. Based on your experience, what are some difficulties an artist might encounter in trying to draw a large area realistically?

2 Practice It!

Analyze as You Read

Read this paragraph from Section 2.

Read to Write

Choose any painting or drawing in this book and analyze, in writing, what is taking place. Use the questions *who*, *what*, *when*, or *how* to help you get started.

> To make their paintings more realistic, Renaissance artists also used a technique called chiaroscuro. Chiaroscuro softened edges by using light and shadows instead of stiff outlines to separate objects. In Italian, *chiaro* means "clear or light," and *oscuro* means "dark." Chiaroscuro created more drama and emotion in a painting.
>
> —*from page 623*

▲ The *Mona Lisa*

Analyze the above paragraph by doing the following:

1. Look at the painting of Mona Lisa from page 622. Do you see the use of chiaroscuro? If so, in what way does it create drama or emotion?

2. Choose another painting in this or a different text. Look at it carefully to see if the technique of chiaroscuro was used. Describe to a partner the light and dark areas that you see.

3. Try your hand at drawing an object or scene using the technique of chiaroscuro.

3 Apply It!

As you read this chapter, choose at least one section to study and analyze for deeper meaning. Exchange your analysis with a classmate who has analyzed a different passage.

Section 1

The Renaissance Begins

Get Ready to Read!

What's the Connection?

Previously, you learned about life in medieval Europe. In this section, you will see how Europeans began to look to the ideals of the ancient Greeks and Romans as they left the Middle Ages behind.

Focusing on the Main Ideas

- The wealthy urban society of the Italian city-states brought a rebirth of learning and art to Europe. *(page 609)*

- Italy's location helped its city-states grow wealthy from trade and banking, but many of the cities fell under the control of strong rulers. *(page 611)*

- Unlike medieval nobles, the nobles of the Italian city-states lived in cities and were active in trade, banking, and public life. *(page 614)*

Locating Places

Florence (FLAWR•uhns)

Venice (VEH•nuhs)

Meeting People

Marco Polo (MAHR•koh   POH•loh)

Medici (MEH•duh•chee)

Niccolò Machiavelli (NEEK•koh•LOH MA•kee•uh•VEH•lee)

Building Your Vocabulary

Renaissance (REH•nuh•SAHNS)

secular (SEH•kyuh•luhr)

diplomacy (duh•PLOH•muh•see)

Reading Strategy

Summarizing Information Complete a chart like the one below showing the reasons Italian city-states grew wealthy.

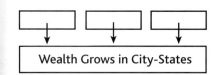

Wealth Grows in City-States

NATIONAL GEOGRAPHIC When & Where?

1350

c. 1350
Renaissance begins in Italy

1450

1434
Medici family begins rule of Florence

1550

1513
Machiavelli writes *The Prince*

The Italian Renaissance

Main Idea The wealthy urban society of the Italian city-states brought a rebirth of learning and art to Europe.

Reading Focus Hollywood makes many of the world's movies. Why is it the center of the movie industry? Read to learn why the city-states of Italy became the center of art during the Renaissance.

Renaissance (REH•nuh•SAHNS) means "rebirth." The years from about 1350 to 1550 in European history are called the Renaissance because there was a rebirth of interest in art and learning.

In some ways the Renaissance was a rebirth of interest in the same subjects the Greeks and Romans had studied. After the horrible years of the Black Death, Europeans began looking to the past when times seemed better. They wanted to learn how to make their own society better.

During the Renaissance, Europeans also began to stress the importance of the individual. They began to believe that people could make a difference and change the world for the better.

People were still very religious during the Renaissance, but they also began to celebrate human achievements. People became more **secular** (SEH•kyuh•luhr). This means they were more interested in this world than in religion and getting to heaven.

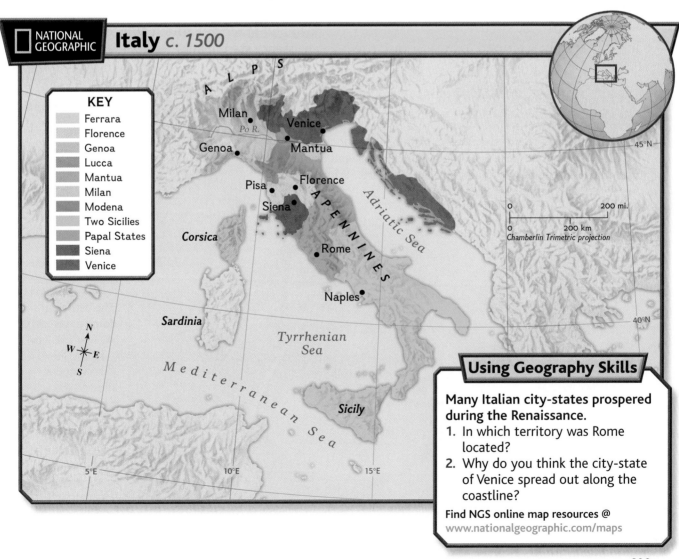

NATIONAL GEOGRAPHIC

Italy c. 1500

KEY
- Ferrara
- Florence
- Genoa
- Lucca
- Mantua
- Milan
- Modena
- Two Sicilies
- Papal States
- Siena
- Venice

0   200 mi.
0   200 km
Chamberlin Trimetric projection

45°N
40°N
5°E   10°E   15°E

ALPS
Po R.
Milan
Venice
Mantua
Genoa
Pisa
Florence
Siena
Corsica
APENNINES
Adriatic Sea
Rome
Naples
Sardinia
Tyrrhenian Sea
Mediterranean Sea
Sicily

N W E S

Using Geography Skills

Many Italian city-states prospered during the Renaissance.
1. In which territory was Rome located?
2. Why do you think the city-state of Venice spread out along the coastline?

Find NGS online map resources @
www.nationalgeographic.com/maps

Why did the Renaissance begin in Italy? First of all, Italy had been the center of the Roman Empire. Ruins and art surrounded the Italians and reminded them of their past. It was only natural that they became interested in Greek and Roman art and tried to make their own art as good.

Another reason the Renaissance began in Italy was because by the 1300s, Italy's cities had become very wealthy. They could afford to pay painters, sculptors, architects, and other artists to produce new works.

A third reason was because the region was still divided into many small city-states. **Florence** (FLAWR•uhns), **Venice** (VEH•nuhs), Genoa, Milan, and Rome were some of the most important cities of the Renaissance.

The Italian city-states competed with each other. This helped bring about the Renaissance. Wealthy nobles and merchants wanted artists to produce works that increased the fame of their cities.

In most of Europe, the vast majority of people lived in the country, including the knights and nobles who owned estates. In Italy's city-states, the population was becoming more urban. That means more people were living in the city, rather than in the country. So many people living together in a city meant more customers for artists and more money for art.

The large number of people living in cities also led to more discussion and sharing of ideas about art. Just as the city-states of ancient Greece had produced many great works of art and literature, so too did urban society in Italy.

✓ **Reading Check** **Explain** Why did the Renaissance start in Italy?

Florence Cathedral

Florence, Italy, was one of the centers of the Renaissance. The Florence Cathedral became a symbol of the city, as well as one of the finest examples of Renaissance architecture. *What were other important Italian Renaissance cities?*

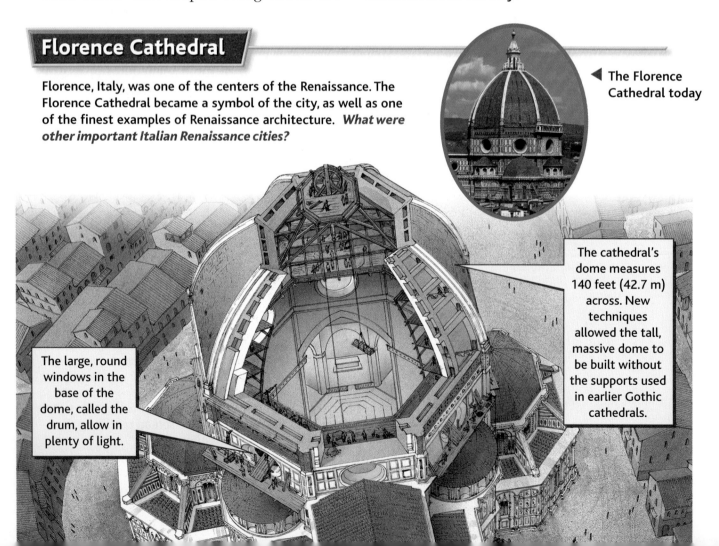

◀ The Florence Cathedral today

The large, round windows in the base of the dome, called the drum, allow in plenty of light.

The cathedral's dome measures 140 feet (42.7 m) across. New techniques allowed the tall, massive dome to be built without the supports used in earlier Gothic cathedrals.

The Rise of Italy's City-States

Main Idea Italy's location helped its city-states grow wealthy from trade and banking, but many of the cities fell under the control of strong rulers.

Reading Focus Do you have a bank account? What are banks for? Read to learn how banking helped to make the Italian city-states wealthy and powerful.

During the Middle Ages, no ruler was able to unite Italy into a single kingdom. There were several reasons for this. First of all, the Roman Catholic Church did everything it could to stop the rise of a powerful kingdom in Italy. Church leaders were afraid that if a strong ruler united Italy, that same ruler would be able to control the pope and the Church.

At the same time, the city-states that developed in Italy were about equal in strength. They fought many wars and often captured territory from each other, but no state was able to defeat all the others.

Probably the most important reason the city-states stayed independent was because they became very wealthy. With their great wealth, they could build large fleets and hire people to fight in their armies. A person who fights in an army for money is called a mercenary. The city-states also loaned money to the kings of Europe. The kings left the city-states alone so they could borrow more money in the future.

Italy's City-States Grow Wealthy

The Italian city-states became wealthy through trade. The geography of the long Italian peninsula meant that most of the city-states had a coastline and ports where merchant ships could dock. They were also perfectly located on the Mediterranean Sea. Spain and France lay to the west, and the Byzantine and Ottoman Empires lay to the east. North Africa was only a short trip to the south.

From the Byzantines, Turks, and Arabs, the Italians bought Chinese silk and Indian spices and sold them to people in Western Europe for very high prices. At the same time, from the Spanish, French, Dutch, and English, they bought goods such as wool, wine, and glass that they could sell in the Middle East. The Italian cities also had many skilled artisans, who could take raw materials the merchants bought and make goods that could be sold for high prices.

Geography was not the only reason for the success of the Italians. Several events led to trade becoming even more important in the city-states. First, the Crusades brought Italian merchants into contact with Arab merchants. Second, the rise of the Mongol Empire united almost all of Asia into one vast trade network.

The Mongols encouraged trade and protected the Silk Road from China to the Middle East. This made it cheaper and easier for caravans to carry goods from China and

▲ This painting shows a wealthy Italian family during the Renaissance. *How did competition between the city-states lead to great works of art?*

India to Muslim and Byzantine cities. As more and more silk and spices were shipped from Asia, the price of these goods fell. More Europeans could afford the luxuries, and demand for the items greatly increased. In turn, business for Italian merchants continued to grow.

Who Was Marco Polo?

Europeans were fascinated with Asia and its goods after reading a book written by **Marco Polo** (MAHR•koh POH•loh), a merchant from the city of Venice. In the 1270s, Marco Polo went on an amazing journey with his father and uncle to China. They set off to meet Kublai Khan, the ruler of the Mongol Empire.

When the Polo family finally made it to the khan's court, the great emperor was impressed with Marco Polo. He sent Marco Polo on business all over China. Marco Polo asked many questions and learned more about Asia than any other European. When he returned to Europe, he published a book about his travels. His stories helped increase interest in China and made many people want to buy China's goods.

The Wealth of Florence

No city was more famous in the Renaissance than Florence. It was the first to grow wealthy, and it produced many famous artists. It sat on the banks of the Arno River surrounded by beautiful hills. It was walled and had many tall towers for defense. Its people were known for their love of elegant clothing.

At first, Florence's wealth came from trading cloth, especially wool. The city's merchants sailed to England to get sheep's wool. Artisans in Florence then wove it into fine fabrics. Florentines also found another way to make money—banking.

With goods pouring into Italy from around the world, merchants needed to know the value of coins from different countries. Florentine bankers became the experts. They used the florin, the gold coin of Florence, to measure the value of other money. Bankers also began lending money and charging interest. Florence's richest

▼ Lorenzo de' Medici

▲ This painting shows bankers in Florence doing business at a counter topped with brightly embroidered cloth. *Why did banking become so important in Florence?*

▲ This painting from Renaissance Italy shows the busy pier and the Ducal Palace in Venice. *What industry provided some of Venice's wealth?*

family, the **Medici** (MEH•duh•chee), were bankers. They had branch banks as far away as London.

The Rise of Venice
The wealthiest city-state of all was Venice, where Marco Polo was born. Venice is at the northern end of the Adriatic Sea. The Venetians were great sailors and shipbuilders. They built their city on many small, swampy islands just off the coast. Early Venetians learned how to drive long wooden poles into mud to support their buildings.

Instead of paving roads, the Venetians cut canals through their swampy islands and used boats to move about. Even today, many of the streets in the older parts of Venice are canals and waterways. Gondolas—a type of long, narrow boat—still carry people along these canals.

Some of Venice's wealth came from building ships. Artisans worked on ships at a shipyard known as the Arsenal. Teams of workers cut the wood, shaped it into hulls, caulked (or sealed) the wood, and made sails and oars. Sometimes Venetians needed ships quickly. When the Turks tried to take a Venetian colony in the Mediterranean, the Arsenal built 100 ships in only two months to prepare for battle.

✓ **Reading Check** **Describe** How did Florence and the Medici family become so wealthy?

The Urban Noble

Main Idea Unlike medieval nobles, the nobles of the Italian city-states lived in cities and were active in trade, banking, and public life.

Reading Focus How does our society measure wealth? Before the Renaissance, wealth was based on the amount of land a person owned. Read to learn how that changed during the Renaissance.

The wealthy men of the Italian city-states were a new type of leader—the urban noble. Before this time, European nobles got their wealth from land, not trade. In fact, they looked down on trade and believed themselves above the town merchants.

In the Italian city-states, old noble families moved to the cities. They mixed with wealthy merchants and decided that money from trade was just as good as money from land.

Meanwhile, wealthy merchants copied the manners and lifestyle of noble families. Soon, the sons and daughters of nobles and rich merchants were marrying each other. Eventually, the old nobles and wealthy merchant families blended together to become the upper class of the city-states.

How Were Italian City-States Run?
At first, many of the city-states were republics. A republic is a government controlled by its citizens. Not everyone was a citizen, however, only the artisans and merchants who had membership in the city's guilds.

From your study of the ancient Romans, you might recall that when their cities faced war or rebellion, they gave power to a dictator. The Italian city-states did something similar. In many cases, the cities were ruled by one powerful man who ran the government.

In Venice, the head of state was the duke, or doge. At first, the doge had great power over his council of nobles. Later, he lost power to a small group of nobles.

In Florence, the powerful Medici family gained control of the government in 1434. The Medici ran Florence for many decades. Lorenzo de' Medici ruled the city from 1469 to 1492. Known as "the Magnificent," Lorenzo used his wealth to support artists, architects, and writers. Many of Italy's Renaissance artists owed their success to his support.

Politics in Italy was complicated. Within each city, the rulers had to keep the poor from

Primary Source

The Prince

In Machiavelli's masterpiece, he explains his theories about human nature.

"You should consider then, that there are two ways of fighting, one with laws and the other with force. The first is properly a human method, the second belongs to beasts. But as the first method does not always suffice [meet your needs], you sometimes have to turn to the second. Thus a prince must know how to make good use of both the beast and the man."

—Niccolò Machiavelli,
The Prince

▲ Niccolò Machiavelli

DBQ Document-Based Question

Why must a good leader know more than one way to fight?

rebelling and prevent other wealthy people from seizing power. They had to make deals with merchants, bankers, landlords, church leaders, and mercenaries. At the same time, they had to deal with the leaders of the other city-states.

To deal with the other states around them, the Italians developed **diplomacy** (duh•PLOH•muh•see). Diplomacy is the art of negotiating, or making deals, with other countries. Each city-state sent ambassadors to live in the other city-states and act as representatives for their city. Many of the ideas of modern diplomacy first began in Italy's city-states.

How could a ruler maintain power in the Italian city-states? **Niccolò Machiavelli** (NEEK•koh•LOH MA•kee•uh•VEH•lee), a diplomat in Florence, tried to answer this question when he wrote *The Prince* in 1513. Machiavelli claimed that people were

▲ This palace served as a government building in Rome for hundreds of years. *What form of government did many of the city-states have at first?*

greedy and self-centered. Rulers should not try to be good, he argued. Rather, they should do whatever is necessary to keep power and protect their city, including killing and lying. Today when we say someone is being Machiavellian, we mean they are being tricky and not thinking about being good.

 **Reading Check** **Compare** How were medieval and Renaissance nobles different?

Section 1 Review

History Online

Homework Helper Need help with the material in this section? Visit jat.glencoe.com

Reading Summary

Review the Main Ideas

• A rebirth of learning called the Renaissance began in wealthy Italian city-states in the 1300s.

• Italian city-states, including Florence and Venice, grew wealthy through trade, manufacturing, and banking.

• In the Italian city-states, a noble's wealth was based on trade, rather than the amount of land owned.

What Did You Learn?

1. Why is the era from 1350 to 1550 in Europe called the Renaissance?

2. Why did the Renaissance begin in Italy?

Critical Thinking

3. **Organizing Information** Draw a diagram like the one below. Add details about the characteristics of the Italian Renaissance.

4. **Economics Link** How did Renaissance cities gain their wealth? Give several examples.

5. **Summarize** Describe the governments of Italian city-states during the Renaissance.

6. **Analyze** Who were the Medicis and why were they important?

7. **Persuasive Writing** Write a letter to the editor of a Renaissance newspaper telling whether you agree or disagree with Machiavelli's beliefs about rulers and power during the Renaissance.

You Decide . . .

The Value of City-States

During the Renaissance, Italy was divided into more than 20 city-states. Some people think that the city-state form of government was a good idea. The leaders and wealthy nobles of the city-states encouraged the arts and sciences. This produced masterpieces by Michelangelo, Raphael, Leonardo, and others. Would this rebirth of arts and sciences have happened if Italy's independent city-states had not existed?

Other people, such as Girolamo Savonarola, were against the city-state form of government. After the fall of the Medici family in Florence, Savonarola spoke out in favor of a new type of leadership:

"I tell you that you must select a good form for your new government, and above all no one must think of making himself head if you wish to live in liberty."

—Girolamo Savonarola,
"This Will Be Your Final Destruction"

Examine the advantages and disadvantages of the city-state form of government. Then decide whether you think this system is primarily beneficial or primarily harmful.

Advantages:
- Because of their independent governments, each territory on the Italian peninsula was able to have its own culture.
- Some city-states were led by wealthy families, but most were led by a single leader. Almost all supported cultural and scientific advancement. The competition among city-states also encouraged the development of art and science.
- City-state rulers helped preserve the values and teachings of the ancient Greeks and Romans. They gave their own artists, architects, scholars, and writers opportunities to study classical works and interpret them in their own ways.

▲ A detail from the ceiling of the Sistine Chapel painted by Michelangelo

▲ Renaissance nobles

Disadvantages:

- Many city-states were led by one man. The common people were often mistreated until they revolted and threw out their leaders. This happened to Florence's Medici family in 1527.

- The divided city-states were weaker than a united Italy would have been, so they were often invaded by foreign groups.

- Smaller territories did not always have enough soldiers to defend their cities and land. They hired mercenaries—generals and armies from outside their city—to help them fight. Sometimes mercenaries took over the city-states that had hired them.

- Many Italians were poor because they had to pay high taxes. This created a lower class and an upper class, but no middle class. It also caused the commoners to revolt against the rich.

- Wealthy families often battled with each other for control of the city-states.

- Some city-state rulers became even wealthier by overseeing banking and trade. These leaders lived in luxury, while many citizens were very poor.

- Many citizens liked their city-state and wanted to help it. This encouraged patriotism.

- Some rulers were generous to the citizens of their city-states. For example, Duke Federigo da Montefeltro (1422–1482), a popular ruler in Urbino, built schools, hospitals, churches, and a library with his own money. He was known for talking to the commoners and helping the poor.

- The city-states helped bring an end to feudalism by making merchants, as well as landowners, wealthy and ending the relationship between lords and vassals.

You Be the Historian

Checking for Understanding

1. Do you think that the art of the Renaissance would have been created if Italy had not been divided into individual city-states? Why or why not?

2. Do you think Italian artists had more artistic freedom under this form of government? Why or why not?

3. Would you have enjoyed living during the Renaissance? Would you have wanted to be a ruler, noble, artist, or commoner? Why?

Section 2

New Ideas and Art

Get Ready to Read!

What's the Connection?

In Section 1, you learned about the growth of Italian city-states. In this section, you will learn how the wealth of the city-states led to an age of artistic achievements.

Focusing on the Main Ideas

- Humanists studied the Greeks and Romans, and the development of the printing press helped spread their ideas. *(page 619)*

- Renaissance artists used new techniques to produce paintings that showed people in an emotional and realistic way. *(page 623)*

- Renaissance ideas and art spread from Italy to northern Europe. *(page 625)*

Locating Places
Flanders (FLAN•duhrz)

Meeting People
Dante Alighieri (DAHN•tay A•luh•GYEHR•ee)

Johannes Gutenberg (yoh•HAHN•uhs GOO•tuhn•BUHRG)

Leonardo da Vinci (LEE•uh•NAHR•doh duh VIHN•chee)

Michelangelo Buonarroti (MY•kuh•LAN•juh•LOH BWAW•nahr•RAW•tee)

William Shakespeare (SHAYK•SPIHR)

Building Your Vocabulary
humanism (HYOO•muh•NIH•zuhm)

vernacular (vuhr•NA•kyuh•luhr)

Reading Strategy
Organizing Information Create a diagram to show features of Renaissance art.

NATIONAL GEOGRAPHIC When & Who?

1400   **1500**   **1600**

c. 1455 Johannes Gutenberg uses printing press to print the Bible

1494 Leonardo begins painting *The Last Supper*

1512 Michelangelo finishes painting Sistine Chapel's ceiling

1601 Shakespeare writes *Hamlet*

Renaissance Humanism

Main Idea Humanists studied the Greeks and Romans, and the development of the printing press helped spread their ideas.

Reading Focus Have you ever tried to draw a copy of a painting you like? Is it harder to copy what other people have done or to come up with new ideas for your own pictures? Read to learn how Renaissance artists borrowed ideas from the past but tried to be original too.

In the 1300s, a new way of understanding the world developed in medieval Europe. This new approach was called **humanism** (HYOO•muh•NIH•zuhm). It was based on the values of the ancient Greeks and Romans. Humanists believed that the individual and human society were important. Humanists did not turn away from religious faith, but they wanted a balance between faith and reason. Their new ideas encouraged men to be active in their cities and achieve great things.

Ancient Works Become Popular
In the 1300s, Italians began to study early Roman and Greek works. For most of the Middle Ages, Western Europeans knew little about ancient Greek and Roman writings. When they went on the Crusades, however, they opened trade with the Middle East and began to get information from the Arabs. Arab scholars knew classic Greek and Roman works very well. In addition, when the Turks conquered Constantinople in 1453, many Byzantine scholars left and moved to Venice or Florence.

One famous scholar of the ancient works was Petrarch (PEH•TRAHRK). Francesco Petrarch was a poet and scholar who lived in the 1300s. He studied Roman writers like Cicero and wrote biographies of famous Romans.

Petrarch encouraged Europeans to search for Latin manuscripts in monasteries all over Europe. In time, his efforts paid off and new libraries were built to keep the manuscripts. The largest was the Vatican Library in Rome.

Italians studied more than ancient books. They studied the old buildings and statues all around them. All over Rome, one could see workers cleaning the dirt and rubble from broken columns and statues. Italian artists eagerly studied the proportions of the ancient works. If they knew how long a statue's arms were compared to its height, they would be able to understand why it looked so perfect.

Ancient Greek manuscript on Archimedes ▼

◀ Francesco Petrarch has been called the father of Italian Renaissance humanism. *How did Petrarch contribute to the preservation of Roman knowledge?*

619

HISTORY MAKERS

Movable Type c. 1450

Johannes Gutenberg, a German goldsmith, built a printing press modeled after a winepress. Once the press was completed, Gutenberg spent two years printing his first book. For each page, he set metal letters in a frame, rolled ink over the frame, and pressed the frame against paper. Around 1455, he completed printing what is now known as the Gutenberg Bible, or the 42 Line Bible. This was the first book printed using movable metal type, sparking a revolution in publishing and reading.

▼ Gutenberg Bible

Changes in Literature During the Renaissance, educated people wrote in "pure" Latin, the Latin used in ancient Rome. Petrarch thought classical Latin was the best way to write, but when he wanted to write poems to the woman he loved, he wrote in the **vernacular** (vuhr•NA•kyuh•luhr). The vernacular is the everyday language people speak in a region—Italian, French, or German, for example. When authors began writing in the vernacular, many more people could read their work.

In the early 1300s, **Dante Alighieri** (DAHN•tay A•luh•GYEHR•ee), a poet of Florence, wrote one of the world's greatest poems in the vernacular. It is called *The Divine Comedy*. As a young man, Dante was active in politics, but when noble families began fighting over power, he had to leave Florence. That was when he wrote his long poem—more than 14,000 lines. *The Divine Comedy* tells the gripping tale of the main character's journey from hell to heaven. The horrible punishments for different sins were vividly described.

Another important writer who used the vernacular was Chaucer. Chaucer wrote in English. In his famous book, *The Canterbury Tales*, he describes 29 pilgrims on their journey to the city of Canterbury. *The Canterbury Tales* describes the levels of English society, from the nobles at the top to the poor at the bottom. The English Chaucer used in his writing is the ancestor of the English we speak today.

The Printing Press Spreads Ideas

The printing press was a key to the spread of humanist ideas throughout Europe. In the early 1450s, **Johannes Gutenberg** (yoh•HAHN•uhs GOO•tuhn•BUHRG) developed a printing press that used movable metal type. This type of printing press made it possible to print many books much more quickly. With more books available, more people learned to read. Scholars could read one another's works and debate their ideas in letters.

Ideas grew and spread more quickly than ever before in Europe.

The Chinese had already invented movable type, but it did not work well with their large alphabet of characters. For Europeans, the printing press was a big improvement. It was easy to use with linen paper, another Chinese invention.

Gutenberg's Bible, printed in the 1450s, was the first European book produced on the new press. Soon books flooded Europe. About 40,000 books were published by 1500. Half of these were religious works like the Bible or prayer books.

How Did Humanism Affect Society?

Humanist scholars studied the Greeks and Romans to increase their knowledge of many different topics. They were curious about everything, including plants and animals, human anatomy and medicine, and the stars and planets. Their study of mathematics helped them in many subjects.

One of the best Renaissance scientists was also a great artist, **Leonardo da Vinci** (LEE•uh•NAHR•doh duh VIHN•chee). Leonardo dissected corpses to learn anatomy and studied fossils to understand the world's history. He was also an inventor and an engineer.

Most of what we know about Leonardo comes from his notebooks. Leonardo filled their pages with sketches of his scientific and artistic ideas. Centuries before the airplane was invented, Leonardo drew sketches of a glider, a helicopter, and a parachute. Other sketches show a version of a military tank and a scuba diving suit.

✔ **Reading Check** **Explain** What was the benefit of writing in the vernacular?

Primary Source

Leonardo's Inventions

Leonardo da Vinci's notebooks contained sketches of inventions that would not be produced for hundreds of years.

DBQ **Document-Based Question**

Compare Leonardo's sketches of a helicopter and subway to their modern counterparts. How accurate was Leonardo?

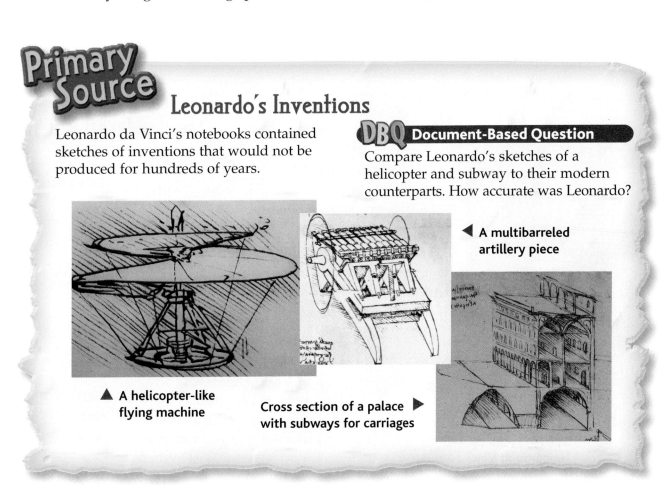

◀ A multibarreled artillery piece

▲ A helicopter-like flying machine

Cross section of a palace ▶ with subways for carriages

Biography

LEONARDO DA VINCI
1452–1519

Leonardo was born in Vinci, Italy, to a peasant woman named Caterina. Shortly after Leonardo's birth, she left the boy in the care of his father. By the time Leonardo was 15 years old, his father knew his son had artistic talent. He arranged for Leonardo to become an apprentice to the famous painter Andrea del Verrocchio.

By 1472, Leonardo had become a master in the painters' guild of Florence. He worked in Florence until 1481, and then he went to the city of Milan. There he kept a large workshop and employed many apprentices. During this time, Leonardo began keeping small pads of paper tucked in his belt for sketching. Later he organized the drawings by theme and assembled the pages into notebooks.

Seventeen years later, Leonardo returned to Florence, where he was welcomed with great honor. During this time, Leonardo painted some of his masterpieces. He also made scientific studies, including dissections, observations of the flight of birds, and research on the movement of water currents.

In 1516 Leonardo accepted an invitation to live in France. The king admired Leonardo and gave him freedom to pursue his interests. During the last three years of his life, Leonardo lived in a small house near the king's summer palace. He spent most of his time sketching and working on his scientific studies.

▲ Leonardo da Vinci

> **"Nothing can be loved or hated unless it is first known."**
>
> —Leonardo da Vinci

▲ The *Mona Lisa* by Leonardo da Vinci

Then and Now

Leonardo's curiosity fueled his creativity and interest in science. What invention created in the last 100 years do you think would impress Leonardo the most? Why?

Artists in Renaissance Italy

Main Idea Renaissance artists used new techniques to produce paintings that showed people in an emotional and realistic way.

Reading Focus Have you ever had trouble making your drawings look real and three-dimensional? Read to learn how Renaissance artists learned to make their art look natural and real.

During the Renaissance, wealthy Italian families and church leaders paid artists to create paintings, sculptures, and buildings for display throughout their cities. The pope himself funded many works of art to decorate the Vatican. Renaissance artists followed the models of the ancient Romans and Greeks but expressed humanist ideas.

What Was New About Renaissance Art?

If you compare medieval and Renaissance paintings, you will see major differences in their styles. Renaissance art tries to show people as they would appear in real life. It also tries to show people's emotions. When a medieval artist depicted the birth of Jesus, he wanted to remind Christians about their belief that Jesus was born to save the world. A Renaissance artist painting the same scene might try to show how tender Mary looked with her tiny baby.

Renaissance painters also used new techniques. The most important was perspective (puhr•SPEHK•tihv), a method that makes a drawing or painting look three-dimensional. Artists had tried to use perspective before, but Renaissance artists perfected it. Using perspective, objects in a scene appear to be at different distances from the viewer. The result is a more realistic image.

To make their paintings more realistic, Renaissance artists also used a technique called chiaroscuro (kee•AHR•uh•SKYUR•oh).

▲ The sculpture, *La Pieta*, by Michelangelo shows Mary holding the body of Jesus after his death. *What did Renaissance artists try to portray in their works?*

Chiaroscuro softened edges by using light and shadows instead of stiff outlines to separate objects. In Italian, *chiaro* means "clear or light," and *oscuro* means "dark." Chiaroscuro created more drama and emotion in a painting.

The Peak of the Renaissance

The artistic Renaissance lasted from about 1350 to 1550, but it hit its peak between 1490 and 1520. At that time, three great artists were producing their masterpieces—Leonardo da Vinci, Raphael Sanzio, and **Michelangelo Buonarroti** (MY•kuh•LAN•juh•LOH BWAW•nahr•RAW•tee).

Although Leonardo also became a great scientist and inventor, he trained as an artist. Born in 1452, he began his training in Florence at a young age. Training in workshops was an old tradition, but during the Renaissance, individual artists began to do something no medieval artist had done— they signed their own work.

One of Leonardo's most famous works is *The Last Supper,* which he began painting in 1494 on a wall behind a church altar. He painted on wet plaster with watercolor paint. A painting done this way is called a

The Way It Was

Focus on Everyday Life

The Life of a Renaissance Artist

If a young boy in Renaissance Italy wanted to be an artist, he would become an apprentice at a workshop run by an established artist. The main job of apprentices was preparing materials for the master artist and his assistants. Apprentices used minerals, spices, egg yolk, and other everyday materials to mix paints. They readied wax and clay for sculpture modeling. Eventually, apprentices became assistants. Talented assistants could become masters of their own workshops.

Master artists could afford to have workshops because of the patronage system in Italy. Patrons—people who pay to support someone else's work—would commission, or hire, an artist to complete a project. That artist was usually helped by his assistants and apprentices. Patrons were usually political and church leaders, organizations, and wealthy bankers and merchants.

▲ Renaissance painter and apprentice

Connecting to the Past

1. What was the main job of apprentices?
2. Does the patronage system or the apprentice system exist today? If so, in what fields?

fresco (FREHS•koh), which in Italian means "fresh." Frescoes were painted in churches all over Italy.

One of Leonardo's great artistic skills is visible in *The Last Supper.* In this painting of Jesus and his disciples, Leonardo was able to show human emotions through small differences in how each apostle held his head or the apostle's position in relation to Jesus. Leonardo showed this skill again in the *Mona Lisa.* People still argue about what the woman in the portrait is thinking—what is the mystery behind her smile?

Although Raphael worked at the same time as Leonardo, he was much younger. Even as a young man, Raphael worked with ease and grace and became known as one of Italy's best painters. Italians especially loved the gentle Madonnas he painted. He also painted many frescoes in the Vatican Palace. Perhaps his best-known painting is the *School of Athens*, which depicts a number of Greek philosophers.

The third great Renaissance artist was Michelangelo. Like many other artists of the time, Michelangelo painted, sculpted, and designed buildings. He painted one of the best-known Renaissance works—the ceiling of the Sistine Chapel in Rome.

Although he painted many outstanding works, Michelangelo was a sculptor at heart. He believed his talents were inspired by God. He carved his statues to show perfect versions of human beings as a symbol of God's beauty and perfection. Michelangelo's best-known sculpture is the 13-foot-tall statue *David.* The sculptor made David seem calm, yet ready for action. Also impressive is Michelangelo's statue of the biblical Moses. The huge figure appears both wise and powerful.

✓ **Reading Check** **Compare and Contrast** What were some of the differences between medieval and Renaissance artists?

The Renaissance Spreads

Main Idea Renaissance ideas and art spread from Italy to northern Europe.

Reading Focus If you were a Canadian artist, would your painting look different than if you lived in Arizona? Read to learn how the Renaissance changed as it moved into northern Europe.

In the late 1400s, the Renaissance spread to northern Europe and later to England. The printing press helped humanist ideas to spread, as did people who traveled.

What Is the Northern Renaissance?

The Northern Renaissance refers to the art in places we know today as Belgium, Luxembourg, Germany, and the Netherlands. Like Italian artists, northern artists wanted their works to have greater realism, but they used different methods. One important method they developed was oil painting. First developed in **Flanders** (FLAN•duhrz)—a region that is in northern Belgium today—oils let artists paint intricate details and surface textures, like the gold braid on a gown.

Jan van Eyck was a master of oil painting. In one of his best-known paintings, a newly married couple stands side by side in a formal bedroom. Van Eyck showed every fold in their rich gowns and every detail of the chandelier above their heads.

Albrecht Dürer (AHL•brehkt DUR•uhr) is perhaps one of the greatest artists of the Northern Renaissance. Dürer was able to master both perspective and fine detail. He is best known for his engravings. An engraving is made from an image carved on metal, wood, or stone. Ink is applied to the surface, and then the image is printed on paper.

Dürer's *Four Horsemen of the Apocalypse* is an outstanding example of a woodcut, a print made from carved wood. In it, four fierce horsemen ride to announce the end of the world.

Globe Theater

William Shakespeare's plays were performed at the Globe Theater in London. It could hold about 3,000 people. Plays were performed every day of the week except Sunday. Performances occurred during the day, since the theater had no lights. *When did the Renaissance spread to northern Europe and England?*

Flags announced the type of play. White flags meant comedies, black flags meant tragedies, and red flags stood for history plays.

Wealthy and important people sat beneath the covered section.

Poor commoners, called groundlings, stood on the ground for the show. They often brought fruit and vegetables to throw at actors they did not like.

Who Was William Shakespeare? In England, the Renaissance took place in writing and theater more than in art. The Renaissance began in England in the later 1500s, during the rule of Elizabeth I.

Theater was popular in England in the 1500s. Admission was only one or two cents, so even the poor could attend. English playwrights, or writers who create plays, wrote about people's strengths, weaknesses, and emotions.

The greatest English writer of that era was **William Shakespeare** (SHAYK•SPIHR). He wrote tragedies, comedies, and historical plays. Some of his great tragedies include *Hamlet, MacBeth,* and *Romeo and Juliet.* In each tragedy, the characters' flaws cause their downfall. Among his most famous comedies are *A Midsummer Night's Dream, Twelfth Night,* and *Much Ado About Nothing.* His best-known historical plays include

▲ Dürer's *Four Horsemen of the Apocalypse*

Henry V and *Richard III*. Shakespeare's plays are still performed today and remain very popular.

✔ **Reading Check** **Compare** How did the northern Renaissance differ from the Italian Renaissance?

History Online

Homework Helper Need help with the material in this section? Visit jat.glencoe.com

Section 2 Review

Reading Summary

Review the Main Ideas

- During the Renaissance, scholars examined the ancient works of the Greeks and Romans, began to write in the vernacular, and explored many scientific fields.

- Italian Renaissance artists employed new techniques and created masterpieces of painting and sculpture.

- As the Renaissance spread to northern Europe and England, artists and writers, such as Dürer and Shakespeare, created great works.

What Did You Learn?

1. Explain the beliefs of humanists during the Renaissance.

2. Explain the artistic technique of perspective.

Critical Thinking

3. **Summarizing Information** Draw a chart like the one below. Use it to describe the artistic work and techniques of each artist listed.

Leonardo da Vinci	
Michelangelo	
Jan van Eyck	
Shakespeare	

4. **Evaluate** What was the importance of the printing press on Renaissance society?

5. **Science Link** Describe the scientific efforts and contributions of Leonardo da Vinci.

6. **Explain** How were the ideals of the Renaissance expressed in England? Provide examples in your answer.

7. **Expository Writing** Choose a painting or sculpture shown in this section. In a short essay, describe the work and explain how it demonstrates Renaissance techniques or characteristics.

A MIDSUMMER NIGHT'S DREAM

By William Shakespeare,
Adapted by E. Nesbit

Before You Read

The Scene: This story takes place in Athens, Greece, in a legendary time when magical creatures lived among humans.

The Characters: Hermia and Lysander are in love. Demetrius loves Hermia, and Helena loves Demetrius. Oberon and Titania are the King and Queen of the Fairies.

The Plot: Hermia and Lysander run away to be married. Demetrius follows them because he loves Hermia. Helena follows Demetrius because she loves him. The fairies they encounter try to use magic to help the four humans.

Vocabulary Preview

betrayed: gave to an enemy

mortal: human

quarrel: argument

glade: grassy open space in a forest

suitor: one who wants to marry another

bade: asked

scheme: plan

Have you ever tried to help someone but made the situation worse? In this story, fairies attempt to help four young people traveling through the woods, but their efforts do not go as planned.

As You Read

Keep in mind that William Shakespeare wrote this story as a play. E. Nesbit
rewrote the story in paragraph form to make it shorter and easier to read.

Hermia and Lysander were [in love]; but Hermia's father wished her to marry another man, named Demetrius.

Now in Athens, where they lived, there was a wicked law, by which any girl who refused to marry according to her father's wishes, might be put to death. . . .

Lysander of course was nearly mad with grief, and the best thing to do seemed to him for Hermia to run away to his aunt's house at a place beyond the reach of that cruel law; and there he would come to her and marry her. But before she started, she told her friend, Helena, what she was going to do.

Helena had been Demetrius' sweetheart long before his marriage with Hermia had been thought of, and being very silly, like all jealous people, she could not see that it was not poor Hermia's fault that Demetrius wished to marry her instead of his own lady, Helena. She knew that if she told Demetrius that Hermia was going, as she was, to the wood outside Athens, he would follow her, "and I can follow him, and at least I shall see him," she said to herself. So she went to him, and betrayed her friend's secret.

Now this wood where Lysander was to meet Hermia, and where the other two had decided to follow them, was full of fairies,[1] as most woods are, if one only had the eyes to see them, and in this wood on this night were the King and Queen of the fairies, Oberon and Titania. Now fairies are very wise people, but now and then they can be quite as foolish as mortal folk. Oberon and Titania, who might have been as happy as the days were long, had thrown away all their joy in a foolish quarrel. . . .

So, instead of keeping one happy Court and dancing all night through in the moonlight, as is fairies' use, the King with his attendants wandered through one part of the wood, while the Queen with hers kept state in another. And the cause of all

---

[1]**fairies:** imaginary beings, usually having small human form and magic powers

this trouble was a little Indian boy whom Titania had taken to be one of her followers. Oberon wanted the child to follow him and be one of his fairy knights; but the Queen would not give him up.

On this night, in a glossy moonlight glade, the King and Queen of the fairies met.

"Ill² met by moonlight, proud Titania," said the King.

"What! jealous, Oberon?" answered the Queen. "You spoil everything with your quarreling. Come, fairies, let us leave him. I am not friends with him now."

"It rests with you to make up the quarrel," said the King. "Give me that little Indian boy, and I will again be your humble servant and suitor."

"Set your mind at rest," said the Queen. "Your whole fairy kingdom buys not that boy from me. Come fairies."

And she and her train rode off down the moonbeams.³

"Well, go your ways," said Oberon. "But I'll be even with you before you leave this wood."

Then Oberon called his favorite fairy, Puck. Puck was the spirit of mischief. . . .

"Now," said Oberon to this little sprite,⁴ "fetch me the flower called Love-in-idleness. The juice of that little purple flower laid on the eyes of those who sleep will make them when they wake to love the first thing they see. I will put some of the juice of that flower on my Titania's eyes, and when she wakes, she will love the first thing she sees, were it lion, bear, or wolf, or bull, or meddling monkey, or a busy ape."

---

²**ill:** causing suffering or distress
³**moonbeams:** rays of light from the moon
⁴**sprite:** fairy

While Puck was gone, Demetrius passed through the glade followed by poor Helena, and still she told him how she loved him and reminded him of all his promises, and still he told her that he did not and could not love her, and that his promises were nothing. Oberon was sorry for poor Helena, and when Puck returned with the flower, he bade him follow Demetrius and put some of the juice on his eyes, so that he might love Helena when he woke and looked on her, as much as she loved him. So Puck set off, and wandering through the wood found, not Demetrius, but Lysander, on whose eyes he put the juice; but when Lysander woke, he saw not his own Hermia, but Helena, who was walking through the wood looking for the cruel Demetrius; and directly he saw her he loved her and left his own lady, under the spell of the crimson flower.

When Hermia woke she found Lysander gone, and wandered about the wood trying to find him. Puck went back and told Oberon what he had done, and Oberon soon found that he had made a mistake, and set about looking for Demetrius, and having found him, put some of the juice on his eyes. And the first thing Demetrius saw when he woke was also Helena. So now Demetrius and Lysander were both following her through the wood, and it was Hermia's turn to follow her lover as Helena had done before. The end of it was that Helena and Hermia began to quarrel, and Demetrius and Lysander went off to fight. Oberon was

enameled[5] skin of a snake. Oberon stooped over her and laid the juice on her eyes. . . .

Now, it happened that when Titania woke the first thing she saw was a stupid clown, one of a party of players who had come out into the wood to rehearse their play. This clown had met with Puck, who had clapped[6] [a donkey's] head on his shoulders so that it looked as if it grew there. Directly Titania woke and saw this dreadful monster, she said, "What angel is this? Are you as wise as you are beautiful?"

"If I am wise enough to find my way out of this wood, that's enough for me," said the foolish clown.

"Do not desire to go out of the wood," said Titania. The spell of the love-juice was on her, and to her the clown seemed the most beautiful and delightful creature on all the earth. "I love you," she went on. "Come with me, and I will give you fairies to attend on you."

So she called four fairies, whose names were Peaseblossom, Cobweb, Moth, and Mustardseed.

"You must attend this gentleman," said the Queen. "Feed him with apricots, and dewberries, purple grapes, green figs, and mulberries. Steal honey-bags for him from the humble-bees, and with the wings of painted butterflies fan the moonbeams from his sleeping eyes." . . .

"Would you like anything to eat?" said the fairy Queen.

very sorry to see his kind scheme to help these lovers turn out so badly. So he said to Puck:

"These two young men are going to fight. You must overhang the night with drooping fog, and lead them so astray, that one will never find the other. When they are tired out, they will fall asleep. Then drop this other herb on Lysander's eyes. That will give him his old sight and his old love. Then each man will have the lady who loves him, and they will all think that this has been only a Midsummer Night's Dream. Then when this is done all will be well with them."

So Puck went and did as he was told, and when the two had fallen asleep without meeting each other, Puck poured the juice on Lysander's eyes. . . .

Meanwhile Oberon found Titania asleep on a bank. . . .There Titania always slept a part of the night, wrapped in the

---

[5]**enameled:** coated with a glassy substance
[6]**clapped:** forcefully put

"I should like some good dry oats," said the clown—for his donkey's head made him desire donkey's food—"and some hay to follow."

"Shall some of my fairies fetch you new nuts from the squirrel's house?" asked the Queen.

"I'd rather have a handful or two of good dried peas," said the clown. "But please don't let any of your people disturb me, I am going to sleep."

Then said the Queen, "And I will wind thee in my arms."

And so when Oberon came along he found his beautiful Queen lavishing kisses and endearments on a clown with a donkey's head. And before he released her from the enchantment, he persuaded her to give him the little Indian boy he so much desired to have. Then he took pity on her, and threw some juice of the disenchanting flower on her pretty eyes; and then in a moment she saw plainly the donkey-headed clown she had been loving, and knew how foolish she had been.

Oberon took off the [donkey's] head from the clown, and left him to finish his sleep with his own silly head lying on the thyme and violets.

Thus all was made plain and straight again. Oberon and Titania loved each other more than ever. Demetrius thought of no one but Helena, and Helena had never had any thought of anyone but Demetrius. As for Hermia and Lysander, they were as loving a couple as you could meet in a day's march, even through a fairy-wood. So the four [mortals] went back to Athens and were married; and the fairy King and Queen live happily together in that very wood at this very day.

Responding to the Reading

1. How did Demetrius and Lysander fall in love with Helena?

2. How did the story get its title, *A Midsummer Night's Dream?*

3. **Cause and Effect** Why were Lysander and Demetrius preparing to fight?

4. **Predict** What do you think might have happened if Oberon had not interfered with the conflict among the four young people?

5. **Reading** **Read to Write** Reread the last paragraph in the story, then write another ending to the story that could replace that paragraph.

Section 3

The Reformation Begins

Get Ready to Read!

What's the Connection?
During the Middle Ages, all of Western Europe's Christians were Catholic. The movement called the Reformation, however, questioned Catholic beliefs and power.

Focusing on the Main Ideas
- The reforms of Martin Luther led to the creation of new Christian churches. *(page 634)*
- Political leaders often supported Protestantism because they wanted more power. *(page 639)*
- John Calvin's Protestant teachings spread across Europe and into North America. *(page 640)*

Locating Places
Wittenberg (WIH•tuhn•BUHRG)
Geneva (juh•NEE•vuh)

Meeting People
Martin Luther
Desiderius Erasmus (DEHS•ih•DIHR• ee•uhs ih•RAZ•muhs)
John Calvin

Building Your Vocabulary
Reformation (REH•fuhr•MAY•shuhn)
indulgence (ihn•DUHL•juhns)
denomination (dih•NAH•muh•NAY•shuhn)
theology (thee•AH•luh•jee)
predestination (pree•DEHS•tuh•NAY•shuhn)

Reading Strategy
Cause and Effect Create a diagram to show some of the reasons for the Reformation.

Reasons for the Reformation

NATIONAL GEOGRAPHIC When & Where?

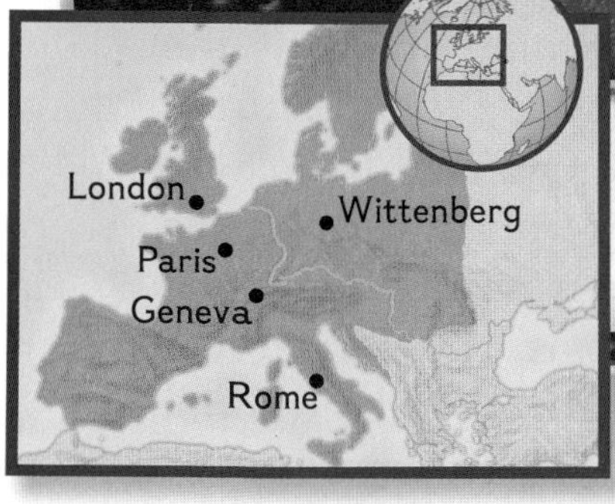

1500 — 1530 — 1560

1517 Martin Luther writes Ninety-Five Theses

1519 Charles V becomes Holy Roman Emperor

1555 Peace of Augsburg signed

London, Paris, Wittenberg, Geneva, Rome

CHAPTER 17   The Renaissance and Reformation   633

Calls for Church Reform

Main Idea The reforms of Martin Luther led to the creation of new Christian churches.

Reading Focus Can you think of any reformers in the United States? Read to learn how some Europeans set out to reform the Catholic Church and ended up starting a new church instead.

In 1517 a young monk named **Martin Luther** challenged the Roman Catholic Church. He publicly argued that the pope could not decide what a person had to do to get into heaven. Eventually, his challenge to the pope's authority led to the creation of new churches in Western Europe.

At first, Luther only wanted to reform the Catholic Church. This is why we call these events the **Reformation** (REH•fuhr•MAY•shuhn). The Reformation, however, became the beginning of a movement in

▲ Desiderius Erasmus, the most famous Christian humanist, criticized the wealth and power of Catholic leaders. *What change did Erasmus want to make to the Bible?*

Christianity known as Protestantism. By the end of the Reformation, many new Christian churches had appeared in Europe. The religious unity the Catholic Church had created in Western Europe, and which had lasted for hundreds of years, had been broken.

What Ideas Led to the Reformation? In the last section, you read about humanism. When humanism spread to northern Europe, it led to a new movement in Christianity called Christian humanism. Its first leader was a scholar and clergyman named **Desiderius Erasmus** (DEHS•ih•DIHR•ee•uhs ih•RAZ•muhs).

Erasmus wrote that human beings could use their reason to become better Christians and thereby improve the Church. He studied ancient Christian works for inspiration.

One of Erasmus's goals was to translate the Bible into the vernacular. He wanted a farmer working in the fields to be able to stop and read the Bible. Erasmus also wrote that what mattered was that people be good in their everyday lives. It was not enough to participate in religious activities, like going to church on Sunday.

The Church Upsets Reformers By the 1300s, many people felt the Church had problems. It taxed peasants heavily, and some bishops behaved like they were kings. They built palaces, spent money on fine art, and made sure that their relatives had good jobs. In many villages, priests could barely read or give a good sermon.

Many Catholics became angry at the Church's focus on money. One Church practice that especially angered them was the selling of indulgences. An **indulgence** (ihn•DUHL•juhns) was a pardon from the Church for a person's sins. The Church had given out indulgences before, but it did not usually sell them. In the 1500s, however, the pope needed money to repair the church of St. Peter's in Rome. To get that money, he decided to sell indulgences in northern Germany.

The sale of indulgences outraged Martin Luther. Luther had looked in the Bible and found nothing that said an indulgence could pardon sin. The whole idea of selling God's forgiveness seemed unholy to him.

Martin Luther was not the first person to question the pope's power. As early as the 1370s, an English priest named John Wycliffe (WIH•KLIHF) had opposed Church policies. He preached that Christians needed only to recognize Jesus Christ as a power above them, not the pope.

Wycliffe and Luther both challenged the pope's power, but they had something else in common—their respect for the Bible. Wycliffe wanted everyone to read the Bible. After Wycliffe died, his followers translated the Bible into English for the first time.

▲ This painting shows indulgences being sold in a village marketplace. *Why was the Church selling indulgences?*

▲ Indulgence box

Who Was Martin Luther?

Martin Luther became one of the most famous men in history. His break with the Catholic Church led to a revolution in Christianity. Why would a religious man disagree with his faith? First of all, Luther was angered by the behavior of Church leaders. Secondly, he was worried about his own soul.

Luther was born in 1483 in a small German village. A bright and sensitive boy, he grew up in a disciplined family. His father wanted him to study law, but Luther often thought about serving the Church. One day, he was out riding when a bolt of lightning knocked him to the ground. According to legend, Luther made up his mind to be a monk at that moment.

When Luther went to Rome on a pilgrimage, he was shocked at the behavior of the Roman clergy. Back home in Germany, he taught at a university in the town of **Wittenberg** (WIH•tuhn•BUHRG). He worried about the Church's problems and also about his own soul. With the plague killing people all around him, it is not surprising that Luther worried about whether he would go to heaven when he died.

The Church said that Luther would be saved and would go to heaven if he performed good works and received the sacraments. Still Luther worried that this was not true. He prayed and fasted long hours as he searched for answers to his

▲ Martin Luther began the Reformation when he made public his Ninety-Five Theses. **How did the Catholic Church react to Luther's actions?**

questions. He prayed so long that sometimes he fell unconscious on the cold church floor.

Luther found his answers by studying the Bible. He concluded that only faith, not good works, brought salvation. He believed that salvation was a gift from God, not something earned by doing good works.

In 1517, when the Church began selling indulgences, Luther was astonished. How could the Church tell peasants that buying an indulgence would save them? He angrily prepared a list of 95 arguments against indulgences and sent them to his bishop. Some accounts say that Luther also nailed them to the door of Wittenberg

Web Activity Visit jat.glencoe.com and click on *Chapter 17—Student Web Activity* to learn more about the Reformation.

Cathedral for everyone to read. The list became known as the Ninety-Five Theses. Thousands of copies were printed and read all across the German kingdoms.

Revolt Leads to New Churches At first the Church did not take Luther very seriously. Soon, though, Church leaders saw that Luther was dangerous. If people believed Luther, they would rely on the Bible, not priests. Who would need priests if the sacraments were not needed to get to heaven?

The pope and Luther argued for several years, but Luther refused to change his position. Finally, the pope excommunicated Luther. This meant Luther was no longer a member of the Church and could no longer receive the sacraments. He was also no longer considered a monk.

In the following years, Luther's ideas led to the creation of a new **denomination** (dih•NAH•muh•NAY•shuhn), or organized branch of Christianity. It was known as Lutheranism and was the first Protestant denomination.

Lutheranism has three main ideas. The first is that faith in Jesus, not good works, brings salvation. The second is that the Bible is the final source for truth about God, not a church or its ministers. Finally, Lutheranism said that the church was made up of all its believers, not just the clergy.

Peasant Revolts Luther's debate with the pope was so famous that even peasants in the countryside had heard about it. They liked what they heard about Luther.

The life of a peasant had always been hard, but in the 1520s, it was terrible. The crops had been poor for several years. On top of that, noble landowners increased the taxes that peasants had to pay.

Because of their suffering, Luther's ideas stirred the peasants to revolt. If

Luther had a right to rebel against an unjust pope, then the peasants must have a right to stand up to greedy nobles.

The peasants began by listing their demands. Like Luther, they based their ideas on the Bible. One leader said the peasants would no longer work for the nobles, "unless it should be shown us from the Gospel that we are serfs."

When the nobles did not give in, huge revolts broke out. It was not long, however, before the peasants were defeated. The nobles had better weapons and horses and won easily, killing at least 70,000 peasants.

At first Luther sympathized with the peasants, but he soon changed his mind. He was afraid of what might happen without a strong government. Luther used his powerful sermons to tell peasants that God had set the government above them and they must obey it.

✓ **Reading Check** **Cause and Effect** What was the result of the Church's decision to sell indulgences in 1517?

Linking Past & Present

The Anabaptists, Amish, and Mennonites

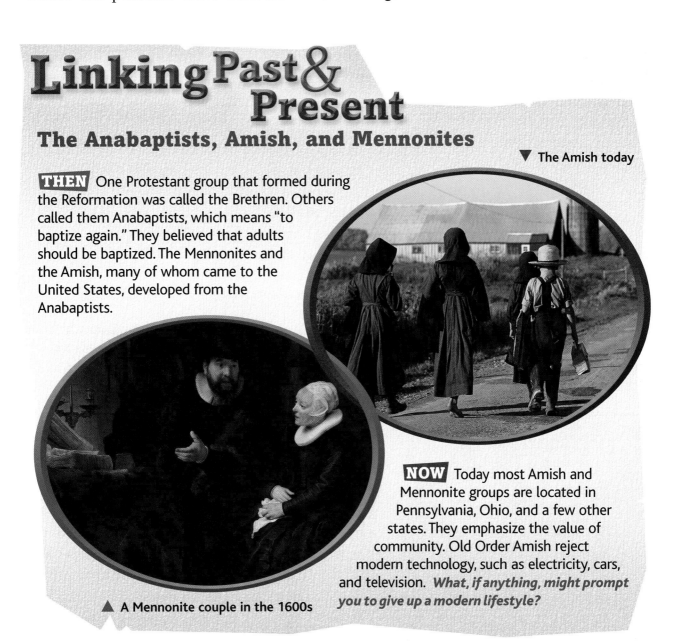

▼ The Amish today

THEN One Protestant group that formed during the Reformation was called the Brethren. Others called them Anabaptists, which means "to baptize again." They believed that adults should be baptized. The Mennonites and the Amish, many of whom came to the United States, developed from the Anabaptists.

NOW Today most Amish and Mennonite groups are located in Pennsylvania, Ohio, and a few other states. They emphasize the value of community. Old Order Amish reject modern technology, such as electricity, cars, and television. *What, if anything, might prompt you to give up a modern lifestyle?*

▲ A Mennonite couple in the 1600s

Biography

MARTIN LUTHER
1483–1546

▲ Martin Luther

Long before Martin Luther struggled with the Catholic Church, he faced difficult issues. Luther was born in Eisleben, Germany, in 1483 to a family of miners. Both his parents beat Luther as a child. Martin Luther and his father had terrible tempers. Luther later said his father's beatings caused him to feel bitter and hateful toward his family.

To avoid his abusive home life, Luther focused on his education. He was a student at the Latin School in Mansfield in 1488. As a teenager he went to two other schools away from home. At his father's urging, he considered studying law but instead earned a degree in philosophy in 1502.

Later, Luther entered a monastery to separate himself from his abusive past. In 1505 he traveled to Erfurt and became a monk. He then went to Wittenberg in 1508 and stayed with a group of Augustinian hermits. There he continued his study of theology.

Luther was a determined young man. Although he was a priest, he began to question the practices of the Catholic Church. His reforms resulted in a break with the Church. In 1525 he married a former nun named Katharine von Bora. They had six children and lived in a former monastery.

> "He who gives to a poor man, or lends to a needy man, does better than if he bought pardons."
>
> –Martin Luther,
> "The Ninety-five Theses (1517)"

Although known for his hot temper—which cost him many friendships—Luther and his wife cared for as many as 20 orphans whose parents died from the plague. In his later years, Luther enjoyed gardening and music, and continued his lifelong love of writing. He died in 1546, probably of a heart attack.

▲ Wittenberg today

Then and Now

Martin Luther was willing to stand up for his beliefs, even if that meant offending people. Can you think of anyone in the news who has shown that same willingness?

Politics and Lutheranism

Main Idea Political leaders often supported Protestantism because they wanted more power.

Reading Focus Under the United States Constitution, the government cannot favor any one religion. Read to learn what happened in Europe during the Reformation when kings decided what faith people had to follow.

In the past, there had been thinkers who challenged Catholic beliefs, but the Church had always remained in control. What had changed in the 1500s that allowed Protestantism to take hold? One reason Protestantism succeeded is that some of Europe's kings realized they could increase their power by supporting Lutheranism against the Catholic Church.

You read earlier about the Holy Roman Empire, which covered much of central Europe. The heart of the empire was made up of about 300 small German kingdoms. In 1519 Charles V became the Holy Roman Emperor. His empire included the lands of the Holy Roman Empire, as well as all of Spain, the Netherlands, parts of Italy, and territories in the Americas.

The local kings and nobles of the Holy Roman Empire were concerned about Charles V's power. They did not want a strong central ruler. They wanted to keep ruling their own little kingdoms.

Many German rulers decided to become Lutherans for religious and political reasons. By doing so, their kingdom also became Lutheran. After breaking with the Catholic Church, these rulers seized lands owned by Catholic monasteries in their kingdoms. Now they, and not the Church, would earn income from those lands.

At the same time, when the Catholic Church left a kingdom, it meant that church taxes no longer flowed out of the kingdom.

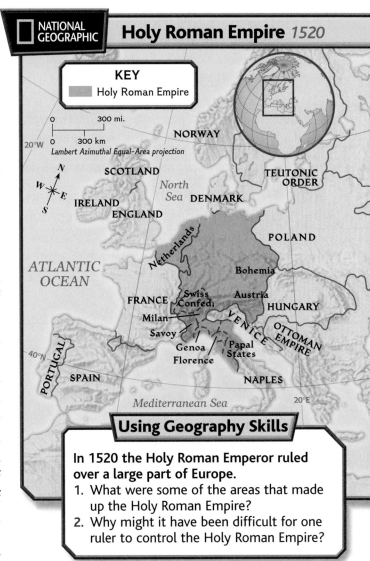

NATIONAL GEOGRAPHIC

Holy Roman Empire 1520

KEY
Holy Roman Empire

300 mi.
300 km
20°W
Lambert Azimuthal Equal-Area projection

NORWAY
SCOTLAND
North Sea DENMARK
IRELAND
ENGLAND
TEUTONIC ORDER
ATLANTIC OCEAN
Netherlands
POLAND
Bohemia
FRANCE Swiss Confed.
Milan
Savoy
Genoa
Florence
Austria
VENICE
Papal States
HUNGARY
OTTOMAN EMPIRE
40°N
PORTUGAL
SPAIN
NAPLES
Mediterranean Sea
20°E

Using Geography Skills

In 1520 the Holy Roman Emperor ruled over a large part of Europe.
1. What were some of the areas that made up the Holy Roman Empire?
2. Why might it have been difficult for one ruler to control the Holy Roman Empire?

Rulers could impose their own church taxes and keep the money for themselves. This made rulers who became Protestants stronger and the Church weaker.

Charles V eventually went to war with the German rulers who converted to Lutheranism, but he was unable to defeat them. In 1555 the fighting ended with the Peace of Augsburg. This agreement let each German ruler decide whether his kingdom would be Lutheran or Catholic. As a result most of northern Germany became Protestant, while the south stayed Catholic.

✓ Reading Check **Explain** Why did many German princes support Martin Luther's ideas?

Calvin and Calvinism

Main Idea John Calvin's Protestant teachings spread across Europe and into North America.

Reading Focus Are there some things you are sure are true? Read to learn how some Protestants developed a faith where everyone agreed that some people were going to heaven and others were not.

Who Was John Calvin?
John Calvin was born in France in the early 1500s. Everyone in his hometown expected that such a dutiful and intelligent boy would become a priest. When he reached the right age, he went off to Paris to study **theology** (thee•AH•luh•jee). Theology is the study of questions about God.

Calvin was very interested in religion. He got up early to read books on theology. During the day, he debated ideas with other students and then went home to read late into the night.

Although Calvin lived in France, he began to hear about the ideas of Martin Luther. Secretly, Calvin began to read about Luther at his college. He and the other students were careful to whisper when they discussed Luther's ideas. The more Calvin read, the more he was convinced by Luther's new ideas.

Eventually, Calvin had to leave Paris because it became too dangerous to talk about Lutheranism. Sometimes he hid out at friends' houses. Once he dared to return to his hometown, but he was arrested and spent months in a damp jail. Calvin finally found safety in **Geneva** (juh•NEE•vuh), Switzerland, a Protestant city. There his powerful preaching convinced many people to follow him.

What Is Calvinism?
Calvin agreed with Luther that faith was more important than good works, but he added other ideas too. Calvinism became the basis of many Protestant churches, including the churches of Puritans and Presbyterians in England and Scotland.

Calvin's main idea was that God's will is absolute and decides everything in the world in advance. God has decided who will go to heaven and who will not. This belief is called **predestination** (pree•DEHS•tuh•NAY•shuhn), meaning that no matter what people do, the outcome of their life is already planned.

Primary Source
Knowledge of God

John Calvin's writings helped Europeans accept Protestantism.

"What help is it . . . to know a God with whom we have nothing to do? Rather, our knowledge should serve first to teach us fear and reverence [respect]; secondly, with it as our guide and teacher, we should learn to seek every good from him, and having received it, to credit it to his account. . . . Again, you cannot behold him clearly unless you acknowledge him to be the fountainhead [source of life] and source of every good."

—John Calvin, *Institutes of the Christian Religion*

▲ John Calvin

DBQ Document-Based Question
According to Calvin, what is needed for believers to understand God clearly?

Some people could say that if their life's outcome were already determined, then why would it matter if they were good or bad? However, most people decided that they were probably among the saved. To prove it, they worked hard, behaved well, and obeyed the laws of their towns. In this way, Calvinism became a powerful tool in society. It encouraged people to work hard at their business and to behave themselves.

Another important idea of Calvinism is that neither kings nor bishops should control the Church. Calvinists believed that congregations should choose their own elders and ministers to run the church for them.

This idea had a strong impact on England and on many of the English settlers in America. The idea that a congregation should be allowed to choose its own

▲ In this picture, John Calvin is shown speaking before leaders in Geneva. *Which Protestant churches were based on Calvinism?*

leaders helped support the idea that the people should also be allowed to elect their own political leaders.

✓ **Reading Check** **Compare** How did Calvin's ideas differ from those of Luther?

History Online

Homework Helper Need help with the material in this section? Visit jat.glencoe.com

Section 3 Review

Reading Summary

Review the Main Ideas

- Many Christians, including Martin Luther, believed the Catholic Church was becoming corrupt. This led people to leave the Church and create new Christian churches.

- Many European rulers and nobles supported Luther's reforms for political as well as religious reasons.

- John Calvin's Protestant teachings inspired his followers to work hard and live good lives.

What Did You Learn?

1. What were indulgences, and why did they become controversial?

2. What were John Calvin's basic beliefs about God's will?

Critical Thinking

3. **Organizing Information** Draw a diagram to list the three main ideas of Lutheranism.

4. **Explain** What were the Ninety-Five Theses?

5. **Cause and Effect** Who was Erasmus, and how were his ideas about Christianity affected by humanism?

6. **Analyze** How did Europe's peasants react to Luther's teachings, and what was Luther's response?

7. **Creative Writing** Write a script for a play about an imaginary meeting between Martin Luther and John Calvin. Think about what the two men may have discussed concerning their beliefs and how they differed.

Section 4

Catholics and Protestants

Get Ready to Read!

What's the Connection?
In the last section, you learned about the rise of Protestantism. In this section, you will read about the Catholic Church's attempts at reform and the struggle between Europe's Protestants and Catholics.

Focusing on the Main Ideas
- Catholics and Protestants fought religious wars across Europe. *(page 643)*

- Henry VIII created the Anglican Church in England. *(page 648)*

- As part of the Counter-Reformation, Catholic kingdoms began sending missionaries overseas to convert people to Christianity. *(page 650)*

Locating Places
Trent
Navarre (nuh•VAHR)
Paris
London

Meeting People
Ignatius of Loyola (ihg•NAY•shuhs uhv loy•OH•luh)
Henry of Navarre
Henry VIII
Mary I
Elizabeth I

Building Your Vocabulary
seminary (SEH•muh•NEHR•ee)
heresy (HEHR•uh•see)
annul (uh•NUHL)

Reading Strategy
Cause and Effect Create a diagram to show the results of the Catholic Church's attempts at reform.

Reform	
Results	Results

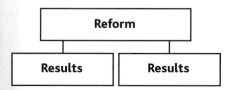

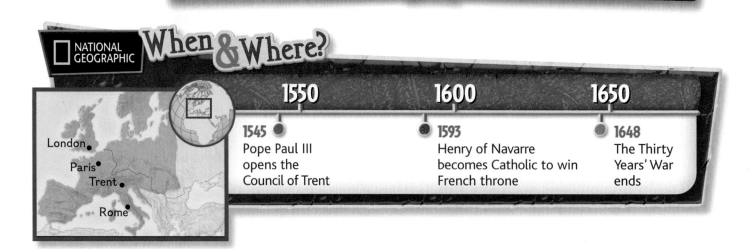

1550   **1600**   **1650**

1545 Pope Paul III opens the Council of Trent

1593 Henry of Navarre becomes Catholic to win French throne

1648 The Thirty Years' War ends

London
Paris
Trent
Rome

Counter-Reformation

Main Idea **Catholics and Protestants fought religious wars across Europe.**

Reading Focus Have you visited Protestant and Catholic churches? Could you see any differences? Read to learn the reasons for those differences.

In the 1500s and 1600s, the Catholic Church set out to defeat Protestantism and convince people to return to the Church. This effort came to be called the Counter-Reformation. As you learned earlier, the Reformation also triggered a series of bloody wars in Europe between Catholic and Protestant rulers. When the last wars ended in 1648, Europe was divided into Catholic and Protestant areas.

The Church Tries to Reform Itself

The Catholic Church waged a war against Protestantism, but it knew it needed to reform itself. Pope Paul III understood this need. After becoming pope, Paul called a church council at **Trent,** near Rome. The council held meetings for 20 years, from the 1540s to the 1560s.

The Council of Trent made Catholic beliefs clear. It also set up strict rules for how bishops and priests should behave. The Catholic clergy were told to work even harder at instructing people in the faith. To train new priests, seminaries were set up. A **seminary** (SEH•muh•NEHR•ee) is a special school for training and educating priests.

In 1540 Pope Paul III took another important step. He recognized a new order of priests, the Society of Jesus, known as the Jesuits. Jesuits were the pope's agents in Europe. They taught, preached, and fought **heresy** (HEHR•uh•see). A heresy is a religious belief that contradicts what the Church says is true.

▲ The Council of Trent is believed to be the basis for the Catholic Counter-Reformation. *What did the Council of Trent accomplish?*

Ignatius and Christianity

Ignatius of Loyola became devoted to the Christian religion while recovering from an injury.

"In everything else he was healthy except that he could not stand easily on his leg and had to stay in bed. As he was much given to reading . . . when he felt better he asked to be given some of them [books] to pass the time. But in that house none of those that he usually read could be found, so they gave him a Life of Christ and a book of the lives of the saints in Spanish. As he read them over many times, he became rather fond of what he found written there."

—*The Autobiography of St. Ignatius Loyola*, Joseph F. O'Callaghan, trans.

▲ **Ignatius of Loyola**

DBQ Document-Based Question

Why do you think Ignatius read the religious books even though they were not the type of book he usually read?

The man who founded the Jesuits was a Spaniard, **Ignatius of Loyola** (ihg•NAY•shuhs uhv loy•OH•luh). He was a daring soldier, but his life changed when he was wounded in battle. While recuperating, he read about Christian saints who performed brave deeds to defend their faith. Ignatius decided he would be a soldier for Jesus Christ.

The Religious Wars in France

John Calvin was originally from France, and many French people became interested in his ideas. As Calvinism spread in France, French Protestants became known as Huguenots.

Only about seven percent of the French people became Protestants, but almost half of France's nobles did, including the Bourbon family. The Bourbons were the second most powerful family in France. They ruled a kingdom in southern France called **Navarre** (nuh•VAHR) and were also in line for the throne of France.

Many French nobles wanted to weaken the king. The Huguenot nobles especially wanted the king weak so they could practice their religion freely. At the same time, France's king, Henry II, wanted to build a strong central government.

Henry II died in 1559, and his son Francis II died the following year. This meant that Francis's brother Charles, a 10-year-old boy, was now king. Since Charles was too young to rule, his mother ran the government for him. His mother was Catherine de' Medici—the daughter of Lorenzo de' Medici, the powerful Italian leader of Florence.

Catherine was determined to keep the French kingdom strong for her son. She believed the Huguenots were a threat to the king's power and refused to compromise with them. In 1562 a civil war that would last more than 30 years began in France between Protestants and Catholics.

In 1589 **Henry of Navarre,** the leader of Huguenot forces and head of the Bourbon family, became King Henry IV of France. For the next few years, the war continued because Catholic nobles would not accept a Protestant as king. Henry won most of his battles but was unable to capture **Paris.**

Henry IV then made a famous deal. He knew most French people were Catholic and that they demanded a Catholic king. Henry agreed to become a Catholic so the French people would accept him as king.

In 1593 Henry went to Paris and put on white satin for the Catholic ceremony. As he passed through the church doors, he smiled and, according to tradition, said that Paris was "worth a mass." He meant it was worth becoming a Catholic to rule all of France.

Henry IV did not forget his Huguenot followers, however. He issued an edict, or order, while visiting the city of Nantes in 1598. The Edict of Nantes said Catholicism was France's official religion, but it also gave Huguenots the right to worship freely.

What Was the Thirty Years' War? The worst religious war of the Reformation era was fought in the Holy Roman Empire in the 1600s. The war began in Bohemia—today known as the Czech Republic. Protestant nobles in Bohemia rebelled against their Catholic king. Other Protestant kings in Germany decided to help the rebels, and the war expanded throughout the empire.

The war lasted 30 years, from 1618 to 1648, and quickly became a war of kingdoms. France, Sweden, Denmark, England, and the Netherlands sent troops to help the

NATIONAL GEOGRAPHIC
Religions in Europe c. 1600

0   300 mi.
0   300 km
Lambert Azimuthal Equal-Area projection

SWEDEN
NORWAY
SCOTLAND
North Sea
Baltic Sea
RUSSIA
IRELAND
DENMARK
ENGLAND
NETHERLANDS
GERMAN STATES
•Wittenberg
POLAND
Canterbury•
SPANISH NETHERLANDS
•Worms
BOHEMIA
ATLANTIC OCEAN
Paris•
Augsburg•
BAVARIA
AUSTRIA
FRANCE Zurich•
•SWITZERLAND
HUNGARY
Geneva•
Trent•
ITALY
Rome•
PORTUGAL
SPAIN
OTTOMAN EMPIRE
Mediterranean

KEY
Dominant religion
Anglican
Calvinist
Eastern Orthodox Christian
Lutheran
Muslim
Roman Catholic
Mixture of Calvinist, Lutheran, and Roman Catholic
Minority religion
Calvinist
Lutheran
Muslim
Roman Catholic

Using Geography Skills

By the late 1500s, many northern Europeans had become Protestants, while most southern Europeans had remained Catholics.
1. Which areas of Europe became dominantly Calvinist?
2. Where in Europe do you think religious conflict might have taken place?

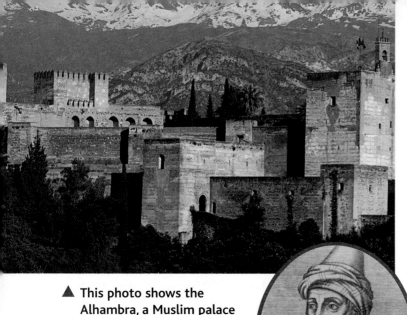

▲ This photo shows the Alhambra, a Muslim palace and fortress in Granada, Spain. *What happened to Spanish Muslims after Ferdinand and Isabella took power?*

Maimonides ▶

Protestants, while Spain and the Holy Roman Empire backed the Catholics.

Town fought against town, and roving troops murdered peasants on the roads. When it was over, only wolves were found wandering where some towns used to be. The war weakened Spain and helped make France one of Europe's most powerful countries.

The Reformation in Spain The ideas of Luther and Calvin never became very popular in Spain. Still, when Protestants began fighting in Europe, it affected Spain. Spanish rulers became suspicious of Protestant countries and of anyone in Spain who was not Catholic.

When the Reformation began in the 1500s, Spain was a young nation. It had been founded in 1469 when King Ferdinand and Queen Isabella married and joined their two kingdoms. These monarchs wanted a strong nation. They felt that all their subjects should be Catholic, because that would keep Spain's citizens loyal and united.

When Ferdinand and Isabella began to rule, many Muslims still lived in Spain. As you read in earlier chapters, Muslims ruled Spain from about A.D. 700 to 1200. During those years, people of different religions lived together in relative harmony.

The Muslims made non-Muslims pay special taxes and limited their rights, but they did not seek to kill or expel nonbelievers. Jews, for example, found life in Muslim Spain better than other places in Europe. As you read in earlier chapters, Jews were persecuted throughout Europe during the Middle Ages.

Muslim Spain during the Middle Ages was a golden age for Jewish thinkers and poets. The most famous Jewish scholar was Maimonides (my•MAH•nuh•DEEZ). He was born in Spain and his books on religion and medicine earned him great respect.

This golden age ended when Catholics took control of Spain. Jews and Muslims were no longer welcome. In 1492 Ferdinand and Isabella ordered all Jews and Muslims to convert to Catholicism or leave the country. To ensure religious unity, they also set up the Spanish Inquisition to investigate people's beliefs.

The Spanish Inquisition was a Catholic court, similar to the one the Catholic Church had set up in Europe to investigate heresy. The Spanish Inquisition was much crueler, however. Charges of heresy were made just to eliminate enemies. Horrible tortures were invented to force confessions of guilt. The head of the Spanish Inquisition, Tomás de Torquemada (TAWR•kuh•MAH•duh), executed some 2,000 Spaniards. Even the pope in Rome could not stop him.

✔ **Reading Check** **Identify** What deal earned Henry of Navarre the French throne?

Biography

CATHERINE DE' MEDICI
1519–1589

▲ Catherine de' Medici

Catherine de' Medici was an Italian woman who played an important role in French history. She was born in Florence to Lorenzo de' Medici and Madeleine de la Tour d' Auvergne. Catherine was orphaned as a baby and was raised by relatives. At age 14, Catherine was married to Henry, a French prince. Catherine took Italian artists, musicians, writers, and dancers with her to the French court. She was never fully accepted in France, however, because she was Italian and was not from a royal family.

In 1547 Catherine's husband became King Henry II. After he died in a jousting accident in 1559, their three oldest sons—Francis II, Charles IX, and Henry III—succeeded each other as king. Although Catherine was no longer queen, she still had much influence over her sons.

Catherine is blamed for many of the conflicts between French Catholics and French Protestants, called Huguenots. In 1568 she outlawed freedom of worship. In 1572 Catherine arranged the murder of a Huguenot adviser. His death sparked the Saint Bartholomew's Massacre, which resulted in the deaths of about 6,000 Huguenots. Catherine was not always opposed to Huguenots. In fact, she arranged the marriage of her daughter Margaret to Henry of Navarre, a former Protestant Huguenot who became King Henry IV of France.

Views on Catherine's accomplishments are mixed. Some blame her entirely for the French religious wars. Others remember her efforts to protect her sons. Still others remember her as a Renaissance woman because she supported the arts, added to the royal library, and sponsored a dance and theater pageant that is considered to be the first ballet. Catherine died in 1589 of pneumonia.

> "God and the world will have reason to be satisfied with me."
>
> —Catherine de' Medici, *Biography of a Family*

◀ Catherine de' Medici meets with foreign ambassadors

Then and Now

If Catherine de' Medici were running for political office today, do you think she would be a popular candidate? Why or why not?

The English Reformation

Main Idea Henry VIII created the Anglican Church in England.

Reading Focus You have probably heard about the Pilgrims. Do you know why the Pilgrims left England to come here? Read to learn how the Reformation came to England and why some Protestants decided to leave England and go to America.

Because England is an island, ideas from Europe sometimes took longer to get there. Surprisingly, though, England broke away from the Catholic Church earlier than the rest of Europe. That change was based on a political decision by the English king. Later, however, the English people strongly debated Reformation ideas.

Henry VIII Starts His Own Church In the history of England, no king is more famous than **Henry VIII.** He ruled England from 1509 to 1547. He was stubborn, impatient, and cruel. Henry married six queens, divorced two, and beheaded two more. He imprisoned bishops and nobles in the Tower of **London** (LUHN•duhn) for disagreeing with him. They also were eventually beheaded.

◄ In his attempt to divorce his wife and marry another woman, Henry VIII broke away from the Catholic Church and created the Church of England. *Why did the pope refuse to annul Henry VIII's marriage?*

Henry and his father were members of the Tudor family. In the 1400s, before the Tudors came to the throne, England's nobles had been at war with each other. Henry was determined to keep the peace and to keep the Tudors on the throne.

To do this he needed a son to succeed him, but Henry had no son. His wife Catherine had given birth only to daughters. Henry asked Pope Leo to **annul** (uh•NUHL), or cancel, his marriage to Catherine.

An annulment is not the same as a divorce. If the pope annulled the marriage, it would be as if the marriage had never happened. It would mean that Henry could find a new wife to give birth to sons. Those sons would be heirs to the throne, not the daughters Catherine had given him.

Popes had annulled marriages before, but this time the pope refused. Catherine was the daughter of Ferdinand and Isabella of Spain. Her nephew was the Holy Roman Emperor. Spain was the strongest Catholic kingdom at that time, and the pope did not want to make Catherine's family angry.

Henry decided to have the archbishop of Canterbury—the highest bishop in England—annul the marriage. In response, the pope excommunicated Henry from the Church. Henry then declared that the king, not the pope, was the head of the Church in England.

Henry ordered all the priests and bishops in England to accept him as the new head of their church. Some refused and were killed. The most famous was Sir Thomas More, who was executed in 1535. Henry then seized the Catholic Church's land in England and gave some of it to his nobles. This kept the nobles loyal to the king and to the Church of England. If they ever let the Catholic Church regain power in England, they would have to give up their land.

Mary I (above) attempted to restore the Catholic religion in England, and she married Philip II (right), the Catholic king of Spain. *Why was Mary I known as "Bloody Mary"?*

How Did Calvinism Affect England?

Although the Catholics were defeated, the religious battles were not over. A new fight began to make the Anglican Church more Protestant in its beliefs and rituals.

By the late 1500s, the ideas of John Calvin had reached England. Many educated people read Calvin's works and became convinced that he was right. They began to demand that the Anglican Church give up its Catholic ways of doing things. These reformers became known as Puritans because they wanted to purify the Anglican Church of Catholic ideas.

Puritans began to form their own congregations. These congregations were independent. They made their own decisions about what their congregations should and should not do. They did not report to a bishop of the Anglican Church, and they chose their own ministers.

Queen Elizabeth I tolerated the Puritans, but when James I became king in 1603, the Puritans faced harder times. James refused to allow anyone to disagree with the Anglican Church. The king headed the Anglican Church and appointed its leaders. The leaders, in turn, chose the priests for the congregations. James believed that by choosing their own ministers, the Puritans were challenging the king's power.

James I and the king who came after him, Charles I, persecuted the Puritans. They shut down Puritan churches and jailed Puritan leaders. Many Puritans decided to move to America to practice their religion freely. There they founded colonies that eventually became the states of Massachusetts, Connecticut, New Hampshire, and Rhode Island.

Who Was Bloody Mary?

The Church of England came to be known as the Anglican Church. It kept most of the rituals and sacraments of the Catholic Church. However, many English Catholics were not satisfied. They wanted to stay Catholic. They backed Henry's daughter Mary when she became Queen **Mary I** in 1553. Mary had been raised Catholic and wanted to make England a Catholic kingdom again.

Mary restored the Catholic Church in England and arrested Protestants who opposed her. In her struggle to make England Catholic again, Mary burned 300 people at the stake. The English were horrified and called her "Bloody Mary."

Mary ruled about five years, then died. Her half-sister Elizabeth took over the throne, becoming Queen **Elizabeth I.** Elizabeth was a Protestant. She restored the Anglican Church and went on to become one of the greatest rulers in English history.

✔️ **Reading Check** **Cause and Effect** Why did Henry VIII create the Anglican Church?

Missionaries Go Overseas

Main Idea As part of the Counter-Reformation, Catholic kingdoms began sending missionaries overseas to convert people to Christianity.

Reading Focus Do you think spreading democracy is important? Read to learn how Catholic missionaries tried to spread their religion to other people in the world.

When the Counter-Reformation began, many Catholics became committed to spreading their faith. As part of this new energy and determination, Catholic kingdoms began sending missionaries overseas to America and Asia.

The Jesuits were active missionaries in the 1500s and 1600s. French and Spanish Jesuits headed to America and Asia. In America, the Native Americans called them the "Black Robes."

The first Jesuit missionary to Japan, Francis Xavier, arrived in 1549. The Japanese at first welcomed the Jesuits. By 1600, the Jesuits had converted thousands of Japanese to Christianity.

Eventually the Jesuits clashed with people who believed in Buddhism and Shintoism. The Japanese Shogun, or military ruler, banned Christianity in Japan and expelled all missionaries.

Spanish missionaries had much greater success in the Philippine Islands. Most of the people there eventually became Catholic. Today the Philippines are the only Asian country with a Catholic majority. French missionaries tried to convert the people of Vietnam but were expelled by Vietnam's emperor.

✓ **Reading Check** **Identify** In what parts of the world did Catholic missionaries teach?

Section 4 Review

History Online
Homework Helper Need help with the material in this section? Visit jat.glencoe.com

Reading Summary
Review the Main Ideas

- Across Europe, religious wars between Catholics and Protestants were fought in the 1500s and 1600s, while the Spanish monarchs tried to make Spain an exclusively Catholic country.

- In England, Henry VIII broke with the Catholic Church and created the Anglican Church. Puritans later tried to reform the Anglican Church and then fled to America.

- Catholic missionaries tried to spread their religion to Asia and America.

What Did You Learn?

1. What was the Council of Trent, and what did it accomplish?

2. Why was the Edict of Nantes important?

Critical Thinking

3. **Organizing Information** Draw a chart like the one below. Fill in details about the steps the Catholic Church took to counter the Reformation.

Church's Efforts to Stop Protestantism

4. **Analyze** Why did Henry VIII form the Anglican Church?

5. **Explain** Who were the Puritans, and what were their beliefs and practices?

6. **Predict** How do you think conflicts over religion affected the world outside of Europe?

7. **Expository Writing** Write a short essay summarizing the history of Catholicism in Spain in the 1400s and 1500s.

Chapter 17 Reading Review

Section 1 The Renaissance Begins

Vocabulary
Renaissance
secular
diplomacy

Focusing on the Main Ideas
- The wealthy urban society of the Italian city-states brought a rebirth of learning and art to Europe. *(page 609)*
- Italy's location helped its city-states grow wealthy from trade and banking, but many of the cities fell under the control of strong rulers. *(page 611)*
- Unlike medieval nobles, the nobles of the Italian city-states lived in cities and were active in trade, banking, and public life. *(page 614)*

Section 2 New Ideas and Art

Vocabulary
humanism
vernacular

Focusing on the Main Ideas
- Humanists studied the Greeks and Romans, and the development of the printing press helped spread their ideas. *(page 619)*
- Renaissance artists used new techniques to produce paintings that showed people in an emotional and realistic way. *(page 623)*
- Renaissance ideas and art spread from Italy to northern Europe. *(page 625)*

Section 3 The Reformation Begins

Vocabulary
Reformation
indulgence
denomination
theology
predestination

Focusing on the Main Ideas
- The reforms of Martin Luther led to the creation of new Christian churches. *(page 634)*
- Political leaders often supported Protestantism because they wanted more power. *(page 639)*
- John Calvin's Protestant teachings spread across Europe and into North America. *(page 640)*

▲ Gutenberg Bible

Section 4 Catholics and Protestants

Vocabulary
seminary
heresy
annul

Focusing on the Main Ideas
- Catholics and Protestants fought religious wars across Europe. *(page 643)*
- Henry VIII created the Anglican Church in England. *(page 648)*
- As part of the Counter-Reformation, Catholic kingdoms began sending missionaries overseas to convert people to Christianity. *(page 650)*

Review Vocabulary

Write **True** beside each true statement. Replace the word in italics to make false statements true.

___ 1. *Diplomacy* is the art of negotiating.

___ 2. When the pope needed money in the 1500s, he sold *indulgences.*

___ 3. The Renaissance belief that the individual and human society were important was known as *theology.*

___ 4. A *heresy* is a special school for training and educating priests.

___ 5. *Predestination* encouraged Calvinists to prove they were among the saved.

___ 6. Writers began to write in the *secular*, the everyday language of a region.

Review Main Ideas

Section 1 • The Renaissance Begins

7. What set the stage for the Renaissance in Italy?

8. What made nobles of the Renaissance different from nobles of previous times?

Section 2 • New Ideas and Art

9. What did the humanists believe?

10. How did Renaissance art differ from the art of the Middle Ages?

Section 3 • The Reformation Begins

11. What happened when Martin Luther tried to reform the Catholic Church?

12. Describe John Calvin's teachings.

Section 4 • Catholics and Protestants

13. Where and why did the Thirty Years' War begin?

14. What changed England from a Catholic to a Protestant country?

Critical Thinking

15. **Analyze** Do you think banking played a role in the wealth and art of the Italian city-states? Explain.

16. **Conclude** Some Puritans moved to North America to practice their religion without interference from European leaders. How was that desire for religious freedom reflected in the U.S. Constitution?

Review

Reading Skill | Analyze and Clarify

Go Beyond the Words

17. Read this passage about the importance of the printing press. Then answer the questions at the right to help you analyze and clarify how the printing press affected Europe.

In the early 1450s, Johannes Gutenberg developed a printing press that used movable metal type. This type of printing press made it possible to print many books much more quickly. With more books available, more people learned to read. Scholars could read one another's work and debate their ideas in letters. Ideas grew and spread more quickly than ever before in Europe.

Who? _____   Where? _____

What? _____   Why? _____

When? _____

To review this skill, see pages 606–607.

Geography Skills

Study the map below and answer the following questions.

18. **Location** What geographical advantage does Venice have over Milan?

19. **Human/Environment Interaction** Why might Mantua have been at a disadvantage in terms of trade?

20. **Movement** If you traveled from the city of Florence to the city of Venice, in what direction would you be going?

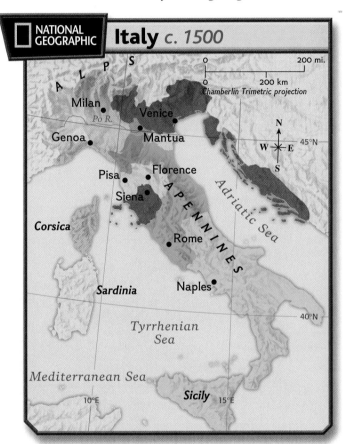

NATIONAL GEOGRAPHIC

Italy c. 1500

Using Technology

23. **Researching** The Renaissance revived the Greek idea that a well-rounded person took part in a variety of activities, including sports. Use the Internet and your local library to research one of the following sports of the Renaissance: javelin hurling, tennis, archery, fencing, boxing, or hunting. Present your findings to your classmates. Discuss who participated and any resemblances to modern-day sports.

Linking Past and Present

24. **Inferring** Renaissance artists, architects, and writers were greatly influenced by ancient Greek and Roman culture. Do you think people in those professions today are equally influenced by artists and writers of the past? Why or why not?

Read to Write

21. **Expository Writing** Research the life of Renaissance nobles, merchants, shopkeepers, or peasants. Then write an essay describing the lifestyle and position of the group you chose.

22. **Using Your FOLDABLES** Use information in your completed foldable to create a poster about one of the changes that occurred during the Renaissance and Reformation. Draw pictures, write captions, create titles, and so on. Present your poster to the class.

Primary Source Analyze

These are two of Luther's Ninety-Five Theses.

"37. Every true Christian, whether living or dead, has a share in all the benefits of Christ and of the Church, . . . even without letters of pardon. . . .

45. Christians should be taught that he who sees any one in need, and, passing him by, gives money for pardons, is not purchasing for himself the indulgences of the Pope but the anger of God. . . ."

—Martin Luther, "Ninety-five Theses"

DBQ Document-Based Questions

25. According to Luther, is the buying of indulgences necessary?
26. What does Luther say is a use for money that will please God?

Chapter 18

Enlightenment and Revolution

◄ A statue of Louis XIV on horseback outside of the palace of Versailles in France

NATIONAL GEOGRAPHIC

When & Where?

1500	1600	1700	1800
1492 Columbus reaches the Americas	**1543** Copernicus supports idea of sun-centered universe	**1690** John Locke writes about government	**1776** Declaration of Independence is signed

Chapter Preview

By the end of the Renaissance, Europe and the rest of the world were entering a time of rapid change. Read this chapter to find out how voyages of exploration and scientific discoveries affected people in different parts of the world.

History Online

Chapter Overview Visit jat.glencoe.com for a preview of Chapter 18.

 View the Chapter 18 video in the *World History: Journey Across Time* Video Program.

The Age of Exploration

In the 1400s, Europeans began to explore overseas and build empires. Trade increased and goods, technology, and ideas were exchanged around the world.

The Scientific Revolution

Scientific ideas and discoveries gave Europeans a new way to understand the universe.

The Enlightenment

During the 1700s, many Europeans believed that reason could be used to make government and society better.

The American Revolution

Britain and France established colonies in North America. Britain's American colonies eventually rebelled against Britain and formed a new nation, the United States.

FOLDABLES™
Study Organizer

Summarizing Information *Make this foldable to help you organize and summarize information about the Enlightenment and era of revolutions.*

Step 1 *Mark the midpoint of a side edge of one sheet of paper. Then fold the outside edges in to touch the midpoint.*

Step 2 *Fold the paper in half again from side to side.*

Step 3 *Open the paper and cut along the inside fold lines to form four tabs.*

Cut along the fold lines on both sides.

Step 4 *Label as shown.*

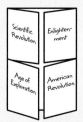
Scientific Revolution | Enlightenment
Age of Exploration | American Revolution

Reading and Writing *As you read the chapter, write information under each appropriate tab. Be sure to summarize the information you find by writing only main ideas and supporting details.*

**Reading
Skill**

Monitor and Adjust

1 Learn It!

Your Reading Strengths

Different people read differently. Some people read and understand something quickly, while other people may need to read something several times to comprehend it fully. It is important to identify your own strengths and weaknesses as a reader.

Read the following paragraph describing the story of how Newton discovered gravity:

> According to tradition, Newton was sitting in his garden one day when he watched an apple fall to the ground. The apple's fall led him to the idea of gravity, or the pull of the earth and other bodies on objects at or near their surfaces.
>
> —*from pages 675–676*

Reading Tip

Depending upon what you are reading, you may need to slow down or speed up. When you study, read more slowly. When you read for pleasure, you can read more quickly.

- Can you visualize this scene in your mind, almost like a movie?
- Are there any words you do not know?
- What questions do you have about this passage?
- What does this scene make you think of based on what you have previously read, seen, or experienced?
- Do you need to reread it?

2 Practice It!

Improve Your Reading

The paragraph below appears in Section 3. Read the passage and answer the questions that follow.

> During the 1600s and 1700s, many European thinkers favored limits on government power. However, powerful kings and queens ruled most of Europe. This system was known as **absolutism.** In this system, monarchs held absolute, or total, power. They claimed to rule by divine right, or by the will of God. This meant that rulers did not answer to their people, but rather to God alone.
>
> —*from page 686*

Read to Write

Choose one explorer, philosopher, or scientist that you were introduced to in this chapter. Write a list of questions that a modern talk-show host might ask if he or she interviewed this person.

▼ **Catherine the Great**

◄ **Peter the Great**

- What words or sentences made you slow down as you read?
- Did you have to reread any parts?
- What questions do you still have after reading this passage?

3 Apply It!

As you read the chapter, identify one paragraph in each section that is difficult to understand. Discuss each paragraph with a partner to improve your understanding.

The Age of Exploration

Get Ready to Read!

What's the Connection?
You have learned how Italy's cities grew rich from trade. In the 1400s, other European states began exploring the world in search of wealth.

Focusing on the Main Ideas

- In the 1400s, trade, technology, and the rise of strong kingdoms led to a new era of exploration. *(page 659)*

- While the Portuguese explored Africa, the Spanish, English, and French explored America. *(page 661)*

- To increase trade, Europeans set up colonies and created joint-stock companies. *(page 666)*

- Exploration and trade led to a worldwide exchange of products, people, and ideas. *(page 668)*

Locating Places
Strait of Magellan (muh•JEH•luhn)
Netherlands (NEH•thuhr•luhnz)
Moluccas (muh•LUH•kuhz)

Meeting People
Vasco da Gama

Christopher Columbus

Magellan (muh•JEH•luhn)

John Cabot (KA•buht)

Jacques Cartier
(ZHAHK kahr•TYAY)

Building Your Vocabulary
mercantilism
(MUHR•kuhn•TUH•LIH•zuhm)

export (EHK•SPOHRT)
import (IHM•POHRT)
colony (KAH•luh•nee)
commerce (KAH•muhrs)
invest (ihn•VEHST)

Reading Strategy
Cause and Effect Complete a diagram like the one below showing why Europeans began to explore.

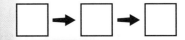

NATIONAL GEOGRAPHIC When & Where?

NORTH AMERICA
EUROPE
CHINA
INDIA
AFRICA
SOUTH AMERICA

1400

1500

1600

1420 Portugal begins mapping Africa's coast

1492 Columbus reaches the Americas

1520 Magellan's crew sails around the world

1588 England defeats the Armada

Europe Gets Ready to Explore

Main Idea In the 1400s, trade, technology, and the rise of strong kingdoms led to a new era of exploration.

Reading Focus Do you like traveling to places that you have never been? Read to see why Western Europeans set off to explore the world.

◀ Early compass

▲ European explorers and traders began to use smaller, faster ships called caravels in the 1400s. *What advantage did triangular sails offer a ship?*

Astrolabe ▲

In the 1400s and 1500s, nations in Western Europe began exploring the world. They soon gained control of the Americas and parts of India and Southeast Asia as well. Why did they begin exploring in the 1400s? Many events came together to create just the right conditions for exploration.

Trade With Asia As you have read, in the Middle Ages, Europeans began buying vast amounts of spices, silks, and other goods from Asia. In the 1400s, however, it became harder to get those goods.

First of all, the Mongol Empire had collapsed. The Mongols had kept the Silk Road running smoothly. When their empire collapsed, local rulers along the Silk Road imposed new taxes on merchants. This made Asian goods more expensive.

Next, the Ottoman Turks conquered the Byzantine Empire and blocked Italian merchants from entering the Black Sea. The Italians had trading posts on the coast of the Black Sea where they bought goods from Asia. Now, they could no longer reach them. They had to trade with the Turks instead, and this drove prices even higher.

Europeans still wanted the spices and silks of East Asia. Anyone who could find a way to get them cheaply would make a lot of money. Merchants began looking for a route to East Asia that bypassed the Middle East. If they could not get there by land, maybe they could get there by sea.

New Technology Even though the Europeans wanted to go exploring, they could not do it without the right technology. The Atlantic Ocean was too dangerous and difficult to navigate.

By the 1400s, they had the technology they needed. From the Arabs, Europeans learned about the astrolabe and the compass. The astrolabe was an ancient Greek device that could be used to find latitude. The compass, invented by the Chinese, helped navigators find magnetic north.

Even with these new tools, the Europeans needed better ships. In the 1400s, they began using triangular sails developed by the Arabs. These sails let a ship zigzag into the wind.

▲ Prince Henry's school for navigation helped make possible the discovery of new water routes and new lands. Here, Prince Henry is shown watching for the return of his ships. *What types of professionals did Prince Henry invite to his research center?*

They also began building ships with many masts and smaller sails to make their ships go faster. A new type of rudder made steering easier. In the 1400s, these inventions came together in a Portuguese ship called the caravel. With ships like the caravel, Europeans could begin exploring the world.

The Rise of Strong Nations
Even with new technology, exploration was still expensive and dangerous. For most of the Middle Ages, Europe's kingdoms were weak and could not afford to explore. This situation began to change in the 1400s.

The rise of towns and trade helped make governments stronger. Kings and queens could tax the trade in their kingdom and then use the money to build armies and navies. Using their new power, they were able to build strong central governments.

By the end of the 1400s, four strong kingdoms—Portugal, Spain, France, and England—had been built in Europe. They had harbors on the Atlantic Ocean and were anxious to find a sea route to Asia. The question was where to go.

Did Maps Encourage Exploration?
By the 1400s, most educated people in Europe knew the world was round, but they only had maps of Europe and the Mediterranean. When the Renaissance began, however, people began to study ancient maps as well as books written by Arab scholars.

Twelve hundred years earlier, a Greek-educated Egyptian geographer named Claudius Ptolemy had drawn maps of the world. His book *Geography* was discovered by Europeans in 1406 and printed in 1475.

With the invention of the printing press, books like Ptolemy's could be printed and sold all over Europe. Ptolemy's ideas about cartography, or the science of mapmaking, were very influential. His basic system of longitude and latitude is still used today.

European cartographers also began reading a book written by al-Idrisi, an Arab geographer. Al-Idrisi had published a book in 1154 showing the parts of the world known to Muslims. By studying the works of al-Idrisi and Ptolemy, Europeans learned the geography of East Africa and the Indian Ocean. If they could find a way around Africa, they could get to Asia.

✔ **Reading Check** **Summarize** What were the main reasons the Europeans began exploring the world in the 1400s?

Exploring the World

Main Idea While the Portuguese explored Africa, the Spanish, English, and French explored America.

Reading Focus Have you ever done something daring or tried something new not knowing how it would turn out? Read to learn how European explorers took chances and went places no Europeans had ever been before.

By the early 1400s, Europeans were ready to explore. England and France were still fighting each other, however, and Spain was still fighting the Muslims. This gave Portugal the chance to explore first.

Who Was Henry the Navigator?

In 1419 Prince Henry of Portugal, known as "Henry the Navigator," set up a research center in southern Portugal. He invited sailors, cartographers, and shipbuilders to come and help him explore the world.

In 1420 Portugal began mapping Africa's coastline and trading with Africa's kingdoms. It also seized the Azores (AY• ZOHRZ), Madeira (muh•DIHR•uh), and Cape Verde islands. Soon after, the Portuguese discovered sugarcane would grow on the islands.

Sugar was very valuable in Europe. To work their sugarcane fields, the Portuguese began bringing enslaved Africans to the islands. This was the beginning of a slave trade that would eventually bring millions of enslaved people to the Americas as well.

In 1488 the Portuguese explorer Bartolomeu Dias reached the southern tip of Africa. Nine years later, **Vasco da Gama** (VAS•koh dah GA•muh) rounded the tip of Africa, raced across the Indian Ocean, and landed on India's coast. A water route to East Asia had at last been found.

Santa María

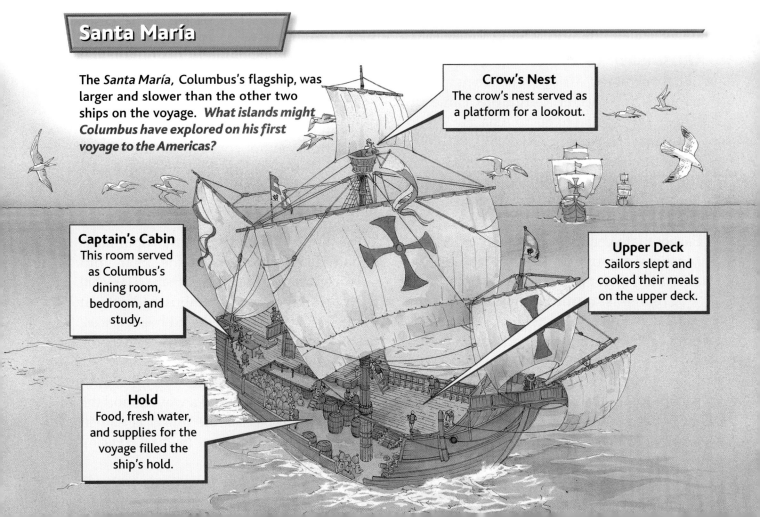

The *Santa María*, Columbus's flagship, was larger and slower than the other two ships on the voyage. *What islands might Columbus have explored on his first voyage to the Americas?*

Crow's Nest
The crow's nest served as a platform for a lookout.

Captain's Cabin
This room served as Columbus's dining room, bedroom, and study.

Upper Deck
Sailors slept and cooked their meals on the upper deck.

Hold
Food, fresh water, and supplies for the voyage filled the ship's hold.

European Exploration of the World

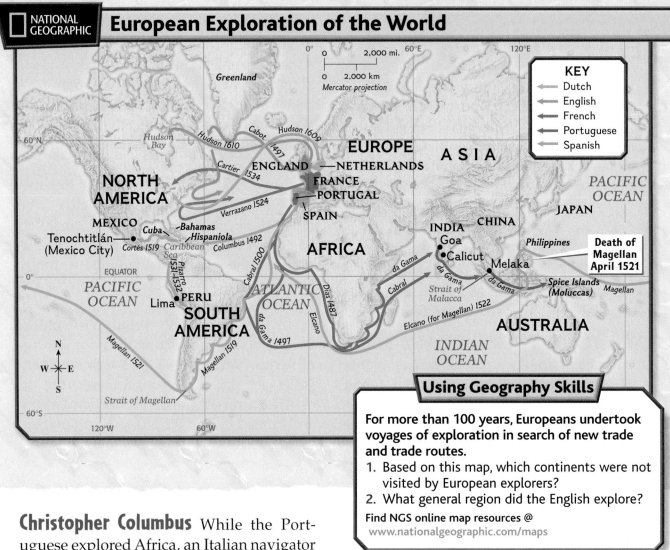

KEY
← Dutch
← English
← French
← Portuguese
← Spanish

Using Geography Skills

For more than 100 years, Europeans undertook voyages of exploration in search of new trade and trade routes.

1. Based on this map, which continents were not visited by European explorers?
2. What general region did the English explore?

Find NGS online map resources @ www.nationalgeographic.com/maps

Christopher Columbus While the Portuguese explored Africa, an Italian navigator named **Christopher Columbus** came up with a daring plan to get to Asia. He would sail across the Atlantic Ocean.

Columbus needed money to make the trip. The rulers of Portugal, England, and France all turned him down. Finally in 1492 Ferdinand and Isabella of Spain said yes. Earlier that year, they had finally driven the Muslims out of Spain. They could now afford to pay for exploration.

Columbus outfitted three ships: the *Santa María,* the *Niña,* and the *Pinta.* In 1492 they left Spain and headed west. As the weeks passed, the crew grew desperate. Finally they sighted land, probably the island of San Salvador. Columbus claimed the land for Spain and then explored the nearby islands of Cuba and Hispaniola.

Columbus thought he was in Asia. He made three more voyages to the region but never realized he had arrived in the Americas. Eventually, Europeans realized they had found two huge continents.

Who Was Magellan? Many Spaniards explored the Americas in the 1500s, but only Ferdinand **Magellan** (muh•JEH•luhn) tried to finish what Columbus had set out to do. In 1520 he left Spain and headed west to sail around the Americas and then all the way to Asia.

Magellan sailed south along South America. Finally, he found a way around the continent. The passage he found is named the **Strait of Magellan** (muh•JEH•luhn).

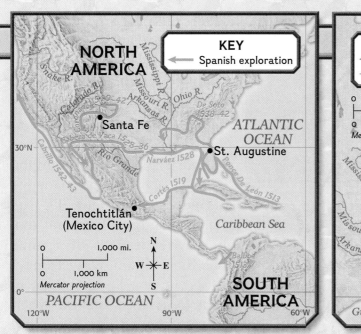

KEY
← Spanish exploration

NORTH AMERICA

Snake R. · Colorado R. · De Soto 1539-42 · Arkansas R. · Ohio R. · Missouri R. · Mississippi R.

ATLANTIC OCEAN

• Santa Fe

30°N · Cabrillo 1542-43 · Cabeza de Vaca 15?8-36 · Rio Grande · Narváez 1528 · St. Augustine · Cortés 1519 · Ponce De León 1513

Tenochtitlán (Mexico City)

Caribbean Sea

Balboa 1513?

0 1,000 mi.
0 1,000 km
Mercator projection

120°W · PACIFIC OCEAN · 90°W · SOUTH AMERICA · 60°W

0°

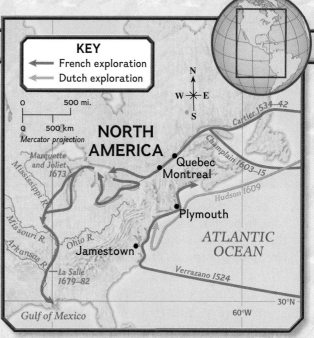

KEY
← French exploration
← Dutch exploration

0 500 mi.
0 500 km
Mercator projection

NORTH AMERICA

Marquette and Joliet 1673 · Mississippi R. · Missouri R. · Arkansas R. · Ohio R.

• Quebec
Montreal
Cartier 1534-42
Champlain 1603-15
Hudson 1609

• Plymouth

• Jamestown

La Salle 1679-82

ATLANTIC OCEAN

Verrazano 1524

Gulf of Mexico · 60°W · 30°N

Important European Explorers

Christopher Columbus

Voyages: 1492, 1493, 1498, 1502

First European to sail west searching for a water route to Asia

Vasco da Gama

Voyage: 1497–1499

First European to sail around the south of Africa and reach India

Ferdinand Magellan

Voyage: 1519–1522

Led the first expedition to sail completely around the world

Jacques Cartier

Voyages: 1534, 1535, 1541

Explored the St. Lawrence River

Henry Hudson

Voyages: 1607, 1608, 1609, 1610

Explored the Hudson River and Hudson Bay

After passing through the stormy strait, his ship entered a vast sea. It was so peaceful, or pacific, that he named the sea the Pacific Ocean.

Magellan then headed west. His sailors nearly starved and had to eat leather, sawdust, and rats. Finally, after four months at sea, they reached the Philippines. After local people killed Magellan, his crew continued west across the Indian Ocean, around Africa, and back to Spain. They became the first

known people to circumnavigate (suhr•kuhm• NA•vuh•GAYT), or sail around, the world.

The First English and French Explorers

As the news spread about Columbus's journey, England decided to search for a northern route to Asia. In 1497 an English ship commanded by **John Cabot** (KA•buht) headed across the Atlantic.

Cabot arrived at a large island he named Newfoundland. He then traveled south

▲ To defeat the Spanish Armada, the English sent ships that had been set on fire toward the Spanish warships. *Why was the defeat of the Spanish Armada important?*

along the coast of present-day Canada but did not find a path through to Asia. Cabot disappeared on his second trip and was never heard from again.

In 1524 France sent Giovanni da Verrazano to map America's coast and find a route through to Asia. Verrazano mapped from what is today North Carolina north to Newfoundland but found no path to Asia.

Ten years later, the French tried again. This time they sent **Jacques Cartier** (ZHAHK kahr•TYAY). Cartier sailed past Newfoundland and entered the St. Lawrence River. Hoping he had found a passage to Asia, Cartier made two more trips to map the St. Lawrence River. After these trips, France stopped exploring. By the mid-1500s, French Protestants and Catholics were fighting a civil war. There was no more exploring until it was settled.

Spain Fights England

After Columbus, the Spanish went on to build a vast empire in America. They forced enslaved Native Americans to grow sugarcane and mine gold and silver. Later they brought enslaved Africans to the region to work on their farms.

Spanish nobles called conquistadors traveled to America in the hopes of becoming rich. Hernán Cortés conquered the Aztec, and Francisco Pizarro conquered the Inca. Soon after their victories, vast amounts of gold and silver began to flow to Europe from Spain's empire in America.

Meanwhile, England had become Spain's enemy. As you have read, in 1527 King Henry VIII of England broke from the Catholic Church and made his kingdom Protestant. By the 1560s, the Dutch had become Protestant, too, even though they were part of Spain's empire at that time. Spain was strongly Catholic and tried to stop Protestantism in the **Netherlands** (NEH•thuhr•luhnz). When the Dutch people rebelled against Spain, England came to their aid.

To help the Dutch, Queen Elizabeth I of England let English privateers attack Spanish ships. Privateers are privately owned ships that have a license from the government to attack ships of other countries. People nicknamed the English privateers "sea dogs." They raided the Spanish treasure ships that were bringing gold back from America.

England's raids frustrated Philip II, the king of Spain. In 1588 he sent a huge fleet known as the Spanish Armada to invade England. In July 1588, the Armada headed into the English Channel—the narrow body of water between England and Europe. The Spanish ships were large and had many guns, but they were hard to steer. The smaller English ships moved much more quickly. Their attacks forced the Armada to retreat north. There a great storm arose and broke up the Armada.

The defeat of the Spanish Armada was an important event. The Spanish were still strong, but England now had the power to stand up to them. This encouraged the English and Dutch to begin exploring both North America and Asia.

☑ **Reading Check** **Identify** Who was the first European to sail to India? Whose crew was first to sail around the world?

Biography

ELIZABETH I

1533–1603

▲ Queen Elizabeth I

Elizabeth I is one of the most popular British rulers—but she was more loved by the people of England than by her father, King Henry VIII. Elizabeth's young life was filled with change and sadness. She was born to Henry VIII and his second wife, Anne Boleyn. The king was upset when Elizabeth was born, because he wanted a boy to inherit the throne.

When Elizabeth became queen, she surrounded herself with intelligent advisers. Together they turned England into a strong, prosperous country. Elizabeth supported Protestantism in England and in the rest of Europe. She sent aid to the French Huguenots and Protestants in Scotland and the Netherlands. She worked well with Parliament but called few sessions during her reign. She was a skilled writer and speaker and won the love and support of the English people.

Elizabeth never married, which was unusual at that time. Many men were interested in marrying her, but she turned down their proposals. One reason Elizabeth probably remained single was to maintain control of the government at a time when most rulers were men. She also used her status to the advantage of England. Many prominent men wanted to marry her, and she sometimes threatened to marry someone's enemy in order to get him to do what she wanted.

Elizabeth's personality also influenced England's society. She loved horse riding, dances, parties, and plays. Her support of the arts resulted in the development of new English literature and music. Elizabeth was so popular by the time of her death that the date she became queen was celebrated as a national holiday for 200 years.

> **"I have the heart and stomach of a king and of a king of England, too."**
> —Elizabeth I, "Armada Speech"

Then and Now

Even though Queen Elizabeth I had an unhappy childhood, she overcame it to become one of England's most popular leaders. Today England's Queen Elizabeth II has also faced sad situations. Research her life and write a short essay comparing her life to the life of Elizabeth I.

The Commercial Revolution

Main Idea To increase trade, Europeans set up colonies and created joint-stock companies.

Reading Focus Do you know anyone who works at home? Read to learn how merchants in the 1600s gave people jobs at home and changed the world trade system.

While Spain built its empire in America, Portugal began building a trading empire in Asia. In 1500, shortly after Vasco da Gama's trip, the Portuguese sent 13 ships back to India. Led by Pedro Alvares Cabral (PAY•throo AHL•vahr•ihs kuh•BRAHL), the Portuguese fought a war against the Muslim merchants in the Indian Ocean.

After defeating the Arab fleet, the Portuguese built trading posts in India, China, Japan, the Persian Gulf, and in the **Moluccas** (muh•LUH•kuhz), or Spice Islands of Southeast Asia. From these bases, they controlled most of southern Asia's sea trade.

What Is Mercantilism?

As Europeans watched Spain and Portugal grow wealthy from their empires, they tried to figure out how they had become rich. They came up with the idea of **mercantilism** (MUHR•kuhn•TUH•LIH•zuhm). Mercantilism is the idea that a country gains power by building up its supply of gold and silver. Mercantilists believe the best way to do this is to **export** (EHK•SPOHRT), or sell to other countries, more goods than you **import** (IHM•POHRT), or buy from them. If you export more than you import, more gold and silver flows in from other countries than goes out.

Mercantilists also thought countries should set up colonies. A **colony** (KAH•luh•nee) is a settlement of people living in a new territory controlled by their home country. Colonists are supposed to produce goods their country does not have at home. That

▲ These ships sailed for the Dutch East India Company, which carried out trade in Asia. *Which European nation did the Dutch replace in the spice trade?*

way, the home country will not have to import those goods from other countries.

Trade Empires in Asia

Mercantilism encouraged Europeans to set up trading posts and colonies in Asia and North America. By the end of the 1500s, Spain had set up a colony in the Philippines. The Spanish shipped silver to the Philippines from America and then used it to buy Asian spices and silk for sale in Europe.

In the 1600s, English and French merchants landed in India and began trading with the people there. In 1619 the Dutch built a fort on the island of Java, in what is now Indonesia. They slowly pushed the Portuguese out of the spice trade.

What Are Joint-Stock Companies?

Trading overseas was very expensive. In the 1600s, however, new ways of doing business developed in Europe. Historians call this the "commercial revolution." **Commerce** (KAH•muhrs) is the buying and selling of goods in large amounts over long distances.

To trade goods long distance, merchants needed a lot of money. They had to buy many goods, store them in warehouses, and ship them over land and sea. They had to know what people in distant lands wanted to buy and what prices were like there.

This new business created a new type of businessperson called an entrepreneur. Entrepreneurs **invest** (ihn•VEHST), or put money into a project. Their goal is to make even more money when the project is done.

Many projects were so large that a group of entrepreneurs had to come together and form a joint-stock company. A joint-stock company is a business that people can invest in by buying a share of the company. These shares are called stocks.

What Is the Cottage Industry?
To trade over a long distance, merchants need a large supply of goods. They also have to buy goods at low prices so they can make money selling them at higher prices elsewhere.

By the 1600s, merchants had become frustrated by artisans and guilds. They charged too much and could not make goods fast enough. So merchants began asking peasants to make goods for them. In particular, they asked the peasants to make wool cloth. The peasants were happy to make extra money and glad to find work they could do in their homes.

This system was called the "putting out" system. Merchants would buy wool and put it out to the peasants. This system is also sometimes called the "cottage industry," because the small houses where peasants lived were called cottages.

✓ Reading Check Explain How did merchants raise the money for overseas trade?

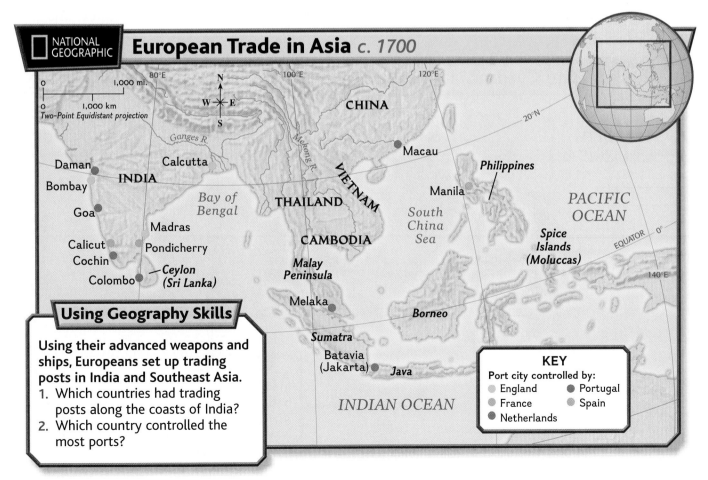

NATIONAL GEOGRAPHIC

European Trade in Asia *c. 1700*

Using Geography Skills

Using their advanced weapons and ships, Europeans set up trading posts in India and Southeast Asia.
1. Which countries had trading posts along the coasts of India?
2. Which country controlled the most ports?

KEY
Port city controlled by:
- England
- Portugal
- France
- Spain
- Netherlands

A Global Exchange

Main Idea Exploration and trade led to a world-wide exchange of products, people, and ideas.

Reading Focus Have you heard about insects from other countries that hurt American crops? Read to learn how the movement of goods and people between America and the rest of the world caused great changes.

After the Age of Exploration, the economies of Europe, Africa, Asia, and America changed. As Europe traded with the world, a global exchange of people, goods, technology, ideas, and even diseases began. We call this transfer the Columbian Exchange, after Christopher Columbus.

Two important foods—corn and potatoes—were taken to Europe from North America. Corn was used to feed animals. Larger, healthier animals resulted in more meat, leather, and wool. The potato was also important. Europeans discovered that if they planted potatoes instead of grain, about four times as many people could live off the same amount of land.

Other American foods, such as squash, beans, and tomatoes, also made their way to Europe. Tomatoes greatly changed cooking in Italy, where tomato sauces became very popular. Chocolate was a popular food from Central America. By mixing it with milk and sugar, Europeans created a sweet that is still popular today.

Some American foods, such as chili peppers and peanuts, were taken to Europe, but they also made their way to Asia and Africa where they became popular. Both Europeans and Asians also began smoking tobacco, an American plant.

Many European and Asian grains, such as wheat, oats, barley, rye, and rice, were planted in the Americas. Coffee and tropical fruits, such as bananas, were brought to America as well. Eventually, coffee and

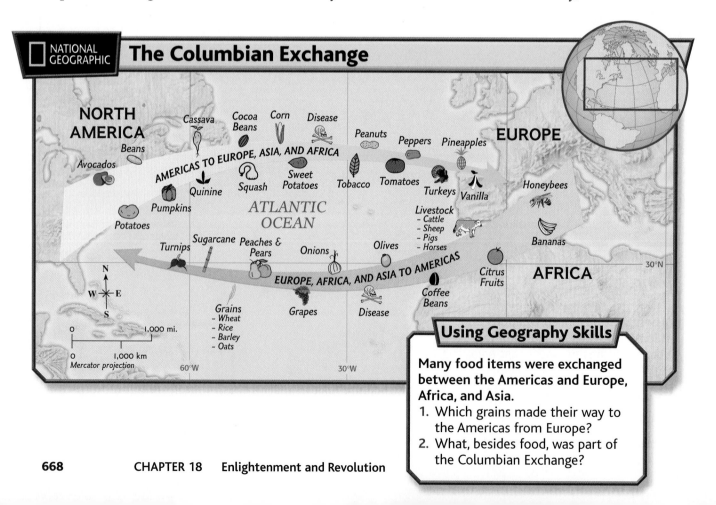

The Columbian Exchange

NORTH AMERICA — Cassava, Cocoa Beans, Corn, Disease, Beans, Avocados, Quinine, Squash, Sweet Potatoes, Tobacco, Pumpkins, Potatoes, Turnips, Sugarcane, Peaches & Pears, Onions

AMERICAS TO EUROPE, ASIA, AND AFRICA

ATLANTIC OCEAN

Peanuts, Peppers, Pineapples, Tomatoes, Turkeys, Vanilla, Olives, Livestock – Cattle – Sheep – Pigs – Horses

EUROPE, AFRICA, AND ASIA TO AMERICAS

EUROPE — Honeybees, Bananas

Grains – Wheat – Rice – Barley – Oats

Grapes, Disease, Coffee Beans, Citrus Fruits

AFRICA

30°N

60°W   30°W

0   1,000 mi.
0   1,000 km
Mercator projection

Using Geography Skills

Many food items were exchanged between the Americas and Europe, Africa, and Asia.

1. Which grains made their way to the Americas from Europe?
2. What, besides food, was part of the Columbian Exchange?

banana farms employed thousands of workers in Central and South America.

New animals such as pigs, sheep, cattle, chickens, and horses were also brought to America. Chickens changed the diet of many people in Central and South America, while horses changed the lives of Native Americans on the Great Plains. Horses provided a faster way to move from place to place. As a result, Native Americans began hunting buffalo as their main food source.

A huge movement of people also took place after Europeans obtained sugarcane from Asia and began growing it in the Caribbean. To plant and harvest the sugarcane, they enslaved millions of Africans and moved them to the Americas.

Europeans also changed Asian society. With their guns and powerful ships, the Europeans easily defeated Arab fleets and Indian princes. Across Asia, the Europeans forced local rulers to let them set up trading posts. Within a short time, the East India Company of England had built an empire in India, and the Dutch East India Company had built an empire in Indonesia.

The arrival of the Europeans in Japan also changed that society. Using guns and cannons imported from Europe, a new shogun was finally able to defeat the feudal lords, the daimyo, and reunite Japan.

Not everything exchanged between Europe and America was good. When Europeans arrived in America, they were carrying germs that could kill Native Americans. Many diseases, including smallpox, measles, and malaria, swept across the Americas killing millions of people.

✓ **Reading Check** **Describe** Describe the Columbian Exchange.

History Online
Homework Helper Need help with the material in this section? Visit jat.glencoe.com

Section 1 Review

Reading Summary

Review the Main Ideas

- Rising prices of Asian goods, strong central governments, and new sailing technology led to European exploration of the world.

- Portugal found a route to India while Spain, England, and France explored America.

- Europeans used joint-stock companies to build colonies and trading posts in Asia following the ideas of mercantilism.

- European exploration and trade brought about a global exchange of goods, technology, and disease.

What Did You Learn?

1. What was a caravel, and why was it important?

2. Describe the accomplishments of Ferdinand Magellan.

Critical Thinking

3. **Organize Information** Draw a chart like the one below. Use it to name the explorers discussed in this section, the country they sailed for, and the places they explored.

Explorer	Country Sailed for	Area Explored

4. **Summarize** Describe the development of the African slave trade.

5. **Understand Cause and Effect** Why did merchants create joint-stock companies and use cottage industries?

6. **Analyze** How did foods imported from the Americas benefit Europe? Identify some of those foods.

7. **Reading** **Monitor and Adjust** Write a 10-question multiple choice test to help you review the important information in this section. Exchange tests with a classmate.

Section 2

The Scientific Revolution

Get Ready to Read!

What's the Connection?
One result of the Renaissance was a new interest in science. During the 1600s, people began to observe, experiment, and reason to find new knowledge.

Focusing on the Main Ideas
- The thinkers of the ancient world developed early forms of science and passed this knowledge to later civilizations. *(page 671)*

- European interest in astronomy led to new discoveries and ideas about the universe and Earth's place in it. *(page 673)*

- The Scientific Revolution led to new discoveries in physics, medicine, and chemistry. *(page 675)*

- Using the scientific method, Europeans of the 1600s and 1700s developed new ideas about society based on reason. *(page 678)*

Meeting People
Ptolemy (TAH•luh•mee)
Copernicus (koh•PUHR•nih•kuhs)
Kepler (KEH•pluhr)
Galileo (GA•luh•LEE•oh)
Newton (NOO•tuhn)
Descartes (day•KAHRT)

Building Your Vocabulary
theory (THEE•uh•ree)
rationalism (RASH•nuh•LIH•zuhm)
scientific method
hypothesis (hy•PAH•thuh•suhs)

Reading Strategy
Compare and Contrast Use a diagram like the one below to show the similarities and differences in the views of Ptolemy and Copernicus.

Ptolemy   Copernicus

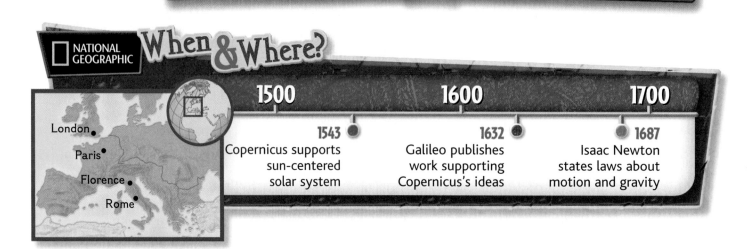

NATIONAL GEOGRAPHIC When & Where?

London
Paris
Florence
Rome

1500   **1600**   **1700**

1543
Copernicus supports sun-centered solar system

1632
Galileo publishes work supporting Copernicus's ideas

1687
Isaac Newton states laws about motion and gravity

The Scientific Revolution

Main Idea The thinkers of the ancient world developed early forms of science and passed this knowledge to later civilizations.

Reading Focus Have you ever taught a skill or passed on an idea to a younger brother or sister? Read in this chapter how the scientific ideas of early thinkers were passed on to later generations.

From earliest times, people have been curious about the world around them. Thousands of years ago, people began to use numbers, study the stars and planets, and watch the growth of plants and animals. These activities were the beginnings of science. Science is any organized study of the natural world and how it works.

Early Scientists

Early civilizations developed different kinds of science to solve practical problems. Among the first sciences were mathematics, astronomy, and medicine. Mathematics was used for record keeping and building projects. Astronomy helped people keep time and figure out when to plant and harvest crops. Early civilizations also developed medical practices, such as surgery, acupuncture, and the use of herbs, for treating illnesses.

The ancient Greeks left behind a large amount of scientific knowledge. They believed that reason was the only way to understand nature. As they studied the world, they developed theories. A **theory** (THEE•uh•ree) is an explanation of how or why something happens. A theory is based on what you can observe about something. It may not be correct, but it seems to fit the facts.

In Ancient Greece, the Greek philosopher Aristotle observed nature and collected vast amounts of information about plants and animals. He then took the facts

▲ This model shows the universe according to the ideas of the Polish astronomer Nicolaus Copernicus, with the sun at the universe's center. *What did Ptolemy's geocentric theory state?*

he gathered and classified, or arranged them into groups, based on their similarities and differences.

The Greeks made many important scientific advances, but their approach to science had some problems. For example, they did not experiment, or test, new ideas to see if they were true. Many of their conclusions were false because they were based on "common sense" instead of experiments.

For example, in the A.D. 100s, the Egyptian-born astronomer **Ptolemy** (TAH•luh•mee) stated that the sun and the planets moved around the earth in circular paths. After all, it did seem like the earth was the center of the universe. Astronomers in Europe accepted Ptolemy's geocentric, or earth-centered, theory for more than 1,400 years.

Science During the Middle Ages

Under Roman rule, Western thinkers continued to accept the scientific knowledge of the Greeks. After the fall of Rome, during the Middle Ages, most Europeans were more interested in theology, the study of God, than in the study of nature. For scientific knowledge, they relied on Greek and Roman writings and saw no need to check their facts or to make their own observations. Many of these ancient works, however, were either lost or poorly preserved. In the writings that survived, errors were added as copies were made.

Meanwhile, Arabs and Jews in the Islamic Empire preserved much of the science of the Greeks and Romans. They carefully copied many Greek and Roman works into the Arabic language. They also came into contact with the science of the Persians and the Indian system of mathematics.

Arabic and Jewish scientists made advances of their own in areas such as mathematics, astronomy, and medicine. However, in spite of these achievements, scientists in the Islamic world did not experiment or develop the instruments necessary to advance their scientific knowledge.

During the 1100s, European thinkers became interested in science again as a result of their contacts with the Islamic world. Major Islamic scientific works were brought to Europe and translated into Latin. The Hindu-Arabic system of numbers also spread to Europe, where it eventually replaced Roman numerals. Christian thinkers, such as Thomas Aquinas, tried to show that Christianity and reason could go together. During the 1100s, Europeans began building new universities. They

A New View of the Universe

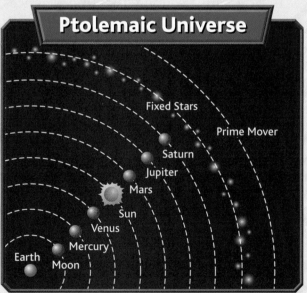

Ptolemaic Universe

Fixed Stars

Prime Mover

Saturn

Jupiter

Mars

Sun

Venus

Mercury

Earth

Moon

The astronomical theory of Ptolemy (left) placed Earth at the center of the universe (above). His theory was accepted for more than a thousand years. *According to the diagram, how many planets besides Earth were known at the time of Ptolemy?*

would play an important role in the growth of science.

Beginning in the 1400s, voyages of exploration further added to Europe's scientific knowledge. Better charts, maps, and navigational instruments helped voyagers reach different parts of the world. Through exploration, the size of oceans and continents became better known. Scientists gathered and classified new knowledge about plants, animals, and diseases in different parts of the world.

As scientific knowledge grew, the stage was set for a new understanding of the natural world that would shake Europe to its foundations.

✓ **Reading Check** **Describe** Describe scientific knowledge during the Middle Ages.

A Revolution in Astronomy

Main Idea European interest in astronomy led to new discoveries and ideas about the universe and Earth's place in it.

Reading Focus What would people on Earth think if life were discovered on other planets? Read to see how Europeans reacted to new discoveries about the universe.

During the 1500s, European thinkers began to break with the old scientific ideas. They increasingly understood that advances in science could only come through mathematics and experimentation. This new way of thinking led to a revolution, or sweeping change, in the way Europeans understood science and the search for knowledge. Astronomy was the first science affected by

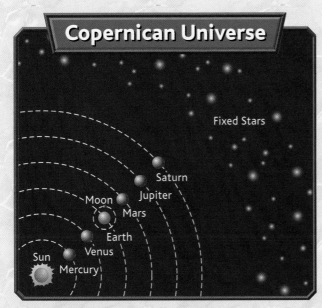

Copernican Universe

Fixed Stars

Saturn
Jupiter
Moon
Mars
Earth
Venus
Sun
Mercury

Nicolaus Copernicus (right), a Polish mathematician, believed that the sun was at the center of the universe. His model (above) placed Earth and the other planets in orbits around the sun. *Why did Europeans again become interested in science in the 1100s?*

the Scientific Revolution. New discoveries brought changes in the way Europeans saw the universe. They challenged traditional thinking that God had made the earth as the center of the universe.

Who Was Copernicus? Leading the Scientific Revolution was a Polish mathematician named Nicolaus **Copernicus** (koh•PUHR•nih•kuhs). In 1543 Copernicus wrote a book called *On the Revolutions of the Heavenly Spheres.* He disagreed with Ptolemy's view that the earth was the center of the universe. Copernicus believed that Ptolemy's theory was too complicated. Instead, he developed a simpler heliocentric, or sun-centered, theory of the universe. Copernicus's theory stated that the Sun, not Earth, was the center of the universe. The planets moved in circular paths around the Sun.

Kepler's Revolution The next step in the march of science was taken by a German astronomer named Johannes **Kepler** (KEH•pluhr). He supported Copernicus's theory but also made corrections to it. Kepler added the idea that the planets move in ellipses (ih•LIHPS•eez), or oval paths, rather than circular

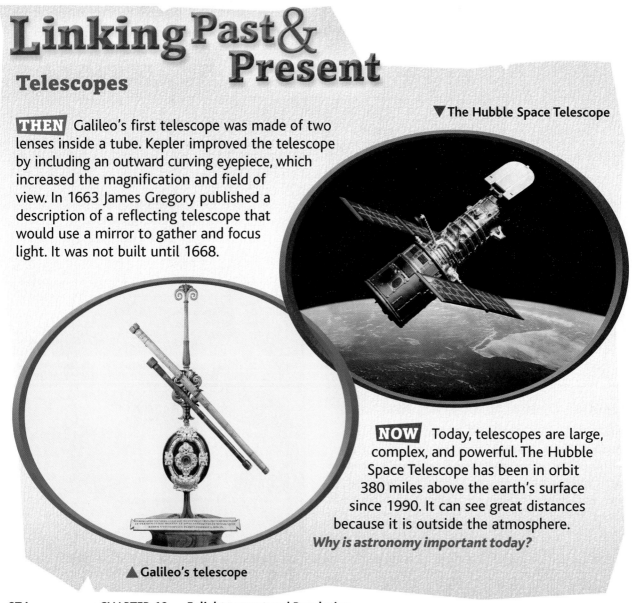

Linking Past & Present

Telescopes

THEN Galileo's first telescope was made of two lenses inside a tube. Kepler improved the telescope by including an outward curving eyepiece, which increased the magnification and field of view. In 1663 James Gregory published a description of a reflecting telescope that would use a mirror to gather and focus light. It was not built until 1668.

▼ The Hubble Space Telescope

NOW Today, telescopes are large, complex, and powerful. The Hubble Space Telescope has been in orbit 380 miles above the earth's surface since 1990. It can see great distances because it is outside the atmosphere.
Why is astronomy important today?

▲ Galileo's telescope

ones. His theory made it easier to explain the movements of the planets. It also marked the beginning of modern astronomy.

Who Was Galileo? An Italian scientist named Galileo Galilei made the third great breakthrough in the Scientific Revolution. **Galileo** (GA•luh•LEE•oh) believed that new knowledge could come through experiments that were carefully carried out. For example, Galileo challenged Aristotle's idea that the heavier the object is, the faster it falls to the ground. Galileo's experiments proved that Aristotle was wrong. Objects fall at the same speed regardless of their weight.

Galileo also realized that scientific instruments could help humans better explore the natural world. He improved instruments, such as the clock and telescope. With the telescope, Galileo found clear evidence supporting Copernicus's view that Earth revolves around the Sun.

Galileo also played an important role in the development of new scientific instruments. In 1593 he invented a water thermometer that, for the first time, allowed temperature changes to be measured. Galileo's assistant, Evangelista Torricelli, then used the element called mercury to build the first barometer, an instrument that measures air pressure.

When Galileo published his ideas in 1632, his work was condemned by the Roman Catholic Church. The Catholic Church held to the geocentric, or earth-centered, view of the universe, believing that it was taught in the Bible. The pope ordered Galileo to come to Rome to be tried for heresy. Church threats finally forced Galileo to withdraw many of his statements. Even so, Galileo's ideas spread throughout Europe and changed people's views about the universe.

Reading Check **Explain** How did Galileo prove Copernicus's theory?

New Scientific Discoveries

Main Idea The Scientific Revolution led to new discoveries in physics, medicine, and chemistry.

Reading Focus Think about all the facts you know about medicine. For example, you know your heart pumps blood, your lungs breathe air, and your body is made of cells. Read to learn how scientists of the 1600s and 1700s made discoveries we often take for granted today.

Throughout the 1600s and 1700s, the Scientific Revolution continued to spread. Many new discoveries were made in physics, medicine, and chemistry.

Who Is Isaac Newton? Despite continuing scientific breakthroughs, the ideas of Copernicus, Kepler, and Galileo needed to be brought together as one system. This feat was accomplished by an English mathematician named Isaac **Newton** (NOO•tuhn).

According to tradition, Newton was sitting in his garden one day when he watched an apple fall to the ground. The

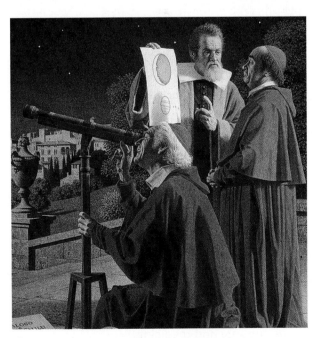

▲ In this painting, Galileo presents his astronomical findings to the Catholic clergy. *How did Galileo respond to the Church's condemnation of his work in astronomy?*

apple's fall led him to the idea of gravity, or the pull of the earth and other bodies on objects at or near their surfaces.

In a book called *Principia*, published in 1687, Newton stated his laws, or well-tested theories, about the motion of objects in space and on Earth. The most important was the universal law of gravitation. It explains that the force of gravity holds the entire solar system together by keeping the sun and the planets in their orbits. Newton's ideas led to the rise of modern physics, or the study of physical properties such as matter and energy.

Medicine and Chemistry

Sweeping changes were made in medicine in the 1500s and 1600s. Since Roman times, European doctors had relied on the teachings of the Greek

History Online

Web Activity Visit jat.glencoe.com and click on *Chapter 18—Student Web Activity* to learn more about early scientific discoveries.

physician Galen. Galen wanted to study the human body, but he was only allowed to dissect, or cut open, animals.

In the 1500s, however, a Flemish doctor named Andreas Vesalius began dissecting dead human bodies for research. In 1543 Vesalius published *On the Structure of the Human Body.* In this work, Vesalius presented a detailed account of the human body that replaced many of Galen's ideas.

Other breakthroughs in medicine took place. In the early 1600s, William Harvey, an English doctor, proved that blood flowed through the human body. In the mid-1600s, an English scientist named Robert Hooke began using a microscope, and he soon discovered cells, the smallest structures of living material.

Beginning in the 1600s, European scientists developed new ideas in chemistry. Chemistry is the study of natural substances and how they change. In the mid-1600s, Robert Boyle, an Irish scientist, proved that all substances are made up of basic elements that cannot be broken down.

European scientists of the 1700s also developed ways to study gases. They discovered hydrogen, carbon dioxide, and oxygen. By 1777, Antoine Lavoisier (AN•twahn luhv•WAH•zee•AY) of France had proven that materials need oxygen to burn. Marie Lavoisier, also a scientist, contributed to her husband's work.

Reading Check **Identify** According to Newton, what force held the planets in orbit?

The Scientific Revolution

Scientist	Nation	Discoveries
Nicolaus Copernicus (1473–1543)	Poland	Earth orbits the Sun; Earth rotates on its axis
Galileo Galilei (1564–1642)	Italy	other planets have moons
Johannes Kepler (1571–1630)	Germany	planets have elliptical orbits
William Harvey (1578–1657)	England	heart pumps blood
Robert Hooke (1635–1703)	England	cells
Robert Boyle (1627–1691)	Ireland	air is made of gases
Isaac Newton (1643–1727)	England	gravity; laws of motion; calculus
Antoine Lavoisier (1743–1794)	France	how materials burn

Understanding Charts

During the Scientific Revolution, scientists made discoveries in many fields, such as astronomy and medicine.
1. What did William Harvey discover?
2. Identify Which scientists' discoveries dealt with chemistry?

Biography

SIR ISAAC NEWTON
1642–1727

Isaac Newton was born into a farming family on December 25, 1642, in Woolsthorpe, England. His father died before Newton was born. His mother remarried when he was three years old. His new stepfather did not want the boy to live with them, so Newton was raised by his grandmother.

Newton earned a degree from Trinity College, part of Cambridge University, in 1664. He planned to work for the university, but from 1664 to 1666, it closed because of the plague. Newton spent the next two years in his hometown. While there, he made some of his most important discoveries. He developed his theory of gravity, invented a new kind of mathematics called calculus, and discovered that white light is made up of all of the different colors of light.

Newton returned to Cambridge, earned a master's degree, and was appointed to several positions there. His life was very stressful because many scientists questioned his calculations. These criticisms made Newton reluctant to publish his discoveries, but eventually he did. His book *Principia* is considered one of the greatest scientific books ever written. In it Newton describes his three laws of motion and his ideas about gravity.

▲ Newton analyzing light rays

"If I have seen farther, it is by standing upon the shoulders of giants."
–Isaac Newton, in a letter to Robert Hooke

During his life, Newton won many awards for his discoveries. In 1705 he became the first scientist ever to be knighted by the English king.

Then and Now

Newton's findings were criticized by some scientists of his time. Do research to find a scientific discovery made in the last 50 years that others have questioned or criticized. Describe your findings to the class.

▲ Trinity College today

The Triumph of Reason

Main Idea Using the scientific method, Europeans of the 1600s and 1700s developed new ideas about society based on reason.

Reading Focus What do modern scientists do in their laboratories? Read to understand how methods of scientific research changed Europeans' understanding of human society in the 1600s and 1700s.

As scientists made new discoveries, European thinkers began to apply science to society. For these thinkers, science had proven that the physical universe followed natural laws. By using their reason, people could learn how the universe worked. Using this knowledge, people also could solve existing human problems and make life better.

Descartes and Reason One of the most important scientific thinkers was the Frenchman René **Descartes** (day•KAHRT). In 1637 he wrote a book called *Discourse on Method*. In this book, Descartes began with the problem of knowing what is true. To find truth, he decided to put aside everything that he had learned and make a fresh start. To Descartes, one fact seemed to be beyond doubt—his own existence. Descartes summarized this idea by the phrase, "I think, therefore I am."

In his work, Descartes claimed that mathematics was the source of all scientific truth. In mathematics, he said, the answers were always true. This was because mathematics began with simple, obvious principles and then used logic to move gradually to other truths. Today, Descartes is viewed as the founder of modern **rationalism** (RASH•nuh•LIH•zuhm). This is the belief that reason is the chief source of knowledge.

What Is the Scientific Method?

Scientific thought was also influenced by English thinker Francis Bacon, who lived from 1561 to 1626. Bacon believed that

The Microscope

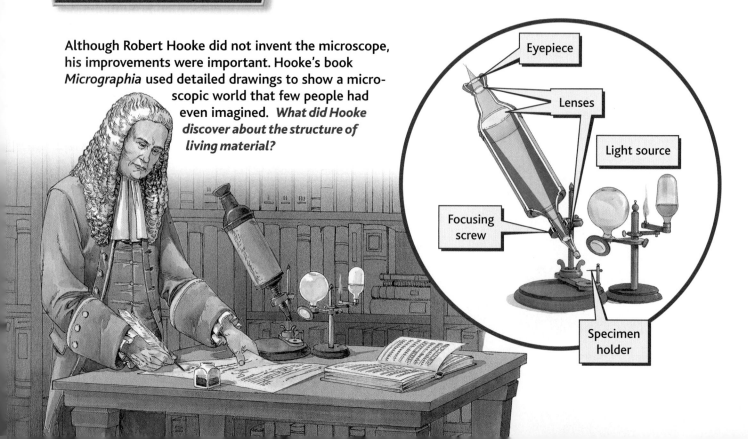

Although Robert Hooke did not invent the microscope, his improvements were important. Hooke's book *Micrographia* used detailed drawings to show a microscopic world that few people had even imagined. *What did Hooke discover about the structure of living material?*

Eyepiece

Lenses

Light source

Focusing screw

Specimen holder

ideas based on tradition should be put aside. He developed the **scientific method,** an orderly way of collecting and analyzing evidence. It is still the process used in scientific research today.

Francis Bacon ▲

The scientific method is made up of several steps. First a scientist begins with careful observation of facts and then tries to find a **hypothesis** (hy•PAH•thuh•suhs), or explanation of the facts. Through experiments, the scientist tests the hypothesis under all possible conditions to see if it is true. Finally, if repeated, experiments show that the hypothesis is true, and then it is considered a scientific law.

✓ **Reading Check** **Explain** What is the scientific method?

The Scientific Method

Observe some aspect of the universe.

⬇

Hypothesize about what you observed.

⬇

Predict something based on your hypothesis.

⬇

Test your predictions through experiments and observation.

⬇

Modify hypothesis in light of results.

Understanding Charts

The scientific method is still important today.
1. What is the next step after predictions are tested through experiments and observation?
2. **Conclude** Why is the scientific method necessary to create scientific law?

History Online
Homework Helper Need help with the material in this section? Visit jat.glencoe.com

Section ② Review

Reading Summary

Review the Main Ideas
- The thinkers of the ancient world developed early forms of science and passed this knowledge to later generations.
- European interest in science led to new discoveries and ideas about the universe and Earth's place in it.
- The scientific revolution led to new discoveries in physics, medicine, and chemistry.
- Descartes invented rationalism, and Bacon developed the scientific method.

What Did You Learn?

1. Who was Copernicus, and what was the heliocentric theory?

2. Describe Francis Bacon's beliefs about scientific reasoning.

Critical Thinking

3. **Summarize** Draw a diagram like the one below. Add details to show some of the new ideas developed during the Scientific Revolution.

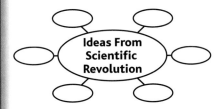

Ideas From Scientific Revolution

4. **Drawing Conclusions** What do you think Descartes meant when he said, "I think, therefore I am"?

5. **Science Link** Explain Kepler's view of the solar system.

6. **Analyze** Why did the Church condemn Galileo's astronomical findings?

7. **Writing Questions** Imagine that you could interview Galileo about his work and his life. Write five questions you would like to ask him. Include possible answers with your questions.

Get Ready to Read!

What's the Connection?

As you have read, the Scientific Revolution led to new discoveries. At the same time, it also led to many new ideas about government and society.

Focusing on the Main Ideas

• During the 1700s, many Europeans believed that reason could be used to make government and society better. *(page 681)*

• The Enlightenment was centered in France, where thinkers wrote about changing their society and met to discuss their ideas. *(page 684)*

• Many of Europe's monarchs, who claimed to rule by the will of God, tried to model their countries on Enlightenment ideas. *(page 686)*

Locating Places

Prussia (PRUH•shuh)
Austria (AWS•tree•uh)
St. Petersburg (PEE•tuhrz•BUHRG)

Meeting People

Thomas Hobbes (HAHBZ)
John Locke
Montesquieu (MAHN•tuhs•KYOO)
Voltaire (vohl•TAR)

Building Your Vocabulary

natural law
social contract
separation of powers
deism (DEE•IH•zuhm)
absolutism (AB•suh•LOO•TIH•zuhm)

Reading Strategy

Summarizing Information Complete a table like the one below showing the major ideas of Enlightenment thinkers.

Thinkers	Ideas

NATIONAL GEOGRAPHIC When & Where?

1600 — 1700 — 1800

1643 Louis XIV becomes king of France

1690 John Locke writes about government

1792 Mary Wollstonecraft calls for women's rights

St. Petersburg · London · Moscow · Paris · Berlin · Vienna

New Ideas About Politics

Main Idea During the 1700s, many Europeans believed that reason could be used to make government and society better.

Reading Focus What makes people get along with each other? Do they need rules, a strong leader, or to learn to work together? Read to learn how thinkers in Europe answered these questions.

During the 1700s, European thinkers were impressed by scientific discoveries in the natural world. They believed that reason could also uncover the scientific laws that governed human life. Once these laws were known, thinkers said, people could use the laws to make society better.

As the Scientific Revolution advanced, many educated Europeans came to believe that reason was a much better guide than faith or tradition. To them, reason was a "light" that revealed error and showed the way to truth. As result, the 1700s became known as the Age of Enlightenment.

During the Enlightenment, political thinkers tried to apply reason and scientific ideas to government. They claimed that there was a **natural law,** or a law that applied to everyone and could be understood by reason. This law was the key to understanding government. As early as the 1600s, two English thinkers—Thomas Hobbes and John Locke—used natural law to develop very different ideas about how government should work.

Who Was Thomas Hobbes?

Thomas Hobbes (HAHBZ) wrote about English government and society. During his life, England was torn apart by civil war. Supporters of King Charles I fought those who backed Parliament. Charles I wanted to have absolute, or total, power as king. Parliament claimed to represent the people

▲ This illustration is from the title page of Hobbes's *Leviathan.* *What sort of government did Hobbes support in* Leviathan?

and demanded a greater voice in running England. The fighting finally led to Charles's execution. This event shocked Thomas Hobbes, who was a strong supporter of the monarchy.

In 1651 Hobbes wrote a book called *Leviathan.* In this work, Hobbes argued that natural law made absolute monarchy the best form of government.

According to Hobbes, humans were naturally selfish and violent. They could not be trusted to make decisions on their own. Left to themselves, people would make life "nasty, brutish, and short." Therefore, Hobbes said, they needed to obey a government that had the power of a leviathan, or sea monster. To Hobbes, this meant the rule of a king, because only a strong ruler could give people direction.

Why Is John Locke Important?

Another English thinker **John Locke** thought differently. He used natural law to affirm citizens' rights and to make government answerable to the people.

The Law of Nations

Montesquieu's beliefs about government are still influential today.

"Again, there is no liberty, if the judiciary power be not separated from the legislative and executive. Were it joined with the legislative, the life and liberty of the subject would be exposed to arbitrary control; for the judge would be then the legislator. Were it joined to the executive power, the judge might behave with violence and oppression."

—Montesquieu,
The Spirit of Laws

▲ Montesquieu

DBQ Document-Based Question

According to Montesquieu, why should judges be independent?

During Locke's life, another English king, James II, wanted to set up an absolute monarchy against Parliament's wishes. In 1688 war threatened, and James fled the country. Parliament then asked Mary, James's daughter, and her husband, William, to take the throne. This event came to be called the "Glorious Revolution."

In return for the English throne, William and Mary agreed to a Bill of Rights. In this document, they agreed to obey Parliament's laws. The document also guaranteed all English people basic rights, like those the Magna Carta had given to the nobles. For example, people had the right to a fair trial by jury and to freedom from cruel punishment for a crime.

In 1690 John Locke explained many of the ideas of the Glorious Revolution in a book called *Two Treatises of Government.* Locke stated that government should be based on natural law. This law, said Locke, gave all people from their birth certain natural rights. Among them were the right to life, the right to liberty, and the right to own property.

Locke believed that the purpose of government is to protect these rights. All governments, he said, were based on a **social contract,** or an agreement between rulers and the people. If a ruler took away people's natural rights, the people had a right to revolt and set up a new government.

Who Was Montesquieu?

England's government after the Glorious Revolution was admired by thinkers in France. They liked it better than their own absolute monarchy. In 1748 Baron **Montesquieu** (MAHN•tuhs•KYOO), a French thinker, published a book called *The Spirit of Laws.*

In this book, Montesquieu said that England's government was the best because it had a separation of powers. **Separation of powers** means that power should be equally divided among the branches of government: executive, legislative, and judicial. The legislative branch would make the laws while the executive branch would enforce them. The judicial branch would interpret the laws and judge when they were broken. By separating these powers, government could not become too powerful and threaten people's rights.

✓ **Reading Check** **Explain** According to Montesquieu, how should government be organized?

Biography

JOHN LOCKE
1632–1704

John Locke was born in Somerset, England. His father was a lawyer but also served as a cavalry soldier. Using his military connections, he arranged for his son John to get a good education. Locke studied classical languages, grammar, philosophy, and geometry at Oxford University. To Locke, the courses were not exciting, so he turned to his true interests—science and medicine.

After graduating, Locke went to work for governments in Europe. He continued to study science and philosophy. He particularly liked the work of Descartes. In 1671 Locke began recording his own ideas about how people know things. Nineteen years later, he published his ideas in *An Essay Concerning Human Understanding.* In this book, Locke argued that people's minds are blank when they are born and that society shapes what people think and believe. This idea meant that if people could make society better, it would also make people better.

▲ John Locke

> "Law is not to abolish or restrain, but to preserve and enlarge freedom."
>
> –John Locke, *Two Treatises of Government*

In 1683 Locke fled to Holland after the English government began to think his political ideas were dangerous. During that time, he was declared a traitor and was not able to return until after the Glorious Revolution of 1688. It was at that time that he wrote his famous *Two Treatises of Government.* Soon afterward, Locke retired to Essex. There he enjoyed frequent visits from Sir Isaac Newton and other friends until his death in 1704.

▲ William and Mary being crowned following the Glorious Revolution

Then and Now

Give examples of how Locke's ideas have influenced our lives and ideas.

The French Philosophes

Main Idea The Enlightenment was centered in France, where thinkers wrote about changing their society and met to discuss their ideas.

Reading Focus What role do writers play in the United States today? Read on to find out what effect writers had on Europe during the Enlightenment.

During the 1700s, France became the major center of the Enlightenment. As the Enlightenment spread, thinkers in France and elsewhere became known by the French name *philosophe* (FEE•luh•ZAWF), which means "philosopher." Most philosophes were writers, teachers, journalists, and observers of society.

The philosophes wanted to use reason to change society. They attacked superstition, or unreasoned beliefs. They also disagreed with Church leaders who opposed new scientific discoveries. The philosophes believed in both freedom of speech and the individual's right to liberty. They used their skills as writers to spread their ideas across Europe.

Who Was Voltaire?
The greatest thinker of the Enlightenment was François-Marie Arouet, known simply as **Voltaire** (vohl•TAR). Born in a middle-class family, Voltaire wrote many novels, plays, letters, and essays that brought him fame and wealth.

Voltaire became known for his strong dislike of the Roman Catholic Church. He blamed Church leaders for keeping

◀ Voltaire

▲ During the Enlightenment, upper-class nobles held gatherings of writers, artists, government officials, and other nobles in their homes to discuss and debate new ideas. *How did the philosophes spread their ideas?*

knowledge from people in order to maintain the Church's power. Voltaire also opposed the government supporting one religion and forbidding others. He thought people should be free to choose their own beliefs.

Throughout his life, Voltaire was a supporter of **deism** (DEE•IH•zuhm), a religious belief based on reason. According to the followers of deism, God created the world and set it in motion. He then allowed it to run itself by natural law.

Who Was Diderot?

Denis Diderot was the French philosophe who did the most to spread Enlightenment ideas. With the help of friends, Diderot published a large, 28-volume encyclopedia. His project, which began in the 1750s, took about 20 years to complete.

The *Encyclopedia* included a wide range of topics, such as science, religion, government, and the arts. It became an important weapon in the philosophes' fight against traditional ways. Many articles attacked superstition and supported freedom of religion. Others called for changes that would make society more just and caring.

The Enlightenment and Women

The Enlightenment raised questions about the role of women in society. Previously, many male thinkers claimed that women were less important than men and had to be controlled and protected. By the 1700s, however, women thinkers began calling for women's rights. The most powerful supporter of women's rights was the English writer Mary Wollstonecraft. Many people today see her as the founder of the modern movement for women's rights.

Primary Source

Natural Rights of Women

Mary Wollstonecraft argued that the natural rights of the Enlightenment should extend to women as well as men.

▲ Mary Wollstonecraft

"In short, in whatever light I view the subject, reason and experience convince me that the only method of leading women to fulfill their peculiar [specific] duties is to free them from all restraint by allowing them to participate in the inherent rights of mankind. Make them free, and they will quickly become wise and virtuous, as men become more so, for the improvement must be mutual."

—Mary Wollstonecraft, *A Vindication of the Rights of Woman: With Strictures on Political and Moral Subjects*

DBQ Document-Based Question

What did Wollstonecraft believe would happen if women were allowed rights?

In 1792 Mary Wollstonecraft wrote a book called *A Vindication of the Rights of Woman.* In this work, she claimed that all humans have reason. Because women have reason, they should have the same rights as men. Women, Wollstonecraft said, should have equal rights in education, the workplace, and in political life.

Rousseau's Social Contract

By the late 1700s, some European thinkers were starting to criticize Enlightenment ideas. One of these thinkers was Jean-Jacques Rousseau (zhahn zhahk ru•SOH).

Rousseau claimed that supporters of the Enlightenment relied too much on reason. Instead, people should pay more attention to their feelings. According to Rousseau, human beings were naturally good, but civilized life corrupted them. To improve themselves, he thought people should live simpler lives closer to nature.

In 1762 Rousseau published a book called *The Social Contract.* In this work, Rousseau presented his political ideas. A workable government, he said, should be based on a social contract. This is an agreement in which everyone in a society agrees to be governed by the general will, or what society as a whole wants.

✓ Reading Check **Describe** Who were the philosophes?

The Age of Absolutism

Main Idea Many of Europe's monarchs, who claimed to rule by the will of God, tried to model their countries on Enlightenment ideas.

Reading Focus If you were given the chance to be a leader, how would you treat the people you ruled? As you read, think about the power of Europe's kings and queens during the 1600s and 1700s.

During the 1600s and 1700s, many European thinkers favored limits on government power. However, powerful kings and queens ruled most of Europe. This system was known as **absolutism** (AB•suh•LOO•TIH•zuhm). In this system, monarchs held absolute, or total, power. They claimed to rule by divine right, or by the will of God. This meant that rulers did not answer to their people, but rather to God alone.

NATIONAL GEOGRAPHIC **The Way It Was**

Focus on Everyday Life

Music of the Enlightenment The 1700s was one of the greatest musical periods in history. Before this time, almost all music was religious in nature and was limited to church performances. During the Enlightenment, music was played in theaters for the first time, and some of the new pieces were not religious.

▲ A string quartet

Many types of music existed in the 1700s. Sonatas were performed with one instrument and a piano, and string quartets were played with four instruments. Concertos and symphonies were longer and involved an orchestra. Operas were full-scale theatrical performances using vocal and instrumental music.

Baroque music emphasized drama and emotion. Johann Sebastian Bach and George Frederick Handel composed baroque music. Bach composed

However, as the Enlightenment spread, many of Europe's absolute rulers turned to philosophes for help in making their governments work better. At the same time, however, they did not want to lose any of their power. Historians have called these rulers enlightened despots. Despots are rulers who hold total power.

Louis XIV: France's Sun King
During the 1600s, France was one of Europe's strongest nations. In 1643 Louis XIV came to the throne. As king, Louis XIV was the most celebrated absolute monarch. His reign of 72 years—the longest in European history—set the style for Europe's kings and queens. Louis was known as the Sun King, because Europe's rulers and nobles all "revolved" around him.

Louis relied on a bureaucracy, but he was the source of all political authority in France. He is said to have boasted, "I am the State."

Louis's army fought and won wars to expand France's territory, but these conflicts were costly in money and soldiers to France. The king's constant wars and excessive spending weakened France and the monarchy.

Frederick the Great
During the 1600s and 1700s, Germany was a collection of over 300 separate states. Of these states, two—**Prussia** (PRUH•shuh) and **Austria** (AWS•tree•uh)—became great European powers.

The most famous Prussian ruler was Frederick II, also called Frederick the Great. He ruled from 1740 to 1786. As Prussia's king, Frederick strengthened the army and fought wars to gain new territory for Prussia. He also tried to be an "enlightened despot." He supported the arts and learning and tried to carry out enlightened reforms. He permitted his people to speak and publish more freely. He also allowed greater religious toleration.

many pieces of music that are still popular today. Handel wrote many operas, but he is best known for *Messiah*, an oratorio, or religious composition that mixes voices, orchestra, and organ.

Classical music emerged in the mid-1700s. Classical composers, inspired by the ancient Greeks and Romans, emphasized balance, harmony, and stability. Franz Joseph Haydn and Wolfgang Amadeus Mozart wrote classical music. Haydn's use of instruments made the symphony more popular. Mozart composed a large number of musical pieces that remain popular today.

Wolfgang Amadeus Mozart ▼

▲ Johann Sebastian Bach

Connecting to the Past
1. What is the difference in tone between baroque and classical music?
2. What factors allowed music to thrive during the 1700s?

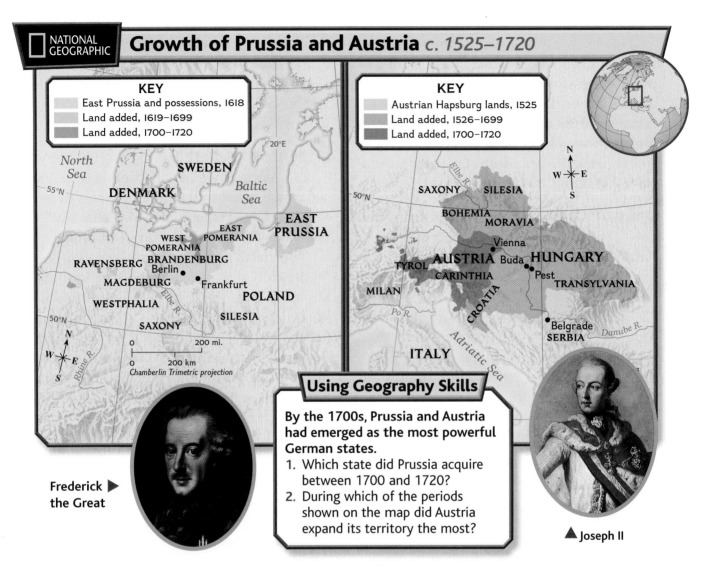

Growth of Prussia and Austria c. 1525–1720

KEY
- East Prussia and possessions, 1618
- Land added, 1619–1699
- Land added, 1700–1720

KEY
- Austrian Hapsburg lands, 1525
- Land added, 1526–1699
- Land added, 1700–1720

North Sea
SWEDEN
DENMARK
Baltic Sea
55°N
20°E
EAST PRUSSIA
WEST POMERANIA
EAST POMERANIA
RAVENSBERG
BRANDENBURG
Berlin
MAGDEBURG
Frankfurt
WESTPHALIA
POLAND
SILESIA
50°N
SAXONY
Elbe R.
Rhine R.
0   200 mi.
0   200 km
Chamberlin Trimetric projection

Elbe R.
SAXONY   SILESIA
50°N
BOHEMIA   MORAVIA
Vienna
AUSTRIA Buda HUNGARY
TYROL
CARINTHIA   Pest
MILAN   TRANSYLVANIA
CROATIA
Po R.
Belgrade
SERBIA   Danube R.
Adriatic Sea
ITALY

Frederick ▶ the Great

Using Geography Skills

By the 1700s, Prussia and Austria had emerged as the most powerful German states.
1. Which state did Prussia acquire between 1700 and 1720?
2. During which of the periods shown on the map did Austria expand its territory the most?

▲ Joseph II

Austria's Hapsburg Rulers

By the 1700s, the other powerful German state—Austria—ruled a large empire of many different peoples, languages, and cultures. This vast Austrian empire spread over much of central and southeastern Europe. It was ruled by a family known as the Hapsburgs.

In 1740 a young Hapsburg princess named Maria Theresa became Austria's ruler. Clever and talented, Maria Theresa worked hard to improve the lot of Austria's serfs, who worked for the nobles. She also tried to make government work better.

After Maria Theresa died in 1780, her son, Joseph II, became ruler. Joseph II admired Enlightenment ideas. He freed the serfs, made land taxes equal for nobles and farmers, and allowed books to be published freely. Most of Joseph's reforms failed, however. The nobles opposed Joseph's changes, and he was forced to back down. However, the former serfs, now farmers, were allowed to keep their freedom.

Russia's Peter I and Catherine II

To the east of Austria stretched the vast empire of Russia. As you read previously, Russia was ruled by all-powerful rulers known as czars. One of the most powerful czars was Peter I, also known as Peter the Great. During his reign from 1689 to 1725, Peter tried to make Russia into a strong and up-to-date European power. He began reforms to make the government work more smoothly.

Peter also improved Russia's military and expanded Russia's territory westward to the Baltic Sea. In 1703 he founded a city called **St. Petersburg** (PEE•tuhrz•BUHRG) in this area. A few years later, Russia's capital was moved to St. Petersburg from Moscow.

After Peter died, conflict erupted among Russia's nobles. Then, in 1762 a German princess named Catherine came to the throne of Russia. Early in her reign, Catherine was devoted to Enlightenment ideas. She studied about and wrote letters to the philosophes. She even thought about freeing the serfs, but a serf uprising changed her mind. In the end, she allowed the nobles to treat the serfs as they pleased.

Under Catherine, Russia gained even more land and increased its power in Europe. As a result, Catherine became known as "the Great." However, by 1796,

Russia grew more powerful ▶ during the reigns of Peter the Great (above) and Catherine the Great (right). *How did Peter try to make Russia a European power?*

the year Catherine died, the ideas of liberty and equality had spread across Europe. These ideas seriously threatened the rule of powerful kings and queens.

✓ **Reading Check** **Explain** How did the ideas of absolute monarchs conflict with the ideas of Enlightenment thinkers?

History Online

Homework Helper Need help with the material in this section? Visit jat.glencoe.com

Section 3 Review

Reading Summary

Review the Main Ideas

- In the 1700s, many Europeans thought reason could make government and society better. Hobbes, Locke, and Montesquieu developed ideas about how to improve government.

- Enlightenment thinkers, such as Voltaire, Diderot, and Rousseau, described ways to make society better.

- By the 1700s, most of Europe's rulers were absolute monarchs. Some, however, tried to create governments based on Enlightenment ideas.

What Did You Learn?

1. Who were the French philosophes?

2. What was the *Encyclopedia*, and what message did it attempt to deliver to its readers?

Critical Thinking

3. **Organizing Information** Draw a chart to list the rulers of the Enlightenment, their countries, and their accomplishments.

Ruler	Country	Accomplishments

4. **Cause and Effect** How did civil war in England affect Hobbes?

5. **Explain** Do you think enlightened despots were really enlightened?

6. **Conclude** Which of the Enlightenment thinkers discussed in this section do you think had the most impact on modern society? Explain your answer.

7. **Civics Link** Describe how beliefs about people and government during the Enlightenment are reflected in our government today.

The American Revolution

Get Ready to Read!

What's the Connection?

Between the 1500s and 1700s, Europeans set up colonies in North America. In the British colonies, English traditions and the Enlightenment gave colonists a strong sense of their rights.

Focusing on the Main Ideas

- European colonies in North America developed differently from each other and from Europe. *(page 691)*

- Great Britain faced problems in North America, because the American colonists objected to new British laws. *(page 695)*

- The American colonies formed a new nation, the United States of America. *(page 698)*

Locating Places

Quebec (kih•BEHK)

Jamestown

Boston

Philadelphia

Meeting People

Pilgrim

George Washington

Tom Paine

Thomas Jefferson

Building Your Vocabulary

representative government

constitution

popular sovereignty
(SAH•vuh•ruhn•tee)

limited government

Reading Strategy

Cause and Effect Complete a cause-and-effect diagram showing why the British colonies declared independence.

	→	
	→	
	→	
	→	

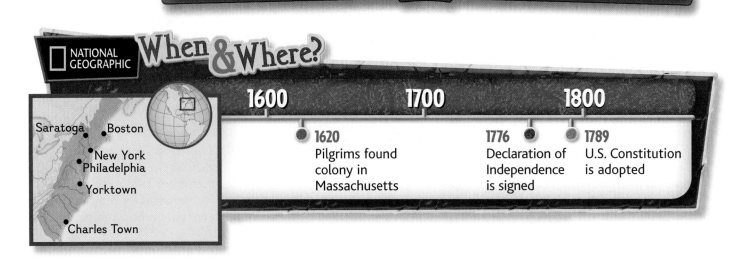

NATIONAL GEOGRAPHIC **When & Where?**

Saratoga, Boston, New York, Philadelphia, Yorktown, Charles Town

1600 — 1700 — 1800

1620 Pilgrims found colony in Massachusetts

1776 Declaration of Independence is signed

1789 U.S. Constitution is adopted

Settling North America

Main Idea European colonies in North America developed differently from each other and from Europe.

Reading Focus What would make you want to move to a new place? In this chapter, you will learn why Europeans settled in North America from the 1500s to the 1700s.

Previously, you learned that Spain and Portugal built colonies in the Americas in the 1500s. Beginning in the 1600s, the French, English, and other Europeans began setting up their own colonies in the Americas. While most of Spain's colonies were in the Caribbean, Mexico, and South America, most of France and England's colonies were in North America.

The Spanish in North America The Spanish did not ignore the lands north of Mexico and the Caribbean. In the 1500s, Spanish conquistadors explored the southeastern corner of North America and the lands north of Mexico. They had hoped to find wealthy empires like those of the Aztec and Inca. Instead, they found only small villages of Native Americans. As a result, Spain remained much more interested in its colonies in Mexico, Peru, and the Caribbean, because they provided large amounts of silver and gold.

The Spanish did not completely ignore the rest of North America. They built settlements and forts along the northern edge of their territory. These settlements, such as St. Augustine in Florida and Santa Fe in New Mexico, were intended to keep other Europeans out of Spanish territory.

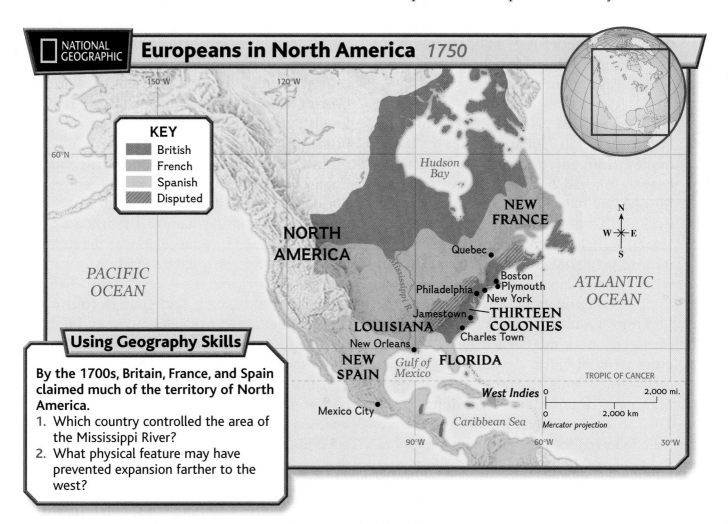

NATIONAL GEOGRAPHIC Europeans in North America *1750*

KEY
- British
- French
- Spanish
- Disputed

Using Geography Skills

By the 1700s, Britain, France, and Spain claimed much of the territory of North America.

1. Which country controlled the area of the Mississippi River?
2. What physical feature may have prevented expansion farther to the west?

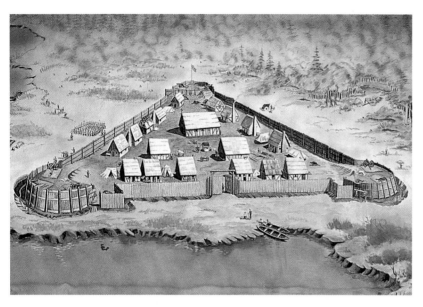

▲ **This painting shows what the original settlement at Jamestown may have looked like in 1607.** *What prevented the Jamestown settlement from collapsing?*

Louisiana in honor of King Louis XIV. The French settlers in southern Louisiana also began bringing in enslaved Africans to grow sugarcane, rice, and tobacco.

The English Settle in America

English settlers came to North America for many reasons. While merchants set up some English colonies to make money, others were set up by people who wanted religious freedom. England's colonies grew rapidly because of economic problems in England. Many people in England wanted to move to America because their landlords had evicted them from their farms. In America, they had a chance to own land for themselves. Still others came because they were unemployed and needed work.

By 1600, England's rulers had accepted the ideas of mercantilism. Colonies and trading posts in Asia and America were making Europe's kingdoms wealthy. The English government believed colonies were needed to keep England strong.

In 1607 the Virginia Company, an English joint-stock company, set up the first permanent English settlement in North America. The settlers named it **Jamestown** after King James I. Jamestown was the first town of a new colony called Virginia.

Life in Virginia was very hard. The colonists could barely find enough to eat. Many settlers died from starvation and the cold winters, and others were killed in clashes with Native Americans.

During those first years, the colony made no money for the merchants who had invested in it. It might have collapsed had not one of the settlers, John Rolfe, discovered that tobacco could grow in Virginia's soil.

Spanish priests also headed north. They set up missions, or religious communities, to teach Christianity and European ways to the Native Americans. Missions were set up in California, New Mexico, Florida, and other areas of North America.

France Settles North America The French came to North America to make money from fur trading. By the 1600s, beaver fur had become very popular in Europe. In 1608 French merchants hired explorer Samuel de Champlain (sham•PLAYN) to help them. Champlain set up a trading post named **Quebec** (kih•BEHK) in what is now Canada. Quebec became the capital of the colony of New France.

From Quebec, French fur trappers, explorers, and missionaries moved into other parts of North America. In 1673 the explorers Louis Joliet and Jacques Marquette found the Mississippi River. Then in 1682 a French explorer named La Salle followed the Mississippi all the way to the Gulf of Mexico. He named the region

Tobacco was popular in Europe in the 1600s. Soon the colonists in Virginia were growing it in large amounts and selling it for a lot of money. Tobacco became the first cash crop of the English colonies. A cash crop is grown in large quantities to sell for profit.

Eventually, tobacco was grown on large farms called plantations. Because plantations need many workers, the English began bringing in enslaved Africans to work the land. The success of Virginia encouraged the English government to set up more colonies in America to grow cash crops. The colony of South Carolina, for example, began growing rice and indigo. The English also began setting up colonies in the Caribbean to grow sugarcane.

Not all English settlers came to North America in search of wealth. Some came to find religious freedom. As you read in the last chapter, many Protestants in England were Puritans. Puritans wanted to rid the Anglican Church of Catholic rituals and allow each congregation to choose its own leaders. King James I and his son King Charles I both believed Puritans were a threat to their authority and persecuted them.

In 1620 a group of Puritans known as the **Pilgrims** decided to go to America so that they could worship freely. In 1620 they boarded a ship called the *Mayflower* and set out for North America. They landed just north of Cape Cod in what is today the state of Massachusetts. They named their settlement Plymouth.

The success of the Pilgrims encouraged other Puritans to begin leaving England for America. Led by John Winthrop, a group of Puritans landed in America and founded the colony of Massachusetts. Others soon followed. By 1643, more than 20,000 Puritans had moved to America. They founded Rhode Island, Connecticut, and New Hampshire.

Primary Source

The Mayflower Compact

The Pilgrims governed themselves according to this document.

"Having undertaken for the Glory of God, and Advancement of the Christian Faith, and the Honour of our King and Country, a Voyage to plant the first colony in the northern Parts of Virginia; Do . . . covenant [agree] and combine ourselves together into a civil Body Politick [political group], for our better Ordering and Preservation. . . . And by Virtue hereof do enact, constitute, and frame, such just and equal Laws, . . . and Offices, from time to time, as shall be thought most meet and convenient for the general Good of the Colony; unto which we promise all due Submission and Obedience."

—Mayflower Compact, November 21, 1620

▲ The Pilgrims sign the Mayflower Compact.

To what do the Pilgrims promise submission and obedience?

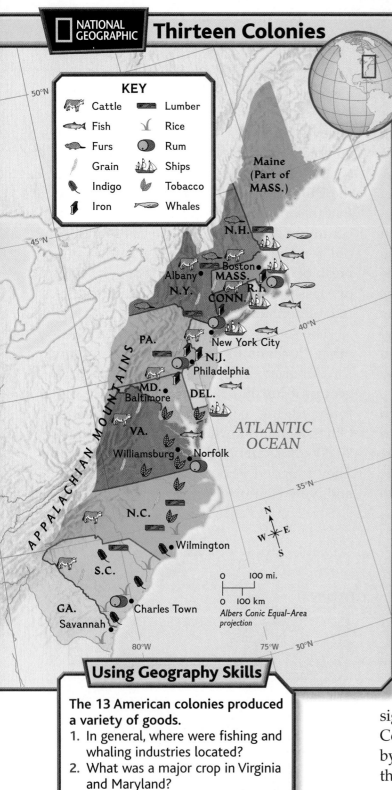

NATIONAL GEOGRAPHIC
Thirteen Colonies

KEY

Cattle		Lumber	
Fish		Rice	
Furs		Rum	
Grain		Ships	
Indigo		Tobacco	
Iron		Whales	

Maine (Part of MASS.)

N.H.
Boston
Albany • MASS.
N.Y. R.I.
CONN.
New York City
PA.
N.J.
Philadelphia
MD. • DEL.
Baltimore
VA. ATLANTIC OCEAN
Williamsburg • Norfolk
N.C.
Wilmington
S.C.
GA.
Savannah Charles Town

APPALACHIAN MOUNTAINS

0   100 mi.
0   100 km
Albers Conic Equal–Area projection

N W E S

50°N   45°N   40°N   35°N   30°N
80°W   75°W

Using Geography Skills

The 13 American colonies produced a variety of goods.
1. In general, where were fishing and whaling industries located?
2. What was a major crop in Virginia and Maryland?

Other people seeking religious freedom set up colonies as well. English Catholics founded Maryland in 1634. The Quakers, another religious group that had been persecuted in England, founded Pennsylvania in 1680.

By the early 1700s, the English had created 13 colonies along the coast of North America. These colonies had different economies and societies, but they had one thing in common: they wanted to govern themselves.

Self-Government in America The tradition of self-government began early in the English colonies. To attract more settlers, the head of the Virginia Company gave the colonists in Virginia the right to elect burgesses, or representatives, from among the men who owned land. The first House of Burgesses met in 1619. It was patterned after the English Parliament and voted on laws for the Virginia colony.

The House of Burgesses set an example for **representative government,** or a government in which people elect representatives to make laws and conduct government. It was not long before other colonies set up their own legislatures as well.

A year after the Virginia House of Burgesses met, the Pilgrims arrived in North America and began their own tradition of self-government. Before going ashore, the Pilgrims signed an agreement called the Mayflower Compact. They agreed to rule themselves by choosing their own leaders and making their own laws.

Over the years, most of the English colonies began drawing up **constitutions,** or written plans of government. These documents let the colonists elect assemblies and protected their rights.

✓ **Reading Check** Compare and Contrast
How was the founding of Jamestown different from the founding of Plymouth?

Trouble in the Colonies

Main Idea Great Britain faced problems in North America, because the American colonists objected to new British laws.

Reading Focus Do you like to make your own decisions, without someone else telling you what to do? Read to find out why the American colonies wanted to make decisions without British interference.

During the early 1700s, there were many changes in England and its overseas colonies. In 1707 England united with Scotland and became the United Kingdom of Great Britain. The term *British* came to mean both the English and the Scots.

By 1750, Great Britain had become the world's most powerful trading empire. It had 13 prosperous colonies along the Atlantic coast of America and others in India and the Caribbean. For years, Britain and its American colonies seemed to get along well. This relationship changed, however, when the British tried to control trade and impose taxes on the colonies. These efforts angered colonists.

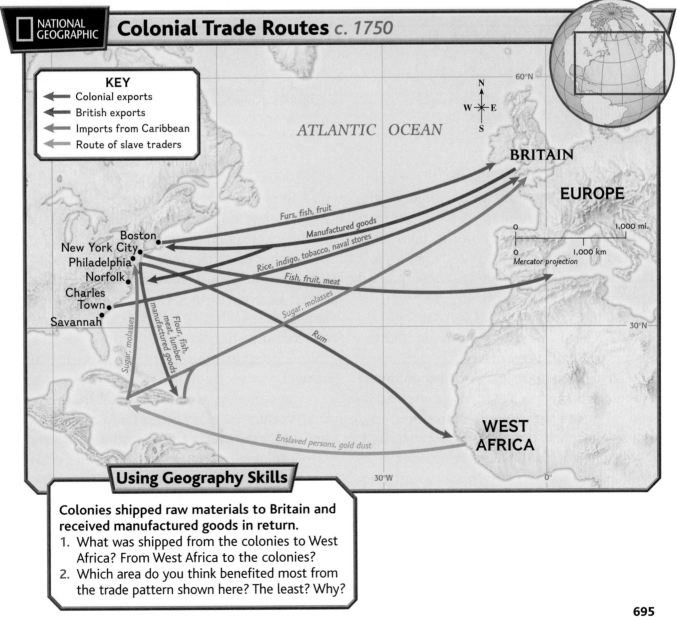

NATIONAL GEOGRAPHIC

Colonial Trade Routes c. 1750

KEY
- Colonial exports
- British exports
- Imports from Caribbean
- Route of slave traders

ATLANTIC OCEAN

BRITAIN

EUROPE

Boston
New York City
Philadelphia
Norfolk
Charles Town
Savannah

Furs, fish, fruit
Manufactured goods
Rice, indigo, tobacco, naval stores
Fish, fruit, meat
Sugar, molasses
Rum
Sugar, molasses
Flour, fish, meat, lumber, manufactured goods
Enslaved persons, gold dust

WEST AFRICA

0   1,000 mi.
0   1,000 km
Mercator projection

60°N
30°N
30°W   0°

Using Geography Skills

Colonies shipped raw materials to Britain and received manufactured goods in return.
1. What was shipped from the colonies to West Africa? From West Africa to the colonies?
2. Which area do you think benefited most from the trade pattern shown here? The least? Why?

695

The Road to Revolution

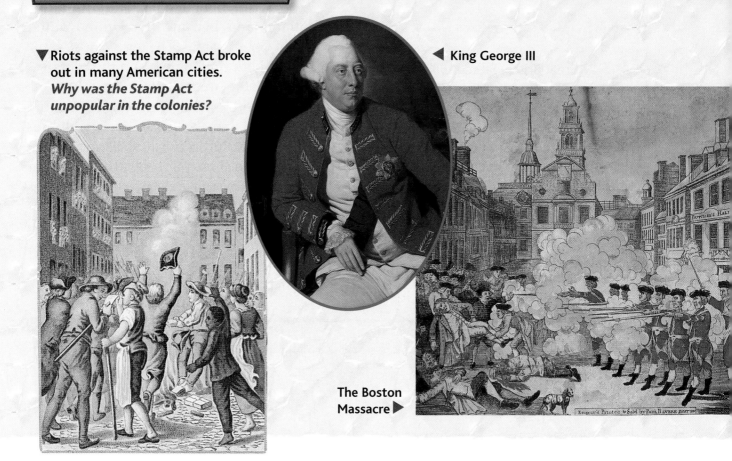

▼ Riots against the Stamp Act broke out in many American cities. *Why was the Stamp Act unpopular in the colonies?*

◄ King George III

The Boston Massacre ▶

Colonial Government and Trade For many years, Great Britain had allowed the American colonies the freedom to run their local affairs. In each colony, men who owned property elected representatives to a legislature. Colonial legislatures passed laws and could tax the people. However, the governor of a colony could veto laws passed by the legislature. The king appointed the governor in most colonies.

Great Britain controlled the colonies' trade according to the ideas of mercantilism. The American colonies produced raw materials, such as tobacco, rice, indigo, wheat, lumber, fur, deerskin leather, fish, and whale products. These were then shipped to Great Britain and traded for manufactured goods such as clothing, furniture, and goods from Asia, such as tea or spices.

To control this trade, Britain passed a series of laws called the Navigation Acts in

the 1600s. Under these laws the colonists had to sell their raw materials to Britain even if they could get a better price elsewhere. Any goods bought by the colonies from other countries in Europe had to go to England first and be taxed before they could be sent to the Americas. The trade laws also said that all trade goods had to be carried on ships built in Britain or the colonies and that the crews had to be British as well.

The colonists at first accepted the trade laws because it guaranteed them a place to sell their raw materials. Later, the colonists came to resent British restrictions. With population in the colonies growing, the colonists wanted to make their own manufactured goods. They also wanted to sell their products elsewhere if they could get higher prices. Many colonial merchants began smuggling, or shipping goods in and

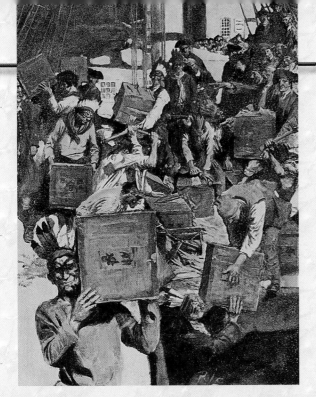

▲ During the Boston Tea Party, a group of colonists, some dressed as Native Americans, dumped chests of tea into Boston Harbor. Many more colonists cheered them on from shore. *What was Britain's response to this event?*

out of the country without paying taxes or getting government permission.

Why Did the British Tax the Colonies?

Between 1756 and 1763, the French and British fought for control of North America. The British won, gaining nearly all of France's North American empire. The war was very costly, however, and left the British government deep in debt. Desperate for money, the British made plans to tax the colonists and tighten trade rules.

In 1765 Parliament passed the Stamp Act, which taxed newspapers and other printed material. All of these items had to bear a stamp showing that the tax was paid. The colonists were outraged. They responded by boycotting, or refusing to buy, British goods.

Finally, delegates from nine colonies met in New York to discuss the Stamp Act. They sent a letter to the British government stating that the colonies could not be taxed except by their own assemblies. The British backed down for a while, but they still needed money. In 1767 Parliament placed taxes on glass, lead, paper, paint, and tea.

Tax Protests Lead to Revolt

The American colonists grumbled about the new taxes. They bullied the tax collectors, and journalists drew ugly cartoons of King George III. Worried, the British sent more troops to **Boston,** Massachusetts, where the largest protests had taken place.

In March 1770, violence broke out. A crowd of colonists began insulting British soldiers and throwing snowballs at them. The soldiers fired into the crowd. Five people were killed. This event came to be called the Boston Massacre. Shortly thereafter, all of the taxes were repealed, or canceled, except the one on tea.

In 1773 Parliament passed the Tea Act. It allowed a British trading company to ship tea to the colonies without paying the taxes colonial tea merchants had to pay. This allowed the company to sell its tea very cheaply and threatened to drive the colonial tea merchants out of business.

In Massachusetts, angry colonists decided to take action. A group of protesters dressed as Native Americans boarded several British ships in Boston Harbor and dumped their cargoes of tea into the water. This event is known as the Boston Tea Party.

To punish the colonists, Parliament in 1774 passed laws that closed down Boston Harbor and put the government of Massachusetts under military rule. It also said that British troops should be quartered, or given a place to live, in colonists' homes. The colonists called these laws the Intolerable Acts, or laws they could not bear.

The Intolerable Acts made the colonists more determined to fight for their liberties.

In September 1774, delegates from 12 colonies met in Philadelphia. They called themselves the First Continental Congress. The Congress spoke out against the Intolerable Acts and called for their repeal.

Colonial leaders, however, were divided about what to do. Some, like George Washington of Virginia, hoped to settle the differences with Great Britain. Others, like Samuel Adams of Massachusetts and Patrick Henry of Virginia, wanted the colonies to become independent.

✓ **Reading Check** **Identify** What was the Boston Tea Party?

The War of Independence

Main Idea The American colonies formed a new nation, the United States of America.

Reading Focus What causes people to go to war? Read to find out how the war between Great Britain and the Americans shaped the course of world history.

Before the colonists could decide what to do, fighting broke out in Massachusetts. The British set out to destroy a store of weapons at Concord. On April 19, 1775, they met colonial troops at Lexington and fought the first battle of the American Revolution.

Primary Source

The Declaration of Independence

On July 4, 1776, Congress approved the Declaration of Independence. The preamble—the first part of the document—explains Congress's reason for issuing the declaration:

"When in the Course of human events, it becomes necessary for one people to dissolve the political bands which have connected them with another. . . . they should declare the causes which impel them to the separation."

The document also explained that people have certain basic rights:

"We hold these truths to be self-evident, that all men are created equal, that they are endowed by their Creator with certain unalienable Rights, that among these are Life, Liberty and the pursuit of Happiness."

—Declaration of Independence, July 4, 1776

DBQ **Document-Based Question**

Why do you think the Congress thought they had to issue a written declaration of independence?

▲ Benjamin Franklin, John Adams, and Thomas Jefferson, shown left to right, worked together to write the Declaration of Independence.

▲ The American leaders who met in Philadelphia in 1787 and wrote the United States Constitution were some of the nation's greatest political minds.
What sort of system of government did the Constitution create?

In May 1775, the Second Continental Congress met in **Philadelphia. George Washington** was named head of a new colonial army. The Congress then tried again to settle their differences with Great Britain. They appealed to King George III, who refused to listen.

More and more Americans began to think that independence was the only answer. In January 1776, a writer named **Tom Paine** made up many minds when he wrote a pamphlet called *Common Sense.* Paine used strong words to condemn the king and urged the colonists to separate from Great Britain.

The Declaration of Independence On July 4, 1776, the Congress issued the Declaration of Independence. Written by **Thomas Jefferson** of Virginia, the Declaration stated that the colonies were separating from Great Britain and forming a new nation, the United States of America.

In the Declaration, Jefferson explained why the colonists were founding a new nation. To do this, Jefferson borrowed the ideas of John Locke. In Section 3, you learned about Locke's idea that people have the right to overthrow governments that violate their rights. The Declaration stated that "all men are created equal" and have certain God-given rights. It said that King

George III had violated colonists' rights, and so they had the right to rebel.

The Declaration also drew from earlier English documents, such as the Magna Carta and the English Bill of Rights. Both documents established the idea that governments are not all-powerful and that rulers had to obey the laws and treat citizens fairly.

How Did the Americans Win the War?

After the Declaration was made, the war between the British and Americans dragged on. The first important American victory came in 1777 at the Battle of Saratoga in New York. This battle marked a turning point in the war. France, Great Britain's old enemy, realized that the United States might actually win. In 1778 France agreed to help the Americans.

The French were very important in the final victory. This came in 1781 at the Battle of Yorktown on the coast of Virginia. The French navy blocked the British from escaping by sea, while American and French forces surrounded and trapped the British inside Yorktown. Realizing they could not win, the British laid down their weapons. Peace negotiations began, and two years later, the Treaty of Paris ended the war.

The United States Constitution In 1783 Great Britain recognized American independence. At first the United States was a confederation, or a loose union of independent states. Its plan of government was a document called the Articles of Confederation. The Articles created a national government, but the states held most powers. It soon became clear that the Articles were too weak to deal with the new nation's problems.

In 1787, 55 delegates met in Philadelphia to change the Articles. Instead, they decided to write a constitution for an entirely new national government. The new United States Constitution set up a federal system, in which powers were divided between the national government and the states. Following the ideas of Montesquieu, power in the national government was divided between executive, legislative, and judicial branches. A system called checks and balances enabled each branch to limit the powers of the other branches.

Under the Constitution, the United States was a republic with an elected president instead of a king. Elections held in 1789 made George Washington the first president of the United States. That same year, a Bill of Rights was added to the U.S. Constitution. The Bill of Rights set out certain rights the government could not violate. These rights included freedom of religion, speech, and press, and the right to trial by jury.

The U.S. Constitution was also shaped by Enlightenment principles. One of these is **popular sovereignty** (SAH•vuh•ruhn•tee), or the idea that government receives its powers from the people. Another is **limited government,** or the idea that a government may use only those powers given to it by the people.

 **Reading Check** **Explain** Why did the colonists decide to separate from Great Britain and create a new nation?

History Online

Homework Helper Need help with the material in this section? Visit jat.glencoe.com

Section 4 Review

Reading Summary

Review the Main Ideas

- In North America, the French settled in Canada and along the Mississippi River, while the British settled along the Atlantic coast.

- Americans protested when the British government attempted to impose more control and more taxes on the colonies.

- The Americans defeated the British in the American Revolution and set up a republican form of government with powers divided among three branches.

What Did You Learn?

1. When and where was the first battle of the American Revolution fought?

2. What is the Bill of Rights?

Critical Thinking

3. **Sequence Information** Draw a time line like the one below. Fill in events related to the American Revolution.

4. **Analyze** Why did England's colonies in America grow quickly?

5. **Civics Link** Which of John Locke's ideas appeared in the Declaration of Independence?

6. **Explain** How did the search for religious freedom affect the founding of colonies in America?

7. **Persuasive Writing** Write two letters to the editor at a colonial newspaper. One should support British involvement in its American colonies. The other should support the colonists' arguments for independence.

Section 1 The Age of Exploration

Vocabulary
mercantilism
export
import
colony
commerce
invest

Focusing on the Main Ideas
- In the 1400s, trade, technology, and the rise of strong kingdoms led to a new era of exploration. *(page 659)*
- While the Portuguese explored Africa, the Spanish, English, and French explored America. *(page 661)*
- To increase trade, Europeans set up colonies and created joint-stock companies. *(page 666)*
- Exploration and trade led to a worldwide exchange of products, people, and ideas. *(page 668)*

Early astrolabe ▼

Section 2 The Scientific Revolution

Vocabulary
theory
rationalism
scientific method
hypothesis

Focusing on the Main Ideas
- The thinkers of the ancient world developed early forms of science and passed this knowledge to later civilizations. *(page 671)*
- European interest in astronomy led to new discoveries and ideas about the universe and Earth's place in it. *(page 673)*
- The Scientific Revolution led to new discoveries in physics, medicine, and chemistry. *(page 675)*
- Using the scientific method, Europeans of the 1600s and 1700s developed new ideas about society based on reason. *(page 678)*

Section 3 The Enlightenment

Vocabulary
natural law
social contract
separation of powers
deism
absolutism

Focusing on the Main Ideas
- During the 1700s, many Europeans believed that reason could be used to make government and society better. *(page 681)*
- The Enlightenment was centered in France, where thinkers wrote about changing their society and met to discuss their ideas. *(page 684)*
- Many of Europe's monarchs, who claimed to rule by the will of God, tried to model their countries on Enlightenment ideas. *(page 686)*

Section 4 The American Revolution

Vocabulary
representative government
constitution
popular sovereignty
limited government

Focusing on the Main Ideas
- European colonies in North America developed differently from each other and from Europe. *(page 691)*
- Great Britain faced problems in North America, because the American colonists objected to new British laws. *(page 695)*
- The American colonies formed a new nation, the United States of America. *(page 698)*

Review Vocabulary

Write the key term that completes each sentence.

a. constitution
b. scientific method
c. separation of powers
d. mercantilism
e. commerce
f. absolutism

1. According to the idea of ___, a country gains power by gathering gold and setting up colonies.
2. A(n) ___ is a written plan for government.
3. Francis Bacon developed the ___.
4. The system in which monarchs held total power was called ___.
5. Montesquieu believed that a(n) ___ was needed for good government.
6. The buying and selling of goods in large amounts over long distances is called ___.

Review Main Ideas

Section 1 • The Age of Exploration
7. What led to the European era of exploration?

8. How were joint-stock companies related to overseas trade?

Section 2 • The Scientific Revolution
9. Describe the scientific discoveries of Newton and Galileo.
10. What was the importance of the scientific method?

Section 3 • The Enlightenment
11. How did the Enlightenment affect Europe's rulers?
12. How did the ideas of Thomas Hobbes and John Locke about government differ?

Section 4 • The American Revolution
13. Why did the American colonists want independence from Britain?
14. How did the new government of America reflect ideas developed during the Enlightenment?

Critical Thinking

15. **Economics Link** How are the ideas of mercantilism reflected in our economy today?

Review

Reading Skill | Monitor and Adjust ⟨ Your Reading Strengths

16. Write five questions you would ask to help you better understand the information in the following paragraph.

To help the Dutch, Queen Elizabeth I of England let English privateers attack Spanish ships. Privateers are privately owned ships that have a license from the government to attack ships of other countries. People nicknamed the English privateers "sea dogs." They raided the Spanish treasure ships bringing gold back from America.

To review this skill, see pages 656–657.

Geography Skills

Study the map below and answer the following questions.

17. **Place** Which city in Europe was the first to receive the potato as part of the Columbian Exchange?

18. **Movement** Why do you think so much time passed before the potato was introduced in Sweden and Finland?

19. **Movement** Does it appear from the map that trade between nations followed a strict pattern?

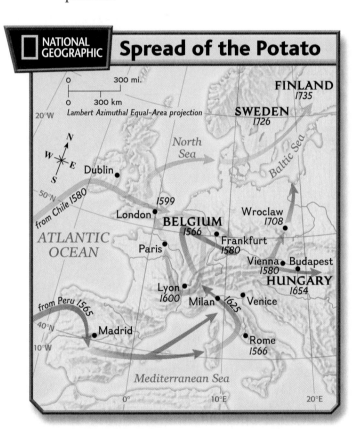

NATIONAL GEOGRAPHIC **Spread of the Potato**

Read to Write

20. **Descriptive Writing** Write a brief essay describing Montesquieu's beliefs about government and explaining how they are reflected in the U.S. Constitution.

21. **Using Your FOLDABLES** Work with a few classmates to create a question and answer game using the information in your foldables. Questions should cover the Scientific Revolution, Enlightenment, Age of Exploration, and American Revolution. Switch groups to play the games.

History Online
Self-Check Quiz To help you prepare for the Chapter Test, visit jat.glencoe.com

Using Technology

22. **Researching** Use the Internet and your local library to research present-day exploration in space and in the depths of the ocean. Find out about the technologies used, how these explorations are funded, and their impact on our knowledge of the universe. Write a report on how present-day explorers and their voyages are similar to and different from those of Europe in the Age of Exploration.

Linking Past and Present

23. **Analyzing** The music, art, and literature of the Enlightenment reflected people's views during that time. Write a description of how present-day music, art, and literature reflect how people currently feel about society. Give examples to support your opinion.

Primary Source — **Analyze**

Portuguese official Duarte Barbosa described the way his country dealt with African kingdoms.

"The king of this city [Mombasa] refused to obey the commands of the King our Lord, and through this arrogance he lost it, and our Portuguese took it from him by force. He fled away, and they slew [killed] many of his people and also took captive many, both men and women, in such sort that it was left ruined and plundered and burned."

—Duarte Barbosa, "The East Coast of Africa"

DBQ **Document-Based Questions**

24. What did the king of Mombasa do that angered the Portuguese?
25. How did the Portuguese handle the conflict?

Comparing Early Modern Civilizations

Compare early modern civilizations by reviewing the information below. Can you see how the people of these civilizations had lives that were very much like yours?

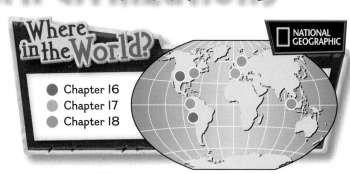

Where in the World?

NATIONAL GEOGRAPHIC

- Chapter 16
- Chapter 17
- Chapter 18

	The Americas Chapter 16	Renaissance and Reformation Chapter 17	Enlightenment and Revolution Chapter 18
Where did these civilizations develop?	• North America • Central America • Caribbean islands • South America	• Europe	• Western Europe • North America • Africa • South Asia • Southeast Asia
Who were some important people in these civilizations?	• Pachacuti, ruled A.D. 1438–1471 • Montezuma II, ruled A.D. 1502–1520 • Atahualpa, ruled A.D. 1525–1533	• Leonardo da Vinci A.D. 1452–1519 • Martin Luther A.D. 1483–1546 • Queen Isabella (Spain), ruled A.D. 1474–1504	• Christopher Columbus A.D. 1451–1506 • Queen Elizabeth I (England), ruled A.D. 1558–1603 • Galileo Galilei A.D. 1564–1642
Where did most of the people live?	• Hunter-gatherers • Farming villages • Cities (Tenochtitlán and Cuzco)	• City-states (Italy) • Commercial cities (London, Paris) • Farming villages	• Port cities (Lisbon, Amsterdam) • Overseas settlements and plantations
What were these people's beliefs?	• Traditional Native American religions	• Northern Europe: Protestant • Southern Europe: Roman Catholic • Jewish communities	• Europeans spread Christianity overseas • Rise of Deism in Europe and America

	The Americas Chapter 16	Renaissance and Reformation Chapter 17	Enlightenment and Revolution Chapter 18
What was their government like?	• Local groups ruled by chiefs and councils • Powerful emperors or kings (Maya, Aztec, and Inca)	• Italian city-states ruled by wealthy families • Most European areas ruled by kings, princes, and nobles	• English king's powers are limited, representative government spreads • United States founded as a republic

What was their language and writing like?	• Native Americans spoke hundreds of languages • Mayan and Aztec languages written in hieroglyphics • Inca had no written language	• Printed books helped spread knowledge • Vernacular used in Protestant worship • Latin remains language of Catholic Church	• Meeting of cultures meant spread of knowledge about languages • European languages brought by settlers to overseas colonies
What contributions did they make?	• Developed trade networks and methods of farming and building 	 • Furthered education • Created lifelike art • Different religions existed side by side	 • Reason seen as a way to truth • General rules developed for scientific study • Beginning of modern democracy
How do these changes affect me? *Can you add any?*	• Native Americans passed on foods (corn, chocolate, potatoes) • Many place names in the Americas are based on Native American words (Chicago, Mississippi)	• Renaissance and Reformation Europeans passed on practice of printing books • School subjects (history, language) are rooted in Renaissance learning	• Supported rights (free speech, religion, press) that we enjoy today • Scientific tools (microscope, telescope) and vaccines for disease developed

Appendix

SkillBuilder Handbook 708

Standardized Test Practice 726

Primary Sources Library 736

Suggested Readings 748

Glossary 750

Spanish Glossary 756

Gazetteer 763

Index 772

Acknowledgements 792

What Is an Appendix?

An appendix is the additional material you often find at the end of books. The following information will help you learn how to use the Appendix in **Journey Across Time: The Early Ages.**

SkillBuilder Handbook

The **SkillBuilder Handbook** offers you information and practice using critical thinking and social studies skills. Mastering these skills will help you in all your courses.

Standardized Test Preparation

The skills you need to do well on standardized tests are practiced in the **Standardized Test Practice** section of this Appendix.

Primary Sources Library

The **Primary Sources Library** provides additional first-person accounts of historical events. Primary sources are often narratives by a person who actually experienced what is being described.

Suggested Readings

The **Suggested Readings** list suggests the titles of fiction and non-fiction books you might be interested in reading. These books deal with the same topics that are covered in each chapter.

Glossary

The **Glossary** is a list of important or difficult terms found in a textbook. Since words sometimes have other meanings, you may wish to consult a dictionary to find other uses for the term. The glossary gives a definition of each term as it is used in the book. The glossary also includes page numbers telling you where in the textbook the term is used.

The Spanish Glossary

The **Spanish Glossary** contains everything that an English glossary does, but it is written in Spanish. A Spanish glossary is especially important to bilingual students, or those Spanish-speaking students who are learning the English language.

Gazetteer

The **Gazetteer** (GA•zuh•TIHR) is a geographical dictionary. It lists some of the largest countries, cities, and several important geographic features. Each entry also includes a page number telling where this place is talked about in your textbook.

Index

The **Index** is an alphabetical listing that includes the subjects of the book and the page numbers where those subjects can be found. The index in this book also lets you know that certain pages contain maps, graphs, photos, or paintings about the subject.

Acknowledgements and Photo Credits

This section lists photo credits and/or literary credits for the book. You can look at this section to find out where the publisher obtained the permission to use a photograph or to use excerpts from other books.

Test Yourself

Find the answers to these questions by using the Appendix on the following pages.

1. **What does *dynasty* mean?**
2. **What is the topic of the first Primary Source reading?**
3. **On what page can I find out about Confucius?**
4. **Where exactly is Roanoke located?**
5. **What is one of the Suggested Readings for Unit 3?**

SkillBuilder Handbook

Contents

Finding the Main Idea 709

Taking Notes and Outlining 710

Reading a Time Line 711

Sequencing and Categorizing
Information 712

Recognizing Point of View 713

Distinguishing Fact From Opinion 714

Analyzing Library and Research
Resources 715

Analyzing Primary Source Documents . . .716

Building a Database 717

Summarizing 718

Evaluating a Web Site 719

Understanding Cause and Effect 720

Making Comparisons 721

Making Predictions 722

Drawing Inferences and Conclusions 723

Recognizing Economic Indicators 724

Interpreting Political Cartoons 725

Finding the Main Idea

Why Learn This Skill?

Understanding the main idea allows you to grasp the whole picture and get an overall understanding of what you are reading. Historical details, such as names, dates, and events, are easier to remember when they are connected to a main idea.

1 Learning the Skill

Follow these steps when trying to find the main idea:

- Read the material and ask, "Why was this written? What is its purpose?"

- Read the first sentence of the first paragraph. The main idea of a paragraph is often found in the topic sentence. The main idea of a large section of text is often found in a topic paragraph.

- Identify details that support the main ideas.

- Keep the main idea clearly in your mind as you read.

2 Practicing the Skill

Read the paragraph in the next column that describes how the culture of the world is changing. Answer the questions, and then complete the activity that follows. If you have trouble, use the graphic organizer to help you.

Cultural diffusion has increased as a result of technology. Cultural diffusion is the process by which a culture spreads its knowledge and skills from one area to another. Years ago, trade—the way people shared goods and ideas—resulted in cultural diffusion. Today communication technology, such as television and the Internet, links people throughout the world.

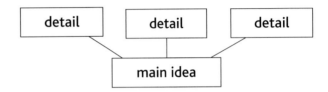

1. What is the main idea of this paragraph?

2. What are some details that support that main idea?

3. Practice the skill by reading three paragraphs in your textbook and identifying their main ideas.

4. Do you agree or disagree with the main idea presented above? Explain.

3 Applying the Skill

Bring a newspaper or magazine to class. With a partner, identify the main ideas in three different articles. Then describe how other sentences or paragraphs in the article support the main idea.

Taking Notes and Outlining

Why Learn This Skill?

If you asked someone for his or her phone number or e-mail address, how would you best remember it? Most people would write it down. Making a note of it helps you remember. The same is true for remembering what you read in a textbook.

1 Learning the Skill

Taking notes as you read your textbook will help you remember the information. As you read, identify and summarize the main ideas and details and write them in your notes. Do not copy material directly from the text.

Using note cards—that you can reorder later—can also help. First write the main topic or main idea at the top of the note card. Then write the details that support or describe that topic. Number the cards to help you keep them in order.

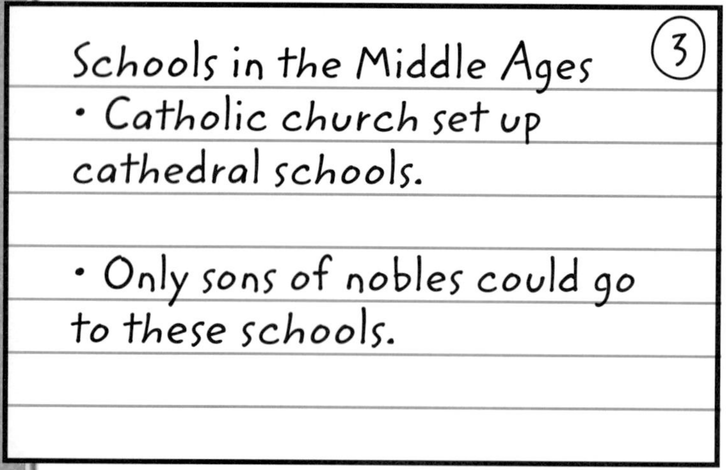

Schools in the Middle Ages ③
• Catholic church set up cathedral schools.

• Only sons of nobles could go to these schools.

You also may find it helpful to use an outline when writing notes. Outlining can help you organize your notes in a clear and orderly way.

First read the material to identify the main ideas. In this textbook, section headings and subheadings provide clues to the main ideas. Supporting details can then be placed under each heading. Each level of an outline must contain at least two items. The basic pattern for outlines is as follows:

Main Topic
   I. First idea or item
  II. Second idea or item
     A. first detail
     B. second detail
       1. subdetail
       2. subdetail
  III. Third idea or item
     A. first detail
     B. second detail

2 Practicing the Skill

Look back at Chapter 2, Section 1. Outline the main ideas of the section as shown above.

3 Applying the Skill

Use the outline that you created in step 2 to write a paragraph with a main idea and at least three supporting details.

Reading a Time Line

Why Learn This Skill?

Have you ever had to remember events and their dates in the order in which they happened? A time line is an easy way to make sense of the flow of dates and events. It is a simple diagram that shows how dates and events relate to one another. On most time lines, years are evenly spaced. Events on time lines are placed beside the date they occurred.

1 Learning the Skill

To read a time line, follow these steps:

• Find the dates on the opposite ends of the time line. They show the period of time that the time line covers.

• Note the equal spacing between dates on the time line.

• Study the order of events.

• Look to see how the events relate to each other.

2 Practicing the Skill

Examine the time line below. It shows major events in the history of early Egypt. Then answer the questions and complete the activity that follows.

1. When does the time line begin? When does it end?

2. What major event happened during the 1500s B.C.?

3. How long did the Hyksos rule Egypt?

4. What happened to Egypt during the 300s B.C.?

3 Applying the Skill

List 10 key events found in Unit 1 and the dates on which these events took place. Write the events in the order in which they occurred on a time line.

Ancient Egypt

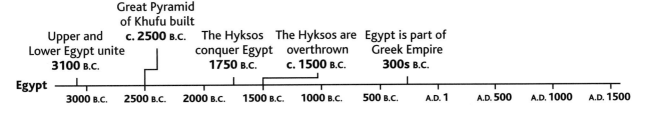

| Upper and Lower Egypt unite 3100 B.C. | Great Pyramid of Khufu built c. 2500 B.C. | The Hyksos conquer Egypt 1750 B.C. | The Hyksos are overthrown c. 1500 B.C. | Egypt is part of Greek Empire 300s B.C. |

Egypt — 3000 B.C. | 2500 B.C. | 2000 B.C. | 1500 B.C. | 1000 B.C. | 500 B.C. | A.D. 1 | A.D. 500 | A.D. 1000 | A.D. 1500

Sequencing and Categorizing Information

Why Learn This Skill?

Sequencing means placing facts in the order in which they happened. *Categorizing* means organizing information into groups of related facts and ideas. Both actions help you deal with large quantities of information in an understandable way.

1 Learning the Skill

Follow these steps to learn sequencing and categorizing skills:

- Look for dates or clue words that provide you with a chronological order: *in 2004, the late 1990s, first, then, finally, after the Great Depression,* and so on.

- Sequencing can be seen in unit and chapter time lines or on graphs where information covers several years.

- If the sequence of events is not important, you may want to categorize the information instead. To categorize information, look for topics and facts that are grouped together or have similar characteristics. If the information is about farming, one category might be *tools of farming.*

- List these categories, or characteristics, as the headings on a chart.

- As you read, look for details. Fill in these details under the proper categories on the chart.

2 Practicing the Skill

Read the paragraph below and then answer the questions that follow.

Buddhism started in India about 500 B.C. but was mostly driven out by 300 B.C. The religion of Islam also influenced India's history. In the A.D. 700s, Muslims from southwest Asia brought Islam to India. In the 1500s, they founded the Mogul empire and ruled India for the next 200 years.

1. What information can be organized by sequencing?

2. What categories can you use to organize the information? What facts could be placed under each category?

3 Applying the Skill

Look at the Geographic Dictionary on pages GH14 and GH15. Record any terms that would fit into the category "bodies of water." Also, find two newspaper or magazine articles about an important local issue. Sequence or categorize the information on note cards or in a chart.

Recognizing Point of View

Why Learn This Skill?

If you say, "Cats make better pets than dogs," you are expressing a point of view. You are giving your personal opinion. Knowing when someone is giving you his or her personal point of view can help you judge the truth of what is being said.

1 Learning the Skill

Most people have feelings and ideas that affect their point of view. A person's point of view is often influenced by his or her age, background, or position in a situation.

To recognize point of view, follow these steps:

- Identify the speaker or writer and examine his or her views on an issue. Think about his or her position in life and relationship to the issue.

- Look for language that shows an emotion or an opinion. Look for words such as *all, never, best, worst, might,* or *should.*

- Examine the speech or writing for imbalances. Does it have only one viewpoint? Does it fail to provide equal coverage of other viewpoints?

- Identify statements of fact. Factual statements usually answer the *Who? What? When?* and *Where?* questions.

- Determine how the person's point of view is reflected in his or her statements or writing.

2 Practicing the Skill

Read the following statement about wildlife in Africa, and answer the questions below.

Mountain gorillas live in the misty mountain forests of East Africa. Logging and mining, however, are destroying the forests. Unless the forests are protected, all of the gorillas will lose their homes and disappear forever. As a concerned African naturalist, I must emphasize that this will be one of the worst events in Africa's history.

1. What problem is the speaker addressing?
2. What reasons does the speaker give for the loss of the forests?
3. What is the speaker's point of view about the problem facing the gorillas in East Africa?

3 Applying the Skill

Choose a "Letter to the Editor" from a newspaper. Summarize the issue being discussed and the writer's point of view about that issue. State what an opposing point of view to the issue might be. Describe who might hold this other viewpoint in terms of their age, occupation, and background.

Distinguishing Fact From Opinion

Why Learn This Skill?

Suppose a friend says, "Our school's basketball team is awesome. That's a fact." Actually, it is not a fact; it is an opinion. Knowing how to tell the difference between a fact and an opinion can help you analyze the accuracy of political claims, advertisements, and many other kinds of statements.

1 Learning the Skill

A **fact** answers a specific question such as: What happened? Who did it? When and where did it happen? Why did it happen? Statements of fact can be checked for accuracy and proven.

An **opinion,** on the other hand, expresses beliefs, feelings, and judgments. It may reflect someone's thoughts, but it cannot be proven. An opinion often begins with a phrase such as *I believe, I think, probably, it seems to me,* or *in my opinion.*

To distinguish between facts and opinions, ask yourself these questions:

- Does this statement give specific information about an event?

- Can I check the accuracy of this statement?

- Does this statement express someone's feelings, beliefs, or judgment?

- Does it include phrases such as *I believe,* superlatives, or judgment words?

2 Practicing the Skill

Read each statement below. Tell whether each is a fact or an opinion, and explain how you arrived at your answer.

(1) The Han dynasty ruled China from 206 B.C. to A.D. 220.

(2) The Han dynasty was a much better dynasty than the Qin dynasty.

(3) The Han divided the country into districts to be better able to manage such a large area.

(4) The government should not have encouraged support for arts and inventions.

(5) The Han kept very good records of everything they did, which helps historians today learn about them.

(6) Han rulers chose government officials on the basis of merit rather than birth.

(7) No other ruling family in the world can compare with the Han dynasty of China.

(8) Han rulers should have defended the poor farmers against the harsh actions of wealthy landowners.

3 Applying the Skill

Read one newspaper article that describes a political event. Find three statements of fact and three opinions expressed in the article.

Analyzing Library and Research Resources

Why Learn This Skill?

Imagine that your teacher has sent you to the library to write a report on the history of ancient Rome. Knowing how to choose good sources for your research will help you save time in the library and write a better report.

1 Learning the Skill

Not all sources will be useful for your report on Rome. Even some sources that involve topics about Rome will not always provide the information you want. In analyzing sources for your research project, choose items that are nonfiction and that contain the most information about your topic.

When choosing research resources ask these questions:

• Is the information up-to-date?

• Does the index have several pages listed for the topic?

• Is the resource written in a way that is easy to understand?

• Are there helpful illustrations and photos?

2 Practicing the Skill

Look at the following list of sources. Which would be most helpful in writing a report on the history of ancient Rome? Explain your choices.

(1) A travel guide to Italy today

(2) A guide to early Roman art and architecture

(3) A children's storybook about ancient Europe

(4) A history of ancient Greece

(5) A study of the rise and fall of the Roman Empire

(6) A book on modern republican ideas

(7) A biographical dictionary of ancient rulers of the world

(8) An atlas of the world

3 Applying the Skill

Go to your local library or use the Internet to create a bibliography of sources you might use to write a report on the history of ancient Rome. List at least five sources.

▲ Roman mosaic showing gladiators in battle

Analyzing Primary Source Documents

Why Learn This Skill?

Historians determine what happened in the past by combing through bits of evidence to reconstruct events. These types of evidence—both written and illustrated—are called primary sources. Examining primary sources can help you understand history.

1 Learning the Skill

Primary sources are sources that were created in the historical era being studied. They can include letters, diaries, photographs and pictures, news articles, legal documents, stories, literature, and artwork.

To analyze primary sources, ask yourself the following questions:

- What is the item?
- Who created it?
- Where did it come from?
- When was it created?
- What does it reveal about the topic I am studying?

2 Practicing the Skill

The primary source that follows comes from *Stories of Rome* by Livy. Livy was a Roman historian who lived from 59 B.C. to A.D. 17. Here he has written a story with a moral, or lesson to be learned. Read the story, and then answer the questions that follow.

Once upon a time, the different parts of the human body were not all in agreement. . . . And it seemed very unfair to the other parts of the body that they should worry and sweat away to look after the belly. After all, the belly just sat there . . . doing nothing, enjoying all the nice things that came along. So they hatched a plot. The hands weren't going to take food to the mouth; even if they did, the mouth wasn't going to accept it. . . . They went into a sulk and waited for the belly to cry for help. But while they waited, one by one all the parts of the body got weaker and weaker. The moral of this story? The belly too has its job to do. It has to be fed, but it also does feeding of its own.

Excerpt from *Stories of Rome*, Livy, c. 20 B.C.

1. What is the main topic?
2. Who did the hands and mouth think was lazy?
3. What did the hands and mouth do about it?
4. What was the moral—or lesson—of the story?

3 Applying the Skill

Find a primary source from your past—a photo or newspaper clipping. Explain to the class what it shows about that time in your life.

Building a Database

Why Learn This Skill?

A database is a collection of information stored in a computer or on diskette files. It runs on software that organizes large amounts of information in a way that makes it easy to search and make any changes. It often takes the form of a chart or table. You might build databases to store information related to a class at school or your weekly schedule.

1 Learning the Skill

To create a database using word-processing software, follow these steps:

- Enter a title identifying the type of information in your document and file names.

- Determine the set of specific points of information you wish to include. As the database example on this page shows, you might want to record data on the imports and exports of specific countries.

- Enter the information categories along with country names as headings in a columned chart. Each column makes up a field, which is the basic unit for information stored in a database.

- Enter data you have collected into the cells, or individual spaces, on your chart.

- Use your computer's sorting feature to organize the data. For example, you might alphabetize by country name.

- Add, delete, or update information as needed. Database software automatically adjusts the cells in the chart.

2 Practicing the Skill

On a separate sheet of paper, answer the following questions referring to the database on this page.

1. What type of information does the database contain?

2. What related fields of information does it show?

3. The author learns that Canada also exports clothing, beverages, and art to the United States. Is it necessary to create a new database? Explain.

3 Applying the Skill

Build a database to help you keep track of your school assignments. Work with four fields: Subject, Assignment Description, Due Date, and Completed Assignments. Be sure to keep your database up-to-date.

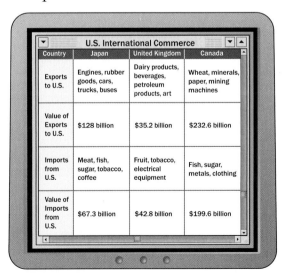

U.S. International Commerce

Country	Japan	United Kingdom	Canada
Exports to U.S.	Engines, rubber goods, cars, trucks, buses	Dairy products, beverages, petroleum products, art	Wheat, minerals, paper, mining machines
Value of Exports to U.S.	$128 billion	$35.2 billion	$232.6 billion
Imports from U.S.	Meat, fish, sugar, tobacco, coffee	Fruit, tobacco, electrical equipment	Fish, sugar, metals, clothing
Value of Imports from U.S.	$67.3 billion	$42.8 billion	$199.6 billion

Summarizing

Why Learn This Skill?

Imagine you have been assigned a long chapter to read. How can you remember the important information? Summarizing information—reducing large amounts of information to a few key phrases—can help you remember the main ideas and important facts.

1 Learning the Skill

To summarize information, follow these guidelines when you read:

- Separate the main ideas from the supporting details. Use the main ideas in a summary.

- Use your own words to describe the main ideas. Do not copy the selection word for word.

- If the summary is almost as long as the reading selection, you are including too much information. The summary should be very short.

2 Practicing the Skill

To practice the skill, read the paragraph below. Then answer the questions that follow.

The Ming dynasty that followed the Mongols tried to rid the country of Mongol influence. The Ming leaders believed that China could become a great empire. They expanded Chinese control over parts of East Asia, including Korea, Vietnam, and Myanmar (Burma). To re-establish the importance of Chinese culture, they encouraged the practices of older Chinese traditions, especially in the arts. Chinese literature during the Ming era followed the styles of ancient Chinese writers. Some of the finest Chinese paintings and pottery were created during this period. Ming rulers also built the Forbidden City.

1. What are the main ideas of this paragraph?
2. What are the supporting details?
3. Write a brief summary of two or three sentences that will help you remember what the paragraph is about.

3 Applying the Skill

Read a newspaper or short magazine article. Summarize the article in one or two sentences.

Evaluating a Web Site

Why Learn This Skill?

The Internet has grown to become a necessary household and business tool as more people use it. With so many Web sites available, how do you know which one will be the most helpful to you? You must look at the details, so you do not waste valuable time in Web searches.

1 Learning the Skill

The Internet is a valuable research tool. It is easy to use, and it often provides fast, up-to-date information. The most common use of the Internet by students is in doing research. However, some Web site information is not really accurate or reliable.

When using the Internet to do research, you must evaluate the information very carefully. When evaluating the Web site, ask yourself the following questions:

- Do the facts on the site seem accurate?

- Who is the author or sponsor of the site, and what is that person's or organization's reason for maintaining it?

- Does the site information explore a subject in-depth?

- Does the site contain links to other useful resources?

- Is the information easy to read and access?

2 Practicing the Skill

To practice the skill, find three Web sites on the shoguns or samurai of Japan. Follow these steps and write your explanation.

1. Evaluate how useful these sites would be if you were writing a report on the topic.

2. Chose which one is the most helpful.

3. Explain why you chose that site.

3 Applying the Skill

If your school had a Web site, what kind of information would be on it? Write a paragraph describing this site.

A Japanese samurai warrior ▶

Understanding Cause and Effect

Why Learn This Skill?

You know if you watch television instead of completing your homework, you probably will not get a good grade. The cause—not doing homework—leads to the effect—not getting a good grade.

1 Learning the Skill

A *cause* is any person, event, or condition that makes something happen. What happens as a result is known as an *effect*.

These guidelines will help you identify cause and effect.

- Identify two or more events.

- Ask questions about why events occur.

- Look for "clue words" that alert you to cause and effect, such as *because, led to, brought about, produced,* and *therefore.*

- Identify the outcome of events.

2 Practicing the Skill

As you read the following passage, record cause-and-effect connections in a chart or graphic organizer.

Around 200 B.C., Mesopotamians were among the first in the world to blend copper and tin to make bronze.

Bronze brought many changes to life in Mesopotamia. For one thing, bronze was much harder than the copper products that were used until that time. Because it was harder, bronze made better tools and sharper weapons. This improvement in technology was a help to farmers, craftworkers, and soldiers alike.

Molten [melted] bronze was also easier to pour than the metals used earlier. Craftworkers were able to make finer arrows, ax-heads, statues, bowls, and other objects.

3 Applying the Skill

Look again at the chapter you are currently reading. Choose a major event that is described and list its causes.

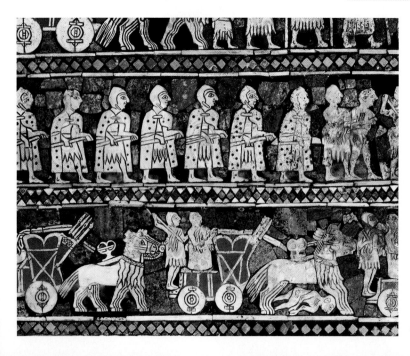

◀ **The Royal Banner of Ur**

Making Comparisons

Why Learn This Skill?

Suppose you want to buy a portable CD player, and you must choose among three models. To make this decision, you would probably compare various features of the three models, such as price, sound quality, size, and so on. By making comparisons, you will figure out which model is best for you. In the study of world history, you often compare people or events from one time period with those from a different time period.

1 Learning the Skill

When making comparisons, you examine and identify two or more groups, situations, events, or documents. Then you identify any similarities (ways they are alike) and differences (ways they are different). For example, the chart on this page compares the characteristics of two ancient civilizations.

When making comparisons, apply the following steps:

- Decide what items will be compared. Clue words such as *also, as well as, like, same as,* and *similar to* can help you identify things that are being compared.

- Determine which characteristics you will use to compare them.

- Identify similarities and differences in these characteristics.

2 Practicing the Skill

To practice the skill, analyze the information on the chart at the bottom of this page. Then answer these questions.

1. What items are being compared?

2. What characteristics are being used to compare them?

3. In what ways were the Phoenicians and Israelites similar? In what ways were they different?

4. Suppose you wanted to compare the two peoples in more detail. What are some of the characteristics you might use?

3 Applying the Skill

Think about two sports that are played at your school. Make a chart comparing such things as: where the games are played, who plays them, what equipment is used, and other details.

Phoenician and Israelite Civilizations

Cultural Characteristic	Phoenicians	Israelites
Homeland	Canaan	Canaan
Political Organization	city-states	12 tribes; later, kingdom
Method of Rule	kings/merchant councils	kings/council of elders
Main Occupations	artisans, traders, shippers	herders, farmers, traders
Religion	belief in many gods and goddesses	belief in one, all-powerful god
Main Contribution	spread of an alphabet	principles of social justice

Making Predictions

Why Learn This Skill?

In history you read about people making difficult decisions based on what they think *might* happen. By making predictions yourself, you can get a better understanding of the choices people make.

1 Learning the Skill

As you read a paragraph or section in your book, think about what might come next. What you think will happen is your *prediction*. A prediction does not have a correct or incorrect answer. Making predictions helps you to carefully consider what you are reading.

To make a prediction, ask yourself:

- What happened in this paragraph or section?

- What prior knowledge do I have about the events in the text?

- What similar situations do I know of?

- What do I think might happen next?

- Test your prediction: read further to see if you were correct.

◀ Aztec shield

2 Practicing the Skill

To practice the skill, read the following paragraph about the Aztec Empire. Then answer the questions.

The Aztec of ancient Mexico built the strongest empire of any Native American group. They mined gold, silver, and other goods for trade. In building their empire, they conquered many other Native American groups. The Aztec fought their enemies using wooden weapons with stone blades.

In the 1500s, a Spanish army seeking gold heard about the Aztec and their riches. Led by Hernán Cortés, the Spaniards were helped by enemies of the Aztec. Armed with steel swords, muskets, and cannons, the Spaniards moved towards the Aztec capital.

1. Choose the outcome below that is most likely to occur between the Aztec and Spaniards.
   a. The Spaniards will avoid the Aztec altogether.
   b. The two groups will become friends.
   c. The Spaniards will conquer the Aztec.
   d. The Aztec will conquer the Spaniards.

2. Explain why you chose the answer you did.

3 Applying the Skill

Watch a television show or a movie. Halfway through the show, write your prediction of how it will end on a piece of paper. At the end of the show, check your prediction.

Drawing Inferences and Conclusions

Why Learn This Skill?

Suppose your teacher brought an artifact to class and a classmate exclaimed, "That came from Greece, didn't it?" You might infer that your classmate had an interest in Greece.

1 Learning the Skill

To *infer* means to evaluate information and arrive at a *conclusion*. Social studies writers do not always spell out everything in the text. When you make inferences you "read between the lines." You must then use the available facts and your own knowledge of social studies to draw a conclusion.

Use the following steps to help draw inferences and make conclusions:

- Read carefully for stated facts and ideas.

- Summarize the information and list the important facts.

- Apply related information that you may already know to make inferences.

- Use your knowledge and insight to develop some conclusions about these facts.

2 Practicing the Skill

Read the passage below and answer the questions.

Many Greek temples were decorated with sculpture. Greek sculpture, like Greek architecture, was used to express Greek ideas. The favorite subject of Greek artists was the human body. Greek sculptors did not copy their subjects exactly, flaws and all. Instead, they tried to show their ideal version of perfection and beauty.

1. What topic is the writer describing?
2. What facts are given?
3. What can you infer about Greek cities from the information?
4. What conclusions can you draw about how the Greeks felt about sculptures?

3 Applying the Skill

Read one of the biographies in this text. What can you infer about the life of the person described? Draw a conclusion about whether or not you would like to meet this person.

◀ Ancient Greek sculptures of Socrates (far left), Plato (middle), and Aristotle (left)

Recognizing Economic Indicators

Why Learn This Skill?

Every day, business and government leaders are faced with the challenge of trying to predict what will happen to the economy in the coming months and years. To help these leaders in making decisions, economists, or scientists who study the economy, have developed ways to measure an economy's performance. These ways are called economic indicators.

1 Learning the Skill

Economic indicators are statistics, or numbers, that tell how well the economy is doing and how well the economy is going to do in the future. They include the number of jobless, the rate at which prices rise over a period of time, and the amount of goods and services that are produced and sold. Each month, the U.S. Department of Commerce gathers data for 78 economic indicators covering all aspects of the state of the United States economy. The chart below lists some common terms for economic indicators that you may read about.

Economic Indicators

Term	Definition
Saving	
Income	
Expenditure	
Consumption	
Inflation	
Debt	
Gross Domestic Product (GDP)	
Interest Rates	
Credit	
Export	
Import	

▲ Prices on the stock market often rise or fall based on changes in economic indicators.

2 Practicing the Skill

Start an Economics Handbook. Using a dictionary, look up each economic term listed on this chart. Write a definition for each term in your Economics Handbook.

3 Applying the Skill

Think about one of the countries you have read about in this text that has grown to be wealthy. Using the terms that you just defined, write a paragraph describing that country's wealth.

Interpreting Political Cartoons

Why Learn This Skill?

Political cartoonists use art to express political opinions. Their work appears in newspapers, magazines, books, and on the Internet. Political cartoons are drawings that express an opinion. They usually focus on public figures, political events, or economic or social conditions. A political cartoon can give you a summary of an event or circumstance and the artist's opinion in a quick and entertaining manner.

1 Learning the Skill

To interpret a political cartoon, follow these steps:

• Read the title, caption, or conversation balloons. Most cartoons will carry at least one of these elements. They help you identify the subject of the cartoon.

• Identify the characters or people shown. They may be caricatures, or unrealistic drawings that exaggerate the characters' physical features.

• Identify any symbols shown. Symbols are things that stand for something else. An example is the American flag that is a symbol of our country. Commonly recognized symbols may not be labeled. Unusual symbolism will be labeled.

• Examine the actions in the cartoon—what is happening and why?

• Identify the cartoonist's purpose. What statement or idea is he or she trying to get across? Decide if the cartoonist wants to persuade, criticize, or just make people think.

2 Practicing the Skill

On a separate sheet of paper, answer these questions about the political cartoon below.

1. What is the subject of the cartoon?
2. What words give clues as to the meaning of the cartoon?
3. What item seems out of place?
4. What message do you think the cartoonist is trying to send?

3 Applying the Skill

Bring a news magazine to class. With a partner, analyze the message in each political cartoon that you find.

Standardized Test Practice

Standardized tests are one way educators measure what you have learned. This handbook is designed to help you prepare for standardized tests in social studies. On the pages that follow, you will find a review of the major social studies critical thinking skills that you will need to master to be successful when taking tests.

Contents

Interpreting a Map 727

Interpreting a Political Map 728

Interpreting Charts 729

Making Comparisons 730

Interpreting Primary Sources 731

Interpreting a Political Cartoon 732

Interpreting a Circle Graph 733

Drawing Inferences and Conclusions 734

Comparing Data 735

Interpreting a Map

Before 1492, people living in Europe in the Eastern Hemisphere had no idea that the continents of North America and South America in the Western Hemisphere existed. That was the year Christopher Columbus first reached the Americas. His voyage of exploration paved the way for other European voyages to the Western Hemisphere. The voyages of the early explorers brought together two worlds. Previously these parts of the globe had no contact with each other. Trade between the hemispheres changed life for people on both sides of the Atlantic Ocean. The trade between the peoples of the Eastern Hemisphere and the Western Hemisphere is referred to as the Columbian Exchange.

Skills Practice

Although globes are the best, most accurate way to show places on the round earth, people can more easily use maps to represent places. A map is made by taking data from a round globe and placing it on a flat surface. To read a map, first read the title to determine the subject of the map. Then read the map key or the labels on the map to find out what the colors and symbols on the map mean. Use the compass rose to identify the four cardinal directions of north, south, east, and west. Study the map of the Columbian Exchange and answer the questions that follow on a separate sheet of paper.

1. What is the subject of the map?

2. What do the arrows represent?

3. What continents are shown on the map?

4. What foods did Europeans acquire from the Americas?

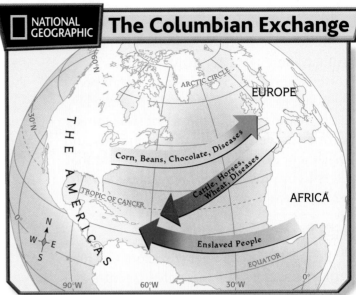

NATIONAL GEOGRAPHIC — The Columbian Exchange

5. What did the Americas acquire from Europe?

6. What people were brought from Africa to the Americas?

7. In what direction is Europe from the Americas?

Standardized Test Practice

DIRECTIONS: Use the map and your knowledge of social studies to answer the following question on a separate sheet of paper.

1. Which of the following statements about the Columbian Exchange is true?

   A Food products were traded only between Africa and the Americas.

   B Europeans acquired cattle from the Americas.

   C Europeans introduced corn, tomatoes, and beans to Native Americans.

   D Enslaved Africans were brought to the Americas.

Interpreting a Political Map

By 1750, or the middle of the eighteenth century, there were 13 British colonies in North America. A colony is a group of people living in one place who are governed by rulers in another place. The British colonists in America were ruled by the monarchy and Parliament of Great Britain. That meant that rulers living 3,000 miles away made laws for the American colonists.

Skills Practice

Political maps illustrate divisions between territories such as nations, states, colonies, or other political units. These divisions are called boundaries. Lines represent the boundaries between political areas. To interpret a political map, read the map title to determine what geographic area and time period it covers. Identify the colonies or other political units on the map. Look at the map key for additional information. Study the map on this page and answer the questions that follow on a separate sheet of paper.

1. List the New England Colonies.
2. Which were the Middle Colonies?
3. Which Middle Colony bordered Pennsylvania to the north?
4. Which was the southernmost early British colony?
5. Name the body of water that formed the eastern border of the colonies.
6. Where was Charles Town located?

NATIONAL GEOGRAPHIC
The Thirteen Colonies *1750*

Standardized Test Practice

DIRECTIONS: Use the map and your knowledge of social studies to answer the following questions on a separate sheet of paper.

1. The New England Colony that covered the largest land area was
   A Virginia.
   B Pennsylvania.
   C Massachusetts.
   D New Hampshire.
2. The northernmost Middle Colony is the present-day state of
   F Maryland.
   G New York.
   H Massachusetts.
   J Pennsylvania.
3. The settlement of Plymouth was located
   A near Jamestown.
   B in Massachusetts.
   C in the Southern Colonies.
   D in Virginia.

Interpreting Charts

Government is a necessary part of every nation. It gives citizens stability and provides services that many of us take for granted. However, governments can sometimes have too much power.

The United States was founded on the principle of limited government. Limited governments require all people to follow the laws. Even the rulers must obey rules set for the society. A democracy is a form of limited government. Not all forms of government have limits. In unlimited governments, power belongs to the ruler. No laws exist to limit what the ruler may do. A dictatorship is an example of an unlimited government.

Skills Practice

Charts are visual graphics that categorize information. When reading a chart, be sure to look at all the headings and labels. Study the charts on this page and answer the questions that follow on a separate sheet of paper.

1. What do the charts compare?

2. Which political systems are forms of limited government?

3. Which form of government often uses military rule?

4. In which political system does the king or queen have complete power?

Limited Governments

Representative Democracy	Constitutional Monarchy
People elect leaders to rule	King or queen's power is limited
Individual rights important	Individual rights important
More than one political party	More than one political party
People give consent to be governed	People elect governing body

Unlimited Governments

Dictatorship	Absolute Monarchy
One person or small group rules	King or queen inherits power
Few personal freedoms	Usually some freedoms
Rule by force, often military	Officials are appointed by king or queen
Ruler does not have to obey rules	Monarch has complete authority

Standardized Test Practice

DIRECTIONS: Use the charts and your knowledge of social studies to answer the following questions on a separate sheet of paper.

1. Information found in the charts shows that the most restrictive form of government is a

   A dictatorship.

   B representative democracy.

   C absolute monarchy.

   D constitutional monarchy.

2. Under which type of government do citizens have the most power?

   F unlimited government

   G limited government

   H absolute monarchy

   J dictatorship

3. An example of an unlimited government is

   A the United States in the 1960s.

   B Libya in the 1970s.

   C the United Kingdom in the 1980s.

   D Mexico in the 1990s.

Making Comparisons

The roots of representative democracy in the United States can be traced back to colonial times. In 1607 English settlers founded the colony of Jamestown in present-day Virginia. As the colony developed, problems arose. Later, colonists formed the House of Burgesses to deal with these problems. Citizens of Virginia were chosen as representatives to the House of Burgesses. This became the first legislature, or lawmaking body, in America.

Today citizens of the United States elect representatives to Congress. The major function of Congress is to make laws for the nation. There are two houses, or chambers, of the U.S. Congress. Legislative bodies with two houses are said to be bicameral. The bicameral Congress of the United States includes the Senate and the House of Representatives. Article I of the U.S. Constitution describes how each house will be organized and how its members will be chosen.

Skills Practice

When you make a comparison, you identify and examine two or more groups, situations, events, or documents. Then you identify any similarities and differences between the items. Study the information presented on the chart on this page and answer the questions that follow on a separate sheet of paper.

1. What two things does the chart compare?

2. How are the qualifications for each house of the U.S. Congress similar?

3. The members of which house are probably more experienced? Why?

The U.S. Congress

House of Representatives	Senate
Qualifications: Must be 25 years old Must be U.S. citizen for 7+ years Must live in the state they represent	**Qualifications:** Must be 30 years old Must be U.S. citizen for 9+ years Must live in the state they represent
Number of Representatives: 435 total representatives; number of representatives per state is based on state population	**Number of Representatives:** 100 total senators; two senators elected from each state regardless of state population
Terms of Office: Two-year terms	**Terms of Office:** Six-year terms

Standardized Test Practice

DIRECTIONS: Use the chart and your knowledge of social studies to answer the following questions on a separate sheet of paper.

1. Which of the following statements best reflects information shown in the chart?

   A The Senate has more members than the House of Representatives.

   B Representatives to the House are elected to two-year terms.

   C House members must be residents of their states for at least 9 years.

   D A state's population determines its number of senators.

2. One inference that can be made from information shown on the chart is that

   F Texas elects more senators than Rhode Island.

   G Texas elects more House members than Rhode Island.

   H Texas elects fewer senators than Rhode Island.

   J Texas elects fewer House members than Rhode Island.

Interpreting Primary Sources

When Thomas Jefferson wrote the Declaration of Independence, he used the term "unalienable rights." Jefferson was referring to the natural rights that belong to humans. He and the other Founders of our nation believed that government could not take away the rights of the people.

Skills Practice

Primary sources are records of events made by the people who witnessed them. A historical document such as the Declaration of Independence is an example of a primary source. Read the passage below and answer the questions that follow on a separate sheet of paper.

> "We hold these truths to be self-evident, that all men are created equal, that they are endowed by their Creator with certain unalienable Rights, that among these are Life, Liberty, and the pursuit of Happiness . . ."
>
> —Declaration of Independence, July 4, 1776

1. What does the document say about the equality of men?

2. List the three natural, or unalienable, rights to which the document refers.

After gaining independence, American leaders wrote the U.S. Constitution in 1787. The Bill of Rights includes the first 10 amendments, or additions, to the Constitution. The First Amendment protects five basic rights of all American citizens. Study the chart on this page and answer the questions that follow.

1. Which right allows Americans to express themselves without fear of punishment by the government?

2. Which right allows people to worship as they please?

3. Which right allows citizens to publish a pamphlet that is critical of the president?

4. What is the Bill of Rights?

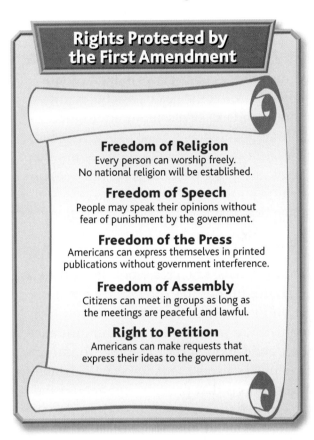

Rights Protected by the First Amendment

Freedom of Religion
Every person can worship freely. No national religion will be established.

Freedom of Speech
People may speak their opinions without fear of punishment by the government.

Freedom of the Press
Americans can express themselves in printed publications without government interference.

Freedom of Assembly
Citizens can meet in groups as long as the meetings are peaceful and lawful.

Right to Petition
Americans can make requests that express their ideas to the government.

Standardized Test Practice

DIRECTIONS: Use the chart and your knowledge of social studies to answer the following question on a separate sheet of paper.

1. Which First Amendment right protects citizens who are staging a protest outside a government building?

   A freedom of speech

   B freedom of the press

   C freedom of assembly

   D freedom of religion

Interpreting a Political Cartoon

Just as the government of the United States is limited in its powers, freedoms extended to Americans also have limits. The First Amendment was not intended to allow Americans to do whatever they please without regard to others. Limits on freedoms are necessary to keep order in a society of so many people. The government can establish laws to limit certain rights to protect the health, safety, security, or moral standards of a community. Rights can be restricted to prevent one person's rights from interfering with the rights of another. For example, the freedom of speech does not include allowing a person to make false statements that hurt another's reputation.

Skills Practice

The artists who create political cartoons often use humor to express their opinions on political issues. Sometimes these cartoonists are trying to inform and influence the public about a certain topic. To interpret a political cartoon, look for symbols, labels, and captions that provide clues about the message of the cartoonist. Analyze these

elements and draw some conclusions. Study the political cartoon on this page and answer the questions that follow on a separate sheet of paper.

1. What is the subject of the cartoon?

2. What words provide clues as to the meaning of the cartoon?

3. Whom does the person in the cartoon represent?

4. What is the person doing?

5. What do the subject's thoughts suggest about the task faced by those involved in planning the new nation's government?

6. What limits are placed on First Amendment rights? Why are these rights limited?

LET'S SEE NOW...WE'LL GIVE THEM FREEDOM, BUT NOT TOO MUCH FREEDOM; LIBERTY, BUT NOT TOO MUCH LIBERTY; RIGHTS, BUT NOT TOO MANY RIGHTS...

P. harris

Standardized Test Practice

DIRECTIONS: Use the political cartoon and your knowledge of social studies to answer the following questions on a separate sheet of paper.

1. The most appropriate title for the cartoon is

   A Limits on Government.

   B Parliament at Work.

   C Limiting Rights.

   D Unlimited Government.

2. The sources of our rights as citizens of the United States come from which of the following?

   F the Declaration of Independence and the U.S. Constitution

   G the will of the president

   H unwritten customs and traditions

   J the United Nations charter

Interpreting a Circle Graph

"E pluribus unum" is a Latin phrase found on United States coins. It means "Out of many, one." The United States is sometimes called a "nation of immigrants." Unless you are a Native American, your ancestors came to America within the last 500 years.

Groups of people who share a common culture, language, or history are referred to as ethnic groups. American neighborhoods include many different ethnic groups. The circle graph on this page shows the major ethnic groups in the United States.

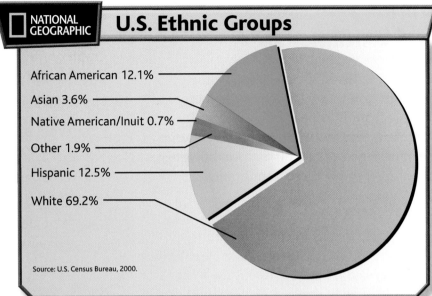

NATIONAL GEOGRAPHIC

U.S. Ethnic Groups

African American 12.1%
Asian 3.6%
Native American/Inuit 0.7%
Other 1.9%
Hispanic 12.5%
White 69.2%

Source: U.S. Census Bureau, 2000.

Skills Practice

A circle graph shows percentages of a total quantity. Each part, or slice, of the graph represents a part of the total quantity. To read a circle graph, first read the title. Then study the labels to find out what each part represents. Compare the sizes of the circle slices. Study the circle graph and answer the questions that follow on a separate sheet of paper.

1. What information does this circle graph present?

2. Which ethnic group includes the largest percentage of Americans?

3. Which groups represent less than 1 percent of the people in the United States?

4. What percentage of the United States population is represented by African Americans?

5. The smallest ethnic group has lived in the United States the longest. What is this ethnic group?

Standardized Test Practice

DIRECTIONS: Use the graph and your knowledge of social studies to answer the following questions on a separate sheet of paper.

1. Which group's population is about three times greater than the number of Asians?

    A African American

    B White

    C Native American/Inuit

    D Other

2. How does the Hispanic population compare to the African American population of the United States?

    F It is greater than the African American population.

    G It is the smallest segment of the United States population.

    H It is less than half the size of the African American population.

    J It is slightly less than the African American population.

Drawing Inferences and Conclusions

During the mid-nineteenth century, immigration to the United States increased. People from European countries such as Germany and Ireland traveled to America seeking new opportunities. Life, however, was not easy for these immigrants.

Skills Practice

To infer means to evaluate information and arrive at a conclusion. When you make inferences, you "read between the lines." You must use the available facts and your own knowledge of social studies to form a judgment or opinion about the material.

Line graphs are a way of showing numbers visually. They are often used to compare changes over time. Sometimes a graph has more than one line. The lines show different quantities of a related topic. To analyze a line graph read the title and the information on the horizontal and vertical axes. Use this information to draw conclusions. Study the graph on this page and answer the questions that follow on a separate sheet of paper.

1. What is the subject of the line graph?

2. What information is shown on the horizontal axis?

3. What information is shown on the vertical axis?

4. Why do you think these immigrants came to the United States?

U.S. Immigration, 1820–1860

Source: *Historical Statistics of the United States: Colonial Times to 1970.*

Standardized Test Practice

DIRECTIONS: Use the line graph and your knowledge of social studies to answer the following questions on a separate sheet of paper.

1. The country that provided the most immigrants to the United States between the years 1820 and 1860 was

   A Great Britain.

   B Ireland.

   C Germany.

   D France.

2. In about what year did the number of German immigrants to the United States reach a peak?

   F 1845

   G 1852

   H 1855

   J 1860

3. Irish migration to the United States increased in the mid-1800s because of

   A a terrible potato famine in Ireland.

   B the failure of a German revolution in 1848.

   C the nativist movement.

   D the availability of low-paying factory jobs.

Comparing Data

The world's earliest civilizations developed more than 6,000 years ago. The discovery of farming led to the rise of ancient cities in Mesopotamia and the Nile River valley. These early cities shared one important characteristic—they each arose near waterways. Since water was the easiest way to transport goods, the settlements became centers of trade.

Since then cities have grown all over the world. Every 10 years, the United States Census Bureau collects data to determine the population of the United States. (A census is an official count of people living in an area.) The first census was conducted in 1790. At that time, there were 3.9 million people in the 13 original states. The most recent census occurred in 2000. The results of that census showed that more than 280 million people reside in the 50 states that make up our nation.

Skills Practice

The charts on this page show populations of the five most populous cities in the United States during different time periods. When comparing information on charts be sure to read the titles and headings to define the data being compared. Study the charts and answer the questions below on a separate sheet of paper.

1. Which U.S. city had the greatest population in 1790?

2. Which U.S. city had the greatest population in 2000?

3. What was the population of Philadelphia in 1790?

4. What was Philadelphia's population in 2000?

5. Which cities are on both lists?

Population of Five Largest U.S. Cities, 1790

City	Number of People
New York City	33,131
Philadelphia	28,522
Boston	18,320
Charleston	16,359
Baltimore	13,503

Population of Five Largest U.S. Cities, 2000*

City	Number of People
New York City	8,008,278
Los Angeles	3,694,820
Chicago	2,896,016
Houston	1,953,631
Philadelphia	1,517,550

*Numbers do not include metropolitan areas.

Standardized Test Practice

DIRECTIONS: Use the charts and your knowledge of social studies to answer the following questions on a separate sheet of paper.

1. One inference that can be made from the charts is that the most populous cities in the United States

   A have good weather.

   B were founded early in our nation's history.

   C are port cities.

   D are in the eastern United States.

2. In 1790 the major cities of the United States were all

   F larger than 20,000 people.

   G located in the East.

   H Northern cities.

   J founded for religious reasons.

Primary Sources Library

Working With Primary Sources

Suppose that you have been asked to write a report on changes in your community over the past 25 years. Where would you get the information you need to begin writing? You would draw upon two types of information—primary sources and secondary sources.

Definitions

Primary sources are often first-person accounts by someone who actually saw or lived through what is being described. In other words, if you see a fire or live through a great storm and then write about your experiences, you are creating a primary source. Diaries, journals, photographs, and eyewitness reports are examples of primary sources. Secondary sources are second-hand accounts. For instance, if your friend experiences the fire or storm and tells you about it, or if you read about the fire or storm in the newspaper, and then you write about it, you are creating a secondary source. Textbooks, biographies, and histories are secondary sources.

Checking Your Sources

When you read primary or secondary sources, you should analyze them to figure out if they are dependable or reliable. Historians usually prefer primary sources to secondary sources, but both can be reliable or unreliable, depending on the following factors.

Time Span

With primary sources, it is important to consider how long after the event occurred the primary source was written. Chances are the longer the time span between the event and the account, the less reliable the account is. As time passes, people often forget details and fill in gaps with events that never took place. Although we like to think we remember things exactly as they happened, the fact is we often remember them as we wanted them to occur.

Reliability

Another factor to consider when evaluating a primary source is the writer's background and reliability. First, try to determine how this person knows about what he or she is writing. How much does he or she know? Is the writer being truthful? Is the account convincing?

Opinions

When evaluating a primary source, you should also decide whether the account has been influenced by emotion, opinion, or exaggeration. Writers can have reasons to distort the truth to

The Roman Colosseum

suit their personal purposes. Ask yourself: Why did the person write the account? Do any key words or expressions reveal the author's emotions or opinions? Compare the account with one written by another witness to the event. If they differ, ask yourself why they differ and which is more accurate.

Interpreting Primary Sources

To help you analyze a primary source, use the following steps:

- **Examine the origins of the document.**
  You need to determine if it is a primary source.

- **Find the main ideas.**
  Read the document and summarize the main ideas in your own words. These ideas may be fairly easy to identify in newspapers and journals, for example, but are much more difficult to find in poetry.

- **Reread the document.**
  Difficult ideas are not always easily understood on the first reading.

- **Use a variety of resources.**
  Form the habit of using the dictionary, the encyclopedia, and maps. These resources are tools to help you discover new ideas and knowledge and double-check other sources.

King Tut's Mask

Classifying Primary Sources

Primary sources fall into different categories:

Printed Publications

Printed publications include books such as autobiographies. Printed publications also include newspapers and magazines.

Songs & Poems

Songs and poems include works that express the personal thoughts and feelings or political or religious beliefs of the writer, often using rhyming and rhythmic language.

Visual Materials

Visual materials include a wide range of forms: original paintings, drawings, sculptures, photographs, film, and maps.

Oral Histories

Oral histories are chronicles, memoirs, myths, and legends that are passed along from one generation to another by word of mouth. Interviews are another form of oral history.

Personal Records

Personal records are accounts of events kept by an individual who is a participant in, or witness to, these events. Personal records include diaries, journals, and letters.

Artifacts

Artifacts are objects such as tools or ornaments. Artifacts present information about a particular culture or a stage of technological development.

Early Civilizations

The people of early civilizations formed societies. These societies had a sense of justice and sets of values. As today, the family was the basic unit of society where values and justice were learned.

Reader's Dictionary

Bull of Heaven: mythical creature sent by the gods to kill Gilgamesh and Enkidu

Humbaba: evil spirit who guards the cedar forest through which Gilgamesh and Enkidu travel

steppe: wide, rolling, grassy plain

reproach: fault

Canaan: an ancient land that lay along the Syrian Desert

The *Epic of Gilgamesh*

 **Printed Publications**

The Epic of Gilgamesh—written c. 2500 B.C.— is one of the most well-known ancient tales. In this passage, Gilgamesh describes his adventures and journeys with his best friend, Enkidu.

We overcame everything: climbed the mountain,
captured the **Bull of Heaven** and killed him,
brought **Humbaba** to grief, who lives in the
   cedar forest;
entering the mountain gates we slew lions;
my friend whom I love dearly underwent with
   me all hardships.
The fate of mankind overtook him.
Six days and seven nights I wept over him
until a worm fell out of his nose.
Then I was afraid.
In fear of death I roam the wilderness. The case of
   my friend lies heavy in me.
On a remote path I roam the wilderness. The case
   of my friend Enkidu lies heavy in me.
On a long journey I wander the **steppe.**
How can I keep still? How can I be silent?
The friend I loved has turned to clay. Enkidu, the
   friend I love, has turned to clay.
Me, shall I not lie down like him,
never again to move?

This Sumerian tablet is covered with cuneiform writing, the language in which the Epic of Gilgamesh *was written.*

An Egyptian Father's Advice to His Son

Personal Records

Upper-class Egyptians enjoyed collecting wise sayings to provide guidance for leading an upright and successful life. This excerpt of instructions from Vizier Ptah-hotep dates from around 2450 B.C.

If you have, as leader, to decide on the conduct of a great number of men, seek the most perfect manner of doing so that your own conduct may be without **reproach.** Justice is great, invariable, and assured; it has not been disturbed since the age of Ptah. . . .

If you are a wise man, bring up a son who shall be pleasing to Ptah. If he conforms his conduct to your way and occupies himself with your affairs as is right, do to him all the good you can; he is your son, a person attached to you whom your own self has begotten. Separate not your heart from him. . . .

If you are powerful, respect knowledge and calmness of language. Command only to direct; to be absolute is to run into evil. Let not your heart be haughty, neither let it be mean. . . .

Ancient Israelites

Printed Publications

Much of the history of the ancient Israelites is recorded in the Bible. The Bible tells about a man named Abraham and his wife Sarah:

The Lord said to [Abraham], 'Leave your own country, your kin, and your father's house, and go to a country that I will show you. I shall make you into a great nation; I shall bless you. . . .'

[Abraham] . . . set out as the Lord had bidden him. . . . He took his wife [Sarah], his brother's son Lot, and all the possessions they had gathered . . . and they departed for **Canaan.**

When Abraham arrived in Canaan, the Bible says that God made a covenant, or special agreement, with him. It is considered by the Jewish people to be the beginning of their history.

When they arrived there, [Abraham] went on as far as the sanctuary. . . . When the Lord appeared to him and said, 'I am giving this land to your descendants,' [Abraham] built an altar there to the Lord who had appeared to him.

An ancient scroll from the Jewish Torah

Document Based Questions

1. What happened to the friend of Gilgamesh?
2. What is shown on the Sumerian tablet?
3. Does any part of the Egyptian father's advice have value today for sons or daughters? Be specific and support your answer.
4. According to the Bible, what did the Lord tell Abraham to do, and why?

The Ancient World

Some of the greatest thoughts in modern civilization came from the ancient world. Important philosophers and religious leaders formed ideas we still express today. These ideas are timeless.

Reader's Dictionary

refinements: improvements

regulations: rules

nurture: upbringing

immortal: never dying

palpable: obvious

The *Analects* of Confucius

 Printed Publications

An analect is a selected thought or saying. The sayings below were written by the Chinese philosopher Confucius in c. 400 B.C.

"If you make a mistake and do not correct it, this is called a mistake."

"Be dutiful at home, brotherly in public; be discreet and trustworthy, love all people, and draw near to humanity. If you have extra energy as you do that, then study literature."

"If leaders are courteous, their people will not dare to be disrespectful. If leaders are just, people will not dare to be [ungovernable]. If leaders are trustworthy, people will not dare to be dishonest."

A certain pupil asked Confucius about government: "What qualifies one to participate in government?"

Confucius said, "Honor five **refinements**. . . . Then you can participate in government."

The pupil asked, "What are the five refinements?"

Confucius said, "Good people are generous without being wasteful; they are hard working without being resentful; they desire without being greedy; they are at ease without being [proud]; they are dignified without being fierce."

Statue of Confucius

The Rights of Women

Printed Publications

In the Republic, Plato presents his ideas on a just society in the form of dialogues, or imaginary conversations, between Socrates and his students. In this dialogue, Socrates has just finished questioning his student about the type of men who might make the best "watchdogs" of Athenian government. He surprises his student by turning to the subject of women.

Let us further suppose the birth and education of our women to be subject to similar or nearly similar **regulations** [as men]; . . .

What do you mean?

What I mean may be put into the form of a question, I said: Are dogs divided into hes and shes, or do they both share equally in hunting and in keeping watch and in the other duties of dogs? [O]r do we entrust to the males the entire and exclusive care of the flocks, while we leave the females at home, under the idea that the bearing and [feeding of] their puppies is labour enough for them?

No, he said, they share alike; the only difference between them is that the males are stronger and the females weaker.

But can you use different animals for the same purpose, unless they are [raised] in the same way?

You cannot.

Then, if women are to have the same duties as men, they must have the same **nurture** and education?

Yes.

The *Rig Veda*

Songs & Poems

The Vedas, written in ancient India, are the oldest writings of the Hindu religion. This song was written c. 1100 B.C.

The goddess Night has drawn near, looking about on many sides with her eyes. She has put on all her glories.

The **immortal** goddess has filled the wide space, the depths and the heights. She stems the tide of darkness with her light.

The goddess has drawn near, pushing aside her sister the twilight. Darkness, too, will give way.

As you came near to us today, we turned homeward to rest, as birds go to their home in a tree.

People who live in villages have gone home to rest, and animals with feet, and animals with wings, even the ever-searching hawks.

Ward off the she-wolf and the wolf; ward off the thief. O night full of waves, be easy for us to cross over.

Darkness—**palpable,** black, and painted—has come upon me. O Dawn, banish it like a debt.

A representation of the Hindu god Siva

Document Based Questions

1. What are the five refinements according to Confucius?
2. What does Plato think will help make men and women more equal?
3. Who is the sister to the goddess Night in the last reading?
4. What does the song say Dawn should do about Darkness?

New Empires and New Faiths

With the growth of new empires came great change. Events occurred that gave people the chance to be great leaders and heroes. New faiths continued to form new ideas.

Reader's Dictionary

cognizant: aware

trifling: insignificant

posterity: future time

allay: calm

incurred: brought upon oneself

Incense burner from the Byzantine Empire in the shape of a church

A Woman on the Throne

*I*n 1081 an able general named Alexius Commenus captured Constantinople. As Emperor Alexius I, he defended the Byzantine Empire against attacks from invaders. His daughter, Anna Comnena, retold the story of his reign in a book called *The Alexiad* (uh • lehk • see • uhd). *She begins her account by describing Alexius's decision to turn the government to his mother Anna Dalassena.*

He really longed that his mother rather than himself should take the helm of the state, but so far he had concealed this design [plan] from her, fearing that if she became **cognizant** of it, she might actually leave the palace [for a convent]. . . . Therefore in all daily business he did nothing, not even a **trifling** thing, without her advise . . . and made her a partner in the administration of affairs, sometimes too he would say openly that without her brain and judgement the Empire would go to pieces.

. . . she was perhaps more devoted to her son than most women. And so she wished to help her son. . . . She ruled . . . with the Emperor, her son, and at times even took the reins alone and drove the chariot of Empire without harm or mishap. For besides being clever she had in very truth a kingly mind, capable of governing a kingdom.

A Heroic Rescue Attempt

Personal Records

Pliny the Elder—a Roman admiral and well-known author and scientist—died attempting to rescue people trapped at the foot of Mt. Vesuvius when it erupted. His nephew, Pliny the Younger, recorded his uncle's death in a letter written to a Roman historian named Tacitus. The letter forms an eyewitness account of the eruption and expresses Roman views of courage and duty.

Thank you for asking me to send you a description of my uncle's death so that you can leave an accurate account of it for **posterity**; . . .

As he was leaving the house he was handed a message from Rectina, . . . whose house was at the foot of the mountain, so that escape was impossible except by boat. She was terrified by the danger threatening her and implored him to rescue her. . . . Ashes were already falling, hotter and thicker as the ships drew near. . . . For a moment my uncle wondered whether to turn back, but when the helmsman advised this he refused, telling him that Fortune stood by the courageous. . . . This wind was . . . in my uncle's favour, and he was able to bring his ship in.

Meanwhile on Mount Vesuvius broad sheets of fire and leaping flames blazed at several points. . . . My uncle tried to **allay** the fears of his companions. . . . They debated whether to stay indoors or take their chance in the open, for the buildings were now shaking with violent shocks, and seemed to be swaying. . . .

. . . A sheet was spread on the ground for him [uncle] to lie down, and he repeatedly asked for cold water to drink. Then the flames and smell of sulphur which gave warning of the approaching fire drove the others to take flight. . . . He stood . . . and then suddenly collapsed, I imagine because the dense fumes choked his breathing. . . . When daylight returned on the 26th—two days after the last day he had seen—his body was found. . . .

The Quran

Printed Publications

The Quran is the holy book of Islam. The verses below come from Chapter 1, verses 2–7.

Praise be to Allah, the Lord of the Worlds,
The Compassionate, the Merciful,
Master of the Day of Judgement,
Only You do we worship, and only You
do we implore for help.
Lead us to the right path,
The path of those You have favoured
Not those who have **incurred** Your wrath or
have gone astray.

Document Based Questions

1. Why did Alexius conceal his plans to turn the government over to his mother?
2. Why did Pliny the Elder sail to Mt. Vesuvius?
3. Does Pliny the Younger consider his uncle a hero? Why or why not?
4. Who is the quote from the Quran praising?

The Middle Ages

During the Middle Ages, civilizations began to develop to be more as we know them in modern times. There were still strong leaders—some good, some bad. But it became a time when the common people began to demand their rights. Women especially started to have a voice in their status and how they would live.

Reader's Dictionary

ebony: a hard, heavy wood

score: twenty

mitqal: an ancient unit of measure

heirs: descendants

abject: low

Drawing of Mansa Musa

The Sultan of Mali

An Arab scholar named Ibn Fadl Allah al Omari describes the West African court and army of Mansa Musa in the 1330s. He refers to Mansa Musa as sultan, *the Arab word for "king."*

The sultan of this kingdom presides in his palace on a great balcony called *bembe* where he has a seat of **ebony** that is like a throne fit for a large and tall person: on either side it is flanked by elephant tusks turned towards each other. His arms stand near him, being all of gold, saber, lance, quiver, bow and arrows. He wears wide trousers made of about twenty pieces [of stuff] of a kind which he alone may wear. Behind him there stand about a **score** of Turkish or other pages which are bought for him in Cairo. . . . His officers are seated in a circle about him, in two rows, one to the right and one to the left; beyond them sit the chief commanders of his cavalry. . . . Others dance before their sovereign, who enjoys this, and make him laugh. Two banners are spread behind him. Before him they keep two saddled and bridled horses in case he should wish to ride.

Arab horses are brought for sale to the kings of this country, who spend considerable sums in this way. Their army numbers one hundred thousand men of whom there are about ten thousand horse-mounted cavalry: the others are infantry having neither horses nor any other mounts. . . .

The officers of this king, his soldiers and his guard receive gifts of land and presents. Some among the greatest of them receive as much as fifty thousand *mitqals* of gold a year, besides which the king provides them with horses and clothing. He is much concerned with giving them fine garments and making his cities into capitals.

The Magna Carta

The Magna Carta, signed in England in 1215, for the first time gave common people some freedoms and protections. It also limited the power of King John.

To all free men of our kingdom we have also granted, for us and our **heirs** for ever, all the liberties written out below. . . .

No widow shall be compelled [forced] to marry, so long as she wishes to remain without a husband. . . .

For a trivial offence, a free man shall be fined only in proportion to the degree of his offence. . . .

No sheriff, royal official, or other person shall take horses or carts for transport from any free man, without his consent. . . .

No free man shall be seized or imprisoned . . . or outlawed or exiled . . . except by the lawful judgement of his equals or by the law of the land.

To no one will we sell, to no one deny or delay right or justice.

All merchants may enter or leave England unharmed and without fear, and may stay or travel within it, by land or water, for purposes of trade. . . .

All these customs and liberties that we have granted shall be observed in our kingdom.

The Tale of Genji

The Tale of Genji is the story of a young man searching for the meaning of life. It was written by Murasaki Shikibu in A.D. 1010. Genji's friend described three classes of women: those of high rank and birth whose weak points are concealed; those of the middle class; and those of the lower class. This is part of Genji's reply.

[Genji said] "It will not always be so easy to know into which of the three classes a woman ought to be put. For sometimes people of high rank sink to the most **abject** positions; while others of common birth rise to . . . think themselves as good as anyone. How are we to deal with such cases?"

Murasaki Shikibu

Document Based Questions

1. What conclusions can you draw about Mansa Musa's power?
2. Why do you think Mansa Musa treated his soldiers so well?
3. According to the Magna Carta, when can a man be imprisoned?
4. What does Genji seem to realize about the social classes that his friend does not?

A Changing World

World exploration expanded as countries looked for new lands to conquer. There was great competition among European countries to claim undiscovered riches. This exploration did not always benefit the people already living in explored lands, however.

Reader's Dictionary

finery: fancier clothes and jewelry

installed: placed in

plunder: stolen goods, usually during war

stench: a very bad smell

scorn: anger

Aztec and Spanish soldiers in battle

Arrival of the Spaniards

Personal Records

Aztec accounts of the Spanish conquest of Mexico in 1519 is recorded in The Broken Spears, edited and translated by Miguel Leon-Portilla. This selection describes the meeting of Montezuma and Cortés.

The Spaniards arrived . . . near the entrance to Tenochititlan. That was the end of their march, for they had reached their goal.

[Montezuma] now arrayed himself in his **finery,** preparing to go out to meet them. . . .

. . . Then he hung the gold necklaces around their necks and gave them presents of every sort as gifts of welcome.

When [Montezuma] had given necklaces to each one, Cortés asked him: "Are you [Montezuma]? Are you the king? . . ."

And the king said: "Yes, I am [Montezuma]." Then he stood up to welcome Cortés; he came forward, bowed his head low and addressed him in these words: "Our lord, you are weary. The journey has tired you, but now you have arrived on the earth. You have come to your city, Mexico. You have come here to sit on your throne. . . ."

When the Spaniards were **installed** in the palace, they asked [Montezuma] about the city's resources. . . . They questioned him closely and then demanded gold.

[Montezuma] guided them to it. . . .

. . . When they entered the hall of treasures, it was as if they had arrived in Paradise. . . . All of [Montezuma's] possessions were brought out: fine bracelets, necklaces with large stones, ankle rings with little gold bells, the royal crowns and all the royal finery—everything that belonged to the king. . . . They seized these treasures as if they were their own, as if this **plunder** were merely a stroke of good luck.

The Life of Olaudah Equiano

Printed Publications

Olaudah Equiano was kidnapped from West Africa and brought to America as a slave. In 1789 he wrote an account of this frightening journey. Here he describes the first part of that trip.

The first thing I saw was a vast ocean, and a ship, riding at anchor, waiting for its cargo. The ocean and the ship filled me with astonishment that soon turned to fear. I was taken to the ship and carried on board! . . .

The crew took me down below decks, into the ship's stinking hold. With the horribleness of the **stench** and my crying I was so sick and low that I couldn't eat. I wanted to die. . . .

That first day, among the poor chained men in the hold, I found some people of Benin.

"What are they going to do to us?" I asked.

"They are taking us away to work for them," a man from Benin explained.

"And do they only live here," I asked, "in this hollow place, the ship?"

"They have a white people's country," the man explained, "but it is far away."

"How can it be," I asked, "that in our whole country nobody ever heard of them?"

"They live *very* far away," another man explained.

Queen Elizabeth's Speech To Her Troops

Oral Histories

In 1588, a Spanish fleet, known as the Spanish Armada, was sent to invade England. Queen Elizabeth I spoke to her troops before the battle.

Let tyrants fear: I have so behaved myself that under God I have placed my chiefest strength and safeguard in the loyal hearts and goodwill of my subjects. Wherefore I am come . . . to live and die amongst you all, to lay down for my God and for my kingdom and for my people mine honor and my blood even in the dust. I know I have the body but of a weak and feeble woman, but I have the heart and stomach of a king and a king of England too—and take foul **scorn** that . . . any prince of Europe should dare to invade the borders of my realm.

Queen Elizabeth I

Drawing of a slave ship

Document Based Questions

1. What gifts did Montezuma give to Cortés?
2. Why do you think Montezuma took Cortés to see his personal treasury?
3. How did Equiano travel from Africa to the Americas?
4. In her speech, is Queen Elizabeth encouraging or discouraging her troops? Explain.

Suggested Readings

If you are interested in reading more about people and events in world history, the following list will help you. The book titles listed for each unit are fiction and nonfiction books you can read to learn more about that time period.

Unit 1:

Arnold, Caroline. *Stone Age Farmers Beside the Sea.* Clarion Books, 1997. A photo-essay describing the prehistoric village of Skara Brae.

Bunting, Eve. *I Am the Mummy Heb-Nefert.* Harcourt Brace, 1997. Fictional story of a mummy recalling her past life as the wife of the pharaoh's brother.

Courlander, Harold. *The King's Drum, and Other African Tales.* Harcourt, 1962. Folktales taken from Africa south of the Sahara.

Deem, James M. *Bodies from the Bog.* Houghton Mifflin, 1998. A photo-essay that looks at information from the well-preserved bodies found in a Danish bog.

Gregory, Kristiana. *Cleopatra VII: Daughter of the Nile.* Scholastic Inc., 1999. A fictional diary written by Cleopatra.

Herrmann, Siegfried. *A History of Israel in Old Testament Times.* Fortress Press, 1975. The Old Testament as a history of early Israel, with evidence from sources other than the Bible.

Lattimore, Deborah Nourse. *Winged Cat: A Tale of Ancient Egypt.* HarperCollins, 1995. A tale of a servant girl and a High Priest using the Book of the Dead to investigate the death of the girl's sacred cat.

Maltz, Fran. *Keeping Faith in the Dust.* Alef Design Group, 1998. Fictional account of a 16-year-old girl whose family is forced to flee their home near the Dead Sea to the fortress of Masada, where Roman forces are held off by the Jews for seven years.

Morley, Jacquelin. Mark Bergin, and John James. *An Egyptian Pyramid.* Peter Bedrick, 1991. Explains how the pyramids were built and their purpose.

Perl, Lila. *Mummies, Tombs, and Treasure: Secrets of Ancient Egypt.* Clarion Books, 1990. An account of what ancient Egyptians believed about death and the afterlife.

Travis, Lucille. *Tirzah.* Herald Press, 1991. Fictional story of a 12-year-old boy who flees from Egypt with Moses during the Exodus.

Trumble, Kelly. *Cat Mummies.* Clarion Books, 1996. Reasons and background examining why ancient Egyptians mummified thousands and thousands of cats.

Wetwood, Jennifer. *Gilgamesh, and Other Babylonian Tales.* Coward, McCann & Geoghegan, 1970. Retells ancient tales of Sumer and Babylon.

Unit 2:

Chang, Richard F. *Chinese Mythical Stories.* Yale Far Eastern Publications, 1990. Legends and myths of China.

Craft, Charlotte. *King Midas and the Golden Touch.* Morrow, 1999. The myth of King Midas and his greed for gold.

Evslin, Bernard. *Heroes and Monsters of Greek Myth.* Scholastic, 1988. A collection of Greek myths.

Fleischman, Paul. *Dateline: Troy.* Candlewick Press, 1996. Author uses modern wars (Persian Gulf, Vietnam) to better understand the Trojan War.

Ganeri, Anita. *Buddhism.* NTC Publishing Group, 1997. Overview of Buddhist history and beliefs.

Ganeri, Anita. *Hinduism.* NTC Publishing Group, 1996. Overview of Hindu history and beliefs.

Hamilton, Edith. *The Greek Way.* Norton, 1983. The story of the Greek spirit and mind told by great writers.

Harris, Nathaniel. *Alexander the Great and the Greeks.* Bookwright Press, 1986. Contributions Alexander made to the Greeks.

Homer and Geraldine McCaughrean. *The Odyssey.* Oxford, 1999. Illustrated retelling of *The Odyssey* using modern language.

Ross, Stewart. *The Original Olympic Games.* NTC Publishing Group, 1999. A history of the Olympics.

Theule, Frederic. *Alexander and His Times.* Henry Holt and Co., 1996. A pictorial and historic account of the life of Alexander the Great.

Unit 3:

Boyd, Anne. *Life in a 15th-Century Monastery (A Cambridge Topic Book).* Lerner Publications, 1979. An account of the daily life of monks in the monastery at Durham, England.

Browning, Robert. *The Byzantine Empire.* Charles Scribner's Sons, 1980. The Byzantine world from A.D. 500 to fall of Constantinople in 1453.

Burrell, Roy. *The Romans: Rebuilding the Past.* Oxford University Press, 1991. A historical outline of ancient Rome.

Comte, Fernand. *Sacred Writings of World Religions.* Chambers, 1992. The history, beliefs, and major figures of more than 20 religions, among them Judaism, Islam, and Christianity.

Dillon, Eilis. *Rome Under the Emperors.* Tomas Nelson, 1975. Views of Roman society and family life in the time of Trajan, as seen by young people of four different families and social classes.

Powell, Anton. *The Rise of Islam.* Warwick Press, 1980. An overview of Islamic culture.

Tingay, Graham. *Julius Caesar.* Cambridge University Press, 1991. An account of the life and achievements of Julius Caesar.

Unit 4:

Giles, Frances and Joseph. *Life in a Medieval Village.* Harper Perennial, 1990. An illustrated look at the way most medieval people passed their lives.

Haugaard, Erik Christian. *The Revenge of the Forty-Seven Samurai.* Houghton Mifflin, 1995. The tale of Jiro, a young boy who must aid 47 samurai who are attempting to avenge the unjust death of their lord. This historical novel provides a detailed look at Japanese feudal society.

Heer, Friedrich. *Charlemagne and His World.* Macmillan, 1975. Large, lavishly illustrated description of the period.

McKendrick, Meveena. *Ferdinand and Isabella.* American Heritage, 1968. Photographs and contemporary paintings help re-create the period.

Sanders, Tao Tao Liu. *Dragons, Gods, and Spirits from Chinese Mythology.* NTC, 1997. Collection of myths, legends, and folktales providing insight into the culture and historic development of China.

Scott, Sir Walter. *Ivanhoe.* Longmans, Green, and Co., 1897. A twelfth-century story of hidden identity, intrigue, and romance among the English nobility.

Wisniewski, David. *Sundiata: Lion King of Mali.* Houghton Mifflin, 1999. Story about the ancient king of Mali and how he defeated his enemies to become the ruler.

Unit 5:

Cowie, Leonard W. *Martin Luther: Leader of the Reformation (A Pathfinder Biography).* Frederick Praeger, 1969. A detailed biography of Luther.

Davis, Burke. *Black Heroes of the American Revolution.* Harcourt, Brace and Jovanovich, 1991. Highlights achievements of African Americans during the Revolution.

Hibbard, Howard. *Michelangelo.* Westview Press, 1985. Biography of Michelangelo told through his paintings, poems, and personal letters.

Hooks, William H. *The Legend of White Doe.* Macmillan, 1998. Tale about Virginia Dare, the first child of English settlers born in the Americas.

Lomask, Milton. *Exploration: Great Lives.* Scribners, 1988. Biographies of explorers.

Mee, Charles L. *Daily Life in the Renaissance.* American Heritage, 1975. Works of art showing people in their daily lives.

O'Dell, Scott. *The Hawk that Dare Not Hunt by Day.* Houghton Mifflin, 1975. Novel about a boy who helps the reformer Tyndale smuggle his translation of the Bible into England.

Stuart, Gene S. *America's Ancient Cities.* National Geographic Society, 1988. An illustrated collection of essays on cultures of North America and Mesoamerica.

Glossary

A

absolutism system of rule in which monarchs held total power and claimed to rule by the will of God (p. 686)

acupuncture Chinese practice of easing pain by sticking thin needles into patients' skin (p. 246)

adobe sun-dried mud brick (p. 591)

agora in early Greek city-states, an open area that served as both a market and a meeting place (p. 122)

alphabet group of letters that stand for sounds (p. 85)

anatomy the study of body structure (p. 305)

animism belief that all natural things are alive and have their own spirits (p. 490)

annul to cancel (p. 648)

anthropologist scientist who studies the physical characteristics and cultures of humans and their ancestors (p. 9)

anti-Semitism hatred of Jews (p. 548)

apostle early Christian leader who helped set up churches and spread the message of Jesus (p. 348)

aqueduct human-made channel built to carry water (p. 291)

archaeologist scientist who learns about past human life by studying fossils and artifacts (p. 9)

aristocrat noble whose wealth came from land ownership (p. 227)

artifact weapon, tool, or other item made by humans (p. 9)

artisan skilled craftsperson (p. 20)

astronomer person who studies stars, planets, and other heavenly bodies (pp. 30, 185)

B

barbarian uncivilized person (p. 435)

barter to exchange goods without using money (p. 319)

bazaar marketplace (p. 389)

Brahman in Hinduism, the universal spirit of which all gods and goddesses are different parts (p. 203)

Buddhism religion founded by Siddhartha Gautama, the Buddha; taught that the way to find truth was to give up all desires (p. 205)

bureaucracy a group of appointed officials who are responsible for different areas of government (p. 229)

C

caliph important Muslim political and religious leader (p. 380)

calligraphy beautiful handwriting (p. 421); the art of producing beautiful handwriting (p. 501)

caravan group of traveling merchants and animals (pp. 30, 373)

caste social group that a person is born into and cannot change (p. 199)

cataract steep rapids formed by cliffs and boulders in a river (p. 39)

census a count of the number of people (p. 432)

city-state independent state made up of a city and the surrounding land and villages (p. 19)

civilization complex society with cities, organized government, art, religion, class divisions, and a writing system (p. 17)

clan group of families related by blood or marriage (pp. 461, 487)

clergy religious officials, such as priests, given authority to conduct religious services (pp. 355, 538)

colony settlement in a new territory that keeps close ties with its homeland (pp. 121, 666)

comedy form of drama in which the story has a happy ending (p. 161)

commerce the buying and selling of goods in large amounts over long distances (p. 666)

concordat agreement between the pope and the ruler of a country (p. 521)

confederation a loose union of several groups or states (p. 592)

Confucianism system of beliefs introduced by the Chinese thinker Confucius; taught that people needed to have a sense of duty to their family and community in order to bring peace to society (p. 236)

conquistador Spanish conqueror or soldier in the Americas (p. 595)

constitution written plan of government (pp. 488, 694)

consul one of the two top government officials in ancient Rome (p. 269)

covenant agreement (p. 82)

crier announcer who calls Muslim believers to prayer five times a day (p. 394)

cuneiform Sumerian system of writing made up of wedge-shaped markings (p. 20)

currency system of money (p. 294)

daimyo powerful military lord in feudal Japan (p. 496)

Dao the proper way Chinese kings were expected to rule under the Mandate of Heaven (p. 230)

Daoism Chinese philosophy based on the teachings of Laozi; taught that people should turn to nature and give up their worldly concerns (p. 238)

deism religious belief based on reason (p. 685)

deity god or goddess (p. 49)

delta area of fertile soil at the mouth of a river (p. 39)

democracy government in which all citizens share in running the government (p. 126)

denomination an organized branch of Christianity (p. 636)

dharma in Hinduism, the divine law that requires people to perform the duties of their caste (p. 204)

dhow an Arab sailboat (p. 453)

Diaspora refers to the scattering of communities of Jews outside their homeland after the Babylonian captivity (p. 96)

dictator in ancient Rome, a person who ruled with complete power temporarily during emergencies (p. 271)

diplomacy the art of negotiating with other countries (p. 615)

direct democracy system of government in which people gather at mass meetings to decide on government matters (p. 139)

disciple close follower of Jesus (p. 344)

doctrine official church teaching (p. 355)

domesticate to tame animals and plants for human use (p. 13)

drama story told by actors who pretend to be characters in the story (p. 160)

dynasty line of rulers from the same family (pp. 44, 210, 226)

economy organized way in which people produce, sell, and buy goods and services (p. 410)

embalming process developed by the ancient Egyptians of preserving a person's body after death (p. 49)

empire group of territories or nations under a single ruler or government (pp. 23, 89)

epic long poem that tells about legendary or heroic deeds (p. 157)

Epicureanism philosophy founded by Epicurus in Hellenistic Athens; taught that happiness through the pursuit of pleasure was the goal of life (p. 184)

excommunicate to declare that a person or group no longer belongs to a church (pp. 361, 521)

exile period of forced absence from one's country or home (p. 94)

export to sell to another country (p. 666)

extended family family group including several generations as well as other relatives (p. 469)

fable short tale that teaches a lesson (p. 158)

feudalism political system based on bonds of loyalty between lords and vassals (pp. 497, 523)

fief under feudalism, the land a lord granted to a vassal in exchange for military service and loyalty (p. 524)

filial piety children's respect for their parents and older relatives, an important part of Confucian beliefs (p. 234)

fjord steep-sided valley that is an inlet of the sea (p. 518)

Forum open space in Rome that served as a marketplace and public square (p. 306)

fossil the trace or imprint of a plant or animal that has been preserved in rock (p. 9)

glacier huge sheet of ice (p. 573)

Glossary

gladiator in ancient Rome, person who fought animals and other people as public entertainment (p. 306)

gospel ("good news") one of the four accounts of Jesus' life, teachings, and resurrection (p. 355)

grand jury group that decided whether there was enough evidence to accuse a person of a crime (p. 537)

griot storyteller (p. 449)

guild medieval business group formed by craftspeople and merchants (pp. 503, 530)

guru religious teacher and spiritual guide in Hinduism (p. 201)

Hellenistic Era period when the Greek language and Greek ideas spread to the non-Greek peoples of southwest Asia (p. 178)

helot person who was conquered and enslaved by the ancient Spartans (p. 126)

heresy belief that differs from or contradicts the accepted teachings of a religion (pp. 547, 643)

hierarchy organization with different levels of authority (p. 355)

hieroglyphics system of writing made up of thousands of picture symbols developed by the ancient Egyptians (p. 42)

Hinduism system of religion that grew out of the religion of the Aryans in ancient India (p. 203)

historian person who studies and writes about the human past (p. 9)

humanism Renaissance movement based on the values of the ancient Greeks and Romans, such as that individuals and human society were important (p. 619)

hypothesis proposed explanation of the facts (p. 679)

icon Christian religious image or picture (p. 359)

iconoclast person who opposed the use of idols in Byzantine churches, saying that icons encouraged the worship of idols (p. 360)

ideograph a character that joins two or more pictographs to represent an idea (p. 228)

igloo dome-shaped home built by the Inuit (p. 590)

import to buy from another country (p. 666)

incense material burned for its pleasant smell (p. 62)

indulgence pardon from the Church for a person's sins (p. 634)

inflation period of rapidly increasing prices (p. 319)

invest to put money into a project (p. 667)

irrigation method of bringing water to a field from another place to water crops (p. 18)

karma in Hinduism, the good or bad energy a person builds up based upon whether he or she lives a good or bad life (p. 204)

knight in the Middle Ages, a noble warrior who fought on horseback (p. 524)

laity church members who are not clergy (p. 355)

latifundia large farming estates in ancient Rome (p. 278)

legacy what a person leaves behind when he or she dies (p. 178)

Legalism Chinese philosophy developed by Hanfeizi; taught that humans are naturally evil and therefore need to be ruled by harsh laws (p. 239)

legion smaller unit of the Roman army made up of about 6,000 soldiers (p. 266)

limited government idea that a government may only use the powers given to it by the people (p. 700)

mandate formal order (p. 230)

martial arts sports, such as judo and karate, that involve combat and self-defense (p. 499)

martyr person willing to die rather than give up his or her beliefs (p. 353)

mass Catholic worship service (p. 546)

matrilineal refers to a group that traces descent through mothers rather than fathers (p. 469)

meditation practice of quiet reflection to clear the mind and find inner peace (p. 499)

mercantilism the idea that a country gains power by building up its supply of gold and silver (p. 666)

messiah in Judaism, a deliverer sent by God (pp. 101, 344)

minaret tower of a mosque from which the crier calls believers to prayer five times a day (p. 394)

missionary person who travels to carry the ideas of a religion to others (pp. 363, 520)

monastery religious community where monks live and work (pp. 362, 413)

monopoly control of all (or almost all) trade or production of a certain good (p. 576)

monotheism the belief in one god (p. 81)

monsoon strong wind that blows one direction in winter and the opposite direction in summer (p. 195)

mosaic picture made from many bits of colored glass, tile, or stone (p. 333)

mosque Muslim house of worship (p. 389)

mummy body that has been embalmed and wrapped in linen (p. 50)

myth traditional story describing gods or heroes or explaining natural events (p. 155)

natural law law that applies to everyone and can be understood by reason (p. 681)

nirvana in Buddhism, a state of wisdom and freedom from the cycle of rebirth (p. 205)

nomad person who regularly moves from place to place (p. 10)

novel long fictional story (p. 432)

oasis green area in a desert fed by underground water (p. 373)

ode poem that expresses strong emotions about life (p. 304)

oligarchy government in which a small group of people holds power (p. 126)

oracle sacred shrine where a priest or priestess spoke for a god or goddess (p. 156)

oral history the stories passed down from generation to generation (p. 470)

P

papyrus reed plant of the Nile Valley, used to make a form of paper (p. 42)

parable story that used events from everyday life to express spiritual ideas (p. 345)

paterfamilias ("father of the family") name for the father as head of the household in ancient Rome (p. 307)

patrician wealthy landowner and member of the ruling class in ancient Rome (p. 269)

Pax Romana ("Roman Peace") long era of peace and safety in the Roman Empire (p. 287)

peninsula body of land with water on three sides (p. 117)

persecute to mistreat a person because of his or her beliefs (p. 353)

pharaoh all-powerful king in ancient Egypt (p. 48)

philosopher thinker who seeks wisdom and ponders questions about life (pp. 140, 169)

philosophy study of the nature and meaning of life; comes from the Greek word for "love of wisdom" (p. 169)

pictograph a character that stands for an object (p. 228)

pilgrim person who travels to go to a religious shrine or site (p. 213)

plague disease that spreads quickly and kills many people (pp. 319, 554)

plane geometry branch of mathematics that shows how points, lines, angles, and surfaces relate to one another (p. 185)

plateau area of high flat land (p. 446)

plebeian member of the common people in ancient Rome (p. 269)

polis the early Greek city-state, made up of a city and the surrounding countryside and run like an independent country (p. 122)

pope the bishop of Rome, later the head of the Roman Catholic Church (p. 356)

popular sovereignty idea that a government receives its power from the people (p. 700)

porcelain type of ceramic ware that is made of fine clay and baked at high temperatures (p. 418)

praetor important government official in ancient Rome (p. 270)

Glossary

predestination belief that no matter what a person does, the outcome of his or her life is already planned by God (p. 640)

prophet person who claims to be instructed by God to share God's words (p. 87)

proverb wise saying (p. 89)

province political district (p. 28)

pyramid huge stone structure built by the ancient Egyptians to serve as a tomb (p. 50)

quipu rope with knotted cords of different lengths and colors (p. 588)

Quran holy book of Islam (p. 377)

rabbi Jewish leader and teacher of the Torah (p. 101)

raja prince who led an Aryan tribe in India (p. 199)

rationalism the belief that reason is the chief source of knowledge (p. 678)

Reconquista ("reconquest") Christian struggle to take back the Iberian Peninsula from the Muslims (p. 558)

reform change that tries to bring about an improvement (pp. 320, 411)

Reformation movement to reform the Catholic Church; led to the creation of Protestantism (p. 634)

regent person who acts as a temporary ruler (p. 334)

reincarnation rebirth of the soul or spirit in different bodies over time (p. 204)

Renaissance ("rebirth") period of renewed interest in art and learning in Europe (p. 609)

representative democracy system of government in which citizens choose a smaller group to make laws and governmental decisions on their behalf (p. 139)

representative government system of government in which people elect leaders to make laws (p. 694)

republic form of government in which the leader is not a king or queen but a person elected by citizens (p. 265)

resurrection the act of rising from the dead (p. 347)

rhetoric public speaking (p. 307)

Sabbath weekly day of worship and rest for Jews (p. 94)

saint Christian holy person (p. 333)

salvation the act of being saved from sin and allowed to enter heaven (p. 350)

samurai class of warriors in feudal Japan who pledged loyalty to a noble in return for land (p. 494)

Sanskrit written language developed by the Aryans (p. 199)

satire work that pokes fun at human weaknesses (p. 304)

satrap official who ruled a state in the Persian Empire under Darius (p. 133)

satrapies the 20 states into which Darius divided the Persian Empire (p. 133)

savanna grassy plain (p. 69)

schism separation (p. 361)

scholasticism medieval way of thinking that tried to bring together reason and faith in studies of religion (p. 550)

scientific method orderly way of collecting and analyzing evidence (p. 679)

scribe record keeper (p. 20)

sect a smaller group with distinct beliefs within a larger religious group (p. 499)

secular interested in worldly rather than religious matters (p. 609)

seminary school for training and educating priests and ministers (p. 643)

separation of powers equal division of power among the branches of government (p. 682)

serf peasant laborer bound by law to the lands of a noble (p. 524)

sheikh leader of an Arab tribe (p. 373)

Shiite Muslim group that accepts only the descendants of Muhammad's son-in-law Ali as rightful rulers of Muslims (p. 382)

shogun military ruler of feudal Japan (p. 495)

shrine holy place (p. 490)

social class group of people who share a similar position in society (p. 233)

social contract agreement between rulers and the people upon which a government is based (p. 682)

Socratic method way of teaching developed by Socrates that used a question-and-answer format to force students to use their reason to see things for themselves (p. 170)

solid geometry branch of mathematics that studies spheres and cylinders (p. 186)

Sophist professional teacher in ancient Greece; believed that people should use knowledge to improve themselves and developed the art of public speaking and debate (p. 169)

specialization the development of different kinds of jobs (p. 15)

steppe wide, rolling, grassy plain (p. 424)

Stoicism philosophy founded by Zeno in Hellenistic Athens; taught that happiness came not from following emotions, but from following reason and doing one's duty (p. 184)

stupa Buddhist shrine that is shaped like a dome or mound (p. 211)

subcontinent large landmass that is part of a continent but distinct from it (p. 195)

sultan military and political leader with absolute authority over a Muslim country (pp. 383, 467)

Sunni Muslim group that accepts descendants of the Umayyads as rightful rulers of Muslims (p. 382)

Swahili refers to the culture and language of East Africa (p. 467)

synagogue Jewish house of worship (p. 94)

tanka Japan's oldest form of poetry; an unrhymed poem of five lines (p. 501)

technology tools and methods used to help humans perform tasks (p. 11)

terror violent actions that are meant to scare people into surrendering (p. 426)

theocracy government headed by religious leaders (p. 208)

theology the study of religion and God (pp. 550, 640)

theory an explanation of how or why something happens (p. 671)

Torah the laws that, according to the Bible, Moses received from God on Mount Sinai; these laws later became the first part of the Hebrew Bible (p. 82)

tragedy form of drama in which a person struggles to overcome difficulties but meets an unhappy end (p. 160)

treason disloyalty to the government (pp. 431, 599)

trial jury group that decided whether an accused person was innocent or guilty (p. 537)

tribe group of related families (pp. 81, 424)

tribute payment made by one group or nation to another to show obedience or to obtain peace or protection (pp. 60, 89)

triumvirate in ancient Rome, a three-person ruling group (p. 280)

tyrant person who takes power by force and rules with total authority (p. 125)

vassal in feudalism, a noble who held land from and served a higher-ranking lord, and in return was given protection (pp. 496, 523)

vault curved structure of stone or concrete forming a ceiling or roof (p. 303)

vernacular everyday language used in a country or region (pp. 552, 620)

veto to reject (p. 270)

warlord military leader who runs a government (p. 409)

Zoroastrianism Persian religion founded by Zoroaster; taught that humans had the freedom to choose between right and wrong, and that goodness would triumph in the end (p. 133)

Spanish Glossary

A

absolutism / absolutismo sistema de gobierno en que los monarcas tiene poder absoluto y alegan gobernar según decreto divino (pág. 686)

acupuncture / acupuntura práctica china para aliviar el dolor clavando la piel de los pacientes con agujas delgadas (pág. 246)

adobe / adobe ladrillo de barro secado al sol (pág. 591)

agora / ágora en las primeras ciudades-estado griegas, un área abierta que servía tanto de mercado como de lugar de reunión (pág. 122)

alphabet / alfabeto grupo de letras que representan sonidos (pág. 85)

anatomy / anatomía estudio de la estructura corporal (pág. 305)

animism / animismo creencia de que todas las cosas naturales están vivas y tienen sus propios espíritus (pág. 490)

annul / anular el acto de invalidar (pág. 648)

anthropologist / antropólogo científico que estudia las características físicas y las culturas de los seres humanos y sus antepasados (pág. 9)

anti-Semitism / antisemitismo odio hacia los judíos (pág. 548)

apostle / apóstol nombre dado a líderes cristianos que ayudaban a establecer iglesias y a difundir el mensaje de Jesucristo (pág. 348)

aqueduct / acueducto canal construido por el hombre para transportar agua (pág. 291)

archaeologist / arqueólogo científico que aprende acerca de la vida humana en el pasado estudiando fósiles y artefactos (pág. 9)

aristocrat / aristócrata noble cuya riqueza provenía de la propiedad de la tierra (pág. 227)

artifact / artefacto arma, herramienta u otro artículo hecho por humanos (pág. 9)

artisan / artesano persona hábil artísticamente (pág. 20)

astronomer / astrónomo persona que estudia las estrellas, a los planetas y a otros cuerpos celestiales (págs. 30, 185)

B

barbarian / bárbaro persona incivilizada (pág. 435)

barter / trueque intercambiar bienes sin utilizar dinero (pág. 319)

bazaar / bazar mercado (pág. 389)

Brahman / Brahman en el hinduismo, el espíritu universal del que todos los dioses y diosas son partes diferentes (pág. 203)

Buddhism / budismo religión fundada por Siddhartha Gautama, Buda; enseñó que la manera de hallar la verdad era renunciar a todo deseo (pág. 205)

bureaucracy / burocracia grupo de funcionarios designados que son responsables de diferentes áreas del gobierno (pág. 229)

C

caliph / califa importante líder político y religioso musulmán (pág. 380)

calligraphy / caligrafía hermosa escritura a mano (pág. 421); el arte de producir tal hermosa escritura (pág. 501)

caravan / caravana grupo itinerante de mercaderes y animales (págs. 30, 373)

caste / casta grupo social en el que una persona nace y que no puede cambiar (pág. 199)

cataract / catarata rápidos empinados formados por precipicios y rocas erosionadas en un río (pág. 39)

census / censo conteo del número de personas (pág. 432)

city-state / ciudad-estado estado independiente compuesto por una ciudad y la tierra y aldeas circundantes (pág. 19)

civilization / civilización sociedad compleja, con ciudades, un gobierno organizado, arte, religión, divisiones de clase y un sistema de escritura (pág. 17)

clan / clan grupo de familias relacionadas por sangre o casamiento (págs. 461, 487)

clergy / clero funcionarios religiosos, como los sacerdotes, con autoridad concedida para llevar a cabo servicios religiosos (págs. 355, 538)

colony / colonia asentamiento en un territorio nuevo que mantiene lazos cercanos con su tierra natal (págs. 121, 666)

comedy / comedia forma de drama en el que la historia tiene un final feliz (pág. 161)

commerce / comercio compra y venta de bienes en cantidades grandes y a través de largas distancias (pág. 666)

concordat / concordato acuerdo entre el Papa y el gobernante de un país (pág. 521)

confederation / confederación unión libre de varios grupos o estados (pág. 592)

Confucianism / confucianismo sistema de creencias introducidas por el pensador chino Confucio; enseñó que las personas necesitaban tener un sentido del deber hacia su familia y la comunidad para llevar paz a la sociedad (pág. 236)

conquistador / conquistador soldado español en las Américas (pág. 595)

constitution / constitución plan de gobierno (págs. 488, 694)

consul / cónsul uno de los dos altos funcionarios en la Roma antigua (pág. 269)

covenant / pacto acuerdo (pág. 82)

crier / almuecín anunciador que llama a los creyentes musulmanes a orar cinco veces al día (pág. 394)

cuneiform / cuneiforme sistema sumerio de escritura compuesto de símbolos con forma de cuña (pág. 20)

currency / moneda sistema monetario (pág. 294)

daimyo / daimyo poderoso señor militar en el Japón feudal (pág. 496)

Dao / Dao manera apropiada en la que se esperaba que los reyes chinos gobernaran bajo el Mandato del Cielo (pág. 230)

Daoism / Daoism filosofía china basada en las enseñanzas de Laozi; enseñó que las personas debían volverse a la naturaleza y renunciar a sus preocupaciones terrenales (pág. 238)

deism / deísmo doctrina religiosa basada en la razón (pág. 685)

deity / deidad dios o diosa (pág. 49)

delta / delta área de tierra fértil en la boca de un río (pág. 39)

democracy / democracia forma de gobierno en la que todos los ciudadanos participan en la administración del gobierno (pág. 126)

denomination / denominación rama organizada del cristianismo (pág. 636)

dharma / dharma en el hinduismo, la ley divina que llama a las personas a realizar los deberes de su casta (pág. 204)

dhow / dhow velero árabe (pág. 453)

Diaspora / diáspora se refiere al esparcimiento de las comunidades de judíos fuera de su tierra natal después del cautiverio babilónico (pág. 96)

dictator / dictador en la Roma antigua, una persona que gobernaba temporalmente con poder absoluto durante emergencias (pág. 271)

diplomacy / diplomacia el arte de negociar con otros países (pág. 615)

direct democracy / democracia directa sistema de gobierno en el que las personas se congregan en reuniones masivas para decidir sobre asuntos de gobierno (pág. 139)

disciple / discípulo seguidor de Jesucristo (pág. 344)

doctrine / doctrina enseñanza oficial de la iglesia (pág. 355)

domesticate / domesticar domar animales y plantas para uso humano (pág. 13)

drama / drama historia contada por actores que pretenden ser personajes en la misma (pág. 160)

dynasty / dinastía línea de gobernantes de la misma familia (págs. 44, 210, 226)

economy / economía manera organizada en la que las personas producen, venden y compran bienes y servicios (pág. 410)

embalming / embalsamado proceso desarrollado por los antiguos egipcios para la conservación del cuerpo de una persona después de muerta (pág. 49)

empire / imperio grupo de territorios o naciones bajo un mismo mandatario o gobierno (págs. 23, 89)

epic / epopeya poema largo que cuenta acerca de actos legendarios o heroicos (pág. 157)

Epicureanism / epicureísmo filosofía fundada por Epicuro en la Atenas helenista; enseñó que la felicidad a través de la persecución del placer era la meta de la vida (pág. 184)

excommunicate / excomulgar declarar que una persona o grupo no pertenece más a la iglesia (págs. 361, 521)

Spanish Glossary

exile / exilio período de ausencia forzada de una persona de su país u hogar (pág. 94)

export / exportar vender a otro país (pág. 666)

extended family / familia extendida grupo familiar que incluye a varias generaciones así como a otros parientes (pág. 469)

fable / fábula cuento corto que enseña una lección (pág. 158)

feudalism / feudalismo sistema político basado en lazos de lealtad entre señores y vasallos (págs. 497, 523)

fief / feudo bajo el feudalismo, la tierra que un señor otorgaba a un vasallo a cambio de su servicio militar y lealtad (pág. 524)

filial piety / piedad filial el respeto de los niños para sus padres y parientes mayores, una parte importante de las creencias confucianas (pág. 234)

fjord / fiordo valle de paredes abruptas que es una bahía del mar (pág. 518)

Forum / Foro espacio abierto en Roma que servía como mercado y plaza pública (pág. 306)

fossil / fósil huella o impresión de una planta o animal que se ha conservado en piedra (pág. 9)

glacier / glaciar masa inmensa de hielo (pág. 573)

gladiator / gladiador en la Roma antigua, persona que peleaba contra animales y otras personas como entretenimiento público (pág. 306)

gospel / evangelio ("buena nueva") uno de los cuatro relatos sobre la vida, enseñanzas y resurrección de Jesucristo (pág. 355)

grand jury / gran jurado grupo que decide si hay suficiente evidencia para acusar a una persona de un delito (pág. 537)

griot / griot narrador en poblados africanos (pág. 449)

guild / gremio grupo medieval de negocios formado por artesanos y mercaderes (págs. 503, 530)

guru / gurú maestro religioso y guía espiritual en el hinduismo (pág. 201)

Hellenistic Era / Era helenista período cuando el idioma y las ideas griegas se esparcieron a los habitantes no griegos del suroeste de Asia (pág. 178)

helot / ilota persona conquistada y esclavizada por los espartanos antiguos (pág. 126)

heresy / herejía creencia que difiere de las enseñanzas aceptadas de una religión o que las contradice (págs. 547, 643)

hierarchy / jerarquía organización con diferentes niveles de autoridad (pág. 355)

hieroglyphics / jeroglíficos sistema de escritura compuesto por miles de símbolos gráficos desarrollados por los antiguos egipcios (pág. 42)

Hinduism / hinduismo sistema religioso que se originó a partir de la religión de los arios en la antigua India (pág. 203)

historian / historiador persona que estudia y escribe acerca del pasado humano (pág. 9)

humanism / humanismo movimiento del renacimiento basado en las ideas y los valores de los antiguos romanos y griegos, de tal manera que los individuos y la sociedad humana eran importantes (pág. 619)

hypothesis / hipótesis explicación que se propone de los hechos (pág. 679)

icon / icono imagen o retrato religioso cristiano (pág. 359)

iconoclast / iconoclasta persona que se oponía al uso de ídolos en las iglesias bizantinas, aludiendo que los iconos alentaban el culto de ídolos (pág. 360)

ideograph / ideógrafo un carácter que une dos o más pictografías para representar una idea (pág. 228)

igloo / iglú casa con forma de domo construida por los inuitas (pág. 590)

import / importar comprar de otro país (pág. 666)

incense / incienso material que al quemarse despide un olor agradable (pág. 62)

indulgence / indulgencia perdonar la iglesia los pecados de una persona (pág. 634)

inflation / inflación período de incremento rápido de precios (pág. 319)

invest / invertir poner dinero en un proyecto (pág. 667)

Spanish Glossary

irrigation / irrigación método para llevar agua de otro lugar a un campo para regar las cosechas (pág. 18)

karma / karma en el hinduismo, la energía buena o mala que una persona desarrolla según si vive una vida buena o mala (pág. 204)

knight / caballero en la Edad Media, un guerrero noble que peleaba a caballo (pág. 524)

laity / laicado miembros de iglesia que no constituyen el clero (pág. 355)

latifundia / latifundios grandes propiedades agrícolas en la Roma antigua (pág. 278)

legacy / legado lo que una persona deja cuando muere (pág. 178)

Legalism / legalismo filosofía china desarrollada por Hanfeizi; enseñó que los humanos son naturalmente malos y por lo tanto necesitaban ser gobernados por leyes duras (pág. 239)

legion / legión unidad más pequeña del ejército romano, compuesta por aproximadamente 6,000 soldados (pág. 266)

limited government / gobierno limitado idea de que un gobierno sólo puede usar los poderes cedidos por los ciudadanos (pág. 700)

mandate / mandato orden formal (pág. 230)

martial arts / artes marciales deportes, como el judo y el karate, que involucran combate y defensa personal (pág. 499)

martyr / mártir persona dispuesta a morir antes que renunciar a sus creencias (pág. 353)

mass / misa servicio de culto Católico (pág. 546)

matrilineal / matrilineal se refiere a un grupo de personas que busca su ascendencia a través de las madres más que de los padres (pág. 469)

meditation / meditación práctica de reflexión silenciosa para aclarar la mente y encontrar la paz interior (pág. 499)

mercantilism / mercantilismo doctrina según la cual un país obtiene poder al amasar un abastecimiento de oro y plata (pág. 666)

messiah / mesías en el judaísmo, un salvador mandado por Dios (págs. 101, 344)

minaret / minarete torre de una mezquita desde donde el almuecín llama a los creyentes a la oración cinco veces al día (pág. 394)

missionary / misionero persona que viaja para llevar las ideas de una religión a otros (págs. 363, 520)

monastery / monasterio comunidad religiosa donde los monjes viven y trabajan (págs. 362, 413)

monopoly / monopolio el control de todo (o casi todo) el comercio o la producción de ciertos bienes (pág. 576)

monotheism / monoteísmo la creencia en un solo dios (pág. 81)

monsoon / monzón viento fuerte que sopla en una dirección en el invierno y en la dirección opuesta en el verano (pág. 195)

mosaic / mosaico figura hecha con muchos trozos de vidrios de colores, azulejo o piedra (pág. 333)

mosque / mezquita casa de culto musulmana (pág. 389)

mummy / momia cuerpo que se ha embalsamado y envuelto en lino (pág. 50)

myth / mito cuento tradicional que describe dioses o a héroes o explica eventos naturales (pág. 155)

natural law / ley natural ley que se aplica a todos y la cual puede entenderse por razonamiento (pág. 681)

nirvana / nirvana en el budismo, un estado de sabiduría y libertad del ciclo del renacimiento (pág. 205)

nomad / nómada persona que regularmente se mueve de un lugar a otro (pág. 10)

novel / novela historia ficticia larga (pág. 432)

oasis / oasis área verde en un desierto, alimentada por agua subterránea (pág. 373)

ode / oda poema que expresa emociones fuertes acerca de la vida (pág. 304)

oligarchy / oligarquía gobierno en el que un grupo pequeño de personas mantiene el poder (pág. 126)

Spanish Glossary

Spanish Glossary

oracle / oráculo templo sagrado en donde un sacerdote o sacerdotisa hablaban a nombre de un dios o diosa (pág. 156)

oral history / historia oral historias transmitidas de generación en generación (pág. 470)

papyrus / papiro planta de juncos del Valle de Nilo, empleada para hacer un tipo de papel (pág. 42)

parable / parábola historia que usa acontecimientos de la vida diaria para expresar ideas espirituales (pág. 345)

paterfamilias / paterfamilias ("padre de la familia") nombre dado al padre como cabeza de la casa en la Roma antigua (pág. 307)

patrician / patricio hacendado poderoso y miembro de la clase gobernante en la Roma antigua (pág. 269)

Pax Romana / Paz Romana era prolongada de paz y seguridad en el Imperio Romano (pág. 287)

peninsula / península extensión territorial rodeada de agua en tres lados (pág. 117)

persecute / perseguir maltratar una persona a causa de sus creencias (pág. 353)

pharaoh / faraón rey todopoderoso en el antiguo Egipto (pág. 48)

philosopher / filósofo pensador que busca la sabiduría y formula preguntas acerca de la vida (págs. 140, 169)

philosophy / filosofía estudio de la naturaleza y significando de la vida; viene de la palabra griega que significa "amor a la sabiduría" (pág. 169)

pictograph / pictógrafo carácter que representa a un objeto (pág. 228)

pilgrim / peregrino persona que viaja para ir a un relicario o sitio religioso (pág. 213)

plague / peste enfermedad que se esparce rápidamente y mata a muchas personas (págs. 319, 554)

plane geometry / geometría plana rama de las matemáticas que muestra cómo se relacionan los puntos, las líneas, los ángulos y las superficies (pág. 185)

plateau / meseta área de tierra alta y plana (pág. 446)

plebeian / plebeyo miembro de las personas comunes en la Roma antigua (pág. 269)

polis / polis antigua ciudad-estado griega, compuesta de una ciudad y las áreas circundantes y gobernada como un país independiente (pág. 122)

pope / Papa el obispo de Roma, posteriormente, la cabeza de la iglesia católica romana (pág. 356)

popular sovereignty / soberanía popular idea de que un gobierno recibe su poder de los ciudadanos (pág. 700)

porcelain / porcelana tipo de artículo de cerámica hecho de arcilla fina y horneado a altas temperaturas (pág. 418)

praetor / pretor importante funcionario de gobierno en la Roma antigua (pág. 270)

predestination / predestinación creencia de que sea lo que sea que haga una persona, el resultado de su vida ya ha sido planificado por Dios (pág. 640)

prophet / profeta persona que declara estar instruido por Dios para compartir Sus palabras (pág. 87)

proverb / proverbio dicho sabio (pág. 89)

province / provincia distrito político (pág. 28)

pyramid / pirámide inmensa estructura de piedra construida por los antiguos egipcios para utilizarse como una tumba (pág. 50)

quipu / quipu lazo con cuerdas anudadas de longitudes y colores diferentes (pág. 588)

Quran / Corán libro sagrado del Islam (pág. 377)

rabbi / rabino líder judío y maestro del Torá (pág. 101)

raja / rajá príncipe que dirigió a una tribu aria en la India (pág. 199)

rationalism / racionalismo la creencia de que la razón es la fuente principal del conocimiento (pág. 678)

Reconquista ("reconquest") / *reconquista* lucha cristiana para recuperar la península Ibérica de los musulmanes (pág. 558)

reform / reforma cambio que intenta producir una mejora (págs. 320, 411)

Reformation / reforma movimiento para reformar la iglesia católica; condujo a la creación del protestantismo (pág. 634)

regent / regente persona que opera como un gobernante temporal (pág. 334)

reincarnation / reencarnación renacimiento del alma o el espíritu en cuerpos diferentes a través del tiempo (pág. 204)

Renaissance / renacimiento ("nacer de nuevo") período en que se renovó el interés en las artes y el conocimiento en Europa (pág. 609)

representative democracy / democracia representativa sistema de gobierno en el que los ciudadanos escogen a un grupo más pequeño para promulgar leyes y tomar decisiones gubernamentales en su nombre (pág. 139)

representative government / gobierno representativo sistema de gobierno en que los ciudadanos eligen a sus líderes para promulgar leyes (pág. 694)

republic / república forma de gobierno en la que el líder no es un rey ni una reina sino una persona elegida por los ciudadanos (pág. 265)

resurrection / resurrección acto de volver a la vida (pág. 347)

rhetoric / retórica hablar en público (pág. 307)

Sabbath / sabbat día semanal de culto y descanso para los judíos (pág. 94)

saint / santo persona cristiana santificada (pág. 333)

salvation / salvación acto de ser salvado del pecado y aceptado para entrar al cielo (pág. 350)

samurai / samurai clase de guerreros en el Japón feudal que prometía lealtad a un noble a cambio de tierra (pág. 494)

Sanskrit / Sánscrito idioma escrito desarrollado por los arios (pág. 199)

satire / sátira obra que hace burla de las debilidades humanas (pág. 304)

satrap / sátrapa funcionario que gobernaba un estado en el Imperio pérsico durante la época de Darío (pág. 133)

satrapies / satrapies los 20 estados en los cuales Darío dividió al Imperio pérsico (pág. 133)

savanna / sabana llanura cubierta de hierba (pág. 69)

schism / cisma separación (pág. 361)

scholasticism / escolástica forma de pensamiento medieval que trató de unir a la razón y a la fe en estudios religiosos (pág. 550)

scientific method / método científico manera organizada de recoger y analizar pruebas (pág. 679)

scribe / escriba conservador de registros (pág. 20)

sect / secta un grupo más pequeño con creencias distintas dentro de un grupo religioso más grande (pág. 499)

secular / secular que se interesa en bienes materiales en lugar de asuntos religiosos (pág. 609)

seminary / seminario escuela en donde se entrenan y se educan a los sacerdotes y los ministros (pág. 643)

separation of powers / separación de poderes división equitativa de los poderes entre las ramas del gobierno (pág. 682)

serf / siervo trabajador campesino atado por ley a las tierras de un noble (pág. 524)

sheikh / jeque líder de una tribu árabe (pág. 373)

Shiite / chiíta grupo musulmán que acepta sólo a los descendientes de Ali, el hijo político de Mahoma, como auténticos líderes de los musulmanes (pág. 382)

shogun / shogun gobernante militar del Japón feudal (pág. 495)

shrine / relicario lugar sagrado (pág. 490)

social class / clase social grupo de personas que comparten una posición semejante en la sociedad (pág. 233)

social contract / contrato social acuerdo entre mandatarios y ciudadanos sobre el cual se basa un gobierno (pág. 682)

Socratic method / método socrático método de enseñanza desarrollado por Sócrates que emplea un formato de pregunta y respuesta para forzar a los estudiantes a utilizar su raciocinio para ver las cosas por sí mismos (pág. 170)

solid geometry / geometría sólida rama de las matemáticas que estudia a las esferas y los cilindros (pág. 186)

Sophist / Sofista maestro profesional en Grecia antigua; creían que las personas deben utilizar el conocimiento para mejorarse a sí mismas y desarrollaron el arte de hablar en público y el debate (pág. 169)

specialization / especialización desarrollo de diferentes tipos de trabajos (pág. 15)

Spanish Glossary

Spanish Glossary

steppe / estepa ancha planicie ondeada cubierta de hierba (pág. 424)

Stoicism / estoicismo filosofía fundada por Zeno en la Atenas Helenista; enseñaba que la felicidad provenía no de seguir a las emociones, sino a la razón y de cumplir con nuestro deber (pág. 184)

stupa / estupa templo budista con forma de cúpula o montículo (pág. 211)

subcontinent / subcontinente gran masa de tierra que forma parte de un continente pero está separada de él (pág. 195)

sultan / sultán líder político y militar con autoridad absoluta sobre un país musulmán (págs. 383, 467)

Sunni / sunní grupo musulmán que sólo acepta a descendientes de los Omeyas como auténticos gobernantes de los musulmanes (pág. 382)

Swahili / suajili se refiere a la cultura e idioma de Africa del Este (pág. 467)

synagogue / sinagoga casa de culto judía (pág. 94)

tanka / tanka forma más antigua de poesía en Japón; poema sin rima de cinco líneas (pág. 501)

technology / tecnología instrumentos y métodos utilizados para ayudar a los humanos a realizar tareas (pág. 11)

terror / terror acciones violentas para atemorizar personas para que rendirse (pág. 426)

theocracy / teocracia gobierno dirigido por líderes religiosos (pág. 208)

theology / teología el estudio de la religión y de Dios (págs. 550, 640)

theory / teoría explicación de cómo o por qué ocurre algo (pág. 671)

Torah / Torá las leyes que, según la Biblia, Moisés recibió de Dios en el monte Sinaí; estas leyes se convirtieron después en la primera parte de la Biblia hebrea (pág. 82)

tragedy / tragedia forma de drama en la que una persona se esfuerza para vencer dificultades pero encuentra un final infeliz (pág. 160)

treason / traición deslealtad al gobierno (págs. 431, 599)

trial jury / jurado grupo que decide si una persona acusada es inocente o culpable (pág. 537)

tribe / tribu grupo de familias relacionadas (págs. 81, 424)

tribute / tributo pago realizado por un grupo o nación a otra para mostrar obediencia o para obtener paz o protección (págs. 60, 89)

triumvirate / triunvirato en la Roma antigua, un grupo gobernante de tres personas (pág. 280)

tyrant / tirano persona que toma el poder por la fuerza y gobierna con autoridad total (pág. 125)

vassal / vasallo en el feudalismo, un noble que ocupaba la tierra de un señor de más alto rango y lo servía, y a cambio le daba protección (págs. 496, 523)

vault / cámara estructura curva de piedra o cemento que forma un techo (pág. 303)

vernacular / vernáculo idioma cotidiano empleado en un país o región (págs. 552, 620)

veto / veta rechazar (pág. 270)

warlord / caudillo líder militar que dirige un gobierno (pág. 409)

Z

Zoroastrianism / zoroastrismo religión persa fundada por Zoroastro; enseñaba que los humanos tenían la libertad de escoger entre lo correcto y lo incorrecto, y que la bondad triunfaría al final (pág. 133)

A Gazetteer (GA•zuh•TIHR) is a geographic index or dictionary. It shows latitude and longitude for cities and certain other places. Latitude and longitude are shown in this way: 48°N 2°E, or 48 degrees north latitude and two degrees east longitude. This Gazetteer lists most of the world's largest independent countries, their capitals, and several important geographic features. The page numbers tell where each entry can be found on a map in this book. As an aid to pronunciation, most entries are spelled phonetically.

Aachen [AH•kuhn] City in Germany near the Belgian and Dutch borders; capital of Charlemagne's Frankish empire. 50°N 6°E (pp. 512, 516)

Acre Region in Brazil. 10°S 68°W (p. 542)

Acre River River chiefly in western Brazil. 10°S 68°W (p. 542)

Actium [AK•shee•uhm] Cape on the western coast of Greece. 37°N 23°E (p. 297)

Aden Port city of the Red Sea in southern Yemen. 12°N 45°E (p. 433)

Aden, Gulf of Western arm of the Arabian Sea, between Yemen, Somalia, and Djibouti. 11°N 45°E (p. 445)

Adrianople [AY•dree•uh•NOH•puhl] Ancient city in northwestern Turkey, now called Edirne. 41°N 26°E (p. 323)

Adriatic [AY•dree•A•tihk] **Sea** Arm of Mediterranean Sea between Italy and the Balkan Peninsula. 44°N 14°E (pp. R2, 117, 134, 144, 149, 176, 263, 269, 274, 293, 352, 361, 367, 516, 548, 609, 653, 688)

Aegean [ih•JEE•uhn] **Sea** Gulf of the Mediterranean Sea between Greece and Asia Minor, north of Crete. 39°N 24°E (pp. R2, 117, 134, 144, 149, 176, 328, 548)

Afghanistan [af•GA•nuh•STAN] Central Asian country west of Pakistan. 33°N 63°E (pp. R2, R3, R19, 176, 198)

Africa Second-largest continent, south of Europe between the Atlantic and Indian Oceans. 10°N 22°E (pp. R2, R3, R5, R20, R21, 33, 109, 262, 263, 269, 274, 293, 297, 352, 358, 361, 367, 380, 385, 433, 444, 446, 449, 460, 463, 468, 469, 473, 479, 518, 554, 565, 573, 662, 658, 668)

Agincourt [A•juhn•KOHRT] Village in northern France. 52°N 6°E (pp. 557, 561)

Agra [AH•gruh] City in northern India, site of the Taj Mahal. 27°N 78°E (p. 394)

Ahaggar [uh•HAH•guhr] **Mountains** Arid, rocky, upland region in southern Algeria in the center of the Sahara. 25°N 6°E (p. 445)

Alaska Largest state in the United States, located in the extreme northwestern region of North America. 65°N 150°W (pp. R2, R4)

Albania [al•BAY•nee•uh] Country on the Adriatic Sea, south of Yugoslavia. 42°N 20°E (p. R3)

Albany Capital city of New York. 42°N 73°W (p. 694)

Alexandria [A•lihg•ZAN•dree•uh] City and major seaport in northern Egypt in the Nile River delta. 31°N 29°E (pp. 176, 179, 182, 189, 246, 293, 323, 329, 352, 361, 367, 374)

Algeria [al•JIHR•ee•uh] Country in North Africa. 29°N 1°E (p. R3)

Algiers [al•JIHRZ] Capital city of Algeria, largest Mediterranean port of northwestern Africa. 36°N 2°E (pp. R3, 385)

Alps Mountain system of south central Europe. 46°N 9°E (pp. R2, 263, 269, 274, 513, 514, 609, 653)

Altay Mountains Mountain range in Asia. 49°N 87°E (pp. R5, 225)

Altun Mountains Range of mountains that are a part of the Kunlun Shan in China. 35°N 83°E (p. 225)

Amazon River River in northern South America, largely in Brazil, second-longest river in the world. 2°S 53°W (pp. R2, R4, 473, 565, 577)

Amsterdam Capital of the Netherlands. 52°N 4°E (p. 548)

Amu Darya [AH•moo DAHR•yuh] Largest river of central Asia. 38°N 64°E (p. 198)

Andes [AN•deez] Mountain range along the western edge of South America. 13°S 75°W (pp. R4, R15, 577)

Angola [ang•GOH•luh] Southern African country north of Namibia. 14°S 16°E (pp. R2, R3)

Anjou [AN•JOO] Former province and duchy of France. 45°N 73°W (p. 538)

Antarctica Fifth-largest of the earth's seven continents; it surrounds the South Pole. 80°S 127°E (pp. R3, R5)

Antioch [AN•tee•AHK] Ancient capital of Syria, now a city in southern Turkey. 36°N 36°E (pp. 246, 352, 361, 367, 542)

Antwerp [ANT•WUHRP] City in northern Belgium. 51°N 4°E (p. 548)

Anyang [AHN•YAHNG] City in northern China, was China's first capital. 36°N 114°E (pp. 224, 226, 251)

Apennines [A•puh•NYNZ] Mountain range that runs through Italy. 43°N 11°E (pp. 263, 269, 609, 653)

Appalachian Mountains Mountain system of eastern North America. 38°N 82°W (pp. R4, R11, 590, 694)

Aquitaine [A•kwuh•TAYN] Former duchy and kingdom in southwest France. 43°N 1°E (pp. 538, 557)

Arabia Desert peninsula of southwestern Asia across the Red Sea to Africa. 27°N 32°E (pp. R2, R18, R19, 17, 28, 70, 109, 246, 329, 374, 380, 385, 425, 433, 435, 554)

Arabian Desert Arid region in eastern Egypt; also called the Eastern Desert. 22°N 45°E (pp. R18, R19, 17, 28, 39, 75)

Arabian Peninsula Great desert peninsula in extreme southwestern Asia. 28°N 40°E (pp. R5, 374, 445, 448, 452)

Arabian Sea Portion of the Indian Ocean between the Arabian Peninsula and the subcontinent of India. 16°N 65°E (pp. R3, R5, R19, 109, 176, 193, 195, 198, 210, 213, 219, 246, 374, 380, 409, 425, 433, 452, 554, 565)

Aragón Region and former kingdom in northeastern Spain. 42°N 1°W (p. 538)

Aral [AR•uhl] **Sea** Large saltwater lake, or inland sea, in central Asia. 45°N 60°E (pp. R3, R5, 132, 198, 246, 380, 383, 397, 424, 425, 554)

Arctic Ocean Smallest of the earth's four oceans. 85°N 170°E (pp. 573, 590)

Argentina [AHR•juhn•TEE•nuh] South American country east of Chile. 36°S 67°W (pp. R2, R14)

Arkansas River River in the western United States, a major tributary of the Mississippi River. 38°N 100°W (pp. R11, 663)

Asia Largest of the earth's seven continents. 50°N 100°E (pp. R22, R23, 13, 17, 33, 255, 295, 409, 424, 429, 435, 439, 518, 565, 573, 662)

Asia Minor Region of the ancient world, roughly corresponding to present-day Turkey. 38°N 31°E (pp. R22, R23, 17, 28, 117, 121, 132, 176, 179, 189, 269, 274, 277, 286, 292, 293, 297, 323, 327, 329, 342, 352, 358, 361, 367, 374, 380, 385, 542)

Assyria [uh•SIHR•ee•uh] Ancient country in Asia that included the Tigris River valley in Mesopotamia. 35°N 42°E (p. 28)

Astrakhan [AS•truh•KAN] City in southern European Russia on the Volga River near the Caspian Sea. 46°N 48°E (p. 554)

Asunción [uh•SOON•see•OHN] Capital city of Paraguay. 25°S 58°W (p. R2)

Athens Capital of Greece, an ancient city-state. 38°N 23°E (pp. 117, 121, 124, 125, 134, 138, 144, 149, 154, 176, 182, 293)

Atlanta Capital city of Georgia in the United States. 33°N 84°W (p. R2)

Atlantic Ocean Second-largest body of water in the world. 5°S 25°W (pp. R2–7, R11, R13–16, R20–22, 13, 121, 269, 293, 323, 329, 337, 352, 361, 385, 463, 469, 473, 479, 513, 514, 516, 518, 538, 542, 555, 557, 561, 565, 573, 577, 590, 639, 645, 662, 663, 668, 691, 694, 695, 703)

Atlas Mountains Mountain range in northwestern Africa on the northern edge of the Sahara. 31°N 5°W (pp. R20, R21, 445)

Augsburg [AWGZ•BUHRG] City in south central Germany. 48°N 10°E (pp. 555, 688)

Australia Island continent southeast of Asia. 25°S 135°W (pp. R3, R5, 13, 33, 658, 662)

Austria [AWS•tree•uh] Country in central Europe. 47°N 12°E (pp. R3, R16, 13, 385, 548, 639, 688)

Avignon [A•veen•YOHN] City in southern France, on the Rhône River. 43°N 4°E (p. 557)

Axum [AHK•SOOM] Ancient kingdom in northeastern Africa. 14°N 38°E (p. 451)

Azores [AY•ZOHRZ] Group of nine islands in the North Atlantic Ocean. 37°N 29°W (pp. R2, R4, R20, R21, 658)

B

Babylon [BA•buh•luhn] Once the world's largest and richest city, on the banks of the Euphrates River in northern Mesopotamia. 32°N 45°E (pp. 16, 17, 26, 28, 86, 93, 132, 174, 176)

Baghdad [BAG•DAD] Capital city of Iraq. 33°N 44°E (pp. R3, 374, 379, 380, 383, 385, 397, 423, 424, 425, 452, 554)

Bahamas [buh•HAH•muhz] Country made up of many islands between Cuba and the United States. 23°N 74°W (pp. R2, R4, R13, 662)

Balkan [BAWL•kuhn] **Peninsula** Peninsula in southeastern Europe bounded on the east by the Black and Aegean Seas, on the south by the Mediterranean Sea, and on the west by the Adriatic and Ionian Seas. 42°N 20°E (pp. 117, 327, 329)

Baltic [BAWL•tihk] **Sea** Sea in northern Europe connected to the North Sea. 55°N 17°E (pp. R3, R5, R16, R18, 513, 518, 538, 548, 555, 645, 688, 703)

Baltimore City in northern Maryland in the United States. 39°N 77°W (p. 694)

Bangkok [BANG•KAHK] Capital of Thailand. 14°N 100°E (pp. R3, 433, 667)

Bangladesh [BAHNG•gluh•DEHSH] South Asian country bounded by Myanmar and India. 24°N 90°E (pp. R3, 198)

Barcelona City in northeastern Spain. 41°N 2°E (p. 555)

Bavaria State in southeastern Germany. 48°N 13°E (p. 688)

Bay of Bengal Arm of the Indian Ocean between India and the Malay Peninsula on the east. 17°N 87°E (pp. R3, R5, R22, R23, 109, 193, 194, 195, 198, 210, 213, 246, 409, 411, 425, 433, 439, 565, 667)

Bay of Naples Inlet of the Tyrrhenian Sea in south central Italy. 40°N 14°E (pp. R16, 293)

Beijing [BAY•JIHNG] Capital of China. 40°N 116°E (pp. R3, 409, 411, 423, 424, 425, 430, 431, 439, 554)

Belgium [BEHL•juhm] Country in northwestern Europe. 51°N 5°E (pp. R3, R16, 703)

Belgrade [BEHL•GRAYD] Capital of Yugoslavia. 45°N 21°E (pp. 548, 555, 688)

Belize [buh•LEEZ] Central American country east of Guatemala. 18°N 89°W (pp. R2, R13, 583)

Benue River [BAYN•way] River, the main tributary of the Niger River, in west central Africa. 8°N 8°E (p. 469)

Beringia [buh•RIHN•jee•uh] A natural land bridge that long ago linked present-day Siberia and Alaska. 66°N 169°W (p. 573)

Bering Sea Part of the North Pacific Ocean, situated between the Aleutian Islands on the south and the Bering Strait, which connects it with the Arctic Ocean, on the north. 55°N 175°E (pp. R2, R3, R4, R5, R23, 573)

Berlin Capital of Germany. 53°N 13°E (p. 688)

Bhutan [boo•TAHN] South Asian country northeast of India. 27°N 91°E (pp. R3, R22, R23, 198)

Bialystok [bee•AH•lih•STAWK] City in northeastern Poland. 53°N 23°E (p. 548)

Black Sea Inland sea between southeastern Europe and Asia Minor. 43°N 32°E (pp. R3, R5, R17, R18, 109, 121, 132, 144, 176, 179, 189, 246, 255, 269, 274, 292, 293, 297, 323, 328, 329, 352, 361, 367, 374, 380, 383, 385, 397, 424, 425, 513, 518, 538, 542, 554, 565, 639, 639, 645)

Bohemia Historical region and former kingdom in what is now the Czech Republic. 49°N 13°E (pp. 639, 645, 688)

Bombay Port city in western India, now called Mumbai. 18°N 72°E (p. 667)

Bordeaux [bawr•DOH] City in southwestern France. 44°N 0°W (pp. 555, 557, 561)

Borneo Third-largest island in the world, located in the Malay Archipelago in southeastern Asia. 0°N 112°E (pp. R3, 246, 425, 433, 554, 667)

Boston Capital of Massachusetts. 42°N 71°W (pp. 691, 694, 695)

Brazil Largest country in South America. 9°S 53°W (pp. R2, 473)

Britain Largest island in the British Isles. 54°N 4°W (pp. R2–3, R4–5, R16, 286, 293, 297, 302, 317, 323, 352, 358, 361, 363, 695)

Brittany Former province and duchy in France. 48°N 3°W (pp. 538, 557)

Bruges [BROOZH] City in northwestern Belgium. 51°N 3°E (pp. 522, 555, 557)

Buda [BOO•duh] Town in Hungary that combined with Pest and Óbuda in 1873 to form Budapest. 47°N 19°E (pp. 555, 688)

Budapest [BOO•duh•PEHST] Capital of Hungary. 47°N 19°E (p. 703)

Bulgaria [BUHL•GAR•ee•uh] Country in southeastern Europe on the Balkan Peninsula. 42°N 24°E (pp. R3, R17, 176)

Burgundy Historic kingdom and province within France. 49°N 4°E (pp. 538, 557)

Burma Country in Southeast Asia, now known as Myanmar. 21°N 95°E (p. 667)

Byblos [BIH•bluhs] Ancient city of Phoenicia on the Mediterranean Sea, near present-day Beirut, Lebanon. 34°N 35°E (pp. 17, 90, 105, 132)

Byzantine [BIH•zuhn•TEEN] **Empire** Eastern part of the Roman Empire that survived after the breakup of the western part of the empire in the A.D. 400s; Constantinople was its capital. 41°N 29°E (pp. 383, 518, 538, 542)

Byzantium [buh•ZAN•tee•uhm] Ancient city that became the capital of the Eastern Roman Empire; was later renamed Constantinople and is now called Istanbul. 41°N 29°E (pp. 293, 397)

Gazetteer

Cahokia [kuh•HOH•kee•uh] City in southwestern Illinois on the Mississippi River near St. Louis; largest city of the Mississippian Mound Builders. 38°N 90°W (p. 572)

Cairo [KY•roh] Capital of Egypt. 31°N 32°E (pp. R3, 380, 385, 452, 479)

Calais [ka•LAY] Seaport in northeastern France on the Strait of Dover. 50°N 1°E (p. 557)

Calakmul [kah•lahk•MOOL] Mayan city-state. (p. 585)

Calcutta City in eastern India, now known as Kolkata. 22°N 88°E (pp. R3, 433, 667)

Calicut Seaport on the Arabian Sea in southwestern India, now called Kozhikode. 11°N 75°E (pp. 433, 662, 667)

California State in the western United States. 36°N 120°W (pp. R2, R6, R7, R8)

Campania [kam•PAY•nyuh] Region in southern Italy on the Tyrrhenian Sea. 41°N 14°E (p. 263)

Canaan [KAY•nuhn] Kingdom in Southeast Asia along the Mediterranean Sea, later called Palestine. 31°N 35°E (p. 81)

Canada Country in North America north of the United States. 50°N 100°W (pp. R2, R4, R6, R7)

Cannae [KA•nee] Ancient town in southern Italy where Hannibal defeated the Romans in 216 B.C. 41°N 16°E (p. 274)

Canterbury [KAN•tuhr•BEHR•ee] City in Kent in southeastern England; site of an early Christian cathedral. 51°N 1°E (pp. 538, 645)

Caribbean [KAR•uh•BEE•uhn] **Sea** Part of the Atlantic Ocean bordered by the West Indies, South America, and Central America. 15°N 76°W (pp. R2, R4, 473, 565, 590, 662, 663, 691)

Carpathian [kahr•PAY•thee•uhn] **Mountains** Mountain system in central and Eastern Europe. 49°N 20°E (p. 513)

Carthage [KAHR•thihj] Ancient city on the northern coast of Africa. 37°N 10°E (pp. 263, 268, 269, 274, 292, 293, 297, 329, 337, 367, 514)

Caspian [KAS•pee•uhn] **Sea** Saltwater lake in southeastern Europe and southwestern Asia, the largest inland body of water in the world. 40°N 52°E (pp. R3, R5, R17, 17, 76, 109, 132, 176, 179, 198, 246, 255, 293, 297, 329, 361, 374, 380, 383, 385, 397, 424, 425, 513, 518, 542, 554, 565)

Castile Former kingdom in Spain. 39°N 3°E (p. 538)

Çatal Hüyük [chah•TAHL hoo•YOOK] Early Neolithic community in present-day Turkey. 38°N 35°E (p. 8)

Caucasus [KAW•kuh•suhs] **Mountains** Range of mountains that forms a boundary between Europe and Asia between the Caspian and Black Seas. 43°N 42°E (pp. R17, 374)

Ceylon [sih•LAHN] Country in the Indian Ocean south of India, now called Sri Lanka. 8°N 82°E (pp. R22, 433, 667)

Chaco Canyon Center of Anasazi civilization in present-day New Mexico. 36°N 108°W (p. 578)

Chaeronea [KEHR•uh•NEE•uh] Ancient town in Greece near Thebes. 38°N 22°E (p. 176)

Champagne Region of northeastern France. 48°N 2°E (p. 557)

Changan [CHAHNG•AHN] Capital of China during the Tang dynasty, now called Xian. 34°N 108°W (pp. 240, 241, 246, 408, 409, 411, 416, 420, 439)

Chang Jiang [CHAHNG JYAHNG] River in China, third-longest in the world; formerly called the Yangtze River. 30°N 117°E (pp. 198, 225, 226, 230, 241, 246, 409, 410, 424, 425, 431, 439)

Charles Town City in southeastern South Carolina, now called Charleston. 33°N 80°W (pp. 694, 695)

Chernigov [chehr•NEE•guhf] Principality in the Kievan Rus. 51°N 31°E (p. 548)

Chichén Itzá [chee•CHEHN eet•SAH] Most important city of the Mayan peoples, located in the northern part of the Yucatán Peninsula. 20°N 88°W (p. 575)

China Country in East Asia, world's largest by population; now called the People's Republic of China. 37°N 93°E (pp. R3, R5, R22–23, 109, 198, 225, 226, 230, 241, 246, 409, 411, 416, 424, 431, 432, 433, 435, 439, 485, 554, 658, 662, 667)

Chittagong [CHIH•tuh•GAHNG] Port city in southeastern Bangladesh. 22°N 90°E (pp. 433, 554)

Clermont City in central France. 45°N 3°E (pp. 534, 542, 544)

Cologne [KUH•LOHN] City in west central Germany on the Rhine River. 50°N 6°E (p. 542)

Congo River River in Central Africa. 2°S 17°E (p. 469)

Connecticut A state in the northeastern United States. 41°N 73°W (p. 694)

Constantinople [KAHN•STAN•tuhn•OH•puhl] City built on the site of Byzantium, now known as Istanbul in present-day Turkey. 41°N 29°E (pp. 246, 302, 317, 323, 327, 329, 337, 351, 352, 358, 361, 367, 374, 379, 380, 424, 425, 518, 542, 555)

Copán Ancient city of the Mayan people, in northwestern Honduras. 14°N 89°W (p. 575)

Cordoba [KAWR•duh•buh] City in southern Spain. 37°N 4°W (pp. 379, 380, 538, 555)

Corinth City of ancient Greece, southwest of the modern city of Corinth. 37°N 22°E (pp. 117, 144, 269, 274)

Corsica Island in the Mediterranean Sea. 42°N 8°E (pp. R5, R16, 121, 263, 269, 274, 293, 329, 337, 542, 538, 555, 609, 653)

Costa Rica [KAHS•tuh REE•kuh] Republic in southern Central America. 11°N 85°W (p. R2)

Crécy [kray•SEE] Site in France of battle in which England defeated France in 1346. 50°N 48°E (pp. 557, 561)

Crete [KREET] Greek island southeast of mainland in the southern Aegean Sea. 35°N 24°E (pp. R17, 116, 117, 121, 132, 134, 149, 179, 189, 269, 274, 293, 329, 337, 385, 542, 548, 555)

Crimea Peninsula in southeastern Ukraine. 45°N 33°E (p. 548)

Cuba Island country in the West Indies. 22°N 79°W (pp. R2, R4, 662)

Cuzco [KOOS•koh] City in southern Peru. 13°S 71°W (pp. 572, 577, 582, 593, 603)

Cyprus [SY•pruhs] Island country in the eastern Mediterranean Sea, south of Turkey. 35°N 31°E (pp. R3, R5, R17, 62, 90, 121, 132, 179, 189, 269, 274, 293, 329, 385, 542)

Damascus [duh•MAS•kuhs] Capital of Syria. 33°N 4°W (pp. 90, 105, 246, 348, 352, 361, 374, 380, 383, 385, 397)

Danube [DAN•yoob] **River** Second-longest river in Europe. 43°N 24°E (pp. R5, 176, 269, 274, 292, 293, 297, 323, 329, 337, 380, 383, 385, 397, 425, 513, 514, 516, 538, 555)

Danzig City in northern Poland. 54°N 18°E (p. 555)

Dead Sea Salt lake in southwestern Asia, bounded by Israel, the West Bank, and Jordan. 31°N 35°E (pp. R5, 17, 39, 75, 90, 105)

Deccan Plateau Region in India. 19°N 76°E (pp. R5, 195, 198)

Delhi [DEH•lee] City in northern India. 28°N 76°E (pp. R3, 117, 379, 385)

Delos [DEE•LAHS] Greek island in the southern Aegean Sea. 37°N 25°E (pp. 138, 144)

Delphi [DEHL•FY] Ancient Greek town and site of Temple of Apollo. 38°N 22°E (pp. 117, 156)

Denmark Scandinavian country in northwestern Europe. 56°N 8°E (pp. R3, 518, 639, 645, 688)

East Africa Region in east Central Africa comprised of Burundi, Kenya, Rwanda, Somalia, Tanzania, and Uganda. 5°N 35°E (pp. R3, R5, R20, R21, 246)

East China Sea Arm of the northwestern Pacific Ocean between the eastern coast of China and the Ryukyu Islands, bounded by the Yellow Sea and Taiwan. 30°N 125°E (pp. R5, 225, 226, 230, 241, 251, 409, 411, 425, 439, 485)

Eastern Desert Arid region in eastern Egypt, also called the Arabian Desert. 22°N 45°E (pp. 39, 75)

East Sea Arm of the Pacific Ocean, lying between Japan and the Asian mainland; also called the Sea of Japan. 40°N 132°E (pp. R5, 225, 485)

Ebro River River in northeastern Spain, emptying into the Mediterranean Sea. 42°N 2°W (p. 516)

Edinburgh Capital city of Scotland. 55°N 3°W (p. 555)

Edo [EH•doh] Village in Japan where the Sumida River joins Tokyo Bay, site of present-day Tokyo. 34°N 131°E (pp. 485, 507)

Egypt Country in North Africa on the Mediterranean Sea. 26°N 27°E (pp. R3, 1, 17, 28, 38, 39, 59, 62, 70, 75, 121, 132, 176, 246, 269, 286, 293, 297, 302, 317, 327, 329, 352, 361, 367, 374, 380, 383, 385, 397, 426, 448, 452, 479)

England Part of the island of Great Britain lying east of Wales and south of Scotland. 51°N 1°W (pp. R2–3, R4–5, R16, 518, 522, 534, 538, 542, 544, 557, 639, 645, 662)

English Channel Narrow sea separating France and Great Britain. 49°N 3°W (pp. 557, 567)

Equator An imaginary circle that divides the earth into the Northern Hemisphere and the Southern Hemisphere; latitude of any single point on the Equator is 0°. (pp. R2, R3, R4, R5, 33, 425, 433, 445, 452, 463, 469, 479, 554, 565, 577, 667)

Eridu [EHR•ih•DOO] Ancient settlement in Mesopotamia. 31°N 46°E (p. 17)

Estonia [eh•STOH•nee•uh] Republic in northeastern Europe, one of the Baltic states. 59°N 25°E (p. 548)

Ethiopia [EE•thee•OH•pee•uh] Country in East Africa north of Somalia and Kenya. 8°N 38°E (pp. 452, 479)

Etruria [ih•TRUR•ee•uh] Ancient region on the Italian peninsula that was home to the Etruscans; area is now called Tuscany. 30°N 46°E (p. 263)

Euphrates [yu•FRAY•teez] **River** River in southwestern Asia that flows through Syria and Iraq and joins the Tigris River near the Persian Gulf. 36°N 40°E (pp. 17, 109, 121, 132, 176, 179, 189, 246, 255, 293, 297, 329, 374, 380, 383, 397, 565)

Europe One of the world's seven continents, sharing a landmass with Asia. 50°N 15°E (pp. R3, R5, R16–17, 13, 28, 33, 109, 255, 426, 429, 473, 565, 573, 633, 642, 662, 658, 668, 695)

Fertile Crescent Region in the Middle East that reaches from Israel to the Persian Gulf, including the Tigris and Euphrates Rivers. 34°N 45°E (p. 17)

Flanders Historic region in present-day Belgium. 50°N 2°E (p. 557)

Florence City in the Tuscany region of central Italy at the foot of the Apennines. 43°N 11°E (pp. 555, 608, 609, 639, 653, 670)

Florida State in the southeastern United States bordered by Alabama, Georgia, the Atlantic Ocean, and the Gulf of Mexico. 30°N 84°W (p. 691)

Formigny [FAWR•mee•NYUH] Site in northern France of a French victory during the Hundred Years' War. 49°N 0°W (pp. 557, 561)

France Third-largest country in Europe, located south of Great Britain. 47°N 1°E (pp. R2–3, R4–5, R16, 380, 385, 518, 522, 534, 538, 542, 544, 548, 557, 639, 645, 662)

Frankfurt Port city in west central Germany on the Main River. 50°N 8°E (pp. 555, 688, 703)

Galilee [GA•luh•LEE] Region of ancient Palestine, now part of northern Israel, between the Jordan River and the Sea of Galilee. 32°N 35°E (pp. 352, 361, 367)

Ganges [GAN•JEEZ] **Plain** Flat, fertile area around the Ganges River. 24°N 89°E (pp. 195, 198)

Ganges [GAN•JEEZ] **River** River in India that flows from the Himalaya to the Bay of Bengal. 24°N 89°E (pp. R3, R5, R22, 193, 195, 198, 210, 213, 219, 246, 409, 424, 667)

Gaugamela [GAW•guh•MEE•luh] Area near Babylon and the Tigris River, site of famous battle in 331 B.C. 36°N 44°E (pp. 174, 176)

Gaul Ancient Roman name for the area now known as France. 45°N 3°E (pp. 269, 274, 277, 286, 293, 297, 302, 317, 323, 352, 358, 361)

Geneva [juh•NEE•vuh] City in western Switzerland. 46°N 6°E (p. 633)

Genoa City and seaport in northwestern Italy. 44°N 9°E (pp. 538, 542, 548, 555, 608, 609, 639, 653)

Germany Western European country south of Denmark. 51°N 10°E (pp. R3, 518)

Ghana [GAH•nuh] Country in West Africa on the Gulf of Guinea. 8°N 2°W (pp. R2, 448, 451)

Ghent City in western Belgium. 51°N 4°E (pp. 555, 557)

Giza City in northern Egypt and site of the Great Pyramid. 29°N 31°E (pp. 17, 39, 47, 62, 75)

Gobi [GOH•bee] Vast desert covering parts of Mongolia and China. 43°N 103°E (pp. R5, 109, 225, 246, 409, 411, 425, 431, 439)

Gomel Port city in southeastern Belarus on the Sozh River. 52°N 31°E (p. 548)

Granada [gruh•NAH•duh] Province on the southern coast of Spain. 12°N 61°W (pp. 380, 394, 553)

Great Plains The continental slope extending through the United States and Canada. 45°N 104°W (p. R4)

Great Rift Valley Depression extending from Syria to Mozambique. 5°S 35°E (p. 445)

Great Wall Wall built in the 200s B.C. to protect China's northern border. 338°N 109°E (pp. 431, 436)

Greece Country in southeastern Europe on the Balkan Peninsula. 39°N 21°E (pp. R3, R5, R17, 6, 117, 121, 124, 125,

132, 134, 138, 149, 154, 176, 263, 268, 269, 274, 277, 286, 292, 293, 297, 302, 317, 323, 351, 352, 358, 361, 367, 385)

Guangzhou [GWAHNG•JOH] Port city in southern China on the Chang Jiang. 23°N 113°W (pp. R3, 246, 409, 411, 424, 431, 439)

Gulf of Mexico Gulf on part of the southern coast of the United States. 25°N 94°W (pp. R2, R4, 565, 575, 590, 663, 691)

Hadrian's Wall Ancient Roman stone wall built to protect the northern boundary of Roman Britain. 55°N 3°W (pp. 293, 297)

Hainan [HY•NAHN] Province in southeastern China and island in the South China Sea. 32°N 120°E (pp. R5, 225)

Hamburg City in north central Germany near the North Sea. 53°N 10°E (pp. 548, 555)

Han [HAHN] Chinese state along Huang He and Chang Jiang. 33°N 112°E (p. 241)

Hanging Gardens Located in Babylon, one of the Seven Wonders of the Ancient World. 32°N 45°E (p. 29)

Hangzhou [HAHNG•JOH] Port city in southeastern China, capital during the Song dynasty. 30°N 120°E (pp. 246, 408, 409, 411, 416, 424, 425, 431, 439, 554)

Harappa [huh•RA•puh] Ancient city in the Indus River valley in present-day Pakistan. (pp. 194, 196, 198, 219)

Heian [HAY•ahn] Ancient capital city of Japan, now called Kyoto. 35°N 135°E (pp. 485, 491, 493, 498, 507)

Himalaya [HIH•muh•LAY•uh] Mountain system forming a barrier between India and the rest of Asia. 29°N 85°E (pp. R3, R5, R22–23, 193, 195, 198, 213, 219, 246, 409, 424, 425, 426, 439)

Hindu Kush Major mountain system in central Asia. 35°N 68°E (pp. 109, 198, 213, 219)

Hispaniola [HIHS•puh•NYOH•luh] Island in the West Indies. 19°N 72°E (pp. R4, 662)

Hokkaido [hah•KY•doh] Second-largest island of Japan. 43°N 142°E (pp. R3, R5, 484, 485, 507)

Holy Roman Empire Lands in western and central Europe, empire founded by Charlemagne. 52°N 15°E (pp. 512, 522, 534, 538, 542, 544, 557, 630, 639)

Honshu [HAHN•shoo] Largest island of Japan, called the mainland. 36°N 138°E (pp. R3, R5, 484, 485, 507)

Huang He [HWAHNG HUH] Second-longest river in China, formerly called the Yellow River. 35°N 113°E (pp. 225, 226, 230, 241, 246, 409, 410, 424, 425, 439)

Hudson Bay Large inland sea in Canada. 60°N 85°W (pp. R2, R4, 565, 590, 662, 691)

Hungary Eastern European country south of Slovakia. 46°N 17°E (pp. R3, R16, 518, 538, 542, 548, 639, 688, 703)

India South Asian country south of China and Nepal. 23°N 77°E (pp. R3, R5, R22, 109, 193, 194, 195, 198, 210, 213, 219, 246, 380, 383, 409, 425, 433, 435, 554, 662, 658, 667)

Indian Ocean Third-largest ocean. 10°S 70°E (pp. R3, R5, 13, 109, 195, 198, 210, 213, 425, 433, 452, 463, 469, 479, 554, 565, 662)

Indonesia [IHN•duh•NEE•zhuh] Island republic in Southeast Asia consisting of most of the Malay Archipelago. 40°S 118°E (pp. R3, R5, R23, 381)

Indus [IHN•duhs] River River in Asia that begins in Tibet and flows through Pakistan to the Arabian Sea. 27°N 68°E (pp. R3, R5, 109, 176, 193, 195, 198, 210, 213, 219, 246, 380, 383, 409, 424, 425, 565)

Ionian [eye•OH•nee•uhn] Sea Arm of the Mediterranean Sea separating Greece and Albania from Italy and Sicily. 38°N 18°E (pp. 117, 144, 149, 193, 195, 198, 210, 213, 219, 246, 263)

Iraq Country in southwestern Asia at the northern tip of the Persian Gulf. 32°N 42°E (pp. R3, R5, R18–19, R22, 176, 263)

Iran Southwest Asian country on the eastern shore of the Persian Gulf, formerly called Persia. 31°N 53°E (pp. R3, 176, 198)

Ireland Island west of Great Britain occupied by the Republic of Ireland and Northern Ireland. 54°N 8°W (pp. R2, R4, R16, 518, 538, 645)

Israel Southwest Asian country south of Lebanon. 32°N 34°E (pp. R3, 1, 90, 105, 176)

Issus Ancient town of Asia Minor located north of the Syrian border. 37°N 36°E (p. 176)

Italy Southern European country south of Switzerland and east of France. 43°N 11°E (pp. R3, R5, R16, 121, 262, 263, 268, 269, 274, 277, 286, 292, 293,

297, 302, 317, 323, 327, 329, 337, 342, 351, 352, 358, 361, 367, 385, 516, 518, 522, 542, 609, 645, 653, 688)

Jamestown First permanent English settlement in North America, in southeast Virginia. 37°N 77°W (p. 691)

Japan Chain of islands in the northern Pacific Ocean. 36°N 133°E (pp. R3, R5, R23, 225, 409, 413, 425, 484, 485, 488, 491, 498, 507, 662)

Java Island of the Malay Archipelago in southern Indonesia. 8°S 111°E (pp. R3, R5, R23, 425, 554)

Jeddah City in western Saudi Arabia. 21°N 39°E (p. 433)

Jericho Oldest Neolithic community, in the West Bank between Israel and Jordan. 25°N 27°E (p. 8)

Jerusalem [juh•ROO•suh•luhm] Capital of Israel and a holy city for Christians, Jews, and Muslims. 31°N 35°E (pp. 17, 28, 80, 86, 89, 90, 92, 93, 105, 132, 329, 342, 343, 351, 352, 358, 361, 367, 374, 380, 383, 385, 397, 534, 542, 544)

Jordan River River flowing from Lebanon and Syria to the Dead Sea. 30°N 38°E (pp. 17, 90, 105, 176)

Judaea [ju•DEE•uh] Territory in southwest Asia and a region of historic Palestine. 31°N 35°E (pp. 342, 352, 361, 367)

Judah [JOO•duh] Southern kingdom of ancient Hebrews in Canaan, renamed Palestine. 25°N 49°E (pp. 90, 105)

K

Kaaba [KAH•buh] Sacred shrine in Makkah. 21°N 39°E (p. 374)

Kamakura [kah•MAH•kuh•RAH] City in Japan, former location of the Shogun military government. 35°N 139°E (pp. 485, 491, 495)

Karakorum [KAR•uh•KOHR•uhm] Capital of the Mongol Empire during most of the 1200s. 47°N 102°E (pp. 193, 195, 423, 424, 425)

Kathmandu [KAT•MAN•DOO] Capital of Nepal. 27°N 85°E (p. 210)

Khanbaliq [KAHN•buh•LEEK] Capital of Kublai Khan's Mongol Empire, now called Beijing. 40°N 116°E (pp. 423, 425, 428)

Khyber Pass Mountain pass in western Asia connecting Afghanistan and Pakistan. 34°N 71°E (p. 194)

Kiev [KEE•EHF] Capital of Ukraine, on the Dnieper River. 50°N 30°E (pp. R3, 425, 518, 534, 538, 544, 548, 555)

Kievan Rus State made of small territories around Kiev, destroyed by Mongols in 1240. 50°N 30°E (pp. 538, 542)

Knossos [NAH•suhs] Ancient city on Crete. 35°N 24°E (pp. 116, 117, 149)

Korea Peninsula in eastern Asia, divided into the Democratic People's Republic of Korea (North Korea) and the Republic of Korea. 38°N 127°E (pp. R3, R5, R23, 225, 409, 411, 413, 429, 484, 485, 491, 498)

Kunlun Shan Major mountain system in western China. 35°N 83°E (p. 225)

Kush [KUHSH] Ancient region in present-day Sudan, formerly called Nubia. 21°N 33°E (pp. 1, 70, 109, 198, 213, 219)

Kyoto [kee•OH•toh] Ancient capital of Japan, formerly called Heian. 35°N 135°E (pp. 485, 491, 498, 507)

Kyushu [kee•OO•shoo] One of the four major islands of Japan. 33°N 131°E (pp. R3, 484, 485, 503, 507)

Latium [LAY•shee•uhm] Region in west central Italy. 42°N 12°E (p. 263)

Lebanon [LEH•buh•nuhn] Southwest Asian country on the eastern coast of the Mediterranean Sea. 34°N 34°E (pp. R3, 176)

Leon Historic region and former kingdom in Spain. 41°N 5°W (pp. 538, 555)

Libya [LIH•bee•uh] North African country west of Egypt. 28°N 15°E (pp. R3, 176)

Lisbon [LIHZ•buhn] Capital of Portugal. 39°N 9°W (p. 555)

London Capital of the United Kingdom, on the Thames River in southeastern England. 52°N 0° (pp. R2, 518, 542, 553, 555, 557, 561, 633, 642, 670, 680, 703)

Luoyang [luh•WOH•YAHNG] City in northern China on the Huang He. 34°N 112°E (pp. 224, 230, 246, 248, 251, 409, 424, 439)

Macao [muh•KOW] Region on the southeastern coast of China. 22°N 24°E (pp. 430, 667)

Macedonia [MA•suh•DOH•nee•uh] Country in southeastern Europe on the Balkan Peninsula. 41°N 22°E (pp. 117, 174, 175, 176, 269, 274)

Machu Picchu [MAH•choo PEE•choo] Incan settlement in the Andes northwest of Cuzco, Peru. 13°S 72°W (p. 577)

Madagascar [MA•duh•GAS•kuhr] Island in the Indian Ocean off the southeastern coast of Africa. 18°S 43°E (pp. R5, 445, 479)

Madinah [mah•DEE•nuh] Holy Muslim city in western Saudi Arabia. 24°N 39°E (pp. 372, 380, 383, 385, 397)

Makkah [MAH•kuh] Holy city of Muslims, also known as Mecca, in western Saudi Arabia. 21°N 39°E (pp. 372, 374, 380, 383, 385, 397, 425, 433, 448, 452, 554)

Mali [MAH•lee] Republic in northwestern Africa. 15°N 0°W (p. 451)

Manchuria Historic region of northeastern China. 48°N 124°E (p. 436)

Marathon Village of ancient Greece northeast of Athens. (p. 134)

Marseille [mahr•SAY] City in southern France. 43°N 5°E (pp. 542, 555)

Massachusetts State in the northeastern United States. 42°N 72°W (p. 694)

Massalia [muh•SAH•lee•uh] Ancient Greek colony on the site of present-day Marseille. 44°N 3°E (p. 293)

Mediterranean Sea Inland sea of Europe, Asia, and Africa. 36°N 13°E (pp. R3, R5, 17, 28, 39, 62, 70, 75, 90, 105, 109, 117, 121, 132, 144, 149, 176, 179, 189, 263, 269, 274, 292, 293, 297, 323, 329, 337, 352, 361, 367, 374, 380, 383, 385, 397, 425, 445, 452, 463, 479, 513, 514, 518, 538, 542, 548, 555, 609, 639, 645, 653, 703)

Mekong [MAY•KAWNG] **River** River in southeastern Asia that begins in Tibet and empties into the South China Sea. 18°N 104°E (pp. 246, 409, 411, 424, 439, 667)

Memphis Ancient capital of Egypt. 29°N 31°E (pp. 38, 39, 47, 59, 62, 70, 75, 80)

Meroë [MEHR•oh•ee] Capital city of Kush. 7°N 93°E (pp. 68, 70, 452)

Mesa Verde National park in southwestern Colorado containing artifacts and cliff dwellings from the Anasazi. 37°N 108°W (p. 578)

Mesoamerica [MEH•zoh•uh•MEHR•ih•kuh] Ancient region including present-day Mexico and most of Central America. 10°N 92°W (pp. 17, 575)

Mesopotamia [MEH•suh•puh•TAY•mee•uh] Early center of civilization, in the area of modern Iraq and eastern Syria between the Tigris and Euphrates Rivers. 34°N 13°E (pp. 1, 17, 26, 28, 132, 380)

Mexico North American country south of the United States. 24°N 104°W (pp. R2, 575, 662)

Mexico City Capital of Mexico. 19°N 99°W (pp. R2, 658, 662, 663)

Milan City in northern Italy. 45°N 9°E (pp. 548, 555, 609, 639, 653, 688, 703)

Mississippi River Large river system in the United States that flows southward into the Gulf of Mexico. 32°N 92°W (pp. R2, R4, 590, 663)

Mogadishu [MAH•guh•DIH•shoo] Capital of Somalia. 2°N 45°E (pp. R3, 433, 452, 460, 479)

Mohenjo-Daro [moh•HEHN•joh DAHR•oh] Ancient settlement in the Indus Valley. 27°N 68°E (pp. 196, 198, 219)

Moluccas [muh•LUH•kuhz] Group of islands in Indonesia, formerly called the Spice Islands. 2°S 128°E (pp. R5, 662, 667)

Mombasa City and seaport of Kenya. 4°S 39°E (pp. 433, 452)

Mongolia [mahn•GOH•lee•uh] Country in Asia between Russia and China. 46°N 100°E (pp. R3, 225, 409, 425, 431, 439)

Morocco [muh•RAH•koh] North African country on the Mediterranean Sea and the Atlantic Ocean. 32°N 7°W (pp. R20, R21, 380, 449, 473, 479)

Moscow [MAHS•koh] Capital of Russia. 55°N 37°E (pp. R3, 234, 425, 540, 544)

Mount Everest Highest mountain in the world, located in the Himalaya between Nepal and Tibet. 28°N 86°E (pp. 193, 195)

Mount Fuji Highest mountain in Japan. 35°N 138°E (pp. 485, 507)

Mount Olympus [uh•LIHM•puhs] Highest mountain in Greece on the border between Thessaly and Macedonia. 41°N 23°E (pp. 117, 154)

Mount Sinai [SY•ny] Part of a rocky mass on the Sinai Peninsula of northeastern Egypt. 29°N 33°E (p. 90)

Mycenae [MY•SEE•nee] Ancient city in Greece. 37°N 22°E (pp. 116, 117, 149)

Nanjing [NAHN•JIHNG] City in eastern China, capital during the Ming dynasty. 32°N 118°E (pp. 430, 431, 433)

Napata [NA•puh•tuh] Ancient capital of Kush. 18°N 32°E (pp. 68, 70)

Naples City in southern Italy. 40°N 14°E (pp. 555, 609, 639, 653)

Nara The first permanent capital of Japan, near Osaka. 34°N 135°E (pp. 485, 491, 507)

Navarre [nuh•VAHR] Former kingdom in southern France and northern Spain. 42°N 1°W (pp. 538, 642)

Nazareth [NA•zuh•ruhth] Ancient town Galilee, now in northern Israel. 32°N 35°E (pp. 352, 361, 367)

Nepal [nuh•PAWL] Mountain country between India and China. 28°N 43°E (pp. R3, 198, 202, 205)

Netherlands [NEH•thuhr•luhnz] Country in northwestern Europe. 53°N 3°E (pp. R2–3, R4–5, R16, 639, 645, 662)

New Carthage City and seaport in southern Spain on the Mediterranean Sea also called Cartagena. 38°N 1°W (pp. 269, 274)

Nile River World's longest river flowing north from the heart of Africa to the Mediterranean Sea. 27°N 31°E (pp. R3, R5, R20, R21, 28, 38, 39, 47, 59, 62, 68, 70, 75, 109, 121, 132, 176, 179, 189, 246, 269, 269, 293, 297, 329, 374, 383, 385, 397, 425, 445, 452, 565)

Nineveh [NIH•nuh•vuh] Ancient capital of Assyria, on the Tigris River. 26°N 43°E (pp. 17, 26, 28, 132)

Ningxia [NIHNG•shee•AH] Region in northwestern China. 37°N 106°E (p. 424)

Normandy Region and former province of France, bordering the English Channel. 49°N 2°E (pp. 518, 538)

North America Continent in the northern part of the Western Hemisphere between the Atlantic and Pacific Oceans. 45°N 100°W (pp. R2, R4, R6–11, 13, 565, 573, 590, 658, 662, 663, 668, 691)

North Sea Arm of the Atlantic Ocean between Europe and the eastern coast of Great Britain. 56°N 3°E (pp. R16, 293, 513, 514, 518, 538, 542, 548, 555, 639, 645)

Norway Northern European country on the Scandinavian peninsula. 63°N 11°E (pp. R3, R16, 518, 538, 639, 645)

Novgorod [NAHV•guh•RAHD] City in western Russia. 58°N 31°E (p. 540)

Nubia [NOO•bee•uh] Region in present-day Sudan on the Nile River, later known as Kush. 21°N 33°E (p. 39)

Nuremburg City in south central Germany. 49°N 11°E (p. 555)

Oder River River in north central Europe, emptying into the Baltic Sea. 52°N 14°E (p. 513)

Olympia Site of the ancient Olympic Games in Greece. 38°N 22°E (pp. 125, 154)

Oman [oh•MAHN] Country on the Arabian Sea and the Gulf of Oman. 20°N 57°E (pp. R3, R5, R19, 198)

Onega City in Russia. 63°N 38°E (p. 540)

Ostia [AHS•tee•uh] Ancient city of Italy in Latium at the mouth of the Tiber River. 44°N 10°E (p. 293)

Orléans [AWR•lay•AHN] City in north central France. 47°N 1°E (pp. 553, 557, 561)

Osaka [oh•SAH•kuh] City and port in Japan. 34°N 135°E (pp. R3, 485, 507)

Ottoman Empire Turkish empire from the late 1200s in Asia Minor, spreading throughout the Middle East. 45°N 25°E (pp. 639, 645)

Pacific Ocean The largest and deepest of the world's four oceans, covering more than a third of the earth's surface. 0° 170°W (pp. R2–3, R4–5, R6–10, R12, R14, R15, 13, 225, 409, 425, 426, 433, 485)

Pakistan [PA•kih•STAN] Officially the Islamic Republic of Pakistan, a republic in South Asia, marking the area where South Asia converges with southwest Asia. 28°N 67°E (pp. R3, 176, 198)

Palestine A historic region, situated on the eastern coast of the Mediterranean Sea. 31°N 35°E (pp. 286, 293, 297, 302, 327, 329, 383, 397, 426, 534, 542, 555)

Papal States A territory in Italy formerly under direct temporal rule of the pope. 43°N 13°E (pp. 538, 639)

Paris Capital of France. 49°N 2°E (pp. 286, 297, 327, 397, 516, 518, 542, 555, 557, 633, 642)

Pataliputra [PAH•tuh•lih•POO•truh] Capital of Maurya. 24°N 86°E (pp. 209, 210, 246)

Peloponnesus [PEH•luh•puh•NEE•suhs] A peninsula in southern Greece. 37°N 22°E (pp. 117, 124, 125, 144)

Pergamum [PUHR•guh•muhm] An ancient city of northwest Asia Minor in Mysia, now Turkey. 39°N 28°E (pp. 179, 189)

Persepolis Ancient capital of Persian empire, now in ruins. 30°N 53°E (pp. 132, 176, 374)

Persia The conventional European designation of the country now known as Iran. 32°N 55°E (pp. 132, 144, 176, 246, 374, 380, 383, 385, 397, 425, 554)

Persian Gulf An arm of the Arabian Sea in southwestern Asia, between the Arabian Peninsula on the southwest and Iran on the northeast. 27°N 50°E (pp. R3, R5, R19, 17, 28, 132, 109, 176, 374, 380, 383, 385, 397, 435, 448, 452, 554, 565)

Philadelphia City in eastern Pennsylvania on the Delaware River. 40°N 75°W (pp. 690, 691, 694, 695)

Philippines [FIH•luh•PEENZ] Island country in the Pacific Ocean southeast of China. 14°N 125°E (pp. R3, R5, 662, 667)

Pinsk City in southern Belarus. 52°N 26°E (p. 548)

Pisa City in central Italy. 43°N 10°E (pp. 542, 609, 653)

Plataea [pluh•TEE•uh] Ancient city of Greece. 39°N 22°N (p. 134)

Plateau of Tibet [tuh•BEHT] World's highest plateau region, bordered by the Himalaya, Pamirs, and Karakoram mountain ranges. (p. 225)

Plymouth Town in eastern Massachusetts, first successful English colony in New England. 42°N 71°W (pp. 664, 663, 691)

Poland Country in central Europe. 52°N 17°E (pp. R3, R16–17, 538, 542, 639, 645, 688)

Po River River in northern Italy, the longest in the country. 45°N 11°E (pp. 263, 274, 513, 514, 653, 688)

Portugal A long narrow country on Atlantic Ocean, sharing the Iberian Peninsula with Spain. 38°N 8°W (pp. R2, 430, 435, 538, 639, 645, 662, 664)

Posen City in western Poland. 52°N 17°E (p. 548)

Prayagal City in central India, part of the Mauryan empire, 321 B.C. 26°N 81°E (p. 210)

Provence Region in southeastern France. 44°N 6°E (p. 548)

Prussia [PRUH•shuh] Former kingdom and state of Germany. (p. 538)

Pyrenees Mountain range in southwestern Europe, extending from the Bay of Biscay to the Mediterranean Sea. 43°N 0°E (pp. 269, 274, 513, 514, 516)

Puteoli [pyu•TEE•uh•LY] Port city on the Bay of Naples. 42°N 14°E (p. 293)

Q

Qin [CHIHN] Chinese state along Huang He and Chang Jiang. 33°N 112°E (p. 241)

Quanzhou [chuh•WAHN•JOH] City in southeastern China. 25°N 111°E (pp. 431, 433)

Quebec [kih•BEHK] Capital city of Quebec Province, Canada, on the St. Lawrence River. 47°N 71°W (pp. 658, 663, 691)

R

Red Sea Narrow, inland sea, separating the Arabian Peninsula, western Asia, from northeastern Africa. 23°N 37°E (pp. R3, R5, R18–19, R20, R21, 28, 70, 121, 132, 179, 246, 247, 293, 329, 352, 361, 367, 374, 383, 385, 397, 425, 433, 445, 448, 554, 565)

Reims [REEMZ] City in the Champagne region of northeastern France. 49°N 4°E (p. 557)

Rhine [RYN] **River** One of the principal rivers of Europe, rising in eastern Switzerland. 50°N 7°E (pp. 292, 293, 513, 514, 538, 542, 557, 688)

Rhodes Island in the Aegean Sea. 36°N 28°E (pp. 183, 269, 274)

Rhone River River of southeastern France. 44°N 4°E (pp. 557, 561)

Rio Grande [REE•oh GRAND] River that forms part of the boundary between the United States and Mexico. 30°N 103°W (pp. R2, R4, 590, 663)

Rocky Mountains Mountain system in western North America. 50°N 114°W (pp. R4, 590)

Rome Capital of Italy. 41°N 12°E (pp. R3, 262, 263, 268, 269, 274, 277, 286, 292, 293, 297, 302, 306, 317, 323, 327, 329, 337, 342, 351, 352, 353, 354, 355, 356, 358, 361, 367, 514, 516, 518, 522, 534, 542, 548, 555, 608, 609, 633, 642, 645, 653, 670, 703)

Rouen [roo•AHN] City in northern France, on the Seine River, near the English Channel, in Normandy. 49°N 1°E (p. 557)

Russia Independent republic in Eastern Europe and northern Asia, the world's largest country by area. 61°N 60°E (pp. R3, R17, 246, 485, 538, 645)

S

Sahara [suh•HAR•uh] Desert region in northern Africa that is the largest hot desert in the world. 23°N 1°W (pp. R5, R20, R21, 70, 374, 444, 448, 449, 479)

St. Augustine City in northeastern Florida on the Atlantic coast; oldest permanent existing European settlement in North America. 30°N 81°W (p. 663)

St. Petersburg Second-largest city and largest seaport in Russia, located in the northwestern part of the country. 59°N 30°E (p. R3)

Salamis [SA•luh•muhs] Island in eastern Greece in the Gulf of Saronikós. 37°N 23°E (p. 134)

Salonica City and port in northeastern Greece. 40°N 23°E (p. 548)

Samarkand Capital of Samarqand Oblast, central Uzbekistan. 39°N 67°E (pp. 424, 425, 554)

Samaria Ancient city and state in Palestine, located north of present-day Jerusalem east of the Mediterranean Sea. 32°N 35°E (pp. 86, 90, 105)

Santa Fe Capital of New Mexico located in the north central part of the state. 36°N 106°W (p. 663)

Sardinia Island off western Italy, in the Mediterranean Sea. 40°N 9°E (pp. R5, 263, 269, 274, 293, 329, 337, 514, 518, 522, 534, 538, 542, 555, 609, 653)

Sardis Ancient city of Asia Minor, now in Turkey. 38°N 28°E (pp. 132, 134)

Saudi Arabia [SOW•dee uh•RAY•bee•uh] Monarchy in southwestern Asia, occupying most of the Arabian Peninsula. 22°N 46°E (pp. R3, R5, R18–19, 176)

Savoy Former duchy lying between Italy and France. 43°N 21°E (p. 639)

Scandinavia Consists of Norway, Sweden, and Denmark in northern Europe. 62°N 14°E (pp. 512, 544)

Scotland One of the four countries that make up the United Kingdom, the mainland occupies the northern part of Great Britain. 57°N 5°W (pp. R16, 518, 538, 639, 645, 664)

Sea of Japan Arm of the Pacific Ocean lying between Japan and the Asian mainland; also called the East Sea. 40°N 132°E (pp. R3, R5, R23, 225, 485)

Seine [SAYN] **River** River in northern France. 48°N 4°E (pp. 513, 514, 516, 518, 557, 561)

Seleucia [suh•LOO•shee•uh] Kingdom extending eastward from Asia Minor

into what is now Pakistan. 36°N 36°E (pp. 179, 189)

Shikoku [shih•KOH•koo] One of the four largest islands of Japan. 33°N 133°E (pp. 484, 485, 507)

Siberia Large region consisting of the Asian portion of Russia as well as northern Kazakhstan. 57°N 97°E (pp. R5, R23, 425, 426)

Sicily [SIH•suh•lee] Largest island in the Mediterranean Sea off the coast of southern Italy. 37°N 13°E (pp. R5, 121, 262, 263, 269, 274, 293, 329, 337, 352, 361, 367, 538, 542, 553, 555, 609, 653)

Sidon City and seaport in southwestern Lebanon on the Mediterranean Sea. 33°N 35°E (pp. 17, 90, 105, 293)

Silk Road Large network of trade routes stretching from western China to southwest Asia. 34°N 109°E (p. 246)

Songhai [SAWNG•HY] Empire located along the Niger River. 13°N 5°E (p. 451)

South America Continent in the southern part of the Western Hemisphere lying between the Atlantic and Pacific Oceans. 15°S 60°W (pp. R2, R4, R14, R15, 13, 473, 565, 573, 577, 658, 662)

South China Sea Arm of the Pacific Ocean, located off the eastern and southeastern coasts of Asia. 15°N 114°E (pp. R3, R5, 109, 225, 241, 246, 409, 425, 433, 439, 554, 565, 667)

Spain Country in southwestern Europe. 40°N 4°W (pp. R2–3, R4–5, R16, 268, 269, 277, 286, 292, 293, 297, 302, 317, 323, 327, 329, 337, 352, 358, 361, 380, 385, 516, 518, 522, 534, 542, 544, 639, 645, 662, 664,)

Sparta City in ancient Greece and capital of Laconia. 37°N 28°E (pp. 117, 121, 124, 125, 134, 138, 144, 149)

Sri Lanka [sree•LAHNG•kuh] Country in the Indian Ocean south of India, formerly called Ceylon. 8°N 82°E (pp. R3, R5, R22, 198, 202, 433, 667)

Stockholm Capital city and seaport of Sweden. 59°N 18°E (p. 555)

Strait of Gibraltar Narrow passage connecting the Mediterranean Sea with the Atlantic Ocean. 35°N 5°W (pp. R2–3, R4–5, R16, 380, 385)

Strait of Magellan Channel between the Atlantic and Pacific Oceans on the southern tip of South America. 52°S 68°W (pp. R2, R4, R14, R15, 662)

Strait of Messina Passage separating mainland Italy from the island of Sicily. 38°N 15°E (p. 263)

Strasbourg City in eastern France. 48°N 7°E (p. 548)

Sumatra Island in western Indonesia. 2°N 99°E (pp. R3, R5, R23, 425, 433, 554, 667)

Susa Persian capital, in the region of southern Mesopotamia between the Tigris and Euphrates Rivers. 34°N 131°E (pp. 17, 132, 176)

Sweden Northern European country on the eastern side of the Scandinavian peninsula. 60°N 14°E (pp. R3, 518, 538, 688, 703)

Syracuse [SIHR•uh•KYOOS] The capital of Syracuse Province, on the southeastern coast of the island of Sicily. 37°N 15°E (pp. 182, 186)

Syria [SIHR•ee•uh] Southwestern Asian country on the east side of the Mediterranean Sea. 35°N 37°E (pp. R3, R18–19, 62, 176, 177, 269, 274, 286, 293, 329, 348, 352, 374, 380, 383, 385, 426, 542)

Syrian [SIHR•ee•uhn] **Desert** Desert of the northern Arabian Peninsula, including northern Saudi Arabia, northeastern Jordan, southeastern Syria, and western Iraq. 32°N 40°E (pp. R18–19, 17, 90, 105)

Taiwan [TY•WAHN] Island country off the southeast coast of China, the seat of the Chinese Nationalist government. 23°N 122°E (pp. R3, R5, R23, 225)

Taklimakan [TAH•kluh•muh•KAHN] **Desert** Desert in northwestern China. 40°N 83°E (p. 225)

Tarsus City in southern Turkey. 37°N 34°E (pp. 352, 361, 367)

Tenochtitlán [tay•NAWCH•teet•LAHN] Aztec city in the Valley of Mexico. 19°N 99°W (pp. 575, 582, 593, 658, 662, 663)

Teotihuacán [TAY•oh•TEE•wuh•KAHN] Site in central Mexico that in ancient times was one of the largest cities in the world. 19°N 98°W (pp. 572, 575)

Thar Desert Desert in northwestern India. 25°W 72°E (p. 219)

Thebes [THEEBZ] Ancient city and former capital of Egypt. 25°N 32°E (pp. 28, 39, 59, 62, 70, 75, 117, 132, 144, 479)

Thermopylae [thuhr•MAH•puh•lee] Mountain pass in ancient Greece. 38°N 22°E (p. 134)

Tian [tee•AHN] **Shan** Mountain range in central Asia. 45°N 85°E (p. 225)

Tiber [TY•buhr] **River** River in north Italy. 42°N 12°E (pp. 263, 269, 274)

Tibet [tuh•BEHT] Country in central Asia. 32°N 83°E (pp. 208, 246, 246, 409, 424, 425, 439, 554)

Tigris River River in southeastern Turkey and Iraq that merges with the Euphrates River. 34°N 44°E (pp. 17, 121, 132, 176, 179, 189, 246, 255, 293, 297, 329, 374, 380, 383, 397, 565)

Timbuktu [TIHM•BUHK•TOO] Trading city of Muslim learning in West Africa. 16°N 3°W (pp. 381, 444, 448, 451, 460, 468, 473, 479)

Tlaxcala [tlah•SKAH•luh] State in east central Mexico. 19°N 98°W (p. 575)

Tokyo Capital of modern Japan, formerly called Edo. 34°N 131°E (pp. R3, 485, 507)

Toledo Historic city in central Spain. 39°N 4°W (p. 555)

Tours City in west central France. 47°N 0°E (p. 516)

Trieste Seaport in northeastern Italy. 45°N 13°E (p. 548)

Tripoli [TRIH•puh•lee] Capital city of Libya. 32°N 13°E (pp. R3, 385, 448, 479)

Tunis Capital city of Tunisia. 36°N 10°E (p. 385)

Turkey Country in southeastern Europe and western Asia. 38°N 32°E (pp. R3, R22, 176, 384)

Turkmenistan [tuhrk•MEH•nuh•STAN] Central Asian country on the Caspian Sea. 40°N 56°E (pp. R3, R22, 176)

Tyre [TYR] Town in southern Lebanon on the Mediterranean Sea. 33°N 35°E (pp. 17, 90, 121, 132, 176, 352, 542)

Tyrrhenian [tuh•REE•nee•uhn] **Sea** Arm of the Mediterranean Sea between Italy and the islands of Corsica, Sardinia, and Sicily. 40°N 12°E (pp. 263, 609, 653)

Ukraine [yoo•KRAYN] Eastern European country west of Russia on the Black Sea. 49°N 30°E (pp. R3, R17, 548)

Ur Ancient city in Mesopotamia. 32°N 47°E (p. 17)

Ural Mountains Mountain chain running from northern Russia southward to the Kirgiz Steppe. 56°N 58°E (pp. R3, R5, 513)

Uruk Ancient settlement in Mesopotamia on the site of present-day Al Warka, Iraq. 33°N 45°E (p. 17)

Valencia City in eastern Spain. 39°N 0°W (p. 555)

Venice City and seaport in northeastern Italy. 45°N 12°E (pp. 522, 538, 542, 548, 555, 608, 609, 639, 653, 688, 703)

Vistula River Longest river in Poland. 52°N 20°E (p. 513)

Volga River River in western Russia, longest in Europe. 47°N 46°E (pp. R3, R5, 424, 425, 513, 540)

Wei He [WAY HUH] River in central China. 34°N 198°E (pp. 225, 226, 230, 241)

West Indies Islands in the Caribbean Sea between North America and South America. 19°N 79°W (p. 473)

Wittenberg [WIH•tuhn•BUHRG] City in east central Germany on the Elbe River. 51°N 12°E (pp. 633, 645)

Xianyang [SHYEHN•YAHNG] City in northern China. 34°N 108°E (p. 241)

Xi Jiang [SHEE•JYAHNG] River in southern China. 24°N 110°E (p. 241)

Yathrib [YA•thruhb] Town in Saudi Arabia, now called Madinah. 24°N 39°E (p. 374)

Yellow Sea Arm of the Pacific Ocean bordered by China, North Korea, and South Korea. 35°N 122°E (pp. R5, R23, 225, 226, 230, 241, 424, 431, 485)

Zama [ZAY•muh] Town in northern Africa southwest of Carthage in present-day northern Tunisia. 35°N 139°E (pp. 274, 276)

Zhou [JOH] Empire in what is now northern China. 34°N 110°E (p. 229)

Index

Italicized page numbers refer to illustrations. The following abbreviations are used in the index:
m = map, c = chart, p = photograph or picture, g = graph, crt = cartoon, ptg = painting, q = quote

A

Aachen, 516, *m516*

abacus, 236, *p236*

Abbasid Dynasty, 382, *m383;* empire, *m383, m397*

abbots, 520

Abraham, 81; leading Israelites to Canaan, *ptg81*

absolute monarchy, 681, 682

absolutism, 686–89

Abu al-Abbas, 382

Abu Bakr, 380, *c381*

Abu Talib, 376

Achilles, 177

Acoma, 591

acropolis, 122, 141, *p141*

Actium, battle of, 282, *p283*

actors, 160, *p160, ptg160,* 501

acupuncture, 246, *c247,* 671

Adams, John, 698, *p698*

Adams, Saumuel, 698

Adena, 580

adobe, 591

Adriatic Sea, 613

Aegean Sea, 120, *m134,* 328

Aeneas, 264

Aeneid (Virgil), 264, 304

Aeschylus, 161

Aesop, 153, *p153,* 154, 158, *p158*

Aesop's fables, 158

Africa, 13, 41, 68–72, *m109, m113,* 121, *m121,* 178, 274, 357, *p357,* 380, 384, 440–77, 594, 660, 661, *m662,* 669; central, 41, 72; culture, 469, 474–76; early civilizations of, 68–72; geography and climate of, *m445,* 445–46, 450; farming in, 13, *m13;* Kush, 70–72; Nubia, 69–70; Ottoman attack of, 384; Portuguese exploration of, 661; religions today, 463, *m463, p463;* rise of civilizations of, 444–53; slave trade and, 472–73, *m473,* 661, 669; society

in, 469–70, 472–73; United States compared to, *c446, m446. See also* Africa, medieval

Africa, medieval, 440–77; Arabic language introduction to, 467; art, 469, 474–75; Banta migrations, 469, *m469;* Christianity and, 452, 463; community in, 470; culture, 469, 474–76; education, 470; families of, 469–70, *p470;* Ghana, 448, 461–62; geography, 445–46, 447, 450; government, 461–62; life in, 469–70; Mali, 448–49, 462; music and dance, *c475, p475,* 475–76; Muslim influence, 467; rain forest kingdoms, 450–51; religion, 452, 463, *m463, c463;* 464–65, 467, 469; rise of civilizations of, 444–53; role of oral tradition, 449, 470, 474, 476; 463; role of women in, 469, 470, 471; slavery and, 472–73, *m473;* society, 469–70, 472–73; Songhai, 449, 462; spread of Islam to, 464–65, 467; trade and, 447, 448, *m448,* 451, *c451. See also* Africa; Axum; East Africa; Ghana, medieval; Mali, medieval; North Africa; Songhai; West Africa

Agamemnon, 120; gold mask of, *p119*

Age of Enlightenment, 681–89. *See also* Enlightenment

Age of Patriarchs, 76

"Age of Pericles," 138–47. *See also* Pericles

agora, 122, 123, *p139,* 143

Agra, India, 394

agricultural revolution, 13, *m13,* 574–75; in first American civilizations, 574–75; in Neolithic times, 13, *m13, c13*

agriculture: development of flood and irrigation systems, 18, 21, 41, 230, 417, 503, 577, 579, 591; development of

techniques in, 18, 41, 199, 230, 417, 526; early, 13, *m13;* food surpluses, 15, 43, 386, 450–51, 503, 577; inventions and, 21, 41, 230; Mesoamerican, 574–75; Neolithic, 13, *m13, c13. See also* farming

Ahmose, prince of Egypt, 61

Akbar, ruler of Mogul, 385, 386, *p386*

Akhenaton, king of Egypt, 64; religious reformer of Egypt, 64

Akihito, emperor of Japan, 487

Akkadians, 23

Alaric, Visigoth leader, 323

Alaska, 573, 590; people and cultures of, *m590*

al Bekri, 462, *q462*

Alcuin, 516

Alexander the Great, 95, 137, 150, 159, 172, 176–79, *p177, p180,* 180–81, *p181, p187,* 210, 252; conquests, 95, 177, 178; control over Judah, 95; empire of, *m176,* 176–78; Hellenistic Era, 178–79; invasion of western India, 210; king of Macedonia, 176; legacy of, 177–78; villain or hero, 180, 181

Alexandria, Egypt, 177, *p178, m178,* 179, 183, 305; modern, *p178*

Alfred, king of Wessex, 535

Algeria, 357

Algonquian, 592

algorithms, 216

Alhambra, 394, 646, *p646*

Ali, 381, *c381,* 382

al-Idrisi, 660

Alighieri, Dante, 620

Allah, 374, 380

alliances, 584, 597

alphabets, 85, 120, 326, 363; Cyrillic, 363, *c363;* Greek, 120, *c120;* Phoenician, 85, *c85,* 120; Roman, 326

Alps, 263, 514

al-Razi, 391, *q391*

Amaterasu, 487, *p487*

ambassadors, 615

Amenhotep IV, pharaoh of Egypt, 64

American Revolution, 690–700; Battle of Saratoga as turning point, 700; Battle of Yorktown, 700; colonial government, 696–97; Declaration of Independence, 700; factors leading up to, 694, 695, 696–97; first battle of, 699; issues of trade and taxation, 696–97; role of France in, 700; Second Continental Congress, 700; Treaty of Paris as end to, 700

Americas, 568–601, 650, 662; Catholic missionaries to, 650; Europeans in North America, *m691,* 691–94; fall of the Aztec and Inca Empires, 594–600; first, 572–81; first American civilizations, 574–81; life in the, 582–92; pathway to the, 573; Spanish arrival in, 594–97, 599–600. *See also* American Revolution; Aztec Empire; humans, early; Inca Empire; Maya; Mesoamerican civilizations; Native Americans; North American civilizations; Olmec Empire

Amida, 499

Amish, 637, *p637*

Amon-Re, 71

Amos, 91

Anabaptists, 637, *p637;* past and present, 637

Anasazi, *m578,* 578–80, 591; art, 579; cliff dwellings, 578–79, 580; farming, 579; trade, 579

anatomy, 305, 676

Andean civilizations: culture, 588; political structure, 588; social structure, 588; religion, 588

Andes, 578

Angles, 514, 535

Anglican Church, 649, 693

Anglo-Saxons, 514, 535, 536

animism, 490

annulment, 648

anthropologist, 9

Antigone **(Sophocles),** 161

Antioch, Syria, 541, 542

Antiochus, 96

anti–Semitism, 48

Antony, 282, 289

Anyang, China, 226, 247

Apache, 591

Apennines, 263

Aphrodite, 155, *p155*

Apollo, 155, *p155*

apostles, 348, 349, *p350*

Appolonius of Rhodes, 183

apprentices, 530

aqueducts, 291, *p291, p303,* 309

Aquinas, St. Thomas, 550, 551, *p551;* biography, 551; concept of "natural law," 550

Arabia, *m109,* 373–74, 380–81, 382–83, 384, *m385;* Bedouins, *p373,* 373–74; culture, 373–74; 380–81; daily life in, 373–74; early, 373–84; empires of, 380–81, 382; fall of Arab Empire, 383; geography of, 373; government, 375; opposition to Islam, 374–75; Ottoman attack of, 384; religion of, 374, 380–81; spread of Islam in, *m380,* 380–81; teachings of Islam, 377–78; trade, 373, 381; tribal organization of, 373. *See also* Islam; Muslims

Arabian Nights, The, 393

Arabian Sea, 195

Arabic language, 381, 388, 390–91, 467; acceptance of, 381, 390–91, 467; spread of, 388, 467; trade and, 388

archaeological dig, 9, *p9;* care and cleaning of artifacts, 9; preservation techniques, 9; use of grids, 9

archaeologists, 9, 10, 20, 486

archbishop of Canterbury, 648

Archimedes, 150, 185, *p185,* 186, *q186;* design of catapult, 186; scientific contributions of, *c185;* solid geometry and, 186

architecture: Aztec, 586, 587; Chaldean, 29; Doric, Ionic, Corinthian columns, *p162,* 163; Egyptian, 50–52, 60, 62, 65, 66; European, 549–50; Gothic styles of, 549; Greek, 154, 162–63, 183; Hellenistic Era of, 183; influences on modern, 326, 467; Japanese, 499–500; Kushite, 71; modern, 325, *p325;* Muslim, 384, *p384,* 386, 389, 393–94, 467; Ottoman, 384, *p384;* Parthenon, *p162, c162;* Renaissance, 619, *p619,* Roman, 303–04, 325, *p325,* 326; Romanesque styles of, 549. *See also* art

Arctic regions, 590

Ares, 155, *p155*

Argonautica **(Appolonius),** 183

Arian, *q181*

Aristarchus, 185; scientific contributions of, *c185*

aristocrats, 227, 229, 230, 233, 236, 242, 244–45, 247

Aristophanes, 161

Aristotle, 168, *p168,* 170, *p170,* 171, 172, *p172,* 550; biography, 172; "golden mean," 170, 171; ideas and influence of, *c109, c170,* 171, 550

Ark of the Covenant, 83, *p83*

Arsenal, 613

art and artisans: African, 474–75; Anasazi, 579, *p579;* Aztec, *ptg586,* 587 Chaldean, 30; Chinese, 229, *ptg421,* 421–22, *p422,* 432, *p432;* Egyptian, 60, *ptg60;* engravings, 625; Etruscan, 265, *p265, ptg265;* European, 549–50, *p550;* frescoes, 624; Greek, 143, 162–63, 183; guilds, 503; Harappan, 197;

Hellenistic Era of, 183; guilds, 503, 530; Incan, 588; Japanese, 499–501, 503; Kushite, 69, *ptg69;* Mayan, *p583;* Muslim, 389, 393–94; Mycenaean, 119; Neolithic, *c14,* 15; oil painting, 625; Paleolithic, 10, *ptg10,* 11, *c14;* Renaissance and, 609–10, 612, 613, 614, 619, 621, 622, *ptg622,* 623–24, 625–26; Roman, 303–04; sculpture, 60, 163, 183, 229, 624; Shang dynasty, 229; Song dynasty, 421, *ptg421;* Sumerian, 20; use of chiaroscuro, 623; use of perspective in, 623; woodcuts, 626

Artemis, 155, *p155*

artifacts, 9, *p9,* 486, 578–79; Anasazi, *p579;* Assyrian, *p28;* Athenian, *p125, p130, p142;* Aztec, *p585, p586, p596;* Benin, *p450;* Byzantine, *p359, p360;* Chinese, *p223, p227, p228, p229, p235, p238, p243, p249;* cleaning and preservation of, 9; Egyptian, *p43, p50, p53, p60, p61, p64, p65, p66;* Etruscan, *p265;* Greek, *p119, p123, p125, p139, p142, p157, p161;* Hopi, *p591;* hunter-gatherer, *p573;* Incan, *p588, p599;* Japanese, *p486, p489, p501;* Jomon, *p486;* Kushite, *p71, p72;* Mayan, *p584, p585;* medieval African, *p450, p470, p473;* Mesopotamian, *p18, p19, p20, p21, p24, p25;* Minoan, *p118;* Moche, *p577;* Mohenjo-Daro, *p196;* Mound Builder, *p580;* Neolothic Age, *p12, p14;* Noh, *p501;* Olmec, *p575;* Paleolithic Age, *ptg10;* Persian, *p132;* Qin dynasty, *p243;* Roman, *p267, p307, p309, p318, p334;* Shang dynasty, *p227, p228, p229;* Yayoi, *p486;* Zhou dynasty, *p223, p229, p249*

artisans, 20, 30, 43, 45, 51, 389, 451, 489–500. *See also* art and artisans

Aryabhata, 215

Aryans, 198–201; caste

system, 200–01; changes brought by, 199; development of Sanskrit, 199, *c199;* Hinduism and, 202, 203; invasion of India, 108, *c194,* 198–99; migration of, *m198;* nomadic life of, 198; religion of, 203; role of men and women, 201; society of, 199–201, *c200*

Ashikaga shogunate, 496, 497

Ashikaga Takauji, 496

Asia, 13, *m13,* 39, 60, 64, 65, 66, *m109,* 178, 276, 343, 411, 418, 554, 573, 594, 611–12, 650, 659, 666; Black Death in, *m554;* Catholic missionaires to, 650; central, 119, 231, 343, 383, 411, 418, 424; early farming in, 13, *m13;* European trade in, *m667;* French control of sea trade of, 666; northwest, 384; search for sea route to, 594; Southeast, 206, 211, 213; southwest, 39, 178, 179, 418, 426; trade and, 231, *m246,* 246–47, 388, 417–18, 435, 659, 666, *m667;* western, 60, 65, *m109,* 121, *m121, m193,* 205, 208. *See also* China; Mongol Empire; Silk Road

Asia Minor, *m117,* 120, *m121,* 132, *m132,* 133, 134, 137, 139, 146, 177, 349, 384, 541, 542

Askia, Muhammad, 465

Asoka, emperor of Mauryan empire, 211, 212, *p212,* 213; biography, 212; first Buddhist king, 211; political and moral achievements of, 211, 212; reign of, *c109,* 211

Aspalta, king of Kush, 71

Aspasia, 144

assembly, government, 129, 130, 139, *c140*

Assyria, 27–28. *See also* Assyrians

Assyrians, *c26,* 27–28, *m28,* 67, 71; Chaldeans and, 28; culture of, 28; empire of, 27, 28, *m28,* 90; fall of empire, 28; fall of Israel and, 91; government of,

Index

28; invasion of Egypt, 71; iron-making, 71; life in, 28; religion of, 28; Samaritans, 91–92; warriors, 27, p27, 28; weaponry of, 27

astrolabe, 391, p391, 659, p659

astronomers, 30, 51, 182, 185, 671, 672, 673–75. *See also* astronomy; science

astronomy, 21, 30, 51, 185, 216, 391, 585, c671, 671, 672, 673–75; astrolabe, 391, p391; building the pyramids and, 51; calendar, 21, 30, 51, 585; Copernican Armillary Sphere, p671; development of scientific instruments, 675; geocentric theory of, 671; helio-centric theory of the universe, 674; planetary movement, 674–75; Scientific Revolution and, 673–75; telescope, 675; used for planting and harvesting, 585; used for predicting eclipses, 585. *See also* science

Athena, 112, p129, p155, 155

Athens, p112, c124, m125, 125–26, 128–30, 139–47, p142; artifacts of, p125, p129, p142; culture of, 128–29, 140, 142–44; democracy and, 126, 129–30, 139–40, c140; economy, 143; education in, 120; fall of, 145–46; "Golden Age," 141; government of, 124, 126, 129–30, 139–40, c140; homes in, 142, p142; life in, 128–29, 142–44; Macedonian invasion of, 175; men of, 143; Peloponnesian War and, m144, 144–46; Persian Wars, m134, 134–37; "school of Greece," 140, 141; slavery in, 142; soldier's oath, 122; Sparta as compared to, 125–30; trade and, 143; tyranny in, 125–26; under rule of Pericles, 139–40, 141; women in, 143, p143, 144

Atahualpa, emperor of Inca, 599–600; defeat of by Pizarro, 600

Aton, 64

Augustine, Saint, 356, p357; biography, 357

Augustus, emperor of Rome, 282–83, q287, 287–88, 289, p289, q289, q297, 343; achievements of, 287–88; biography, 289; government of, 288; legal system and, 288

Augustulus, Romulus, emperor of Rome, 324

Austria, 687, 688, m688; growth of, m688; Hapsburg rulers of, 688

Axum, 72, c451, m451, c451, 452; economy, c451, 452; government, 452; location, c451; religion, c451, 452; rise of, 452; trade, c451, 452

Aztec Empire, 576–77, 585–87, 596–97; architecture of, ptg586, 587, p587; city of Tenochtitlán, 586, 587, p587; class structure, 587; culture, 585–87, p587; daily life, c586, p586, 587; defeat of by Spanish, 596–97, 598; disease and, 597; government, 585–86; oral tradition of, 586; religious beliefs and practices, 586, 587, 597; rise of empire, 585–86; role of men and women, 587; slavery, 587; social classes, 587; trade, 576–77; warfare, 587, 596; weapons, p585, p596

B

Babylon, 22, 23, 29–30, 94, 95, 101, 132, m132, m176, 177; building of city, 23; capture of, 30, 132; center of science, 30; city of, 23, 29–30; exile of Jews to, 94; Hanging Gardens of, 29, p29; Ishtar Gate as main entrance to, p30; life in, 29–30; trade, 30

Bach, Johann Sebastian, 686–87, p687

Bacon, Francis, 678–79; development of scientific method, 679

Baghdad, 382, 383, 388, 391, 426

Balboa, Vasco Nunez de, 599

Balkan Peninsula, m117

Baltic Sea, 539, 555

banking, 549, 612–13

Bantu, 469–70; culture, 469; families, 469–70; migrations, m469; oral history of, 470

barbarians, 435

barter, 319, 529

Basil, 363

bazaar, p388, 389

Bedouins, p373, 373–74

Beijing, China, 428

Belgium, 625; Northern Renaissance in, 625

Belize, 583

Belorussians, 539

Benedict, 363, q367

Benin empire, 450, 451; artists, 451; farming, 450; trade, 451

Benue River, 469

Berbers, 447, 448, 449

Beringia, 573, m573

Bering, Vitus, 573

Bernard of Clairvaux, 545

Bethlehem, 346

Bhagavad Gita, "Song of the Lord," 214

Bible: Christian, 344, 346, 349; first English translation of, 635; Gutenberg, 620, 621; Hebrew, 81, 82, 94, 95, 96, 99, 348, 350; moral teachings of, 377; New Testament, 356; Reformation and, 636, 637; stained glass as picture, 550; translation of into vernacular, 634; written copies of, 520. *See also* Hebrew Bible

Bill of Rights: English, 682, 700; United States, 700

bishops, 355, c355, 363, 641, 649

Black Death, m554, c554, ptg554, 554–55, m555, 609; impact on global population, 555; spread of, m554, 554–55, m555

Black Sea, 328, 659

Bodhidharma, 500, p500

bodhisattvas, 208

Bologna, Italy, 550

Book of Epodes, The (Horace), 304

Book of the Dead, 49, 50

Boston, Massachusetts, 697

Boston Massacre, 697, p696

Boston Tea Party, 697, ptg697

boyars, 539

Boyle, Robert, 676, c676

Brahma, 204

Brahman, 203–04

Brahmans, 200, p200

Brethren, 637

Britain, 291, 363–64, 514, 520, 700; invasion of, 363, 364, 514; spread of Christianity to, 363. *See also* England

Bronze Age, 15

Brutus, 281, p281

bubonic plague, 554–55. *See also* Black Death

Buddha, the, 205–06, p207, 207, p211, q219, p412, p431, p493

Buddhism, 205–06, 208, 248, 412–13, 489, 492–93, 499; Eightfold Path, 206, 208; "Enlightened One," 205; first Buddhist king, 211; Four Noble Truths of, 206; government and, 208; in China, 248, 412–13; in India, 205–06; in Japan, 413, 489, 492–93, 499; in Korea, 413; Mahayana, 208, 499; moral teachings of, 205–06; nirvana, 205, 208; Noh plays used to teach, 501; Pure Land, 499; reincarnation and, 206, 208; sects of, 499; in Southeast Asia, 206, 208; spread of, c109, 206, 208, 412–13; Theravada, 206; Zen, 499

building techniques, 19, 28, 29, 51, 52, 162, 196, 197, 303, 325, 326, 333. *See also* architecture

Buonarroti, Michelangelo, p618, 623, 624; *La Pieta,* p623; painting of the Sistine Chapel ceiling, 624

bureaucracy, 229, 687

Bushido, 494, 495, 496

Byzantine Church, 359–61; iconoclasts, 360; pope as

Index

head of, 360. *See also* Byzantine Empire

Byzantine Empire, 324, 327–34, 359–60, *m383,* 539, 541, 543, 611, 659; art and architecture of, 333, *p333;* culture of, 328, 334; Eastern Orthodox view of church-state relations, 359; economy, 333; education in, 334; government, 329–30; Hagia Sophia, *p332,* 333; icons, 359–60; importance of Constantinople, 328; influences of Greek culture on, 328–29, 334; Justinian, emperor of, 329–30; military, 330; mosaics, 333; Muslim attack of, 541; political structure, 328, 329–30; 334; rise of, 328; religion and government, 359, 360; Roman Catholic view of church-state relations, 359; rulers of, 329–30, 331; social structure, 328, 333–34; trade in, 332–33; women of, 333–34

Byzantium, Greece, 320

Cabot, John, 663–64

Caesar, Julius, 280–82, *p281, ptg284,* 284–85; assassination of, 281, *ptg284;* creation of Julian calendar, 281; dictator of Rome, 281, 285; military campaigns of, 280–81, *p281;* reformer, 281, 284; rise to power, 281

Caffa, Italy, 555

Cahokia, 581; mounds, *p581*

Cahuilla, 591

Cairo, Egypt, 52, 388, 392, 646

Calakmul, 585

calendar: Chaldean seven-day, 30; development of, 21, 30, 51, *p118, p147,* 281; Egyptian 365-day, 51; Julian 12-month, 365-day, leap year, 281; Mayan, 365-day, 585; Minoan, *p118, p147;* Muslim, 376; Sumerian 12-month, 21

California, *m590,* 591; natural resources of, 591; people and cultures of, *m590,* 591

Caligula, emperor of Rome, 288, *p288;* reign and accomplishments of, *c288*

caliphs, 380, *c381,* 382, 383; achievements of, *c381;* Rightly Guided, *c381*

calligraphy, 421, 501

Calvinism, 640–41, 644, 646, 649

Calvin, John, *q640, p640,* 640–41, *p641,* 644, 646; ideas of, 640–41, 646

camels, 447, *p447,* 465; trade and, 447, *p447*

Canaan, 81, 82, 84–85, 132; battle, 84; Promised Land, 84–85

Canaanites, 84

Canada, 590

Canterbury, England, 364, 520

Canterbury Tales, The **(Chaucer),** 620

Capet, king of France, 538

caravans, 30, 373, 388, 447, *p447,* 465

caravel, 660

Caribbean Sea, 594

Carpathian Mountains, 539

Carpathians, 514

Carter, Howard, 65

Carthage, state of, *m274,* 274–76, 357

Catherine the Great, queen of Russia, 689, *ptg689*

Cartier, Jacques, 664

cartography, 660; impact of printing press and, 660

Cassius, 281, *p281*

caste, 199

caste system, *c200,* 200–01; Buddhism and, 206; Hinduism and, 204; social levels of, *c200,* 200–01

catacombs, 353, *p353*

Çatal Hüyük, 14

cataracts, 39, 40

cathedrals, 549

Catherwood, Frederick, 583

Catholic Church. *See* Christian Church;
Christianity; Roman Catholic Church

cats, in ancient Egypt, 64

cause and effect, understanding, 482–83

Cayuga, 592

Celts, 514, 535

censors, government, 241

census, *c381,* 432, 492, 536; Domesday Book, 536; for military service, 492; for taxation, 492

Central America, climate and geography, 575, 577, 578; development of trade in, 575, 576, 577; development of urban societies in, 575–76. *See also* Aztec Empire

Chaco Canyon, New Mexico, 579; Anasazi settlement of 579

Chaeronea, battle of, 176

Chaldeans, 29–30; Babylon, 29–30; Babylonian captivity of the Jews and, 92; empire of, 29–30, 90; fall of, 30; first calendar, 30; rulers of Judah, 92; science and, 30

Champlain, Samuel de, 692

Changan, Tang, *p418*

Changan's Royal Palace, 418, *p418*

Chang Jiang (Yangtze River), 225, *m225,* 242, 410

Charlemagne, emperor of Rome (Charles the Great), 360, *ptg515,* 515–16, *p516,* 517, *p517;* biography, 517

Charles I, king of England, 681, 693

Charles V, Holy Roman emperor, 639

Chaucer, 620

chemistry, 391, 676; discovery of basic elements of substances, 676; discovery of hydrogen, carbon dioxide, oxygen, 676; founder of, 391

Cherokee, 592; law code of, 592

chiaroscuro, 623

China: art of, 229, *ptg421,* 421–22, *p422, p432, p436;* Buddhism in, 248, 412–13; changes in, 248; Christian missionaries to, *p435,* 435–36; cities, 412, *p412,* 418, *p418;* civil service examinations in, 244, 414–15, 432; civil war, 248; Confucianism, 235, *c109, c236,* 236–39, *c239,* 413–14; culture of, 226–29, 230–31, *c247,* 420–22, 432; Daoism, *c236,* 238, *c239;* development of flood control systems and irrigation systems, 230, *c247,* 417; discovery of coal and steel, 418–19; discovery of gunpowder, 420; discovery of the compass, 420, 659; dynasties, 226–29, 229–31, 241–43, 244–49, *m409, c409,* 409–12; early, 14, *c108, c109, m109, c220,* 220–48; economic structures of, 411, 417–19; European arrival in, 435–46; explorations of the world, 433–36; families of, 234–35; farming in, 227, 230, 233–34, 417, 432; first civilizations, 224–31; four Chinese dynasties, *c247;* geography, *m225,* 225–26; Han dynasty, *m214,* 244–46; Huang He valley, 225, 226, *m226;* important leaders of, *c247;* inventions of, 230–31, 245–46, 419–21, 659; language of, 228, *c247;* Legalism, *c236,* 238–39, *c239;* life in ancient China, 232–39, *p234, p235,* 248; literature of, 420–21; major changes in, 248; Mandate of Heaven, 230; middle ages, 404–37; military, 231, 234; Ming dynasty, 430–36; Mongol invasion and rule of, *m424,* 424–29; Neolithic Age villages, 14; numbering system, *c236;* outbreak and spread of Black Death in, 554–55; papermaking and, 245; philosophers and thinkers, 235–39, *c238;* political structures of, 227, 229–30, 234, 235, 238–39, 247, *c247,* 248; printing, 419–20; Qin

Index

dynasty, *m214*, 241–43; religion and, *c109*, 227–28, 230, *c247*; reunification of, 409–11; roles of men and women, 227, 234–35; scholar officials in, 414–15, *p415*; Shang dynasty, 226–29; Silk Road, *c109*, 246–47, *c247*, 417; society of, 233–34, 415, 416–22; Song dynasty, *c409*, *m411*, 411–12; Sui dynasty, *c409*, 409–11; Tang dynasty, *m409*, *c409*, 411, 412, 413; technological innovations, 418–20; trade, 231, *m246*, 246–47, 388, 417–18, 435; use of pest control, 235; villages of, *p233*, 233–34; writing, 228; Xia dynasty, 226; Zhou dynasty, 229–31. *See also* individual listings for dynasties

Chin dynasty. *See* Qin dynasty

chocolate, 595, *c595*; making, 595, *p595*

Christian Church, 351–56; *c351*, *m351*, *m352*, *c355*, 545–48; archbishops, 355, *c355*; bishops, 355, *c355*; Byzantine Church, 359–61; clergy, 355; diocese, 355, *c355*; early, 355–56; gospels, 355–56; hiearchy, 355; laity, 355, *c355*; medieval, 546–47; organization of, 355, *c355*; patriarchs of, 355, *c355*; persecution of Jews, 547; persecution of Muslims, 558; pope, 356; preservation of knowledge and, 520; priests, 355, *c355*; Reformation and, 634–37, 639, 640–41, 642–46, 648–50; role of monks and missionaries, 362, 363, 364, 435–36, 519–21, 539, 650; schism in, 361. *See also* Byzantine Church; Christianity; Eastern Orthodox Church; religion; Roman Catholic Church

Christianity, 81, 83, 91, 326, 338–65, 545–47, 635–37, 639–41, 643–46, 648–50; apostles and, 348, 349; Battle of Tours and, 515; beliefs of, 350, 550; Christian humanism, 634; first Christians, 348–50; growth and spread of, 348, *m352*, 361–64, 359, 519–21, 650; influence of Judaism on, 81, 83, 91, 95; Jesus of Nazareth and, 344–47, 350; legalization of, 354; martyrs, 353; missionaries, 362, *p362*, 363, 364, 435–36, 520–21, 539, 650; origins of, 326; persecution of Christians, 353; Reformation and, 648–50; religious orders in, 545–46; revolution in, 635–37, 639–41, 643–46; Rome's adoption of, 354, 519; salvation and, 350, 636. *See also* Byzantine Church; Christian Church; Eastern Orthodox Church; religion; Roman Catholic Church

Christmas, 346

Chumash, 591

Church of England, 648–49

Cicero, 282, *p282*, *q228*, 283; ideas as influence on U.S. Constitution, 283

Cincinnatus, Lucius, Quinctius, dictator of Rome, 271, 272, *p272*; biography, 272

Cistercian order, 545

cities: councils, 530; danger of fire in, 531; emergence and rise of, 18, 196, 581; government of, 197, 530; growth of, 528–29; life in, 530–31; medieval European, 528–30; planning of, 196–97, 575; pollution of, 531. *See also* city-states

citizens, 123, 140, 700; Bill of Rights and, 700; fair treatment of, 700; natural law and, 681–82; responsibilities of, 145, 326; rights of, 122–23, 129, 130, 140, 145, 681, 682; Roman ideas about, 326

citizenship, 122–23; comparing American and Athenian, *c140*; development of idea of, 122; Greek, 122; qualifying for, 122–23, 130; soldiers and, 123

City of God, The **(Augustine),** 356

city-states: government of, 20, 126, 127, 128, 129–30, 614–15, 616, 617; Greek, 122–23, 125–30, 134–37, 139, 144–46, 157, 175; East African, 452, 453; geography, 19, 122, 611, 613; Italian, *m609*, 611–13, 614–15, 616–17; Mayan, 583–84; Mesopotamian, 19–20; oligarchies versus democracies in, 126, 129–30; Persian Wars and, 134–37; Philip II and, 175; Sumerian, 19; trade and, 20, 452, 453, 611–14; value of, 616–17; wealth of, 611–12

civilization, 17

civilizations, first, *c4*, 4–16, 17; comparing Neolithic and Paleolithic Ages, *c14*; early human, *c8*, *m8*, 8–15; first empires, *c26*, *m26*, 26–30; hunter-gatherers, 10, *c14*, 573, 574, *p574*, 580; Mesopotamian, *c16*, *m16*, 16–23, *m17*; Neolithic people, 12, *m13*, 13–15, *c14*; Paleolithic people, 10–11, *c14*. *See also* humans, early Neolithic Age; Paleolithic Age

civil service exam, 244, 411, 414, 415; taking the, *ptg244*, *p414*

clans, 487, 493, 494; war between, 494–95

Claudius, emperor of Rome, 288, *p288*; reign and accomplishments of, *c288*

Cleisthenes, 130

Cleopatra VII, queen of Egypt, 282

clergy, 35, 546–47

Cloud Messenger, The **(Kalidasa),** 215

Clovis, king of Franks, 514–15

coal, 418–19; discovery of, 418–19; coal-mining industry, 419

code of chivalry, 526

Code of Hammurabi, 23, 24–25, *p25*; fair or cruel, 24–25. *See also* Hammurabi

Code of Justinian. *See* Justinian Code

colonies: English, 692–94; French, 692; Greece, ancient 121, *m121*, 179; mercantilism and, 666; Roman, 281; Spanish, 662, 691–92

Colorado, 578

Colosseum, 303–04, 305, *p305*

Columbian Exchange, *m668*, 668–69

Columbus, Christopher, *p594*, 594–95, 662

comedies, 160–61, 183, 304

commerce, 666

Common Sense **(Paine),** 699

comparing: American and Athenian and democracy, *c140*; jury system, past and present, *c536*; Neolithic and Paleolithic ages, *c14*

comparing and contrasting, 442–43

compass, 420, 659, *p659*

concordat, 521

confederations, 592

Confessions **(Augustine),** 356, 357

Confucianism, 235, 236, *q236*, 238, *c238*, 413–15, 488; neo-, 414–15

Confucius (Kongfuzi), 236, *q236*, 237, *p237*, *q237*, 238, *p238*, 413, 414; biography, 237; develops philosophy in China, *c109*

Congo River, 446

connections, making, 114–15

"Conquest and Aftermath" (Diaz), *q596*

conquistadors, 595, 664

Constantine, emperor of Rome, 320, 321, *p321*, 354, *ptg354*; biography, 321; Edict of Milan, 354; first Christian emperor, 321, 354

Constantinople, 320, *p328*, 384, 543; importance of, 328; location of, 328

constitutions, 488, 694, 700. *See also* United States Consitution

consuls, 269–70

context clues, using, 152–53

convents, 545

Copernicus, Nicolaus, 674, *c676*

Cortés, Hernán, 596–97, 598, *p598,* 664; biography, 598; defeat of the Aztec, 597; invasion of Cuba and Mexico, 596–97, 598

cottage industry, 667

Council of Trent, 643, *p643*

councils, 530, 614

Counter-Reformation, 643–46

counts, 516

courts, 516

court token, *p129*

covenant, 82

Coyas, 588

Crassus, 280, *p280*

Crete, 118, 119, 120, *m121,* 164, 165, 166

crier, 394

Croesus, king of Lydia, 156

crop rotation, 526

crucifixion, 347

Crusades, 541–43, *m542*; causes of, 541; course of, 541–43; creation of Christian states during, 542; First Crusade, 541; Fourth Crusade, 543; impact on feudalism, 543; impact on trade, 543; Second Crusade; 542; Seige of Jerusalem, *p541*; Third Crusade, 542–43

culture: African, medieval, 469, 474–76; Athenian, 128–29, 140, 142–44; Aztec, 585–87; Chinese, 226–29, 230–31, *c247,* 420–22, 432; Eastern Woodlands, *m590,* 592; Egyptian, 39–40, 41–42, 43–44, *c44,* 45, 46, 51, 60, 61; Europe, medieval, 526–28, 549–50, 552; Greek, ancient, 118, 119, 120, 154–63, 168–73, 182–87; Gupta, 213, 214–16; Inca, 588; Indian, 213, 214–16; Japan, medieval, 499–500, 503; Ming dynasty, 432; Minoan, 118, 119; Muslim, 388–90, *p389, p390*; Neolithic, *c14*; Paleolithic, *c14*; spread of, 178, 183–86; Shang dynasty, 227–28; Sparta, 126–27, *p127*; Sumerian, 19, 20–21; Tang dynasty, 420–21

cuneiform writing, 20, 21, *p25*; tablet, *p21*

Cuzco, 578, 588, 589

Cyrillic alphabet, 363, *c363*

Cyrus the Great, *p131,* 132–33

Cyrus, king of Persia, 94

da Gama, Vasco, 662

Dahia al-Kahina, queen of Africa, 470

daimyo, 496–97, 503

Dalai Lama, 208

Damascus, Syria, 348, 380, 382, *m383,* 388, 392

Daniel, 95, *p95*

Dante. *See* Alighieri, Dante

Danube River, 292, 513, 539

Dao (Tao), 230, 238, 249

Dao De Jing (Laozi), 238, *q251*

Daoism, *c238,* 238–39, 421

Darius, king of Persia, *p133,* 133–35, 137

Dark Age, of Greece, 120; recovery from, 121, 122

David, king of Israel, 87, *ptg87,* 88, *p88,* 89, 99, 343; anointing of with oil, *ptg87*; biography, 88; unification of tribes of Israel, 88; warrior, 88, 89

David (Michelangelo), 624

da Vinci, Leonardo, *p618,* 621, 622, *p622,* 623–24; artist, 621, 622, *ptg622,* 623–25; biography, 622; notebooks of, 621, *p621,* 622; scientist, 621, 622

Dead Sea Scrolls, 100, 101; restoration of, *p100*

Deborah, 84

Deccan Plateau, 195

Declaration of Independence, 698, *q698,* 699–700

deism, 685

deity, 49

Delhi, India, 385

Delian League, 139, 140

Delos, *c138,* 139

Delphi, 150, 156; oracle of Apollo, 156, *p156*; temple at, *p150*

delta, 39

Demeter, 155

democracy, 126, 129–30; American vs. Athenian, *c140*; Athenian, 128–30, 139–40, *c140,* 145; direct, 138, 139, *c140*; power of, 145; representative, 138, 139, *c140,* 537, 538

Demosthenes, 175, *p175, q175*

denomination, 636; creation of new 636

Descartes, Rene, 678

despots, 687

dharma, 204; as divine law, 204; in literature, 215

dhow, *p452,* 453

Diamond Sutra, 419

Diaspora, 95, 474

dictator, 271, 272

Diderot, 685

diocese, 355

Diocletian, emperor of Rome, 320, 354

diplomacy, 615; Italian city-states as basis for modern, 615

direct democracy, 138, 139, *c140*

Discourse on Method (Descartes), 678

Divine Comedy, The (Dante), 620

doctrine, 355

doge, 614

domesticate, 13

Dominican Republic, 594

Dominicans, 546, 550, 551

Dorians, 120, 126

drama, 160; actors in, 160, *p160, ptg161,* 501; Greek, 160–61; Japanese, 501; playwrights, 161, 626; tragedies and comedies, 160–61, 626

duke, 614

Duo Fu, 420–21, *q421*

Dürer, Albrecht, 625–26; *Four Horsemen of the Apocalypse, ptg626*

dynasty, 44, 226. *See also* individual listings

East Africa, 451–53; city-states of, 452–53; economy, *c451*; location, *c451*; religion, 452, 467; trade, *c451,* 453

Eastern Desert, 40

Eastern Orthodox Church, 359, 360, 363, 540; in Russia, 540; view of church-state relations, 359

Eastern Woodlands, *m590,* 592; geography and climate of, 592; governments of, 592; life in, 592; Northeast Woodlands, 592; people and cultures of, *m590*; Southeast Woodlands, 592

economics: barter, 319, 529; Columbian Exchange, *m668,* 668–69; commerce, 666; cottage industries, 667; entrepreneurs, 667; exports, 666; global exchange, 668–69; imports, 666; inequality in, 294; inflation, 319; investments, 667; joint-stock companies, 667; monetary exchange and, 121, 529; profits, 667; "putting out" system, 667; Roman economy, 292–93, 319, 320; single monetary system, 242, *c245*; specialization and, 15, 121; stocks, 667; supply and demand, 612; surpluses in early civilizations, 15, 43, 386, 450–51, 503, 577. *See also* trade

economy, 410

Edessa, 542

Edict of Milan, 354

Edict of Nantes, 645

edubba, 21, *p21*

education: ancient Mesopotamian, 21, *c21*; Byzantine, 334; comparing past and present, 21; Europe, medieval, 516, 550; first universities, 550; Greek, 128–29; Jewish, 97, 98; medieval European, 516, 550; Roman, 334; under

Charlemagne, 516, 517

Egypt, *m3,* 14, *p34,* 81, 82, 92, 95, 101, *m132,* 133, 177, 178, 179. *See also* Egypt, ancient

Egypt, ancient, *c34,* 34–74, *m39, ptg40, c44, m62;* art and architecture of, 43, *c44,* 46, 60; "the Black Land," 41; capture of Nubia, 60; cats in, 64; comparing Mesopotamia to, *c44;* culture of, 39–40, 41–42, 43–44, *c44,* 45, 46, 51, 60, 61; decline and fall of, 67; economic structures, 40, 41–42, 43, *c44;* empire of, *c59, m59,* 59–67; family life in, 46; farming, 41–42, *p42, p43,* 46; geography and location, *m39,* 39–40, 41; government in, 43; Israelites and, 81, 82; kingdoms and dynasties of, 43–44, *m62;* life in, 45–46; Lower Egypt, 43; medicine of, 50; Middle Kingdom, 44, 60–61; Neolithic Age villages, 14; New Kingdom, 44; Nile River valley, 38–46; Old Kingdom, 44, 47–52; political structures, 43–44, 48, 60, 63, 64–65, 66; pyramids, 50–52, *p51, c51, p52;* religion, 48, 49–50, 64, 67; rulers of, 43–44, 48, 60, 62, 63, 64–65, 66; science and, 41–42, 51; slavery in, 62; social structures, *c45,* 45–46; temples of, 63, 65, 66, 67; trade, 40, 43, 62, 63, 69; united kingdom of, 44; Upper Egypt, 43

Elements (Euclid), 185–86

Elijah, 91

Elizabeth, I, queen of England, 649, 664, 665, *p665;* biography, 665

ellipses, 674–75

El Salvador, 583

embalming, process of, 49–50, *p49*

empires, 89; first, 26–31. *See also* individual listings for

Encyclopedia (Diderot), 685

England, 535–37, 648–49, 660, 690–99; absolute monarchy, 681, 682;

American Revolution and, 690–99; development of legal and constitutional practices in, 536, *c536,* 537; English Bill of Rights, 682, 700; English Reformation, 648–49; "Glorious Revolution," 682; government of, 681–82; Henry VIII, 648, *p648;* Hundred Years' War, 557, *m557;* invasion of by Angles and Saxons, 514, 535; medieval, 535–37; Norman rule of, 535–36; Parliament, 537, 682, 697; rise of modern democratic thought, 537; search fo sea route to Asia, 660; taxation of American colonies, 697; trade restrictions on American colonies, 696–97; war with Spain, 664

English Bill of Rights, 682, 700

English Channel, 513

engravings, 625

Enlightenment, 680–89; absolutism, 681, 686–89; concept of natural law, 681–82; concept of natural rights, 682; criticism of ideas of, 685–86; divine right of kings, 681, 687–89; influence of on current times, 682, 700; music of, 686–87; philosophies of, 681–82, 683, 684–89; reason in, 681–83, 685–86; rise of democratic ideas, 682, 700; scientific experimentalism and, 671–79; spread of ideas of, 685; women and, 685

entrepreneurs, 667

ephors, 127

Epic of Gilgamesh, 20

epics, 20, 157, 159, 183, 215, 304, 552. *See also* literature

epicureanism, 184

Epicurus, 184

Equiano, Olaudah, 463, *q463*

Erasmus, Desiderius, 634, *p634;* Christian humanism and, 634

Eratosthenes, 185; scientific

contributions, *c185*

Essenes, 100

Estates-General, 538

Ethelbert, king of Kent, 364, 520

Ethiopia, 72, 451

Etruria, Italy, 265, *m265*

Etruscans, 264–66; art, 265, *ptg265;* culture, 265; shaping of Roman civilization, 264–65

Euclid, 185–86, *p186;* plane geometry and, 185–86; scientific contributions of, *c185*

Euphrates River, 18, 22, 23; Hammurabi and, 22

Euphrates River valley, 18. *See also* Mesopotamia

Euripides, 161

Europe, 14, 384, 389, 435–36, 472–73, 659–64; arrival of Europeans in China, 435–36; geography of, *m513,* 513–14, *m514;* Huns, 322, *m323;* invasions of, 320, 322–24, *m323;* Neolithic Age villages, 14; Renaissance, 608–17, 619–26; search for a sea route to Asia, 659-60; slave trade of, 472–73, *m473;* world exploration, 659–64, *m662. See also* Europe, medieval; Renaissance

Europe, medieval, 508–59; Angles, 514, 535; art and architecture, 549–50; Black Death and, 554–55; cities of, 530, 531; Crusades, 541–43; culture, 526–28, 549–50, 552; early Middle Ages, 512–21; education, 516, 550; farming, 525–26; feudalism, 522–33; geography, *m513,* 513–14, *m514;* Franks, 360, 514–19; Germanic kingdoms, 514–16, 518–19; government in, 520, 530, 532–33, 536, 537, 550; Hundred Years' War, 557; invasions of, 514–15, *m518,* 518–19; inventions of, 525–26; late Middle Ages, 553–59; life in, 526–28, 531; literature, 552; Magyars, 518, 519;

manorial system, 524–25; Muslim and, 515, 519, 541–43, 646, 666; people of, *m513,* 513–16, 518–21; political systems of, 520, 530, 532–33, 536, 537, 550; religion and, 519–21, 528, 545–48; Saxons, 513, 514; Spanish Inquisition, 558; trade and, 528–29, 554–55; Vikings, 518–19, 535, 539; Visigoths, 322–24, 514; women of, 526

Evans, Arthur, 118

Ewuare, king of Benin, 450

excommunication, 361, 521, 636, 648; of Henry VIII, 648; of Martin Luther, 636

exile, 94

Exodus, 82

exploration, age of, 654–69; explorers, 661–64; innovations in technology, 659–60; maps, 660; rise of strong nations, 660; trade with Asia, 659. *See also* Americas

exports, 666

extended families, 469

Extremadura, 596, 598, 599

Ezana, king of Axum, 452

Ezekiel, 91

Ezra, 94

fable, 158

families: African, 469; Chinese, 234–35; Egyptian, 46; extended, 469; Greek, 129, 143; of matrilineal villages, 469; paterfamilias, 307, 308; Roman, 307

farming: Aryans and, 199; Chinese, 227, 230, 233–34, 244–45, 417, 432; crop rotations, 526; crops, 13, *m13,* 574–75, 577, 579; early, 13, *m13,* 15, 574–75; early North American, 591, 592; Egyptian, 41, 42, *p42;* food from, 42–43; harvesting, plowing, planting, 42–43, *p42, p43,* 591; Greek, 119, 120, 125,

129, 143; Harappan, 197; in early India, 196; medieval European, 525–26; Muslim, 389; Nile River valley, 41; rise of cities and, 581; Roman, 293; surpluses in, 15, 43; techniques in, 18, 234–35, 579, tenant, 244–45; terrace, *p234*, 234–35; Zhou dynasty, 230. *See also* agriculture

Ferdinand, king of Spain, 558, 646

Fertile Crescent, 18

feudalism, 522–33, *c523*; cities of feudal Europe, 528–31; Japanese, 497; knights and vassals, 523–24; life of nobles, *p526*, 526–27, *p527*; life of peasants, 527–28; manorial system, 524–25; political system, 523–24; trade, 528–29

fief, 524

filial piety, 234, 249

fire, 10–11, 531; danger of in medieval cities, 531; discovery of, 10–11

First Continental Congress, 698

First Triumvirate, 280

Five Pillars of Islam, 378, *c378*

Flanders, 529, 625; devlopment of oil painting technique in, 625

floods, 41, *c44*

Florence Cathedral, 610, *p610*

Florence, Italy, 610, 612–13; banking and trade in, 612–13; city–state of, 610; importance of in Renaissance, 610; wealth of, 612–13

Forbidden City, 432; Imperial Palace at, *p404*

Forum, the, 306

fossils, 9

Four Noble Truths, 206

France, 121, 538, 557, 644–45, 660, 684–85, 687, 700; center of the Enlightenment, 684–85; Estates-General, 538; exploration and, 660; Huguenots, 644; Louis XIV, 687; Middle Ages, 538; philosophers of,

684–85; religious wars in, 644–45; role in American Revolution, 700

Franciscans, 546

Francis of Assisi, 546, *p546*, *q546*

Franklin, Benjamin, 698, *p698*

Franks, 360, 514–16, *m516*, 518–19; Frankish kingdoms, *m516*; Holy Roman Empire and, 519; rulers of, 514–17, 518, 519

Frederick I, emperor of Holy Roman Empire, 519

Frederick II, emperor of Holy Roman Empire, 519, 542–43

Frederick the Great, king of Prussia, 687, *p688*

fresco, 624; painting of during Renaissance, 624

friars, 546

Fu Hao, 227

Fujiwara clan, 493–94, 502

Galen, 305, 676; study of anatomy, 305, 676

Galilee, 344, 346

Galileo, 674, 675, *ptg675*, *c676*; scientific contributions of, 674, 675, *c676*; telescope, 674, *p674*, 675

Ganesha, 204, *p204*

Ganges River, 195, 199

Gaul, Caesar's battles in, 280, *p280*

Gempei War, 494–95

Geneva, Switzerland, 640, 641

Genoa, Italy, 555

Gentiles, 349

Geography (Ptolemy), 660

geography: Africa, *m445*, 445–46; Arabia, 373; China, *m225*, 225–26; Greece, ancient, 117; Egypt, ancient, *m117*; *m39*, 39–40, 41; Europe, medieval, *m513*, 513–14, *m514*; India, *m109*, 133, 191, 193, 194, *m195*, 195–96, 199; influence on settlement patterns and, 39–40, 117, 196, 445–46,

448; Japan, medieval, 485, *m485*; Mali, *c451*; Mayan location and, 575, 583; Native American settlements, 590, 591, 592; Nile River valley, 39–40; Rome, *m263*, 263–64

geometry, 21, 42, 182, 185–86; plane, 185–86; solid, 186; used by Egyptians to survey land, 42

George III, king of Englad, *p696*, 697

Georgia, 592

Germanic kingdoms, *m514*, 514–16, *m516*, 518–19

Germany, 519, 639; Lutheranism and, 639

Ghana, medieval, 448, *c451*, 461–62; economy, 448, *c451*; government, 461–62; growth of empire in, 448; location, *c451*; religion, 463, 464–65; 467; ruler and subjects, 461, *p461*; trade, *c451*, 461, 462

Gilgamesh, 20–21

Giza, Egypt, 42, 52

glaciers, 573

gladiators, 306–07, 309, 319

gladius, 266, *p266*

Globe Theater, 625, *p625*, *c625*

Glory of Kings, 451

Gobi, *m109*, 429

God, 350, 374, 377, 463, 640, 685, 686; Allah as one true, 374; belief in one, 374, 377, 463; deism, 685; in three persons, 350; monotheism, 81, 83; will of as absolute, 640, 686

gods and goddesses: Aztec, 586, 587; Greek, 155, *c155*, *p155*, 156, *c310*; Hindu, 203, *c204*, 213; Inca, 588; Mayan, 584; Roman, 309, *c310*; Sumerian, 19

gold: mercantilism and, 666; trade, *c451*, 447, 449

gold mines, 448, *m448*, 449

Good Samaritan, parable of, 345; preaching, *p345*

gospel, 355–56

government: absolute monarchy, 681; abuse of power in, 270; advantages and

disadvantages of city-state, 616–17; ambassadors, 615; Aristotle and, 171; Articles of Confederation, 700; Bill of Rights and, 700; balance of power in, 682, 700; centralized, 210, 241, 488, 588; city–state, 20, 126, 127, 128, 129–30, 614–15, 616, 617; colonial, 696; comparing, *c140*, 171; confederations, 592, 700; constitution as plan of, 488; councils, 530, 614; democracies, 139, *c140*, 171; dictatorship, 271, 272, 281, 285, 614; diplomacy, 615; duke, doge as head of state in, 614; English Bill of Rights and, 700; House of Burgesses, 694; influences on, 171, 537, 550, 700; Iroquois League, 592; legislatures, 696; limited, 700; Magna Carta and, 700; mayors in, 515; military, 495; monarchies, 171; Montesquieu and, 700; national government, 700; Native American, 592; natural law and, 681–82; natural rights and, 682; oligarchies, 171; Parliament, 537; popular sovereignty, 700; power in, 700; ranks of importance in, 492; reforms, 411, 488, 492, 681–83; 688–89; regents, 493; religion and, 48, 208, 212, 228, 230, 354, 355, 360, 376, 492–93; representative, 283, 537, 538, 694; republics, 614, 700; Roman, 269–73; veto, 270; self-, 694; separation of powers, 682, 700; shogunates, 495; social contracts in, 682; well-organized, 28; women in, 235, 334, 470, 471, 504, 585. *See also* politics

Gracchus, Gaius, 279, *p279*

Granada, Spain, 394, 646

Grand Canal, 410, *p410*

Grand Council, 592

grand jury, 537

Granicus, battle of, 177

gravity, theory of, 675–76, *c676*, 677

Great Britain. *See* Britain, England

Great Charter, 537

Great Council, 537

Great Mosque in Makkah, *p368*

Great Peace, 592

Great Pyramid, 52

Great Rift Valley, 446

Great Serpent Mound, 580, *p580*

Great Sphinx, *p34, 48, p48*

Great Temple, 587, *p587*

Great Wall of China, 220, *p220,* 242; first, 220

Greece, ancient: *m109,* 112–47, *p123, m125, m132,* 150–87; "Age of Pericles," 138–47; Alexander the Great, 174–81; alphabet, 120, *c120;* amphitheater, ruins of, 160, *p160;* art and architecture, 162–63; capture of Troy, 157–58, 264; Christianity and, 356; citizenship in, 122–23, 124, 139; city-states, 113, 116, 122–23, 124, 125–26, 128, 129, 135, 136, 139, 144, 146, 157, 175; civilization, 113, 116–23, 150–89, 232–39; colonies of, 121, *m121;* culture of, 118, 119, 120, 154–63, 168–73, 182–87; Dark Age, *c112, c116,* 120; democracy in, 126, 129–30, 139–40; drama, 160–61, 183; early Greeks, 113, 116–23; economy of, 121; first kingdoms, *p119,* 119–20; geography of, 117, *m117;* gods and goddesses, 155, *c155, p155,* 156; governments of, 119, 125, 126, 127–28; Jews and, 95–96; literature of, 155–58, 160–61, 164–67, 183; Macedonian attack of, 175–76; medicine, 184; military, *p122,* 123, *p144,* 266; Minoans, 118; Mycenaeans, *p119,* 119–20; mythology, 155–56; oligarchy, 126, 129, 147; Olympics, 128, *p128;* oracle, 156; Peloponnesian War, 112; Persian War and, 134–37; philosophy and history, 168–73, 187; Polis, 122–23;

power structure of, 125; religion, 155, *c155, p155,* 156, 184; representative democracy and, 139, *c140;* science and math, 185–86, *c185;* slavery and, 121, 125, 126, 129, 142; soldier's oath, *q122;* Sparta and Athens, 113, 124–30; trade, 118, 121, *m121,* 125; tyranny in city-states, 112, 125–26; Xerxes' invasion of, 112

Greece, classical. *See* Greece, ancient

Gregory the Great, 364, *p519,* 520

Gregory VII, Pope, 520–21

griots, 449, 450, 470, 476, *p476*

Guangzhou, 242

Guatemala, 583

guilds, 503, 530, 550

gunpowder, 420, 426, 429; invention of, 420; Mongol use of, 426; trade in, 429

Gupta empire, *m213,* 213–14; cities of, 213; culture, 213, 214–16; discoveries and inventions of, 215–16; economy, 213; founding of, 213; religion of, 213; tourism in, 213; trade, 213

guru, 201

Gutenberg, Johannes, *p618,* 620–21; development of printing press, 620–21; Gutenberg Bible, 620, 621

Hades, 155, *p155*

Hadrian, emperor of Rome, 291–92, *p292*

Hagakure: The Book of the Samurai **(Tsunetomo),** 495, *q495*

Hagia Sophia, *p332, 333*

Haiti, 594

Halcyon bird, 166

Hammurabi, king of Babylon, *p22,* 22–23, 24–25; biography, 22; code of (laws), 23, 24–25; control of Euphrates and, 22

Handel, 686–87

Han dynasty, *c109,* 244–45; artifact, *p109;* civil service exam, 244, *ptg244;* diffusion of Buddhism during, 248; empire of, 244–45; government, 244; inventions, *p245,* 245–46; papermaking, *p245,* 245; Silk Road, *m246,* 246–47; trade, *m246,* 246–47

Hanfeizi, 238, *p238,* 239; Legalism and, 238, 239

Hanging Gardens of Babylon, 29, *p29;* as one of Seven Wonders of the Ancient World, 29

Hannibal, general of Rome, 275–76

Hanukkah, 96, *c96*

Han Wudi, emperor of China, 244–45

Han Yu, 413, *p413, q413*

Hapi, 49

Harappa, 196–97; collapse of, 198; planned city, 196–97; priest-king of, *p196;* society, 197; trade, 197

Harvey, William, 676, *c676*

Hatshepsut, queen of Egypt, 62, 63, *p63;* biography, 63; expansion of trade and, 62, 63

Haydn, Franz Joseph, 687

head coverings: past and present, 97, *c97*

Hebrew Bible, 81, 82, 94, 95, 96, 99, 348, 350; Christian study of, 348, 350; influence of, 95, 96; Torah as first part of, 82

Hebrews, ancient, 76–77, 80–85, 86–92, 93–102; early, 81–83; movements of, 81, 82, 84, 90, 92; religion, 81, 82–83, 87, 94–95; social structure of, 97–98. *See also* Israelites, ancient

Heian, Japan, 493, 495

Helena, 354

Hellenistic Era, 178–79, 183–86; spread of culture and, 178, 183–86. *See also* Greece, ancient

Hellenistic kingdoms, 178–79, *m179. See also* Hellenistic Era

helots, 126, 127, 147

Henry IV, king of France (Henry of Navarre), 644–45

Henry VIII, 648, *p648,* 664

Henry, Patrick, 698

Henry, prince of Portugal (Henry the Navigator) 661

Hera, 155, *p155*

heresy, 547, 643, 646, 675

heretics, 547; questioning of, *ptg547*

Hermes, 155, *p155*

Herod, king of Judaea, 100

Herodotus, *q75,* 135, *p135, q135, p168,* 173; "father of history," 173

Hestia, 155, *p155*

hierarchy, 355

hieroglyphics, 42, 61, *p61, c61,* 70, 585; comparing computer icons to, 61, *c61;* Mayan, 585; Nubian, 70

hijab, 390, *p390*

Hildegard of Bingen, 545

Himalaya, 195, 196

Hinduism, 203–04, 213; Aryans and, 203; Brahman, 203–04; caste system and, 204; dharma, 204; early, 203; gods and goddesses, 203, *c204,* 213; Gupta empire and, 213; Hindu temple, *p203;* karma, 203–04; reincarnation, 204; Upanishads, 203

Hindu Kush, India, *m109*

Hindus, 385

Hipparchus, 185; scientific contributions of, *c185*

Hippocrates, 184, 185; scientific contributions of, *c185*

Hippocratic Oath, 184

Hippodrome, 320

Hispaniola, 594

historians, 28, 173, 304, 326, 666; Greek, 173; Muslim, 393; Roman, 304

History of Rome **(Livy),** 272, 304

History of the Jewish War **(Josephus),** 343

History of the Peloponnesian War **(Thucydides),** 173, 189

History of the Persian Wars (Herodotus), 135

Hittites, 27, 64, 66

Hobbes, Thomas, 681

Hohokam, 579

Hokkaido, 485, *m485*

Holy Roman Empire, 519, 639, *m639*; Thirty Years' War, 645–46

Homer, 154, 157, 158, 159, *p159, q159*, 177, 304; biography, 159

Honduras, 583

Honshu, 485, *m485*

Hooke, Robert, 676, *c676*

Hopewell, 580

hoplites, 123, *p123*

Horace, 304, *q304*, 326

Horyuji temple, 488, *p489*

Hosea, 91

House of Burgesses, 694

House of Commons, 537

House of Lords, 537

House of Wisdom, 391

Huang He (Yellow River), 225

Huang He valley, 225. *See also* China

Huguenots, 644; religous wars of France, 644–45

Huitzilopochtli, 587

humanism, 619–21, 634; beliefs of, 619; Christian, 634; Petrarch as father of, 619–20; printing press as key to spread of ideas of, 620–21; societal impact, 621; study of ancient works, 619

humans, early, *c8*, 8–15, 573, *p574*, 574–75; adaptations to the environment, 10, *c14*, 573, 574–75, 580; archaeology and, 9–10, 578–79; artifacts, 9, *p10, p11, p14, p573, p575*; art of, *ptg10*, 10, 11, 14, *c14*; comparing, *c14*; development of spoken language, 11; domestication of plants and animals, 580; farming revolution, 13, *c14*, 574–75; food surpluses, 15; hunter-gatherers, 10, *c14*, 573, 574, *p574*, 580; Ice Ages and, 10–11, 573, 574; invention of tools, 11;

migration of, 573, *m573*; Neolithic people, 12, 13–15, *c14*; Paleolithic people, 10–11, *c14*; religion, 14; roles of men and women, 10, *c14*; specialization, 15; technological advances, 15; trade, 15. *See also* Neolithic Age; Özti; Paleolithic Age

Hundred Years' War, 557

Huns, 322, *m323*

hunter-gatherers, 10, *c14*, 573, 574, *p574*, 580; adaptations for the environment, 10, *c14*, 573, 574–75, 580; migration of, 573, *m573*. *See also* humans, early

Hyksos, 60–61

"Hymn to the Nile," 41

Hypatia, 185; scientific contributions of, *c185*

hypothesis, 679

Iberian Peninsula, 558

Ibn Battuta, 464–65

Ibn Khaldun, 382, *q382*, 392, *p392*; biography, 392

Ibn Sina, 391

Icarus and Daedalus, 164–67

Ice Ages, 10–11, 573, 574

icons, 359–60

ideographs, 228

Idylls, 183

Igbo, 463

igloos, 590

Illiad (Homer), 152, 157–58, 159, 177

Immortals, 133

Imperial City, China, 432

imports, 666

Inca Empire, 578, 588–89, 599–600; artistic, engineering, mathematical achievements of, 588, 589; culture, 588; defeat of, 599–600; government, 588; life in, 588; oral traditions, 588; record keeping in, 599; religion, 588; social structure, 588; spread of smallpox in, 599; unification through

roads and language, 588; warfare, 599–600

incense, 62

India, 14, *m109*, 133, 177, 190–217, 373, 380, 385, *m386*, 388, 392, 412, 418; Aryans and, 198–201, 202, 203; astronomy, 216; British control of, 386; Buddhism, 202, 205–08; caste system, 199–201, *c200*, 206; creation of Muslim empire in, 385–86; culture, 196, 197, 214–15; early, 190–217; economy, 196; first civilizations of, 196–201, first empires, 209–17; geography, *m109*, 133, 191, 193, 194, *m195*, 195–96, 199; government, 191, 197; Gupta empire, *m213*, 213–14; Hinduism, 203–204; Indus River valley, 196–97; influence of Moguls on, 386; intellectual tradition of, 214–15; invasion of by Alexander the Great, 177; language, 199; life in, 199–201; literature, math, science in, 214–16; marriage in, 201; Mauryan dynasty of, 210–12; Mohenjo-Daro, 196–97, *p197*; nations of modern Indian subcontinent, 195; Neolithic villages of, 14; political system, 197; religions of, 202–05; river systems, 195, 199; role of men and women, 201; social system of, 197, *c200*, 199–201; trade, 211, 373, 386, 388; Varnas, *c200*, 200–01; vedas of, 214; western, 133

Indian Ocean, 195, 388

Indonesia, 381

Indra, 204

indulgences, 634–35, 636; box, *p635*; pardons for sins, 634–35, 636; selling of, 634–35, 636

Indus River, 177, 195, 196, 198; settlements of, 108

Indus River valley, 195. *See also* India

inferences, making, 406–07

inflation, 319

Innocent III, Pope, 543

Inquisition, 547, 558

inspiration, 152

Inti, 588

Intolerable Acts, 697–98

Inuit, 590

inventions: compass, 420, 659, *p659*; Leonardo's, 621; gunpowder, 420; heavy wheeled plow, 525; horse collar, 525; iron drill bits, 245; iron plow, 230, *p235*; movable type, 419, 621; paper, 245, 621; plow, 21; printing press, 620–621; printing process, 419–20; saddle and stirrup, 231; sailboat, 21, 453; shadoof, 41; steel, 419; waterwheels, 245; wagon wheel, 21; water mills, 526. *See also* math; science

invest, 667

Iran, 382, 383

Iraq, 382

Ireland, 363, 364, 519

iron, 71; iron weapons, 27; ironworking, 419, 448

Iroquois, 592

Iroquois League, 592; law code of of, 592

irrigation, 18, 21, 22, 29, 41, 230, 234, 247, 389, 417, 503, 577, 579, 591. *See also* agriculture; farming

Isabella, queen of Spain, 558, 594, *p594*, 646

Isaiah, 91

Ishtar Gate, *p30*

Isis, 49

Islam: acceptance of and impact on medieval Africa, 448, 464–65, 467; arts and literature, 389, 391, 392, 393–94; beliefs, 378, *c378*, 467; civilization of, 368–95; economic structures, *c331*, 386; empires of, 379–86; Five Pillars of Islam, 378, *c378*; Hijrah, 376; India and, 385–86; law code and rules of, 378; meaning of, 374; medicine, 391; Muhammad, prophet of, 374–77; opposition to, 375; preservation of ancient texts, 391; Quran as holy book of, 377–78; Rightly Guided Caliphs,

Index

380, c381; rise of, 372–78; science and mathematics, 391; Shiites, 382; social structures, 389–90; spread of, m380, 380–81, 448, 464–65, 467; state of, 374; struggles within, 382–83; Sufis, 381; Sunnis, 382; teachings of in connection with Judaism and Christianity, 81, 83, 91, 95; Umayyad caliphs, 380; women and, 390. *See also* Muslims

Israel, 14, 81, 90, 91, 92, 102, 343; creation of Jewish nation of, 102; education in ancient, 97, 98; fall of, 91, 92; kingdom of, 90; prophets of, 91, c91, 344; twelve tribes of, 81. *See also* Israelites, ancient; Jews; Judaism; Judah; Judaea

Israelites, ancient, 76–77, 80–85, 86–92, 93–102, m105; Assyrians and, 91–92; Canaan, as Promised Land, 84; Chaldeans and, 92; early, 81–83; education of, 97, 98; fall of Israel and Judah, 90–92; fighting judges, 84; first Israelites, 80–85; growth of Judaism, 93–102; King David, 88, 89; kingdom of Israel, kingdoms, m105; King Saul, 87, 89; King Solomon, 89–90; religion of, 81–85; temple of, 89, 91, 92, 100; Ten Commandments as "rule of law," 83; twelve tribes of, 81, 84, 87, 91. *See also* Hebrews, ancient; Israel; Jews; Judah; Judaism

Istanbul, 320, 384

Italy, 121, m121, 263, m263, 519; city-states of, m609, 611–13, 614–15, 616–17; geography of, 263, m263, 611; Ostrogoths in, 514; Renaissance in, 609–17, 619–24. *See also* Florence, Italy; Renaissance; Venice, Italy

Ivan I, 540

Ivan III, czar of Russia, 540

Ivan IV, czar of Russia, 540

Jacob, 81; family tribes of, 81

James I, king of England, 649, 692, 693

Jamestown, Virginia, 692, *ptg692*

Japan, 413, 480–504; art and architecture, 499–501, 503; Buddhism in, 413, 488, 489, 492–93, 499; Christianity in, 650; culture, 499–500, 503; daimyo, 496–97; drama, 501; early, 484–90; economy, 503; feudalism in, 497; first settlers, 486–87; geography, 485, m485; government of, 488, 492–94, 495, 496, 497; Jomon, 486; Kamakura, 495; life in, 498–504; literature, 501; medieval, 480–504; myth of creation of, 487; religion in, 489, 490, 492–93, 499; religons of, 488, 489, 490, 492–93, 650; rise of military society in, 494–97; role of women, 501, 504; samurai, 494–95; Shinto, 490; shoguns, 494–97, 650; social structures, 495, 503, 504; trade, 503; Yamato, 487–88; Yayoi, 486–87; wars, 494–95, 497

Jefferson, Thomas, 698, *p698*, 699

Jeremiah, 91

Jericho, 14, 84, *p84*; battle for, *p84*

Jerome, Saint, 322, *p322*, *q322*, 362

Jerusalem, 89, 90, 92, 94, 101, 132, m132, 343, 347, 547; rebuilding of, 94; temple in, 100, 101

Jesuits (Society of Jesus), 643, 644, 650; Ignatius of Loyola as founder of, 644

Jesus of Nazareth, *p344*, 344–47, *p345*, *p346*, *q346*, *ptg347*; 348; biography, 346; crucifixion of, 347; disciples of, 344; life of, 344–45, 347; resurrection as foundation for Christianity, 347, 350; teachings of, 344–45, 346, 348; use of parables,

p344, 345, *p345*

Jews, 90, 91, 92, 94–102, 343, 547–58, 558; anti-Semitism, 548; clothing, 98; Diaspora, 96; diet of, 98; education and, 97, 98; Essenes, 100, 101; exile and return of to Judah, 94; expulsion of, 548, m548; family, importance of, 97–98; fortress at Masada, *p343*; Greeks and, 95–96; holidays celebrated by, c96; Jesus' teachings about religious laws of, 344–45; Maccabees and, 96; messianic prophecies, 344; Muslim rule of, 646; Nebuchadnezzar and, 92; persecution of, 81, 82, 96, 101, 646; Pharisees, 100; rebellions of, 92, 343; Romans and, 100–01, 343; Sabbath as day of worship and rest, 94; Sadducees, 100; Spanish Inquisition and, 558; spread of ideas and values, 81, 96; way of life, 97, c97, 98

Jimmu, emperor of Japan, 487

Joan of Arc, 556, *p556*, *q556*, 557; biography, 556

John, king of England, 537

joint-stock company, 667

Jomon, 486

Jordan, 14, 81

Joseph II, king of Austria, 688, *p688*

Josephus, 105, *q105*, 343

Joshua, 84; battle for Jericho, 84, *ptg84*

journeyman, 530

Judaea, 100, 343, 344, 347; Judah becomes, 343; rule of King Herod, 100

Judah, 90, 92, 94, 96, 98, 100, 343; education in, 98; fall of, 92; founding of, 90; return of Jews to, 94; Roman conquer and rule of, 100, 343

Judaism: as first monotheistic religion, 81; beliefs, 82, 83, 95; destruction of Temple, 101; ethical teachings, 82, 83, 95; God as moral lawgiver, 82; growth of, 93–102; Hanukkah, 96;

Hebrew Bible, study in, 81, 82, 83, 95; justice in, 95; major Jewish holidays, c96; observance of law in, 82, 83; origins of, 81, 94;

jury system, 536, c536, 537; grand jury, 537; linking past and present, c536; trial jury, 537

Justinian Code, 330

Justinian, emperor of Byzantine Empire, 329–30; conquests of, 330; law code, 330

Kaaba, 374, *p377*; pilgrimages to, 377, *p377*

Kalidasa, 215

Kamakura, Japan, 495

kami, 490

kamikaze, 495

Kammu, emperor of Japan, 493

Karakorum, Mongolia, 428

karma, 203–04

Kashta, king of Kush, 71

Kente clothe, 474, *p474*

Kepler, Johannes, 674–75, c676

Kerma, kingdom of, 69

Khadija, 375

Khanbaliq, China, 428

Khan, Genghis, *p424*, 424–27, *p427*, *q427*; Mongol Empire under, m424, 424–27, m425

Khan, Kublai, ruler of Mongol, *p428*, 428–29, 495

Khufu, king of Egypt, 52

Kievan Rus, 539–40

Kitab al-lbar (Khaldun), 392

knights, 524, 526; code of chivalry, 526

Knossos, palace at, 118

kofun, 487

Kongo, kingdom of, 450–51

Korea, 409–10, 411, 413, 429; China and, 409–10; Mongol control of, 429; spread of Buddhism to, 413

Korean Peninsula, 409

Index

kosher foods, 98

Krishna, 204, 214

Krishna and Maidens, ptg214

Kshatriyas, 200, *c200*

Kush, civilization of, 67, *c68, m68,* 68–72, *m70;* art of, 69; capitals of, 70, 71; economy of, 69, 70; Egyptian influence on 70, 71; geography, 68, 69, 70; importance of iron to, 71; kingdom of Kerma, 69; military, 71; Nubia, 69–70; rise of, 70–71; rule of Egypt, 67; rulers of, 71, 72; slavery, 72; trade in, 69, 70, 71, 72

Kyoto, Japan, 480, 493, 497, 503

Kyushu, 485, *m485*

laity, 355, *c355*

Lakshmi, 204

lamas, 208

language: Arabic, 381, 388, 390–91, 467; Bantu, 469; development of, 120, 199, *c199,* 229; evolution of written forms of, 85, 120, 228; Hebrew, 81; Latin, 292, 304, 326, 328, 352, 552; Quechua, 588; Sanskrit, *c199,* 214; Swahili, 469; vernacular, 552, 620, 634

Laozi, *p238,* 238, *q239;* Daoism and, *c238,* 238–39

latfundia, 278

La Salle, 692

Last Supper, 347, *ptg347*

Last Supper, The **(Leonardo),** 624–25;

Latin, 292, 304, 326, 328, 352, 552; as basis for modern European languages, 304, 326; manuscripts, 619, *p619,* 620

Latins, 264, 266

Latium, Italy, 263, 265

Lavoisier, Antoine and Marie, 676, *c676*

law: belief in moral, 81, 378; Code of Hammurabi, 23, 24–25; common, 537; courts of, 537; from God in Torah, 82; ideas about, 681–82, 683; influence of

Justinian Code, 330; juries and, 536, *c536,* 537; Legalism and, *c238,* 239; natural, 550, 681–82; Qin dynasty, 243; Quran, 378; rights of citizens and, 273; Roman influence on, 325–26; Roman system of, 273, 325–26; "rule of," 273; standards of justice, 273; U.S. system of as compared to Roman, 273; veto of, 696; written, 273

Lebanon, 81, 542

legacy, 178, 187

Legalism, *c238,* 239, 241

legionaries, Roman, 266, *p266, p267;* armor, shield, spear, 266, *p266*

legions, 266

Leo III, emperor of Byzantine, 360

Leonidas, king of Sparta, 135–36

Leviathan **(Hobbes),** 681

Li Bo, 420, *p420, q420*

Libyans, 67; conquerors of ancient Egypt, 67

limited government, 700

Li Po. *See* Li Bo

literature: changes in during Renaissance, 620; Chinese, 420–21; Egyptian, 60; epics, 20, 157, 159, 183, 215; European, 552; fables, 158; Greek, 155–56, 157–58, 160–61, 164–67, 183; Hellenistic Era, 183; Indian, 214–15; Japanese, 501; influence of Greek and Roman writings on later thought, 619, 621; moral and religious references of, 158, 214, 215, 619; Muslim, 393; mythology, 155–56; odes, 304; oral tradition of, 158, 159, 214, 449, 470, 474, 476; plays, 304, 626; poetry, 157–58, 214, 304, 420–21, 626; Renaissance, 620, 626; Roman, 304; satires, 304; Tang dynasty, 420-21; written in the vernacular, 620

Liu Bang, emperor of Han, 244, *c247, p247*

Livia, empress of Rome, 308

Livy, 304, 326; historian of Rome, 304

Locke, John, 681–82, 683, *p683, q683,* 700; biography, 683

London, tower of, 648

lords, 523–26, 532–33

lord-vassal system, 523–26, 532–33

Louis XIV, king of France, 687, *q687*

Loyola, Ignatius of, 644, *p644, q644;* founder of Jesuits, 644

Luoyang, 248

Lutheranism, 636–37, 639, 640; creation of, 636–37; Germans and, 639; politics and, 639

Luther, Martin, 634–37, *p636,* 638, *p638, q653;* biography, 638; creation of Lutheranism, 636; Ninety-Five Theses as beginning of Reformation, 636

Luxembourg, Germany, 625

Maccabees, 96

Maccabeus, Judas, 96

Macedonia, *m117,* 146, 174, 175, 178–79; attack on Greece, 175–76; empire breaks apart, 178–79; geography and culture, 175

Machiavelli, Niccolò, 614, *p614, q614,* 615

Machu Picchu, 588, 589, *p589*

Madinah, 376, *m383*

Magna Carta, 537, *q537, 682,* 700 ; historical importance of, 537, 682, 700

Magyars, 518, 519

Mahabharata, 214–15

Mahayana Buddhism, 208, 499

Maimonides, 646, *p646*

main idea, understanding, 78–79, 340–41; and supporting details, 370–71

Makeda, queen of Sheba, 451-52

Makkah, 373, 374, 375,

m383, m385, 389, 465, 555; Black Death in, 555; pilgrimage to, *p375,* 465

Mali, medieval, 448–49, *c451;* economic structures, 449, *c451,* 462; government and political structure of, 462; location, *c451;* Mansa Musa, 462, 465, 466; religion, 65; 467; trade and 449, *c451,* 462

Malintzin, 597; translator for Cortes, 597

Mamun, 390

mandate, 230

Mandate of Heaven, 230

manorialism. *See* manorial system

manorial system, 526–27

manors, 526–27, *p527*

Mansa Musa, 449, 462, 465, *p465,* 466, *p466;* biography, 466; rule of, 462, 465, 466; strenthening of Islam, 465

manuracturing, 530; quality standards in, 530

Marathon, 134–35; battle of, *c108,* 134–35, *m134*

Martel, Charles, 515, 523; ideas as basis for feudalism, 523

martial arts, 499, 500, *p500, c500;* linking past and present, 500, *c500*

martyr, 353

Mary I, queen of England, 649, *p649*

Mary Magdalene, 347

Mary, Saint (mother of Jesus), 546

Masada, Israel, 343; ruins at, *p343*

math: algebra, 391; algorithms, 216; Chinese numbering system, 236; counting based on 10, *c44,* 51; fractions, *c44,* 51; geometry, 21, 42, 182, 185–86; Greek, *c185,* 185–86; Gupta, 215; Indian, 215–16; Indian-Arabic numerical system, 215–16, 391; method of number caluclations, 588; number system based on 50, *c44;* Mayan, 585; number system based on 10, *c44,* 51; number system based on 20, 585; number system based on 60, 21, *c44;* quipu, 588, *p599;* Sumerian number system, 21; 360-degree circle, 21

matrilineal, 469

Matthew, Saint, 355, *p355*

Maurya, Chandragupta, 210; centralized government of, 210; founder of India's first empire, 210

Mauryan dynasty, *m210,* 210–11; fall of, 211; first empire of India, *m210,* 210–11; religion and, 211, 212; rulers of, 210, 211; trade and, 211

Maya, 583–85, 596; art and architecture, *p583,* 584; culture, 584–85; development of mathematical system, 585; development of 365-day calendar, 585; development of written language, 585; geographic location of, 575, 583; government, 583–84, 585; political system of, 584–85; religious beliefs and practices, 584; role of women, 585; social structure, 584; sports, 584, *p584;* study of astronomy, 585; trade, 575–76, 584; warfare, 584

Mayflower, 693

Mayflower Compact, 693, 694, *q693*

mayors, 515

measles, 597, 669

Medici family, 613, 614

Medici, Catherine, de', 644, 647, *p647*

Medici, Lorenzo de', 614

medicine: acupuncture, 246, 671; study of anatomy, blood circulation, 391, 676; bone-setting, 216; Chinese, 245; discovery of cells, 676; Egyptian, 50; Greek, 184; Gupta, 216; herbal treatments in, 50, 216, 245, 671; Hippocratic oath, 184; medical drawings, 391, *p391;* identification of disease, 391; invention

of tools for, 216; medical books, *c44,* 50; Muslim, 391; plastic surgery, 216, 671; specialization in, 50; surgery, 216; spread of disease, 391; study of anatomy, 305, 676

meditation, 499, *p499*

Mediterranean region, 263, *m263,* 287, 291, 348; spread of Christianity to, 348

Mediterranean Sea, 40, 81, 95, *m117,* 118, *m132,* 213, 246, 373, 384, 388, 611

Memphis, Egypt, 44, 60

Menander, 183

Mennonites, 637

mercantilism, 666, 692, 696

mercenaries, 611

Meroë, Kush, 71, 72

messiah, 101, 344, 347, 348; Jewish prophecy and, 344

Mesa Verde National Park, 578–79

Mesoamerican civilizations, 574–76, *m575,* 583–87; achievements of, 585; agricultural systems, 575; art and architecture, 583, *ptg583,* 587; development of calendar, 585; develpment of written language, 585; economic structures, 575; geographic structures, 575–76, 583; government and political structures, 583–84, 585–86; knowledge of seasonal changes, 585; oral tradition, 586; religious beliefs, 584, 585, 586, 587; slavery and, 587; social structures, 584–85, 587

Mesopotamia, *m3,* 16–23, 27, 30, 81, 132, *m132,* 197, 291, 384; artisans of, *c44;* Assyrians, 27–28; Babylon, 23; Chaldeans, 29; city-states, 19, *p19,* 23; comparing to Egypt, *c44;* "cradle of civilization," 20; cuneiform writing, 20, *c44;* development of writing, 20; early civilizations of, 16–25, *m17;* economic structure of, *c44;* economy of, *c44;* education in, 21, *c21;*

geography, 17, *m17,* 18, 20; government of, 19, 20; Hammurabi, 22, 23, 24–25; inventions of, 21; laws of, 23, 24–25; life in, 20; literature, 20; Ottomans conquer, 384; political structure of, 19–20; religion, 19; rulers, 19–20, 22, 23, 24, 25; Sargon, 23; scientific and mathematic advances, 21, *c44;* society in, 20; Sumerians, 18–21; students today in, 21, *p21;* writing, 20

metalworking, 486

Mexico, 13, *m13,* 14, 574, 575, *m575,* 583, 596–97; climate and geography of, 574, 575, 583; farming in, 13, *c13, m13,*575 ; Mayan ancestors, 583–85; Neolithic villages of, 14; trade, 575, 576. *See also* Aztec Empire; Maya

Micah, 91

Michelangelo. *See* Buonarroti, Michelangelo

microscope, 676, 678, *p678*

Middle Ages: China in, 404–37; early, 512–21; Europe, medieval, 508–59; Japan, medieval, 480–504; late, 553–58. *See also* Europe, medieval; Japan, medieval

Middle East, 14, *c381,* 389

Middle Kingdom, Egypt's, 60–61; arts and literature, 60; culture of, 60; Hyksos, 60–61

"A Midsummer Night's Dream, " 627–32

migrations: to America, 573, *m573;* Bantu, 469, *m469*

military: Greek, 122–23, 126–27, 134–37, *p144;* Japan, 494–97; Kushite, 71; Mongol, 424, 425–26, *p426,* 427, 429, 540; Mycenaean, 120; Persian, 133, 134–37; Roman, 266–67, 279, 280–81, 287–88; Shang dynasty, 227; Sparta, military, 115, *p115,* 126–27, *p127*

Minamoto clan, 494–95

Minamoto Yoritomo, 495

minaret, 394, *p394*

Ming dynasty, *c430, m431,* 430–36; beginnings and rise of, 431–32; culture, 432; fall of, 436; maritime expeditions, 433, 434, 435; reforms of China, 432; shipbuilding technology, 433, 435; trade and, 434, 435

Minoans, 113, 118, *ptg118,* 119; calendar, *p118, p147;* civilization, *c108;* collapse of civilization, 118; control of eastern Mediterranean, *c116,* 118; culture, 118, 119; trade, 116, 118, 119

Minos, king of Crete, 165

missionaries, 362, *p362,* 363, 364, 435–36, 520–21, 539, 650; past and present, 362, *c362*

Mississippi, 592

Mississippians, 580–81; architecture of, 581; farming, 581; rise of cities in, 581

Mississippi River, 592

Moche, 577–78; agricultural techniques, 577; art, 577, *p577,* 578; engineering, 577; geography, 577; trade, 577

Moguls, 385–86; economy of, 386; Muslim empire of, 385–86; trade, 386

Mohawk, 592; government of, 592

Mohenjo-Dara, 196; artifacts and ruins, *p196*

Moluccas, 666

Mona Lisa (Leonardo), *ptg622,* 624,

monasteries, 357, 362, *p362,* 413, 519, 520; Mont St. Michel, *p520*

monastic religious orders, 363

money: as form of exchange, 121; coins, 121, 388, 529; common currency, 293–94; distrust of, 320; euro based on Roman, 294, *p294;* single monetary system, 242, *c245*

Mongol Empire, 383, *m424,* 424, *m425,* 425–26, 428–29, 495, 540; Black Death and, 554;

conquests of, 425–26; invasion of Kievan Rus, 539–40; maritime expedition, 429; nomadic life of, 424; religion of, 426, 428; rule in China, 428–29; rulers of, 425–27, 428–29; trade and, 426, 429, 611–12; use of terror, 426; warriors of, 424, 425–26, *p426*, 427, 429, 540. *See also* Khan, Genghis; Khan, Kublai

Mongolia, 424. *See also* Mongol Empire

monks, 362, *p362*, 366, 520

Monks Mound, 581

monopoly, 576

monotheism, 81

monsoons, 195–96

Montesquieu, 682, *p682*, *q682*, 700; concept of separation of powers, 682

Montezuma II (Moctezuma), 596–97, 598, *p598*; biography, 598; Cortés defeat of, 597

Moore, Sir Thomas, 648

mortal, 164

mosaics, 333, *p333*

Moscow, Russia, 540, *m540*, 689; growth of, 540

Moses, 82, 83, *p83*; parting of the Red Sea, *ptg82*

Mosque of the Prophet, 376; tomb of Muhammad, 376, *p376*

mosques, *p384*, 389, 393, *p393*

Mound Builders, 580–81; domesticaion of plants, 580; trade, 580

Mount Olympus, 155, 156

Mount Sinai, 82, 83, *p83*

Mount Vesuvius, 290, *p290*; eruption of, 290, *p290*; modern-day, 290, *p290*

Mozart, Wolfgang Amadeus, 687, *p687*

Muhammad, 374–76; biography, 376; prophet of Islam, 374–76; relationship of caliphs to, *c381*; government of, 375, 377; opposition to, 374–75; teachings of, 374, 377

mummy, 50, 51, 64, 65; cat, 64

Muqaddimah **(Khaldun),** *q382*, 392

Murasaki Shikibu, 501, 502, *p502*, *q502*; biography, 502

Muscovy. *See* Moscow; *see also* Russia

music: African, 475–76, *c475*, *p475*; 476, 545

Muslims, *c387*, 387–94, 433, 448, 515, 519, 541–43, 646, 666; achievements of, 390–92, 393–94, 433; art and architecture, 389, 393–94; attack of Japan, 495; cities of, 388–89; Crusades and, 541–43; culture, 388–90, *p389*, *p390*; decline of rule of, 384, 386; empires of, 380–81, 384–86; everyday life of, 388–90; French defeat of fleet, 666; inventions, 391; language, 390; Moguls, 385–86; religion and, 377, 381, 392; role of men and women, 390; rule of Spain, 646; slavery of non-, 389–90; social structure, 389–90; split into Sunnis and Shiites, 382; trade and, 388, 396; ways of life, *c387*, 387–94, *p389*, *p390*, *p391*, *p393*. *See also* Islam

Mycenae, 119; ruins at, *p119*

Mycenaeans, 118, 119–20; culture, 119; Dark Age of, 121; decline and collapse of civilization, *c116*, 121; kingdoms and government of, 119–20; religion, 119; spread of culture, 120; trade, 119–20; war and, 120, 121, 157–58

mythology, Greek, *c155*, 155–56

myths, 155, 156, 165, 487

Naomi, 99, *ptg99*; biography, 99

Napata, Kush, 70

Nara, Japan, 492

Narmer, 43–44

Natchez, 592; social classes of, 592

Native Americans, 578–81; Acoma, 591; Adena, 580; Algonquian, 592; Anasazi, 579–80; Apache, 591; Cahuilla, 591; California, 591; Cayuga, 592; Cherokee, 592; Chinook, 591; Chumash, 591; Columbian Exchange and, *m668*, 668–69; confederations, 592; disease and, 596; early civilizations of, 578–81; enslavement of, 664; geography, climate and, 590, 591, 592; governments of, 592; Grand Council of, 592; Great Peace, 592; Haida, 591; Hidatsa, 591; Hohokam, 579; Hopewell, 580; Inuit, 590; Iroquois League, 592; Jesuit missionaries and, 650; laws of, 592; life in the Eastern Woodlands, 592; life in the Pacific Northest, 591; life in the Southwest, 591; life on the Great Plains, 591–92; life on the West Coast, 591; Mandan, 591; Mississippians 580–81; Mohawk, 592; Mound Builders, 580; Natchez, 592; Navajo, 591; Oneida, 592; Onondaga, 592; Pawnee, 591; people and cultures of, *m590*, 590–92; people of the Far North, 590; Pomo, 591; Pueblo, 591; Seneca, 592; Tlinkit, 591; Zuni, 591

natural law, 550, 681

natural rights, 681–82, 685; of women, 685

Navigation Acts, 696

Nazareth, 344, 346

Nebuchadnezzar, Chaldean king, 29, 92

Nefertari, queen of Egypt, 66

neo-Confucianism, 414

Neolithic Age (New Stone Age), 12, *m13*, 13–15, *c14*; arts and crafts of, *c14*; benefits of settled life, 15; compared to Paleolithic Age, *c14*;

domestication of plants and animals, 13; economic specialization, 15; farming revolution, 13, 15; growth of villages during, 14; human adaptations, *c14*; life in, 12, 14–15; Ötzi, man of, 12, *p12*; role of men and women, *c14*

Nerfertiti, queen of Egypt, 64

Nero, emperor of Rome, 288, *p288*; reign and accomplishments of, *c288*

Netherlands, 625, 664

New Kingdom, 61–62

New Testament, 355–56

Newton, Isaac, 675–76, *c676*, 677, *p677*, *q677*; biography, 677; scientific contributions of, 675–76

Niger delta, 450

Nigeria, 469

Niger River, *m469*

Nile River, 39, *m39*, 40, 49, 60, 69, 446

Nile River valley, 38–46, *m39*; geography of, 39–40, 41; life in, 45–46; river people, 41–42; settlement of, 39–40, today, 40, *p40*; united Egypt and, 43–44. *See also* Egypt, ancient

Ninety-Five Theses, 636, *q653*

Nineveh, 28; one of world's first libraries, 28

nirvana, 205

Noah, 95

nobles, 45, 46, 60, 125, 129, 492, 493, 494, 503, 516–19, 523–26, 537, 557, 614–15, 684, *p684*, 688; Frankish, 515, 519; samurai as warriors for, 494; shift of power to, 523; urban, 614-15; War of the Roses and, 557

Noh plays, 501; used to teach Buddhism, 501

nomads, 10, 132, 198, 199, 242, 245, 373–74, 383, 409, 424, *p424*, 445, 469–70, 518, 576, 579, 585; Aztec, 585; Bantu, 469–70; Bedouins, 373–74; hunter-gatherers as, 10; Magyars, 518; Mongols, 424, *p424*; Seljuk Turks,

383; Toltec, 576; Xiongnu, 242, 245

Norman conquest, 535–36

Normandy, 535–36, 557

North Africa, *m121,* 121, 178, 274, 357, *p357,* 380, *c381,* 384, 448, *m448,* 611; trade of, 448, *m448*

North America, *m13,* 578–81, 590–92; early civilizations of, 578–81; early farming in, *m13, c13,* 578, 579; people and cultures of, *m590,* 590–92. *See also* American Revolution; Americas; Native Americans

North Carolina, 592

Northern Renaissance, 625–26

note taking, 260–61

novels, 432

Novgorod, Russia, 540

Nubia, 69–70. *See also* Kush, civilization of

numbering systems: Chinese, *c236;* based on 10, *c44,* 51; based on 20, 585; based on 60, 21, *c44;* Indian-Arabic, 215–16, 391; Sumerian, 21

nuns, 362, 363, 545

Nzinga, queen of Matamba, 470, *p471;* biography, 471

oases, 373, 445

Ocatavian, emperor of Rome, 282–83, 287–88, 289. *See also* Augustus, emperor of Rome

odes, 304

Odoacer, 324

Odysseus, 158

***Odyssey* (Homer),** 157, 158, 159

***Oedipus Rex* (Sophocles),** 161

Old Kingdom, Egypt's, 47–52; pyramids, 50–52; religion, 49–50; rulers of, 48

Old Stone Age, 10

Old Testament, 88

oligarchy, 126–27, 129, 147

Olmec Empire, *m575,* 575–76; first planned city, 575; trade, 575

Olympics, 128, *p128;* first, 108, *p108;* past and present, 128

Omar Kyayyam, 392, *p392,* 393, *q393;* biography, 392

Oneida, 592; government of, 592

Onin War, 497

Onondaga, 592; government of, 592

***On the Structure of the Human Body* (Vesalius),** 676

oracle, 156; bones, 228, *p228;* Greek at Delphi, 156, *ptg156*

oral history, 470

***Oresteia* (Aeschylus),** 161

Osiris, 49, 50, *p50*

Ostia, Italy, 293

Ostrogoths, 322, *m513,* 514

Otto I, emperor of Holy Roman Empire, 519

Ottoman empire, 384–85, *m385,* 611, 659; architecture, 384, *p384;* expansion of, *m385;* government, 385; religion, 385

Ötzi, 12, *p12;* biography, 12; weapons of, 12, *p12*

Oxford, England, 550

oxygen, 676

Pachacamac, 588

Pachacuti, Inca king, 588, 589, *p589, q589;* biography, 589

Pacific Northwest, 590; life in, 590; Native American people of, *m590,* 591; natural resources, 591

Pacific Ocean, 599

Paine, Tom, 699

Paleolithic Age, 10–11, *c14;* adaptations to the environment, 10, *c14;* arts and crafts, *ptg10, 14;* importance of fire and, 10; nomadic life of, people, 10; roles of men and women, 10, *c14*

Palestine, 101, 102, *m383,* 384, 542

Panama, 599

Panchantantra, 215

Panchen Lama, 208

Papacy. *See* pope

Papal States, 515

papermaking, 42, 245, *p254;* China, 245; Egyptian, 42; linking past and present, 245

papyrus, 42

parables, 345; Jesus teaching, *p344, p345*

Pariahs (Untouchables), *c200, p200,* 200–01

Paris, France, 538, 550, 644

Parliament, 537, 681, 697

Parthenon, *p112,* 141, *p141, c162, p162,* 163

Parvati, 204

Passover, celebration of, 82, *p82, c96,* 347

Pataliputra, 210

paterfamilias, 307, 308

patriarchs, 355

patricians, 269, 270–71, 278

Patrick, 364, 519

Paul III, Pope, 643

Paula, 362

Paul of Tarsus, 348, 349, *p349,* 362

Pax Romana, 287; good emperors of, *c292*

Peace of Augsburg, 639

peasants, 636–37

Peisistratus, 129

Peloponnesian War, *c112, c138, m144,* 144–46, 146, 176; impact of, 176

Peloponnesus, *m117,* 120, *m125*

peninsula, 117

Pepin, king of Franks, 515

Pergamum, 178

Pericles, 113, 140, 141, *q141, p141, p145, q145;* achievements of, 140–41; "Age of," 138–47; biography, 141; democracy and, 141, 145; funeral oration, 145; ruler, leader, general, statesman, 140–41

persecution, 353

Persia, *m132, p132,* 132–37, 382, 383, *m383,* 392

Persian Empire, 30, *m132,* 94, 132–33; defeat of Chaldeans and, 94; expansion and rise of, 132–33; fall of, 137;

government and political organization of of, 133–34; military of, 133; religion of, 133; rulers of, 132–33, 134–35; Spartans and, 146. *See also* Persian Wars

Persian Gulf, 28

Persian Wars, *m134,* 134–37, *p136,* 177

perspective, 623; use of in art, 623

Peru, 578. *See also* Inca Empire

Petén, 583

Peter, the Apostle, 348

Peter the Great, 688–89, *ptg689*

Petrarch, Francesco, *p619,* 619–20; humanism and, 619–20

pharaohs, 45, 48, 49, *p49,* 50, 60, 62, 63, 64–66, *p66,* 67; embalming of, 49, *p49,* 50

Pharisees, 100

Pheidippides, 135; modern marathon and, 135

Philadelphia, Pennsylvania, 699

Philip II, king of France, 538, 543

Philip II, king of Macedonia, 175–76

Philip II, king of Spain, 649, *p649,* 664

Philip IV, king of France, 538

Philippine Islands, 650

Philistines, 87, 88, 89, 101

philosophers, 140, 684, *p684;* Chinese, 235–39; French, 684–86; Greek: 140, *ptg169,* 169–70, *c170, p172,* 184; important contributions of, *c170,* 184; influences on today, *c170,* 184

philosophy, 169, 235–39; freedom of speech and, 684; idea of absolute right and wrong, 170; Socratic method, 170; use of reason, 684–85

Phoenicia, 132, *m132*

Phoenicians, 84; alphabet, 85, *c85,* 120

pictographs, 228

pilgrimage, 376, *p376,* 378, *c378,* 465, 466; of Mansa Musa, 465, 466

pilgrims, 213, 546–47

Pilgrims, 693

pilium, 266, p266

Pi Sheng, 419

Piye, king of Kush, 71

Pizarro, Francisco, 599–600, 664; defeat of Inca, 600

plague, 82, 319, 554; bubonic, 554; ten plagues, 82. *See also* Black Death

plane geometry, 185–86

Plataea, battle of, 137, 139

plateau, 446

Plato, 144, 170, p170, 171, 172; biography, 172; ideas of, 170, c170

Plautus, 304

playwrights, 161, 183, 304, 625

plebeians, 269, 270–71, 273, 278; Council of the Plebs, 270; political reforms by, 270–71

Plutarch, 126, q126

poetry, 88, 157–58, 214–15, 392, 393, 420–21, 470, 501, 552, 620; epics, 20, 157, 159, 183, 215, 304, 552; Greek, 157–58; Indian, 214; of King David, 88; Muslim, 392, 393; Renaissance, 620; Tang, 420–21; tanka, 501; troubadour, 552

polis, 122–23

***Politics* (Aristotle),** 171

politics and political systems: absolutism, 681, 686–89; Assyrian, 28; Lutheranism and, 639; natural law and, 681–82; provinces as political districts, 28; reason and, 681–82, 683, 685–86; Roman, 278–79; separation of powers in, 682. *See also* government

Polo, Marco, p428, q428, 428–29, p429; 612;

Pompeii, Italy, 290, p290

Pompey, 280, p280

pope, 356, 359, 360, 361, 515, 519, 623, 636, 643, 648

popular sovereignty, 700

population: migrations, 469, m469; 573, m573; shifts, 120, 230, 417, 555, m573; 576; urban, 610.

See also migrations

porcelain, 418, 421-22, p422

Portugal, 435, 472, 473, 558, 660; exploration, 660, 661; slave trade and, 472–73, 661; trading empire of, 666; war with Muslims, 558, 666

Poseidon, 155, p155

Praetorian Guard, 287–88

praetors, 270

predestination, 640–41

predicting, 36–37

prehistoric people, 9–15, 573–75, p574; migrations of, m573. *See also* humans, early

prehistory, 9

previewing, 6–7

***Prince, The* (Machiavelli),** 614, 615

Prince Who Knew His Fate, The, 53–58

***Principia* (Newton),** 676, 677

printing, 419–20, 620–21, 660; impact on spread of ideas, 620, 621; invention of movable type, 419, 620; invention of the printing press, 620–21

privateers, 664

procurator, 343

prophecies, 156

prophets, 87, 91, 377; major Hebrew, 91, c91

Protestantism, 639, 643–45, 664, 665

Protestants, 636, 640, 693; Calvinism and, 640; Catholics and, 643–45; Lutheranism and, 636

proverbs, 89, 470

provinces, 28

Prussia, 687

Ptolemy, 305, 660, 671, 672, p672; scientific contributions of, 305, 660

pueblos, 579–80

Punic Wars, m274, 274–76;

Pure Land Buddhism, 499

Puritans, 649, 693

Puteoli, Italy, 293

pyramids, 34, p34, 50–52, c51, p51, p52, p70, 71, p576, 577, 584, 587, p587; astronomy, math and

building of, 51; Great Pyramid, 52; Great Temple, 587, p587; inside, p51, c51; Kushite, p70, 71; Mayan, p576, 584; Moche, 577; Pyramid of the Sun, 577; Tikal, p576

Pythagoras, 169, 185, c185; scientific contributions of, c185; Pythagorean theorem, 169

Q

Quebec, 692

Qin dynasty, m241, 241–43; government, 241–42, 243; Great Wall, 242

Qin Shihuangdi, emperor of China, 241–42, 243, p243, q243; biography, 243; government of, 241–42, 243; legalism and, 241, c247

Quechua, 588

Quetzalcoatl, 597

Quran, 377–78, 393, 465, 472; influence on Muslims' daily life, 378; source of Islamic beliefs and practices and law, 377; slavery and, 472; study of, p378, 465

R

rabbis, 101

rain forests, p445, 445, 450–51; kingdoms of, 450–51; Mayan civilization in, 575–76

raja, 199

Rama, 215

Ramayana, 214–15

Ramses II, king of Egypt, 65, 66, p66, 67

Raphael. *See* Sanzio, Raphael

rationalism, 678

Re, 49

reading skills: analyze and clarify, 606–07; building vocabulary, 192–93; cause and effect, 482–83; compare and contrast, 442–43; context clues, 152–53; inferences, 406–07; main idea, 78–79, 340–41; main idea

and supporting details, 370–71; making connections, 114–15; monitor and adjust, 656–57; predicting, 36–37; previewing, 6–7; questioning, 510–11; responding and reflecting, 300–01; sequence clues, 340–41; taking notes, 260–61; text structure, 222–23; summarizing, 570–71

reason, 678–79, 681

Reconquista, 558

Red Sea, 40, 60, 82, 446; parting of by Moses, ptg82

Reformation, 634–37, 638, 639–41, 642–46, 647, 648–50; Counter-, 643–46; English, 648–49

reforms, 411

regents, 493

reincarnation, 204, 206; caste system and, 204, 206

religion: African, 463, m463, c463, 464–65, 467; Aryan, 203; Aztec, 586, 587; Bantu, 469; based on reason, 685; Buddhism, 205–06, 208, 248, 412–13, 489, 492–93, 499; Calvinism, 640–41, 649; Christianity, 81, 83, 91, 326, 338–65, 545–47, 635–37, 639–41, 643–46, 648–50; common beliefs of Christians, Jews and Muslims, 377; Counter-Reformation, 643–46; deism, 685; Egyptian, 49–50, 64; English Reformation, 648–50; European, m645; 644–46; freedom of, 354, 381, 385, 412–13, 645, 685, 692, 693; government and, 48, 208, 212, 228, 230, 462; Greek, 155–56; Hinduism, 203–04, 213; humanism and, 619; human sacrifice in, 584, 587, 588; Incan, 588; influences on society, 81; Islam, 368–95, m380; Jewish, 81–85, 95, 96, 133; Lutheranism, 636–37, 639; Mayan, 584; Mesopotamian, 19;

monotheism in, 64, 81; music and, 476, 545; persecution based on, 81, 82, 96, 101, 646, 649; popular, 546; Reformation, 633–50; religous orders, 363, 545–46; religious texts, 81, 82, 91, 94, *p94*, 95, 96, 98, 99, 100, 101, 334, *p334*; Roman, 309–10, *c310*, 324, 326; sacraments in, 546; Samaritans, 91; Shang dynasty and, 227–28; Shinto, 490; Tang dynasty and, 412–13; Vedas as hymns and prayers for, 214; wars about, 643, 644–45; worship of gods and goddesses, 81, 309–10, *c310*; worship of one God, 64, 81; Zorastrianism, 133. *See also* individual listings

Remus, 264

Renaissance, 608–17, 619–26; art, 609–10, 612, 613, 614, 619, 621, 622, *ptg622*, 623–24, 625–26; beginnings of, 609–10, 614–15; cartography and, 660; crusades and, 611, 619; emphasis on the secular, 609; impact of printing press on spread of ideas, 620, 621; influence of Greek and Roman thought on, 619, 621; humanism and, 619–21; Italian, 609–15; life of an artist, 624; literature, 620, 626; meaning of, 609; Northern, 625; scientific study and, 621; spread of, 620–21, 625–26

representative democracy, 138, 139, *c140*, 537, 538

republic, 265–66

Republic **(Plato),** 170

responding and reflecting, 300–01

resurrection, 347, 348

rhetoric, 307, 357

Rhine River, 292, 323

Richard I, king of England, 542–43

Rightly Guided Caliphs, 380, *c381*

rights. *See* citizens; government; natural rights

Rim-Sin, 22

Rolfe, John, 692

Roman Catholic Church, 356, 359, 360–61, 515, 519–21, 546, 634–36, 638, 639, 643–46, 648, 649, 650; condemnation of Galileo, 675; Council of Trent, 643, *p643*; Counter-Reformation and, 643–46; English Reformation and, 648–49; Inquisition and, 547; Martin Luther and, 634–36, 638, monastic religious orders, 363; missionaries, 650; political roles of clergy, 355, 360; practices, rituals, sacraments of, 546; Protestants and, 643–46; punishment of Jews, 547; Reformation and, 633–39, 648–50; religious orders of, 545–46; rise of, 519–21; role of in preservation of Latin language and religious texts, 520; scientific discoveries and, 675, 684; selling of indulgences, 634–35; spiritual roles of clergy, 360; split from Eastern Orthodox Church, 361; spread of Christianty and, 519–21; view of church-state relations, 359; Voltaire and, 684–85. *See also* Christian Church; Christianity; religion

Roman civilization of, 298–335; art and architecture, 303, 326, 333, *p333*; Byzantine Empire, 327–34; culture of, 303–05, 326; economy of, 292–93, 319, 320; education in, 334; emperors, 287–89, *c288*, 291, 320, 321; expansion of, *m293*; fall of, 317–26; fall of Rome, 322–24; family life in, 307–08, *p309*; Germanic invasion of, 322–24; inflation in, 319; influence in the modern world, 325–26; legacy of, 325–26; Latin, 304; life in ancient, 302–10; literature, 304;

religion, 309–10; sculpture, 303; slavery during, 308–09; sports and contests, *p306*, 306–07, *p307*; trade, 332–33; women in, 308, 333–34

Roman Empire, 100–01, 286–94; Augustus, rule of, *q287*, 287–88, 289, *p289*, 356; Christianity in, 348, 352, *m352*, 354, 355, 356; conflict with Jews, 100–01; Diocletian's reforms, 320; decline and fall of, 319–24; early, 286–94; economy of, 292–93, 319, 320; good emperors of *Pax Romana*, 292–93, *c292*, *p292*; government of, 292–93, 288; Jewish migration in; Julio-Claudian emperors, 288, *c288*; location of territories in; military, 319; persecution of Christians and, 353; prosperity and unity of, 290–94; road system, 293; slavery in, 319

Roman Republic, 265–267, 268–76, 277–85; Assembly of Centuries, 270; birth of, 265–66; citizenship and, 281; corruption in, 278–79; Council of the Plebs, 270–71, 279; dictators of, 271, 279, 281, 284–85; expansion of, 274–76; fall of, 277–83; government of, 269–73, 287–88; Julius Caesar, 280–81; Law of Nations, 273; law, system of, 273; legacy of, 273; military of, 266–67, 279, 280–81, 287–88; patricians, 269, 270–71, 278; plebians, 269, 270–71, 273, 278; political reforms, 279, 281, 284; politics of, 278–79; poverty in, 278–79; Punic Wars, *m274*, 274–76; Senate, 270, 271, 272, 278; trade, 293, *m293*; transition to empire, 286–94; triumvirates in, 280–81, 282; Twelve Tables, 273; unification of, 267

Rome, 343–44, 352; beginnings of, 262–67;

culture, 271; civilization of, 298–335; early influences on, 264–65; First Triumvirate of, 280; geography, *m263*, 263–64; Germanic influence on, 514; gods and goddesses of, *c310*; law, 273; legacy of, 325–26; origins of Roman civilization, 263–65; Second Triumvirate of, 282; Senate, 270; spread of Christianity to, 348, 352, *m352*. *See also* Roman, civilization of; Roman Empire; Roman Republic

Romulus, 264

Rosh Hoshana, *c96*

Rousseau, Jean–Jacques, 685–86

Royal Standard of Ur, 19, *p19*

Rubaiyat **(Khayyam),** 392

Rubicon River, 280; "crossing the Rubicon," 281

"rule of law," 273

Russia, 539–40, *m688*, 688–89; in Middle Ages, 539–40; expansion of, 539; government of, 539; growth of, *m688*; Kievan Rus, 539–40; Moscow, 540, 689; Mongol conquest of, 540

Ruth, 98, 99, *ptg99*; biography, 99

Sabbath, 94

sacraments, 546

Sadducees, 100

Sahara, 40, 381, 445, 446, 447

sailboats, 21, 453

saints, 546

Saladin, king of Egypt, 542

Salamis strait of, 136; battle of, *p136*, 136–37

salt mines, *m448*, 449, *p449*

salt trade, 448, 449, *c451*

salvation, 350, 636

Samaria, 90

Samaritans, 91

Samuel, 87

samurai, 494

Index

Sanskrit, 199, *c199*, 214

Sanzio, Raphael, 623, 624

Saraswati, 204

Saratoga, Battle of, 700

Sargon, king of Akkadians, 23

satires, 304

Satraps, 133, 177

Satrapies, 133

Saul, king of Israelites, 87, 88

savannas, 69, 445, *p445*, 446

Savonarola, Girolamo, 616, *q616*

Saxons, *m513*, 514

Scandinavia, 518

scapegoats, 548

schism, 361; bewteen Catholic and Eastern Orthodox Churches, 361

Schliemann, Heinrich, 119

scholasticism, 550

School of Athens **(Raphael),** 624

science: Arabic language and, 672; astronomy, 21, 30, 51, 185, 216, 391, 585, *c671*, 671, 673–75; barometer, 675; chemistry, 391, 676; classification of substances, 391, 671, 673; contributions of scientists, *c185*, 185–86, 216, 391, 674–79; development of instruments of, 675, 676; discovery of cells, 676; discovery of gases, 676; early scientists, 671; establishment of physics, 185, 186; gunpowder, 420; hypothesis in, 679; impact of exploration on, 673; influence on Greeks and Romans on, 671–72; Islamic, 672; Latin and, 672; math and, 21, 42, 51, 151, *c185*, 185–86, 216–17, 585, 672; medicine, 183, 216, 391, 671; Middle Ages, 671–73; rationalism, 678; reason and, 678–79; scientific method, 678–79; Scientific Revolution, 670–79; seven-day calendar, 30; standardization of weights and measures, 243, 294; telescope and,

674, *p674*, 675; 365–day calendar, 51, 585. *See also* astronomy; inventions; math; medicine

scientific method, 679, *c679*

Scientific Revolution, 670–79, *c676. See also* science

Scipio, 276

scribes, 20, 21, 42, 45

sculpture, 163, 183, 229

Second Continental Congress, 700

sects, 499

secular, 609; interests during Renaissance, 609

Seine River, 513

Seljuk Turks, 383, 384, 385

Seleucid Empire, 178

Selimiye Mosque, 384; prayer at, *p384*

seminary, 643

Senate, Roman, 270, 271, 272, 278

Seneca, 304

Seneca people, 592; government of, 592

separation of powers, 682, 700

sequence clues, using, 340–41

serfs, *p524*, 525, 688, 689

Sermon on the Mount, 344, *p344*, 348

"The Seventeen Article Constitution" (Shotoku), 488, *q488*

Shakespeare, William, *p618*, 626, 627–32

Shang dynasty, *m226*, 226–29; artists, *p229*, *p231*; cities of, 226–27; culture, 227–28; development of language and writing, 228; military, 227; religion, 227–28, *c247*; role of women, 227; social structure, 226–27

sheikh, 373

Shiite Muslims, 382

Shikoku, 485, *m485*

Shinto, 490

shipbuilding, 518, 529, 613, 659–60

shogunate, 495, 496, 650

shoguns, 494–497, 650, 669

Shotoku, prince of Japan,

488, *q488*, 489, *p489*; biography, 489; creation of a constitution, 488; government reforms of, 488

shrines, 19, 490, 499, 500

Shushruta, 216

Sicily, island of, 263, *m263*, 274, 275, 555

Siddhartha Gautama, prince, 205, 206, 207, *p207*, *q207. See also* Buddha

silk farming, 417, *p417*

Silk Road, *m246*, 246–47, 411, 428, 429, *p429*, 554, 611

sinkholes, 583

Sirua, 204

Sita, 215

Siva, 204, *p204*

slavery, 389–90, 472–73, *m473*, 693; Egyptian, 62; European trade in, 472–73, *m473*; Greek, 121, 122, 125, 126, 129, 142; Kushite, 72; Muslim of non-Muslims, 389–90; Roman, 308–09, 319, *p319*; slave ships, *p472*; Sumerian, 20; within Africa, 472

Slavs, 539–40

smallpox, 596, 597, 599, 669; impact on Americas, 596, 597, 669

social class, 233, 249

social contract, 682, 685–86

Socrates, *p109*, 150, 168, *p168*, *p170*, 170–71; ideas of, 170, *c170*

Socratic method, 170, *c102*

solid geometry, 182, 186

Solomon, king of Israelites, *p89*, *q89*, 89–90, 343, 452; meeting with Queen Makeda, 452; temple built by, 89, *p90*

Solon, 124, 129; government reforms of, 129

Song dynasty, *m411*, 411–12

Songhai, medieval, 449, *c451*, 462, 465; economy, *c451*; government, 462; location, *c451*; religion, 465; trade, *c451*

Song of Roland, 552, q552

Sophists, 169–70

Sophocles, 161

South America, *m13*, *c13*; civilization of, *m577*, 577–78; economy, 577–78; early farming in, *m13*, *c13*; food surpluses, 577; geography, 577. *See also* Inca Empire

South Tyrol Museum of Archaeology, 12

Spain, 121, 343, 380, 514, 515, 558, 594–95, 646, 660, 664; arrival in the Americas, 594–95; conquer of Mexico, 595–97; Extremadura, 596; impact of Reformation on, 646; Jewish settlement of, 343; Muslim rule of, 646; search for a sea route to Asia, 594; spread of Islam to, 380; Visigoths, 514; war with England, 664; war with Muslims, 558

Spanish Armada, 664; defeat of, *p665*

Spanish Inquisition, 558, 646

Sparta, 113, *p113*, 115, *p115*, 124–30, *m125*, *p126*, 127, *p127*; compared to Athens, 125–30: culture, 126–27, *p127*; government, 126, 127; life in, 126–27; military, 115, *p115*, 126–27, *p127*; wars and, 135–36, 144–46

Spartacus, 309; slave revolt in Rome, 309

specialization, 15

Spirit of the Laws, 682, *q682*

"Spring Landscape," 421

Stamp Act, 697; riots against, *p696*

steppes, 424

Stevens, John Lloyd, 583;

stocks, 667

Stoicism, 184

stoics, 184

Stone Age, 9, 10

St. Petersburg, 689

Stupas, 211, *p211*

subcontinent, 195

Sudan, 69

Sudras, 200, *c200*

Sufis, 381

Sui dynasty, 409–11;

building of the Grand Canal, 410, *p410, c410*

Suleiman, sultan of Ottoman, 384

sultan, 383, 384, 385

Sumer, 18, *p18,* 19, *p19,* 20, 21; building techniques of, 19; city-state, 19, 21, *p21;* culture, 19, 20–21; development of writing, 20, 21; economy, 20; geography, 19; inventions, 21, 22; life in, *p19,* 20; literature, 20–21; rise of, 18; religion of, 19; roles of men and women, 20; scientific and mathematical advances, 21; slavery in, 20; social classes of, 20

summarizing, 570–71

Summa Theologica **(Aquinas),** 550, 551

Sundiata Keita, king of Mali, 449, 463

Sundiata: The Hungering Lion, 454–59

Sunna, 352; as source of Islamic beliefs, practices, law, 352

Sunni Ali, emperor of Songhai, 449, 462, 463

Sunni Muslims, 382

Susa, 133

Susanowo, 487

Suttee, 201

Swahili, 469

synagogues, 94, 98, 100

Syria, 60, 132, 177, 380, 384, 426, 541

Tabascans, 597; defeat of Aztec and, 597

Taharqa, king of Kush, 72, *p72*

Taino, 595; arrival of the conquistadors, 595

Taj Mahal, 394, *p394*

Takamatsu castle, 497

Tale of Genji, The **(Shikibu),** 501, 502

Talmud, 102, *q102*

Tang dynasty, *m409,* 411, 412, *p412;* culture of, 420–21; Empress Wu, female ruler of, 411; government, 411, 414; life

in, 412, *p412;* military, 411; neo-Confucianism in, 214-15; religion in, 412–13, 414–15;

tanka, 501

Taoism. *See* Daoism

Tarquins, ruling family of Rome, 265

taxes and taxation, 28, 48, 89, 94, 234, 243, 247, 288, *c381,* 381, 382, 385, 386, 411, 426, 436, 448, 488, 492, 494, 530, 537, 540, 543, 634, 636, 646, 660, 688, 697

Tea Act, 697

technology, 11, 41, 418–20; Chinese, 418–20, 422; first use of, 11, navigation, 659. *See also* inventions; science

telescopes, 674, 675; Galileo's, 674, *p674;* Hubble, 674, *p674*

Temple of Delphi, *p150*

Temple of Karnak, *p65,* 66, 67

Ten Commandments, 83, *q83;* Ark of the Covenant, 83, *p83;* as basic moral laws, 83; Moses with, *p83*

Tenochtitlán, 587, *p587,* 594, 597; largest city of Americas, 594

Teotihuacán, 575–76; first planned city of Americas, 575

terror, 426; Mongol use of, 426

text structure, understanding, 222–23

theater, 160, *p160,* 161, *p161,* 501 ; actors' masks, *p161, p501;* Hellenistic Era of, 183; modern, 160, *p160;* ruins of a Greek, *p160*

Thebes, Egypt, 60, 67

Themistocles, 135–36

theocracy, 208

Theocritus, 182, 183, *q183*

Theodora, empress of Byzantine, 330, *p330, q330,* 331, *p331;* biography, 331

Theodosius, emperor of Rome, 322, 354

theology, 550, 640; scholasticism and, 550

theory, 671

Theravada Buddhism, 206

Thermopylae, 136

Thousand and One Nights, The, 393

Thrace, *m121,* 133

Three Gorges Dam Project, 419, *p410*

Thucydides, *q141, q146,* 172–73, *q173, q189*

Thutmose III, pharaoh of Egypt, 62

Tiberius, emperor of Rome, 288, *p288, c288*

Tiber River, 263, *m263,* 264, 293

Tibet, 208, 411

Tigris River, *m17,* 18, 27, 382

Tikal, 576; pyramid in, *p576*

Timbuktu, 381, 449, 465, 467; center of Muslim learning, 381, 465

time lines: Africa, medieval, *c440, c444, c460, c468;* Americas, *c568, c572, c582, c593;* rise of China, early *c220, c224, c232, c240;* China in the Middle Ages, *c404, c408, c416, c423, c430,* Christianity rise of, *c338, c351, c358;* Egypt, ancient, *c34, c38, c47, c53, c68;* Enlightenment and Revolution, *c654, c658, c670, c680, c690,* Europe, medieval *c508, c512, c522, c534, c544, c553;* first civilizations, *c4, c8, c16, c26;* Greeks, ancient, *c112, c116, c124, c131, c138;* Greek civilization, *c150, c154, c168, c174,* c182; India, early *c190, c194, c202, c209;* Islamic civilization, *c368, c372, c379, c387;* Israelites, ancient, *c76, c80, c86, c93;* Japan, medieval *c480, c484, c491, c498;* Renaissance and Reformation, *c604, c608, c618, c633, c642;* Roman civilization, *c298; c302, c317, c327;* Rome, rise of, *c258, c262, c268, c277, c286*

Titus, emperor of Rome, 290

Todaji temple, 493, *p493*

token, jurors, *p129*

Toltec, 576

tools: artifacts, 9, 11, *p11,*

12, *p12,* 14, *p14;* invention of, 11, 15, 230, 231, 235

Torah, 82, 91, 94, *p94,* 98, 100, 101; children studying, *p98*

Toricelli, Evangelista, 675

torii, 500

Torquemada, Tomas de, 646

"Tortoise and the Hare, The" (Aesop), 158

Tours, battle of, 515

trade: African trading empires, 447, 448, 451, *c451, m452;* Anasazi, 579; Arabic as language of, 388; camels and, 447; colonial trade routes, *m695;* "death road," 445; Greek colonies and, 121; gold and salt, 447, 448, 449; growth of industry and, 121; Gupta Empire and, 213; Harappan, 197; impact of Crusades and, 611; Italian city–state, 611–12; Marco Polo and, 612; Mayan, 576, 584; mercantilism and, 696; Minoan, 118, 119; Moche, 577; Mongol Empire and, 426, 429, 611–12; monopoly, 576; Muslim, 388, 396; Mycenaean, 119; North African trade routes, *m448;* product specialization and, 121; river, 449, *c451;* restrictions, 696; routes, 213, *m246,* 246–47, *m448;* Silk Road, *m246,* 246–47, 411, 428, 429, *p429,* 554, 611; slave, 472–73, *m473;* Toltec, 576; Zhou dynasty, 231, 247; Zimbabwe, *c451*

tragedy, Greek, 160

treason, 431, 599

Treaty of Paris, 700

trial jury, 537

tribes, 81, 373, 424

Tribonian, 330

tribunes, 270

tribute, 60, 89, 411, 540, 586

Tripoli, 542

triumph, Roman, 270

triumvirate, 280, *p280,* 282

Trojan Horse, *p157,* 157–58

Trojan War, 120

Troy, *m117,* 157–58; battle of 157–58

Tu Fu. *See* Duo Fu

Tudors, 648

Turkey, 384–85

Tutankhamen, king of Egypt, 65; gold mask of, *p65*

Twelve Tables, 273, *p273*

Two Treatises of Government **(Locke),** 682

tyranny, *c112, c124,* 125–26

tyrant, 125–26, 147

Ukranians, 539

Umar, *c381*

Umayyad caliphs, 380, 382

United States: comparing Africa and, *c446;* comparing Athenian democracy and, *c140*

United States Constitution, 700

universities, 550

Untouchables, *p200,* 200–01; today, 200, p200

Upanishads, 203, 213

urban, 610; population, 610

Urban II, Pope, 541, *p541*

urban nobles, 614–15; in city–states, 614

Uthman, *c381*

Vaisyas, 200, *c200*

Valley of the Kings, 60, 62

vandalism, 32, 412, *p412*

Vandals, 323–24

van Eyck, Jan, 625

varnas, 200–01

vassals, 523, 496

vault, 303

Vedas, the, 214

Venice, Italy, 529, 610, 613, *ptg613, p613;* art of, 613; city-state, 610, importance of in Renaissance, 610; shipbuilding, 613; trade and, 610–11

Vera Cruz, Mexico, 575

vernacular, 552, 620, 634; translation of Bible into, 634

Verrazano, Giovanni da, 664

Vesalius, Andreas, 676

Vespasian, emperor of Rome, 290

veto, 270

Vikings, 518–19, 535, 539

Virgil, 304, 326

Virginia, 692, 693, 694

Virginia Company, 692

Vischer, Hans, 445

Visigoths, 322, 323, 324, 514

Vistula River, 513

vocabulary, building, 192–93

Volga River, 513, 539

Voltaire, *p684,* 684–85

voting: rights, *c140*

warlords, 409

War of the Roses, 557

warrior codes, 122, 494, 495; Bushido, 494, 495; influence on modern thought, 494

wars: American Revolution, 699–700; Crusades, 541–43; Hundred Years', 557; Mycenaean, 120, 121, 157–58; Peloponnesian, *c112, c138, m144,* 144–46, 146, 176; Persian, *m134,* 134–37, *p136,* 177; Punic *m274,* 274–76; religious, 541–43, 644–45; Thirty Years' War, 645; Trojan, 120; War of the Roses, 557

Washington, George, 698, 700

Wendi, emperor of China, 409–10

West Africa, 447–49; eonomies, *c451;* empires of, 447–49; European arrival in, 472; influence of Islam on 464–65, 467; location of, 448, *c451;* slave trade, 472–73; trade, 447, 448–49, *c451,* 472–73

West Bank, 14

Western Wall, 101

"A Wild-Goose Chase: The Story of Philemon and Baucis," 311–16

William, king of England (William the Conqueror), 535–36

Winthrop, John, 693

Wittenberg, Germany, 635

women: Aztec, 587; Byzantine, 333; Christianity and, 353; composers, 545; education of, 308; Enlightenment and, 685; government and, 235, 334, 470, 471, 504, 585; Greek, 129, 143; Japanese, 501, 504; judges, 84; Mayan, 584–85; Muslim, 390; natural rights of, 685; novelist, 502; regents, 334; religions communities of, 362; rights of, 46, 308, 331, 333–34, 585, 685; role of in Aryan culture, 201; role of in early China; 227, 234–35; role of in medieval Africa, 463; religious, 84, 545, 556, 557; role of in Neolithic and Paleolithic Ages, *c14;* role of in Shang dynasty, 227; rulers, 330, 331, 452, 470, 471, 504, 558, 585, 594, 664, 665, 688, 689; Roman, 308; sports and, 127; warriors, 470, 504

Wollstonecraft, Mary, 685, *p685, q685*

woodblock printing, 419

Wood, Michael, *q180*

wool, 529, 611, 612

writing: calligraphy, 501; cuneiform, 20, *c44;* development of, 42, 61, 70, 585; hieroglyphics, 42, 61, 70, 585; Japanese, 501; Mayan, 585; Muslim, 393; Nubian, 70

Wu, empress of China, 411

Wu Wang, 229

Wycliffe, John, 635

Xavier, Francis, 650

Xenophon, 143, *q143*

Xerxes, king of Persia; *p131,* 135; invasion of Greece, *c112*

Xia dynasty, 226

Xiongnu, 242, 245

Yamoto, 487, 488; Taika and, 488

Yangdi, emperor of China, 410–11

Yayoi, 486–87

Yom Kippur, *c96*

Yong Le, emperor of China, 431–32

Yoruba, 470, *q470*

Yuan dynasty, 428

Yucatán, 583

Zakkai, Yohanen ben, 101

Zama, battle of, 276

Zealots, 101, 343

Zen Buddhism, 499; monk meditating, *p499*

Zeno, 184

zero, invention of, 215

Zeus, 155, *p155,* 156

Zheng He, 433, *p434,* 434, 435; biography, 434; voyages of, *m433,* 433, 434, 435

Zheng Zhenxiang, 227

Zhou dynasty, 108, 229–31, *m230;* agriculture, 230; discoveries and inventions, 230; fall of, 231; government, 229–30; 230; religion, 230; trade and manufacturing, 231, 247

Zhu Yuanzhang, emperor of China, 432

ziggurat, 18, *p18,* 19, *p21,* 29; ruins of, *p4*

Zimbabwe, *c451,* 453; ruins of, *p453, m468;* trade and, *c451,* 453

Zoroaster, 131, *p131,* 133

Zoroastrianism, 133

Zuni, 591

Index

Acknowledgements

Glencoe would like to acknowledge the artists and agencies who participated in illustrating this program: Mapping Specialists, Inc.; Studio Inklink; WildLife Art Ltd.

Photo Credits

238 (tl)Robert Frerck/Odyssey Productions, (tc)ChinaStock, (tr)Dennis Cox, (b)Giraudon/Art Resource, NY; 243 (t)ChinaStock, (b)Robert Harding Picture Library; 244 Bibliotheque Nationale, Paris; 245 (l)Ontario Science Centre, (r)Dean Conger/CORBIS; 247 (l)The Art Archive/National Palace Museum Taiwan, (others)The Art Archive/British Library; 249 (t)file photo, (b)Giraudon/Art Resource, NY; 252 (l)Scala/Art Resource, NY, (c)Ancient Art & Architecture Collection, (r)Burstein Collection/CORBIS; 253 (tl)Erich Lessing/Art Resource, NY, (c)Victoria & Albert Museum, London/Art Resource, NY, (bl)Ronald Sheridan/Ancient Art & Architecture Collection, (br)The British Museum, London/Bridgeman Art Library; 254 (l)Cott Nero DIV f.25v Portrait of St. Matthew/British Library, London/Bridgeman Art Library, (tr)Scala/Art Resource, NY, (br)Ancient Art & Architecture Collection; 255 (t)Pierre Belzeaux/Photo Researchers, (c)Brian Lawrence/SuperStock, (l)Nik Wheeler; 256–257 ©Worldsat International Inc. 2004, All Rights Reserved; 256 (t)Ric Ergenbright, (c)Sean Sexton Collection/CORBIS, (bl)Robert Emmett Bright/Photo Researchers, (bcl)Scala/Art Resource, NY, (bcr)Danita Delimont/Ancient Art & Architecture Collection, (br)Werner Forman/Art Resource, NY; 257 (t to b)Brian Lawrence/SuperStock, Richard T. Nowitz/CORBIS, Nabeel Turner/Getty Images, (l to r)Scala/Art Resource, NY, Scala/Art Resource, NY, Earl & Nazima Kowall/CORBIS, Bettmann/CORBIS; 258–259 Roy Rainford/Robert Harding/Getty Images; 261 Ronald Sheridan/Ancient Art & Architecture Collection; 264 Francis Schroeder/SuperStock; 265 (t)file photo, (b)Scala/Art Resource, NY; 266 Stock Montage; 267 Prenestino Museum, Rome/E.T. Archives, London/SuperStock; 269 Michael Holford; 270 Ronald Sheridan/Ancient Art & Architecture Collection; 271 The Art Archive/Archeological Museum Beirut/Dagli Orti; 272 North Wind Picture Archives; 273 Alinari/Art Resource, NY; 278 The Art Archive/Archeological Museum Aquileia/Dagli Orti; 279 Scala/Art Resource, NY; 280 (tl)Archaeological Museum, Venice/E.T. Archives, London/SuperStock, (bl)Louvre, Paris/Bridgeman Art Library, (c)Reunion des Musees Nationaux/Art Resource, NY, (r)Ronald Sheridan/Ancient Art & Architecture Collection; 281 (l)SuperStock, (c)Museo e Gallerie Nazionali di Capodimonte, Naples, Italy/Bridgeman Art Library, (r)Mary Evans Picture Library; 282 Bettmann/CORBIS; 283 North Wind Picture Archive; 284 Nimatallah/Art Resource, NY; 285 Bridgeman Art Library; 287 Victoria & Albert Museum, London/Bridgeman Art Library; 288 (t)C. Hellier/Ancient Art & Architecture Collection, (tc)Ronald Sheridan/Ancient Art & Architecture Collection, (bc)The Art Archive/Museo Capitolino Rome/Dagli Orti, (b)The Art Archive/Staatliche Glypothek Munich/Dagli Orti; 289 Robert Emmett Bright/Photo Researchers; 290 (l)Seamus Culligan/ZUMA/CORBIS, (r)Jonathan Blair/CORBIS; 291 Ric Ergenbright; 292 (l)Roma, Museo Nazion/Art Resource, NY, (cr)Staatliche Glypothek, Munich, Germany/E.T. Archive, London/SuperStock, (others)Archivo Iconografico, S.A./CORBIS; 294 (tl)B. Wilson/Ancient Art & Architecture Collection, (tr)Erich Lessing/Art Resource, NY, (others)The Newark Museum/Art Resource, NY; 295 Michael Holford; 298–299 Picture Finders Ltd./eStock; 301 Erich Lessing/Art Resource, NY; 303 Nik Wheeler/CORBIS; 304 Bibliotheque Nationale, Paris, France, Giraudon/Bridgeman Art Library; 306 Pierre Belzeaux/Photo Researchers; 307 (t)Scala/Art Resource, NY, (b)Erich Lessing/Art Resource, NY; 308 Scala/Art Resource, NY; 309 (l)Stanley Searberg, (r)Giraudon/Art Resource, NY; 310 Reunion des Musees Nationaux/Art Resource, NY; 318 CORBIS; 319 Scala/Art Resource, NY; 320 The Newark Museum/Art Resource, NY; 321 (t)Hagia Sophia, Istanbul, Turkey/E.T. Archives, London/SuperStock, (b)C. Boisvieux/Photo Researchers; 322 Scala/Art Resource, NY; 324 Mary Evans Picture Library; 325 (l)Sean Sexton Collection/CORBIS, (r)Donald Dietz/Stock Boston/PictureQuest; 328 Stapleton Collection, UK/Bridgeman Art Library; 330 Scala/Art Resource, NY; 331 Andre Durenceau/National Geographic Society Image Collection; 332 (l)Giraudon/Art Resource, NY, (c)Brian Lawrence/SuperStock, (r)Ronald Sheridan/Ancient Art & Architecture Collection; 333 The Art Archive/Haghia Sophia Istanbul/Dagli Orti; 334 Ancient Art & Architecture Collection; 335 Giraudon/Art Resource, NY; 338–339 Richard T. Nowitz/CORBIS; 341 akg-images/Orsi Battaglini; 343 Nathan Benn/CORBIS; 344 (l)Reunion des Musees Nationaux/Art Resource, NY, (r)Scala/Art Resource, NY; 345 (l)Erich Lessing/Art Resource, NY, (r)Tate Gallery, London/Art Resource, NY; 346 (t)Elio Ciol/CORBIS, (b)Scala/Art Resource, NY; 347 Louvre, Paris/Bridgeman Art Library; 348 The New York Public Library/Art Resource, NY; 349 (t)Danita Delimont/Ancient Art & Architecture Collection, (b)Victoria & Albert Museum, London/Art Resouce, NY; 350 akg-images/Orsi Battaglini; 353 Scala/Art Resource, NY; 356 Cott Nero DIV f.25v Portrait of St. Matthew/British Library, London/Bridgeman Art Library; 357 (t)Scala/Art Resource, NY, (b)Alinari/Art Resource, NY; 359 Scala/Art Resource, NY; 360 (t)Scala/Art Resource, NY, (b)Michael Holford; 362 (l)Galleria dell' Accademia, Florence, Italy/Bridgeman Art Library, (r)PRAT/CORBIS; 363 C.M. Dixon/Photo Resources;

364 Giraudon/Art Resource, NY; 365 Cott Nero DIV f.25v Portrait of St. Matthew/British Library, London/Bridgeman Art Library; 368–369 Nabeel Turner/Getty Images; 371 Paul Dupuy Museum, Toulouse, France/Lauros-Giraudon, Paris/SuperStock; 373 (l)DiMaggio/Kalish/CORBIS; (r)Kevin Fleming/CORBIS; 375 Bibliotheque Nationale, Paris/Bridgeman Art Library; 376 (t)C. Hellier/Ancient Art & Architecture Collection, (b)George Chan/Photo Researchers; 377 (l)AFP/CORBIS, (r)ARAMCO; 380 The Art Archive/Hazem Palace Damascus/Dagli Orti; 381 Burstein Collection/CORBIS; 382 Alison Wright/CORBIS; 383 Nik Wheeler; 384 James L. Stanfield/National Geographic Society Image Collection; 385 Bettmann/CORBIS; 386 Chester Beatty Library, Dublin/Bridgeman Art Library; 387 (l)Mary Evans Picture Library, (c)Bettmann/CORBIS; 388 Richard Bickel/CORBIS; 389 (t)Jeff Greenberg/Photo Researchers, (b)The Art Archive/Harper Collins Publishers; 390 (l)Stapleton Collection, UK/Bridgeman Art Library, (r)David Turnley/CORBIS; 391 (t)R & S Michaud/Woodfin Camp & Assoc., (b)Paul Dupuy Museum, Toulouse, France/Lauros-Giraudon, Paris/Super-Stock; 392 Bettmann/CORBIS; 394 Galen Rowell/CORBIS; 395 ARAMCO; 398 (t)Scala/Art Resource, NY, (bl)Smithsonian Institution, (bc)Michael Holford, (br)Giraudon/Art Resource, NY; 399 (tl)Stock Montage, (tr)Michael Holford, (c)Scala/Art Resource, NY, (bl)Roy Rainford/Robert Harding/Getty Images, (br)Bibliotheque Nationale, Paris/Bridgeman Art Library; 400 (tl)The British Museum/Topham-HIP/The Image Works, (c)Angelo Hornak/CORBIS, (bl)Ronald Sheridan/Ancient Art & Architecture Collection, (br)Erich Lessing/Art Resource, NY; 401 (tl)Aldona Sabalis/Photo Researchers, (tc)National Museum of Taipei, (tr)Werner Forman/Art Resource, NY, (c)Ancient Art & Architecture Collection, (bl)Ron Dahlquist/SuperStock, (br)akg-images; 402–403 ©Worldsat International Inc. 2004, All Rights Reserved; 402 (t)Stock Boston, (c)Peter Adams/Getty Images, (bl)Art Resource, NY, (bcl)Ali Meyer/CORBIS, (bcr)Mary Evans Picture Library, (br)Kadokawa/Ancient Art & Architecture Collection; 403 (t to b)Tom Wagner/Odyssey Productions, Greg Gawlowski/Lonley Planet Images, Jim Zuckerman/CORBIS, (l to r)Museum of Fine Arts, Houston, Texas, USA, Robert Lee Memorial Collection, gift of Sarah C. Blaffer/Bridgeman Art Library, Courtesy Museum of Maritimo (Barcelona); Ramon Manent/CORBIS, ChinaStock, Christie's Images/CORBIS; 404–405 CORBIS; 407 Kadokawa/Ancient Art & Architecture Collection; 410 (l)The Art Archive/Bibliothèque Nationale Paris, (r)Christopher Liu/ChinaStock; 412 Ira Kirschenbaum/Stock Boston; 413 Bettmann/CORBIS; 414 Snark/Art Resource, NY; 415 Michael Freeman/CORBIS; 417 (l)Keren Su/CORBIS, (r)Philadelphia Free Library/AKG, Berlin/SuperStock; 419 Werner Forman/Art Resource, NY; 420 The Art Archive/British Library; 421 (l)The Art Archive/National Peace Museum Taiwan, (c)Naomi Duguid/Asia Access, (r)Private Collection/Bridgeman Art Library; 422 (l)The British Museum/Topham-HIP/The Image Works, (c)Laurie Platt Winfrey, (r)Seattle Art Museum/CORBIS; 424 (t)National Museum of Taipei, (b)J. Bertrand/Photo Researchers; 425 James L. Stanfield; 426 Werner Forman Archive; 427 (t)Kadokawa/Ancient Art & Architecture Collection, (b)Bibliotheque Nationale, Paris, France/Bridgeman Art Library; 428 The Bodleian Library, Oxford, Ms. Bodl. 264, fol.219R; 429 Hulton/Getty Images; 431 Christie's Images/CORBIS; 432 SEF/Art Resource, NY; 433 ChinaStock; 434 ChinaStock; 435 The Art Archive; 436 Bonhams, London, UK/Bridgeman Art Library; 437 Laurie Platt Winfrey; 440–441 Peter Adams/Getty Images; 443 Werner Forman/Art Resource, NY; 445 (t)Christine Osborne/ Lonely Planet Images, (tc)Frans Lemmens/Getty Images, (bc)Brand X Pictures, (b)Michael Dwyer/Stock Boston/PictureQuest; 449 Volkmar Kurt Wentzel/National Geographic Society Image Collection; 450 (l)Werner Forman/Art Resource, NY, (c)The Metropolitan Museum of Art, The Michael C. Rockefeller Memorial Collection, Gift of Nelson A. Rockefeller, 1964 (1978.412.310), (r)The British Museum, London/Bridgeman Art Library; 452 (t)Nik Wheeler/CORBIS, (b)Merilyn Thorold/Bridgeman Art Library; 453 MIT Collection/CORBIS; 461 (t)Werner Forman/Art Resource, NY, (b)HIP/Scala/Art Resource, NY; 462 Giraudon/Art Resource, NY; 464 Charles & Josette Lenars/CORBIS; 465 Giraudon/Art Resource, NY; 466 (t)Courtesy Museum of Maritimo (Barcelona); Ramon Manent/CORBIS, (b)Steven Rothfeld/Getty Images; 470 Jason Laure; 471 (t)National Maritime Museum, London, (b)Maggie Steber/CORBIS SABA; 472 Art Resource, NY; 473 Michael Holford; 474 (l)Dennis Wisken/Lonely Planet Images, (r)Lawrence Migdale/Getty Images; 475 (l)Werner Forman/Art Resource, NY, (r)Andy Sacks/Getty Images; 476 Jason Laure; 477 Jason Laure; 480–481 Orion Press/Getty Images; 485 Masao Hayashi/Dunq/Photo Researchers; 486 (l)Scala/Art Resource, NY, (cl)The Art Archive, (others)Sakamoto Photo Research Laboratory/CORBIS; 487 Asian Art & Archaeology/CORBIS; 489 (t)Art Resource, NY, (b)mediacolor's/Alamy Images; 490 Frederic A. Silva/Lonely Planet Images; 492 Angelo Hornak/CORBIS; 493 (t)AFP/CORBIS, (b)Tom Wagner/Odyssey Productions; 495 Ancient Art & Architecture Collection; 496 Bettmann/CORBIS; 497 Dave

Bartruff/The Image Works; **499** Nicholas Devore III/Photograhers/ Aspen/PictureQuest; **500** (l)Private Collection, Paul Freeman/Bridgeman Art Library, (r)Keren Su/CORBIS; **501** (l)T. Iwamiya/Photo Researchers, (r)Werner Forman/Art Resource, NY; **502** (t)Mary Evans Picture Library, (b)Private Collection/Bridgeman Art Library; **503** Erich Lessing/Art Resource, NY; **505** Mary Evans Picture Library; **508–509** Greg Gawlowski/Lonley Planet Images; **511** Museo del Prado, Madrid, Spain/Giraudon, Paris/SuperStock; **515** Scala/Art Resource, NY; **516** Giraudon/Art Resource, NY; **517** (t)Ali Meyer/CORBIS, (b)Vanni/Art Resource, NY; **518** Private Collection/Bridgeman Art Library; **519** Hulton/Getty Images; **520** (l)Abbey of Montioliveto Maggiore, Sienna/E.T. Archives, London/SuperStock, (c)Jim Zuckerman/CORBIS, (r)Ronald Sheridan/Ancient Art & Architecture Collection; **526** Scala/Art Resource, NY; **528** (l)Scala/Art Resource, NY, (r)Guildhall Library, Corporation of London, UK/Bridgeman Art Library; **529** (l)Archivo Iconografico, S.A./CORBIS, (r)Ancient Art & Architecture Collection; **530** (l)akg-images, (r)Ronald Sheridan/Ancient Art & Architecture Collection; **531** akg-images; **532** Giraudon/Art Resource, NY; **533** Erich Lessing/Art Resource, NY; **535** Tom Lovell/National Geographic Society Image Collection; **536** (l)Bildarchiv Preussischer Kulturbesitz/Art Resource, NY, (r)John Neubauer/PhotoEdit; **537** Ronald Sheridan/Ancient Art & Architecture Collection; **539** Jim Brandenburg/Minden Pictures; **541** (l)Archivo Iconografico, S.A./CORBIS, (r)Robert W. Nicholson/ National Geographic Society Image Collection; **542** Scala/Art Resource, NY; **545** Scala/Art Resource, NY; **546** Scala/Art Resource, NY; **547** Borromeo/ Art Resource, NY; **549** (l)Ancient Art & Architecture Collection, (tr)akg-images/Schutze/Rodemann, (br)SuperStock; **550** Staatliche Museen, Berlin, Photo ©Bildarchiv Pressicher Kulturbesitz; **551** (t)Museum of Fine Arts, Houston, Texas, Robert Lee Memorial Collection, gift of Sarah C. Blaffer/Bridgeman Art Library, (b)The Art Archive/Dagli Orti; **554** Museo del Prado, Madrid, Spain/Giraudon, Paris/SuperStock; **556** A. Woolfitt/ Woodfin Camp & Assoc./PictureQuest; **562** (t)Laurie Platt Winfrey, (b)The Metropolitan Museum of Art, The Michael C. Rockefeller Memorial Collection, Gift of Nelson A. Rockefeller, 1964 (1978.412.310); **563** (cw from top)Scala/Art Resource, NY, Erich Lessing/Art Resource, NY, Vanni/ Art Resource, NY, Private Collection, Paul Freeman/Bridgeman Art Library, Seattle Art Museum/CORBIS, The British Museum, London/ Bridgeman Art Library, CORBIS; **564** (t)akg-images/Ulrich Zillmann, (cl)The Pierpont Morgan Library/Art Resource, NY, (cr)Vatican Museums & Galleries, Rome/Fratelli Alinari/SuperStock, (bl)Peabody Essex Museum, Salem, MA, (br)North Wind Picture Archives; **565** (t)Christie's Images/CORBIS, (c)National Portrait Gallery, London/SuperStock, (bl)Bluestone Production/SuperStock, (br)Independence National Historical Park; **566–567** ©Worldsat International Inc. 2004, All Rights Reserved; **566** (t)Jeremy Horner/Getty Images, (c)David Hiser/Getty Images, (bl)The Art Archive/Museo Pedro de Osma Lima/Mireille Vautier, (bcl)Timothy McCarthy/Art Resource, NY, (bcr)SuperStock, (br)The Art Archive/ National History Museum Mexico City/Dagli Orti; **567** (t to b)SuperStock, Dave G. Houser/CORBIS, Buddy Mays/CORBIS, (l to r)Victoria & Albert Museum, London/Art Resource, NY, National Portrait Gallery, London/SuperStock, National Portrait Gallery, London, North Wind Picture Archives; **568–569** Robert Fried; **571** HIP/Scala/Art Resource, NY; **573** file photo; **575** Werner Forman/Art Resource, NY; **576** (l)Bowers Museum of Cultural Art/CORBIS, (r)David Hiser/Getty Images; **577** Nathan Benn/CORBIS; **579** (t)Charles & Josette Lenars/CORBIS, (c)Dewitt Jones/CORBIS, (b)Richard A. Cooke/CORBIS; **580** (l)Richard A. Cooke/CORBIS, (r)Mark Burnett; **581** Jim Wark/Index Stock; **583** Doug Stern & Enrico Ferorelli/National Geographic Society Image Collection; **584** Gianni Dagli Orti/CORBIS; **585** (tl)Boltin Picture Library, (c)Michel Zabe/Museo Templo Mayor, (br)Museum of Ethnology, Vienna; **586** Gianni Dagli Orti/CORBIS; **587** (r)E.T. Archive, (others)Michel Zabe/Museo Templo Mayor; **588** akg-images/Ulrich Zillmann; **589** (t)The Art Archive/Museo Pedro de Osma Lima/Mireille Vautier, (b)Jeremy Horner/Getty Images; **591** (l)Addison Doty/Morning Star Gallery, (r)J. Warden/SuperStock; **594** The City of Plainfield, NJ; **595** (l)Mary Evans Picture Library, (r)Dave Bartruff/CORBIS; **596** (l)The Oakland Museum, (others)Biblioteca Colombina, Sevilla, Spain; **597** HIP/Scala/Art Resource, NY; **598** (t)Archivo Iconografico, S.A./CORBIS, (b)The Art Archive/ National History Museum Mexico City/Dagli Orti; **599** Werner Forman/Art Resource, NY; **601** Gianni Dagli Orti/CORBIS; **604–605** Bill Ross/CORBIS; **607** Musee du Louvre, Paris/Giraudon, Paris/SuperStock; **610** akg-images; **611** Palazzo Ducale, Mantua, Italy/M. Magliari/ Bridgeman Art Library, London/SuperStock; **612** Scala/Art Resource, NY; **613** (l)Scala/Art Resource, NY, (r)Kindra Clineff/Index Stock; **614** Archiv/Photo Researchers; **615** Araldo de Luca/CORBIS; **616** Super-Stock; **617** Archivo Iconografico, S.A./CORBIS; **618** (cr)Erich Lessing/Art Resource, NY, (r)Art Resource, NY, (others)Mary Evans Picture Library; **619** (l)Maiman Rick/CORBIS Sygma, (r)Giraudon/Bridgeman Art Library;

620 The Pierpont Morgan Library/Art Resource, NY; **621** (l)The Art Archive/Manoir du Clos Luce/Dagli Orti, (c)Baldwin H. Ward & Kathryn C. Ward/CORBIS, (r)Alinari Archives/CORBIS; **622** (t)Timothy McCarthy/ Art Resource, NY, (b)Musee du Louvre, Paris/Giraudon, Paris/SuperStock; **623** Vatican Museums & Galleries, Rome/Canali PhotoBank; **624** Erich Lessing/Art Resource, NY; **626** Snark/Art Resource, NY; **634** Scala/ Art Resource, NY; **635** (t)Michael Hampshire/National Geographic Society Image Collection, (b)Sammlungen des Stiftes, Klosterneuburg, Austria/ Erich Lessing/Art Resource, NY; **636** akg-images; **637** (l)Bildarchiv Preussischer Kulturbesitz/Art Resource, NY, (r)Getty Images; **638** (t)SuperStock, (b)Dave G. Houser/CORBIS; **640** Erich Lessing/Art Resource, NY; **641** Hulton/Getty Images; **643** Giraudon/Art Resource, NY; **644** Mary Evans Picture Library; **646** (t)Nik Wheeler/CORBIS, (b)CORBIS; **647** (t)Victoria & Albert Museum, London/Art Resource, NY, (b)The Art Archive/Chateau de Blois/Dagli Orti; **648** Scala/Art Resource, NY; **649** (t)Scala/Art Resource, NY, (b)Michael Holford; **651** The Pierpont Morgan Library/Art Resource, NY; **654–655** Buddy Mays/CORBIS; **657** (t)Hermitage, St. Petersburg, Russia/Bridgeman Art Library, (b)Michael Holford; **659** (t)Peabody Essex Museum, Salem, MA, (c)SuperStock, (b)Michael Holford; **660** Bettmann/CORBIS; **663** (l)The Metropolitan Museum of Art, Gift of J. Pierpont Morgan, 1900(00.18.2), (cl)Stock Montage, (c)Collection of The New-York Historical Society, (cr)Reunion des Musees Nationaux/Art Resource, NY, (r)North Wind Picture Archives; **664** National Maritime Museum, London; **665** National Portrait Gallery, London/SuperStock; **666** Reunion des Musees Nationaux/Art Resource, NY; **671** Scala/Art Resource, NY; **672** Louvre, Paris/Bridgeman Art Library; **673** Bettmann/CORBIS; **674** (l)Scala/Art Resource, NY, (r)Denis Scott/ CORBIS; **675** Jean-Leon Huens/National Geographic Society Image Collection; **677** (t)North Wind Picture Archives, (b)Mike Southern; Eye Ubiquitous/CORBIS; **679** Snark/Art Resource, NY; **681** Bettmann/CORBIS; **682** Stefano Bianchetti/CORBIS; **683** (t)National Portrait Gallery, London, (b)Bettmann/CORBIS; **684** (l)Giraudon/Art Resource, NY, (r)Erich Lessing/ Art Resource, NY; **685** Tate Gallery, London/Art Resource, NY; **686** Mozart Museum, Prague, Czech Republic, Giraudon/Bridgeman Art Library; **687** (t)The Art Archive/Society Of The Friends Of Music Vienna/Dagli Orti, (b)akg-images/SuperStock; **688** (l)Giraudon/Art Resource, NY, (r)Reunion des Musees Nationaux/Art Resource, NY; **689** (l)Michael Holford, (r)Hermitage, St. Petersburg, Russia/Bridgeman Art Library; **692** Association for the Preservation of Virginia Antiquities; **693** Private Collection/Picture Research Consultants; **696** (c)The Royal Collection, ©Her Majesty Queen Elizabeth II, (others)The Library of Congress; **697** North Wind Picture Archives; **698** ©Virginia Historical Society. All Rights Reserved; **699** Frances Tavern Museum, New York, NY; **701** Michael Holford; **704** (t)Vatican Museums & Galleries, Rome/Canali PhotoBank, (b)Boltin Picture Library; **705** (tl)Werner Forman/Art Resource, NY, (tc)Scala/Art Resource, NY, (tr)Betmann/CORBIS, (bl)Michel Zabe/ Art Resource, NY, (bc)The Pierpont Morgan Library/Art Resource, NY, (br)©Virginia Historical Society. All Rights Reserved; **706** (bkgd)CORBIS, (l)Picture Finders Ltd./eStock, (r)Sylvain Grandadam/Getty Images; **707** CORBIS; **715** Pierre Belzeaux/Photo Researchers; **720** Michael Holford; **722** Museum of Ethnology, Vienna; **723** Museo Capitolino, Rome/E.T. Archives, London/SuperStock, Scala/Art Resource, NY; **724** Tim Flach/ Getty Images; **725** Jerry Barnett; **732** Sidney Harris; **736** Getty Images; **737** Egyptian National Museum, Cairo/SuperStock; **738** Scala/Art Resource, NY; **739** SuperStock; **740** Vanni/Art Resource, NY; **741** Victoria & Albert Museum, London/Art Resource, NY; **742** Scala/Art Resource, NY; **744** Giraudon/Art Resource, NY; **745** Mary Evans Picture Library; **746** Biblioteca Colombina, Sevilla, Spain; **747** (l)Art Resource, NY, (r)National Portrait Gallery, London/SuperStock

One-Stop Internet Resources

This textbook contains one-stop Internet resources for teachers, students, and parents. Log on to jat.glencoe.com for more information. Online study tools include Chapter Overviews, Self-Check Quizzes, an Interactive Tutor, and E-Flashcards. Online research tools include Student Web Activities, Beyond the Textbook Features, Current Events, Web Resources, and State Resources. The interactive online student edition includes the complete Interactive Student Edition along with textbook updates. Especially for teachers, Glencoe offers an online Teacher Forum, Web Activity Lesson Plans, and Literature Connections.